THE EXPOSITOR'S BIBLE COMMENTARY

with the New International Version

VOLUMES AND CONTRIBUTORS

Volume 1
Introductory Articles: General, Old Testament, New Testament

Volume 2
Genesis: *John H. Sailhamer*
Exodus: *Walter C. Kaiser Jr.*
Leviticus: *R. Laird Harris*
Numbers: *Ronald B. Allen*

Volume 3
Deuteronomy: *Earl S. Kalland*
Joshua: *Donald H. Madvig*
Judges: *Herbert Wolf*
Ruth: *F. B. Huey Jr.*
1, 2 Samuel: *Ronald F. Youngblood*

Volume 4
1, 2 Kings: *Richard D. Patterson and Hermann J. Austel*
1, 2 Chronicles: *J. Barton Payne*
Ezra, Nehemiah: *Edwin Yamauchi*
Esther: *F. B. Huey Jr.*
Job: *Elmer B. Smick*

Volume 5
Psalms: *Willem A. VanGemeren*
Proverbs: *Allen P. Ross*
Ecclesiastes: *J. Stafford Wright*
Song of Songs: *Dennis F. Kinlaw*

Volume 6
Isaiah: *Geoffrey W. Grogan*
Jeremiah: *Charles L. Feinberg*
Lamentations: *H. L. Ellison*
Ezekiel: *Ralph H. Alexander*

Volume 7
Daniel: *Gleason L. Archer Jr.*
Hosea: *Leon J. Wood*
Joel: *Richard D. Patterson*
Amos: *Thomas E. McComiskey*
Obadiah: *Carl E. Armerding*
Jonah: *H. L. Ellison*
Micah: *Thomas E. McComiskey*
Nahum, Habakkuk: *Carl E. Armerding*
Zephaniah: *Larry Walker*
Haggai: *Robert L. Alden*
Zechariah: *Kenneth L. Barker*
Malachi: *Robert L. Alden*

Volume 8
Matthew: *D. A. Carson*
Mark: *Walter W. Wessel*
Luke: *Walter L. Liefeld*

Volume 9
John: *Merrill C. Tenney*
Acts: *Richard N. Longenecker*

Volume 10
Romans: *Everett F. Harrison*
1 Corinthians: *W. Harold Mare*
2 Corinthians: *Murray J. Harris*
Galatians: *James Montgomery Boice*

Volume 11
Ephesians: *A. Skevington Wood*
Philippians: *Homer A. Kent Jr.*
Colossians: *Curtis Vaughan*
1, 2 Thessalonians: *Robert L. Thomas*
1, 2 Timothy: *Ralph Earle*
Titus: *D. Edmond Hiebert*
Philemon: *Arthur A. Rupprecht*

Volume 12
Hebrews: *Leon Morris*
James: *Donald W. Burdick*
1, 2 Peter: *Edwin A Blum*
1, 2, 3 John: *Glenn W. Barker*
Jude: *Edwin A. Blum*
Revelation: *Alan F. Johnson*

THE EXPOSITOR'S BIBLE COMMENTARY

with the New International Version

Romans through *Galatians*

VOLUME 10

Romans - Everett F. Harrison

1 Corinthians - W. Harold Mare

2 Corinthians - Murray J. Harris

Galatians - James Montgomery Boice

Frank E. Gæbelein general editor

ZONDERVAN®

GRAND RAPIDS, MICHIGAN 49530

ZONDERVAN.COM/
AUTHORTRACKER

ZONDERVAN®

The Expositor's Bible Commentary, Volume 10

Requests for information should be addressed to:

Zondervan, *Grand Rapids, Michigan 49530*

ISBN-10: 0-310-60900-3
ISBN-13: 978-0-310-60900-1

This edition is printed on acid-free paper.

Printed in the United States of America

06 07 08 09 10 11 12 • 10 09 08 07 06 05 04 03 02 01

CONTENTS

CONTRIBUTORS TO VOLUME 10

Romans: Everett F. Harrison

A.B., University of Washington; A.M., Princeton University; Th.B., Princeton Theological Seminary; Th.D., Dallas Theological Seminary; Ph.D., University of Pennsylvania

Professor Emeritus of New Testament, Fuller Theological Seminary

1 Corinthians: W. Harold Mare

A.B., M.A., Wheaton College; B.D., Faith Theological Seminary; Ph. D., University of Pennsylvania

Professor of New Testament, Covenant Theological Seminary

2 Corinthians: Murray J. Harris

B.A., M.A., University of New Zealand; Dip.Ed., University of Auckland; B.D., University of Otago; Ph.D., University of Manchester

Lecturer in New Testament, Bible College of New Zealand

Galatians: James Montgomery Boice

A.B., Harvard University; B.D., Princeton Theological Seminary; D. Theol., University of Basel

Pastor of Tenth Presbyterian Church, Philadelphia, Pennsylvania

PREFACE

The title of this work defines its purpose. Written primarily by expositors for expositors, it aims to provide preachers, teachers, and students of the Bible with a new and comprehensive commentary on the books of the Old and New Testaments. Its stance is that of a scholarly evangelicalism committed to the divine inspiration, complete trustworthiness, and full authority of the Bible. Its seventy-eight contributors come from the United States, Canada, England, Scotland, Australia, New Zealand, and Switzerland, and from various religious groups, including Anglican, Baptist, Brethren, Free, Independent, Methodist, Nazarene, Presbyterian, and Reformed churches. Most of them teach at colleges, universities, or theological seminaries.

No book has been more closely studied over a longer period of time than the Bible. From the Midrashic commentaries going back to the period of Ezra, through parts of the Dead Sea Scrolls and the Patristic literature, and on to the present, the Scriptures have been expounded. Indeed, there have been times when, as in the Reformation and on occasions since then, exposition has been at the cutting edge of Christian advance. Luther was a powerful exegete, and Calvin is still called "the prince of expositors."

Their successors have been many. And now, when the flood of new translations and their unparalleled circulation have expanded the readership of the Bible, the need for exposition takes on fresh urgency.

Not that God's Word can ever become captive to its expositors. Among all other books, it stands first in its combination of perspicuity and profundity. Though a child can be made "wise for salvation" by believing its witness to Christ, the greatest mind cannot plumb the depths of its truth (2 Tim. 3:15; Rom. 11:33). As Gregory the Great said, "Holy Scripture is a stream of running water, where alike the elephant may swim, and the lamb walk." So, because of the inexhaustible nature of Scripture, the task of opening up its meaning is still a perennial obligation of biblical scholarship.

How that task is done inevitably reflects the outlook of those engaged in it. Every biblical scholar has presuppositions. To this neither the editors of these volumes nor the contributors to them are exceptions. They share a common commitment to the supernatural Christianity set forth in the inspired Word. Their purpose is not to supplant the many valuable commentaries that have preceded this work and from which both the editors and contributors have learned. It is rather to draw on the resources of contemporary evangelical scholarship in producing a new reference work for understanding the Scriptures.

A commentary that will continue to be useful through the years should handle contemporary trends in biblical studies in such a way as to avoid becoming outdated when critical fashions change. Biblical criticism is not in itself inadmissible, as some have mistakenly thought. When scholars investigate the authorship, date, literary characteristics, and purpose of a biblical document, they are practicing biblical criticism. So also when, in order to ascertain as nearly as possible the original form of the text, they deal with variant readings, scribal errors, emendations, and other phenomena in the manuscripts. To do these things is essential to responsible exegesis and exposition. And always there is the need to distinguish hypothesis from fact, conjecture from truth.

The chief principle of interpretation followed in this commentary is the grammatico-historical one—namely, that the primary aim of the exegete is to make clear the meaning of the text at the time and in the circumstances of its writing. This endeavor to understand what in the first instance the inspired writers actually said must not be confused with an inflexible literalism. Scripture makes lavish use of symbols and figures of speech; great portions of it are poetical. Yet when it speaks in this way, it speaks no less truly than it does in its historical and doctrinal portions. To understand its message requires attention to matters of grammar and syntax, word meanings, idioms, and literary forms—all in relation to the historical and cultural setting of the text.

The contributors to this work necessarily reflect varying convictions. In certain controversial matters the policy is that of clear statement of the contributors' own views followed by fair presentation of other ones. The treatment of eschatology, though it reflects differences of interpretation, is consistent with a general premillennial position. (Not all contributors, however, are premillennial.) But prophecy is more than prediction, and so this commentary gives due recognition to the major lode of godly social concern in the prophetic writings.

THE EXPOSITOR'S BIBLE COMMENTARY is presented as a scholarly work, though not primarily one of technical criticism. In its main portion, the Exposition, and in Volume 1 (General and Special Articles), all Semitic and Greek words are transliterated and the English equivalents given. As for the Notes, here Semitic and Greek characters are used but always with transliterations and English meanings, so that this portion of the commentary will be as accessible as possible to readers unacquainted with the original languages.

It is the conviction of the general editor, shared by his colleagues in the Zondervan editorial department, that in writing about the Bible, lucidity is not incompatible with scholarship. They are therefore endeavoring to make this a clear and understandable work.

The translation used in it is the New International Version (North American Edition). To the International Bible Society thanks are due for permission to use this most recent of the major Bible translations. The editors and publisher have chosen it because of the clarity and beauty of its style and its faithfulness to the original texts.

To the associate editor, Dr. J. D. Douglas, and to the contributing editors—Dr. Walter C. Kaiser, Jr. and Dr. Bruce K. Waltke for the Old Testament, and Dr. James Montgomery Boice and Dr. Merrill C. Tenney for the New Testament—the general editor expresses his gratitude for their unfailing cooperation and their generosity in advising him out of their expert scholarship. And to the many other contributors he is indebted for their invaluable part in this work. Finally, he owes a special debt of gratitude to Dr. Robert K. DeVries, executive vice-president of the Zondervan Publishing House; Rev. Gerard Terpstra, manuscript editor; and Miss Elizabeth Brown, secretary to Dr. DeVries, for their continual assistance and encouragement.

Whatever else it is—the greatest and most beautiful of books, the primary source of law and morality, the fountain of wisdom, and the infallible guide to life—the Bible is above all the inspired witness to Jesus Christ. May this work fulfill its function of expounding the Scriptures with grace and clarity, so that its users may find that both Old and New Testaments do indeed lead to our Lord Jesus Christ, who alone could say, "I have come that they may have life, and have it to the full" (John 10:10).

FRANK E. GAEBELEIN

ABBREVIATIONS

A. General Abbreviations

A	Codex Alexandrinus
Akkad.	Akkadian
א	Codex Sinaiticus
Ap. Lit.	Apocalyptic Literature
Apoc.	Apocrypha
Aq.	Aquila's Greek Translation of the Old Testament
Arab.	Arabic
Aram.	Aramaic
b	Babylonian Gemara
B	Codex Vaticanus
C	Codex Ephraemi Syri
c.	*circa*, about
cf.	*confer*, compare
ch., chs.	chapter, chapters
cod., codd.	codex, codices
contra	in contrast to
D	Codex Bezae
DSS	Dead Sea Scrolls (see E.)
ed., edd.	edited, edition, editor; editions
e.g.	*exempli gratia*, for example
Egyp.	Egyptian
et al.	*et alii*, and others
EV	English Versions of the Bible
fem.	feminine
ff.	following (verses, pages, etc.)
fl.	flourished
ft.	foot, feet
gen.	genitive
Gr.	Greek
Heb.	Hebrew
Hitt.	Hittite
ibid.	*ibidem*, in the same place
id.	*idem*, the same
i.e.	*id est*, that is
impf.	imperfect
infra.	below
in loc.	*in loco*, in the place cited
j	Jerusalem or Palestinian Gemara
Lat.	Latin
LL.	Late Latin
LXX	Septuagint
M	Mishnah
masc.	masculine
mg.	margin
Mid	Midrash
MS(S)	Manuscript(s)
MT	Masoretic text
n.	note
n.d.	no date
Nestle	Nestle (ed.) *Novum Testamentum Graece*
no.	number
NT	New Testament
obs.	obsolete
OL	Old Latin
OS	Old Syriac
OT	Old Testament
p., pp.	page, pages
par.	paragraph
‖	parallel passage(s)
Pers.	Persian
Pesh.	Peshitta
Phoen.	Phoenician
pl.	plural
Pseudep.	Pseudepigrapha
Q	Quelle ("Sayings" source in the Gospels)
qt.	quoted by
q.v.	*quod vide*, which see
R	Rabbah
rev.	revised, reviser, revision
Rom.	Roman
RVm	Revised Version margin
Samar.	Samaritan recension
SCM	Student Christian Movement Press
Sem.	Semitic
sing.	singular
SPCK	Society for the Promotion of Christian Knowledge
Sumer.	Sumerian
s.v.	*sub verbo*, under the word
Syr.	Syriac
Symm.	Symmachus
T	Talmud
Targ.	Targum
Theod.	Theodotion
TR	Textus Receptus
tr.	translation, translator, translated
UBS	The United Bible Societies' Greek Text
Ugar.	Ugaritic
u.s.	*ut supra*, as above
viz.	*videlicet*, namely

vol.	volume
v., vv.	verse, verses
vs.	versus
Vul.	Vulgate
WH	Westcott and Hort, *The New Testament in Greek*

B. Abbreviations for Modern Translations and Paraphrases

AmT	Smith and Goodspeed, *The Complete Bible, An American Translation*
ASV	American Standard Version, American Revised Version (1901)
Beck	Beck, *The New Testament in the Language of Today*
BV	Berkeley Version (The Modern Language Bible)
JB	The Jerusalem Bible
JPS	*Jewish Publication Society Version of the Old Testament*
KJV	King James Version
Knox	R.G. Knox, *The Holy Bible: A Translation from the Latin Vulgate in the Light of the Hebrew and Greek Original*
LB	The Living Bible
Mof	J. Moffatt, *A New Translation of the Bible*
NAB	The New American Bible
NASB	New American Standard Bible
NEB	The New English Bible
NIV	The New International Version
Ph	J. B. Phillips *The New Testament in Modern English*
RSV	Revised Standard Version
RV	Revised Version — 1881–1885
TCNT	Twentieth Century New Testament
TEV	Today's English Version
Wey	*Weymouth's New Testament in Modern Speech*
Wms	C. B. Williams, *The New Testament: A Translation in the Language of the People*

C. Abbreviations for Periodicals and Reference Works

AASOR	*Annual of the American Schools of Oriental Research*
AB	*Anchor Bible*
AIs	de Vaux: *Ancient Israel*
AJA	*American Journal of Archaeology*
AJSL	*American Journal of Semitic Languages and Literatures*
AJT	*American Journal of Theology*
Alf	Alford: *Greek Testament Commentary*
ANEA	*Ancient Near Eastern Archaeology*
ANET	Pritchard: *Ancient Near Eastern Texts*
ANF	Roberts and Donaldson: *The Ante-Nicene Fathers*
ANT	M. R. James: *The Apocryphal New Testament*
A-S	Abbot-Smith: *Manual Greek Lexicon of the New Testament*
AThR	*Anglican Theological Review*
BA	*Biblical Archaeologist*
BASOR	*Bulletin of the American Schools of Oriental Research*
BAG	Bauer, Arndt, and Gingrich: *Greek-English Lexicon of the New Testament*
BC	Foakes-Jackson and Lake: *The Beginnings of Christianity*
BDB	Brown, Driver, and Briggs: *Hebrew-English Lexicon of the Old Testament*
BDF	Blass, Debrunner, and Funk: *A Greek Grammar of the New Testament and Other Early Christian Literature*
BDT	Harrison: *Baker's Dictionary of Theology*
Beng.	Bengel's *Gnomon*
BETS	*Bulletin of the Evangelical Theological Society*
BJRL	*Bulletin of the John Rylands Library*
BS	*Bibliotheca Sacra*
BT	*Babylonian Talmud*
BTh	*Biblical Theology*
BW	*Biblical World*
CAH	*Cambridge Ancient History*
CanJTh	*Canadian Journal of Theology*
CBQ	*Catholic Biblical Quarterly*

CBSC	*Cambridge Bible for Schools and Colleges*
CE	*Catholic Encyclopedia*
CGT	*Cambridge Greek Testament*
CHS	Lange: *Commentary on the Holy Scriptures*
ChT	*Christianity Today*
Crem	Cremer: *Biblico-Theological Lexicon of the New Testament Greek*
DDB	*Davis' Dictionary of the Bible*
Deiss BS	Deissmann: *Bible Studies*
Deiss LAE	Deissmann: *Light From the Ancient East*
DNTT	*Dictionary of New Testament Theology*
EBC	*The Expositor's Bible Commentary*
EBi	*Encyclopaedia Biblica*
EBr	*Encyclopaedia Britannica*
EDB	*Encyclopedic Dictionary of the Bible*
EGT	Nicoll: *Expositor's Greek Testament*
EQ	*Evangelical Quarterly*
ET	*Evangelische Theologie*
ExB	*The Expositor's Bible*
Exp	*The Expositor*
ExpT	*The Expository Times*
FLAP	Finegan: *Light From the Ancient Past*
GR	*Gordon Review*
HBD	*Harper's Bible Dictionary*
HDAC	Hastings: *Dictionary of the Apostolic Church*
HDB	Hastings: *Dictionary of the Bible*
HDBrev.	Hastings: *Dictionary of the Bible,* one-vol. rev. by Grant and Rowley
HDCG	Hastings: *Dictionary of Christ and the Gospels*
HERE	Hastings: *Encyclopedia of Religion and Ethics*
HGEOTP	Heidel: *The Gilgamesh Epic and Old Testament Parallels*
HJP	Schurer: *A History of the Jewish People in the Time of Christ*
HR	Hatch and Redpath: *Concordance to the Septuagint*
HTR	*Harvard Theological Review*
HUCA	*Hebrew Union College Annual*
IB	*The Interpreter's Bible*
ICC	*International Critical Commentary*
IDB	*The Interpreter's Dictionary of the Bible*
IEJ	*Israel Exploration Journal*
Int	*Interpretation*
INT	E. Harrison: *Introduction to the New Testament*
IOT	R. K. Harrison: *Introduction to the Old Testament*
ISBE	*The International Standard Bible Encyclopedia*
ITQ	*Irish Theological Quarterly*
JAAR	*Journal of American Academy of Religion*
JAOS	*Journal of American Oriental Society*
JBL	*Journal of Biblical Literature*
JE	*Jewish Encyclopedia*
JETS	*Journal of Evangelical Theological Society*
JFB	Jamieson, Fausset, and Brown: *Commentary on the Old and New Testament*
JNES	*Journal of Near Eastern Studies*
Jos. Antiq.	Josephus: *The Antiquities of the Jews*
Jos. War	Josephus: *The Jewish War*
JQR	*Jewish Quarterly Review*
JR	*Journal of Religion*
JSJ	*Journal for the Study of Judaism in the Persian, Hellenistic and Roman Periods*
JSOR	*Journal of the Society of Oriental Research*
JSS	*Journal of Semitic Studies*
JT	*Jerusalem Talmud*
JTS	*Journal of Theological Studies*
KAHL	Kenyon: *Archaeology in the Holy Land*
KB	Koehler-Baumgartner: *Lexicon in Veteris Testament Libros*
KD	Keil and Delitzsch: *Commentary on the Old Testament*
LSJ	Liddell, Scott, Jones: *Greek-English Lexicon*
LTJM	Edersheim: *The Life and Times of Jesus the Messiah*

MM	Moulton and Milligan: *The Vocabulary of the Greek Testament*
MNT	Moffatt: *New Testament Commentary*
MST	McClintock and Strong: *Cyclopedia of Biblical, Theological, and Ecclesiastical Literature*
NBÇ	Davidson, Kevan, and Stibbs: *The New Bible Commentary*, 1st ed.
NBCrev.	Guthrie and Motyer: *The New Bible Commentary*, rev. ed.
NBD	J. D. Douglas: *The New Bible Dictionary*
NCB	*New Century Bible*
NCE	*New Catholic Encyclopedia*
NIC	*New International Commentary*
NIDCC	Douglas: *The New International Dictionary of the Christian Church*
NovTest	*Novum Testamentum*
NSI	Cooke: *Handbook of North Semitic Inscriptions*
NTS	*New Testament Studies*
ODCC	*The Oxford Dictionary of the Christian Church*, rev. ed.
Peake	Black and Rowley: *Peake's Commentary on the Bible*
PEQ	*Palestine Exploration Quarterly*
PNFl	P. Schaff: *The Nicene and Post-Nicene Fathers* (1st series)
PNF2	P. Schaff and H. Wace: *The Nicene and Post-Nicene Fathers* (2nd series)
PTR	*Princeton Theological Review*
RB	*Revue Biblique*
RHG	Robertson's *Grammar of the Greek New Testament in the Light of Historical Research*
RTWB	Richardson: *A Theological Wordbook of the Bible*
SBK	Strack and Billerbeck: *Kommentar zum Neuen Testament aus Talmud und Midrash*
SHERK	*The New Schaff-Herzog Encyclopedia of Religious Knowledge*
SJT	*Scottish Journal of Theology*
SOT	Girdlestone: *Synonyms of Old Testament*
SOTI	Archer: *A Survey of Old Testament Introduction*
ST	*Studia Theologica*
TCERK	Loetscher: *The Twentieth Century Encyclopedia of Religious Knowledge*
TDNT	Kittel: *Theological Dictionary of the New Testament*
TDOT	*Theological Dictionary of the Old Testament*
Theol	*Theology*
ThT	*Theology Today*
TNTC	*Tyndale New Testament Commentaries*
Trench	Trench: *Synonyms of the New Testament*
UBD	*Unger's Bible Dictionary*
UT	Gordon: *Ugaritic Textbook*
VB	Allmen: *Vocabulary of the Bible*
VetTest	*Vetus Testamentum*
Vincent	Vincent: *Word-Pictures in the New Testament*
WBC	*Wycliffe Bible Commentary*
WBE	*Wycliffe Bible Encyclopedia*
WC	*Westminster Commentaries*
WesBC	*Wesleyan Bible Commentaries*
WTJ	*Westminster Theological Journal*
ZAW	*Zeitschrift für die alttestamentliche Wissenschaft*
ZNW	*Zeitschrift für die neutestamentliche Wissenschaft*
ZPBD	*The Zondervan Pictorial Bible Dictionary*
ZPEB	*The Zondervan Pictorial Encyclopedia of the Bible*
ZWT	*Zeitschrift für wissenschaftliche Theologie*

D. Abbreviations for Books of the Bible, the Apocrypha, and the Pseudepigrapha

OLD TESTAMENT

Gen	2 Chron	Dan
Exod	Ezra	Hos
Lev	Neh	Joel
Num	Esth	Amos
Deut	Job	Obad
Josh	Ps(Pss)	Jonah
Judg	Prov	Mic
Ruth	Eccl	Nah
1 Sam	S of Songs	Hab
2 Sam	Isa	Zeph
1 Kings	Jer	Hag
2 Kings	Lam	Zech
1 Chron	Ezek	Mal

NEW TESTAMENT

Matt	1 Tim
Mark	2 Tim
Luke	Titus
John	Philem
Acts	Heb
Rom	James
1 Cor	1 Peter
2 Cor	2 Peter
Gal	1 John
Eph	2 John
Phil	3 John
Col	Jude
1 Thess	Rev
2 Thess	

APOCRYPHA

1 Esd	1 Esdras
2 Esd	2 Esdras
Tobit	Tobit
Jud	Judith
Add Esth	Additions to Esther
Wisd Sol	Wisdom of Solomon
Ecclus	Ecclesiasticus (Wisdom of Jesus the Son of Sirach)
Baruch	Baruch
Ep Jer	Epistle of Jeremy
S Th Ch	Song of the Three Children (or Young Men)
Sus	Susanna
Bel	Bel and the Dragon
Pr Man	Prayer of Manasseh
1 Macc	1 Maccabees
2 Macc	2 Maccabees

PSEUDEPIGRAPHA

As Moses	Assumption of Moses
2 Baruch	Syriac Apocalypse of Baruch
3 Baruch	Greek Apocalypse of Baruch
1 Enoch	Ethiopic Book of Enoch
2 Enoch	Slavonic Book of Enoch
3 Enoch	Hebrew Book of Enoch
4 Ezra	4 Ezra
JA	Joseph and Asenath
Jub	Book of Jubilees
L Aristeas	Letter of Aristeas
Life AE	Life of Adam and Eve
Liv Proph	Lives of the Prophets
MA Isa	Martyrdom and Ascension of Isaiah
3 Macc	3 Maccabees
4 Macc	4 Maccabees
Odes Sol	Odes of Solomon
P Jer	Paralipomena of Jeremiah
Pirke Aboth	Pirke Aboth
Ps 151	Psalm 151
Pss Sol	Psalms of Solomon
Sib Oracles	Sibylline Oracles
Story Ah	Story of Ahikar
T Abram	Testament of Abraham
T Adam	Testament of Adam
T Benjamin	Testament of Benjamin
T Dan	Testament of Dan
T Gad	Testament of Gad
T Job	Testament of Job
T Jos	Testament of Joseph
T Levi	Testament of Levi
T Naph	Testament of Naphtali
T 12 Pat	Testaments of the Twelve Patriarchs
Zad Frag	Zadokite Fragments

E. Abbreviations of Names of Dead Sea Scrolls and Related Texts

CD	Cairo (Genizah text of the) Damascus (Document)
DSS	Dead Sea Scrolls
Hev	Nahal Hever texts
Mas	Masada Texts
Mird	Khirbet mird texts
Mur	Wadi Murabba'at texts
P	Pesher (commentary)
Q	Qumran
1Q,2Q,etc.	Numbered caves of Qumran, yielding written material; followed by abbreviation of biblical or apocryphal book.
QL	Qumran Literature
1QapGen	Genesis Apocryphon of Qumran Cave 1
1QH	*Hodayot* (Thanksgiving Hymns) from Qumran Cave 1
1QIsa [a, b]	First or second copy of Isaiah from Qumran Cave 1
1QpHab	Pesher on Habakkuk from Qumran Cave 1
1QM	*Milhamah* (War Scroll)
1QS	*Serek Hayyahad* (Rule of the Community, Manual of Discipline)
1QSa	Appendix A (Rule of the Congregation) to 1QS
1QSb	Appendix B (Blessings) to 1QS
3Q15	Copper Scroll from Qumran Cave 3
4QFlor	Florilegium (or Eschatological Midrashim) from Qumran Cave 4
4Qmess ar	Aramaic "Messianic" text from Qumran Cave 4
4QPrNab	Prayer of Nabonidus from Qumran Cave 4
4QTest	Testimonia text from Qumran Cave 4
4QTLevi	Testament of Levi from Qumran Cave 4
4QPhyl	Phylacteries from Qumran Cave 4
11QMelch	Melchizedek text from Qumran Cave 11
11QtgJob	Targum of Job from Qumran Cave 11

TRANSLITERATIONS

Hebrew

א = ʾ	ד = ḏ	י = y	ס = s	ר = r
בּ = b	ה = h	כּ = k	ע = ʿ	שׂ = ś
ב = ḇ	ו = w	כ = ḵ	פּ = p	שׁ = š
גּ = g	ז = z	ל = l	פ = p̄	תּ = t
ג = ḡ	ח = ḥ	מ = m	צ = ṣ	ת = ṯ
דּ = d	ט = ṭ	נ = n	ק = q	

(ה)ָ = â (h)	ָ = ā	ַ = a	ֲ = ^{a}
ֵי = ê	ֵ = ē	ֶ = e	ֱ = ^{e}
ִי = î	ֹ = ō	ִ = i	ְ = ^{e} (*if vocal*)
וֹ = ô		ָ = o	ֳ = ^{o}
וּ = û		ֻ = u	

Aramaic

ʾ b g d h w z ḥ ṭ y k l m n s ʿ p ṣ q r ś š t

Arabic

ʾ b t ṯ ǧ ḥ ḫ d ḏ r z s š ṣ ḍ ṭ ẓ ʿ ǵ f q k l m n h w y

Ugaritic

ʾ b g d ḏ h w z ḥ ḫ ṭ ẓ y k l m n s s̀ ʿ ǵ ṗ ṣ q r š t ṯ

Greek

α	—	*a*	π	—	*p*	αι	—	*ai*
β	—	*b*	ρ	—	*r*	αὐ	—	*au*
γ	—	*g*	σ,ς	—	*s*	ει	—	*ei*
δ	—	*d*	τ	—	*t*	εὐ	—	*eu*
ε	—	*e*	υ	—	*y*	ηὐ	—	*ēu*
ζ	—	*z*	φ	—	*ph*	οι	—	*oi*
η	—	*ē*	χ	—	*ch*	οὐ	—	*ou*
θ	—	*th*	ψ	—	*ps*	υι	—	*hui*
ι	—	*i*	ω	—	*ō*			
κ	—	*k*				ῥ	—	*rh*
λ	—	*l*	γγ	—	*ng*	‛	—	*h*
μ	—	*m*	γκ	—	*nk*			
ν	—	*n*	γξ	—	*nx*	ᾳ	—	*ā*
ξ	—	*x*	γχ	—	*nch*	ῃ	—	*ē*
ο	—	*o*				ῳ	—	*ō*

ROMANS

Everett F. Harrison

ROMANS

Introduction

1. Background
2. Authorship
3. Date and Place of Origin
4. Destination
5. Occasion and Purpose
6. Literary Form
7. Theological Values
8. Canonicity
9. Special Problems
10. Bibliography
11. Outline

1. Background

By common consent, Romans is the greatest of Paul's letters, and the Roman church became one of the major centers of Christendom, yet next to nothing is known about the circumstances surrounding the founding and early history of this church. The apostle does not deal with these things in the course of his letter. Luke provides no help beyond mentioning that Aquila and Priscilla, with whom Paul lived and labored at Corinth, had recently come from Italy (Acts 18:2). He says nothing about Paul's witnessing to them, so the presumption is that they were already believers. The expulsion of Jews from Rome by order of the emperor Claudius was dictated, according to the historian Suetonius (*Claudius* 25), by "disturbances at the instigation of Chrestus." Since the confusion of "i" and "e" was not unknown in Latin renditions of Greek, it is possible to conclude from this statement that the Roman Jews had become unusually agitated and disorderly over the proclamation in their midst of Jesus as the Christ (Christus), provoking the emperor to take action against them. But the stir could have been caused by messianic fervor with revolutionary overtones. At any rate, it is probable that by the fifth decade of the first century the Christian faith had gained a foothold in the capital of the empire. According to Ambrosiaster (4th century), the Roman church was not established by an apostle (which removes Peter from consideration) but by unnamed Hebrew Christians. By the time Paul wrote, it had become famous far and wide for its faith (1:8).

2. Authorship

From the postapostolic church to the present, with almost no exception, the Epistle has been credited to Paul. If the claim of the apostle to have written the Galatian and Corinthian letters is accepted, there is no reasonable basis for denying that he wrote

Romans, since it echoes much of what is in the earlier writings, yet not slavishly. A few examples must suffice: the doctrine of justification by faith (Rom 3:20–22; Gal 2:16); the church as the body of Christ appointed to represent and serve him through a variety of spiritual gifts (Rom 12; 1 Cor 12); the collection for the poor saints at Jerusalem (Rom 15:25–28; 2 Cor 8–9). Understandably, Paul makes fewer references to himself and to his readers in Romans than in 1 and 2 Corinthians and Galatians, since he had not founded the Roman church and guided its struggles to maturity as he had the others.

3. Date and Place of Origin

Fixed dates for the span of Paul's labors are few, but one of them is the summer of A.D. 51, when Gallio arrived in Corinth to serve as proconsul of Achaia. After this the apostle stayed in the city "some time" (Acts 18:18). Possibly in the spring of 52 he went to Caesarea and Jerusalem, stopping at Antioch on the way back and probably spending the winter of 52 there. Presumably, his return to Ephesus was in the spring of 53, marking the beginning of a three-year ministry there (Acts 20:31). At the end of 56 he spent three months in Corinth (Acts 20:3), starting his final trip to Jerusalem in the spring of 57. When he wrote Romans the fund for the Jerusalem church seems to have been finally completed (Rom 15:26ff.). This may indicate a date in early 57 rather than late 56 for the writing of the letter. (The fund was incomplete when Paul, on the way from Ephesus to Corinth, wrote 2 Cor 8–9.)

Corinth is the most likely place of composition, since Phoebe of nearby Cenchrea was apparently entrusted with the carrying of the letter (Rom 16:1, 2). The mention of Gaius as Paul's host (Rom 16:23) confirms this conclusion, Gaius having been one of the most prominent of converts during the apostle's mission at Corinth (1 Cor 1:14). Cenchrea is a less likely possibility. Paul would not naturally have gone there except to board ship. At that juncture a plot against his life forced him to change his plan (Acts 20:3). Thus it is hard to imagine Paul finding time or peace of mind at Cenchrea for composing a book like Romans. A Macedonian origin has also been claimed for the books, with Romans 15:25 as support (cf. NEB). But the verb can be understood futuristically: "I am about to go."

4. Destination

The titles of the Pauline Epistles are not part of the text, so the superscription "The Letter of Paul to the Romans" cannot be attributed to the apostle but must be taken as reflecting the understanding of the church as a whole sometime during the second century. Yet, since the intended readers are located at Rome by the writer (Rom 1:7, 15), all doubt about the destination would seem to be removed.

Strange to say, however, a few manuscript authorities (G, Origen, Ambrosiaster) lack the words "in Rome." One important witness, P^{46}, has the closing doxology of 16:25–27 at the end of chapter 15. This feature, plus the failure of the words "in Rome" to appear in a few manuscripts, as noted above, has led some scholars to follow the suggestion of T.W. Manson.[1] He thinks that P^{46} reflects the letter as Paul wrote it to the Roman church,

[1] *Studies in the Gospels and Epistles* (Philadelphia: Westminster Press, 1962), pp. 225–241.

but that the apostle at the same time sent a copy, minus the indication of Roman destination and with chapter 16 added, to the church at Ephesus. This would mean that the people mentioned in the closing chapter were living at Ephesus rather than at Rome. Attractive though this view is, it has not been universally received, because a good case can be made for a Roman destination for chapter 16.[2]

5. Occasion and Purpose

These two items are so closely related as to warrant considering them together. When Paul's Ephesian ministry had continued for more than two years, with tremendous impact on the city and province, he sensed that it would soon be time for him to move to another field of labor. It may be that for some time he had been looking westward toward Rome (see "many years" in Rom 15:23). Now the conviction grew that he must act by beginning to plan for work in the West (Acts 19:21). He had already preached the gospel in the strategic centers of population in the East and his restless spirit yearned to reach out to places where Christ was not known. He would go through Rome to Spain to plant the gospel there (Rom 15:22–24).

The question naturally arises, Why did this plan dictate the writing of a letter such as Romans? Why not send a note by Phoebe simply to inform the church that he would be coming to them in a short time? Two things should be said about this.

First, since Paul hoped to go beyond Rome even as far as Spain, he evidently expected to have in the Roman church a base of missionary operation comparable to Antioch in the East. If this was to be realized, he needed to share with the church a rather complete exposition of the gospel he had been preaching for over twenty years. By putting this exposition in writing and sending it ahead, he would give the Christian community in Rome an opportunity to digest the message and be ready to share in the extension of the gospel to the West.

Another factor may have entered in. The very passage that sets forth his plan and purpose is followed by one requesting prayer for his safety and success as he went on to Judea prior to leaving for Rome. Particularly ominous is his expressed need to be delivered from unbelievers in Judea (Rom 15:31). The plot by Jews at Corinth against his life (Acts 20:3) may already have been made and become an omen of future events. Possibly at this point intimations from the Holy Spirit began to warn him about the imprisonment and afflictions that awaited him (Acts 20:23). What if he should not live to declare the gospel in the West? Then he must write a letter so systematic and comprehensive that the church would be able intelligently to continue his work, proclaiming the very gospel he was spelling out for them, taking it in his stead to the farthest reaches of the empire. For all he knew at the time, this letter might be in a sense his last will and testament, a precious deposit bequeathed to the church and through it to the community of the faithful everywhere.

Manson's theory that the apostle provided a copy of the letter to go to Ephesus would fit into this concept, such a copy being intended as a lasting memorial to him and a blueprint for intensified evangelization by his friends in the yet unreached regions of the East. But believers at Ephesus must already have been well informed about the

---

[2]For a fuller discussion, see the present writer's *Introduction to the New Testament* (Grand Rapids: Eerdmans, 1971 ed.), pp. 307–311.

gospel after Paul's long ministry in their midst. So Manson's conclusion is speculative.

We should not overlook the distinct possibility that in addition to its evangelistic function Romans may have been designed to meet needs within the congregation, for, alongside its kerygmatic materials, it abounds in teaching. The degree to which Paul was familiar with conditions within the church at Rome may be debatable, but it is highly probable that he knew a good deal about them. Beginning at least from the time of his contact with Priscilla and Aquila at Corinth, he doubtless had a fairly continuous stream of information about the church, especially during his stay at Ephesus, since travel to and from Rome was relatively easy. The number of people listed in chapter 16 suggests many individual sources of information.

Yet for Paul to exhibit on the surface too intimate a knowledge of conditions in the church would be indelicate and might even betray the confidence of his informers. Likewise, to deal with these problems too directly and pointedly would be unseemly in view of his personal detachment from the Roman situation. Consequently, the interpreter is tempted to see in passages that are broad and general in their statement a penetrating relevance the Christians at Rome could hardly avoid seeing as a reference to themselves, compelling them to wonder at the unexpected discernment of an apostle who had not set foot in their city. Especially pertinent in this connection is the tension between Jew and Gentile within the church, two groups that may be approximately identified with the weak and the strong (see 15:1–8). Then there is the warning not to be lifted up with pride because of Israel's being set aside (11:20, 21), followed by a reminder that this setting aside is temporary (11:25, 26). The very fact that Jew and Gentile (rather than mankind) are given so much prominence in the main theme (1:16) and in the section that demonstrates the need for salvation (1:18–3:20) argues for the impact on the apostle of this tension at the time of writing.

6. Literary Form

Of the four types of writing found in the NT (Gospel, Acts, Epistle, Apocalypse) the epistle is by far the most common. The word itself is a transliteration of the Greek *epistolē*, meaning a communication, usually of a written nature. Romans bears this label in 16:22. Paul uses the word fairly often in reference to his correspondence with churches (e.g., 1 Cor 5:9; Col 4:16; 1 Thess 5:27). There is also a reference to his writings in 2 Peter 3:16.

The appropriateness of using "epistle" to describe Paul's written works has been challenged in modern times by Adolph Deissmann,[3] who contended for a distinction between epistle and letter, based not on the form but on the intent of the author. He reasoned that the epistle has a public character, often being of an official nature, intended to be preserved for posterity, whereas the letter is a private communication, dealing with matters of the moment and not expected to survive for scrutiny by future generations. Furthermore, Deissmann pictured Paul as a rough artisan possessed of little literary skill and requiring the aid of a secretary in composing his letters. Such a view is certainly not in accord with the judgment even of Paul's opponents (2 Cor 10:10). C.H. Dodd exposed the fallacy of this view when he acutely observed, "That [Paul] was not born to a proletarian status seems clear from the tone of his letters. A man born to manual

[3]*Bible Studies* (Edinburgh, 1901), pp. 3–59; *Paul* (London, 2nd. ed., 1926), pp. 3–26.

labour does not speak self-consciously of 'labouring with my own hands.'"[4] The very fact that we can speak of a Pauline style shows in itself that even when Paul used an amanuensis the mold of his thinking was well preserved. A passage such as 1 Corinthians 13 can hardly be attributed to an assistant.

Deissmann's weakness was his failure to recognize the wide gap between the letters found in the nonliterary papyri and the letters of Paul. The latter are not properly classed as private correspondence; indeed, even the most personal, the letter to Philemon, was directed also to the church that met in his house. So we must conclude that so far as Paul's writings are concerned, the line between private and public letters cannot be sharply drawn. One may with perfect propriety describe them either as letters or as epistles. As letters, they are direct, unstilted, relevant to the needs of the moment; as epistles they convey in elevated and beautiful expression the timeless truth of the gospel intended by God for all generations.

Many have observed that Romans is almost like an essay, showing comparatively little attention to the personal needs and pressing problems of the readers, and in this respect is strikingly different from 1 Corinthians, for example. Such a difference is not unexpected, since Paul did not found the Roman church and was doubtless acquainted with only a limited number of its constituency (ch. 16). But the difference should not be overstated, because there are indications that Paul is to some extent addressing himself to the situation of his readers. For example, he would hardly have allowed himself to discuss the problem of the strong and the weak (14:1–15:7) at such length had he not learned that this was a matter of concern to the Roman church. Again, his warning about "those who cause divisions and put obstacles in your way" (16:17) could reflect awareness of actual threats to the unity and soundness of the church. The source of his information could have been one or more of the friends listed by name in the closing chapter.

7. Theological values

Romans satisfies the craving of the human spirit for a comprehensive exposition of the great truths of salvation set out in logical fashion, supported and illumined by OT Scripture. The systematic element includes due attention to doctrine and life—in that order, because right relations must be established with God before one can live so as to please him and mediate his blessings to others.

The question as to what is most central to the Pauline theology has been long debated. Some have said that it is justification by faith. Others have insisted that the life "in Christ" is the secret, for it lifts one out of the rigidity and barrenness of legal terminology, disclosing the positive and dynamic relationship the believer may have with God's Son. Fortunately, we do not have to choose between these two, because both are important in Paul's presentation. Without justification there can be no life in Christ (5:18), and such life in turn confirms the reality of the justification.

Salvation is the basic theme of Romans (cf. 1:16)—a salvation presented in terms of the righteousness of God, which, when received by faith, issues in life (1:17). It is helpful to realize that salvation, righteousness, and life are eschatological terms. The apostle talks about salvation with a future reference (13:11). Righteousness, too, in the absolute sense, belongs only to the perfected state. Again, life comes to fullness of meaning only in terms

---

[4] *New Testament Studies* (Manchester, England: Manchester Univ. Press, 1953), p. 71.

of the future (6:22; cf. Mark 10:29, 30). Yet all these future realities are to be entered into and enjoyed during the earthly pilgrimage of the saints. Salvation is a present reality (10:10). So is righteousness (4:3–5). So is life (6:23; 8:2). In the last analysis, only the grace of God permits us to participate now in that which properly belongs to the future.

Though Romans does not give special instruction about the Trinity, it clearly delineates the respective responsibilities of the members of the Godhead. The gospel, which is the theme of the letter, is called the gospel of God at the very beginning (1:1) before it is called the gospel of his Son (1:9). God's righteousness must be reckoned with, both by sinner and by saint, for it is the basis of judgment as well as of salvation. The Son of God is held up to view also from the first, because the gospel centers in him (1:3). He is the one through whom the grace of God is mediated to sinful humanity in justification, reconciliation, and redemption. The man Christ Jesus is set over against the first Adam as the one who has succeeded in undoing the ruin wrought by the fall (5:12–21) and who now sustains and preserves all who put their trust in him (5:10). The Spirit's role is to nurture the new creation life of the children of God by providing assurance of their sonship (8:16), release from the bondage of sin (8:2–4), effectiveness in prayer (8:26, 27), experience of the love of God (5:5) and of other joys of spiritual life (14:17), crowned by a confident hope that the bliss of the better state that is to come will be realized (8:23; 15:13). The Spirit also provides the dynamic for Christian service (15:19).

It is not possible, however, to claim for the Epistle a complete coverage of doctrine. Though salvation is central in Romans, its climax in terms of the coming of the Lord is not unfolded to any extent (13:11), though the glorification of the saints is included (8:18, 19, 23). Furthermore, though the word "church" appears five times in chapter 16, it is not a theme for definitive instruction per se. Too much can be made of this seeming incompleteness, however. From chapters 9 to 11 it appears that Paul is deeply concerned about the composition of the church, how Jew and Gentile relate to it in the divine plan. Again, any attempt to deal with the concept of "covenant" is lacking, for the two references (9:4; 11:27) say nothing about the new covenant in Christ (contrast with 2 Cor 3 and Gal 3–4). That there should be no mention of the Lord's Supper may seem strange, especially since baptism is mentioned (6:4). But in Romans Paul is not concerned with ecclesiology, at least not in the sense of giving it specific (as opposed to incidental) treatment. Despite these omissions, it remains true that nowhere else in Scripture is the subject of salvation dealt with in such breadth and thoroughness.

In the so-called practical section of the Epistle (chs. 12–15) the effect of these great truths ("the mercies of God") is set forth in terms of transformed conduct. Christians have a life to live in this world as well as a faith to hold and a fellowship to enjoy. Paul was pastor as well as preacher. In Romans, as in his other letters, his theological teaching was given not merely for the sake of information, but to build up and encourage the people of God.

8. Canonicity

Since ancient authorities regularly include Romans without question, no problem exists in this area. Marcion had it in his list, as did the Canon of Muratori. Although its position in the various lists is not uniform, from the fourth century onward and even in the third (P^{46} of the Chester Beatty Papyri collection), Romans stands at the head of the Pauline Epistles. Since it was not the first to be written, its position may be taken as testimony to a growing awareness in the church of its cardinal importance.

9. Special Problems

Only one problem will be dealt with here, a question that has divided students of Romans through the years. It is the problem of the composition of the church at Rome. Were the believers mainly Gentiles or were Jewish Christians in the majority? At the outset, Paul considers his readers Gentiles (1:13) and this should be decisive unless contrary evidence of the strongest sort can be adduced. Such evidence is sometimes held to be available at the point where the apostle speaks of Abraham as "our forefather" (4:1) and in the passage where he treats the law (presumably Mosaic) and says that his readers know it (7:1ff.). Neither of these constitutes compelling evidence.

As to the former item, it means no more than does the apostle's allusion to "our forefathers" in 1 Corinthians 10:1, an obvious reference to Israel in a letter intended for a Gentile church. Paul was careful to teach the spiritual kinship that existed between the Israel of the past and the people of God in the Christian dispensation. In the case of Abraham, this is spelled out clearly when he calls Abraham "the father of all who believe but have not been circumcised" (Rom 4:11). As to the familiarity of Roman Christians with the Mosaic law, two things need to be observed. One is that Paul feels perfectly free to quote the law and other portions of the Hebrew Scriptures even when writing to Gentile churches—e.g., Galatians and Corinthians. Many Gentile converts to the gospel had previously attended the synagogue as God-fearers and there had heard the OT read and expounded.

The second consideration is that in writing to the Galatian churches about the purpose of the law, Paul affirms that it "was put in charge to lead us to Christ" (Gal 3:24). Though Gentiles were not under the law, they were to profit from it as a guide leading and impelling them to Christ as Savior. With consistency, Paul preserves the same stance in writing to the church at Rome.

There remains, however, the awkward fact that the apostle devotes three chapters (9–11) to the nation of Israel. The failure of this people as a whole to turn to Jesus as the Messiah was a source of deep grief to him. One may well ask, Was it not to inform and comfort a church essentially in the same position as himself that he discusses this matter at such length? Not necessarily. Here one can ask a counter question: Would Paul be at pains to warn Gentile believers in direct terms not to take their position for granted and lapse into a false security (11:13ff.) if he were writing for the benefit of a chiefly Hebrew-Christian group?

Going back to the solid fact that Paul addresses the church as Gentile in character (1:13), we must ask ourselves whether chapters 9 to 11 might have a special purpose as addressed to Gentile believers. These people could certainly learn much from the passage—viz., the obvious advantages God had given the Jew, his own sovereignty in setting them apart as his chosen people, his righteousness in cutting them off so far as national privilege was concerned, and his faithfulness to covenant commitments to be seen when the nation by repentance and faith would be restored. Gentile believers could find much here to warn them and much to lead them to prayer and witness on behalf of Israel. When these considerations are added to the generous use of the OT in the development of the theme of Romans, it becomes clear that Paul is concerned lest Gentile Christianity should lose sight of its heritage in OT history and revelation.

10. Bibliography

BOOKS

Barclay, William. *The Letter to the Romans.* Philadelphia: Westminster Press, 1955.
Barrett, C.K. *A Commentary on the Epistle to the Romans.* New York: Harper and Brothers, 1957.
Barth, Karl. *A Shorter Commentary on Romans.* Richmond: John Knox Press, 1959.
______. *The Epistle to the Romans.* Oxford University Press, E.T. 1933.
Best, Ernest. *The Letter of Paul to the Romans.* Cambridge: Cambridge University Press, 1967.
Black, Matthew. *Romans.* NCB. Greenwood: Attic Press, 1973.
Bruce, F.F. *The Epistle of Paul to the Romans.* TNTC. Grand Rapids: Eerdmans, 1963.
Calvin, John. *Commentary on the Epistle of Paul the Apostle to the Romans.* Grand Rapids: Eerdmans, 1947.
Cranfield, C.E.B. *A Commentary on Romans 12–13.* Edinburgh: Oliver and Boyd, 1965.
Denney, James. *St. Paul's Epistle to the Romans.* EGT (vol. II). London: Hodder and Stoughton, 1917.
Dodd, C.H. *The Epistle of Paul to the Romans.* Moffatt NT Com. New York: Harper and Brothers, 1932.
Field, Frederick. *Notes on the Translation of the New Testament.* Cambridge: Cambridge University Press, 1899.
Gifford, E.H. *The Epistle of St. Paul to the Romans.* London: John Murray, 1886.
Godet, F. *Commentary on St. Paul's Epistle to the Romans.* Edinburgh: T. & T. Clark, 2 vols. E.T. 1883–84.
Haldane, Robert. *Exposition of the Epistle to the Romans.* New York: Robert Carter and Bros., 1860.
Hodge, Charles. *A Commentary on the Epistle to the Romans.* New York: Armstrong, 1896.
Hunter, A.M. *The Epistle to the Romans.* London: SCM Press, 1955.
Käsemann, Ernst. *An die Römer.* Handbuch z. NT. Tübingen: J.C.B. Mohr, 1973.
______. *New Testament Questions Today.* Philadelphia: Fortress Press, E.T. 1969.
Knox, John. *The Epistle to the Romans.* IB vol. 9. New York: Abingdon Press, 1954.
Lagrange, M.J. *Épître aux Romains.* Paris: Gabalda. 6th ed., 1950.
Leenhardt, Franz J. *The Epistle to the Romans.* London: Lutterworth Press, E.T. 1961.
Liddon, H.P. *Explanatory Analysis of St. Paul's Epistle to the Romans.* London: Longman, Green and Co., 1893.
Luther, Martin. *Commentary on the Epistle to the Romans.* Grand Rapids: Zondervan, E.T. 1954.
Meyer, H.A.W. *Critical and Exegetical Handbook to the Epistle to the Romans.* New York: Funk and Wagnalls, E.T. 1884.
Michel, Otto. *Der Brief and die Römer.* Göttingen: Vandenhoeck & Ruprecht, 1955.
Moule, Handley C.G. *Epistle of St. Paul to the Romans.* 5th ed. New York: Armstrong, 1902.
Munck, Johannes. *Christ and Israel; an Interpretation of Romans 9–11.* Philadelphia: Fortress Press, E.T. 1967.
______. *Paul and the Salvation of Mankind.* Richmond: John Knox Press, E.T. 1959.
Murray, John. *The Epistle to the Romans.* NIC. Grand Rapids: Eerdmans, 1968.
Nygren, Anders. *Commentary on Romans.* Philadelphia: Muhlenberg Press, E.T. 1949.
Richardson, Peter. *Israel in the Apostolic Church.* Cambridge: Cambridge University Press, 1969.
Sanday, William and Headlam, Arthur C. *A Critical and Exegetical Commentary on the Epistle to the Romans.* ICC. Edinburgh: T. & T. Clark, 5th ed., 1925.
Schlatter, A. *Gottes Gerechtigkeit.* Stuttgart: Calwer Verlag, 1952.
Shedd, William G.T. *A Critical and Doctrinal Commentary upon the Epistle of St. Paul to the Romans.* New York: Scribner's, 1879.
Stifler, James M. *The Epistle to the Romans.* New York: Revell, 1897.
Thomas, W.H. Griffith. *St. Paul's Epistle to the Romans.* 3 vols. London: The Religious Tract Society, n.d.
Ziesler, J.A. *The Meaning of Righteousness in Paul.* Cambridge: Cambridge University Press, 1972.

ARTICLES

Borg, Marcus. "A New Context for Romans xiii." NTS 19 (Jan. 1973) 205–218.
Bring, Ragnar. "Paul and the Old Testament." ST 25 (1971) 21–60.
Danker, F.W. "Romans V.12: Sin under Law." NTS 14 (April 1968) 424–439.
Dinkler, Erich. "The Historical and Eschatological Israel in Romans Chapters 9–11: A Contribution to the Problem of Predestination and Individual Responsibility." JR 36 (1956) 109–127.
Donfried, Karl Paul. "A Short Note on Romans 16." JBL 89 (1970) 441–449.
Reumann, John. "The Gospel of the Righteousness of God." INT 20 (1966) 432–452.

11. Outline

I. Introduction (1:1–15)
   A. Salutation (1:1–7)
   B. Paul and the Church at Rome (1:8–15)
II. Theme: The Gospel As the Revelation of God's Righteousness (1:16, 17)
III. The Need for Salvation: The Plight of Mankind (1:18–3:20)
   A. In the Pagan World (1:18–32)
   B. Principles of Judgment (2:1–16)
   C. Specific Guilt of the Jew (2:17–3:8)
   D. Summary (3:9–20)
IV. Justification: The Imputation of Righteousness (3:21–5:21)
   A. The Description of Justification (3:21–26)
   B. The Availability of Justification Through Faith Alone (3:27–31)
   C. The Illustration of Justification From the Old Testament (4:1–25)
      1. The case of Abraham (4:1–5)
      2. The case of David (4:6–8)
      3. The promise to Abraham—apart from circumcision (4:9–12)
      4. The promise to Abraham—apart from the law (4:13–17)
      5. Abraham's faith the standard for every believer (4:18–25)
   D. The Benefits of Justification (5:1–11)
   E. The Universal Applicability of Justification (5:12–21)
V. Sanctification: The Impartation of Righteousness (6:1–8:39)
   A. The Believer's Union With Christ in Death and Resurrection Life (6:1–14)
      1. The statement of the fact (6:1–10)
      2. The appeal based on the fact (6:11–14)
   B. Union With Christ Viewed As Enslavement to Righteousness (6:15–23)
   C. Union With Christ Viewed As Deliverance From Law (7:1–6)
   D. The Relationship Between Law and Sin (7:7–25)
   E. The Blessings of Life in the Spirit (8:1–39)
      1. Liberation by the Spirit from the law of sin and death (8:1–11)
      2. Additional ministries of the Spirit (8:12–27)
      3. The security and permanence of the life of the redeemed (8:28–39)
VI. The Problem of Israel: God's Righteousness Vindicated (9:1–11:36)
   A. Paul's Sorrow Over Israel's Condition (9:1–5)
   B. God's Choice of Israel Based on Election, not on Natural Generation or Works of Merit (9:6–13)
   C. God's Freedom to Act in His Own Sovereign Right (9:14–29)

- D. Israel's Failure to Obtain Righteousness Due to Reliance on Works Rather Than Faith (9:30–10:21)
- E. Israel Not Entirely Rejected; There Is a Remnant of Believers (11:1–10)
- F. Israel's Temporary Rejection and the Salvation of Gentiles (11:11–24)
- G. Israel's Future Salvation (11:25–32)
- H. Praise to God for His Wisdom and His Ways (11:33–36)

VII. Our Spiritual Service: The Practice of Righteousness (12:1–15:13)

- A. The Appeal for Dedication of the Believer (12:1, 2)
- B. Varied Ministries in the Church, the Body of Christ (12:3–8)
- C. Principles Governing Christian Conduct (12:9–21)
- D. The Duty of Submission to Civil Authority (13:1–7)
- E. The Comprehensive Obligation of Love (13:8–10)
- F. The Purifying Power of Hope (13:11–14)
- G. Questions of Conscience in Which Christians Differ (14:1–15:13)
  1. Brethren must refrain from judging one another (14:1–13)
  2. Brethren must avoid offending one another (14:14–23)
  3. The unity of the strong and the weak in Christ (15:1–13)

VIII. Conclusion (15:14–16:27)

- A. Paul's Past Labors, Present Program, and Future Plans (15:14–33)
- B. Personal Greetings, Warning Concerning Schismatics, and Doxology (16:1–27)

Text and Exposition

I. Introduction

A. *Salutation*

1:1–7

[1]Paul, a servant of Christ Jesus, called to be an apostle and set apart for the gospel of God—[2]the gospel he promised beforehand through his prophets in the Holy Scriptures [3]regarding his Son, who as to his human nature was a descendant of David, [4]and who through the Spirit of holiness was declared with power to be the Son of God by his resurrection from the dead: Jesus Christ our Lord. [5]Through him and for his name's sake, we received grace and apostleship to call people from among all the Gentiles to the obedience that comes from faith. [6]And you also are among those who are called to belong to Jesus Christ.

[7]To all in Rome who are loved by God and called to be saints:

Grace and peace to you from God our Father and from the Lord Jesus Christ.

1 As in all his letters, Paul uses his Roman name. The shift from "Saul" occurs in the biblical context where he came in contact with a Roman official (Acts 13:6–12). Paul's relation to Christ is primary, so to express his attachment to his Lord he uses the term "servant." Some prefer the rendering "slave," but this could suggest an unwilling attachment. In Israel the citizenry regarded themselves as servants of their king, even though they were free men. Since this word *doulos* is used of Christ in relation to the Father (Phil 2:7), where "slave" would be inappropriate, the translation "servant" is altogether fitting here. By beginning in this fashion, the writer is putting himself on the same plane as his readers. He does not seek to dominate them. If "servant" expresses Paul's commitment to Christ, "apostle" sets forth his authority as Christ's appointee—his right not only to preach the gospel (believers in general could do that) but to found and supervise churches and if necessary discipline them. But this authority carries with it responsibility, for he must give account of the conduct of his mission (1 Cor 4:1–4).

Paul has been "set apart" for the gospel of God. As a Pharisee he had been set apart to a life of strict observance of Jewish law and custom. Now his life work is to further the gospel, the good news that God has for man. It is most natural to locate the time of this setting apart at Paul's conversion and commission (Acts 9:15; Gal 1:12).

2 Before the historic events providing the basis for the gospel message unfolded, God "promised" the good news in the prophetic Scriptures. Promise means more than prophecy, because it commits the Almighty to make good his word, whereas a prophecy could be just an advance announcement of something that would happen. The concept permeates this Epistle (4:13–25; 9:4; 15:8). God did not invent the gospel to cover up disappointment over Israel's failure to receive the Lord Jesus. Nor did Paul create the gospel, which was "his" (2:16; 16:25) in an entirely different sense. The reference to Scripture prepares the reader for rather copious use of the OT, beginning with 1:17.

3,4 The gospel centers in God's Son, who had this status before he took "human nature" and who, in becoming man, became not only an Israelite (9:5) but a son of David (Matt 1:1; Luke 1:32; Acts 13:22, 23; 2 Tim 2:8), a qualification he needed as Messiah (Isa 11:1).

By beginning with the sonship, Paul guards his whole statement from doing service for a heretical adoptionist Christology. The period of Christ's earthly life and ministry was followed by another phase—that which resulted from his resurrection. "With power" may belong with "declared," but may with greater warrant be joined with "Son of God," indicating the new quality of life Jesus had after his resurrection (Phil 3:10; Col 1:29).

"Spirit of holiness" is a unique expression generally regarded as a Semitism conveying the same concept as "Holy Spirit." There may be a suggestion here that Jesus, anointed and sustained by the Holy Spirit in the days of his flesh, was acknowledged by the fact of resurrection to have successfully endured the tests and trials of his earthly life, having been obedient even to death. By resurrection he has become a life-giving spirit (1 Cor 15:45). His rising was indeed "from the dead." But Paul says more, namely, "of the dead," suggesting that Christ is the forerunner of others in this transformation (cf. 1 Cor 15:20, 21).

Another approach emphasizes the balanced construction of *kata pneuma* placed over against *kata sarka*, suggesting that the person of the Son is in view throughout (cf. 1 Tim 3:16). This could yield the conclusion that the human nature of Jesus was so holy, so absolutely free of sin, that death could not hold him (cf. Acts 2:24). On this view, there is no mention of the Holy Spirit.

Appropriately, Jesus Christ is now described as "our Lord." Though the title was fitting during his earthly ministry, it attained more frequent use and greater meaning following the resurrection (Acts 2:36; 10:36). Notable is the fact that in this initial statement about the gospel nothing is said concerning the redeeming work of Christ, which is reserved for later consideration (3:21–26; 4:25; 5:6–21). It was the infinite worth of the Son that made his saving work possible.

5–7 Now the apostle returns to his responsibility to proclaim the good news (cf. v.1). Two problems present themselves here, and they are somewhat related. Who is indicated by "we," and how should one understand the phrase "all the Gentiles"? Clearly, in using "we," Paul cannot be including his readers, because they did not possess apostleship. Could he be referring to other apostles, of whom the Roman believers must have heard? This is a possibility, though it is an unexpected development and is not amplified. The problem is complicated by the mention of the intended sphere of labor—"among all the Gentiles." This wording makes the limitation of the "we" to Paul (as a literary plural) natural, since the Gentiles constituted his special field of labor (cf. 15:16, 18, where the word "obey" corresponds to the word "obedience" in this passage). On the other hand, "all the Gentiles" can equally well be rendered, "all the nations" or "all peoples" (cf. Matt 28:19). This would favor the wider reference of "we" to all the apostles, since Israel would be included as one of the peoples. It is difficult to decide this question.

The desired response to the gospel message is "obedience that comes from faith." (For obedience, see 15:18; 16:26 and for faith, 1:16, 17; 10:17.) Paul's readers were not called, as he was, to apostleship; they were called "to belong to Jesus Christ" and to be "saints," the common term designating believers. This term has almost the same force as the expression Paul uses for himself—"set apart" (v.1). While it does not indicate actual condition (as opposed to position), it carries the aroma of holiness to which every child of God is called (6:19, 22).

At length the apostle is ready to extend a greeting to his readers—"grace and peace." Ordinary letters of that period usually contained a single word meaning "greeting" (as in James 1:1). Paul, however, is partial to terms with theological import. He desires for his readers a continuing and deepening experience of spiritual blessing that only God can bestow. Father and Son are the joint benefactors. While the NT contains several explicit statements of the deity of our Lord, in addition it has many that imply his godhood, as in this case. People may long for grace and peace, but only God can grant such gifts. The rich meaning of these terms will emerge as Paul uses them in the body of his work.

Notes

3,4 A frequently expressed opinion holds that Paul is here making use of a Christological formula not original with him but presumably known to the Roman church. This judgment is based on the absence of mention of the Davidic descent in the Pauline Epistles (2 Tim 2:8 is regarded as deutero-Pauline), the unparalleled use of "Spirit of holiness," and likewise the use of ὁρίζω (*horizō*—a word attributed to Paul in Acts 17:31 but not appearing in his writings), the absence of any reference to the death of Christ, etc. Unquestionably, there are brief creedal statements in Paul (e.g., 1 Cor 8:6), and there may be enough data to warrant the conclusion in this case that the passage is pre-Pauline. However, it is worth noting that in Acts 13:33–35 Paul is credited with emphasizing in close connection with each other three items found in Romans 1:3, 4, namely, the sonship of the Messiah, his relation to David, and his resurrection from the dead.

B. *Paul and the Church at Rome*

1:8–15

8First, I thank my God through Jesus Christ for all of you, because your faith is
being reported all over the world. 9God, whom I serve with my whole heart in
preaching the gospel of his Son, is my witness how constantly I remember you 10in
my prayers at all times; and I pray that now at last by God's will the way may be
opened for me to come to you.

11I long to see you so that I may impart to you some spiritual gift to make you
strong—12that is, that you and I may be mutually encouraged by each other's faith.
13I do not want you to be unaware, brothers, that I planned many times to come
to you (but have been prevented from doing so until now) in order that I might have
a harvest among you, just as I have had among the other Gentiles.

14I am obligated both to Greeks and non-Greeks, both to the wise and the
foolish. 15That is why I am so eager to preach the gospel also to you who are at
Rome.

8–10 The salutation has been unusually long and now, instead of moving to his theme at once the apostle still lingers over introductory matters. Doubtless he felt the need of getting acquainted, so to speak, by unburdening his own heart about what his readers mean to him. It is a shining example of his pastoral concern mingled with gracious sensitivity in dealing with the saints.

First of all, Paul must express his thanks to God for his readers. This was customary, and he omitted an expression of thanks only in writing the Galatians. His thanksgiving for the Roman believers is based on their faith (cf. Eph 1:15, 16; Col 1:3, 4; and 1 Thess 1:3).

Not without reason Paul has become known in Christendom as the apostle of faith. To him, faith was the basic Christian virtue, and he was eager to commend it. Here the commendation is exceedingly generous, even hyperbolic. The whole world has heard of their faith (cf. 1 Thess 1:8). It was Paul's habit to praise believers when this was in order. If rebuke had to be given, it would find a more ready reception if the way was prepared by heartfelt appreciation. Paul's statement about his thanksgiving is followed by a statement concerning his prayer—both intercession for them and a special plea that his hope of coming to be with them, providing it is God's will, shall be realized.

But why should Paul find it necessary to summon God as his witness that he had been faithful in praying for the Roman believers? There are two reasons. For one thing, he had been praying "constantly." The Greek word denotes "repeatedly," meaning that there is no great length of time between prayers. This seems almost too much to expect of a man who did not know most of these people. Furthermore, as he will tell his readers later (15:25), he is about to leave for Jerusalem, and this could give the appearance of his not putting the Roman believers first in his plans. Here, as elsewhere, when Paul calls God as his witness, it is because the thing he is claiming seems difficult to believe.

11–13 The apostle confesses to a great desire to see his readers, not simply that he might come to know them personally, but that he might minister to them. By "spiritual gift" we are probably not to understand something charismatic (the purpose, "to make you strong," is not favorable to such a view), since Paul does not specify any particular gift and avoids the plural (cf. 1 Cor 12:1). Moreover, his own prominence in the contemplated bestowal hardly makes room for the specialized gifts of the Spirit (cf. 1 Cor 1:7). But no sooner has this sentiment been expressed than it is halfway recalled, being revised because it seems to suggest that blessing will flow only one way, from Paul to the church. So he alters his language to make room for mutual encouragement and upbuilding. Faith is basically one, but to see it at work in one individual after another, in various ways, adds zest to Christian fellowship. Paul himself needed this.

As he had prayed constantly for the Romans, so he had planned many times to visit them, but again and again the plan had to be set aside. There is no intimation of Satanic opposition as in the case of the Thessalonian church (1 Thess 2:18), so we are left with the supposition that his work in the East had involved him so completely that he did not see his way clear to break away for the projected trip to Rome.

His hope to have "a harvest" among his readers should not be interpreted narrowly, as though he is hinting that some in their ranks are not genuinely saved. His use of the word "Gentiles" instead of "churches" may be a pointer for us, hinting that "among you" is a reference to the community rather than to the church specifically, and that the fruit he envisions is the reaching of the unsaved. This would not exclude fruit-bearing in the sense of the development of the saints in character (Gal 5:22, 23), but the other meaning seems the more obvious.

14,15 Paul looks forward to his visit, but he also considers it an obligation. On what is this based? He has already laid the groundwork for such a statement by acknowledging that he is Christ's servant (v.1) and that he has been given a charge to take the gospel to all peoples (v.5). In mentioning "Greeks and non-Greeks" he seems to have in mind all non-Jewish members of the human race. He is carrying forward the term he has just used at the end of the previous verse—*Gentiles*.

The Hellenistic writers Philo and Josephus tended to think of the Jews as a third group. Philo in particular had the concept that the Jews, with their special religious advantages, were destined to be the people who, by means of their universal faith, could unify these two diverse groups. In classical and even in early Hellenistic times, the Greeks were prone to include the Latins among the *barbaroi.* But by the time of Paul this was no longer the case. The Romans had become the caretakers of Hellenic civilization. This being so, it is probable that in using *barbaroi* Paul had in mind the territory beyond Rome to the West, where he hoped to go. At the same time, when v.15 is taken into account, it should be granted that he would not have to look beyond Rome itself with its diverse population to find representatives of both groups.

The "wise" are not being equated with the Greeks, for this would mean that non-Greeks are being dubbed "foolish," which would be unwarranted. The wise are perishing in the midst of their worldly wisdom (1 Cor 1:18–21), and the foolish in their abject simplicity. Both need the gospel.

How heartwarming is the apostle's attitude toward his obligation! Instead of considering it a burden he must bear, a duty he must carry out, he is "eager" to fulfill it. If one has the finest intellectual and formal preparation for preaching but is lacking in zeal, he cannot hope for much success. The call to preach and the need for the message together constitute the preacher's compelling incentive to proclaim the message of salvation.

Notes

14 When the word rendered "non-Greeks" is transliterated, it yields "barbarians" (*βάρβαροι, barbaroi*). As one can see, the first two syllables are the same, which points to the original force of this word as indicating a stammerer. Later it came to mean non-Greeks, those who did not use the Greek language. A further development was its application to uncivilized people, taking on the meaning of savage, which is the usual connotation of the word "barbarian" todav

II. Theme: The Gospel As the Revelation of the Righteousness of God

1:16,17

[16]I am not ashamed of the gospel, because it is the power of God for the salvation of everyone who believes: first for the Jew, then for the Gentile. [17]For in the gospel a righteousness from God is revealed, a righteousness that is by faith from first to last, just as it is written: "The righteous will live by faith."

16 Having confessed his fervent desire to preach the gospel at Rome, Paul goes on to give a reason for his zeal. He has no sense of reserve about his mission. He does not in any way consider his task unworthy or one that will prove to be illusory. He is ready to challenge the philosophies and religions in Rome that vie for the attention of men, because he knows on the basis of his experience in the East that God's power at work in the proclamation of the good news is able to transform lives. The Greek word for "power" (*dynamis*) has sometimes elicited the reaction that the gospel is dynamite! This is quite out of place, for the emphasis is not on blowing false religions out of the way or blasting a trail of success for the true faith or even on delivering people from habits they have been unable to shake off. Paul himself goes on to explain in what sense "power" is to be understood. The stress falls not on its mode of operation but on its intrinsic efficacy. It offers something not to be found anywhere else—a righteousness from God. More about that directly.

Closer at hand is the linkage between power and salvation. Judaism was prone to think of the law as power, but this is not affirmed in Scripture. As for salvation, the OT is clear in its teaching that whether it is conceived of physically as deliverance (Exod 14:13) or spiritually (Ps 51:12), it comes from the Lord. This is maintained in the NT as well, and is affirmed in Paul's statement that the gospel is "the power of God" for salvation. So if the apostle permits himself to say that if he himself saves anyone (1 Cor 9:22), it is only in the sense that he is Christ's representative who is able to point out the way to his fellowmen.

Salvation is a broad concept. It includes the forgiveness of sins, but involves much more, because its basic meaning is soundness or wholeness. It promises the restoration of all that sin has marred or destroyed. It is the general term that unites in itself the particular aspects of truth suggested by justification, reconciliation, sanctification, and redemption. But its efficacy depends on man's willingness to receive the message. "Everyone who believes" will benefit equally. This sweeping declaration ties in with the previous statement (concerning Greeks and non-Greeks) and now includes both the Jew and the Gentile. The Jew receives "first" consideration. This does not mean that every Jew must be evangelized before the gospel can be presented to Gentiles. But it does mean that God, after having dealt in a special way with the Jew in OT days and having followed this by sending his Son to the lost sheep of the house of Israel, could not pass by this people. To them was given the first opportunity to receive the Lord Jesus, both during his ministry (John 1:11) and in the Christian era (Acts 1:8; 3:26). Paul himself followed this pattern (Acts 13:45, 46: 28:25, 28). It is a case of historical priority, not essential priority, for the Jew who is first to hear the gospel is also the first to be judged for his sins (2:9).

17 Next, the apostle passes to an explanation of his statement that the gospel means salvation for those who receive it by faith. The reason given is that this salvation discloses "a righteousness from God." Paul is dependent here on the OT (Isa 46:12, 13, KJV, NASB; 61:10). "In the Hebrew tradition, early and late, God's righteousness is the way he acts, and notably the way he acts in maintaining the covenant" (Ziesler, p. 186). Such an idea was quite foreign to Greek thought. Clearly, the character of God is involved in the sense that what he does and provides must be in keeping with his nature (cf. 3:26). But just as clearly, the expression must go beyond this to include the activity of God. The gospel would not be the good news if it simply disclosed the righteousness of God. Such a message would scarcely demand faith. In view of man's sinful state, it could well create fear. But if salvation as God provides it and offers it is fully in keeping with his righteous character, then it has integrity. If it satisfies God, man can be content with it.

Returning to the idea of activity, we should look at Paul's statement in Philippians 3:9, where he contrasts his pre-Christian state, in which he had a righteousness based on observance of the law, with his present situation, in which he rests on a righteousness which is of (from) God, based on faith. In summary, God's righteousness in this context, while it has an implied reference to his character, stresses divine provision. What this entails will be unfolded in due course. Paul had already taught that Christ was the medium for the bringing of righteousness from God to sinful man (1 Cor 1:30; 2 Cor 5:21).

Somewhat baffling is the twofold reference to faith—lit. "from faith to faith" (Gr., *ek pisteōs eis pistin*); cf. NIV "by faith from first to last." We should try to determine first of all whether these two prepositional phrases are to be joined to the verb "revealed," or whether they should be taken with God's righteousness as indicating how that righteousness is to be received. Position in the sentence may be said to favor the former alternative, but the resultant sense is obscure. Furthermore, when Paul restates the theme of his letter (3:21, 22) in such a way as to take account of the intervening material, he mentions God's righteousness as manifested (answering to "revealed" in 1:17), then repeats the word "righteousness" and characterizes it as a righteousness through faith (*dia pisteōs*) and for all who believe. These phrases are probably to be understood as a recapitulation of what has been said in 1:17.

Assuming, then, that we are to connect the statement about faith with God's righteousness, we must still inquire into the distinctives of the two phrases involving faith. Among the numerous suggestions are these: from the faith of the preacher to the faith of the hearer; from OT faith to NT faith (based on the quotation immediately following); entirely from faith; and from faithfulness (God's) to faith (man's), as Barth interprets it (*The Epistle to the Romans,* 1933). These various renderings understand "from" as a point of departure. This would be entirely legitimate if the preposition were *apo,* but it is *ek,* which Paul uses repeatedly with faith when indicating the basis on which God grants justification (3:26; 5:1; Gal 2:16) or righteousness (9:30; 10:6), a fact that incidentally shows how readily the term "righteousness" can take on the force of "justification." The really troublesome element here is the second phrase—"for faith." Perhaps what it conveys is the necessity of issuing a reminder to the believer that justifying faith is only the beginning of Christian life. The same attitude must govern him in his continuing experience as a child of God.

It remains to treat the quotation from another standpoint—the order of the words. Is it "The righteous shall live by faith" or "The one who is just by virtue of faith shall live"? Since the apostle quotes the same passage in Galatians 3:11 to show that one is not justified by law but rather by faith, it is probable that he intends the reference in the same way here. Since the quotation is used in Romans at the very beginning, where he confronts the problem of man's getting right with God, the wording that fits most closely the movement of thought should be chosen. At this point Paul is not concerned with how the justified man lives, but how the sinner can be considered just (righteous) in the sight of God. Righteousness as a matter of ethical conduct is reserved for later treatment (chs. 6–8). Ethical righteousness depends on right relation to God, so the latter merits priority of treatment.

It could be argued, of course, that Paul ought to have changed the order of the words to bring this out, and since he did not, the wording of the quotation, "The righteous will live by faith," should be retained. Apparently he was not desirous of disturbing the form of a familiar quotation. We know that he would endorse the truth that the Christian is not only justified by faith but is also expected to live by faith in order to please God. Such an emphasis has its place, but only when the initial problem of the sinner has been met. The liberty involved in using a quotation in a way somewhat different from its original setting is necessitated by the progress of revelation. It was practiced also in Judaism before Paul's time, as we know from the Dead Sea Scrolls. The Qumran group applied Habakkuk 2:4 to their own situation by an interpretative elaboration. "But the righteous through his faithfulness shall live. This refers to all in Jewry who carry out the Law" (*Commentary on the Book of Habakkuk*). Here the passage is made to do service in behalf of the special type of piety, grounded in the study of the Torah, which distinguished the Qumran community.

Notes

17 Of the various efforts to handle the two phrases, Barth's is the most intriguing. It has an element of plausibility in that πίστις (*pistis*) can mean "faithfulness" as well as "faith," and this could be the sense of the LXX rendering of Habakkuk 2:4, the passage from which Paul proceeds to quote. The LXX reading can be translated, "The just shall live by my faithfulness" or "The just shall live by faith in me" (cf. the construction in Rom 3:26). There is no doubt that the Hebrew אמונה (*'emunāh*) means "faithfulness," but the Hebrew text reads "his faithfulness" and refers this to the just man, not to God. It is likely that Paul is reaching beyond faithfulness to what underlies it, namely, faith. He uses *pistis* in Romans 3:3 when writing of God's faithfulness, but when he states his theme, the argument requires him to insist on the more fundamental concept of faith. The very fact that in the previous verse he has posited faith (in its verbal form) as the necessary condition for receiving salvation creates a presumption that faith in v.17 will have the same connotation.

III. The Need for Salvation: The Plight of Mankind (1:18–3:20)

Instead of plunging at once into an exposition of the gospel, Paul launches into a lengthy exposure of the sinfulness of man. This is sound procedure, for until men are persuaded of their lost condition they are not likely to be concerned about deliverance. So Paul undertakes to demonstrate in the human situation a grievous lack of the righteousness God requires. "Within the action of the divine righteousness there is a place for deliverance and for condemnation, a place for salvation and for punishment" (David Hill, *Greek Words and Hebrew Meanings* [Cambridge: Cambridge University Press, 1967], p. 90).

A. *In the Pagan World*

1:18–32

18The wrath of God is being revealed from heaven against all the godlessness
and wickedness of men who suppress the truth by their wickedness, 19since what
may be known about God is plain to them, because God has made it plain to them.
20For since the creation of the world God's invisible qualities—his eternal power
and divine nature—have been clearly seen, being understood from what has been
made, so that men are without excuse.

21For although they knew God, they neither glorified him as God nor gave thanks
to him, but their thinking became futile and their foolish hearts were darkened.
22Although they claimed to be wise, they became fools 23and exchanged the glory
of the immortal God for images made to look like mortal man and birds and animals
and reptiles.

24Therefore God gave them over in the sinful desires of their hearts to sexual
impurity for the degrading of their bodies with one another. 25They exchanged the
truth of God for a lie, and worshiped and served created things rather than the
Creator—who is forever praised. Amen.

26Because of this, God gave them over to shameful lusts. Even their women
exchanged natural relations for unnatural ones. 27In the same way the men also
abandoned natural relations with women and were inflamed with lust for one
another. Men committed indecent acts with other men, and received in themselves
the due penalty for their perversion.

> [28]Furthermore, since they did not think it worthwhile to retain the knowledge of God, he gave them over to a depraved mind, to do what ought not to be done. [29]They have become filled with every kind of wickedness, evil, greed and depravity. They are full of envy, murder, strife, deceit and malice. They are gossips, [30]slanderers, God-haters, insolent, arrogant and boastful; they invent ways of doing evil; they disobey their parents; [31]they are senseless, faithless, heartless, ruthless. [32]Although they know God's righteous decree that those who do such things deserve death, they not only continue to do these very things, but also approve of those who practice them.

18 At the outset it is important to observe the correlation between righteousness and wrath. Both are represented as *being* revealed. As previously observed, full salvation in terms of divine righteousness awaits the future, being eschatological in nature; but it also belongs to the present and is appropriated by faith. Similarly, wrath is an even more obviously eschatological concept, yet it is viewed here as parallel to the manifestation of righteousness, belonging therefore to the present age. It is "being revealed." This means that the unfolding of history involves a disclosure of the wrath of God against sin, seen in the terrible corruption and perversion of human life. This does not mean that the price of sin is to be reckoned only in terms of the present operation of wrath, for there is a day of judgment awaiting the sinner (2:5). But the divine verdict is already in some measure anticipated. "We think that Paul regards the monstrous degradation of pagan populations, which he is about to describe, not as a purely natural consequence of their sin, but as a solemn intervention of God's justice in the history of mankind, an intervention which he designates by the term *paradidonai—to give over*" (Godet, in loc.).

"God's wrath is being revealed from heaven." The two factors, the designation of the wrath as God's and the addition of the words "from heaven" make it difficult to accept the view of C.H. Dodd (pp. 20–24). He observes that Paul never uses the verb *be angry* with God as its subject. Further, in the Pauline corpus "the wrath of God" appears elsewhere only in Ephesians 5:6 and Colossians 3:6. Otherwise we encounter "wrath" or "the wrath," which appear intended to describe "an inevitable process of cause and effect in a moral universe" (p. 23). But it is precarious to make much of the fact that God is not linked with wrath in every Pauline reference. The context usually makes it clear when the divine wrath is intended. In the passage before us the words "from heaven" are decisive. As G. Dalman points out, the phrase as used in the Gospels means *from God* (*The Words of Jesus* [Edinburgh: T. & T. Clark, 1909], p. 219). Furthermore, since there is a wrath to come that will inevitably involve God, there is no reason why he should not involve himself in manifesting his wrath in the present. Human objection to the idea of the wrath of God is often molded, sometimes unconsciously, by human experience of anger as passion or desire for revenge. But this is only a human display of wrath, and one that is corrupted. God's wrath is not temperamental (cf. 13:4, 5, where its judicial character is evident).

The object of the divine wrath is twofold—"all the godlessness and wickedness of men." Paul explicates the first term in vv.19–27 and the second in vv.28–32. "Godlessness" means a lack of reverence, an impiety that arrays man against God, not simply in terms of neglect but also of rebellion. "Wickedness" means injustice, relating to the vitiating of man's conduct toward his fellows. The two together serve to denote the failure of mankind in terms of the requirements of the two tables of the Decalogue. No distinction is made here between Jews and Gentiles, since "men" is broad enough to include the human race. These are the very areas in which the prophets found fault with Israel. But as the thought unfolds, the culprit appears much more sharply in terms of Gentiles than of Jews.

They "suppress the truth by their wickedness." R.C.H. Lenski observes, "Whenever the truth starts to exert itself and makes them feel uneasy in their moral nature, they hold it down, suppress it. Some drown its voice by rushing into their immoralities; others strangle the disturbing voice by argument and by denial" (*The Interpretation of St. Paul's Epistle to the Romans* [Columbus: Wartburg Press, 1945]). Presumably, the truth referred to here is basically the truth about God (cf. v.25). Suppression of the truth implies knowledge of the truth, and what this involves is explained in the sequel.

19,20 The creation bears clear witness to its Maker, and the evidence is "plain to them." Here Paul enters upon a discussion of what is usually designated natural revelation in distinction from the special revelation that comes through the Scriptures. Four characteristics are noted. First, it is a clear testimony set before the eyes of men, as the word "plain" implies. Second, from the use of "understood," the revelation does not stop with perception, but is expected to include reflection, the drawing of a conclusion about the Creator. Third, it is a constant testimony, maintained "since the creation of the world" (cf. Acts 14:17). Fourth, it is a limited testimony in that it reflects God in certain aspects only—namely, "his eternal power and divine nature." One has to look elsewhere for the disclosure of his love and grace—i.e., to Scripture and especially to the revelation of God in his Son (John 1:14). Natural revelation is sufficient to make man responsible, but is not by itself sufficient to accomplish his salvation. The element of power is common to the two spheres of nature (v.20) and grace (v.16). Acquaintance with it in the former area should prepare men to expect it in the latter. But they have failed and are left without excuse. It is characteristic of man in his sinful state that he knows much more truth than he translates into fitting response.

21–23 Despite the knowledge of God conveyed to them through the creation, men failed to act on it. They "neither glorified him as God nor gave thanks to him." Liddon affirms that these two obligations "embrace the whole cycle of the soul's duty towards God" (in loc.). Man is a religious being, and if he refuses to let God have the place of preeminence that is rightfully his, then he will put something or someone in God's place.

"Their thinking became futile." The suggestion that emerges from this statement is that mythology and idolatry grew out of man's insistent need to recognize some power in the universe greater than himself, coupled with his refusal to give God the place of supremacy. He had to make a substitution. It is highly suggestive that the verb "to become futile" yields a noun form that was used for idols (Acts 14:15). Idols are unreal and unprofitable, and their service can only lead to futility and further estrangement from the true and living God. Pertinent is Daniel's rebuke of Belshazzar (Dan 5:23).

This abandonment of God in favor of inferior objects of worship is traced in a descending scale. "Mortal man" is the first substitution. The Creator is forsaken in preference for the creature. Scripture shows us the deification of man in the case of Nebuchadnezzar. The colossus that appeared in his dream was interpreted by Daniel as pointing to the king himself so far as the head of gold was concerned (Dan 2:38). Wasting no time, the monarch erected an immense statue of gold and compelled his subjects to prostrate themselves before it (Dan 3:1). In Paul's day the cult of Caesar had spread throughout the empire. Before long, Caesar and Christ would be competing for the homage of society. In modern times the western world has outgrown crass idolatry, but humanism has subtly injected the worship of man without the trappings. God is quietly ruled out and man is placed on the throne.

The next stage is worship of the animal kingdom. Verse 23 owes its wording largely to Psalm 106:20. The immediate context refers to the sin of Israel in making a calf at Horeb and bowing down to this molten image. Paul makes one change in the text of the psalm, which reads: "And they changed their glory for the likeness of an ox that eats grass." To the psalmist God is the glory of the Israelites. Paul seems to make the glory of God his spirituality, in contrast to any attempt to express his excellence in physical terms. God's majesty may well be included here. Whereas Paul is dealing with a characteristic sin of paganism, he resorts to OT history for an illustration. God did not and could not condone idolatry in the people he had chosen. His judgment fell heavily when there was no repentance, even to the point of desolation and deportation from the land he had given Israel.

According to the prophetic word, the worship of man and beast will merge during the tribulation period. We read of the beast who will control the world, and we encounter this significant statement; "If anyone has insight, let him calculate the number of the beast, for it is man's number" (Rev 13:18).

24,25 The opening word "therefore" carries the reader all the way back to the mention of the revelation of God's wrath, taking in also what lies between. The false worship just pictured is God's judgment for abandoning the true worship. Man's religion in its various cultic forms is a species of punishment for spurning the revelation God has given of himself in nature.

This should dispose of the naive notion that religion as such is necessarily a beneficial thing for mankind. On the contrary, it is in many cases a means of keeping people so occupied that they never arrive at a confrontation with the true God.

"God gave them over" becomes a refrain (vv.24, 26, 28). For a nuance of the term, see 1 Corinthians 5:5; 1 Timothy 1:20. The same expression is used of God's judgment on Israel for idolatry (Acts 7:42). In our passage the reference is principally to Gentiles (Israel was largely purged of this sin by means of the captivity in Babylon). We are not told how this giving over was implemented, but most likely we are to think of it in negative terms—i.e., that God simply took his hands off and let willful rejection of himself produce its ugly results in human life. There is no suggestion here of direct intervention such as was granted to Israel by sending prophets to expostulate with God's people concerning their unfaithfulness.

At this point a problem must be faced. How is it that we have a reference to sexual immorality in v.24 and again in vv.26, 27? Is this a case of repetition? No, the immorality lies in different areas. The earlier reference is to cultic prostitution, the latter to immoral relations in ordinary life. In reading the OT it is sometimes difficult to determine which type is intended. Fertility cults made use of prostitutes, based on a definite rationale. "This religion was predicated upon the belief that the processes of nature were controlled by the relations between gods and goddesses. Projecting their understanding of their own sexual activities, the worshipers of these deities, through the use of imitative magic, engaged in sexual intercourse with devotees of the shrine, in the belief that this would encourage the gods and goddesses to do likewise. Only by sexual relations among the deities could man's desire for increase in herds and fields, as well as in his own family, be realized" (O.J. Baab, *IDB* 3:932–933). How true is the observation that "their foolish hearts were darkened." Paul was no stranger to the matter he discusses here. Writing from Corinth, where the temple of Aphrodite housed hundreds of cult prostitutes, he must have been keenly aware of this scourge that affected the moral life of the city so adversely.

"They exchanged the truth of God for a lie." Many versions are content to render it thus, but the definite article precedes "lie" and probably should be brought out in the translation. This is *the* lie above all others—the contention that something or someone is to be venerated in place of the true God. Bengel in his *Gnomon* makes the laconic observation that this is "the price of mythology." According to the prophetic word, history will repeat itself in that when the man of lawlessness is revealed and demands to be worshiped, men will follow him and reap ruin because they have refused the truth and have believed the lie (2 Thess 2:3–12). There, too, God gives them over to strong delusion (v.11).

In the passage we are considering, the indictment is that by a wretched exchange men came to worship and serve "created things rather than the Creator." An alternative translation is possible: "more than" in place of "rather than." But the flow of the argument demands the latter. It is not that men grant God a relative honor in their devotion, but none at all. They have wholly rid themselves of him by substituting other objects in his place. This should be sufficient to banish the notion that in the practice of idolatry men simply use the idol as a means of worshiping God (cf. Hos 14:3). Contemplating this abysmal betrayal, the apostle cannot resist an outburst to counteract it. The Creator "is forever praised." God's glory remains, even though unacknowledged by many of his creatures.

26,27 For the second time the sad refrain is sounded—"God gave them over"—this time to immorality, with emphasis on perversion in sexual relations. The sequence Paul follows—idolatry, then immorality—raises a question as to the possibility that a connection between the two is being suggested. What is that connection? Sanday and Headlam make a helpful suggestion. "The lawless fancies of men invented their own divinities. Such gods as these left them free to follow their own unbridled passions" (in loc.). Men went so far as to project their own license onto their gods, as a perusal of the Homeric poems readily reveals. Gifford observes, "The sin against God's nature entails as its penalty sin against man's own nature" (in loc.). Paul's use of "exchanged" is suggestive. The first exchange, that of the truth for the lie, is followed by another—the upsetting of the normal course of nature in sexual relations. Instead of using the ordinary terms for men and women, Paul substitutes "males" and "females." The irony is that this sort of bestiality finds no counterpart in the animal kingdom. Perversion is the unique contrivance of the human species. In bringing this discussion to a close, the apostle uses two expressions, "received" and "due penalty," which in the original involve the idea of recompense, the punishment being in keeping with the offense. These terms serve to underscore the principle of *lex talionis* contained in the words "Because of this, God gave them over. . . ." Sexual deviation contains in itself a recompense, a punishment for the abandonment of God and his ways. This need not demand the conclusion that every homosexual follows the practice in deliberate rebellion against God's prescribed order. What is true historically and theologically is in measure true, however, experientially. The "gay" facade is a thin veil for deep-seated frustration. The folly of homosexuality is proclaimed in its inability to reproduce the human species in keeping with the divine commandment (Gen 1:28). To sum up, what men do with God has much to do with their character and life style. Godet put it well when he said, "A law broods over human existence, a law which is at the same time a divine act: Such as thou makest thy God, such wilt thou make thyself" (in loc.). Throughout the passage man is represented as active—seeing, thinking, doing. He is not represented as victimized, as taken captive against his will, as the dupe of evil influences from outside himself. "Sin comes from the mind, which perverts the judgment. The effect of retribution is to abandon the mind to that depravity" (Henri Maurier, *The Other Covenant* [New York: Newman Press, 1968], p. 185).

28–32 Here the second key word of v.18 ("wickedness" or "injustice") reappears, indicating that this section is to be given over almost totally to a picture of the havoc wrought in human relations because of suppressing the knowledge of God. In the original there is a word play—men disapproved of retaining God in their knowledge, so God in turn gave them over to a "depraved" (lit. "disapproved") mind, which led them in turn to commit all kinds of sin. It is God's function to judge, but men have usurped that prerogative in order to sit in judgment on him and dismiss him from their lives. Sometimes this has taken the form of open and public expression, as in the French and Bolshevik revolutions. The prior emphasis on the mind is in accord with our Lord's appraisal, who traced the wellspring of sinful acts to the inner life rather than to environmental factors (Mark 7:20–23). The depraved mind is explained in terms of what it approves and plans—"to do what ought not to be done," that is, what is "offensive to man even according to the popular moral sense of the Gentiles, i.e., what even natural human judgment regards as vicious and wrong" (H. Schlier, TDNT 3:440).

Scholars have found it difficult to detect any satisfactory classification in the long list of offenses included here, which only confirms the fact that sin is irrational in itself and disorderly in its effects. It can be pointed out, however, that the initial group contains broad, generic descriptions of sin. The first of these, "wickedness" (*adikia*), by its derivation, is the antithesis of righteousness, denoting the absence of what is just. The term "iniquity" expresses it rather well. It necessitates the creation of laws to counteract its disruptiveness, lest society itself be rendered impossible. The next term, "evil," denotes what is evil not in the sense of calamity, but with full ethical overtones, signifying what is sinister and vile. This is the term used when the devil is called "the evil one." The third word, "greed," indicates the relentless urge to acquire more (cf. Col 3:5). "Depravity" is an attempt to render *kakia,* a term which indicates a condition of moral evil, emphasizing its internal and resident character or as Trench describes it, "the evil habit of mind." It is related to the word translated "malice" in our text, but the latter goes further, denoting malignity, a mind-set that attributes evil motives to others without provocation. Among the final twelve descriptions, "God-haters" stands out, since it alone is related directly to an attitude toward the Almighty. But it is not isolated, not introduced without reason. The hatred that vents itself on God readily finds objects of its displeasure among his creatures. When man comes to the place of worshiping himself, overweening and insolent pride is the inevitable attitude assumed toward his fellows. Some of the descriptions Paul uses here are not found again in his writings or elsewhere in the NT, but four of them occur in 2 Timothy 3:2, 3 in predictions of the state of society in the last days.

The final item in the indictment is climactic (v.32). It is prefaced by the reminder that men have not lacked a sufficient knowledge of God's "righteous decree" or requirement (for this word see 2:26; 8:4). If the knowledge of his power and deity (v.20) was sufficient to obligate men to worship God with gratitude for his benefits, the knowledge of his righteousness, innate in their very humanity, was sufficient to remind them that the price of disobedience would be death. Yet men were not deterred from their sinful ways by this realization. In fact, they were guilty of the crowning offense of applauding those who practiced wickedness in its various manifestations. Instead of repenting of their own misdeeds and seeking to deter others, they promoted wrongdoing by encouraging it in their fellows, allying themselves with wanton sinners in defiant revolt against a righteous God.

Some questions need to be raised about vv.18–32. Since the use of the past tense predominates in this section, are we to conclude that Paul has in view some epoch in the past when sin manifested itself with special intensity? This is unlikely, for he moves now and again to the present tense also. The conclusion is that the description fits his own time as well as earlier ages. If this were not so, the passage could scarcely deserve a place in the development of the theme.

Another problem is raised by the sweeping nature of the charge made in this portion of the letter. Are we to think Paul is accusing every pagan of this total list of offenses? Such a conclusion is unwarranted. Sinful man is capable of committing all of them, but not every individual is necessarily guilty of every one.

A further query concerns the originality of the presentation. Was the apostle dependent on earlier sources? Somewhat the same ground is covered in the intertestamental work entitled *Wisdom,* a product of Hellenistic Judaism. It reproaches the nations for their idols and, like Paul, notes a connection between idolatry and fornication (14:12). But the development of the thought is not fully the same, for a resort to idolatry is related to men's ignorance of God (13:1), whereas Paul emphasizes a limited knowledge of God gleaned from his works. In another Jewish source the forsaking of the Lord by the Gentiles is noted as resulting in sexual perversion.

> Sun and moon and stars change not their order; so do ye also change not the law of God in the disorderliness of your doings. The Gentiles went astray, and forsook the Lord, and changed their order, and obeyed stocks and stones, spirits of deceit. But ye shall not be so, my children, recognizing in the firmament, in the earth, and in the sea, and in all created things, the Lord who made all things, that ye become not as Sodom, which changed the order of nature (*Testament of Napthali* 3:2–4).

Undoubtedly, the synagogues of the Dispersion made use of material of this kind in trying to proselytize Gentiles.

B. *Principles of Judgment*

2:1–16

1You, therefore, have no excuse, you who pass judgment on someone else, for
at whatever point you judge the other, you are condemning yourself, because you
who pass judgment do the same things. 2Now we know that God's judgment
against those who do such things is based on truth. 3So when you, a mere man,
pass judgment on them and yet do the same things, do you think you will escape
God's judgment? 4Or do you show contempt for the riches of his kindness, tolerance and patience, not realizing that God's kindness should lead you to repentance?

5But because of your stubbornness and your unrepentant heart, you are storing
up wrath against yourself for the day of God's wrath, when his righteous judgment
will be revealed. 6God "will give to each person according to what he has done."
7To those who by persistence in doing good seek glory, honor and immortality, he
will give eternal life. 8But for those who are self-seeking and who reject the truth
and follow evil, there will be wrath and anger. 9There will be trouble and distress
for every human being who does evil: first for the Jew, then for the Gentile; 10but

glory, honor and peace for everyone who does good: first for the Jew, then for the
Gentile. 11 For God does not show favoritism.

12 All who sin apart from the law will also perish apart from the law, and all who
sin under the law will be judged by the law. 13 For it is not those who hear the law
who are righteous in God's sight, but it is those who obey the law who will be
declared righteous. 14 (Indeed, when Gentiles, who do not have the law, do by
nature things required by the law, they are a law for themselves, even though they
do not have the law, 15 since they show that the requirements of the law are written
on their hearts, their consciences also bearing witness, and their thoughts now
accusing, now even defending them.) 16 This will take place on the day when God
will judge men's secrets through Jesus Christ, as my gospel declares.

In turning to this section, one can recognize considerable resemblance to 1:18–32. Human inadequacy in the light of divine standards continues to characterize the discussion (cf. 2:1, "no excuse," with 1:20, "without excuse"). The indictment continues to be stated first in broad terms, with no indication whether the people in view are Jews or Gentiles (cf. 1:18; 2:1), but as the picture unfolds, the Jew takes shape before our eyes just as the Gentile has come into focus in the previous section. Likewise, in both portions, general terms for sin are followed by very specific accusations (cf. 1:18 with 1:23, 26–32 and 2:1–16 with 2:17–29).

1–4 A stylistic change occurs here as the apostle enters into dialogue with an imagined interlocutor who has absorbed what was said up to this point and shows by his attitude that he is in hearty agreement with the exposure of Gentile wickedness. That Paul had experienced such encounters in his missionary preaching is hardly open to doubt. We have an echo here of just such occasions.

The implication in the opening verse is that a Jewish auditor, heartily endorsing the verdict rendered concerning the Gentiles, fails to realize his own plight. True judgment rests on the ability to discern the facts in a given case. If one is able to see the sin and hopelessness of the Gentile, he should logically be able to see himself as being in the same predicament. But he is so taken up with the faults of others that he does not consider his own failures (cf. Matt 7:2, 3). The charge that he who passes judgment does the same things he sees in others is enlarged in 2:17–24. There is a real sting in the allegation "you . . . do the same things," for the word "do" is the term used in 1:32 for the practices of the benighted Gentile. Paul repeats it in v.2. As he moves to state the first of the principles of divine judgment, he carries the observer with him. Surely this man will agree ("we know") that when God pronounces judgment on those who make a practice of indulging in sin, his judgment is based on truth. This has no reference to the truth of the gospel, but simply means that the judgment is reached on the basis of reality, on the facts of the case, not on the basis of appearances or of a man's pretensions. "Do you think you will escape God's judgment?" Two words are emphatic here, "think" and "you." Paul is reading the inmost thoughts of the Jew, whom he understands thoroughly from his own pre-Christian experience. That Judaism could be guilty of such complacency is clear from a passage in *Wisdom* that follows immediately on the portion already noted about pagan idolatry and immorality. "But thou, our God, art gracious and true, longsuffering, and in mercy ordering all things. For even if we sin, we are thine, knowing thy dominion; but we shall not sin, knowing that we have been accounted thine: for to be acquainted with thee is perfect righteousness" (15:1–3).

Paul carries the probing deeper still (v.4), suggesting that in addition to self-righteousness with its accompanying false security there is an ignoring and despising of the fact that God, to be true to himself, must bring sin into judgment. There is even a scornful attitude toward God's forbearance with his people Israel, as though that forbearance were but a confirmation of their security, if not a sign of weakness on God's part. "Because sentence against an evil deed is not executed speedily, the heart of the sons of men is fully set to do evil" (Eccl 8:11). God's kindness toward Israel, noted here, is noted again at a later point in Romans (11:22).

In this passage "tolerance" and "patience" seem to be explanatory of "kindness," which is repeated as the governing thought. The word rendered "tolerance" has the idea of self-restraint. In classical Greek it is used of a temporary truce. "Patience" is literally "longspiritedness." The intent of the kindness is to give opportunity for repentance (cf. 2 Peter 3:15), a term that occurs only here in Romans, though it must have been often on Paul's lips in preaching (Acts 20:21). In this Epistle he places greater emphasis on faith.

5–11 The apostle speaks plainly in order to startle the Jew out of his lethargy of self-deception. What the nation is doing by its stubbornness and impenitence is to invite retribution, which is slowly but surely building up a reservoir of divine wrath that will be crushing when it breaks over the guilty in the day of reckoning. Then the judgment will be revealed, patent to all, in contrast to the indirect working of God's wrath in the present scene, as depicted in chapter 1. At that time a second principle of divine judgment will become apparent, emphasizing performance: "to each person according to what he has done," literally, "according to his works." Profession does not take the place of production. This is very close in sense to the first principle. In view of the comprehensiveness of the passage as a whole, it will hardly do to explain this day of wrath as the destruction of Jerusalem in A.D. 70. The explicit statement that God "will give to each person according to what he has done" points to the final reckoning. National judgment fits into a temporal scheme, but personal judgment belongs to the frontier of the ages to come. The use of the word "day" is decisive enough to settle the issue.

In amplifying this second principle of judgment Paul makes room for only two broad classes—those who persist in doing good and those who follow an evil course (vv.7, 8, 9, 10). The first group, pictured as seeking glory, honor, and immortality, are promised eternal life. Because of the further statement of v.10 that some are to receive glory, honor, and peace, it is tempting to suppose that in v.7 the corresponding three items stated there are the things to be received and that the seeking has eternal life as its object, but this is not permitted by the construction in the Greek. What can the apostle mean by his breathtaking assertion about attaining eternal life? At the very least, it is safe to say that he is not contradicting what he says later about the impossibility of having salvation by means of the works of the law (3:20). Far from teaching a system of salvation by works, the statement of v.7, rightly understood, teaches the opposite. "The reward of eternal life . . . is promised to those who do not regard their good works as an end in themselves, but see them as marks not of human achievement but of hope in God. Their trust is not in their good works, but in God, the only source of glory, honour, and incorruption" (Barrett, in loc.). Paul is simply portraying the motivation and the tenor of the life that will culminate in eternal fellowship with God. As applied to the "seeker" (cf. Acts 17:27), the principle commits God to honor the moral aim and provide the means for making a decision, as we see in the case of the Ethiopian eunuch (Acts 8) and Cornelius (Acts 10). Both were seekers making use of the light they had. The good works the believer performs do not bring him salvation, but they attest the salvation he has received by faith (6:22), and therefore have an essential function (cf. Eph 2:8–10).

On the other side of the ledger we find a pattern of evil defined in terms of self-seeking and rejection of the truth leading to divine wrath in terms of trouble and distress. In the statement "who reject the truth and follow evil" (better, "wickedness") we detect a distinct echo of 1:18. Destiny does not depend on whether one is Jew or Gentile. The Jew is mentioned first simply because of God's prior dealing with him in history. Mention of the two divisions of mankind leads naturally to the pronouncement of the third principle: God's judgment is impartial. He "does not show favoritism" (v.11). This is the truth that Peter learned in the Cornelius incident (Acts 10:34). Paul's explanation of what it involves belongs to the following paragraph.

12–16 The principle of impartiality has to face a problem as soon as the two groups, Jews and Gentiles, are considered together. God has not dealt with them in similar fashion. To the Jew he has given a revelation of himself in Scripture that has been denied the Gentile. But in this section Paul will show that the Gentile does have *a* law, and this suffices as a basis for judgment. Before discussing this law, however, Paul sees in it no power to save, for "all who sin apart from the law will also perish apart from the law." The Gentile does not perish for the reason that he lacks the law which the Jew possesses, but because he sins. In speaking of the Jew, Paul says he "will be judged" by the law, but this does not imply exoneration, for no Jew has succeeded in keeping the law.

The expression "all who sin under the law" could strike a Jewish reader as incongruous, but Paul is linking sin with law deliberately in order to prepare the way for his next statement to the effect that the righteous are not those who "hear the law." We have a reminder in James 1:22–24 of the ease with which the Jew could hear the law read and go away without any effect on his life and conduct. Those who will be "declared righteous" are the doers of the law (v.13). This is the first occurrence in Romans of the important expression "be declared righteous." Full treatment of this matter must wait until we encounter the term again in chapter 3. Sometimes the verb *dikaioō* may have a general, as opposed to a theological, frame of reference, as in the statement "Wisdom is proven right by all her children" (Luke 7:35), where vindication is clearly intended. But the passage before us is dealing with law, sin, and judgment, so that the full theological significance of the word should be retained.

Paul's purpose is to undercut the position of the Jew who is counting on his (limited) obedience to the law for acceptance with God. His compliance would have to be perfect if he were to be declared righteous by an absolutely righteous God (cf. Luke 10:28; contrast Luke 8:12). By analogy, the Gentile is in essentially the same position, seeing that he also is not without law, as Paul goes on to indicate. The future tense of the verb ("will be declared righteous") favors the conclusion that final judgment is in view. Paul is not raising false hopes here; on the contrary, he is dashing them—in keeping with the movement of thought. Only after the flimsy edifice of humanly contrived righteousness has been leveled will the apostle be ready to put in its place the sturdy foundation of the justification provided by God in Christ. Though Paul usually uses the verb "justify" in a realized and positive sense (e.g., 3:24), here the frame of reference is eschatological and negative.

The opening word of v.14—"indeed"—is important as showing that in the discussion of the Gentile situation to which Paul now turns he has in mind a presentation designed to counter the boastfulness of the Jew. He seems anxious to avoid the impression that he is discussing the Gentiles in their entirety (he says "Gentiles," not "the Gentiles"). He is thinking of them in individual terms, not as masses. Furthermore, if he encompassed all men save the Jews in his statement, the contrast with the adverse picture of pagans in chapter 1 would be so startling as to suggest contradiction. There are Gentiles who, despite their apparent disadvantage in not possessing the Mosaic law, "do by nature" what the law requires.

What are these things? Presumably, they are not matters peculiar to the law of Moses, but moral and ethical requirements widely recognized and honored in mankind generally. It is a commonplace of rabbinic teaching that Abraham kept the laws of Sinai long before they were given. Philo taught a correspondence between the law and nature, saying that Moses "wished to show that the enacted ordinances are not inconsistent with nature" (*On Abraham,* 5). Again, Philo notes that Moses begins his work with an account of the creation of the world, "implying that the world is in harmony with the Law, and the Law with the world, and that the man who observes the law is constituted thereby a loyal citizen of the world, regulating his doings by the purpose and will of Nature, in accordance with which the entire world itself also is administered" (*On the Creation,* 3).

Paul states that such men as he has in mind are "a law for themselves." By no means does he intend to say that they are indifferent to any law except that which they invent in their self-interest. On the contrary, he goes on to say that they are governed by the law that is written on their hearts. This ought not to be confused with the promise of the law written in the heart as depicted in Jeremiah 31:33, because if that were the case, as Nygren observes, Gentiles "would indeed have the law, and that in a more intimate way than the Jew had it" (in loc.). Paul is not asserting this. Rather, he is insisting that the basic requirements of the law are stamped on human hearts. Presumably, he can say this because man is made in the image of God. C.S. Lewis begins his argument in *The Case for Christianity* by pointing out that when quarrels develop between people, the thing to be determined is who is in the right and who is in the wrong. The parties may differ radically as to their respective positions on this issue, but they are very clear that there is a right and there is a wrong. Similarly, despite the great differences in laws and customs among peoples around the world, what unites them in a common humanity is the recognition that some things are right and others are wrong.

An additional element that belongs to the equipment of the Gentiles is conscience (v.15). The translation speaks of their consciences as "bearing witness." In the Greek text there is an emphasis that does not appear in the translation—bearing witness *with;* so one must ask, With what? Only one answer seems possible, namely, with the requirements of the law written on the heart. The two function together. In the OT the word "conscience" does not appear. Perhaps this is due to the Jews' overwhelming awareness of the regulating power of revealed truth. However, the operation of conscience is recognized (e.g., Gen 42:21; 2 Sam 24:10), even though the word is lacking.

Paul's fairly frequent use of the term "conscience" indicates his indebtedness to his Greek environment and the desirability of capitalizing on a concept that was familiar to his Gentile churches. With reference to the passage we are considering, C.A. Pierce writes, "That the everyday language of the Gentiles contains a word for confessing to feelings of pain on commission or initiation of particular acts—feelings which carry with them the conviction that the acts ought not to have been committed—is first-hand evidence that the Gentiles are subject, by nature, to a 'natural law' as the Jews, by vocation, to the Torah" (*Conscience in the New Testament* [London: SCM Press, 1955], p. 86). So it can be maintained that the function of conscience in the Gentile is parallel to the function of the law for the Jew. The way conscience operates is described as a process of accusation or defense by the thoughts of a man, the inner life being pictured as a kind of debating forum, so that at times he finds himself exonerated at the bar of conscience, at other times convicted of wrong.

"This will take place on the day when God will judge men's secrets" (v.16). The difficulty to be faced here is the determination of *what* will take place. Does Paul mean that only at the judgment will conscience be engaged in the manner he has just indicated? This would seem to be a severe limitation, unless the intent is to indicate a heightened operation of this God-given monitor as the soul faces the divine assize. It is possible that vv.14, 15 should be regarded as a parenthesis, in which case what takes place on the day of judgment is the declaration of righteousness (or otherwise) referred to in v.13. This interpretation makes good sense, but it has the disadvantage of making a rather unexpected connection, because of the length of the intervening material.

God's judgment will include men's "secrets" (cf. 1 Cor 4:5). This is the only court able to assess them. Many an act that seems entirely praiseworthy to those who observe it may actually be wrongly motivated, and contrariwise some things that seem to men to merit stern disapproval may pass muster in this supreme court because the intention behind the deed was praiseworthy. The Jew theoretically admitted judgment and certainly welcomed it in the case of the Gentile, while trying to shield himself behind his privileged position. The non-Jew admitted the reality of judgment implicitly by the very process of reasoning that either accused or excused his conduct. What the Gentile did not know was the item included here—that God will judge "through Jesus Christ" (John 5:27; Acts 17:31).

Some interpreters have seen in the closing statement, "as my gospel declares," a fourth principle of judgment intended to be linked with the three we have noted. This is more understandable if one works from a literal rendering of the text—"according to my gospel." But to make the gospel, in the sense of its content, to be the criterion for judgment *in this context* is clearly wrong, for Paul is not dealing with the gospel in this chapter. What he is saying is that the gospel he preached includes the prospect of judgment and that it will be conducted through the mediation of Christ.

C. *Specific Guilt of the Jew*

2:17–3:8

17Now you, if you call yourself a Jew; if you rely on the law and brag about your relationship to God; 18if you know his will and approve of what is superior because you are instructed by the law; 19if you are convinced that you are a guide for the blind, a light for those who are in the dark, 20an instructor of the foolish, a teacher of infants, because you have in the law the embodiment of knowledge and truth—
21you, then, who teach others, do you not teach yourself? You who preach against stealing, do you steal? 22You who say that people should not commit adultery, do you commit adultery? You who abhor idols, do you rob temples? 23You who brag about the law, do you dishonor God by breaking the law? 24As it is written: "God's name is blasphemed among the Gentiles because of you."

25Circumcision has value if you observe the law, but if you break the law, you have become as though you had not been circumcised. 26If those who are not circumcised keep the law's requirements, will they not be regarded as though they were circumcised? 27The one who is not circumcised physically and yet obeys the law will condemn you who, even though you have the written code and circumcision, are a lawbreaker.

28A man is not a Jew if he is only one outwardly, nor is circumcision merely outward and physical. 29No, a man is a Jew if he is one inwardly; and circumcision is circumcision of the heart, by the Spirit, not by the written code. Such a man's praise is not from men, but from God.

3:1What advantage, then, is there in being a Jew, or what value is there in circumcision? 2Much in every way! First of all, they have been entrusted with the very words of God.

3What if some did not have faith? Will their lack of faith nullify God's faithfulness? 4Not at all! Let God be true, and every man a liar. As it is written:

"So that you may be proved right in your words and prevail in your judging."

5But if our unrighteousness brings out God's righteousness more clearly, what shall we say? That God is unjust in bringing his wrath on us? (I am using a human argument.) 6Certainly not! If that were so, how could God judge the world? 7Someone might argue, "If my falsehood enhances God's truthfulness and so increases his glory, why am I still condemned as a sinner?" 8Why not say—as we are being slanderously reported and as some claim that we say—"Let us do evil that good may result"? Their condemnation is deserved.

Two main developments are discernible in this passage. In 2:17–29 the advantage of the Jew in terms of his possession of the law and the distinctive mark of circumcision is seen as offset by his boastfulness and his fruitlessness. In 3:1–8 a new factor is introduced: Israel's failure to respond to God in terms of trust and obedience, justifying the visitation of his wrath upon them.

17–20 Here Paul begins to engage in dialogue with a representative Jew, and his razor-sharp irony is superb for its deftness. He proceeds to build up the Jew, citing his various distinctives and appearing to appreciate them (vv.17–20), only to swing abruptly into a frontal assault by exposing the inconsistency between his claims and his conduct (vv.21–24). The Jew was characterized by his reliance on the law, given by God through Moses. It came as the result of a relationship with God enjoyed by no other people. In Paul's time some of the leaders of Judaism were making such extravagant statements about the law as to put it virtually in the place of God. Many Jews were trying to keep the law for its own sake, to honor the law rather than its giver. This tendency was even more developed after the fall of Jerusalem, when the law became the rallying point for a nation that had lost its holy city and its temple.

Paul concedes that the use of the law will bring knowledge of God's will and a recognition of its superior teaching. But this is not all, for the Jew thinks that this advantage makes *him* superior to the Gentile. We can paraphrase here: "You come to the Gentile and propose yourself as a guide for his blindness (when, as a matter of fact, as I have already shown, he has a light and a law as well as you). You come to the Gentile as though he were dumb and childish, giving you the whip hand, which you thoroughly relish. To you they are mere infants, knowing next to nothing." By employing terms actually used by the Jews for the Gentiles, one after the other, not once suggesting that the Gentile has anything to his credit, but invariably magnifying the Jew, Paul has succeeded in exposing Jewish pride and boasting as utterly ridiculous.

21–24 Abruptly the shadow-boxing turns aggressive and the blows become lethal as the Jew is confronted by the disparity between what he teaches others as the will of God and his own manner of life. The thrust loses nothing of its forthrightness by being posed in a series of questions, for the effect is to turn the complacent Jew back on himself to search his own soul.

The indictment is summarized by the general charge of breaking the very law the Jew boasts of (v.23). In fact, the failure is so notorious that even non-Israelites notice the discrepancy. At this point Paul introduces a quotation from Isaiah 52:5. God has been obliged to chasten his disobedient people by permitting them to go into captivity, where their captors make sport of their God who was apparently unable to prevent their deportation (cf. Ezek 36:20, 21). But there also the fault lay not with God but with his people who had refused to take his law seriously.

25–27 If the law was the major distinctive of the Jews, a close second was circumcision. As with the law, so with circumcision, the nation was guilty of placing unwarranted confidence in the rite. Jewish tradition pictures Abraham as sitting at the gate of Gehenna to insure that no circumcised person be allowed to enter perdition (Gen R xlviii). The view that only circumcised children shared in the world to come was commonly held. Circumcision was to Jewry what baptism is to those who maintain baptismal regeneration. In dividing men into two classes, circumcised and uncircumcised, the Jews were in effect indicating those who were saved and those who were not.

But Paul's contention is that circumcision and observance of the law cannot be separated. If one has the symbol of Judaism and lacks the substance, of what value is the symbol? Society has laws that demand that the labeling of a can or bottle match the contents. How much more should there be correspondence in the spiritual realm! If a Gentile should manifest success in observing the law, the lack of circumcision is surely not so important as to discount his spiritual attainment (cf. the line of thought in 2:14). In fact, says Paul, one can go a step further (v.27) and say that the circumcised may find himself on a lower plane than the despised Gentile, because if the latter obeys the law that the Jew takes for granted instead of taking it seriously, then the Gentile will "condemn" him. This does not involve the bringing of any charge, but is a specialized use of the word "condemn" to indicate the effect created by one who surpasses another despite his inferior status or limited advantage (cf. Matt 8:11, 12; 12:41). The Gentile appears in a more favorable light than the Jew.

Some difficulty besets the attempt to understand the phrase in the Greek, which reads, "through letter and circumcision" (v.27). Calvin's attempt to handle the matter by combining the two to make them mean a literal circumcision in contrast to what is spiritual (in loc.) is hardly satisfactory. When Paul wants to make explicit the fact of literal circumcision, he uses the qualifying phrase "in the flesh"—NIV, "physically" (v.28). The basic problem, however, centers in the force of the preposition *dia,* which is normally rendered "through" in a construction such as the verse presents. But does it mean "through" in the sense of instrumentality or in the less common sense of indicating attendant circumstance? An example of the latter usage is in Romans 4:11, where Abraham is spoken of as the father of all who believe "through" circumcision. Clearly, this refers not to instrumentality but to the status of these people at the time they believe. NIV adopts this understanding in v.27—"even though you have . . ."—and this is the common interpretation. The factor that makes one hesitate is Paul's shift from *nomos* (law) to *gramma* (letter). One can detect in Paul's use of the latter term in v.29 and in 2 Corinthians 3:6 a somewhat pejorative connotation—what is written, laid down as law, but lacking any accompanying enablement. If taken in this sense in the passage before us, something of the force of instrumentality may be detected. G. Schrenk writes,

> When we are told in v.27 that the Jew *dia grammatos kai peritomēs* is a transgressor of the law, the *dia* cannot just be translated 'in spite of' as though to denote an accompanying circumstance; it must also be given an instrumental significance. It is precisely through what is written and through circumcision that the Jew is a transgres-

> sor. He is to see that his true position involves possession of the *gramma* and the *peritomē,* but with no genuine fulfilment of the Law, since neither what is written nor circumcision leads him to action (TDNT, 1:765).

In the immediate context (v.23) Paul uses *dia* with the instrumental sense in raising the question of the Jew's dishonoring of God "through the transgression of the law." The transgression of the law is common to both statements.

28,29 That this portion is intended as a conclusion to the discussion of the law and circumcision is evident, for both are mentioned, though the law is referred to in terms of "letter," as in v.27. There was plenty of background for Paul's appeal for circumcision of the heart (e.g., Deut 30:6; Jer 4:4; 9:25, 26). A real Jew, says Paul, is one who has circumcision of the heart, accomplished "by the Spirit, not by the written code" (cf. 2 Cor 3:6). How striking this is! The law is part of the Scripture that the Spirit has inspired, yet there is no hint here that the true Jew is one in whom the Spirit has made the teaching of the law dynamic. By the avoidance of any such suggestion Paul prepares the way for his treatment of the law in chapter 7. He goes on to note that a Jew transformed by the Spirit would really be living up to the name he bears, for "Jew" comes from Judah, which means "praise." He would be praiseworthy in the eyes of God, fulfilling what the law requires but cannot produce (cf. 8:3, 4). Paul writes, of course, as a Christian, as one who has suffered much for his faith from his countrymen. But these closing verses of the chapter show that for all the bluntness of his references to the Jew he is not motivated by a desire to belittle his nation on account of the treatment he has received. He rather seeks their highest good (cf. 9:1–3; 10:1).

In 3:1–8 the subject of the guilt of the Jew is continued, but now with an emphasis on the element of unbelief and also on a sophistical claim of immunity from divine judgment on the plea that God's faithfulness is thrown into bolder relief by human failure. What reasonable basis remains for acting in judgment?

3:1–4 These opening words reflect the devastating attack the apostle has launched. "What advantage, then, is there, in being a Jew"? Although the term "the circumcision" (the definite article is used) is one that could serve to denote Israel (cf. 4:9), clearly that is not the case here, for that would involve tautology. The previous context makes the reference to the rite of circumcision natural. "Much in every way" suggests a manifold advantage, made explicit by "first of all." There seems no doubt that this suggests an enumeration, but Paul proceeds no further than his first point. The reader is kept waiting a long time for any resumption, but eventually the full list is provided (9:4, 5).

For present consideration the chosen advantage is that this nation has been "entrusted with the very words of God." The Greek *logia* is related to *logoi* (e.g., John 14:24) but has a specialized meaning. "Oracles" is the usual rendering. It has this meaning in classical Greek, where it is used especially for divine utterances, often for those preserved and handed down by earlier generations. Jewish writers used it both for pagan oracles, which they considered false, and for revelations from the God of Israel. LXX usage makes it evident that two elements could belong to a *logion:* a disclosure of what God proposes to do (especially in terms of prediction, as in Num 24:16ff.) or a pronouncement of the duty laid upon man in view of the divine will or promise (e.g., Ps 119:67).

To be "entrusted" with the divine oracles obviously means more than to be the recipient of them. Actually it means more even than to be the custodian and transmitter of them. What is called for, in the light of the meaning of *logia,* is faith and obedience.

Just at this point the Jew failed (v.3). Paul has already dealt sufficiently with Jewish failure in terms of the law, but here he deals with it in terms of God's revealed purpose. He is considerate in saying that "some did not have faith." One is reminded of 1 Corinthians 10, where the same author says that some became idolaters, some murmured, etc. Actually, only two men of the exodus generation pleased God and were permitted to enter the promised land. Paul is recognizing the concept of the faithful remnant in Israel. Is the rendering "did not have faith" acceptable here, or should one regard the RSV translation, "were unfaithful," as preferable? The problem is to determine which fits better with the contrasting term, "God's faithfulness." We should recall that the oracles of God summon both to faith (in their promissory character) and to faithfulness (in their legislative aspect). From the Jewish standpoint, a *logion* could involve both *halakhah* and *haggada*—something to be done and something to be believed (*haggada* embraced the promises and much else). But since Paul has dealt with obligation already in chapter 2, we should probably think here in terms of emphasis on the area of belief. Of course, the two concepts of faith and faithfulness are closely related. Barrett's rendering, "proved unbelieving," fits the context.

We should understand "the faithfulness of God" in terms of the covenant aspect of God's dealings with Israel. There are really two sides to this faithfulness, the one positive, the other negative, in line with a similar duality in connection with the righteousness of God (1:17, 18). That the negative aspect is before us here is evident from the mention of his wrath (v.5). This is in harmony with a frequent emphasis in the prophets. When Israel fractured the Sinaitic covenant, God's very faithfulness compelled him to judge his people by sending them into captivity. The positive aspect (which we might have expected from v.1 but which is deferred) will appear in the sustained discussion of God's dealings with Israel (chs. 9–11).

As might be expected, Paul vigorously rejects any suggestion that God could fail in terms of his faithfulness (v.4). The concept of his fidelity is carried forward by the use of a closely related term. He is "true" to his covenant promises because he is true in himself. If one had to choose between the reliability of God and of man, he would have to agree with the psalmist when he declared in his disillusionment concerning his fellows, "Every man [is] a liar" (Ps 116:11). One of the best men in Israel's history, declared to be the man after God's own heart, proved a disappointment. After being chastened for his sin and refusal to confess it for a long period, David was ready to admit that God was in the right and he was in the wrong (Ps 51:4).

5–8 The supposition that human wrong could serve to display the righteousness of God may have been suggested by the passage from Psalm 51 that has just been cited. Is it not possible (so the question goes) that since human failure can bring out more sharply the righteousness of God, the Almighty ought to be grateful for this service and soften the judgment that would otherwise be due the offender? The question is one a Jew might well resort to in line with his thought that God would go easy on his covenant people. So Paul speaks for a supposed interlocutor. The mention of wrath ties in with 2:8, 9.

Paul's explanatory statement, "I am using a human argument," is due to his having permitted himself to use the word "unjust" of God, even though it is not his own assertion. "If that were so," that is, if God were unjust, he would not be qualified to judge the world. There is no attempt to establish his qualifications, since the readers, at least, are not in doubt on a point of this sort about which Scripture is so clear.

Once more the apostle entertains a possible objection (vv.7, 8). The thought is closely related to what has been stated in v.4, as the similarity in language indicates. Though the construction is somewhat rough, the general sense is clear enough. Speaking for an objector, Paul is voicing the hoary adage that the end justifies the means. He has evidently had to cope with this in his own ministry, and he will be dealing with it again in a different context (6:1). Here he is content to turn the tables on the objector. If anyone claims that his falsehood, which throws into sharp relief the truthfulness of God, promotes his glory and should therefore relieve the sinner of condemnation, let him ponder the apostolic verdict—his "condemnation is deserved."

Notes

2:22 One item calls for investigation, namely, the query "Do you rob temples?" (ἱεροσυλεῖς, *hierosyleis*). A cognate of the same word occurs in Acts 19:37 (ἱεροσύλους, *hierosylous*), where it covers sacrilege in the general sense of desecrating sacred things. But in this passage in Romans a precise, strong contrast is intended. The Jew who has been taught to abhor idols is charged with laying hands on them for the sake of profit. This may sound inconceivable, but if the robbery was directed at the offerings brought to the idol, this was tantamount to robbing the idol and thereby desecrating the temple. Ancient temples were repositories of treasure and were therefore a source of temptation to the avaricious (cf. Jos. Antiq. 4:207).

3:5 David Daube has examined the expression κατὰ ἄνθρωπον λέγω (*kata anthrōpon legō*, "I speak according to man") in the light of rabbinic usage and has concluded that it is a technical term in Paul's writing. "It constitutes an apology for a statement which, but for the apology, would be too bold, almost blasphemous" (*The New Testament and Rabbinic Judaism* [London: The Athlone Press, 1956], p. 396).

D. *Summary*

3:9–20

9 What shall we conclude then? Are we any better? Not at all! We have already
made the charge that Jews and Gentiles alike are all under sin. 10 As it is written:

"There is no one righteous, not even one;
11 there is no one who understands,
no one who searches for God.
12 All have turned away
and together become worthless.
There is no one who does good,
not even one."
13 "Their throats are open graves;
their tongues practice deceit."
"The poison of vipers is on their lips."
14 "Their mouths are full of cursing and
bitterness."
15 "Their feet are swift to shed blood;
16 ruin and misery mark their paths,
17 and the way of peace they do not know."
18 "There is no fear of God before their eyes."

19 Now we know that whatever the law says, it says to those who are under the
law, so that every mouth may be silenced and the whole world held accountable

to God. [20]Therefore no one will be declared righteous in his sight by observing the law; rather through the law we become conscious of sin.

9 Questions both of text and of punctuation confront us at this point. (Concerning punctuation, see Note.) As to text, we need have no hesitation in accepting *proechometha,* rendered "Are we any better?" Other renderings of this word are possible. The basic idea of the verb is "to stand out," "excel," or "surpass," and this is the most likely sense here. There is a difficulty, to be sure, in that the word could be either middle or passive voice. If it is to be taken as middle in force as well as in form, the sense will be, "Do we have a defense?" or "Do we excuse ourselves?" But the middle may well be used here in an active sense, as is often done with other verbs. If taken as a passive, the sense will be, "Are we excelled?"

Assuming that Paul is identifying himself here with the Jews, of whom he has been speaking, the question would suggest that the indictment of the Jew has been so severe as to open the possibility that the Gentile is actually in a better position. But insufficient ground has been provided in the foregoing passage to suggest such a possibility. So the best conclusion is that Paul intends to question whether the Jew has an edge over the Gentile. His answer, "Not at all," registers an emphatic denial. Such a denial may seem to be in conflict with the statements in vv.1, 2, and for this reason some would render it, "Not absolutely." But there he deals with the distinctive position of the Jew in the divine economy; here he is dealing with the Jew's moral and spiritual fitness, how he stands before God in terms of fulfilling his God-given role.

Paul backs up his denial of Jewish superiority by reminding his readers of the charge he has been bringing, "that Jews and Gentiles alike are all under sin." To be under sin is to be under its sway and condemnation. It is noteworthy that in his discussion of sin up to this point Paul does not charge the Jew with the death of Christ as he does in 1 Thessalonians 2:15. He could have included the Gentile also (cf. Acts 4:27, 28) and made this a clinching factor in the case against mankind, but he did not. Perhaps this is because few Jews and still fewer Gentiles were involved in effecting the death of the Lord Jesus. Paul is basing his case on a much wider sampling of human character and conduct. The specific episode of Calvary is not needed to make the verdict certain, but can be held in reserve to be used with objectors, if need be.

10–18 However, there is another argument waiting to be brought into play to seal the verdict. It is the testimony of Scripture. Writing to those who are for the most part Gentiles, Paul does not set down Scripture first and then work from that as a base for exposition (which is the method used in the Epistle to the Hebrews), but he uses only a minimum of reference to the OT to substantiate what he has established. Leaving Scripture to the conclusion of the argument is calculated to increase the respect of the Gentile for it as being able to depict man's condition accurately and faithfully. Both Jews and early Christians were in the habit of drawing up collections of Scripture passages relating to various topics in order to use them as proof texts for instruction or argumentation. It is not known whether the present collection, taken mostly from the Psalms, is the work of Paul or whether he is utilizing something previously formulated.

The present catena serves a double purpose: to affirm the universality of sin in the human family and to assert its inroads upon every facet of individual and corporate life. "There is no one righteous, not even one." The language is devastatingly clear and sharp. No exception is allowed. Again, it can be put positively: "All have turned away," which seems to echo the thought of chapter 1 that men had opportunity to know God but discarded him to their own detriment and confusion. Paul wants the full impact to register. He does not turn aside to answer the objection that the OT speaks of righteous men and in fact recognizes them as a class over against the wicked (Ps 1) or as individuals (Job 1:8). From the standpoint of the divine righteousness, they all fall short, as Paul has affirmed of both the Jew and the Gentile, whether under the law or lacking it.

The latter half of the catena, beginning with v.13, reflects the second emphasis, namely, the ramifications of sin in human life. So far as relationship with God is concerned, the rupturing power of sin has been noted (vv.11, 12). But what effect does sin have on the sinner? The effect is total, because his entire being is vitiated. Observe at this point the various members of the body referred to: the throat, the tongue, and the lips (v.13); the mouth (v.14); the feet (v.15); and the eyes (v.18). This list serves to affirm what theologians speak of as total depravity, i.e., not that man in his natural state is as bad as he can possibly be, but rather that his entire being is adversely affected by sin. His whole nature is permeated with it. Human relations also suffer, because society can be no better than those who constitute it. Some of the obvious effects—conflict and bloodshed—are specified (vv.15–17).

The chain of Scriptures closes with a statement of the root difficulty: "There is no fear of God before their eyes" (v.18). This is the same observation gleaned from the study of chapter 1. Getting out of step with God is the cause of conflict and chaos in human relations.

19,20 In these closing statements of the indictment, the apostle may be reading the mind of a Jew who questions the legitimacy of appealing to passages of the sort he has used, on the ground that men in general are in view—or at any rate, Jews who by their very godlessness are not representative of the nation as a whole. But the stubborn fact is that whatever the law says, it says to those who are under the law (v.19). The first clause must refer to the law in the broad sense of the OT revelation (cf. 1 Cor 14:21), for to refer it to the Pentateuch or to its legislative portions would destroy the continuity of thought in the passage. As already observed, the string of quotations derives from the hagiographa and the prophets. "Under the law" is more literally "in the law"; so the thought is probably not so much that the Jew is under the law's authority and dominion in the legal sense as that he is involved in Scripture, which has relevance to him at every point. Otherwise the shift in meaning of *nomos* (law) is very abrupt. Yet the legislative aspect of the law is involved by virtue of being a part of Scripture.

"So that every mouth may be silenced." When human achievement is measured against what God requires, there is no place for pride or boasting but only for silence that lends consent to the verdict of guilty. In the various biblical scenes of judgment, the silence of those who are being judged is a notable feature (e.g., Rev. 20:11–14). Questions may be raised for the sake of clarification of the reason for the verdict (Matt 25:41–46), but when the explanation is given, no appeal is attempted. The Judge of all the earth does right (Gen 18:25).

In making these statements (v.19) the apostle has been occupied with the Jew because Scripture has been at issue, but suddenly he makes a statement that involves all mankind. He pictures the "whole world" as "accountable to God." This seems to be a *non sequitur*. How can Jewish failure in terms of what Scripture requires lead to the involvement of the remainder of the human race? Two possibilities come to mind. One is that the Jewish nation is being regarded as a test case for all peoples. If given the same privileges enjoyed by Israel, the rest would likewise have failed. Their human nature is no different from that of the sons of Abraham. Another possibility, which is the more likely explanation, is that the failure of the non-Jews is so patent that it is not a debatable subject; it can be taken for granted as already established (1:18–32). Once it has been determined that the record of the Jew is no better, then judgment is seen as universally warranted.

The final word to the Jew (v.20) is designed to rob him of any fancied support in the Mosaic law, the word "law" being used as in the second occurrence in v.19. Justification before God cannot be attained by attempted observance of the law, however much man may take satisfaction in that. As Jesus pointed out, no one had succeeded in keeping the law (John 7:19).

For the first time in Romans we encounter the expression "by works of law" (cf. v.28) which has such prominence in Galatians (2:16; 3:2, 5, 10). Part of the verse—"no one will be declared righteous in his sight"—is a quotation from Psalm 143:2, in which a change in the Greek text is made from "no one living" to "no flesh" (NIV simply has "no one"), an alteration designed to bring out the frailty and inability of man with respect to meeting God's requirements (cf. 8:3). The practical result of working seriously with the law is to "become conscious of sin" (cf. 5:20; 7:7–11). How startling it is to contemplate the fact that the best revelation man has apart from Christ only deepens his awareness of failure. The law loudly proclaims his need for the gospel.

Notes

9 As far as punctuation is concerned, the first three words of the Gr. text could be taken together, yielding some such tr. as "Wherein, then, are we excelled?" But οὐ πάντως (*ou pantōs*, "not at all") does not properly answer this question, so the double question should be retained. Uncertainty as to the meaning of προεχόμεθα (*proechometha*) accounts for the interpretative variant reading προκατέχομεν περισσόν (*prokatechomen perisson*), supported principally by D* G ψ 104 and having the meaning, "Why, then, are we especially superior?"

IV. Justification: The Imputation of Righteousness (3:21–5:21)

A. *The Description of Justification*

3:21–26

[21]But now a righteousness from God, apart from law, has been made known, to which the Law and the Prophets testify. [22]This righteousness from God comes through faith in Jesus Christ to all who believe. There is no difference, [23]for all have sinned and fall short of the glory of God, [24]and are justified freely by his grace through the redemption that came by Christ Jesus. [25]God presented him as a sacrifice of atonement, through faith in his blood. He did this to demonstrate his justice, because in his forbearance he had left the sins committed beforehand unpunished—[26]he did it to demonstrate his justice at the present time, so as to be just and the one who justifies the man who has faith in Jesus.

To help his readers follow his train of thought, the apostle reverts to the term he used in stating the theme of the letter in 1:17—God's righteousness. He repeats also the necessity for faith (cf. 1:16) and then summarizes the material from 1:18–3:20 by the reminder that there is no difference between Jew and Gentile so far as sin is concerned. Having done this, he goes on to give a rich exposition of salvation through the use of various theological terms, with principal attention to justification.

21 God's righteousness, that is, his method of bringing men into right relation to himself, is "apart from law," which is agreeable to the declaration that the law operates in quite another sphere—viz., to make those who live under it conscious of their sin (v.20). God's righteousness "has been made known" (literally, "has been manifested"). The perfect tense, in contrast to the present tense in 1:17, where the current proclamation of the gospel requires it, draws attention to the appearing of Jesus Christ in the arena of history (cf. 2 Tim 1:10) or, more specifically, points to the fulfillment of God's saving purpose in him. Yet even before the initial appearing of the Savior, this method of making men right with himself was operating in principle, as "the Law and the Prophets"—a summary term for the OT—testify. This observation prepares the reader for the recital of God's dealings with Abraham and David to be considered in the following chapter.

22 God's righteousness becomes operative in human life "through faith in Jesus Christ." This statement is more explicit than the initial mention of faith in connection with the gospel (1:16, 17), since it specifies the necessary object of faith, even Jesus Christ. A problem lies beneath the surface, however, in that the literal wording is "through faith of Jesus Christ." This raises the possibility that our Lord's own faith, or more precisely, his faithfulness in fulfilling his mission, is the thought intended (G. Howard in ExpT 85 [April 1974] 212–15). The word *pistis* evidently means faithfulness in 3:3. However, a glance at Mark 11:22 makes it clear that the *pistis* of God may mean faith *in* God, as the situation there requires. What should settle the matter in this passage (Rom 3:22) is the precedent in Galatians 2:16, where we find the identical phrase "through faith of Jesus Christ" followed by the explanatory statement, "we believed in Christ Jesus." Consequently, the NIV translation should be regarded as legitimate and preferable.

Incidentally, it is never said that men are saved on account of their faith in Christ, a construction that might encourage the notion that faith makes a contribution and has some merit. On the contrary, faith is simply "the hand of the heart" (Godet). It takes what God bestows but adds nothing to the gift. All recipients of salvation are shut up to faith, for "there is no difference," a repetition of the verdict of 3:9.

23 The reason all must come to God through faith in Christ is that "all have sinned and fall short of [or 'lack,' as in Mark 10:21] the glory of God." This glory cannot be eschatological, as in 5:2, since even believers, for whom the sin problem has been solved, lack the future glory now. The suggestion that the glory is God's approbation or praise (Denney) is unlikely, since this meaning of *doxa,* common in Luke, is somewhat rare in Paul. C.H. Dodd seeks to link the glory with the image of God in man (cf. 1 Cor 11:7) which is marred by sin. This is suggestive, but it would be more acceptable if Paul had used the past tense ("have fallen short") to match the sense in the previous statement about sin. Possibly the best interpretation is to associate the glory with the divine presence and the privilege man originally had of direct communion with God. This ever-present deprivation is depicted in the restriction of the glory to the holy of holies in the tabernacle and the denial of the right of access to the people save through the high priest once a year. God's glory is the majesty of his holy person. To be cut off from this fellowship is *the* great loss occasioned by sin.

24 At first glance it seems that Paul is committing himself to a doctrine of universal salvation, that all who have sinned are justified. That impression is certainly incorrect. The problem can be handled in either of two ways. One method is to suppose that the reader is intended to supply something along this line. "Since all have sinned, all must be justified—if they are to be saved—by God's free grace." The other method is to understand that the last statement in v.22 and all of v.23 should be regarded as semi-parenthetical, so that the statement about being justified is to be joined to "all who believe."

In confronting justification, we encounter the leading doctrinal contribution of Romans. How to be just in God's sight has been the age-old problem of man (Job 9:2; 10:14). To get at the meaning of the doctrine, some attention must be given to terminology. In classical Greek the verb *dikaioō* was sometimes used to mean "do right by a person, give him justice." As a result, it could be used in the sense of "condemn." But in its biblical setting it is used in the opposite sense, namely, "to acquit" (Exod 23:7; Deut 25:1). It is clear both from the OT and the NT that *dikaioō* is a forensic term; it is the language of the law court. But to settle on "acquittal" as the meaning of justification is to express only a part of the range of the word, even though an important part (Acts 13:39).

There is a positive side that is even more prominent in NT usage—"to consider, or declare to be, righteous." The word does not mean "to make righteous," that is, to effect a change of character. Because he considered it ethically deplorable that God should account righteous those who have been and to some extent continue to be sinful, Goodspeed defied the linguistic evidence and rendered *dikaioō* "to make upright." He failed to realize that the question of character and conduct belongs to a different area, namely, sanctification, and is taken up by Paul in due course, whereas justification relates to status and not to condition. For a clear statement on this, see R. Bultmann, *Theology of the New Testament* (New York: Scribner, 1951), 1:276.

In the background is the important consideration, strongly emphasized by Paul, that the believer is "in Christ," a truth to be unfolded at a later stage in Paul's presentation and summarized by him in 8:1 (cf. 1 Cor 1:30; 2 Cor 5:21). Nowhere is this better stated than in his declaration, ". . . that I may gain Christ and be found in him, not having a righteousness of my own that comes from the law, but that which is through faith in Christ" (Phil 3:8, 9). To be justified includes the truth that God sees the sinner in terms of his relation to his Son, with whom he is well pleased.

Though justification has much in common with forgiveness, the two terms ought not to be regarded as interchangeable, because even though forgiveness of sins can be stated in comprehensive fashion (Eph 1:7; 4:32) its continuing aspect, related to confession (1 John 1:9), sets it somewhat apart from justification, which is a once-for-all declaration of God on behalf of the believing sinner.

Sinners are justified "freely," i.e., as a gift. The same word is used in John 15:25, where it bears a somewhat different but not unrelated meaning—"without reason." God finds no reason, no basis, in the sinner for declaring him righteous. He must find the cause in himself. This truth goes naturally with the observation that justification is offered by God's grace. Perhaps the best synonym we have for it is "lovingkindness" (*passim* in the Psalms, KJV). It is a matter not simply of attitude but also of action, as the present verse attests. Grace (*charis*) lies at the basis of joy (*chara*) for the believer and leads to thanksgiving (*eucharistia*). If "freely" is the manner in which justification operates, and grace is its basis, "the redemption that came by Christ Jesus" is the means a gracious God employed to achieve this boon for mankind. The benefit that redemption brings in this life, according to Ephesians 1:7, is forgiveness of sins, and this is applicable in our passage. Another aspect, belonging to the future, is the redemption of the body, which will consummate our salvation (8:23; Eph 4:30).

25 "God presented him as a sacrifice of atonement." Some would object to the rendering "presented" on the ground that a public exhibition of the person of Jesus has something almost theatrical about it, and that for this reason the alternative rendering "purposed" (literally, "set before himself") might be preferred. However, there are words in the passage that express manifestation: "made known" (v.21) and "demonstrate" (vv.25, 26); so the objection is unwarranted. Also it should be pointed out that the emphasis on faith (v.25) suggests that the real force in "presented" is not so much the actual exhibition of Christ on the cross as in the proclamation of the gospel that makes his saving work central. That very proclamation emphasizes that Christ, under God, has become "a sacrifice of atonement." This language is an attempt to render the Greek *hilastērion,* which in form is an adjective that could be taken either as masculine or neuter. If the former, it refers back to "him" (Christ); if the latter, it requires something to be supplied, unless the liberty is taken to give it the force of a noun, as is done when it is considered the equivalent of "propitiation" (*hilasmos*), which occurs in 1 John 2:2; 4:10.

In LXX the first occurrence of *hilastērion* (Exod 25:17) has reference to a propitiatory lid or cover, usually translated "mercy seat." In the following context of Exodus 25 it occurs several times, each time without the word "lid." The only other occurrence in the NT (Heb 9:5) is a clear allusion to the mercy seat of the tabernacle. But can we be sure that Romans 3:25 has the same frame of reference? For one thing, the Hebrews passage has the definite article, whereas the reference in Romans does not. This is not an insuperable objection, for if Paul is intent on stressing that Christ is the antitype of the OT mercy seat, he would naturally omit the article so as to avoid identifying Christ with a material object.

More significant is the objection that whereas Hebrews is filled with references to the sanctuary and its ritual, Romans is not. This is true, but the contrast should not be overdrawn (cf. Rom 12:1). Again, it has been objected that any reference to the mercy seat is incongruous, since that article was withheld from public view and access. But the objection ignores the movement of thought in Hebrews 9, which emphasizes that the death of Christ opened up what had formerly been concealed and inaccessible to the people. As far as Romans is concerned, the word "presented" is a signpost suggesting a similar concept here. T.W. Manson remarks, "The mercy-seat is no longer kept in the sacred seclusion of the most holy place: it is brought out into the midst of the rough and tumble of the world and set up before the eyes of hostile, contemptuous, or indifferent crowds" (JTS 46 [1945] 5). Indeed, Christ has become the meeting place of God and man where the mercy of God is available because of the sacrifice of the Son.

Nygren supports the mercy seat interpretation by noting that the very terms used by Paul in the passage before us tally with the OT setting in Exodus 25—the manifestation of God, his wrath, his glory, the blood, and the mercy seat or propitiatory (p. 157).

Some scholars prefer the view that "propitiatory" requires a complement such as "sacrifice," which the reader is expected to supply, especially since the blood of Christ is mentioned here. But the very phrase "in his blood" tends to make such an addition needless. It remains, however, a viable option.

On the basis of the use of the word *hilastērion* on inscriptions of the *koine* period, A. Deissmann maintained that the word should be rendered "a votive offering" or "a propitiatory gift" (*Bible Studies* [Edinburgh: T. & T. Clark, 1901], pp. 124–135). His comment is, "The crucified Christ is the votive gift of the Divine Love for the salvation of men." But the examples he gives from pagan sources are all concerning votive gifts brought by men, designed to propitiate the deity, whereas Christ is set forth by God as propitiatory. The difference is very real.

In recent years considerable attention has been given to the conclusions of C.H. Dodd on the word in question (*The Bible and the Greeks* [London: Hodder and Stoughton, 1935], pp. 82–95). Dodd's contention is that when the LXX translators used the verb *hilaskesthai* ("to make propitiation") and its derivatives to render the Hebrew root *kipper* they did not attach to the word the classical sense of propitiation but rather gave it the force of expiation, that which is involved in the removal of sin's guilt (in contrast to the appeasement of wrath, which is inherent in the concept of propitiation). Admitting faint traces of propitiation in the OT data, he nevertheless advocates that when the subject of the verb is human, the idea is simply that of making expiation, and when the subject is divine, the concept is that of forgiveness.

Leon Morris (*The Apostolic Preaching of the Cross* [Grand Rapids: Eerdmans, 1955]) worked through the same OT materials and came out with different results, which may be summarized in two observations. First, Dodd ignored the fact that the verb *hilaskesthai*, which he would render "forgive" in reference to God, is used repeatedly in situations where the context makes it clear that the wrath of God is a factor, so that propitiation is actually involved (p. 138). Second, the argument from context is also important for the interpretation of the Romans passage, because the first main section of the book (1:18–3:20) is permeated with the concept of the divine wrath along with the emphasis on judgment. The word "wrath" (*orgē*) is found four times here (1:18; 2:5, 8; 3:5). Under these circumstances it would be strange for Paul to give a statement of the remedy for man's sin and unrighteousness without indicating that the wrath of God has been satisfactorily met by his own provision. There is no term in 3:21–26 that conveys this idea if it is not to be found in *hilastērion* (p. 169). An independent study by David Hill (*Greek Words*, pp. 23–48) leads to conclusions substantially in agreement with Morris's position.

The phrase "through faith in his blood" (v.25) poses a problem. This translation suggests that the believer's faith is to be placed in the blood of Christ, and the sequence of terms favors this. However, it has been pointed out that there is no example of Paul's calling for faith in a thing rather than a person, unless we allow the gospel to be included in this category. So if the translation is allowed to stand, it has to be regarded as anomalous. Furthermore, in the immediate context the idea of putting faith *in* is expressed without a preposition by using the genitive case (3:22, 26). The alternative suggestion is to place a comma after "faith," thus separating the clauses and making both dependent on *hilastērion*.

The remainder of v.25 deals with the necessity of the propitiatory provision in terms of God's justice (the same word in the original as "righteousness"). The character of God needs justification for his passing over "sins committed beforehand"—that is, in the ages prior to the cross. His "forbearance" is not to be thought of as sentimentality or weakness but as an indication that meeting the demands of his righteous character would be accomplished in due season. This happened at the cross. The Greek *paresis* (rendered "left . . . unpunished") is close to *aphesis* ("forgiveness") in meaning, but with an appreciable difference in that *paresis* denotes a temporary remission of a debt (see Milligan and Moulton under *paresis*), which fits the situation here exactly. The full penalty for sin was not exacted, in line with God's forbearance.

26 Now the bearing of the cross on God's dealings with men "at the present time" is unfolded. It amounts to a declaration that God is at once just in himself and justifying in his activity on behalf of mankind. "It is something new, when absolute justice is said to be shown in the atonement through the sacrificial death of Jesus . . . and when God is called 'faithful and just to forgive our sins' (1 John 1:9), *dikaios* combining the ideas of judgment and salvation" (G. Schrenk, S.V. "Righteousness" in *Bible Key Words.* [New York: Harper and Brothers, 1951], p. 21).

Notes

21–24 In his important study of righteousness in Paul, Ziesler (in loc.) concludes that whereas the verb δικαιόω (*dikaioō*) is essentially forensic in meaning ("to justify"), the noun δικαιοσύνη (*dikaiosynē*) and the adjective δίκαιος (*dikaios*) describe "behaviour within relationship" and so are basically ethical in their import. This position is open to the criticism that it too sharply distinguishes the force of the noun and the adjective from that of the verb. In other words, the noun and the adjective are capable of carrying the forensic connotation also. See the review article by Nigel M. Watson in NTS 20 (Jan. 1974) 217–228.

22 Instead of "unto all" (εἰς πάντας, *eis pantas*), a few Fathers have "upon all" (ἐπὶ πάντας, *epi pantas*). A group of MSS (א plus many cursives and Fathers) combine the two readings (cf. KJV).

24 We are confronted by a major theological concept. The Gr. term ἀπολύτρωσις (*apolytrōsis*) has as its kernel the word λύτρον (*lytron*), "ransom," used by Jesus of his own self-giving in behalf of the many (Mark 10:45). Paul does not use this word, though ἀντίλυτρον (*antilytron*) appears once (1 Tim 2:6). The word "redemption" has its OT background chiefly in the deliverance of Israel from Egypt (Exod 6:6; 15:13) and is used often without any reference to sin or the payment of a ransom. But something of the idea of the cost involved continues to cling to the word even though unexpressed. In our passage, the term may be said to connote "deliverance through the *substitutionary* death of Jesus, the emphasis being all the time on liberation" (David Hill, *Greek Words and Hebrew Meanings* [Cambridge: Cambridge University Press, 1967], p. 76).

B. *The Availability of Justification Through Faith Alone*

3:27–31

[27]Where, then, is boasting? It is excluded. On what principle? On that of observing the law? No, but on that of faith. [28]For we maintain that a man is justified by faith apart from observing the law. [29]Is God the God of Jews only? Is he not the God of Gentiles too? Yes, of Gentiles too, [30]since there is only one God, who will justify the circumcised by faith and the uncircumcised through that same faith. [31]Do we, then, nullify the law by this faith? Not at all! Rather, we uphold the law.

27–30 The opening words suggest that the paragraph is designed especially for the Jew, for even though boasting is not confined to the Jew, it has already been noticed as a distinct tendency in his case (2:17, 23). Paul asks on what principle (literally, "through what sort of law") boasting is excluded. But does "principle" convey the idea adequately? Certainly *nomos* is used in this sense later on (e.g., 7:21, 23). The use of the word *nomos*, so familiar to the Jew and so treasured by him, is calculated to catch his eye and make him think. Perhaps something between "law" and "principle" is needed here, something special in the sense of what is ordained by God (see TDNT IV, p. 1071). God has ordained faith as the sole condition of receiving salvation, and that provides no basis for boasting, seeing that in the last analysis it, like the salvation it embraces, is the gift of God (Eph 2:8, Gr.). Paul could speak of the righteousness he sought through law keeping as his own righteousness (Phil 3:9), but he cannot so speak of the righteousness he has in Christ. Once more he insists on justification by faith apart from law keeping. This may appear to bring him into contradiction with his assertion in 2:13. Paul would no doubt respond by saying that everything depends on the right motive. To glory over one's achievement ruins the whole enterprise: it becomes an affront to God, its value is gone. Read Galatians 3:12 in this connection.

Again Paul moves to catch the eye of his Jewish reader by appealing to his awareness that God is one (vv.29, 30; cf. Deut 6:4). The Jew, surrounded by pagan idolatry, proudly repeated his monotheistic confession. Paul now turns it to good account. Logically, if God is one, if he alone is God, then we can expect him to employ only one method to bring humanity to himself. Faith is the condition for receiving salvation on the part of Jew and Gentile alike (v.30). Neither has any advantage over the other. The Gentile must come "by that same faith" required of the Jew (cf. 1:16; Gal. 2:15, 16). It is doubtful that the difference in prepositions used with faith implies any basic distinction in God's dealings with the two groups.

31 The final verse of the chapter has elicited many interpretations, attesting its difficulty. That view is most likely to be correct that accords most closely with the foregoing material.

Paul has twice mentioned law observance (vv.27, 28) as not entering at all into justification, which is by faith apart from works of the law. May we draw the conclusion, then, that the law is useless? By no means, the apostle would answer, for the operation of faith really upholds or establishes the law. The gospel establishes the law in that the latter is vindicated. The law has fulfilled a vital role by bringing an awareness of sin (v.20). A broken law made the redeeming work of Christ at the cross necessary (vv.24, 25). One who sees that the cross was a divine necessity will never feel that he can make himself approved by God by fulfilling the law's demands. If that were possible, Christ would have died in vain. Since the death of Christ was in terms of God's righteousness (v.26), this means that the demands of the law have not been set aside in God's plan of salvation. It is not damaging to this position that "law" lacks the article here, for the same is true in 5:20.

Other views should be noticed briefly. One is that v.31 is intended to provide a transition to chapter 4, where Abraham's justification is explained. On this view "law" simply means Scripture, or more specifically, the Pentateuch. This view gets support from v.21 with its mention of "the Law and the Prophets." Something of a disadvantage is involved, however, in that v.31 in Greek speaks of "law" rather than of "*the* law" (the article is omitted). Further, it is doubtful that the material of the following chapter can be said to uphold the law.

Another possibility is that Paul is striking out against antinomianism. If his statement had occurred in the course of his argument in chapters 6 to 8, this would be quite apparent, but it is less likely here. Still another view is that Paul means to say that the moral standards of the law are maintained under the gospel, thus anticipating the truth stated in 8:4. In line with this is Luther's interpretation that to establish the law means to fulfill it through faith. But again, this anticipates what is developed only later on. The view that Paul means to say that we establish the law because under the gospel Christ keeps it for us is unsupported by anything in the passage. Doubtful also is the contention of H.J. Schoeps that Paul "implies that faith is the true content of the law" (*Paul* [Philadelphia: Westminster Press, 1961], p. 210). This runs counter to the argument in the preceding context.

C. *The Illustration of Justification From the Old Testament* (4:1–25)

The fact that in the gospel a righteousness from God is *revealed* (1:17) could suggest that justification is a new thing, peculiar to the Christian era. To discover that it was already present in the OT serves to engender confidence in an ongoing purpose of God and in the basic unity of the Bible. "It is essential for the structure of faith that behind the appearance of Christ in an historical perspective a preceding activity of God appears" (L. Goppelt, "Paul and Heilsgeschichte," INT 21 [1967] 325).

Paul's fourth chapter is devoted almost exclusively to Abraham and God's dealings with him. The NT writers seem to turn to Abraham almost instinctively when discussing faith (Heb 11; James 2). If Paul can establish as true that the father of the nation of Israel was justified by faith rather than by works, he will have scored heavily, especially with his Jewish readers.

1. *The case of Abraham*

4:1–5

[1]What then shall we say that Abraham, our forefather, discovered in this matter? [2]If, in fact, Abraham was justified by works, he had something to boast about—but not before God. [3]What does the Scripture say? "Abraham believed God, and it was credited to him as righteousness."

[4]Now when a man works, his wages are not credited to him as a gift, but as an obligation. [5]However, to the man who does not work but trusts God who justifies the wicked, his faith is credited as righteousness.

1–5 In calling Abraham "our forefather," the apostle is not turning aside to address Jewish believers only, because he makes the point in this chapter that Gentile believers also have a stake in Abraham (v.16). What had Abraham "discovered" about getting into right relation to God? Since the word is in the perfect tense, there is a hint that what he learned or experienced has value for future generations. Picking up the matter of boasting from 3:27, Paul naturally links works with it, but denies that it is possible to boast of works "before God." Abraham was not guilty of pharisaic folly. Justification is for the glory of God, not of man. To show that Abraham's close relation to God was not based on works, a simple appeal to Scripture is sufficient. That appeal was the more necessary because Judaism even before Paul's day was laying great store by Abraham's piety and was grounding it in his obedience. "Was not Abraham found faithful in temptation and it was reckoned unto him for righteousness?" (1 Macc 2:51). Judaism mingled things that Paul was careful to keep apart. "Law and works, faith and obedience, obedience and merit, reward and blessing are a unity in the rabbinic theology" (Michel, in loc.). The appeal to Scripture rather than to current teaching is decisive. "Abraham believed God, and it was credited to him as righteousness" (v.3). Nothing whatever is said about his obedience in leaving country and kindred in response to God's call. Faith was required for such a response, and that faith was of the same sort that

Abraham exercised later, but since the incident recounted in Genesis 15 had special bearing on justification, it alone is utilized here.

At the time referred to in the quotation (Gen 15:6) Abraham was in the promised land but had as yet no progeny. Reminding God of this fact, he protested, "a slave born in my house will be my heir" (Gen 15:3). The reference is to Eliezer of Damascus. As revealed by the Nuzi tablets, in the society of Ur of the Chaldees, out of which Abraham had come, a couple could adopt a son to help them in their old age and to see that they were properly buried. In consideration of these services, the one adopted was named the heir. As time went on, Abraham saw no prospect other than this. But God directed him to look up into the heavens and count the stars, promising that his descendants would be as numerous. Abraham accepted this promise, relying on God to fulfill it. This was the basis on which God pronounced him righteous.

The nature of Abraham's faith was essentially the same as that of the NT believer despite the difference in time. (Abraham looked forward to something God would do, whereas the Christian looks back to what God has provided in Christ.) Can we go further and say that the object of faith is the same, implicit in the promise to Abraham, explicit in the gospel? It does seem that we are warranted in concluding that Abraham trusted in a promise that pointed to Christ (John 8:56; Gal 3:16), though at this time this may not have been clear to the patriarch. Much depends on how he understood the promise in Genesis 12:3. Abraham's faith was credited to him "as righteousness," which means that faith itself is not righteousness.

Paul goes on to contrast faith with works (vv.4, 5), noting that work yields wages that must be treated as an obligation for an employer, whereas faith means that the one who exercises it receives a righteous standing simply as a gift (literally, "grace") from God. So grace is pitted against obligation and faith against works (cf. 11:6). It is possible that Paul has borrowed the term "wage" (Gr. *misthos*) from the LXX of Genesis 15:1, where reward or recompense is assured to Abraham.

How far grace goes beyond justice is seen in the statement that God justifies the wicked (or ungodly). Not only does God justify men apart from works but he does so contrary to what they deserve. OT law required the judge to condemn the wicked and justify the righteous (Deut 25:1), but where God is both Judge and Savior the wicked have an opportunity denied to them in human reckoning. The prophetic word anticipated this result through the work of the Servant (Isa 53:5, 6, 11). In saying that God justifies the ungodly, the text is not singling out Abraham as the sinner par excellence but rather is pointing to the type of man who is desperately in need of justification, which actually embraces all (cf. 5:6), including Abraham.

Notes

1 There is a textual problem in this verse. The Gr. infinitive εὑρηκέναι (*heurēkenai*), rendered "discovered " in NIV, is placed after "our forefather" in some MSS, in which case it is naturally taken with κατὰ σάρκα (*kata sarka*), "according to the flesh" or "by his own powers." A more important group of MSS place the infinitive after "shall we say," in which contruction the words *kata sarka* go with "our forefather" to indicate a natural or blood relationship. Then a small group of witnesses, including the important MS B, omit the infinitive. The uncertain position of the infinitive in some witnesses tends to support the omission. A few tr., including the NEB, reflect the omission in their wording.

2. *The case of David*

4:6–8

[6]David says the same thing when he speaks of the blessedness of the man to whom God credits righteousness apart from works:

> [7]"Blessed are they whose offenses have been forgiven
> and whose sins have been covered.
> [8]Blessed is the man whose sin the Lord will never
> count against him."

Though the case of David is not strictly parallel to that of Abraham, and though it is treated only briefly, it is clear from the opening word (Gr. *kathaper*) that the general theme remains the same. What strikes one as peculiar is the apparent lack of harmony between what Psalm 32 states and what Paul announces as the bearing of the quotation. Whereas Paul indicates that the quotation has to do with the reckoning of righteousness apart from works, the passage itself contains neither of these terms. Instead, it speaks of offenses that have been forgiven and of sins that have been covered. As we compare v.6 with vv.7, 8, one word stands out as common to both passages. It is the word translated "credit" in v.6 and "count" in v.8 (*logizesthai*). In fact, this word dominates the early part of the chapter, occurring in vv.3, 4, 5, 6, 8, 9, 10, 11.

Paul's training under Gamaliel shows through here, since it is evident that he is utilizing a principle of rabbinic interpretation made famous by Hillel, namely the principle of analogy. This means that in situations where the same word occurs in two passages of Scripture, the sense in one may be carried over to explain the meaning in the other. In the case of Abraham, righteousness was credited to him, apart from works, on the basis of faith. In the case of David. obviously no good work is involved, but on the contrary, sin has been committed. So the far-reaching nature of justification is seen to still greater advantage.

One may add that since David was actually already a justified man, known as the man after God's own heart, in his case we learn the truth that sin in the life of a believer does not cancel justification. God is able to forgive. His gifts are irrevocable (11:29). At the same time, God showed his displeasure regarding David's sin, severely chastening him until the sin had been fully confessed. Even afterward, his sins produced havoc in his family. David suffered the humiliation of the revolt led by Absalom. Yet God did not withdraw his favor and support, as seen by a succession of events: Absalom's setting aside of Ahithophel's counsel, the triumph of David's forces in the battle, the ignominious death of Absalom, and the resurgence of desire on the part of the people for David's return as their king. In contrast to Abraham, David lived under the regimen of the Mosaic law. Though the law is not mentioned, the text says that David "speaks of the blessedness of the man to whom God credits righteousness apart from works" (v.6). There may be a suggestion here that after having sinned, David could not rectify his situation by means of works. He was completely shut up to God's mercy exhibited in the forgiveness of his transgressions.

3. *The promise to Abraham—apart from circumcision*

4:9–12

[9]Is this blessing only for the circumcised, or also for the uncircumcised? We have been saying that Abraham's faith was credited to him as righteousness. [10]Under what circumstances was it credited? Was it after he was circumcised, or before?

It was not after, but before! 11And he received circumcision a sign and seal of the
righteousness that he had by faith while he was still uncircumcised. So then, he
is the father of all who believe but have not been circumcised, in order that
righteousness might be credited to them. 12And he is also the father of the circum-
cised who not only are circumcised but who also walk in the footsteps of the faith
that our father Abraham had before he was circumcised.

9–12 The issue discussed here is the importance of the time of God's declaration of righteousness on behalf of Abraham in relation to the time of his circumcision. By using the term "blessedness" from the opening of Psalm 32 Paul makes the transition from David back to Abraham. Are the uncircumcised able to share in this blessedness? As Strack and Billerbeck point out, the answer of the synagogue to such a question was that the blessedness was properly confined to the circumcision (*Kommentar zum Neuen Testament aus Talmud und Midrasch*, 3:203). Paul dissents, arguing skillfully that the benefit David enjoyed was enjoyed by Abraham, and Abraham received it when he was still uncircumcised! To all intents and purposes, he was like one of the Gentiles. This opens the door to the extension of the blessedness of justification to the Gentiles. Paul is still using the method of analogy regarding *logizesthai* ("credited"). As Genesis 15:6 had been explained with the aid of Psalm 32:1, 2, now the apostle reverses direction and explains Psalm 32 with the aid of Genesis 15. David, of course, was circumcised, but Abraham was not circumcised at the time of his being credited with righteousness on the basis of faith. According to the record, it was fourteen years later that he received the rite (Gen 17:24–26). Circumcision, then, was really a sign of what he previously had. It was a testimony to justifying faith, not something in which to take any pride (cf. 2:25–29). "We cannot doubt that circumcision was delayed in order to teach the believing Gentiles of future ages that they may claim Abraham as their father, and the righteousness of faith as their inheritance" (J.A. Beet, *A Commentary on St. Paul's Epistle to the Romans* [New York: Thomas Whittaker, 1892[8]]). It could even be said that the Gentile has first claim on the patriarch, who was just like himself when justified. The Jew stands rebuffed for his pride and exclusiveness (cf. Acts 15:11; Gal 2:16). Obviously the apostle is not speaking in v.12 of two groups, Jews and Gentiles, for he has finished speaking of Gentiles in the preceding verse. Here he refers to Jews in two categories—not only as circumcised but, what is more important, as believers who share the faith Abraham had before he was circumcised.

4. *The promise to Abraham—apart from the law*

4:13–17

13It was not through law that Abraham and his offspring received the promise
that he should be heir of the world, but through the righteousness that comes by
faith. 14For if those who live by law are heirs, faith has no value and the promise
is worthless, 15because law brings wrath. and where there is no law there is no
transgression.

16Therefore, the promise comes by faith, so that it may be by grace and may
be guaranteed to all Abraham's offspring—not only to those who are of the law
but also to those who are of the faith of Abraham. He is the father of us all. 17As
it is written: "I have made you a father of many nations." He is our father in the
sight of God, in whom he believed—the God who gives life to the dead and calls
things that are not as though they were.

13–17 The thought moves on to the consideration that Abraham's justification was apart from the law or legal considerations. Paul speaks of a promise received by "Abraham and his offspring" that "he should be heir of the world." Nothing so precise can be detected in the text of Genesis. Meyer suggests that the possession of the land of promise, in accordance with God's gift, is here looked on as the foil for a greater inheritance, namely, the messianic kingdom, in which the descendants of Abraham would have a special stake. The objection to this is certainly not that no place for a messianic kingdom can be found in Paul (8:17; 1 Cor 6:2; cf. Matt 19:28), but rather that the subject of the chapter has not changed. Abraham's justification came in connection with the promise of offspring comparable in number to the stars of the heavens. Nothing in the section we are considering suggests the thought of dominion. To be sure, Abraham received a promise that his descendants would possess the gate of their enemies (Gen 22:17) but that concept is not introduced here. Furthermore, "world" lacks the article, so that it is not likely intended to denote the physical world but the multitude of those who will follow Abraham in future generations in terms of his faith. These he can claim as his own. Finally, it is not said that Abraham's offspring will be heirs of the world but that he will be such an heir. This is not favorable to the eschatological interpretation of a millennial kingdom involving the renewed nation of Israel as its core element. The theme is still that vast influence of the man of faith upon succeeding generations and peoples. He will be the father of many nations in the sense that he is the father of their faith, since by that means rather than by some other they will be justified (cf. Gen 12:3; 22:18).

But we must return to Paul's main thrust, that the promise is not conditioned "through law." The thought is not developed in quite the same way as in Galatians 3:17, 18, where it is recognized that the Mosaic law was several hundred years in the future when God was dealing with Abraham, and that the law was not designed to upset the promise or qualify it.

Here, however, the point is made that if inheritance of the promise comes to those "who live by law," then faith is emptied of value and the promise has effectively been put out of operation. As soon as a promise is hedged about with conditional elements, it loses its value. Particularly is this true of the law because of its inflexible character. As Paul puts it, "The law brings wrath." To make the promise conditional on law observance would pit the God of grace against the God of judgment, an intolerable impasse. Where there is no law, there may indeed be sin, but not transgression. In case the promise had been conditioned by law keeping, the human inability to observe the law with complete fidelity would have occasioned disobedience and consequently the operation of wrath, resulting in forfeiture of what was promised. In summary, to introduce law keeping as a condition for receiving the promise would have two disastrous effects. It would put a question mark over the character of God for adding a condition and it would make the realization of the promise impossible for men, since no one has been able fully to keep the law (see vv.14, 15).

The promise, on the other hand, belongs to the realm of faith and grace (v.16). By mentioning faith first, due to its prominence in the whole passage, Paul appears to put grace in a secondary position, but it cannot have been his intent to make grace depend on faith (cf. Eph 2:8). Faith is put forward as a reaffirmation of v.13, after vv.14, 15 have ruled out law. Hence its prominence in the sentence. The only ground for certainty in relation to the promise is grace (as opposed to attempted legal obedience). Probably the element of certainty ("guaranteed") is intended to apply to faith as well as to grace. This is just another way of saying that the ultimate guarantee must be God and his faithfulness.

"Those who are of the law" are not excluded from Abraham's offspring. This means that a person who happened to live during the Mosaic era was not thereby excluded from the blessing of the Abrahamic covenant, provided he had faith. The expression cannot refer to legal obedience without bringing Paul into contradiction with himself. But the blessing of Abraham is also for those who, though not belonging to the Mosaic epoch, yet share the faith of the patriarch. Both groups are in view in the statement "He is father of us all." This is followed by an appeal to the prediction that Abraham would be a father of many nations (Gen 17:5), which could not refer to the twelve tribes of Israel, since they constituted but one nation. Only God could foresee the course of history that was to include the coming of Christ, his finished work, his command to evangelize all nations (Matt 28:9, 20), and the response of faith to the gospel around the world.

God is described by two terms. First, he is one "who gives life to the dead." It is perhaps natural to think of such an expression in terms of resurrection (vv.24, 25), but hardly with reference to receiving Isaac back, as it were, from the dead, when Abraham was ready to offer him to God (a subject pursued in Heb 11:19 but not mentioned here). The thought seems to move rather along the line of making possible the provision of offspring despite the deadness of Abraham and Sarah as producers of offspring (cf. v.19, where the word "dead" occurs twice). This conclusion is favored by the second affirmation in which God is said to be the one who "calls things that are not as though they were." The word "calls" in this case does not mean to describe or designate, but rather "summon," perhaps "call into being." It may be used in this sense for his creative activity (see Isa 48:13, NEB; 2 Baruch 21:4). Isaac was real in the thought and purpose of God before he was begotten.

It is entirely foreign to the context and to all of Paul's teaching to understand him as meaning that God pronounces a man righteous when he really is not. Justification is not a fiction. In the sight of God the justified sinner has a righteous standing that cannot be challenged (8:33, 34).

5. *Abraham's faith the standard for every believer*

4:18–25

> 18Against all hope, Abraham in hope believed and so became the father of many
> nations, just as it had been said to him, "So shall your offspring be." 19Without
> weakening in his faith, he faced the fact that his body was as good as dead—since
> he was about a hundred years old—and that Sarah's womb was also dead. 20Yet
> he did not waver through unbelief regarding the promise of God, but was strength-
> ened in his faith and gave glory to God, 21being fully persuaded that God had
> power to do what he had promised. 22This is why "it was credited to him as
> righteousness." 23The words "it was credited to him" were written not for him
> alone, 24but also for us who believe in him who raised Jesus our Lord from the
> dead. 25He was delivered over to death for our sins and was raised to life for our
> justification.

18–22 The final value of Abraham in respect to justification is that his faith becomes the standard for all believers. "Against all hope," this man believed. In view of his "deadened" condition (and that of Sarah likewise) because of advanced age, the situation seemed past hope. Nevertheless, he believed the promise of God that offspring would be given. "In hope" takes account of the great change that came over his outlook due to the pledge God gave him. After making the original promise (Gen 15:5), God waited until it was physically impossible for this couple to have children. Then he repeated his pledge (Gen 17:5). Abraham's act of faith was essentially the same as on the previous occasion, but meanwhile circumstances had made the fulfillment of the promise impossible apart from supernatural intervention. He was shut up to God and was able to rest his faith there.

He "faced the fact" of his physical condition and that of Sarah and "did not waver through unbelief." The refusal to waver answers to the refusal to weaken in faith. Abraham apparently suffered a momentary hesitancy (Gen 17:17), but it passed and was not held against him. That he really trusted God for the fulfillment of the promise is seen in his readiness to proceed with circumcision for himself and his household before Isaac was conceived (Gen 17:23–27). This act in itself could be construed as giving "glory to God," an expression of trust in the power of the Almighty to make good his promise. Moreover, it was an open testimony to others of his trust in God's faithfulness to his word. If God should fail in this matter, Abraham would be an object of pity by some, of ridicule by others.

As far as Abraham was concerned, he was not taking a chance. He was "fully persuaded" that God's power would match his promise. This man of God was called on to believe in a special divine intervention—not after it occurred, as the Jews were challenged to do concerning the resurrection of Jesus (Acts 2–5), but before. His faith is the more commendable because it was exercised in the face of apparent lack of necessity. Would not Ishmael do as the desired progeny? He had been born to Abraham through Hagar in the interval between the original promise (Gen 15) and its renewal (Gen 17). Abraham was willing to rest in the wisdom as well as in the will of God. Verse 22 probably refers to the original statement of Abraham's justification, emphasizing that his ability to meet the renewed promise of God by unwavering faith was strictly in line with the faith that brought justification at an earlier point (v.3).

23–25 Having dealt with Abraham's situation, the apostle turns finally to applying God's dealings with the patriarch to the readers of the Epistle. This procedure accords with his observation that "everything that was written in the past was written to teach us, so that through endurance and the encouragement of the Scriptures we might have hope" (15:4). There are differences between Abraham's case and the position of the readers. Yet the basic similarity in God's dealings with both is unmistakable. Both believe in God as the one who acts in their behalf; both receive justification. Of course, the mention of the resurrected Jesus (v.24) is an element that could not belong to the OT as history, but the intended parallel with Abraham's experience is fairly evident. The same God who raised Jesus our Lord from the dead quickened the "dead" body of Abraham so as to make parenthood possible.

Death and resurrection were the portion of the Savior (v.25). One can hardly fail to notice the carefully balanced character of this final statement, relating as it does the death of Jesus to our sins and his resurrection to our justification. Beyond question, the statement owes much to Isaiah 53, where in LXX the Servant is pictured as delivered up on account of the sins of the many. Justification appears in the Hebrew text of that chapter (v.11). Moreover, the resurrection, though not stated in so many words, is implied in vv.10, 12. Whether Paul's statement is one he has taken over from Christian tradition (cf. 1 Cor 15:3, 4), as some think, or is entirely his own composition, may be an open question. But at least one can affirm that this passage shows the early tendency to phrase redemptive truth in brief, creedlike formulations.

The chief difficulty for interpretation lies in the preposition "for" that is common to both clauses. In itself our word "for" is ambiguous. It can mean "because of" or "with a view to." So "delivered over to death for our sins" can mean "because our sins were committed" and it was on account of them that Jesus had to die if salvation were to be procured. Similarly, "raised to life for our justification" can mean that Jesus was resurrected because our justification was accomplished in his death (cf. "justified by his blood," 5:9). On the other hand, one can interpret the "for" as meaning that Christ was delivered to death to deal with our sins, to atone for them, and that he was raised in order to achieve our justification. In justice to the Greek text it should be granted that the former alternative is the more natural. The idea of "with a view to" is not readily associated with *dia*, whereas Greek has another preposition (*eis*) that expresses that idea more clearly and is in fact used in the expression "justification that brings life" (literally, "justification with a view to life" (5:18). Furthermore, if one looks for a strict parallel between the passage and the situation of Abraham, he will see that Abraham's justification did not depend on the factor of resurrection, because he believed and was justified before the quickening of his deadened condition. One could reply, of course, that we should not look for complete similarity in the situation of Abraham and that of believers in the Christian era.

It may be helpful to recognize that justification, considered objectively and from the standpoint of God's provision, was indeed accomplished in the death of Christ (5:9) and therefore did not require the resurrection to complete it. Paul does not mention the resurrection in his definitive statement on justification in 3:21–26. Subjectively, however, the resurrection of Christ was essential for the exercise of faith, since his continuance under the power of death would create serious doubts about the efficacy of his sacrifice on the cross. Furthermore, justification is not simply a forensic transaction, important as that aspect is, but involves also a living relationship with God through Jesus Christ (5:18).

Finally, as Murray reminds us (in loc.), the justification to which Paul refers is justification by faith (cf. 5:1) and this applies as definitely to us as to Abraham. To believe in a Christ who died for our sins is only half the gospel. The resurrection cannot be omitted: observe how Paul includes both aspects in 6:3, 4 when showing how the work of Christ provides the foundation for Christian living.

Notes

19 ℵ A B C, among others, have the reading κατενόησεν (*katenoēsen*), meaning "he considered well." Another reading, which puts a negative before this verb, is supported by D G K P Ψ 33, etc. It is a rare situation to have two opposite readings that nevertheless yield much the same sense. The former reading has the stronger attestation.

D. *The Benefits of Justification*

5:1–11

1Therefore, since we have been justified through faith, we have peace with God
through our Lord Jesus Christ, 2through whom we have gained access by faith into
this grace in which we now stand. And we rejoice in the hope of the glory of God.
3Not only so, but we also rejoice in our sufferings, because we know that suffering
produces perseverance; 4perseverance, character; and character, hope. 5And

hope does not disappoint us, because God has poured out his love into our hearts by the Holy Spirit, whom he has given us.

6You see, at just the right time, when we were still powerless, Christ died for the ungodly. 7Very rarely will anyone die for a righteous man, though for a good man someone might possibly dare to die. 8But God demonstrates his own love for us in this: While we were still sinners, Christ died for us.

9Since we have now been justified by his blood, how much more shall we be saved from God's wrath through him! 10For if, when we were God's enemies, we were reconciled to him through the death of his Son, how much more, having been reconciled, shall we be saved through his life! 11Not only is this so, but we also rejoice in God through our Lord Jesus Christ, through whom we have now received reconciliation.

Here the discussion of justification goes beyond the exposition of what it is in itself, for that has been sufficiently covered. At this point we hear no more of the law or of fancied merit built up through obedience to it. Justification is now viewed in the light of the wealth of blessings it conveys to the child of God. Many indeed are the gifts that lie enfolded in this cardinal truth. It becomes a serious thing, then, to say, as some have done, that justification is not a central teaching with Paul but just an illustration of salvation drawn from the law court, or to call it merely a line of argumentation worked out to save his Gentile converts from the ignominy of being circumcised for their admission to the fellowship of the church. If this general appraisal had any truth in it, we should expect the apostle to make much more sparing use of the term "justify" than he does. Indeed we should look for him to be satisfied with "salvation" terminology.

Some would contend that we are already on the ground of sanctification in this chapter, and in support of this opinion they are able to point to the strong emphasis on experience in vv.2–5. No doubt the elements mentioned there do have an important bearing on Christian life, but the overall emphasis still remains on justification (vv.9, 16) along with reconciliation as seen against the background of enmity occasioned by sin (vv.10, 11). Perhaps even more decisive is usage of prepositions, a small but significant indicator. The emphasis in chapter 5 is on what has been done for the believer *through* Christ and his saving work (5:1, 2, 9, 10, 11, 17, 18, 19, 21; cf. 3:24), whereas in chapter 6 Paul deals with what has happened to the believer together *with* Christ (6:4, 5, 6, 8) and what he enjoys *in* Christ (6:11, 23). Furthermore, it is in chapter 6 (vv.19, 22), not in chapter 5, that sanctification (or holiness) first makes its appearance. Nevertheless, it is true that chapter 5, (especially in vv.12–21) prepares for chapters 6 to 8. In this passage the union of the people of Christ with him, as over against their former union with Adam, furnishes the needed context for the development of the various aspects of sanctification.

1–5 "Therefore" suggests that the whole argument from 3:21 on is the background for what is now set forth. Paul is assuming the reality of justification for himself and his readers ("we have been justified"). This could have been inferred from 4:24, 25, but Paul is careful to emphasize that justification is an assured fact before going on to show what is involved in it. So he includes the part that faith plays also, though this too has been affirmed in 4:24.

Before considering the items that come spilling out of the cornucopia of justification, we must confront a textual problem in v.1. NIV reads, "We have peace with God," but NEB, for example, has "let us continue at peace with God." These two renderings reflect two slightly different forms of the same word "have." (For data regarding the textual support for each, see notes at the end of this section.) The second rendering, the cohortative subjunctive, has the stronger attestation in the manuscripts. However, exhortation seems out of place here, especially since the construction demands that this same hortatory thrust be carried to a point midway through v.3. This is particulary awkward in v.2, because the text says that through Christ we have also gained access—and this is fact, not exhortation. The word "also" (*kai*), which is not indicated in many translations, including NIV, seems clearly to point to something mentioned earlier that we also have through Christ. This decidedly favors the rendering "we have peace."

Again, it is well known that short and long *o* of Greek were often confused in pronunciation during the Hellenistic period. J.H. Moulton writes, "It is indeed quite possible that the apostle's own pronunciation did not distinquish o and ō sufficiently to give Tertius a clear lead, without his making inquiry" (*A Grammar of New Testament Greek* [Edinburgh: T. & T. Clark, 1906]. Vol. I, p. 35). This means that it is precarious to lay too much store by the superior manuscript testimony for the *ō* reading. Another consideration is pointed out by Field, who notes that "*echomen* may have been changed into *echōmen* to correspond with *kauchōmetha* ('we rejoice'), which was supposed to be subjunctive mood" (p. 155).

The first of the blessings conveyed by justification is "peace." We have encountered the word in the salutation (1:7) and in an eschatological setting (2:10). Here, however, the milieu is the estrangement between God and man because of sin. Peace takes its meaning from the emphasis on divine wrath in the first section of the Epistle. Observe also, in the present chapter, the occurrence of "wrath" (v.9) and "enemies" (v.10). Peace in this setting means harmony with God rather than a subjective state in the consciousness of man.

That the objective meaning is to be adopted in the present passage is put beyond all doubt by the fact that the kind of peace in view is "peace with God." The same expression "with God" is used in John 1:1 to indicate the unity and perfect harmony between the Father and the Son. Since this particular boon is placed first among the benefits of justification, it should be evident how central is the wrath of God to Paul's exposition of the plight of man that God has moved to remedy. Man's plight could be dealt with only through the mediation of our Lord Jesus Christ. Related passages tell the same story. Christ made peace through the blood of his cross (Col 1:20). "He is our peace," writes Paul in Ephesians 2:14, and then he goes on to show how this peace works in two directions, removing the enmity between Jew and Gentile to make them one in the body of Christ and reconciling both in one body to God through the cross. In his lexicon, Bauer remarks that the term "peace" is nearly synonymous with the messianic salvation (cf. Acts 10:36).

The second benefit is "access" (v.2). Here also faith is mentioned as the essential instrumentality, as in justification itself. Since the word rendered "access" can also mean "approach" or "introduction," it is probable that the latter meaning is the more appropriate here, for introduction is fundamental to the access that is gained thereby. We are to think of the Father in his exaltation and glory as the one approached, with the Lord Jesus introducing us as those who belong to him and so to the Father. There is a striking similarity in thought between our passage and Ephesians 2:17, 18, where Paul asserts that Christ came and preached peace to those far away (Gentiles) and to those near (Jews), "for through him we both have access to the Father by one Spirit." Later in that Epistle Paul shows that this access enables one to approach God in prayer with freedom and confidence (Eph 3:12ff.).

The "grace in which we now stand" sums up the privilege of the saints in this present time, enjoying every spiritual blessing in Christ, and the possession of this grace gives warrant for the hope that we shall share the glory of God (v.2). In this prospect believers exult. Grace gives a foothold in the door that one day will swing wide to permit the enjoyment of the glorious presence of the Almighty, a privilege to be enjoyed forevermore. Grace is the only sure basis for the expectation of sharing eternity with God. Worth noting is the close relationship between faith and hope. As with Abraham (4:18), so with the believer in this age, the two virtues have much in common (cf. 1 Peter 1:21; Heb 11:1).

The word "rejoice," which was used to characterize the hope of the Christian for participating in the glory yet to be revealed (v.2), now carries over to another area totally different in nature as well as in time—namely, that of "sufferings." Peace with God does not necessarily bring peace with man. The actual conditions of life, especially for believers in the midst of a hostile society, are not easy or pleasant, but the knowledge of acceptance with God, of grace constantly supplied, and the prospect of future glory enable believers to exult in the face of sufferings. The word "sufferings" is often rendered "tribulations" and emphasizes the element of pressure. As a result, the usual setting for the term is external suffering such as persecution, but it is used occasionally for distress, a natural extension of the application of the word, since external events tend to affect the human spirit.

We do not expect to find a full treatment of the subject of suffering here, since sufferings are viewed simply as one link in a chain of events and interactions designed to show what profit they bring to Christian experience, not what they are in themselves. Elsewhere Paul stresses that they are an extension of the sufferings experienced by Christ in the days of his flesh, rightly to be experienced now by those who make up his body (Phil 3:10). Believers rejoice when by their suffering they can show their love and loyalty to the Savior (Acts 5:41).

Suffering has this value, that it produces "perseverance," or "steadfast endurance." This is a suitable element to go along with tribulation, because it denotes resistance to pressure, literally "a bearing up under it." One does not take the pressure passively by abjectly giving in to it, as much Oriental philosophy counsels its devotees to do. Christ "endured" the cross and thus triumphed over it. Right here lies one of the distinctives of the Christian faith, in that the believer is taught to glory and rejoice in the midst of suffering rather than to sigh and submit to it as a necessary or inevitable evil.

The value of perseverance is that it develops "character." Job sensed its worth, saying in the midst of his troubles, "When he has tried me, I shall come forth as gold" (Job 23:10 RSV). The word rendered "character" indicates tested value. The newborn child of God is precious in his sight, but the tested and proven saint means even more to him because such a one is a living demonstration of the character-developing power of the gospel. When we stand in the presence of God, all material possessions will have been left behind, but all that we have gained by way of spiritual advance will be retained. This progress is a testimony to God, so it rightly has a place in glory.

This helps to explain Paul's statement that character produces "hope." Looking back, we see that hope consummates a series of items beginning with sufferings. But just prior to that Paul has considered hope from the standpoint of another series—faith, peace, access, grace, and then hope of the glory of God. So we are entitled to say that just as our present access gives hope of sharing the divine glory, so with our sufferings. They help to produce character, and approved Christian character finds its ultimate resting place in the presence of God, not in a grave. By the tutelage of suffering the Lord is fitting us for his eternal fellowship.

Next, Paul makes it plain that this hope is not just a pious wish, for it does not put one to shame. It does not disappoint, because it is coupled with the love of God (v.5). Human love may bring disappointment and frustration, but not the love of God. "The Holy Spirit produces in the believer an immediate and overflowing consciousness that he is the object of God's redeeming love, and this is the guarantee that this hope will not disappoint him" (Shedd, in loc.). Subjective desire is supported by an objective divine gift guaranteeing the realization of an eternal fellowship with God.

This passage, then, contains an intimation of the importance of the believer's possession of the Holy Spirit as a certification concerning the future aspects of his salvation. In chapter 8 this is developed more fully. But even in the limited treatment given the Spirit in the present passage we get a glimpse of something that specially characterizes the Spirit. By him God's love is poured out in our hearts. The initial outpouring at Pentecost (Acts 2:33; cf. Ezek 39:29; Joel 2:28; Zech 12:10) is followed by a maintenance of the flow in individuals who receive the Spirit at conversion. The verb "poured out" speaks of the inexhaustible abundance of the supply, being reminiscent of the copious provision for the thirsty children of Israel in the wilderness (Num 20:8, 11). This is particularly impressive in view of Paul's identification of the rock with Christ (1 Cor 10:4). The blessings found in Christ are mediated to the people of God by the Spirit. Looking back over the paragraph, we see that the thought has advanced from faith to hope and from hope to love (the same order as in 1 Cor 13:13).

Notes

1 Support for the subjunctive ἔχωμεν (*echōmen,* "let us have") among the uncials includes B ℵ A C D E K L, in addition to cursives, versions, and patristic citations. Support for the indicative ἔχομεν (*echomen,* "we have") is provided by correctors of B ℵ FGP, besides cursives, versions, and patristic citations.

However, the discovery of a vellum fragment of part of Romans in 1950 has altered the situation considerably. It supports the text of B everywhere (through some thirty verses) except at 5:1. The Wyman fragment, designated 0220, is dated by W.H.P. Hatch in the latter part of the third century, whereas B dates from the first third of the fourth century. He writes, "This evidence for *echomen* is probably pre-Hesychian. Therefore the argument for the indicative is greatly strengthened, and the claim of the subjunctive to be the correct reading is correspondingly weakened" (HTR 45 [1952] 83).

6–8 Having dwelt on the powerful influence of the divine love ministered to the hearts of believers by the Spirit, Paul goes on to explore the depths of that love, finding it in the cross of Christ. The demonstration of God's love in Christ came "at just the right time." This recalls Paul's placing of the incarnation and redeeming work of our Lord in the fullness of time (Gal 4:4). Since the argument of Romans has included the purpose of the law as bringing clear knowledge of sin (3:20) and as working wrath (4:15), the connection with the Galatians material is fairly close. The law had operated for centuries and had served to expose the weakness and inability of man to measure up to the divine standard of righteousness. No further testing was needed. It *was* the right time. One may ask, perhaps, Suppose it be granted that Galatians and Romans have the same emphasis on this point, why then do they not have the same term for "time" (Rom has *kairos* and

Gal *chronos*)? Actually there is no perceptible difference, since the word "fulness" (*plērōma*) in Galatians introduces the very emphasis of *kairos*—time as to its character rather than as to its duration.

"Powerless" is the translation of a word that commonly means "weak" or "sickly," but here it has a somewhat specialized force well expressed by Sanday and Headlam as "incapable of working out any righteousness for ourselves (in loc.)." A still more uncomplimentary description of those who needed the intervention of Christ's death on their behalf is "ungodly." The same term was used in the striking statement of 4:5 that such are the people God justifies.

A third word descriptive of those for whom Christ died is "sinners." The verb "to sin" has been used in 3:23 to summarize the human predicament traced in the opening chapters. We need to see how Paul prepares the way for the impact of this term by contrasting it with both "righteous" and "good." He puts aside for the moment the technical theological force of the word "righteous" in the sense of "justified" and uses it as it is used in ordinary parlance. Likewise, he ignores the fact that in 3:12 he has quoted "There is no one who does good" from Psalm 14:3, and then proceeds to use "good" as we do when recognizing kindness and benevolence in one another. In other words, Paul is illustrating a point from ordinary life. It is a rare thing, he says, to find a person ready to die for an upright man, but conceivably it would be easier to find one willing to die for a good man. Evidently the "good man" stands on a higher plane than the "righteous man."

Lightfoot berates those who profess to see no substantial difference between the two, quoting extensively from the Fathers to show that they are not synonymous. The righteous man is righteous, but nothing more. He lacks feeling for others. He may be so severely just that he is unattractive, if not actually repellent. On the other hand, the good man, while not lacking righteousness, goes beyond the other by being kind and benevolent (*Notes on Epistles of St. Paul* [London: Macmillan, 1895], pp. 286, 287). The interpretation is slightly complicated by the absence of the article with "righteous," whereas "good" has it. This opens the possibility that the reference is not to a good man but to "the good cause," especially the public good (so Leenhardt, in loc.). But the context requires that all three words—righteous, good, and sinners—be treated as personal.

Now Paul is ready to proceed to his point. It was for "sinners" Christ died, for men who were neither "righteous" nor "good." The contrast is between the tremendous worth of the life laid down and the unworthiness of those who stand to benefit from it. Back of the death of Christ for sinners is the love of God (v.8): God loved; Christ died. No attempt is made to deal with the Savior's reaction or motivation. Paul leaves much to Christian awareness of the intimate bond between Father and Son, the whole truth about God being in Christ (2 Cor 5:19) and Christ being motivated by love for the lost (John 15:12, 13). What he puts in the foreground is the love of God, and this Paul underscores by designating it as "his [God's] own love." It is distinctive, unexpected, unheard of (cf. John 3:16).

Four times in these three verses the expression "die for" occurs, and in each instance the preposition is *hyper* (on behalf of), commonly employed by Paul in such contexts. He could have used *anti* in the place of, which would stress the substitutionary aspect of the death of Christ. He probably avoids it, however, because he is desirous of stressing something else as well, in line with the emphasis on the divine love. For this purpose *hyper* is eminently suited; it can express the substitutionary character of the sacrifice of Christ (as papyri usage indicates) plus the additional element of action on behalf of another in line with the loving empathy of God in Christ.

9–11 Whereas the preceding paragraph dealt with the depth of the love of God as seen in the cross, the present section moves on to declare the height of that love, its refusal to stop short of effecting final and everlasting salvation in which the enmity created by sin has been completely overcome.

We are invited to take our stand on the fact of an achieved justification (the terminology is identical with that found in v.1), then turn to face the far-reaching effects of this justification on our future. Lest it be taken lightly, the means of that justification is repeated also—"by his [Christ's] blood." NEB has "by Christ's sacrificial death," and Barrett renders it, "at the cost of his blood." We were reconciled when we were enemies. Surely, then, since God no longer looks on us as enemies subject to his wrath, he will find it possible to maintain the status quo and not suffer us to lapse back into the unreconciled position and, furthermore, will carry us on to the full end of our salvation. The agency of Christ continues to be crucial, only now with this difference, that, whereas our justification was achieved by his death, our preservation is secured by his life. This is a clear reference to his postresurrection life rather than to his life in the days of his flesh. Here Paul conjoins justification and salvation as he did in the theme (1:16, 17).

No doubt, the pivotal word for the right understanding of vv.10, 11 is *echthroi* (enemies), the fourth term Paul has used for those in the unsaved state. (See vv.6–8 for the others.) Is "enemies" used in an active sense to mean those who have enmity toward God (cf. 8:7) or in the passive sense, meaning those who are reckoned as enemies by God? Several reasons dictate that the latter is the intended force of the word. First, that the word is capable of conveying this meaning is evident from 11:28, where the people of Israel are spoken of as enemies in the reckoning of God and yet loved by him, involving the same combination as in the passage we are considering. The enmity in 11:28 is not temperamental but judicial. Second, the mention of "God's wrath" in v.9 points to the conclusion that the *echthroi* are the objects of the wrath. Third, the tenor of the argument leads one to the same conclusion. Paul reasons from the greater to the lesser. If God loved us when we were enemies, now that he has made provision for us at infinite cost, much more will he go on to see us through to the final goal of our salvation. But if the sense is that God loved us and saved us when we were enemies in our attitude toward him, the "much more" loses its point. "He is not arguing that if we have begun to love God we may reckon on his doing so and so for us, but because He has done so much, we may expect Him to do more" (Archibald McCaig in ISBE, 1930, vol. IV, p. 2537a). Fourth, Paul not only states that we have been reconciled (v.10) but that we have *received* the reconciliation (v.11). He avoids saying that we have done anything to effect the reconciliation. God provided it through the death of his Son. The matter is made even clearer, if anything, in the companion statement that God has reconciled us "to himself" (2 Cor 5:18). The appropriate response of the saved community is exultation (cf. vv.2, 3).

E. *The Universal Applicability of Justification*

5:12–21

12Therefore, just as sin entered the world through one man, and death through sin, and in this way death came to all men, because all sinned—13for before the law was given, sin was in the world. But sin is not taken into account when there is no law. 14Nevertheless, death reigned from the time of Adam to the time of Moses, even over those who did not sin by breaking a command, as did Adam, who was a pattern of the one to come.

[15]But the gift is not like the trespass. For if the many died by the trespass of the
one man, how much more did God's grace and the gift that came by the grace
of the one man, Jesus Christ, overflow to the many! [16]Again, the gift of God is not
like the result of the one man's sin: The judgment followed one sin and brought
condemnation, but the gift followed many trespasses and brought justification.
[17]For if, by the trespass of the one man, death reigned through that one man, how
much more will those who receive God's abundant provision of grace and of the
gift of righteousness reign in life through the one man, Jesus Christ.

[18]Consequently, just as the result of one trespass was condemnation for all
men, so also the result of one act of righteousness was justification that brings life
for all men. [19]For just as through the disobedience of the one man the many were
made sinners, so also through the obedience of the one man the many will be
made righteous.

[20]The law was added so that the trespass might increase. But where sin in-
creased, grace increased all the more, [21]so that, just as sin reigned in death, so
also grace might reign through righteousness to bring eternal life through Jesus
Christ our Lord.

This difficult portion of the Epistle, packed with close reasoning and theological terminology, stands at the very heart of the development of Paul's thought. He has presented all men as sinners and Christ as the one who has died to redeem them. Now he delves into the question How does it come about that all men—with no exception but Jesus Christ—are in fact sinners? In answer, he goes all the way back to the first man Adam to affirm that what he did has affected the whole of mankind, involving everyone in sin and death. But over this record of disaster and loss he puts the countermeasures taken on behalf of the race by another man, Jesus Christ, of which all are potential beneficiaries.

12 The one man through whom sin entered the world is not immediately named (reserved till v.14). The same procedure is followed with the other man to be considered: he is called a man before he is named (v.15). Except for two nontheological references (Luke 3:38; Jude 14), every mention of Adam in the NT comes from the pen of Paul. In 1 Timothy 2:14 he makes the point that Adam, unlike Eve, was not deceived, but sinned deliberately. In 1 Corinthians 15, as in the Romans passage, he institutes a comparison between the first and the last Adam, but confines the treatment to the issue of death and resurrection, even though sin is dealt with somewhat incidentally (vv.17, 56), whereas in Romans 5 both sin and death are named immediately and are woven into the texture of the argument throughout. In the earlier letter Paul makes the significant statement "For as in Adam all die, so in Christ all will be made alive" (1 Cor 15:22) in line with Romans 5:12. Paul has already referred to the inevitable connection between sin and death in the only previous mention of death in Romans (1:32) exclusive of the death of Christ (5:10). But here in v.12 he pictures sin and death as entering the world through one man, with the result that death permeated the whole of mankind. It was the opening in the dike that led to the inundation, the poison that entered at one point and penetrated every unit of man's corporate life.

If Paul had stopped with the observation that death came to all men because all sinned, we would be left with the impression that all sinned and deserved death because they followed the example of Adam. But subsequent statements in the passage make it abundantly clear that the connection between Adam's sin and death and what has befallen the race is far closer than that. Paul can say that the many died because of "the trespass of the one man" (v.15). Clearly the gist of his teaching is that just as mankind has become involved in sin and death through Adam, it has the remedy of righteousness and life only in Christ.

What, then, is the precise relation of Adam in his fall to those who come after him? Paul does not say, unless he provides the information in the last clause of the verse. NIV uses the word "because," which is certainly the meaning of *eph' hō* in 2 Corinthians 5:4 and probably also in Philippians 3:12. The Vulgate rendering of the Greek is *in quo*, which could be understood as meaning "in which" (i.e., death) or "in whom" (i.e., Adam). The former does not make sense and the latter is so far removed from the antecedent ("man") as to be dubious, though this was Augustine's conclusion.

Now if the correct translation is "because all sinned," why did not Paul go on and say specifically that all sinned in the first man? That he could have done so seems clear from v.19: "For just as through the disobedience of the one man the many were made sinners, so also through the obedience of the one man the many will be made righteous." Was it the sudden breaking off to follow another line of thought (vv.13, 14) that prevented the full statement? Or was it his reluctance to gloss over human responsibility, which he had already established in terms of universal sin and guilt (3:23)? Experience demonstrates that despite the inheritance of a sinful nature from Adam, people are convicted of guilt for the sins resulting from it—the sins they themselves commit. Conscience is a factor in human life and the Holy Spirit does convict of sin (John 16:8). Perhaps, then, as some hold, while the emphasis on original sin is primary in the light of the passage as a whole, there is a hint that personal choice and personal sin are not entirely excluded (cf. "many trespasses" in v.16).

That we could have sinned in Adam may seem strange and unnatural to the mind of Western man. Nevertheless, it is congenial to biblical teaching on the solidarity of mankind. When Adam sinned, the race sinned because the race was in him. To put it boldy, Adam *was* the race. What he did, his descendants, who were still in him, did also. This principle is utilized in Hebrews 7:9, 10, "One might even say that Levi, who collects the tenth, paid the tenth through Abraham, because when Melchizedek met Abraham, Levi was still in the body of his ancestor."

If one is still troubled by the seeming injustice of being born with a sinful nature because of what the father of the race did and being held accountable for the sins that result from that disability, he should weigh carefully the significance of reconciliation as stated by Paul: ". . . that God was reconciling the world to himself in Christ, *not counting men's sins against them*" (2 Cor 5:19). The sins committed, that owe their original impetus to the sin of the first man, are not reckoned against those who have committed them provided they put their trust in Christ crucified and risen. God takes their sins and gives them his righteousness. Would we not agree that this is more than a fair exchange?

13,14 The dash at the end of v.12 is intended to indicate that the comparison upon which Paul has launched with his "just as" is not carried through. In view of what follows, the complete statement, if given here, would have run something like this: "Just as sin entered the world through one man, and death through sin, and in this way death came to all men, because all sinned, so righteousness entered the world by one man, and life through righteousness." Grammatically, the conclusion is not formally stated at all, although in KJV it is assumed that vv.13–17 are parenthetical, with v.18 stating the conclusion of v.12. As Meyer puts it, in v.18 and following we have recapitulation but not resumption. The necessary conclusion to v.12 has really been stated already in vv.15–17 in various ways. Throughout the passage the thought is so tremendous as to prove intractable from the standpoint of expressing it in orderly sequence. The thought outruns the structural capacity of language.

Judging from the use of "for" at the beginning of v.13, these two verses are intended to support and explicate v.12. The point is made that from Adam to Moses the law was not yet given, so sin was not present in the sense of transgression. Men did not have a charge from God similar to that which Adam had and violated. But the very fact that death was regnant during this period is proof that there was sin to account for it, seeing that death is the consequence of sin. The sin in view was the sin of Adam, which involved all his descendants. Death in this case rather obviously means physical death, which suggests that the same is true in v.12. This agrees with Paul's treatment of the subject of death in 1 Corinthians 15 (see especially v.22).

Adam is described as "a pattern of the one to come." Pattern translates the work *typos*, ordinarily rendered "type." It may seem strange that Adam should be designated as a type of Christ when the two are so dissimilar in themselves and in their effect on mankind. But there is justification for the parallél. "The resemblance, on account of which Adam is regarded as the type of Christ, consists in this, that Adam communicated to those whom he represented what belonged to him, and that Christ also communicated to those whom he represented what belonged to him" (Haldane, in loc.). This amounts to saying that what each did involved others. "The one to come" is to be taken from the perspective of Adam and his time, and has no reference to the second coming of Christ (cf. Matt 11:3). Barrett is of the opinion that since Paul has just mentioned Adam, the word "one" should be thought of in terms of the Adam to come, the last Adam, as Christ is explicitly termed in 1 Corinthians 15:45.

In his book, *Christ and Adam* (Harper, 1956), Karl Barth has advanced a provocative interpretation of Adam as a type of Christ. He has attempted to reverse the order: "Man's essential and original nature is to be found . . . not in Adam but in Christ. In Adam we can only find it prefigured. Adam can therefore be interpreted only in the light of Christ and not the other way round" (p. 29). It should be evident, however, that Paul's thought here is not moving in the orbit of man as made in the image of God and therefore in the image of Christ who is the image of God. To import the preexistence of Christ is to introduce an element foreign to Paul's purpose and treatment in this passage. For a careful review of Barth's position and its weaknesses, one may consult Murray, pp. 384–90.

15–17 In this section Christ's effect on men is seen as totally different from that of Adam, and vastly superior. Note the repeated expression "how much more." Any hint of parallelism suggested by "pattern" is replaced by the element of contrast. True, there appears to be similarity in one point, in that the work of Adam and that of Christ relate to the many. It will readily be seen by comparing v.15 with v.12 that "the many" is the same as "all men" ("death came to all men" and "the many died"). The use of "the many" has this advantage, that it underscores the importance of Adam and Christ respectively. What one did, in each case, affected not one but many. The expression goes back to Isaiah 53:11, 12, which underlies our Lord's use in Mark 10:45.

Another notable feature of the passage is the expression "how much more" (vv.15, 17). The force of this seems to be bound up with the recurring use of "grace" and "gift," suggesting that the work of Christ not merely cancelled the effects of Adam's transgression so as to put man back into a state of innocence under a probation such as their progenitor faced, but rather gives to man far more than he lost in Adam, more indeed than Adam ever had. The gift, prompted by grace, includes righteousness (v.17) and life (v.18) which is later defined as eternal life (v.21). Paul makes a further observation to the effect that in Adam's case, a single sin was involved, and that was sufficient to bring condemnation, but in the work of Christ a provision is found for the many acts of sin that have resulted in the lives of his descendants (v.16).

Whereas up to this point Paul's train of thought has been concerned with developing the concept of sin taken over from v.12, now it turns to its companion factor, death, likewise mentioned in v.12, with a view to enlarging upon it (v.17). The point of the "much more" appears to be this—that in Christ not only is the hold of death, established by Adam's sin, effectively broken, but because of Christ's redeeming work the believer is able to look forward to reigning in life through Christ. This, of course, implies participation in the resurrection. Believers will have a share in the Lord's kingdom and glory.

18,19 At this point, as noted above, Paul provides something of a conclusion to v.12, but in such a way as to take account of the intervening material. The opening word, "consequently," shows his intent to summarize. Notice the careful balancing of the clauses. One trespass brought condemnation for all humanity and one act of righteousness brought justification for all. Adam's sin is labeled "trespass," indicating that it was deliberate (cf. "breaking a command" in v.14). The basic meaning of the word rendered "trespass" is to convey the idea of falling aside or going astray. "It refers directly to the disruption of man's relation to God through his fault" (Michaelis in TDNT VI, p. 172).

The reference is clearly to the violation of the divine restriction laid down in Genesis 2:17, with resulting condemnation for the entire human race. His act involved others directly; it did not merely set a bad example. Over against Adam's act, Paul put another of an entirely different character—an act of righteousness. The same Greek word occurs at the end of v.16, where it is rendered "justification." Perhaps "act" is a bit narrow for this context. "Work of righteousness" might be better. In fact, the whole scope of the ministry of our Lord could be in view. He came "to fulfill all righteousness" (Matt 3:15). The word "justification" is set over against "condemnation," but something is added, namely, the observation that justification is more than the antithesis of condemnation, more than the setting aside of an adverse verdict due to sin, more than the imputation of divine righteousness. It is the passport to life, the sharing of the life of God (cf. v.21).

Impressed by the fact that the word "one" is regularly used either of Adam or of Christ in 5:12–21, Leenhardt suggests that consistency demands that in v.18, instead of "one act of righteousness" we should render "one man's act of righteousness" (in loc.). To do this, however, would destroy the balance between this clause and the opening statement, where "one trespass" is inescapably the correct rendering rather than "the trespass of one."

Another term for Adam's failure occurs in v.19, namely, "disobedience." This accents the voluntary character of his sin. Matching it is the obedience of Christ. This concept was highly meaningful for Paul, as we know from Philippians 2:5–11. The interpretation of that passage along the lines of a latent comparison between Adam (unnamed, but in the background) and Christ is most satisfactory. Instead of grasping after equality with God, as Adam had done, the Lord Jesus humbled himself and became obedient even to the point of accepting death on a cross.

The result of Christ's obedience is that "the many will be made righteous." Does this refer to righteous character? Possibly so, if the future tense is definitely eschatological in its thrust, pointing to the consummation in glory, when imputed righteousness will have become righteousness possessed in unblemished fullness. But "will be made righteous" may simply be the equivalent of "will become righteous" in the forensic sense, as in 2 Corinthians 5:21, in which case the future tense need not be thought of as eschatological but as embracing all who in this age are granted justification. Most of these were indeed future to Paul's time. The milieu of thought has not shifted from the forensic.

Does the sweeping language used ("the many" being all men) suggest that all mankind will be brought within the circle of justification, so that none whatever will be lost? Some have thought so. But if the doctrine of universalism were being taught here, Paul would be contradicting himself, for he has already pictured men as perishing because of sin (2:12; cf. 1 Cor 1:18). Furthermore, his entire presentation of salvation has emphasized the fact that justification is granted only on the basis of faith. We must conclude, therefore, that only as "the many" are found in Christ can they qualify as belonging to the righteous.

20,21 At the conclusion of the chapter, Adam as a figure fades from view. Yet his influence is still present in the mention of sin and death. Paul now introduces another factor—the Mosaic law—to show its bearing on the great issues of sin and righteousness. There is scarcely a subject treated by Paul in Romans that does not call for some consideration of the law. The closest affinity to the thought in v.20 is found in 3:20, "Through the law we become conscious of sin." Also, chapter 7 traces the relationship between the law and sin in rather elaborate fashion.

The apostle is not maintaining that the purpose of the giving of the law is exclusively "that the trespass might increase," because he makes room for the law as a revelation of the will of God and therefore a positive benefit (7:12). The law also serves to restrain evil in the world (implied in 6:15; stated in 1 Tim 1:9–11). Paul says the law "was added." Similar language is used in Galatians 3:19, where the law is regarded as something temporary, designed to disclose the transgression aspect of sin and prepare the way for the coming of Christ by demonstrating the dire need for his saving work. This function of the law—viz., to increase transgression—was not recognized in rabbinic Judaism (H.J. Schoeps, *Paul* [Philadelphia: Westminster Press, 1961], p. 174). From the Sermon on the Mount, however, it appears that Jesus sought to apply the law in just this way, to awaken a sense of sin in those who fancied they were keeping the law tolerably well but had underestimated its searching demands and the sinfulness of their own hearts.

Lest someone raise a charge against the Almighty that to make possible an increase in sin is not to his credit, Paul insists that only where sin is seen in its maximum expression can divine grace truly be appreciated. "Grace increased all the more." The apostle waxes almost ecstatic as he revels in the superlative excellence of the divine overruling that makes sin serve a gracious purpose. In only one other passage does he use this verb (*hyperperisseuō*), which expresses "super-increase," and there the theme is not sin but trouble—"in all our troubles my joy knows no bounds" (2 Cor 7:4).

With great effect Paul brings the leading concepts of the passage together in the final statement (v.21). "Sin reigned in death" picks up vv.12, 14; "grace" looks back to vv.15. 17; "reign" reflects vv.14, 17; "righteousness" harks back to v.17 as well as to 1:17 and many other passages; "eternal life" completes and crowns the allusion to "life" in vv.17, 18. Sin and death are virtually personified throughout. Sin poses as absolute monarch, reigning through death as its vicar, but in the end it is exposed as a pretender and is obliged to yield the palm to another whose reign is wholly absolute and totally different, being as much a blessing as the other is a curse.

The treatment of sin, death, and salvation in terms of righteousness is crucial to our understanding of our relation to God. It loudly proclaims that no sinner, whether a mystic aspiring to direct contact with God or a legalist counting on his good works to approve him in God's sight, is able in his own way to find acceptance with God. Because another man, Adam, has intervened between him and the Creator, still another, even Jesus Christ, must be the medium of his return as a sinner to a righteous God. The claim of Jesus of Nazareth resounds through the passage: "I am the way—and the truth and the life. No one comes to the Father except through me" (John 14:6).

Notes

12 Entering the debate about the meaning of ἐφ' ᾡ (*eph' hō*), Nigel Turner does not attach great importance to the fact that Paul uses (epi) with the dative rather than ἐν (en), the preposition that appears in 1 Cor 15:22. He remarks that "even in classical Greek, and much more so in the New Testament period, the distinctions between the cases with this preposition are difficult to maintain" (*Grammatical Insights into the New Testament* [Edinburgh: T. & T. Clark, 1965], p. 118). He goes on to suggest that man is "under the power of" and "within the jurisdiction of" Adam. He does not deal with the problem of the remoteness of ἐφ' ᾡ (*eph' hō*) from its alleged antecedent **ἀνθρώπου** (*anthrōpou*).

A new departure in the attempted understanding of *eph' hō* has been made by F.W. Danker, NTS 14 (April 1968) 424–439. He interprets Paul to mean that death passed to all men "on the basis of what law [*eph' hō*] they committed their sins under." He relies both on the previous teaching about law as involving Jew and Gentile (2:12–16) and on the immediate context in 5:13, 14. He is able to make out a plausible case, but one is left with the uneasy feeling that if scholars have missed this down through the years, the chances that the Roman church caught the meaning are rather slim.

V. Sanctification: The Impartation of Righteousness

Up to this point the letter has answered such questions as these: Why does man need salvation? What has God done to effect it? How can we appropriate it? The answers have come in terms of sin, condemnation, the gift of Christ, faith, and justification. Is there need for anything more? Yes, there is. For the saved man cannot safely be turned over to his own wisdom and his own devices, seeing that he has not yet reached the perfect state. He must still contend with sin and must depend on divine resources. God's plan of salvation does not stop with justification but continues on in sanctification. A diagram may help to clarify the relationship between the two.

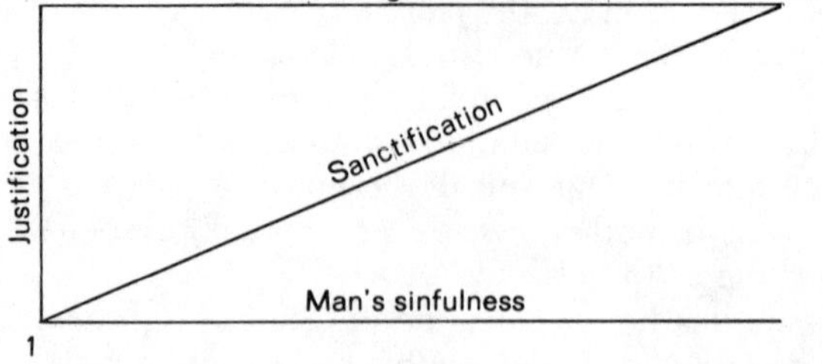

Point 1 marks conversion, or, if we think objectively rather than subjectively, regeneration. It is here that justification takes place. The line from 1 to 2 is not to be thought of as a process but as a change of position effected by God—his declaration of righteousness on behalf of the condemned sinner. Justification by faith means that one is lifted once-for-all to the level of God's righteousness. His standing before God is complete and perfect, because Christ has been made his righteousness (1 Cor 1:30; cf. 2 Cor 5:21). At no time in this life or in the life to come will his status in terms of righteousness be any greater. It will neither diminish nor fade, "for God's gifts and his call are irrevocable" (11:29).

Of course, God is concerned not only with the believer's status but also with his state, his actual condition. No sooner has he justified a person than he begins a process of growth that we know as sanctification. It is represented by the diagonal line between 1 and 3. This is a process, to be sure, but it should be observed that the term "sanctification" is used in Scripture also to express a setting apart that is basic to any progress in the Christian life. Consider the description of the Corinthian believers as (already) "sanctified" (1 Cor 1:2) in seeming contradiction to the unholy state of many of them as evidenced by Paul's exposure of their shortcomings as the letter unfolds. The puzzle is solved by his observation about what happened at their conversion. "You were washed, you were sanctified, you were justified in the name of the Lord Jesus and by the Spirit of our God" (1 Cor 6:11). Mention of their sanctification is actually given priority over their justification, which reverses the expected order. But this is initial or positional sanctification, a setting apart of the sinner to God, which is basic to any improvement in his manner of life (cf. 1 Peter 1:2). This aspect of sanctification cannot be distinguished from justification in respect to time. But sanctification as a process is naturally dependent upon and subsequent to justification.

The significance of point 3 should be noted also. This is the juncture at which the process of sanctification reaches its consummation, when the saint will experience complete sanctification because his sinful nature is left behind and his life is fully conformed to the divine standard as seen in God's Son (8:29). This occurs at death (Heb 12:23) or at the return of Christ in the case of the saints who are alive at that time (1 John 3:2). Then for the first time the believer's actual state in terms of righteousness will conform to the status conferred on him at his justification (Gal 5:5). His standing and his state will be identical.

A. *The Believer's Union With Christ in Death and in Resurrection Life*

6:1–14

1What shall we say, then? Shall we go on sinning so that grace may increase?
2By no means! We died to sin; how can we live in it any longer? 3Or don't you know
that all of us who were baptized into Christ Jesus were baptized into his death?
4We were therefore buried with him through baptism into death in order that, just
as Christ was raised from the dead through the glory of the Father, we too may
live a new life.

5If we have been united with him in his death, we will certainly also be united
with him in his resurrection. 6For we know that our old self was crucified with him
so that the body of sin might be rendered powerless, that we should no longer be
slaves to sin—7because anyone who has died has been freed from sin.

8Now if we died with Christ, we believe that we will also live with him. 9For we
know that since Christ was raised from the dead, he cannot die again; death no
longer has mastery over him. 10The death he died, he died to sin once for all; but
the life he lives, he lives to God.

11In the same way, count yourselves dead to sin but alive to God in Christ Jesus.

> [12]Therefore, do not let sin reign in your mortal body so that you obey its evil desires. [13]Do not offer the parts of your body to sin, as instruments of wickedness, but rather offer yourselves to God, as those who have returned from death to life; and offer the parts of your body to him as instruments of righteousness. [14]For sin shall not be your master, because you are not under law, but under grace.

In this section we will see that Christ passed through certain epochal experiences—namely, death, burial, and resurrection. Viewed from the standpoint of his substitutionary sacrifice for sin, these events do not involve our participation, though our salvation depends on them. Our Lord was alone in enduring the cross, in being buried, and in being raised from the dead. But his redeeming work is not only substitutionary; it is also representative. "One died for all, and therefore all died" (2 Cor 5:14). So Christians are viewed as being identified with Christ in his death, burial, and resurrection. And as truly as he, having borne our sin, is now removed from any claim of sin against him—because he died to sin and rose again—we also by virtue of being joined to him are delivered from any claim of sin to control us. This line of thought is what Paul proceeds to develop in the passage before us. It is evident that God has a plan for dealing with the power of sin as well as with its guilt. The way has been prepared for this emphasis by the presentation of the solidarity between Christ and the redeemed in 5:12–21.

1. *The statement of the fact* (6:1–10)

1–4 It is notable that Paul begins this discussion by raising an objection and answering it. The objection grows out of his presentation of justification, especially the teaching that where sin increased, grace increased all the more (5:20). The query, then, is to this effect: "Are we not able, or even obliged, by the logic of justification, to continue on in sin, now that we are Christians, in order to give divine grace as much opportunity as possible to display itself? The more we sin, the more will God's grace be required to meet the situation, and this will in turn contribute the more to his glory."

The apostle shows his horror at such a suggestion: "By no means!" Other renderings are possible, such as "Away with the notion!" or "Perish the thought!" Paul has already repudiated a similar suggestion in a somewhat different context (3:8). It is probable that in the past, as he taught justification, objections of this sort were raised from time to time by those who feared that his teaching opened the door to libertinism by encouraging indifference to the ethical demands of the law. If so, his answer is not something recently developed, but rather forged out in years of reflection under divine guidance.

His answer is crisp: "We died to sin; how can we live in it any longer?" He does not say that sin is dead to the Christian. Chapter 7 is a sufficient refutation of any such notion. At this point Paul does not explain when or how we died to sin, being content to state the fact and its obvious implication, that to go on sinning is logically impossible. What he does present here is not the impossibility of committing a single sin, but the impossibility of continuing in a life dominated by sin. Death to sin is not something hoped for or resolved upon by the believer; it is something that has already taken place. It is a simple fact basic to the living of the Christian life. The explanation of our death to sin follows immediately (vv.3, 4).

It was accomplished by being "baptized into Christ Jesus." What is being described is a spiritual reality of the deepest import—not a ceremony, not even a sacrament. The metaphor of baptism is clearly used in a relational sense elsewhere, as in the case of the Israelites baptized into Moses by reason of the crossing of the Red Sea (1 Cor 10:2). They became united to him as never before, recognizing his leadership and their dependence on him. Union with Christ means union with him in his death. It is significant that although Jesus emphasized discipleship throughout his ministry, he did not speak of union with himself till he was on the verge of going to the cross (John 14–16). Earlier he spoke of his death under the figure of baptism (Luke 12:50).

Paul uses baptism to illustrate this vital union with Christ in his death (v.4), though baptism does not accomplish it. Apparently, he pictures burial with Christ, however momentarily, in the submergence of the body under the baptismal waters. The importance of burial is that it attests the reality of death (1 Cor 15:3, 4). It expresses with finality the end of the old life governed by relationship with Adam. It also expresses the impossibility of a new life apart from divine action. The God who raised Jesus Christ from the dead has likewise imparted life to those who are his. The expression "to live a new life" is literally "to walk in newness of life," the walk being the evidence of the new type of life granted to the child of God. This is a distinctive type of life realized only by one united to Christ (cf. 2 Cor 5:17), so that Christ is its dynamic. In this connection the question arises, Why should the resurrection of Christ be described as accomplished "through the glory of the Father?" It is because "glory" here has the meaning of power, as in the resurrection of Lazarus (John 11:40).

The latter half of v.4 has a noticeably balanced structure ("just as Christ . . . we too"), recalling the pattern in 5:12, 18, 21. This suggests that the principle of solidarity advanced in 5:12–21 is still thought of as operating here in the significance of baptism. There is no explicit statement that in baptism we were raised with Christ as well as made to share in his death. Resurrection is seen rather as an effect that logically follows from the identification with Christ in his death. However, resurrection is verbally connected with baptism in the parallel passage—Colossians 2:12.

There is a certain awkwardness in the statement that we were buried with Christ through baptism into death, seeing that in human experience burial follows rather than precedes death. However, as Sanday and Headlam point out (in loc.), this awkwardness disappears in the prominence given death in the whole passage. It is not into Christ's *burial* that believers are baptized but into his *death*, because it was there that he dealt with sin.

5–7 In v.5 we encounter a problem concerning resurrection. Is Paul referring to the future bodily resurrection of the saints? Many expositors think so, and they can point to the future tense of the verb ("we will . . . be"). Ordinarily, the future tense relates to something that will happen. Occasionally, however, it indicates what must logically or inevitably occur (cf. Gal 6:5). So if there are other grounds on which to question a future bodily resurrection here, the tense of the verb is not an insuperable obstacle. But a second factor to consider is that Christ's resurrection, mentioned in the previous verse, was indeed a bodily resurrection. This is true enough. But it should be observed that Paul does not say that just as Christ was raised, so we too shall be raised. Instead, he connects the resurrection of Christ with the possibility of a new life for those who are his. And that life belongs to the present time. Furthermore, it is evident from the use of "for" at the beginning of v.6 that what follows is intended to relate closely to the mention of resurrection at the end of v.5. Yet one looks in vain for anything in v.6 that relates to future bodily resurrection. Instead, Paul returns to consider the matter of participation in Christ's death in its bearing on freedom from the bondage of sin. Consequently, one is led to conclude that resurrection in v.5 has to do with spiritual resurrection—raised with Christ—as in Ephesians 2:6; Colossians 2:12, 3:1.

The certainty of our present participation in this new resurrection life is grounded on the truth that "we have been united with him in his death." Paul uses an expression here, translated "united with," that strictly means "grown together," virtually with the force of "fused into one." Clearly this union is not something gradually arrived at through a process of sanctification. Rather it is something established by God that becomes the very basis of sanctification in which the Christ life is expressed through the individuality of the one joined to him.

However, the problem of sin continues to dominate the thought of this section, and Paul returns to this theme by insisting that "our old self was crucified with him" (v.6). While the relation to v.5 is close, the language now becomes sharper and more realistic—e.g., "united with him in his death" becomes "crucified with him" (cf. Gal 2:20). Our spiritual history began at the cross. We were there in the sense that in God's sight we were joined to him who actually suffered on it. The time element should not disturb us, because if we sinned in Adam, it is equally possible to have died to sin with Christ. At this stage of the teaching it is not a question of our personal, conscious participation, but simply of our position as God has arranged it and as he sees it.

But what was it that was crucified? "Our old self" is literally "our old man." The same truth is taught in Colossians 3:9. In Ephesians 4:22, however, the putting off of the old man is a matter of exhortation. In some sense, then, the old man has been crucified; in another sense he may still claim attention. Since "man" has been used of Adam (5:12, 17, 19), it is possible that what has been crucified with Christ is our place in Adam, our position in the old creation, which is under the sway of sin and death. For the Christian, the old is gone; he belongs to the new creation order (2 Cor 5:17).

Yet the old order seeks to dominate the believer, as Ephesians 4:22 implies and experience confirms. Though the seeming inconsistency between that passage and this is not easy to resolve, it may be that in his Epistle to the Ephesians Paul, while presupposing the supplanting of the old Adam, is desirous of exhorting his readers to refuse to live in terms of the old man and instead to live deliberately and consciously in the reality of the new creation. It is necessary to distinguish between the old creation—namely, our inheritance from Adam—and our old nature, or the flesh. The latter still persists in the life of the redeemed and can become a prey to the operation of sin unless countered by the powerful influence of the new life in Christ.

The purpose behind the crucifixion of our old man is that sin should be rendered powerless so far as we are concerned. But the expression "body of sin" is a phrase that needs clarification. It should not be regarded as equivalent to "sinful body," for the body itself is not sinful. Scripture is clear in its teaching that sin arises from the heart, the inner life (Mark 7:21). Should we settle for "sinful self" (NEB)? This is suggestive, since the word *sōma* ("body") sometimes conveys the idea of man in his totality, not simply his physical organism. But this may be going too far in the present passage. The term "body" glances at the fact of crucifixion, which Christ endured in the body. Our body can become the instrument of sin, thus negating the truth of crucifixion with Christ. So "body of sin" seems to mean body insofar as it may become the vehicle of sin. Its previous slavery to the dictates of sin is broken. This annulling of the power of sin is based on a recognized principle—that death settles all claims. Our union with Christ in his death, which was designed to deal with sin once for all, means that we are free from the hold of sin. Its mastery is broken (v.7).

8–10 Union with Christ continues to be the theme in vv.8–10, but attention shifts from its effect on the problem of sin to a consideration of its bearing on the problem of death.

Consequently, resurrection comes into focus. Though there is considerable similarity with the close of v.4, the note of futurity ("we will also live with him") makes it apparent that future bodily resurrection is in view. For a brief time, death, as the executor of sin, held the Savior, but not for long. Since he was not guilty of personal sin, death had no right to hold him indefinitely (Acts 2:24). Likewise, it had no right to recall him to experience death again. Once having been raised from the dead, our Lord is alive for ever and ever (Rev. 1:18).

It was important for Paul to emphasize this truth, for the believer must have full confidence that the captain of his salvation will never again come under the power of sin and death. If he lacks that assurance, the teaching about union with Christ will be of little help to him. "He died to sin once for all." As Meyer puts it, "He submitted Himself to its power in His death, but through that death *He has died to its power*" (in loc.). In his risen life our Lord is set free to resume his face-to-face fellowship with God (John 1:1) and his preoccupation with the consummation of God's eternal purpose. In this respect he presents a pattern for the believer in his expectation of the future and also in his motivation for life in the present time (2 Cor 5:15).

2. *The appeal based on the fact* (6:11-14)

11–14 In the previous section Paul has been imparting information on the subject of union with Christ, and agreeable to this he has three times used the word "know" (vv.3, 6, 9). Now he employs a different key word—"count" or "reckon" (the same term used so often in chapter 4 in connection with righteousness). Reckoning does not create the fact of union with Christ but makes it operative in one's life. The charge to count oneself dead to sin but alive to God in Christ Jesus is in the present tense, indicating a necessity to keep up the process if one is to avoid reactivating the body of sin. Paradoxically, the Christian is dead and alive at the same time, as in Galatians 2:20, dead to sin and self but alive and responsive to God. He is to give no more response to sin than a dead man can give. On the other hand, all the potential that redeemed life affords is to be channeled Godward.

Since Paul seems to lay considerable stress on the importance of this process of counting or reckoning, we should inquire about its value—especially in view of the objection that such a process smacks of attempting to convince oneself of something unrealistic in terms of actual experience and so amounts to self-deception. The justification for the use of this terminology is at least threefold. First, this is a command freighted with apostolic authority. God is speaking through his servant, and what God commands must be efficacious. It must never be treated as frivolous. Second, the command is psychologically sound, for what we think tends to be carried out in action. The thought is father to the act. Third, this process must not be undertaken in a mechanical fashion, as though there were some sort of magic in going through the motions. One must really desire to have freedom from sin and to live responsibly to God. To that end he must avail himself of the means of grace, particularly the diligent use of Scripture and faithfulness in prayer.

This element of willing cooperation receives emphasis in v.12. The implication is that sin has been reigning. The believer must do his part by refusing obedience any longer to sin's enticements. The word "obey" has as its root idea "listening" or "heeding." If the body is kept mortified, it will have no ear for the subtle suggestions of evil. Paul here describes the body as "mortal"—a reminder that despite the glorious asset of being united to Christ, we are still living in a frail instrument subject to the ultimate call of death.

Turning from the body as a whole to its separate members, Paul admonishes his readers not to hand these over to sin (the old master). But this is only half of the Christian's obligation. On the positive side, he is to offer himself (his personality and life-potential) to God with, as a corollary, the separate bodily capacities "as instruments of righteousness." The word "offer," by virtue of its tense, "implies a critical resolve, a *decision* of surrender" (Moule). This passage prepares the way for a similar emphasis in 12:1.

Paul concludes this portion of text with encouragement and an incentive. He promises the Roman Christians that if they will do as he has enjoined, sin will not be their master, and he adds, "because you are not under law, but under grace" (v.14). What is the relevance of this closing observation? Why should law be injected here? Surely because under law sin increases (5:20; cf. 1 Cor 15:56). The inference is that law lords it over its subjects. It condemns and brings them into virtual slavery. It faces them with their guilt and uses that guilt as a manacle to keep them in helpless subjection. But under grace there is liberty to live in accord with a higher principle—the resurrection life of the Lord himself.

It is worthy of attention that Christians are said to be *under* grace. Usually grace indicates a principle of divine operation, a moving out in kindness and love to lift the sinful and unworthy to God. Occasionally it is used of the sphere of the believer's life of privilege (5:2). But here in 6:14 it appears as a disciplinary power, in line with the apostle's effort to show that grace is not license (6:1ff.). Somewhat parallel is the word of Jesus to the weary and burdened, promising rest, but followed up with mention of his yoke (Matt 11:28–30). Related also is Paul's reminder that God's grace has appeared for the salvation of all, *training* us to live sober, upright, and godly lives (see Titus 2:11, 12).

B. *Union With Christ Viewed As Enslavement to Righteousness*

6:15–23

15What then? Shall we sin because we are not under law but under grace? By no means! 16Don't you know that when you offer yourselves to someone to obey him as slaves, you are slaves to the one whom you obey—whether you are slaves to sin, which leads to death, or to obedience, which leads to righteousness? 17But thanks be to God that, though you used to be slaves to sin, you wholeheartedly obeyed the form of teaching to which you were committed. 18You have been set free from sin and have become slaves to righteousness.

19I put this in human terms because you are weak in your natural selves. Just as you used to offer the parts of your body in slavery to impurity and to ever-increasing wickedness, so now offer them in slavery to righteousness and holiness. 20When you were slaves to sin, you were free from the control of righteousness. 21What benefit did you reap at that time from the things you are now ashamed of? Those things result in death! 22But now that you have been set free from sin and have become slaves to God, the benefit you reap leads to holiness, and the result is eternal life. 23For the wages of sin is death, but the gift of God is eternal life through Christ Jesus our Lord.

15–17 Paul has just affirmed, "You are not under the law." He goes on to show that this does not mean that they are free from the demands of righteousness. It would be strange and contradictory if those who are under grace should evidence a manner of life inferior to the standard held by those who are under law. As a matter of fact, the believer must face the fact that his salvation actually means a change of bondage. As he once served sin, he is now committed to a life of practical righteousness.

At first glance, the opening question seems virtually a repetition of v.1. The difference, however, lies in the tense of the verb. In v.1 the question was "Shall we go on sinning so that grace may increase?" Now the question is "Shall we sin [in any given case, or sin at all] because we are not under law but under grace?" Law is supposed to be a restraining influence. If one moves out from under that umbrella, will he not be exposing himself to the danger of committing sin even more than in his previous situation?

In answer, Paul appeals first of all to a fact familiar to all—namely, that whatever one submits to becomes his master. Jesus had taught this by saying, "Everyone who sins is a slave to sin" (John 8:34). To commit sin, then, puts one into bondage to sin, and the sequel is death (cf. 5:12; 8:13). The other option is a life of obedience resulting in righteousness (cf. 5:19). Paul is happy to acknowledge that his readers have renounced the service of sin and are now wholeheartedly obeying Christian teaching (v.17). Let us take special note of the way he puts the matter, especially because of KJV's mistranslation at this point: "that form of doctrine which was delivered you." In some other context Paul might have expressed himself that way, because he frequently spoke of Christian tradition, that which had been handed down to the church as apostolic teaching. But here the normal order is reversed—"you wholeheartedly obeyed the form of teaching to which you were committed." By virtue of becoming Christians, the believers had obligated themselves to obey what we might call the law of Christ (Gal 6:2). Even though he had not founded the Roman church, Paul was confident that those who had preached the gospel there and taught the converts had reproduced the characteristic teaching that had been standard from the beginning (Acts 2:42). Just as the gospel had certain ingredients (they are the substratum of 6:1–5, namely, Christ's death, burial, and resurrection, as in 1 Cor 15:3, 4), so the teaching relating to the life the believer was expected to live was standard throughout the church (cf. C.H. Dodd, *Gospel and Law* [Cambridge: Cambridge University Press, 1951]). Though the language may vary somewhat, the content is the same from writer to writer. This is the point being made in the use of the word "form."

The teaching of Jesus and the apostles, especially in terms of the demands of discipleship, the ethical requirements of the faith, and the principles that must guide believers in their relations one to the other and to the world became in time so definite and fixed that one could go from one area of the church to another and find the same general pattern. The law was a fixed, definite entity with precepts and prohibitions. Grace has its norms also.

18 The term that most adequately describes the standard Christian instruction is "righteousness." Here Paul arrives at the full answer to the question raised in v.15. To be set free from obligation to serve sin means entrance upon the service of righteousness. There is no middle ground, no place in Christian experience where one is free to set his own standards and go his own way. So it is idle to object that on becoming a believer one is simply exchanging one form of slavery for another. There is no alternative. The psalmist perceived this long ago when he wrote, "O Lord, I am thy servant; I am thy servant, the son of thy handmaid. Thou hast loosed my bonds" (Ps 116:16). Let no one say, however, that the two bondages are on the same plane. The one is rigorous and relentless, leading to death; the other is joyous and satisfying, leading to life and peace. To be free from the bondage to sin is a great boon in itself. But life cannot be lived in a vacuum. Service to righteousness means positive achievement that adds meaning to life.

19,20 Reviewing his own remarks, Paul grants that he has spoken "in human terms" (v.19). This is really a kind of apology (see comments on 3:5) for having described Christian life in terms of servitude to righteousness. "There is not a single Old Testament or Rabbinic text with the phrase 'slaves of righteousness' or anything like it—say, 'slaves of the Law' or 'slaves of good deeds.' The faithful are 'slaves of God'; they could be slaves to no one and nothing else" (David Daube, *The New Testament and Rabbinic Judaism* [London: Athlone Press, 1956], p. 284).

Paul gives as a reason for using the reference to slavery, "because you are weak in your natural selves." The nature of the weakness is not expressed—whether it relates to comprehension, so needing an illustration such as slavery, or whether it refers to moral fiber. At any rate, the weakness of the Roman Christians has called for strong language to drive the point home. The remainder of the verse may be said to favor somewhat the second alternative because the apostle enlarges on his earlier description of their pre-Christian life as slaves of sin, going so far as to speak of their "impurity" and "ever-increasing wickedness" (uncleanness within and lawlessness without). The readiness and zeal with which they once served sin now become the basis for a challenge. Surely the new master is worthy of at least equal loyalty and devotion! That new master is not described in personal terms but in personification—righteousness and holiness. The latter word suggests not so much a state of sanctity as an activity, a progression in the life of sanctification. This is also implied by the parallel with "ever-increasing."

To be a slave of sin, Paul affirms, is to be free from the control of righteousness. Under the circumstances, this is a most undesirable freedom. It would be a misunderstanding to interpret these words as meaning that a sinner has no obligation with respect to righteousness. The intent is simply to maintain that one cannot serve two masters. Each bondage is so rigorous, so exacting, that it demands the whole of one's attention.

21,22 So far is the pre-Christian state from being a desirable one that it yields no benefit. In fact, it leaves behind memories that produce shame (v.21). On the other hand, the Christian state of freedom from the necessity of serving sin and the corresponding commitment to God has produced a harvest of holiness (sanctification). At the end of this process is eternal life (cf. Gal 6:8). Paul is not denying the present possession of eternal life, as the following verse makes plain, but is simply presenting eternal life as the inevitable conclusion of the process of sanctification (see chart at the beginning of the chapter). Jesus similarly taught that eternal life was the sequel to genuine discipleship (Mark 10:29, 30).

23 In a fitting conclusion, Paul puts God (and his mastery) over against sin, gift over against wages, eternal life over against death—crowning it all with the acknowledgment that the mediation of Christ Jesus our Lord accounts for the shift from the one camp to the other. The term "wages" is found mostly in a military context to indicate the pay of the soldier. Something of that background is retained in the present passage. (See notes.)

Looking back over 6:15–23, we see that truth has been taught by means of contrast. Obedience is the one concept common to both sides of the contrast; otherwise, all is different:

sin — fruitlessness and shame — death
righteousness — sanctification — life

Notes

23 In his study of the word "wages" in this context, H.W. Heidland (TDNT 5:592) finds a threefold connotation: (1) since ὀψώνια (*opsōnia*) means provision for one's living expenses, sin turns out to be a wretched paymaster, promising life but meting out death; (2) since in practice wages are paid not in a lump sum but regularly and periodically, death is not to be regarded merely as the final payment, but as that which already casts its dark shadow over life, a portent of the deeper darkness to come; and (3) inasmuch as *opsōnia* is a legal term, in contrast to χάρισμα (*charisma*, "gift"), we are to see a pitting of law over against grace. "Man has rights only in relation to sin, and these rights become his judgment. When he throws himself on God without claim, salvation comes to him" (ibid.).

C. *Union With Christ Viewed As Deliverance From Law* (7:1–6)

As already observed, sin and death in their correlation have occupied Paul to a great degree from 5:12 on, with an occasional reference to a third element, the law. In chapter 6 he has sought to explain that the believer's crucifixion with Christ has brought freedom from enslavement to sin's dominion. Since the law has served to promote sin (5:20), it is expedient now to show that Christ's death, which involved the death of those who are his, effected release from the law also. At the same time Paul is careful to indicate that this emancipation from the law is in order to permit a new attachment, namely, to the risen Lord and his Spirit, so that from this union might flow a fruitfulness of life unattainable under the law. Since union with Christ has already been shown to be so powerful a factor in its intended result as to warrant the figure of slavery (to righteousness), the way has been made clear to teach deliverance from the law as not opening the door to irresponsible and sinful conduct.

7:1–6

Do you not know, brothers—for I am speaking to men who know the law—that the law has authority over a man only as long as he lives? [2]For example, by law a married woman is bound to her husband as long as he is alive, but if her husband dies, she is released from the law of marriage. [3]So then, if she marries another man while her husband is still alive, she is called an adulteress. But if her husband dies, she is released from that law and is not an adulteress, even though she marries another man.

[4]So, my brothers, you also died to the law through the body of Christ, that you might belong to another, to him who was raised from the dead, in order that we might bear fruit to God. [5]For when we were controlled by our sinful nature, the sinful passions aroused by the law were at work in our bodies, so that we bore fruit for death. [6]But now, by dying to what once bound us, we have been released from the law so that we serve in the new way of the Spirit, and not in the old way of the written code.

1 The readers are described as those who know "the law." Some would question this wording, since the definite article is lacking in the original. Could it be that since the recipients of the letter reside at Rome, the seat of legislation and government for the

empire, Paul is referring to secular law? This conclusion is not necessary, since "law" occurs without the article in passages that clearly have to do with the Mosaic legislation (e.g., 5:20). At the same time, it is quite possible that Paul is not interested so much in identifying the law he has in mind as in pointing to its character as law, that which has binding force. The word "man" should not suggest that males only are in view, since this is the broad term used for mankind and here has the force of "person." In this opening statement, where the principle is being laid down that law imposes a lifelong obligation on its subjects, this is the natural word to use. The situation is different in the next verse, where the word for "man" is not the same, since a husband is in view.

Already in this initial statement we have a clue for determining the thought that Paul is about to develop. The law has authority over a person only for his lifetime. Since it has been established that the believer died with Christ, one can anticipate the conclusion—that whatever authority the law continues to exercise over others, for the believer that power has been abrogated. "Only for him who in faith appropriates the righteousness of God in Christ is the law abolished" (W. Gutbrod in TDNT 4:1075). It remains, of course, as an entity that expresses the will of God. The life under grace does not belittle the ethical demands of the law.

2,3 To illustrate the binding character of the law, Paul presents the case of a woman who is married to a husband and remains bound by law in this relationship as long as the husband is living. During this time she is not free to seek another attachment. This may be done only in the event that the husband dies. By design, the status of the wife as subject to the husband is presented by the term *hypandros,* a rather rare word meaning literally "under a husband." This pictures more readily than "married woman" what Paul is seeking to bring out. Particularly in Jewish life this was the actual legal status of the wife, for she could not divorce her husband; divorce was a privilege granted only to the man. If the husband died, she was then released from "the law of marriage" (literally, "the law of the husband"). This may sound as though the husband instituted the marriage law, but this is not the idea intended. Hence, the translators have wisely avoided a literal rendering. NEB has a somewhat fuller wording: "She is discharged from the obligations of the marriage-law."

4–6 The opening word "so" indicates that illustration is now giving way to application. But the reader is apt to be somewhat disturbed in that there is a measure of inconsistency in the way the illustration is applied. Note that in the case under consideration three essential statements are made: a woman is married to a man; the man dies; then the woman is free to be married to another. In the application three statements likewise appear or can be readily inferred: the readers have had a binding relation to the law; they have died to the law; and they are now free to be joined to another, even the risen Lord. A glance at these two triadic propositions shows that the parallel breaks down at the second item, for the law, which is the assumed master or husband in the application, is not represented as dying, since the readers are said to have died to the law. Paul avoids saying that the law died, something that is never affirmed in Scripture, though the law had a certain course to run (Gal 3:19). All he is concerned with is continuing the emphasis already made in chapter 6, that death ends obligation. It was not feasible in the illustration to have the woman die, because then she would not have been available for marriage to another, which is vital to the application in which a new relationship is set up between the believer and Christ. Paul was no doubt aware of a certain incongruity between illustration and application, but counted on the understanding of his readers that he was seeking merely to underscore the truth that death with Christ brought to an end the sway of the law over those who are in him and ushered in a new relationship as superior to the old as Christ is superior to the law.

Death to the law is said to have occurred "through the body of Christ" (v.4). This is a reference to the personal body of the Savior in his crucifixion. Through the same means believers became dead both to the law and to sin. "The body of Christ" should not be interpreted as a reference to the church, since the word has not been used in the corporate, mystical sense so far in the Epistle, and when it is so used (12:4, 5) Paul brings in the human body as an analogy in order to make his meaning clear, as he had done in an earlier letter (1 Cor 12:12, 13).

Death to the law occurred so that believers "might belong to another." To belong to Christ involves participation not only in his death but also in his resurrection. Severance from obligation to serve the law is only part of the truth. We are married, as it were, to the risen Lord, with a view to bearing fruit to God. Perhaps an analogy is intended here—as a marriage produces progeny, so the believer's union with Christ results in spiritual fruit. It should be recalled that in our Lord's teaching the secret of fruit bearing is union with himself (John 15:1ff.), the very truth emphasized in the passage before us. A somewhat different background for fruit bearing is predicated in Galatians 5:22, 23, where the fruit is attributed to the Spirit, in contrast to the output of the flesh and of the law. Since Paul speaks of the Spirit in Romans 7:6, the parallel with Galatians 5 is close. The attribution of fruit to Christ in one instance and to the Spirit in another is not disturbing, because there is much common ground in their relationship to believers (cf. Eph 3:16, 17).

In the pre-Christian state there was fruit of a sort, but it was corrupt and perishable, emanating from the sinful nature and produced by the sinful passions as these were aroused by the law (v.5). The contrast between the two types of fruit is striking (cf. 6:21). The phrase "controlled by our sinful nature" is an attempt to render "in the flesh." Paul has used "flesh" in several senses thus far: (1) the humanity of Jesus Christ (1:3); (2) the physical body (2:28), (3) mankind—"all flesh" (3:20); and (4) moral, or possibly intellectual, weakness (6:19). Now he adds a fifth: the so-called "ethical" meaning of flesh, which is the most common use of the word in his writings and denotes the old sinful nature. It is this sense of the word that pervades chapters 7 and 8, together with a final use in 13:14. Paul did not employ the word "flesh" in this sense when exposing in his earlier chapters the universality of sin. In noting that the passions are aroused by the law, Paul is anticipating his fuller statement in vv.7–13 about the manner in which the law promotes sin.

Release from the law has as its objective a bond service to God "in the new way of the Spirit" in contrast to the old way of the written code (literally "letter"). This contrast is not between a literal mode of interpreting Scripture and one that is free and unfettered. The written code, which has special reference to the law rather than to Scripture in general, has no power to give life and to produce a service acceptable to God. Only a person can beget human life, and only a divine person can impart spiritual life, which is then fostered and nurtured by the Spirit. The word "new" has in it not so much the idea of newness in time as freshness and superiority. This is the only mention of the Spirit in the chapter. It anticipates chapter 8 with its unfolding of the wealth of blessing to be experienced in this relationship.

Notes

6 Although γράμμα (*gramma*, "letter") comes from the same root as γραφή (*graphē*), the word for Scripture, the two are not treated by Paul as equivalents. The very fact that *gramma* is pitted against πνεῦμα (*pneuma*, "Spirit") is revealing. It becomes a surrogate for law in its written form. G. Schrenk notes that "*gramma* is not used when he [Paul] speaks of the positive and lasting significance of Scripture. This positive task is always stated in terms of *graphē*. When the reference is to *gramma*, Paul is always thinking of the legal authority which has been superseded, while *graphē* is linked with the new form of authority determined by the fulfilment in Christ and by His Spirit, the determinative character of the new no longer being what is written and prescribed" (TDNT 1:768).

Considerable affinity can be detected between the presentation here and that in 2 Corinthians 3:6, where the *gramma/pneuma* tension likewise appears. In both passages the concepts of death and life occur; also the verb καταργεῖσθαι (*katargeisthai*) occurs (7:6; 2 Cor 3:7, 11, 13, 14) with the meaning "to be discharged from" in Romans and "to fade or disappear" in the 2 Corinthian passage, except for v.14, where it has the force of "to be taken away." In both passages the subject is the abrogation of the law, though the matter is put somewhat differently in Romans, where believers are said to have been discharged from service to the law. But the thought is essentially the same in both places (see Bernardin Schneider, CBQ 15 [1953] p. 203).

Not all translations allow for mention of the Holy Spirit here. NEB, for example, has "to serve God in a new way, the way of the spirit, in contrast to the old way, the way of a written code" (JB is similar). However, it is probable that we have in 7:6 an anticipation of that fullness of treatment of the Spirit that comes out in chapter 8. Also, the parallelism between Romans 7:6 and 2 Corinthians 3, noted above, favors a reference to the Holy Spirit, since there is no doubt that *pneuma* refers to the Spirit in the latter passage.

D. *The Relationship Between Law and Sin* (7:7–25)

This matter requires clarification if for no other reason than that Paul has flatly stated that the believer has died to sin (6:2) and to the law (7:4). Are these, then, so similar as to be in some sense equated? The explanation has been touched on briefly in 7:5, but Paul now expands it. In essence, the solution of the problem is this: the law cannot be identified with sin, because it is the law that provides awareness of sin (cf. 3:20). Can one say of an X-ray machine that revealed his disease that the machine is diseased because it revealed a diseased condition? That would be utterly illogical.

As Paul has appealed to the experience of his converts to support Christian truth (Gal 3:1–5; 4:1–7), so he now appeals to his own experience (vv.7–13). This personal reference then broadens into a more general picture of the soul-struggle of a person who tries to serve God by obeying the law but finds himself checkmated by the operation of sin within himself (vv.14–25).

The observation that consciousness of sin is produced by the law is sharpened by a specific example. Paul seizes on the tenth commandment, which says, "Do not covet." This is of the highest importance for our understanding of the meaning of law in 7:1–6, the law from which the believer has been released. What the apostle has in mind includes the moral law. While students of Scripture find it convenient at times to distinguish between the ceremonial law and the moral law, Paul regards the law as a unit. To one who may be disturbed by the thought that the divine standard for one's life is abandoned by maintaining release from the law, Paul will reply in due course that no such danger exists (8:4).

7:7–25

[7]What shall we say, then? Is the law sin? Far from it! Indeed I would not have
known what sin was except through the law. For I would not have known what it
was to covet if the law had not said, "Do not covet." [8]But sin, seizing the opportu-
nity afforded by the commandment, produced in me every kind of covetous desire.
For apart from law, sin is dead. [9]Once I was alive apart from law; but when the
commandment came, sin sprang to life [10]and I died. I found that the very com-
mandment that was intended to bring life actually brought death. [11]For sin, seizing
the opportunity afforded by the commandment, deceived me, and through the
commandment put me to death. [12]So then, the law is holy, and the commandment
is holy, righteous and good.

[13]Did that which is good, then, become death to me? By no means! But in order
that sin might be recognized as sin, it produced death in me through what was
good, so that through the commandment sin might become utterly sinful.

[14]We know that the law is spiritual; but I am unspiritual, sold as a slave to sin.
[15]I do not know what I am doing. For what I want to do I do not do, but what I hate
I do. [16]And if I do what I do not want to do, I agree that the law is good. [17]As it
is, it is no longer I myself who do it, but it is sin living in me. [18]I know that nothing
good lives in me, that is, in my sinful nature. For I have the desire to do what is
good, but I cannot carry it out. [19]For what I do is not the good I want to do; no,
the evil I do not want to do—this I keep on doing. [20]Now if I do what I do not want
to do, it is no longer I who do it, but it is sin living in me that does it.

[21]So I find this law at work: When I want to do good, evil is right there with me.
[22]For in my inner being I delight in God's law; [23]but I see another law at work in
the members of my body, waging war against the law of my mind and making me
a prisoner of the law of sin at work within my members. [24]What a wretched man
I am! Who will rescue me from this body of death? [25]Thanks be to God—through
Jesus Christ our Lord!

So then, I myself in my mind am a slave to God's law, but in my sinful nature a slave to the law of sin.

7 "Sin" is an oft-repeated word in this paragraph. It does not refer here to an act of sin, but to the sin principle, to that mighty force man cannot tame, but which lurks dormant or relatively inactive in a person's life, then is brought to the fore by prohibition and proceeds to rise up and slay its victim, whom it has utterly deceived. Sin, then, has the same meaning here as in 5:12ff. The same conditions of prohibition and desire, leading to a fall, are latent in both passages. But whereas in 5:12ff. sin is further defined as *paraptōma,* which has in it the very word for "fall," here *hamartia* alone is used. This is suggestive, for since the fall of man there is an inability to get back to God. Man is always "falling short," which is the precise meaning of *hamartia.*

The words "for I would not have known" could be translated, "I did not know," giving them a fully historical setting, but the hypothetical construction is no doubt preferable. The subject in hand is the awareness of sin in a personal, existential sense—an awareness created by the law's demands. To come to grips with this the apostle selects an item from the Decalogue, the very last of the Ten Commandments. Is he selecting more or less at random one of the ten for an illustration? Could he have chosen just as readily the prohibition against stealing or bearing false witness? Possibly he saw something basic here, for "to covet" is more precisely "to desire." If one gives rein to wrong desire, it can lead to lying, stealing, killing, and all the other things prohibited in the commandments. The sin indicated here is not so much a craving for this or that wrong thing, but the craving itself (note that Paul does not bother to spell out the particulars of the tenth commandment, such as the possessions or wife of one's neighbor). In analyzing sin, one must go behind the outward act to the inner man, where desire clutches at the imagination and then puts the spurs to the will.

8 In the background is the Genesis story of the temptation and the fall. Eve was faced with a commandment—a prohibition. When desire was stirred through the subtle suggestion of the serpent, a certain rebelliousness came into play that is the very heart of sin—a preference for one's own will over the expressed will of God. The warning "Don't" to a small child may turn out to be a call for action that had not even been contemplated by the child. A sure way to lose blossoms from the garden is to post a sign that says, "Don't pick the flowers." The word "opportunity" in the original is a military term meaning a base of operations. Prohibition furnishes a springboard from which sin is all too ready to take off. The possibilities for seeking satisfaction through giving way to wrong desire are manifold. In the KJV the word for "desire" is rendered "lust" in v.7 and "concupiscence" in v.8. Since both of these renderings are readily associated with sexual desire, they unduly restrict the frame of reference.

"For apart from law, sin is dead." It appears from a comparison of "dead" with "sprang to life" in v.9 that the word "dead" is intended to be taken in a relative sense, namely, quiescent, dormant, inactive. The statement appears to be an axiom, a broad principle. But since the verb "is" does not appear in the original, a possibility exists that "was" should be supplied, making the reference personal to Paul rather than a general statement (so Murray). On the other hand, when some part of the verb "to be" is left for the reader to supply, as here, it is more apt to be a generalization than a specific historical allusion.

9–11 Paul's statement that he was once alive apart from the law should be taken in a relative sense, for there was actually no time in his life before his conversion when he was unrelated to the law. He was the son of a Pharisee (Acts 23:6) and lived in strictest conformity to the regulations of his sect (Acts 26:5). He seems to mean, then, that there was a time when he was living in a state of blissful indifference to the intensely searching demands that the law made on the inner man. He was careless and self-deceived as to his own righteousness. This state is reflected in Philippians 3:6, where he speaks of his preconversion days when he was "faultless" with respect to legalistic righteousness. Paul's struggle before and at the time of his conversion was intellectual rather than moral. He was convinced that Jesus could not be the Messiah, for God had permitted him to die as a criminal. His conversion meant a complete reversal in this matter. "I died" is subjective in its force. He felt within himself the sentence of death, becoming bogged down in hopelessness and despair in contrast to the blithe self-confidence he had had before. It goes without saying that this dying is entirely unrelated to dying with Christ, of which we have been informed in chapter 6. It was not a death to sin but a death because of sin.

The commandment referred to, like the others, "was intended to bring life." That is to say, its design and ideal were to promote observance that would lead to divine blessing and consequent human happiness. "You shall therefore keep my statutes and my ordinances, by doing which a man shall live: I am the Lord" (Lev 18:5 RSV). The practical difficulty, of course, is that sinful man fails to do the will of God as set forth in the commandments.

In v.11 sin is strongly personified, being represented as acting as a person would act.

The language is reminiscent of the fall, with sin taking the place of the tempter and provoking a deception that led to death (the spiritual death that occurred then and there was prophetic of the physical death to follow in due time). The word "deceive" occurs here in a strong form indicating utter deception. Paul uses the same word on two other occasions when speaking of the deception effected by the serpent in relation to Eve (2 Cor 11:3, 1 Tim 2:14; cf. Exod 8:25, LXX). Sin within him led Paul to do the very thing the commandment forbade, thus bringing him under condemnation as a lawbreaker. Recall his statement about the law in 2 Corinthians 3:6—"the letter kills."

> Bornkamm's insight is helpful: What constitutes this deception and death? The deception of sin can only consist in the fact that it falsely promises life to me. This it cannot do by itself, but only with the help of the divine commandment. Deceptively it appropriates the call to life, which actually declares God's law: do that, and you shall live. What it quietly and deceptively conceals from me is simply this, that it has now usurped this call to live, and therefore the encounter with the divine commandment is no longer direct. Sin always stands in between and has fundamentally perverted my relationship to God's commandment. This perversion is both deception and death (Günther Bornkamm, *Early Christian Experience* [New York: Harper & Row, 1969], pp. 91, 92).

12 It is time for the apostle to give a decisive answer to the question he had raised in v.7: "Is the law sin?" So far from being identifiable with sin, the law is holy, as are the individual commandments it contains. It is possible to understand "the commandment" as a reference to every single precept of the law, but the singular form leads one to think that Paul is casting a backward glance at the tenth commandment. The law is holy because it comes from a holy God and searches out sin. It is righteous in view of the just requirements it lays upon men, righteous also because it forbids and condemns sin. It is good (beneficent) because its aim is life (v.10). The misuse of the law at the hands of sin has not altered its own essential character. Its goodness is reaffirmed in v.13.

13 Having detached the law from any wrongful association with sin, Paul still has the necessity of treating the problem of the law's relation to death, the other great enemy of the race. Continuing to present the case in personal terms, he protests that the responsibility for incurring death must be assigned to sin rather than to the law. Its use of the law to bring death shows how "utterly sinful" sin is. "How evil must that thing be which works the greatest evil through that which is the perfection of righteousness" (Haldane, in loc.). At the same time, the law, which seemed to be victimized by being taken over by sin, emerges as having gained an important objective. It has exposed sin for the evil thing it is.

From this point on to the end of the chapter, the personal emphasis continues, and with increased intensity, as the powerful forces of law and sin are depicted as producing a struggle that ends in a confession of despair relieved only by the awareness that in Jesus Christ there is deliverance. Paul does not shrink from putting himself prominently in this arena of conflict if only his doing so will help others (cf. 1 Cor 4:6).

If his portrayal of the struggle of the soul to observe the law despite the enticement of sin is presented at greater length and with greater intensity than the struggle with the powers of darkness (cf. Eph 6:10ff.), it is not necessarily because the former is intrinsically more important (seeing that the powers are evil also), but because it is so immediately and desperately personal. The other is equally so only in cases of demonic possession.

A shift of emphasis is discernible on moving from vv.7–13 to vv.14–25. In the former section Paul has shown that the fault lay not with the commandment of God but with sin in its use of the commandment. In the latter section he will maintain that the responsible party, ultimately speaking, is not "I" but the sin that dwells within.

14–20 At the outset Paul wants it understood that he is not depreciating the law, for it is "spiritual"—that is, emanating from God (vv.22, 25) who is Spirit (John 4:24). Of course, it is true also that the law as a part of Scripture is the product of the Holy Spirit, who inspired the writers. But that aspect is not prominent here. The law is a reflection of the character of God. Godly people recognize this fact ("we know").

"But I am unspiritual." What a stark contrast! The word "unspiritual" is literally "fleshly," what I am in myself. I am not subject to the law and therefore I am in rebellion against God, since the law is from him. (The problems as to whether Paul speaks individually or universally here and whether as a saved or an unsaved man will be dealt with at the close of the chapter.) Here he moves on to a second description more wretched than the first: "sold as a slave to sin." This strikes the keynote of what follows, down to the anguished cry, "Who will rescue me . . . ?" (v.24). The slavery extends to the totality of his being. It numbs and blinds him, for he confesses that he does not know what he is doing (v.15). It is a graphic picture of many an action carried out by a slave, going through certain motions under the authority and direction of a master. If there appears to be obedience, it is really not a matter of volition, but something almost mechanical. Paul's figure of slavery is cogent here, since he is forced to carry out what he does not want to do, what he really hates, whereas what he would like to do never seems to materialize (v.15).

The failure to do what he desires to do is not to be attributed to a wrong attitude toward the law, since he concurs in the verdict that the law is praiseworthy. It inculcates the right kind of conduct, the things that are beneficent in their results (v.16). If the failure does not come from a wrong attitude toward the law, such as indifference or defiance, then the doing of things contrary to the law must be traced to the power of sin working within him (v.17). Paul is not attempting to escape responsibility, but rather putting his finger on the real culprit—indwelling sin. The invader has managed to secure more than a foothold; he roams the place, considering it his home. In putting the matter like this, Paul has moved from a consideration of outward acts to an emphasis on the unwanted tenancy of sin. With this alien master in control, no matter how strongly he wants to do the good, he finds himself checkmated. He cannot carry it out (v.18). Verse 19 is a virtual repetition of v.15 and the same is true of v.20 in relation to v.17.

Since Paul was a Jew, it is natural to inquire if there was anything in his Jewish inheritance he may have been drawing upon to depict the struggle against sin. A strong case can be made, simply on the basis of similarity, for the conclusion that Paul was indeed dependent on rabbinic teaching at this point so far as the formal framework of his presentation is concerned (W.D. Davies, *Paul and Rabbinic Judaism* [London: SPCK, 1948], pp. 20–27). The Rabbis taught that within man there are two impulses, both attributable to God. One is evil (usually understood as present from birth but inactive during the early years); the other good, making itself felt at the time a Jewish lad at thirteen became a "son of the law." Thereafter the two impulses contend for mastery within the person. The rabbinic remedy suggested for this situation was a devoted study and application of the law. At this point, however, Paul's presentation differs radically from the rabbinic view, for he stoutly maintains that the law, despite its divine origin and intrinsic excellence, cannot counteract the power of sin.

21–25 "So I find this law at work." The language clearly indicates a purpose to summarize what has gone before. So far, the law under discussion is the law of Moses, but here a specialized meaning—that of principle (cf. 3:27; 8:2)—is intended. This usage makes it necessary, when speaking once more of the (Mosaic) law, to call it "God's law" (v.22) for the purpose of differentiation. In Paul's inner being the divine law is welcome and brings delight, but that which manifests itself in the bodily members (what may be called the outward man) is the law (principle, or perhaps authority) of sin. It is a state of war and he finds himself a captive (cf. the earlier figure of a slave in v.14) to the imperious operation of sin. The agony of this unhappy condition comes out in the cry "What a wretched man I am!" It is a powerful and moving cry, recalling the words of Isaiah when he became aware of his sin (Isa 6:5). Since Paul is unable to help himself he must look elsewhere. In this verse and the next one the "I" is clearly the man himself, which warns us against trying to analyze the "I" at earlier points in the chapter in schizophrenic terms. "The source of Paul's wretchedness is clear. It is not a 'divided self,' but the fact that the last hope of mankind, religion, has proved to be a broken reed. Through sin, it is no longer a comfort but an accusation. Man needs not a law but deliverance" (Barrett).

In line with this, the apostle does not say, "What will rescue me?" but "Who . . . ?" There is deliverance, provided by God through Jesus Christ. The appeal from self to the Lord Jesus is meaningless if the latter has the same problem as the tormented suppliant. Jesus' sinlessness and triumph over evil are assumed. Further, "if Christ is my Deliverer, it is implied that '*I myself*' without Christ cannot get beyond the state of distraction and self-contradiction already described in vv.14–23" (Gifford, in loc.).

The final statement of the chapter is another summary. Coming as it does after the cry of thanksgiving for deliverance through Christ, it seems strange that there should be a reversion to the state of tension described earlier. Because of this, some students have ventured the opinion that this part of the verse has somehow been misplaced in the course of the transmission of the text. In his translation Moffatt actually puts it after v.23, despite the fact that there is no manuscript authority for this. As Gifford points out, the reason for the expression "I myself" in the concluding verse is to establish a contrast with "Jesus Christ" in the same verse (in loc.). How then shall we account for the strange order? Apparently Paul felt the desirability of stating once more the essence of the struggle he had depicted in order to prepare the reader to appreciate the more the grand exposition of the deliverance in terms of Christ and the Spirit in the following chapter.

Before moving on to that portion, we must return to the overall problems of interpretation in chapter 7. First of all, is Paul giving a truly autobiographical sketch, or is the "I" a vehicle to present man in his extremity, a means to universalize the experience treated here? It is difficult to decide. The first person ("I") was occasionally used in antiquity as a rhetorical device for expressing something applicable to others. It was so used somewhat by the Rabbis (W.G. Kümmel, *Römer 7 und die Bekehrung des Paulus* [Leipzig: J.C. Hinrich, 1929], pp. 128–131). That Paul could think and write in this fashion is apparent from Romans 3:7. Romans 7, however, is unique in its extent. Perhaps the personal and the universal are intended to mingle here. It has even been suggested that the "I" is a projection of Adam, the man who had so much to do with sin and death.

The more strenuously debated issue is the question of interpretation of the material itself, especially vv.14–25. Are we to regard the state pictured here as that of the unsaved man or of the Christian? The case for the unsaved condition is as follows: (1) It was the prevailing view among the Greek Fathers of the early church. (2) Such expressions as "sold as a slave to sin" and "unspiritual" seem more fitting as a description of the unsaved than of the genuine believer. Donald M. Davies writes, "The main message of chapter six is that in Christ a man is free from sin. How then could Paul, describing a situation of tension in his Christian experience, say that he was sold under sin? Where then is the freedom from sin which he insists on in the previous chapter?" (Int 7 [1953] 159). (3) If the "now" of 8:1 means what it seems to mean, Paul is passing from a consideration of the unsaved to the saved condition. (4) The absence of the Holy Spirit from the discussion and even of Christ (until the very close) is hard to understand if a redeemed experience is under review.

The other interpretation, in contrast, holds that a Christian is being depicted, despite his wretchedness. (1) This was the conclusion of Augustine and of the Reformed interpreters. (2) Appeal is made to the change from the use of the past tense in vv.7–13 to the use of the present tense in vv.14–25. This is understandable if the former section relates to Paul's pre-Christian experience and the rest of the chapter to his postconversion experience. (3) The author's description of his pre-Christian life in Philippians 3:6 as a blameless condition in terms of the law does not jibe with the passage before us. Paul counted this faultlessness as one of the things that could be listed as gain. Both pictures cannot readily apply to the same period. It has been replied that he is speaking in Philippians of his standing with men and not, as in Romans 7, of his relation to God. However, Paul was not a devious person, but transparent. Would he represent himself as possessing what he recounts in Philippians in a merely manward frame of reference if everything within him protested against it as a hollow unreality? (4) The progress of thought in Romans needs to be taken into consideration. Paul has passed beyond his description of the unsaved state and is now giving attention to sanctification and its problems; so the theme is really relevant only to believers. (5) That conflict of the sort described here can and does characterize the Christian life is apparent elsewhere in Paul, especially in Galatians 5:17. (6) The power of self-diagnosis at the penetrating level found here (see vv.22, 23) is beyond the capacity of the natural man. Advocates of the other view suggest that the explanation here is that Paul is writing as a Christian who naturally has gained in perception, and this colors his presentation. (7) A person desiring holiness of life, as pictured here, could only be a believer, for the unsaved person does not long for God but is hostile toward him. (8) The close of the chapter, in terms of the text as it stands and without attempted rearrangement, acknowledges the deliverance in Christ, yet goes on to state the very problem sketched in vv.14–24 as though it continues to be a problem for one who knows the Lord.

The wide difference between these two views puts the general reader in a dilemma. Which view is correct? Which has the better of the argument?

Another and more satisfying approach is possible—namely, that the experience pictured here is not wholly autobiographical but is deliberately presented in such a way as to demonstrate what would indeed be the situation if one who is faced with the demands of the law and the power of sin in his life were to attempt to solve his problem independently of the power of Christ and the enablement of the Spirit. This viewpoint has been well expressed by William Manson:

> It is in this way, I think, that we grasp the actual character of Romans VII. It is an unreal, in the sense of non-historical, a hypothetical situation which is called up before us. It corresponds to no actual phase either of Jewish-Christian or of Pauline-Christian existence, for in neither of these situations can we suppose the soul's darkness to have been unrelieved by some ray of heavenly grace. St. Paul has set the stage for an enquiry dictated by a purely argumentative necessity. *What is life under the law according to the logic of its nature?* St. Paul presents the case from the standpoint of Christianity,

> but a Christianity not present in all its terms. We are contemplating an abstraction developed by dialectic, not the actual situation either of the regenerate or of the unregenerate man, but only the hypothetical condition of a Christian under Law (*Jesus and the Christian* [Grand Rapids: Eerdmans, 1967], p. 159).

A parallel use of methodology may be detected in Ecclesiastes. The writer knows God but purposely and deliberately views life from the standpoint of the natural man in order to expose it as vanity, empty of lasting value.

Romans 7 performs a service by calling into question certain popular notions that lack biblical foundation: that the soul's struggle is essentially against specific sins or habits (Paul talks here not of sins but of sin); that human nature is essentially good (cf. v.18); that sanctification is by means of the law; that if one will only determine to do the right, he will be able to do it. These are some of the misconceptions that must be removed, and they might not have been removed had the apostle proceeded directly from chapter 6 to chapter 8. Without chapter 7 we would not be able to appreciate to the full the truths presented in chapter 8.

Notes

18 The final clause of the sentence ends in οὔ (*ou,* "not") unaccompanied by a verb. Some MSS add "find"; others, "know." NIV accurately conveys the sense.

E. *The Blessings of Life in the Spirit* (8:1–39)

It is altogether too narrow a view to see in this portion simply the antidote to the wretched state pictured in chapter 7. Actually the chapter gathers up various strands of thought from the entire discussion of both justification and sanctification and ties them together with the crowning knot of glorification. Like chapter 5, it presents the blessings of the justified life, grounded in the removal of condemnation. Like chapter 6, it stresses freedom from the bondage of sin and ultimately from the bondage of death. Like chapter 7, it deals with the problem of the flesh, finding the solution in the liberating and productive ministry of the Spirit. The chapter begins with instruction, rises to consolation, and culminates in jubilation. This is high and holy ground indeed for the Christian pilgrim to tread.

1. *Liberation by the Spirit from the law of sin and death*

8:1–11

1Therefore, there is now no condemnation for those who are in Christ Jesus,
2because through Christ Jesus the law of the Spirit of life set me free from the law
of sin and death. 3For what the law was powerless to do in that it was weakened
by our sinful nature, God did by sending his own Son in the likeness of sinful man
to be a sin offering. And so he condemned sin in sinful man, 4in order that the
righteous requirements of the law might be fully met in us, who do not live according to our sinful nature but according to the Spirit.

5Those who live according to their sinful nature have their minds set on what that
nature desires; but those who live in accordance with the Spirit have their minds

set on what the Spirit desires. 6The mind of sinful man is death, but the mind controlled by the Spirit is life and peace, 7because the sinful mind is hostile to God. It does not submit to God's law, nor can it do so. 8Those controlled by their sinful nature cannot please God.

9You, however, are controlled not by your sinful nature but by the Spirit, if the Spirit of God lives in you. And if anyone does not have the Spirit of Christ, he does not belong to Christ. 10But if Christ is in you, your body is dead because of sin, yet your spirit is alive because of righteousness. 11And if the Spirit of him who raised Jesus from the dead is living in you, he who raised Christ from the dead will also give life to your mortal bodies through his Spirit, who lives in you.

1,2 The reader is hardly prepared by the contents of chapter 7 for the glorious pronouncement that there is no condemnation at all for those who are in Christ Jesus, and he finds it hard to associate the "therefore" with anything in the immediately preceding context. The connection must be sought in the entire sweep of the thought as developed from chapter 3 on. The natural antithesis to condemnation is justification. It can be replied, of course, that Paul has already covered this truth and would not be likely to revert to it here. However, this is such a basic truth that Paul brings it even into his discussion of the Christian life (8:33, 34; cf. 8:10). Justification is the basis and starting point for sanctification. One must be assured of acceptance with God before he can grow in grace and conformity to Christ. At the same time, one must grant that the construction of vv.2–4 carries us beyond the thought of freedom from condemnation in the sense of guilt. What is developed is the application of the redeeming work of Christ by the Spirit to the believer's life in such a way that the dominion of sin is broken and the reign of godliness assured. The noun "condemnation" has its counterpart in the verb "condemned" (v.3), which is followed immediately, not by a statement about the standing of the believer, but by one concerning his manner of life (v.4). Consequently, there is both a forensic and a practical force in "no condemnation."

Verse 2 immediately picks up this practical, dynamic aspect by concentrating on the freedom from the imperious rule of sin and death, a freedom now available to the believer through the operation of the Spirit. The word "law" is used figuratively here (cf. 7:21, 23). Clearly it would be impossible for Paul to refer to the law of Moses as "the law of sin and death," even though it provokes sin (7:7, 8) and produces death (7:9–11; 2 Cor 3:6, 7). The law in itself is holy (7:12). In the present passage, therefore, "law" is used to indicate the certainty and regularity of operation that characterizes sin (which leads to death) on the one hand and the Spirit on the other. Whereas the word "law" emphasizes regularity, "life" emphasizes both supernaturalness and spontaneity. Hence the superiority of the Spirit's operation over that of sin.

The NIV differs from the familiar wording "the Spirit of life in Christ Jesus" by stating that "through Christ Jesus the law of the Spirit of life set me free." The former wording points to the Spirit as the life-giver (cf. 2 Cor 3:6) but only as mediating that which is in Christ (Col 3:4). Yet the construction is somewhat cumbersome, a disadvantage not shared by the other wording. Either is possible syntactically. Paul has already noted the enslaving power of sin and the freedom from it achieved by Christ (6:18, 22). This truth was anticipated in the teaching of Jesus (John 8:34–36).

3,4 But how was this freedom gained (v.3)? The opening statement about the powerlessness of the law because of the weakness of the sinful nature to which its commands are addressed is an obvious reminder of the major thrust of chapter 7. The law makes demands, and it condemns when those demands are not met, but it cannot overcome sin. This inability of the law required the personal action of God in Christ. He sent "his own Son." The mission could not be entrusted to anyone else or anyone less than his Son. While the preexistence of the Son is not formally taught here, it is implied, as it frequently is in the Gospel of John where the sending of the Son is mentioned (e.g., 3:17; 7:33; 17:18; 20:21). When vv.2, 3 are taken together, they bear a close resemblance to Galatians 4:4–6, where Father, Son, and Spirit are pictured as involved in the mission of Christ.

The Son was sent "in the likeness of sinful man" ("man" is literally "flesh"). Observe with what care the incarnation is stated. Paul does not say "in sinful flesh," lest the Son's sinlessness be compromised, nor "in the likeness of flesh," which would convey a docetic idea and thereby deny the reality of the humanity of our Lord, making it only an appearance of corporeality. As it stands, the terminology is in full agreement with Philippians 2:7: "being made in human likeness."

So much for Christ's person. What about his work? "To be a sin offering" is the purpose of his coming. The proper translation here is a matter of some controversy. Certainly, "sin offering" is a possible rendering (as in 2 Cor 5:21), but this may be more than Paul intends to say, since he does not surround the expression with sacrificial language. And if it were his intent to stress expiation, a more natural expression would have been "*as* a sin offering." If we translate literally, "for sin," then we are adopting the view that Paul is simply stating that the mission of Christ was to deal effectively with sin, making possible among his people the type of life presented in the following verse. This does not exclude expiation but goes beyond it. Certainly it would be wrong to interpret the passage merely as a reference to the perfection of Christ's life as a rebuke to sin in humanity. This would only tantalize and frustrate those who supposedly were the beneficiaries of his mission.

"So he condemned sin in sinful man." It should be noted again that, in the Greek, "sinful man" is simply "flesh." It is possible that "in the flesh" is intended to be correlated with "through the flesh" at the beginning of the verse, in which case the NIV translation is justified. However, since "flesh" can be used of Christ apart from any sinful connotation (e.g., Col 1:22), it is also possible to refer the phrase to the Savior rather than to sinful humanity (TDNT 7:133). The viewpoint is well expressed by John Murray:

> In that same nature which in all others was dominated and directed by sin, God condemned sin and overthrew its power. Jesus not only blotted out sin's guilt and brought us nigh to God. He also vanquished sin as power and set us free from its enslaving dominion. And this could not have been done except in the "flesh." The battle was joined and the triumph secured in that same flesh which in us is the seat and agent of sin. (in loc.)

This brings the teaching in line with 6:5–11. The words "for sin" create a difficulty for those (e.g., Godet) who see the condemnation of sin as accomplished (according to this passage) simply in the spotless life of the Son. Rather, the entire Christ-event is intended.

The purpose of the incarnation, so far as the believer's life is concerned, is stated in v.4 in such a way as to indicate that the apostle has not allowed the agonizing struggle of chapter 7 to fade from view. There the law was pictured as faultless in itself, a revelation of a holy God, but agonizingly elusive for the man who tries to keep it in his own strength. The self-satisfied man will minimize the law's demands by magnifying his own achievement, whereas the conscientious man will end up in despair. In God's plan, however, the law is to be honored not simply in lip service or in desire but in reality. Its righteous requirement is to be fully met. This can be done only by living according to the Spirit rather than according to the flesh, i.e., the sinful nature of man (cf. "Spirit of life" in v.2). Divine aid is needed to meet the divine requirement.

Paul makes no attempt to particularize the divine requirement but later on he significantly depicts love as the fulfillment of the law (13:10). That love is the primary item in the fruit of the Spirit (Gal 5:22) is surely no happenstance. Observe the balance in this passage between the divine and human elements in Christian life. Paul recognizes that the believer has a life to live; he is not a robot, but a person accountable for his redeemed life as a stewardship. At the same time Paul pictures the requirement of the law as fulfilled (passive) *in* the believer, not *by* him, as though to remind him that the redeemed person does not possess spiritual power he can control and utilize on his own. Rather, the Spirit is always channeling that power and never releases it to those he dwells in for them to use independently of him. The power resides in the Spirit, not in the one he indwells.

It would be a mistake to ground the Christian "walk" solely on the enabling ministry of the Spirit. The close connection with v.3 demands that we include the saving work of Christ. In a previous passage Paul has observed that identification with the Savior in his death and resurrection has this very objective, that "we too may live [Gr., 'walk'] a new life" (6:4).

5–8 At this point Paul launches upon a fairly extended statement contrasting the terms "flesh" and "Spirit," which he has used in v.4. Both terms are difficult because they can have more than one meaning. For example, "flesh" can be used of ordinary physical life shared by believer and unbeliever alike (cf. 2 Cor 10:3). But usually in Paul the ethical force of the word, referring to human nature as corrupted and weakened by sin, is dominant. Because the variety of expressions about the flesh may be confusing, some explanation is necessary. To be in the flesh, as the word is used here (v.8), is to be in the unregenerate state. To be (*ontes,* v.5) according to the flesh is to have the flesh as the regulating principle of one's life. To walk (*peripatousin,* v.4) according to the flesh is to carry out in conduct those things dictated by the flesh.

Less complicated is the use of "Spirit," but even here there is some question as to whether the word used in contrast to "flesh" may not properly be considered as referring to the (redeemed) human spirit. This much is clear, that in the passage under consideration *pneuma* does not mean "spirit" simply as an element in the constitution of man. (It has this meaning in 1 Cor 5:3.) The problem is to determine whether *pneuma* in this passage means the divine life-principle (the new nature communicated to the believer) or whether it should be understood to mean the Spirit of God.

The presence or absence of the definite article does not decide the question, since a reference to the Holy Spirit, considered as a proper name, would not require the article. Neither does the contrast (flesh versus spirit) necessitate a reference to the new nature on the ground that if flesh has a human reference, the same must be true of spirit, for the context of Galatians 5:16, 17, where the two terms are in evident contrast, requires that this be understood as a reference to the Holy Spirit.

Two considerations strongly favor the view that this is a reference to the Holy Spirit. One is the fact that the chapter has begun with an obvious allusion to the divine Spirit (v.2), so that unless there is clear indication to the contrary, one should expect this to be the intended meaning of *pneuma* in the verses that follow. The other is the likelihood that in stating the ground of Christian victory over sin the apostle would assign the basis of that victory to the highest source rather than to a lower, intermediate factor. " 'The Spirit' here regarded as the regulating principle (*kata*) cannot be man's own spirit however renewed and sanctified, but the Divine power itself which renews and sanctifies, i.e., the indwelling Spirit of God" (Gifford, in loc.). The decision on the meaning of *pneuma* in v.10 is more difficult and will be deferred until we come to that verse.

The statements made about the flesh or man's sinful nature in vv.5–8 are to be understood as referring to the unregenerate man, judging by the care with which Paul excludes his readers in v.9. This is not sufficient ground, however, for claiming that the Christian has nothing to do with the flesh. The warning of 8:12ff. would be meaningless if that were the case. But for the moment Paul wishes to expose the flesh in its stark reality as being totally alien to God and his holy purposes. He makes the point that there is a correspondence between a man's essential being and what interests him. The fleshly are occupied with fleshly things, whereas those who possess the Spirit and are controlled by him are concerned with the things of the Spirit. Paul had already taught (1 Cor 2:14) that the fleshly man does not welcome the things of the Spirit. They are foolishness to him. He neither comprehends them nor desires to do so. His mind-set is otherwise. This expression ("to set the mind on") denotes far more than a mental process. It includes not only concentration of thought but also desire (cf. Phil 2:5ff.; Col 3:2).

The same root word appears again (v.6), only in the noun form: "The mind of sinful man is death." Because he is unsaved, this man is cut off from God, and this amounts to death in the sense of separation from God. The spiritual man, on the contrary, enjoys life from God (cf. v.2) and the peace such life affords (cf. 14:17). The dead state of the natural man, both present and future, is traced to the inveterate opposition to God that characterizes "flesh." This hostility manifests itself in the natural man's attitude toward the law of God. The fact that it is God's law does not move him or soften him. He refuses to obey it and thereby puts himself into the position of a rebel against God, since the law is an expression of God's will.

Note the sharp contrast to the response of the believer to the law (v.4). There is a contrast too with the "I" in chapter 7, where there is at least a desire to fulfill the law's demands, even if doing this is grossly deficient. Sinful man (generically understood) is plagued by a double limitation; he neither submits to God's law nor is able to do so (cf. a similar twofold limitation of the natural man respecting spiritual knowledge as stated in 1 Cor 2:14). He neither can nor will receive the things of the Spirit. In summary, Paul has named four characteristics of sinful man: hostility toward God, insubordination to his law, failure to please God, and death. It is no wonder that when Jesus spoke to Nicodemus of the flesh, he went on to declare, "You must be born again" (John 3:7).

9–11 Turning now to his readers, Paul reminds them of the basic difference between themselves and those he has been describing, those who have nothing more than sinful human nature. As believers, they have, in the Spirit, an antidote for the flesh. Furthermore, the Spirit of God "lives" in them. They are his dwelling-place. The "if" is not intended to raise doubt, as though to suggest that some of Paul's readers might have to be excluded. The "if" in this type of construction presupposes the truth of the statement. Previously (v.2) the Spirit has been called the Spirit of life because of his regenerating and renewing power; here he is set forth as the Spirit of God and as the Spirit of Christ, indicating that he carries out the purposes of God and applies the fruits of Christ's redemptive mission to the lives of believers (cf. "the Spirit of his [God's] Son" in Gal 4:6).

No one who lacks the Spirit belongs to Christ. Everyone who trusts Christ has the

Spirit (Eph 1:13). The title "Spirit of Christ" is justified and made meaningful by the deliberate way in which Paul says essentially the same thing about both the Spirit and Christ in relation to the believer: the Spirit lives in you (v.9) and Christ is in you (v.10). The presence and fullness of Christ are realized in the life of the Christian by means of the indwelling Spirit (Eph 3:16, 17). Clearly, the notion that "the Spirit of Christ" is a reference to our Lord's disposition, his kindness, etc., is entirely wide of the mark.

Paul's observation (v.10) about those in whom Christ lives—"your body is dead because of sin, yet your spirit is alive because of righteousness"—has proved difficult for interpreters. Translation is to some extent interpretation, and NIV stands in line with most leading modern translations in making "spirit" refer to the spirit of the Christian rather than to the Spirit of Christ. On the other hand, able commentators in increasing numbers (e.g., Michel, Barth, Barrett, Murray, and Leenhardt) are coming to a different conclusion. Two factors seem decisive. One is the unlikelihood that in a passage that has consistently referred to *pneuma* in terms of the Spirit of God, the word would be given a different frame of reference in this one instance. To be sure, the use of "body" over against "spirit" might seem to be sufficient ground for assuming that Paul is talking about two contrasting elements of the human constitution. But whereas such a sharp contrast is congenial to Greek thought, it is alien to the Hebraic concept of life that characterizes both Testaments. In fact, it has been recognized that in Paul's usage, "body" usually means the totality of one's being, "man as a whole, not a part which may be detached from the true I" (TDNT 7:1064). Can we really suppose that when he speaks of "this body of death" (7:24) he has reference merely to the physical organism? In the passage before us he is asserting that sin necessitated our dying with Christ and that even so we must expect physical death in the future. The second reason for choosing the rendering "Spirit" over "spirit" is found in the last clause, where the *pneuma* is said to be alive because of righteousness. Actually Paul says more than this, for he does not use "alive" but "life." This is more than can be properly said of the human spirit. It has been said, however, of the Spirit at the beginning of the chapter (v.2).

So the best conclusion is that *pneuma* refers to the Holy Spirit. The very fact that the first part of the following verse refers to the living presence of the Spirit in the believer seems to indicate that Paul is repeating what he sought to say at the end of v.10 in order to build on it for a further observation—namely, that the same Spirit will provide resurrection life in due season. The close of v.10 teaches that the Spirit who is life in himself brings life to the person he indwells only because that person has already been granted God's righteousness (justification). So the presence of the Spirit in the redeemed life is at once the evidence of salvation bestowed and the earnest of that final phase of salvation that belongs to the future (v.11). In this passage righteousness cannot be understood in any other light than as imputed righteousness (cf. 1 Cor 1:30).

In v.11 the Spirit is given yet another title: "the Spirit of him who raised Jesus from the dead." The reference is, of course, to God (cf. 4:24). Paul is not asserting, as some claim, that the Spirit raised Jesus from the dead. The title is simply a specialized variation of the Spirit of God. His future work on behalf of the saints will be to "give life" to their mortal (i.e., subject-to-death) bodies. This accords with Paul's description of the glorified bodies of believers as "spiritual" (1 Cor 15:44). "The Spirit is both the instrumental cause of the resurrection-act and the permanent substratum of the resurrection-life" (G. Vos, *The Pauline Eschatology* [Princeton, 1930], p. 169). The life bestowed by the Spirit in that coming day is beyond the power of death or any other agency to vitiate or destroy. It is the very life of God, blessedly spiritual and indestructibly eternal.

Notes

1 In v.1 KJV has a longer wording than NIV, concluding the verse with "who walk not after the flesh, but after the Spirit." This addition is not warranted, being absent from the leading MSS; clearly it has been introduced by scribal zeal from the end of v.4.

2 A decision must be made between two readings: "me" or "you"—με (*me*) or σε (*se*). "You" has the stronger MS support, and for this reason a number of versions follow this reading. On the other hand, there are two factors that warrant retaining "me." For one thing, it is the logical term for Paul to have used, in agreement with the personal thrust of ch. 7. Also, the close of the preceding word in the Gr. text ("set free") has in it the letters *se,* so that a copyist could easily have transcribed *se* for *me* by visual error. If this is what happened, it must have occurred early in the transmission of the text, since σε (*se*) appears in many of our early and most reliable MSS. A mistake of this kind was more easily made in the earlier copies because for several centuries the text was written without any space between the words.

5 The argument of Lenski (*The Interpretation of St. Paul's Epistle to the Romans* [Columbus: Wartburg Press, 1945], p. 503) that "the decisive point is the fact that the Spirit is not a norm (κατὰ, *kata*) as are flesh and spirit," is not convincing, for the same preposition is used with the Spirit elsewhere (Gal 4:29) as well as with God (8:27) and with Christ (15:5).

2. *Additional ministries of the Spirit*

8:12–27

12Therefore, brothers, we have an obligation—but it is not to our sinful nature,
to live according to it. 13For if you live according to the sinful nature, you will die;
but if by the Spirit you put to death the misdeeds of the body, you will live.
14Those who are led by the Spirit of God are sons of God. 15For you did not
receive a spirit that makes you a slave again to fear, but you received the Spirit
who makes you sons. And by him we cry, "*Abba,* Father." 16The Spirit himself
testifies with our spirit that we are God's children. 17Now if we are children, then
we are heirs—heirs of God and co-heirs with Christ, if indeed we share in his
sufferings in order that we may also share in his glory.
18I consider that our present sufferings are not worth comparing with the glory
that will be revealed in us. 19The creation waits in eager expectation for the sons
of God to be revealed. 20For the creation was subjected to frustration, not by its
own choice, but by the will of the one who subjected it, in hope 21that the creation
itself will be liberated from its bondage to decay and brought into the glorious
freedom of the children of God.
22We know that the whole creation has been groaning as in the pains of childbirth
right up to the present time. 23Not only so, but we ourselves, who have the firstfruits
of the Spirit, groan inwardly as we wait eagerly for our adoption as sons, the
redemption of our bodies. 24For in this hope we were saved. But hope that is seen
is no hope at all. Who hopes for what he already has? 25But if we hope for what
we do not yet have, we wait for it patiently.
26In the same way, the Spirit helps us in our weakness. We do not know how
we ought to pray, but the Spirit himself intercedes for us with groans that words
cannot express. 27And he who searches our hearts knows the mind of the Spirit,
because the Spirit intercedes for the saints in accordance with God's will.

12,13 The apostle turns now from instruction to exhortation, from what God has done through Christ and the Spirit to what the believer is expected to do by way of response. But even with a strong emphasis on human responsibility, we see behind the human effort that which can be accomplished only "by the Spirit." The special ministry described here is *mortification.* It is the message of 6:11–14 all over again except for the reminder that no one can hope to deal effectively with the sinful nature simply by determination alone. The Holy Spirit is needed, and he is the Spirit of power.

"Obligation" is the keynote. Only the negative side is stated; the positive side—that we are debtors to the Spirit—must be inferred. If we do not have an obligation to live in terms of the sinful nature, the conclusion must be that our obligation is to live and serve God in terms of the Spirit. It is tremendously important to grasp the import of v.12, because it teaches beyond all question that the believer still has the sinful nature within himself, despite having been crucified with Christ. The flesh has not been eradicated. But we are obliged not "to live according to it." There is really no option, for the flesh is linked to death as life is linked to the Spirit. Sanctification is not a luxury but a necessity. As Bishop Handley Moule stated, "It is not an ambition; it is a duty" (in loc.). Life in accordance with the flesh is doomed to suffer death (cf. v.6). The solicitations of the fleshly nature are constant; hence the necessity of continually putting to death (that is the force of the verb) the deeds of the body. Here "body" is equivalent to "the flesh" as in 6:6. Though this may seem to give a negative emphasis to the life of sanctification, it should be emphasized that this is only part of the divine plan. The positive is just as important—the putting on of the Lord Jesus in such complete preoccupation with him and his will that the believer does not make provision for the flesh (cf. 13:14). Yet since the Spirit is the Spirit of life, he cannot do otherwise than oppose the flesh and its desires, the things that lead inevitably to death.

14–17 The Spirit's ministry set forth in these verses may be thought of as his *attestation*, in which he confirms for the believer the reality of his position as a son of God based on adoption into the heavenly family. Though this ministry is mentioned after that of mortification, it is basic to it, because to be successful in contending against the flesh one must be assured that he has been claimed by God and equipped with his infinite resources. Later (v.23) Paul will move on to set forth another aspect of adoption that belongs to the future, identified with redemption in its ultimate realization.

The relation of the Spirit to the sons of God is presented as being much like that of a shepherd to his sheep. They are "led" by him as their guide and protector. In Galatians 3:24 the law is pictured as having a responsibility to "lead" men to Christ. Once this goal is achieved, the law must hand over the guiding role to the Spirit, who guides into the truth (John 16:13) and, as in the present passage, into holiness. Unlike sin, which may at first only gently seduce, then deceitfully begin to drive as a hard taskmaster, the Spirit relies on persuasion rather than force. In fact, Paul goes to some pains to avoid misunderstanding on this very point, assuring us that the Spirit's leadership does not involve a new bondage that is no improvement over the old in which fear ruled the life (probably a fear of the consequences of sin and a fear of death, as in Heb 2:15). The new title given to the Spirit, namely, "the Spirit who makes you sons" (literally, "Spirit of adoption"), emphasizes the vast gulf between slavery and family relationship. By the Spirit believers cry, "*Abba*, Father." The two terms are equivalents, the first being the Aramaic word Jesus used in prayer (Mark 14:36). Paul's use of the Aramaic alongside the Greek both here and in Galatians 4:6, a closely related passage, may well indicate that the tradition concerning the prayer life of Jesus filtered down through the church even before Mark wrote his Gospel. J. Jeremias notes that in permitting the Twelve to use the Lord's

Prayer, Jesus "authorizes his disciples to follow him in saying *Abba.* He gives them this address as the token of their discipleship" (*The Central Message of the New Testament* [New York: Scribner's, 1965], p. 28). The "cry" refers to calling on God in prayer.

The important term "adoption" bears a relationship to justification in that it is declarative and forensic (inasmuch as it is a legal term). Adoption bestows an objective standing, as justification does; like justification, it is a pronouncement that is not repeated. It has permanent validity. Like justification, adoption rests on the loving purpose and grace of God (Eph 1:5). Though the term is used of Israel in relation to God (9:4; cf. Hos 11:1), it is doubtful that adoption was practiced in OT days. Much more likely is the conclusion that Paul was drawing on the background of Roman law both here and in Galatians 4:5. The readers of both Epistles would be familiar with adoption in their own society (Francis Lyall, "Roman Law in the Writings of Paul—Adoption," JBL 88 [Dec. 1969] 458–66).

Paul's readers are called sons (v.15) and children (v.16), without any appreciable distinction. Both are family terms. "Children" emphasizes family relationship based on regeneration, while "sons" stresses legal standing. (This is not according to the usage of the apostle John, since John uses "children" for believers and reserves "son" for the Son of God.)

Here (v.16), as in Galatians 4:6, the Spirit is represented as bearing witness together with the redeemed spirit in man to the reality of membership in the family of heaven, that is, to the actuality of salvation through Christ. Hebrew law prescribed that at the mouth of two or three witnesses every matter was to be established (Deut 17:6; cf. Matt 18:16). Similarly, there are two witnesses to one's salvation, the person himself in his inmost being and the Holy Spirit, who confirms the believer's realization that he has indeed been made God's child through faith in Christ. Because this witness takes place in the heart (Gal 4:6), it is not a witness others receive, though it may be the basis for testifying to others about the reality of salvation. It may be aided by Scripture (John 20:31; 1 John 5:13) but is not dependent on the written word. It is a secret inner witness (see Bernard Ramm, *The Witness of the Spirit* [Grand Rapids: Eerdmans, 1959]).

A comparison of vv.15 and 16 will bring out an important truth concerning the assurance of salvation. All too often a believer may come to the point of doubting his salvation because his sanctification has proceeded so slowly and so lamely. The Spirit, however, does not base his assuring testimony on progress or the lack of it in the Christian life. He does not lead us to cry, "I am God's child." Rather, he leads us to call upon God as Father, to look away from ourselves to him who established the relationship.

A final truth about adoption is that it involves an inheritance (v.17). In line with current legal provisions that enabled even a slave, once adopted, to inherit his master's possessions, Paul teaches that the Christian follows a similar course: a slave (to sin), a child, then an heir (vv.15–17; cf. Gal 4:6, 7). How unexpected and how breathtaking is the gracious provision of God! The marvel increases with the news that we are co-heirs with Christ. Sharing his sufferings may be looked at as simply the cost of discipleship. Yet it has a brighter aspect, because it is the prelude to partaking with him of the coming glory (cf. 1 Peter 4:13).

18–25 Before passing to the final ministry of the Spirit (vv.26, 27) Paul lingers over the concept of future glory in relation to present suffering. His presentation may be seen as an expansion of what he had already written to the Corinthians (2 Cor 4:17). Weighed in the scales of true and lasting values, the sufferings endured in this life are light indeed, compared with the splendor of the life to come—a life undisturbed by anything hostile or hurtful. Scripture does not tell us much of *what* that glory will be, but it assures us *that* it will be. The glory will be revealed "in us." Another rendering, adopted by several versions, has "to us," which is the more usual force of the construction used here. Possibly the idea is that the glory will be manifested or made available to us, becoming our possession.

Instead of considering the future simply from the standpoint of the redeemed, Paul enlarges the perspective to include the whole creation, which is here personified as longing for the time when the sons of God will enjoy the consummation because the creation's own deliverance from the frustration imposed on it by the fall cannot come until that time. This accords with the superior place given man in the creation (Gen 1:26–28; Ps 8:5–8). "Eager expectation" is a picturesque term describing a person leaning forward out of intense interest and desire. Most of its occurrences relate to the Christian's attitude toward the Lord's coming (e.g., Gal 5:5; Phil 3:20; Heb 9:28). The personification is continued by the use of "frustration," which, as Sanday and Headlam note, "is appropriately used of the *disappointing* character of present existence, which nowhere reaches the perfection of which it is capable" (in loc.).

The one who subjected the creation is not named. Some early Fathers assumed that Adam is in view. Others (e.g., Godet) incline to the notion that Satan is meant. But by far the most natural interpretation is that which postulates God as the one who did the subjecting. The personification is sustained, with the creation being pictured as not willingly enduring the subjection yet having hope for something better, i.e., liberation from its "bondage to decay." The creation longs to share the glorious freedom of the children of God. Shedd remarks, "The restoration of material nature is a condition similar, in its own lower sphere, to the restoration of man's spiritual nature, in its higher sphere. St. Paul here teaches, not the annihilation of this visible world, but its transformation" (in loc.). The apostle is concerned with the creation only as it relates to man. How gracious of God to retain for believers the habitat they have long been accustomed to, only so changed and beautified as to harmonize with their own glorified state.

From v.22 it appears at first sight that "the whole creation" includes man. But v.23 alters this impression, for it sets the entire creation over against the whole body of the redeemed ("we ourselves") and therefore does not include in it the people of God. The groaning of the creation looks back to its subjection to frustration (v.20), whereas the pangs of childbirth anticipate the age of renewal. In other words, the same sufferings are at once a result and a prophecy. Christ spoke of the renewing of the world and called it a "rebirth" (*palingenesia*, Matt 19:28).

Paul makes a parallel between the saints and the material creation. In at least two respects their situation is the same—groaning (cf. 2 Cor 5:2) and eagerly awaiting the new age (v.23). Perhaps a third element of comparison is intended: "the redemption of our bodies," answering to the transformation of the earth. But in one respect no parallel can be made. Only the people of God have "the firstfruits of the Spirit."

The concept of firstfruits (v.23) is prominent in the OT, where, according to the law, Israelites were expected to bring the first-ripe elements of grain, fruit, etc., to the Lord as an offering (Exod 23:19; Neh 10:35). By this observance of worship the offerer acknowledged that all produce was the provision of God and was really his. Implicit also in the ritual was the assurance from the divine side that the general harvest to be enjoyed by the offerer would providentially follow. As applied to our passage, the concept may appear to be somewhat out of place, for if the Spirit is truly a person, how can any more of him be given in the future than has been given at conversion? Clearly, this is not the line of thought intended. On the contrary, we are to understand that the gift of the Spirit to the believer at the inception of Christian life is God's pledge of the completion of the process of salvation, which is here stated as "adoption as sons, the redemption of our bodies." Recall that previously Paul has described the finished product as the spiritual body (1 Cor 15:44). The future bodily resurrection of believers will be the full harvest of redemption. Our bodies will be like that of the glorified Lord (Phil 3:20, 21).

In this connection we encounter adoption for the second time (cf. v.15). The saints already have an adoption: they are acknowledged as God's children. They are sealed by the Spirit for the day of redemption (Eph 1:13, 14; 4:30). Then will take place the second and final adoption. Between the two, there stretches the course of sanctification; but only at the final adoption will the child of God be fully conformed to the likeness of God's Son (v.29; cf. 1 John 3:2). As the physical body is admirably suited to life in this world, the promised spiritual body will be seen to be wonderfully congruent with the realm of light and freedom and limitless movement. But most important of all, it will be like the body of him who has provided redemption from sin and death. This is the Spirit's work of *glorification*.

In keeping with the eager waiting of those who long for their complete salvation (v.23) is the emphasis on hope (vv.24, 25). The connection between hope and suffering should not be overlooked either (cf. 5:4). NIV's "in this hope" is correct, suggesting that from the very moment of the reception of the gospel one must look forward to the final phase set forth in v.23. KJV's "we are saved by hope" unnecessarily makes hope encroach on the sphere of grace (Eph 2:8). The translation of JB, "For we must be content to hope that we shall be saved," is both inaccurate (Paul says we *have* been saved) and unfortunate, suggesting that one cannot in this life be sure of his salvation. The Christian pilgrim is on the road to glory, assured that the promises of the word and the spiritual energy provided for his "walk" are not illusory. As he sees the dark tunnel of death ahead of him, he is confident that beyond it the road leads on to his destination, though it remains unseen. Simply because an element of our salvation—the redemption of the body—is held in reserve, we have a legitimate exercise of hope. If all were ours now, there would be no place for it. Since the object of our hope is not yet realized, "we wait for it patiently." Whether to translate *di' hypomonēs* "patiently" or "with endurance" or "with fortitude" is a difficult decision. If God's promise is chiefly in view (cf. Abraham in 4:18), then "patiently" is appropriate, but if the hardships and sufferings that remain to be faced are in view (note the emphasis on suffering in the context), then the more usual force of the word as "endurance" should be preferred. One can understand the reason for the combined rendering sometimes chosen here, namely, "we wait with patient endurance."

26,27 At length Paul arrives at the final ministry of the Spirit mentioned in this chapter, his work of *intercession*. "In the same way" seems to link this ministry with hope. Both help to sustain the believer amid the burdens and disappointments of life. It is uncertain whether the weakness spoken of here is a general expression for the Christian's limitations while still in the flesh, or whether it is intended to point to his weakness in the specific area of prayer. We know that the apostle had long before discovered his weakness and along with it the compensating factor of the power of God (2 Cor 12:9, 10). The broader interpretation of weakness may well be correct here. Paul may be saying that we do not know how to pray so as to get help for our many-sided weakness. The word "how" could suggest that we do not know the art of prayer—how to phrase our petitions properly. But this is not the Greek word commonly used for "how." Even the wording "what we should pray for" is questionable, since "for" has no equivalent in the original text. So we come by elimination to the more literal wording "what we should pray," that is, the content of our prayers rather than simply the topics. Do we know our real needs as God sees them, and do we know the needs of others? Going deeper, do we know the will of God respecting these things? In the last analysis, it is that that will determine how our prayers will be answered.

Standing over against this severe limitation is the gladdening information that "the Spirit helps us." This word for help occurs in the NT in only one other passage (Luke 10:40). Martha had more than she could handle in the preparation of the meal and asked the Lord to bid her sister Mary come to her aid. We can paraphrase the request like this: "Tell her to help me by taking hold of her end of the task." This picture is useful, because it helps solve a rather vexing problem—viz., that we fail to find in the remainder of this passage any statement about *our* praying. Everything that is said relates to the activity of the Spirit on our behalf, culminating in the declaration that he intercedes "for the saints." Added to this is the fact that when we refer to intercessory prayer, we mean prayer for others rather than for ourselves. On the other hand, the word picture in "help" cannot lightly be dismissed. Furthermore, a previous mention of prayer and communion with God makes it a joint activity of the Spirit and the children of God (vv.15, 16). Since "our hearts" (v.27) suggests immediate personal involvement as well as the residence and operation of the Spirit, the best conclusion seems to be that prayer activity on the part of the believer goes on in the background, though overshadowed by the part played by the Spirit of God. Elsewhere (Eph 6:18) this is called praying in the Spirit.

Verse 27 is needed to clarify something referred to in v.26, i.e., the inexpressible groanings. How can such prayer, if it be called prayer at all, be answered? Are not such prayers unintelligible? Not for God! He is no stranger to the intent of the Spirit. He knows what the inexpressible meaning is, because the petitions the Spirit voices are strictly in accord with the will of God. Barth observes that God "makes himself our advocate with himself, that he utters for us that ineffable groaning, so that he will surely hear what we ourselves could not have told him, so that he will accept what he himself has to offer" (*A Shorter Commentary on Romans*, p. 102). It is a mistake to associate the inexpressible groanings with glossolalia. As Leenhardt notes, the passage is intended to include all Christians, whereas speaking in tongues is a special charismatic gift not possessed by all. In addition, tongues are not mentioned elsewhere in connection with intercession.

Notes

---

24 A twofold problem is encountered here. Some good authorities, including ℵ and A, read ὑπομένει (*hypomenei*, "endures") instead of ἐλπίζει (*elpizei*, "hopes"). Also the reading τίς (*tis*, "who") faces several competing readings. NIV follows τίς . . . ἐλπίζει (*tis* . . . *elpizei*, "who hopes").

---

3. *The security and permanence of the life of the redeemed* (8:28–39)

God's provision for his own is spelled out in exalted and fervent language—reaching back into the past to include his eternal purpose and its implementation in the love and sacrifice of Christ, moving into the present to proclaim God's keeping power, and sweeping down the years to defy any power to separate the saint from the abiding love of God in Christ.

8:28–39

[28]And we know that in all things God works for the good of those who love him, who have been called according to his purpose. [29]For those God foreknew he also predestined to be conformed to the likeness of his Son, that he might be the firstborn among many brothers. [30]And those he predestined, he also called; those he called, he also justified; those he justified, he also glorified.

[31]What, then, shall we say in response to this? If God is for us, who can be against us? [32]He who did not spare his own Son, but gave him up for us all—how will he not also, along with him, graciously give us all things? [33]Who will bring any charge against those whom God has chosen? It is God who justifies. [34]Who is he that condemns? Christ Jesus, who died—more than that, who was raised to life—is at the right hand of God and is also interceding for us. [35]Who shall separate us from the love of Christ? Shall trouble or hardship or persecution or famine or nakedness or danger or sword? [36]As it is written:

> "For your sake we face death all the day long;
> we are considered as sheep to be slaughtered."

[37]No, in all these things we are more than conquerors through him who loved us. [38]For I am convinced that neither death nor life, neither angels nor demons, neither the present, nor the future, nor any powers, [39]neither height nor depth, nor anything else in all creation, will be able to separate us from the love of God that is in Christ Jesus our Lord.

28–30 Verse 28 has problems of text, of connection with the context, and of interpretation. As to the text, some manuscripts make "all things" the subject; others include God as the subject (see note). The problem is not crucial, since even without God being named, there could be no thought in Paul's mind that all things by themselves worked for the good of believers. The entire chapter protests against any such impersonal notion. As to the context, the thought may be connected with the foregoing after this fashion—that we now have a broad, general statement after a more specific one relating to the work of the Spirit as intercessor. So, for example, NEB reads, "And in everything, as we know, he cooperates for good with those who love God." The difficulty with this lies in the remainder of the sentence, where "purpose" must then be referred to the Spirit, whereas elsewhere this is regularly the function of God.

We must also try to settle the meaning of "all things." It is unlikely that the items in vv.29, 30 are intended to provide the content of the "all things," which is deliberately general and suggests especially those things that, while themselves adverse, are turned to good account by the sovereign operation of God on our behalf. This line of thought agrees with 5:3–5 as well as with the mention of sufferings and opposition in the present chapter. The "good" is not defined, but should be sought in the intended conformity to God's Son. The beneficiaries are those who on the human side love God and on the divine side are called according to God's purpose. Paul seldom refers to love for God on the part of the saints (1 Cor 2:9; 8:3). Nor does he introduce it here as the ground for the benefit he has been describing, for it is not meritorious but simply a response to the divine love and grace. The "called" are not those who are merely invited to respond to the proclamation of the gospel; they are called according to God's (electing) purpose.

This calling is further explained in terms of foreknowledge and predestination (v.29).

The former term does not indicate advance awareness or knowledge of someone; it refers to God's choice, his electing decision. This is rendered crystal clear in 1 Peter 1:20. God's calling is not a haphazard thing, nor is it something cold and formal. It is filled with the warmth of love, as in the Hebrew word "to know" (Gen 18:19; Amos 3:2). Though foreknowledge is not mentioned in Deuteronomy 7:6–8, that passage illumines the concept. The antecedent character of God's choice precludes any possibility of human merit as entering into the decision (cf. Eph 1:4). Observe also that we are called according to purpose, not according to foreknowledge, hence foreknowledge must be included in the electing purpose.

If "predestined" stood by itself without any amplification, one might conclude that all that is involved is an action by God whereby one is chosen to salvation. But the remainder of the sentence indicates otherwise, pointing to much more than deliverance from sin and death. The background is adoption, but now presented not as in v.15 (where it is related to the Father and the Spirit) but as related to the Son. Paul presents two aspects of this conformity. By a sharing in the sufferings of Christ (Phil 3:10) that is based on having the mind of Christ (Phil 2:5–8), the believer is gradually being made into his likeness. This is the essence of sanctification. Its second and final aspect is conformity of the body to that of the risen Lord, to be realized at the resurrection (Phil 3:21), which is the culmination of a growth in likeness to Christ based on the Spirit's work in the believer (2 Cor 3:18).

From these passages we learn that fellowship with Christ in his sufferings is the prelude to sharing with him in his glory. God sent his Son in our likeness (v.3) that we might eventually be like him. This makes understandable and legitimate the use of "brothers" as a description of believers in relation to the Son. The likeness will be complete except for the fact that glorified humanity never, of course, becomes deity.

Verse 30 states the various steps involved in the realization of the divine purpose: the call (cf. v.28), justification, and glorification. The marvel is that the final item is stated as though it had already occurred. This led Denney to declare (in loc.) that this is "the most daring verse in the Bible." One is reminded of the so-called prophetic perfect used occasionally in the OT, as for example, in Isaiah 53, where the work of the Servant of Jehovah is spoken of as though his sacrifice had already been made.

Why is sanctification not mentioned in this verse? It is probably left out deliberately because sanctification is the one area in which human cooperation is essential. There is no appeal anywhere to be called or justified or glorified, but there are numerous appeals to cooperate with God in the realization of the life of holiness.

31–36 From this point on to the end of the chapter Paul expounds the impregnable position of the believer. The key lies in the sentence "If God is for us, who can be against us?" (v.31). God has not given empty promises. He has acted, and what he has done in Christ and by the Spirit constitutes all the proof we need that the glorification will be ours in due season. This is precisely the point of v.32. God's activity has cost him dearly—he did not spare "his own Son." In the background is the readiness of Abraham to give up his son Isaac (Gen 22). But whereas a substitute was found for Isaac and he was restored to his father without dying, no other than God's own Son could take away the world's sin and provide reconciliation. So Jesus had to endure the cross. In all of this God was with him (2 Cor 5:19). Moreover, the Son was not an unwilling victim pressed into sacrificial service. "God gave him up" expresses the Father's participation, but the same verb is used of the Son's involvement (Gal 2:20). With the cross before us as the mighty demonstration of God's grace in giving his dearest to help the neediest, it naturally follows that the same gracious spirit will not withhold anything from those who are his. Such is the assurance given us in 2 Peter 1:3 that everything we need for life and godliness has been given.

Paul does not deny that the Christian faces foes and hardships. Yet his challenging question stands: "If God is for us, who can be against us?" Amplifying it, he proceeds to ask a series of questions, and provides answers to them. First, "Who will bring any charge against those whom God has chosen?" (v.33) No one can successfully press charges, no matter how hard he may try. Satan is busy doing just that (Rev 12:10), no doubt pointing out the discrepancy between the profession of believers and their "walk," but he gets nowhere with his pretended zeal for righteousness. Ultimately, as David also perceived (Ps 51:4), all sin is committed against God, no matter how much it affects others. Logically, therefore, God is the only one in position to bring charges against us. This, Paul is saying, God refuses to do, because he is for us, not against us.

The second question, "Who is he that condemns?" (v.34), finds its answer in Christ. He will never renounce the efficacy of his own work on our behalf. Paul packs four aspects of that work into one great sentence (v.34b). (1) Christ died and thereby secured the removal of sin's guilt; (2) he was raised to life and is able to bestow life on those who trust him for their salvation (John 11:25; 14:19); (3) he was exalted to God's right hand, with all power given to him both in heaven, so as to represent us there, and on earth, where he is more than a match for our adversaries; (4) and he intercedes for us at the throne of grace, whatever our need may be (Heb 4:4–16; 7:25).

A third question is "Who shall separate us from the love of Christ?" (v.35). Can there conceivably be a contradiction between Christ's love for his own and his allowing suffering to overtake them? Should the saints question whether Christ's love has grown cold? Severance from his love is no more thinkable than that the Father ceased to love his Son when he allowed him to endure the agonies of the cross, apparently forsaken. Christ predicted trouble for his people who are left in the world, but told them to be of good cheer because he had overcome the world (John 16:33). The quotation from Psalm 44:22 (v.36) reminds believers that suffering has always been the lot of the godly, and therefore their own situation is not peculiar. Whereas the people of God in the OT were often perplexed about the reason for their trials, the saints of NT times can trace their sufferings back to identification with Christ and rejoice that they are counted worthy to suffer for his name (cf. Acts 5:41).

37–39 Here Paul bursts into a magnificent piece of eloquence. This passage, like 1 Corinthians 3:21–23, is notable for largeness of conception and majesty of expression: "No, in all these things we are more than conquerors through him who loved us" (v.37).

Some have found "more than conquerors" puzzling. It could mean that believers turn their enemies into helpers as indicated in 5:3–5. But this is rather conjectural. Bauer affirms that the verb *hypernikaō* used here is a heightened form of "conquer" and suggests the translation "We are winning a most glorious victory." Bauernfeind (TDNT 4:945) renders it, "We win the supreme victory through him who loved us."

By saying "loved us," Paul does not intend to restrict Christ's love to the past, but rather he is emphasizing the historic demonstration of this love that gives assurance of its continuing under all circumstances. Death cannot separate the believer from that love (cf. Phil 1:21; 2 Cor 5:8). Neither can life, with all its allurements and dangers and trials.

Surprisingly, Paul includes angels here (v.38). Since he uses other terms for hostile supernatural powers, the angels should be understood as good ones. Perhaps the meaning is that no angel of this sort would seek to come between Christ's love and the object of that love. Demons are evil spirits such as those often mentioned in the Gospels. Being agents and underlings of the devil, they would delight to separate Christians from Christ, but they cannot do so. Time is equally powerless to do this, whether it be the present with its temptations and sufferings or the future with its uncertainties. "Powers" probably has reference to hostile spiritual intelligences who, though conquered by Christ (Eph 1:21), are nevertheless permitted to carry on spiritual warfare against the saints of God (Eph 6:12).

Nor can space come between us and the love of Christ (v.39). If there are other possibilities, Paul is sure they are all equally impotent. For he declares that there is nothing in all creation that can drive a wedge between the love of the Savior and his redeemed people. After all, the creation itself is his handiwork and cannot thwart the will of the Creator. God is love, and that love has been manifested in the redemption of man.

S. Angus translates "neither height nor depth" as "neither the ascension of the stars nor their declinations," considering that Paul has in mind the fatalism of astral religion (*The Religious Quests of the Graeco-Roman World* [New York: Scribners, 1929], p. 254).

Notes

---

28 The KJV rendering "all things work together for good" is based on the text attested by ℵ C D G and the great bulk of MSS and many quotations from the Fathers. The rendering "in all things God works for the good" is supported by P^{46} A B, among others. It is probable that the second form of the text came into being at an early date to clarify the meaning by tracing this activity definitely to God. Otherwise it is hard to explain how "God" could have dropped out of the majority of witnesses to the text.

VI. The Problem of Israel: God's Righteousness Vindicated (9:1–11:36)

This section contains "unfinished business." Although Paul has insisted on the priority of the Jew (1:16) and has noted in part his advantages (3:1ff.), he has also been obliged to expose the Jews' failure and guilt, despite their being the chosen people of God. Those who have been under divine tutelage for centuries in preparation for the coming of the Messiah have failed to receive him. Has the purpose of God been frustrated? What does the future hold for this people? The problem faced here was underscored in Paul's own ministry. He had been faithful in going to the Jew first, but in place after place he had been rebuffed by Jewish unbelief. In Rome itself his strenuous effort to win a favorable verdict for the Lord Jesus Christ was to prove largely unsuccessful (Acts 28). Was his earlier statement about the power of the gospel (1:16) too hasty, too optimistic? Or were his own labors among his people inadequate? Paul could not subscribe to either conclusion. He had to face the problem from the standpoint of God's purposes and ways.

Jew and Gentile are distinguished in the first three chapters and are still distinguished, as the circumcised and the uncircumcised, in chapter 4. In chapters 5 to 8 the Jew/Gentile tension drops out of sight, only to be renewed in chapters 9 to 11 and brought under searching examination. Notable is the shift in terminology. Although "Jew" occurs twice in this section, Paul prefers "Israel," using it ten times here and nowhere else in the letter. The reason for the change will be noted later.

In line with the nature of the problem Paul is dealing with, he frequently mentions God in chapters 9 to 11 (twenty-six times). References to Christ are limited (seven times), and the Holy Spirit has no place except in 9:1.

For all its distinctiveness, this section does not lose continuity with the foregoing material. "Salvation" (cf. 1:16) and "save" are prominent. "Righteousness" (cf. 1:17) is found nine times; "believe" (cf. 1:16), eight times; and "faith," six times.

Not only is there a connection with the theme of the letter, but also a tie-in with the close of chapter 8; for election, which is treated on an individual basis in 8:28–30, 33, is now viewed from the national perspective of Israel. Adoption is an element common to both portions (8:15; 9:4), as is also the concept of "call" or "calling" (8:28–30; 5 times in ch. 9).

Another feature is the liberal use of OT quotations, partly to emphasize the sovereignty of God and his covenant faithfulness and partly to substantiate the apostle's exposure of Israel's failure. Unfaithfulness to God in OT times has its parallel in rejection of his Son in recent times. Israel according to the flesh has not materially changed.

A survey of the movement of thought in these chapters warrants the conclusion that Paul, who has written so penetratingly on the justification of sinners, now turns to write on the justification (vindication) of God himself (cf. 3:3, 4). He reminds us that the Almighty is free and sovereign in what he does (ch. 9). Then he turns the discussion to the Jews' mistake in trying to establish their own righteousness before God in terms of meritorious obedience to law instead of responding to the gospel of Christ by faith. They have not lacked opportunity to hear (ch. 10). So God did not set Israel aside arbitrarily. This matches the great section on condemnation at the beginning of the Epistle.

In chapter 11 Paul introduces further considerations. One is that Israel's rejection was not complete, for there was a believing remnant in Paul's day. This answers to the treatment on justification in chapters 3 to 5. Also, the rejection is not final, for a mass conversion of Israel will occur, answering roughly to the glorious future pictured in chapter 8. In addition, Paul weaves in the observation that during the time Israel is set aside God continues his work of grace by saving a host of Gentiles. In the end, God is found faithful to his covenant promises in spite of the unfaithfulness of Israel. Moreover, he has turned to good account the failure of the Jew by bringing in the Gentiles during the period of Israel's hardening. This grand achievement embracing both Jew and Gentile leads Paul to conclude with a worshipful note of praise for this unfathomable divine wisdom. It is a testimony to the divine mercy (11:32) which, along with God's righteousness, provides the insight needed to appreciate his ways.

A. *Paul's Sorrow Over Israel's Condition*

9:1–5

> I speak the truth in Christ—I am not lying, my conscience confirms it in the Holy Spirit—2I have great sorrow and unceasing anguish in my heart. 3For I could wish that I myself were cursed and cut off from Christ for the sake of my brothers, those of my own race, 4the people of Israel. Theirs is the adoption as sons; theirs the divine glory, the covenants, the receiving of the law, the temple worship and the promises. 5Theirs are the patriarchs, and from them is traced the human ancestry of Christ, who is God over all, forever praised! Amen.

1–3 The apostle begins on a personal note, expressing his concern for his own people.

His soul is burdened over their condition, as were the prophets of old. Since he has left Judaism behind, this sorrow might be interpreted as somewhat less than sincere. Hence the solemn introduction in which he summons two witnesses—his union with Christ who is the truth (cf. Eph 4:21) and his conscience as aided by the Holy Spirit (cf. 8:16). As though that were not enough, he declares himself ready to accept severance from Christ (cf. 8:39) if that would avail to bring his countrymen into the fold of the Savior (cf. Exod 32:32). The phrase "I could wish" (v.3) faithfully brings out the idiomatic construction used here for stating an impossible wish. Paul could not actually become anathema from Christ (chapter 8 proclaims the impossibility of that). Yet if it were possible, he would gladly make the sacrifice. This readiness takes on poignancy in light of the fact that Paul had suffered the loss of all things in order to gain Christ (Phil 3:8). So he would be facing a double loss.

Paul's longing for the salvation of his people comes out in the way he speaks of them—"my brothers." To avoid misunderstanding, he has to qualify this by noting that the bond is one of "race" rather than of a common faith in Christ. But more than a blood relationship is involved, because he goes on to cite the spiritual heritage of his people that he shares with those of them who have not become Christians. This use of "brothers" appears elsewhere (e.g., Acts 2:29; 3:17; 22:1; 28:17).

4,5 It is notable that the apostle avoids the term "Jews" in v.4, for ordinarily that would stress merely the racial, political, and ritualistic aspects of his nation, unless qualified in some way, as in 2:29, where the description of the true Jew is equivalent to "Israelite." By referring to his countrymen as "the people of Israel," he is emphasizing that they are the covenant people of God, different from every other people on earth. This distinctiveness explains Paul's avoidance of the term "Israel" when speaking of the church (TDNT 3:387). Such is the case even in Galatians 6:16 (Richardson, pp. 74–84).

It is only when the distinctives of Israel are spelled out that the full implication of the word can be appreciated. Probably Paul has in mind his implied promise to enlarge on the advantages of his people (3:2). In the forefront in v.4 he puts "the adoption as sons." The Greek word *hyiothesia* ("adoption as sons"—used also in 8:15) does not occur in LXX, but the idea is certainly present, especially in Deuteronomy 14:1, 2 (cf. Exod 4:22; Hos 11:1). "Paul uses the word, as though to say that even the status of Israel was not something necessary and inherent, but the result of an act of graciousness on the part of God" (IDB 1:48b). This explains Israel's enjoyment of "the divine glory" or "the splendour of the divine presence" (NEB), that which was symbolized by the pillar of cloud that settled over the sanctuary in the wilderness and filled the temple at its dedication.

"The covenants" could be the arrangements God entered into with Abraham, with the nation of Israel at Sinai, and with David. On the other hand, the reference could be to the covenant made with Abraham (Gen 15), then renewed with Isaac (Gen 17), and with Jacob (Gen 28). There is rather good manuscript evidence for "covenant" rather than "covenants," but this reading can hardly be original, for it would most naturally suggest the Mosaic covenant (2 Cor 3:6, 14), which would render the next item, the reception of the law, quite unnecessary. The word "covenant" used here implies divine initiative rather than a mutual agreement between equals.

"The receiving [literally, 'giving'] of the law" refers, of course, to what was communicated through Moses to the children of Israel at Sinai. In Paul's time the nation tended to look upon this as its most prized possession (2:17), the most precious portion of the OT. A closely related item is "the temple worship," since the sacrificial cultus maintained by the priests is meant, and all this was prescribed in the law. "The promises" have a close relationship to the covenants (cf. Eph 2:12) and represent various aspects of the messianic salvation promised in the OT.

The importance of "the patriarchs" (v.5) can be seen in 11:28. They are the men to whom the promises were given prior to the giving of the law. God is pleased to announce himself as the God of Abraham, Isaac, and Jacob (Exod 3:15).

"From them is traced the human ancestry of Christ" (v.5). By "them" we are probably to understand the people of Israel (v.4) rather than the patriarchs. Account is taken of the intervening generations prior to the advent of the Messiah (cf. the genealogies in Matthew and Luke). A subtle distinction is to be noted between "theirs" and "from them." Israel cannot lay claim to Christ in the same way she can claim the patriarchs, even though he entered the human family through the Israelitish gate (cf. 1:3). Christ is much more than the patriarchs. Only in his earthly origin does he belong to the one nation. Because of his heavenly origin and mission he cannot be claimed exclusively by any segment of the race, seeing he is "God over all."

But is "God over all" the correct translation? On the ground that elsewhere Paul avoids such a stark identification, despite his high Christology, some scholars reject the traditional rendering, preferring something on the order of NEB: "May God, supreme above all, be blessed for ever." This involves taking the closing portion of the verse as a doxology and referring it to God (the Father).

Several considerations favor the traditional wording, which refers "God" to Christ: (1) Christ's relationship to Israel on the human side has been stated in such a way as to call for a complementary statement on the divine side. This is provided by the usual translation but not by the other rendering. (2) "Who" can properly be coupled only with the foregoing subject (Christ). If another subject (God) is being introduced, there is no reason at all for the "who." (3) A doxology to God can hardly be intended, since in doxologies the word "blessed" is regularly placed before the one who is praised. Here it comes after. (4) A doxology to God would be singularly out of place in a passage marked by sorrow over Israel's failure to recognize in Christ her crowning spiritual blessing. (5) The definite article, "the," is not linked in the text with "God," but with the foregoing words (literally, "the one being over all"), so Paul is not trying to displace God with Christ, but is doing what John does in saying that the Word was God (John 1:1), that is, has the rank of God. In any case, this is really implied in recognizing him as "over all" (it is very awkward, with NEB, to refer this to God in distinction from Christ).

Looking back over vv.1–5, one is bound to conclude from the combination of Paul's sorrow and the extended enumeration of Israel's privileges that the subject of his nation's spiritual condition must have constantly weighed on him. His statement of the advantages of Israel anticipates the fuller discussion of her election and serves to accent the element of tragedy in her current state. A double purpose is served by the culminating statement concerning the Messiah: it not only underscores the blindness of Israel but is also calculated to keep believing Gentiles from gloating over Israel's fall (11:20), seeing that Israel has been the channel by which God gave Christ to the world.

Notes

---

5 An alternative wording has been favored by a few scholars, arrived at by emendation of the text (reading ὧν ὁ, *hōn ho,* instead of ὁ ὢν, *ho ōn*) and yielding the following: "whose is the God over all, blessed for ever." This would make Israel's possession of the true God her climactic blessing, and it would be a fitting close to the paragraph. However, this conjecture lacks any MS authority.

Those who wish an exhaustive and scholarly study of the punctuation and interpretation of Romans 9:5, should see B.M. Metzger's article "The Punctuation of Rom. 9:5" in *Christ and Spirit in the New Testament,* ed. by B. Lindars and S.S. Smalley (Cambridge: Cambridge University Press, 1973), pp. 95–112.

B. *God's Choice of Israel Based on Election, Not on Natural Generation or Works of Merit*

9:6–13

6It is not as though God's word had failed. For not all who are descended from
Israel are Israel. 7Nor because they are his descendants are they all Abraham's
children. On the contrary, "Through Isaac shall your offspring come." 8In other
words, it is not the natural children who are God's children, but it is the children
of the promise who are regarded as Abraham's offspring. 9For this was how the
promise was stated: "At the appointed time I will return, and Sarah shall have a
son."

10Not only that, but Rebecca's children had one and the same father, our
ancestor Isaac. 11Yet, before the twins were born or had done anything good or
bad—in order that God's purpose in election might stand: 12not by works but by
him who calls—she was told, "The older will serve the younger." 13Just as it is
written: "Jacob I loved, but Esau I hated."

6–9 At once the atmosphere of tragedy is qualified by Paul's forthright denial that the course of events has taken God by surprise. If there is failure, it must be attributed to men, not to God. By "God's word" (v.6) we are to understand "the declared purpose of God" (Sanday and Headlam). This certainly involves the element of promise (cf. vv.8, 9). God's saving purpose does not include all who belong to Israel in the biological sense. This distinction is similar to that drawn concerning the use of the term "Jew" (2:28, 29). Though unnamed, Ishmael is apparently in view, in contrast to Isaac, when a contrast is made between merely being a descendant of Abraham in a physical sense and enjoying God's call to spiritual destiny—belonging to the godly line of descent that would culminate in the Messiah himself (Gal 3:16). It was not true of Isaac that he was born in due course, by natural processes, and that God then acknowledged him for the reason that he belonged to Abraham. Such was the case with Ishmael insofar as it provided a ground for bestowing on him material blessings (Gen 17:20; 21:13). Isaac was unique in that he was the child who was promised. God's purpose was centered in him before he was born. It was God, in fact, not man, who set the time of his birth. Apart from divine enablement to the parents, Isaac would never have been born, for Abraham was impotent and Sarah was no longer able to bear children.

10–13 "Not only that" (v.10). Something more needs to be said, for it could be pointed out that the nation of Israel looked back to its origin in Isaac rather than in Ishmael or the sons of Abraham by Keturah. After all, it was only natural that the son of Sarah should be chosen rather than the son of Hagar the bondwoman. So Paul feels impelled to cite the case of the twin brothers, both of them sons of Isaac and Rebecca, with nothing in the least lacking regarding their parentage. According to ordinary human expectation, they should stand on equal terms before God in his dealings with them. But it was not so. Natural generation from Isaac, the promised seed of Abraham, did not assure them of the same place in the divine economy. God made a distinction between them before they were born—before their characters had been shaped or any deeds had been performed that might form a basis for evaluation. The freedom and sovereignty of God were thus safeguarded. He deliberately disturbed the normal pattern of the culture into which the children were born by decreeing that the elder should serve the younger.

In this connection, by quoting Malachi 1:2, 3, Paul lifts the discussion from what might appear to be a purely personal one to the plane of corporate, national life. God's love for Jacob and hatred for Esau ought not to be construed as temperamental. Malachi is appealing to the course of history as fulfilling the purpose of God declared long before. Hatred in the ordinary sense will not fit the situation, since God bestowed many blessings on Esau and his descendants. The "hatred" is simply a way of saying that Esau was not the object of God's electing purpose (cf. the use of hate in Luke 14:26, where discipleship is stated to involve "hatred" for one's own family and one's own life; they are simply put out of consideration when one takes on himself the responsibility of following Christ). The value of the account of the two brothers is to make clear that in election God does not wait until individuals or nations are developed and then make a choice on the basis of character or achievement. If he did so, this would make a mockery of the concept of election, because it would locate the basis in man rather than in God and his purpose. God's love for Jacob, then, must be coupled with election rather than explained by some worthiness found in him (cf. Deut 7:6–8).

C. *God's Freedom to Act in His Own Sovereign Right*

9:14–29

14What then shall we say? Is God unjust? Not at all! 15For he says to Moses,

"I will have mercy on whom I have mercy,
and I will have compassion on whom I
have compassion."

16It does not, therefore, depend on man's desire or effort, but on God's mercy.
17For the Scripture says to Pharaoh: "I raised you up for this very purpose, that
I might display my power in you and that my name might be proclaimed in all the
earth." 18Therefore God has mercy on whom he wants to have mercy, and he
hardens whom he wants to harden.
19One of you will say to me: "Then why does God still blame us? For who resists
his will?" 20But who are you, O man, to talk back to God? "Shall what is formed
say to him who formed it, 'Why did you make me like this?' " 21Does not the potter
have the right to make out of the same lump of clay some pottery for noble
purposes and some for common use?
22What if God, choosing to show his wrath and make his power known, bore with
great patience the objects of his wrath—prepared for destruction? 23What if he did
this to make the riches of his glory known to the objects of his mercy, whom he
prepared in advance for glory—24even us, whom he also called, not only from the
Jews but also from the Gentiles? 25As he says in Hosea:

"I will call them 'my people' who are not my people:
and I will call her 'my loved one' who
is not my loved one,"

26and,

"It will happen that in the very place where
it was said to them,
'You are not my people,'
they will be called 'sons of the living God.' "

27Isaiah cries out concerning Israel: "Though the number of the Israelites should be like the sand by the sea, only the remnant will be saved. 28For the Lord will carry out his sentence on earth with speed and finality." 29It is just as Isaiah said previously:

"Unless the Lord All-powerful had left us
descendants,
we should have become like Sodom,
and would have been like Gomorrah."

14–18 God's dealings with Jacob and Esau might be challenged as arbitrary, on the ground that Esau was the object of injustice. To demonstrate that this is not God's character, Paul goes further into the history of Israel, focusing on the golden calf incident at Sinai. There the people sinned grievously. If God had acted simply in justice, he could have blotted out his people. Instead, he recalled Moses to the mount and for a second time gave him the tables of commandments, yet not until he had proclaimed to his servant Moses, "I will have mercy on whom I will have mercy" (Exod 33:19). That mercy was seen in sparing a sinful nation. And lest that mercy be construed as depending on man's "desire" or "effort," Paul denies any such qualification (v.16). Mercy, like grace, stands over against human worth and effort whenever salvation is concerned. It is free, because God is not bound to show mercy to any.

The thought moves from Moses to Pharaoh, the king of Egypt at the time of the Exodus—from the leader of Israel to its oppressor (v.17). The Scripture is represented as speaking, a vivid reminder that it is God's word. "I raised you up" is not strictly a reference to Pharaoh's emergence in history, but to God's providence in sparing him up to that time. Pharaoh deserved death for his oppression and insolence, but his life would not be taken during the series of plagues, so that the full extent of his hardness of heart might be evident and the glory of God in the deliverance of his people enhanced (cf. Josh 9:9). The fame of this Pharaoh actually depended on the mercy of God in sparing him. God can be glorified through those who oppose him as well as through those who trust and serve him. The wrath of man can contribute to the praise and glory of God (Ps 76:10).

Paul concludes the Pharaoh episode with this observation: "Therefore God has mercy on whom he wants to have mercy, and he hardens whom he wants to harden" (v.18). He does not so much as bother to indicate that Pharaoh hardened his own heart, an evidence of unbelief and rebellion, because he is emphasizing the freedom of God's action in all cases. The hardening of Pharaoh's heart can profitably be related to the principle laid down in Romans 1, that God's method of dealing with those who reject the revelation of himself in nature and history (and in Pharaoh's case also in miracles) is to abandon them to still greater excess of sin and its consequences.

19–26 Paul, continuing the review of God's sovereign activity, presents another problem. If God acts unilaterally, according to his own will and purpose, does this not remove all basis for judgment, since man is not in a position to resist the divine will? Why, then, should man be blamed? In reply, Paul first points out the inappropriateness of the creature talking back to God (v.20) as though he had sufficient wisdom to judge the Almighty. The illustration of the potter and the clay (v.21) shows how ridiculous this is.

Two of Israel's prophets had made the same point (Isa 29:16; Jer. 18:6). Some interpreters have concluded that Paul has in mind the creation. While it is true that Genesis 2:7 contains the word "formed" which is the same root word as "potter," it is clear that Paul envisions the clay as a "given," and the real problem is what the potter does with the clay, namely, fashioning one type of vessel or another. The apostle is insisting on the right of the potter to make whatever type of vessel he chooses. Those made for "noble purposes" are valuable for their beauty and decorative function, while those made for "common use" are not admired, though they are actually more essential to the household than the other ones. Pharaoh was useful in fulfilling God's purpose. Apart from this, he would not even have appeared on the pages of sacred history.

In v.22 the crucial problem is to interpret correctly the expression "prepared for destruction." Is Paul teaching a double predestination? This is improbable, because he avoids involving God in this case, whereas he *is* involved in showing mercy to the objects of his mercy (v.23). Furthermore, God's patience in bearing with the objects of his wrath suggests a readiness to receive such on condition of repentance (cf. 2:3, 4; 2 Peter 3:9). So "prepared for destruction" designates a ripeness of sinfulness that points to judgment unless there is a turning to God, yet God is not made responsible for the sinful condition. The preparation for destruction is the work of man, who allows himself to deteriorate in spite of knowledge and conscience.

Presumably, and in view of what follows, when Paul speaks of "the objects of his [God's] wrath" (v.22), he has in mind those in Israel who have remained obdurate in opposing the gospel, yet are still the objects of the divine longsuffering. In contrast to them are "the objects of his mercy" (v.23) in whom God wills to show the riches of his glory (in contrast to his wrath). These, whom he has prepared for glory, include both Jews and Gentiles (v.24), in line with the previous teaching (1:16; 2:10, 11; 3:22) and with the prophetic announcement. The same God who declared to Israel through Amos: "You only have I known of all of the families of the earth" (Amos 3:2) declared through Hosea his freedom to call others to be his people (v.25). In all strictness, this passage from Hosea 2:23 refers to the reversal in Israel's status from being called "not my people" (Hos 1:9) to being restored, but in both Romans 9:25 and 1 Peter 2:10 the application is apparently broadened to include Gentiles, as Romans 2:24 intimates. Gentiles, who are not actually a people but only masses of humanity, are called by the grace of God to a distinctive role—that of being the people of God. This was happening in Paul's day.

The second quotation is from Hosea 1:10, omitting the first half of the verse, which refers to the prophesied increase in the number of the people of Israel. Here also the background is the Lo-ammi prophecy of Hosea 1:9, which is now seen to be revoked when Israel will once again be called "sons of the living God." Since Peter uses the Hosea 2:23 passage as applying to Gentiles, Paul's intimation of a similar application is the more understandable. It is just possible that he does not intend the second passage (Hos 1:10) to apply to Gentiles (though this is by no means certain), in which case by the sequence of the passages he may be giving a hint of something developed in chapter 11—namely, the influx of Gentiles during Israel's temporary rejection, to be followed by the turning of Israel to the Lord in great numbers (11:25–27).

27–29 As Paul has used Scripture to show that it teaches God's purpose to extend his mercy to Gentiles, so now he uses Scripture again to make clear that the election of Israel does not preclude her reduction through chastening judgments, yet in the sparing of the remnant his mercy and faithfulness are to be seen. Both passages are from Isaiah. The former anticipates the depletion of the nation by reason of the Assyrian invasion under Sennacherib, described from God's viewpoint as "the rod of my anger, the staff of my fury" (Isa 10:5). Without softening his decree and without delay, God will permit the judgment to fall. Jacob, now numerous, will be reduced to a remnant (Isa 10:22). Thus far, judgment is emphasized, but the remainder of the sentence underscores the divine mercy—"the remnant will be saved." The Hebrew text has ". . . will return" (i.e., after deportation). Paul, however, sees the promise of a greater deliverance, for he says, "will be saved." Even as he wrote, there was a remnant of Israel to be found in the church. In view of the nation's rejection of Jesus as Israel's Messiah, Messianic Jews should be grateful for the minority of Jews who have embraced the gospel of Christ. In 11:5 Paul returns to this theme. If God's judgment had been unsparing, the nation would have become as truly wiped out as Sodom and Gomorrah (v.29). But the divine judgment is tempered by unfailing mercy, of which the remnant is the eloquent proof. This dual theme of the kindness and severity of God comes into focus again at 11:22.

D. *Israel's Failure to Attain Righteousness Due to Reliance on Works Rather Than Faith*

9:30–10:21

30What then shall we say? That the Gentiles, who did not pursue righteousness,
have obtained it, a righteousness that is by faith; 31but Israel, who pursued a law
of righteousness, has not attained it. 32Why not? Because they pursued it not by
faith but as if it were by works. They stumbled over the "stumbling stone." 33As
it is written:

"See, I lay in Zion a stone that causes
men to stumble
and a rock that makes them fall,
and the one who trusts in him will never
be put to shame."

10:1 Brothers, my heart's desire and prayer to God for the Israelites is that they
may be saved. 2For I can testify about them that they are zealous for God, but their
zeal is not based on knowledge. 3Since they disregarded the righteousness that
comes from God and sought to establish their own, they did not submit to God's
righteousness. 4Christ is the end of the law so that there may be righteousness
for everyone who believes.
5Moses describes in this way the righteousness that is by the law: "The man who
does these things will live by them." 6But the righteousness that is by faith says:
"Do not say in your heart, 'Who will ascend into heaven?' " (that is, to bring Christ
down), 7or " 'Who will descend into the deep?' " (that is, to bring Christ up from
the dead). 8But what does it say?

"The word is near you;
it is in your mouth and in your heart";

that is, the word of faith we are proclaiming: 9that if you confess with your mouth,
"Jesus is Lord," and believe in your heart that God raised him from the dead, you
will be saved. 10For it is with your heart that you believe and are justified, and it
is with your mouth that you confess and are saved. 11As the Scripture says, "He
who believes in him will not be put to shame." 12For there is no difference between
Jew and Gentile—the same Lord is Lord of all and richly blesses all who call on
him, 13for, "Everyone who calls on the name of the Lord will be saved."
14How, then, can they call on the one they have not believed in? And how can
they believe in the one of whom they have not heard? And how can they hear
without someone preaching to them? 15And how can they preach unless they are
sent? As it is written, "How beautiful are the feet of those who bring good news!"

[16]But not all the Israelites responded to the good news. For Isaiah says, "Lord, who has believed our message?" [17]Consequently, faith comes from hearing the message, and the message is heard through the word of Christ. [18]But I ask, did they not hear? Of course they did:

"Their voice has gone out into all the earth,
their words to the ends of the world."

[19]Again I ask, did Israel not understand? First, Moses says,

"I will make you envious by means of those
who are not a nation;
I will make you angry by a nation that
has no understanding."

[20]Then Isaiah boldly says,

"I was found by those who did not seek me;
I revealed myself to those who did not
ask for me."

[21]But concerning Israel he says, "All day long I have held out my hands to a disobedient and obstinate people."

9:30–33 Here Paul introduces a contrast between Gentiles and Israel, emphasizing that what has come to the former by the exercise of faith has been denied the latter by their insistence on seeking righteousness on the basis of works.

There is no blanket inclusion of all Gentiles; only those are included who meet the description laid down here—that of not pursuing righteousness in the manner followed by the children of Israel. So far as the construction of the sentence (v.31) is concerned, it follows the pattern of 2:14 in the way Gentiles are referred to, despite the difference in theme. The figure of a foot race is introduced, as indicated by "pursue" and "obtained." The paradox is sharp, picturing Gentiles who are unconcerned about acquiring righteousness actually getting the prize, even though not competing in the race with the Jews. The prize is justification by faith. It is a pitiful picture of the nation of Israel struggling intensely to perfect their religious life and coming up empty-handed. Hodge puts the matter well: "The Gentiles, sunk in carelessness and sin, have attained the favor of God, while the Jews, to whom religion was a business, have utterly failed" (in loc.). It would be a mistake to suppose that Paul is putting a premium on carelessness regarding moral and spiritual considerations. Gentile success is attributed to their avoidance of the false approach of the Jew and their willingness to receive righteousness as a gift. Hardly a passage in the NT is stronger than this one in its exposure of the futility of works as a means of justification.

Verse 31 presents a difficulty. NIV reads, "But Israel, who pursued a law of righteousness, has not attained it." What is the "it"? The Greek has the word "law" in this verse. Yet the reader naturally looks for a repetition of the word "righteousness." Perhaps we can translate, "has not attained to such a law" (namely, the law of righteousness in the sense of righteousness gained by means of the law). Ragnar Bring suggests, "Paul means that they did not attain the kind of righteousness that the law speaks of" (ST 25 [1971] 46). They confusedly identified their own works, in which they took pride, with the absolute standard the law requires. Their whole effort was not grounded in faith but in works designed to gain acceptance (v.32).

"They stumbled over the stumbling stone" (v.32). Doubtless, the analogy of the race continues to influence Paul's thought. Absorbed in their own efforts, the Israelites did not recognize in Christ the stone of their prophetic Scripture, the sure foundation for their faith and life, and fell headlong over him. By failing to receive him, they denied also their own election of which he was the fulfillment and crown. The passage Paul quotes is a combination of Isaiah 8:14 and 28:16. From it we glean that the Lord himself, provided as a foundation stone, was actually to become for Israel a stumbling stone. This became especially true with respect to his cross (1 Cor 1:23). The misdirection of Israel's thinking became painfully clear in that the preaching of the cross, the event that was at once the quintessence of her sin and the sole hope of her salvation, left her defiant in her self-righteousness.

The chapter division does not mark a break in the thought, for the key words, such as "righteousness," "law," and "faith," continue to appear, especially in the beginning of the chapter.

10:1–4 Paul has spoken pointedly about Israel's failure, but not censoriously. He feels for his countrymen. He knows their plight because their condition was his own condition prior to his conversion. His desire for their salvation is reflected in his going to the Jews first (Acts 13:46; 18:5, 6; cf. Rom 1:16) but also in praying to God on their behalf. His preaching may be earnest, but it alone cannot convert. God must move in their hearts.

Paradoxically, it is Israel's zeal for God that constitutes their greatest barrier (v.2). The apostle knows whereof he speaks, for his zeal on behalf of Judaism had been notorious (Acts 22:3; Gal 1:14). That very zeal so preoccupied him that he felt bound to consider Jesus and his followers as traitors to the faith of his fathers. But he persecuted in ignorance (1 Tim 1:13). So here he diagnoses the zeal of Israel as lacking in "knowledge." His people have ignored "the righteousness that comes from God" (cf. 1:17). In trying to establish their own righteous standing before God, they have refused submission to God's righteousness. By looking forward to v.4, where the law is mentioned, we see that this attempt of Israel to achieve a standing in righteousness was related to finding satisfaction in their imagined success in meeting the demands of the law of Moses. Paul is able to analyze their trouble in expert fashion, for he has been over the same route in his spiritual pilgrimage. It was a great day for him when he gave up his cherished righteousness, based on service to the law, in exchange for the righteousness that comes from God and depends on faith (Phil 3:9).

Israel's covenant relation to God and reliance on law keeping do not add up to salvation (John 14:6; Acts 4:12). For this reason Paul points to Christ and his righteousness as Israel's great need (v.4). The proof that Israel was out of line with respect to the will of God, to the extent of rebelling against him, lies in the fact that when he sent his Son as the bringer of a salvation in full accord with the divine righteousness, the nation rejected him. The same kind of revolution in thinking that was necessary for Paul is required for his people.

Considerable debate has centered on the interpretation of v.4, especially on the intended meaning of the word translated "end." Just as in English we speak of "the end of the matter" and use the expression "to the end that"—the one expression meaning conclusion or termination, and the other purpose—the same dual possibility lies in the Greek word *telos.* The second meaning has some plausibility here, because the statement "Christ is the end of the law" (NIV; also KJV, RSV), rather than "Christ brought to an end the law," fits in with the teaching of Paul about the law as the child-leader to bring men to Christ (Gal 3:24). Favorable to the first meaning (Christ brought to an end the law) is the fact that the law had a certain course to run (Luke 16:16; Gal 3:19, 23) in the economy of God. Both concepts seem to fit rather well in our passage. However, the decisive factor that favors "termination" rather than "purpose" as the main idea is the contrast in 9:30ff. between the law and God's righteousness. Though the law is righteous in its requirements, it fails as an instrument of justification (cf. 8:3, 4). Paul's contention regarding the Jew (v.3) is not the incompleteness of his position, which needed the coming of Christ to perfect it, but the absolute wrong of that position, because it entailed an effort to establish righteousness by human effort rather than by acceptance of a divine gift. This consideration makes improbable the view that "end" is used in the sense of fulfillment, as though the thought were aligned with Matthew 5:17.

Paul adds a certain qualification to the statement about Christ as the end of the law for righteousness. He is that "for everyone who believes." This seems to suggest that the law is still applicable to those who do not believe. "Those who have not yet passed from the being-in-the-Law to the being-in-Christ, and those who allow themselves to be misled into exchanging the being-in-Christ for the being-under-the-Law, are under the Law and are made to feel its power" (A. Schweitzer, *The Mysticism of Paul the Apostle* [New York: Henry Holt and Company, 1931], p. 189).

5–13 The thread of the discourse is a continuation of the emphasis on "everyone who believes." This is developed in two ways: first, by showing that the principle of faith is amply set forth in the OT, in fact, in the pages of Moses, and then by expressly indicating, in line with 1:16, that "everyone" includes the Gentile as well as the Jew.

5–8 Paul deals first with the negative side of the attainment of righteousness. He does this by citing a passage from Moses (Lev 18:5) that calls for obedience and performance of the will of God as contained in his statutes and ordinances. The one who complies will live. Paul adds "by it" (So RSV, NEB, et al.; NIV—"by them"), which apparently refers back to the word "righteousness" earlier in v.5 (see Note). Fortunately for our understanding, this passage had already been cited in Galatians 3:12, "The law is not based on faith; on the contrary, 'The man who does these things will live by them.' " In both letters the emphasis falls on *doing* if one expects to live, the very thing insisted on earlier in Romans 2:13. The dark side of the picture is that a curse rests on the one who fails to meet the law's demands. The upshot of the matter is that the course being pursued by Israel, the attempt to gain righteousness for themselves by law keeping (v.3) cannot bring life because of man's weakness and imperfection. It can only lead to self-deception and pride.

Next Paul addresses himself to the positive approach, for which purpose he makes use of another passage from Moses (Deut 30:11–14), this one designed to describe "the righteousness that is by faith." At first sight, the selection of this portion seems inappropriate, since neither "righteousness" nor "faith" can be found here, and there is heavy emphasis on doing, as in Leviticus 18:5. But the context helps us, for the passage presupposes a heart attitude of loving obedience (Deut 30:6–10) rather than a legalistic attempt to attain righteousness. The whole burden of the passage is to discourage the idea that the doing of God's will means to aspire after something that is too difficult and out of reach. Actually, if the life is attuned to God, his will is as near as the mouth and heart (the mouth as the organ to repeat the word of God and turn it back to him in prayer and praise, the heart as the source of desire to please him).

Paul makes his own application of the reference to heaven (v.6) in order to emphasize aspects of the gospel. There is no need to try to ascend to heaven to gain spiritual knowledge or acceptance, for Christ has come from heaven to proclaim and effect salvation for the world. He has come within human reach by his incarnation. In v.7 Paul substitutes "the deep" (abyss) for "the sea" in the Deuteronomy passage, changing the figure from one of distance to one of depth, which makes the contrast with heaven sharper. This affords opportunity to think of Christ as going down into death as a prelude to resurrection. Apparently lost to us by death, he has been returned to us by resurrection. This means that our grasp of the righteousness of God, with his Son as the object of our faith, is not difficult. We have had no part in bringing about the Lord's resurrection any more than in effecting his incarnation. All has been of God. Our part is to believe. There is no place in Christianity, as in some religions, for meritorious pilgrimages. The saving message lies at hand, waiting to be received.

9–13 Building on the Deuteronomy passage, especially its use of "mouth" and "heart," Paul goes on to speak directly of the Christian gospel as to its content and its availability to Jew and Gentile alike.

9,10 "The word of faith" or gospel message is something to confess as well as to believe (cf. 2 Cor 4:13, 14). "Confess" (**ὁμολογέω**, *homologeō*) when used of sin means to say the same thing about it that God says; when used in the creedal sense, as here in v.9, it means to say the same thing that other believers say regarding their faith. This was done within the Christian group especially by new converts in connection with their baptism; when it was done "before men" (Matt 10:32) it had an evangelizing function. The oddity that in our passage confession is given prior mention over believing is simply due to Paul's preservation of the order given in Deuteronomy 30:14, which he had just quoted, where "mouth" is mentioned before "heart." The influence of the OT passage is likewise evident in that, whereas it provided a point of contact for citing the resurrection of our Lord (vv.7, 9), there was nothing to provide a basis for mention of the saving death of Christ (contrast 1 Cor 15:3, 4). The concentration on the resurrection is understandable also when it is recognized that the creedal statement before us pertains to the person of Christ rather than to his redeeming work. "Jesus is Lord" was the earliest declaration of faith fashioned by the church (Acts 2:36; 1 Cor 12:3). This great truth was recognized first by God in raising his Son from the dead—an act then acknowledged by the church and one day to be acknowledged by all (Phil 2:11).

It was natural for the church to have a fundamental confession of this sort, since at the beginning it was Jewish/Christian in its composition and therefore had in its background the example of confession in Israel, "The Lord our God is one Lord" (Deut 6:4). The incarnation necessitated the enlargement of the confession to include the Lord Christ. "For us there is but one God, the Father, from whom all things came and for whom we live; and there is but one Lord, Jesus Christ, through whom all things came and through whom we live" (1 Cor 8:6).

Paul's statement in vv.9, 10 is misunderstood when it is made to support the claim that one cannot be saved unless he makes Jesus the Lord of his life by a personal commitment. Such a commitment is most important; however, in this passage, Paul is speaking of the objective lordship of Christ, which is the very cornerstone for faith, something without which no one could be saved. Intimately connected as it was with the resurrection, which in turn validated the saving death, it proclaimed something that was true no matter whether or not a single soul believed it and built his life on it.

11–13 Scripture indicates how faith can be transforming for one's life, replacing fear and hesitation with bold confidence that rests on the sure promises of God. For this purpose Paul uses Isaiah 28:16 (cf. the close of 9:33). This belief and its blessing is open to Jew and Gentile alike. Whatever "difference" there may be in the two groups in some respects, there is no difference when it comes to the need for Christ and the availability of his salvation (cf. 3:22). The source of their spiritual life is found in "the same Lord," whose blessings are richly bestowed upon them without partiality. The all-embracing blessing is salvation. In support of this, Paul cites Joel 2:32. Peter used the same passage in his Pentecost sermon to indicate to his Jewish audience that the door of salvation was open to them all, despite their shared guilt in rejecting the one whom God had sent (Acts 2:21). This calling on the Lord is the echoing within the human heart of the call of God according to his gracious purpose (8:28–30). The prayer promises of Scripture are restricted to the people of God, with one notable exception—namely, that God will hear the cry of any who call upon him for salvation. When v.13 is compared with v.9, it becomes evident that the Lord of Joel 2:32 is being identified with the Lord Jesus Christ. This poses a problem for those who refuse to ascribe full deity to the Savior.

14,15 Now the apostle turns from the responsibility of the seeker after salvation to emphasize the role that believers are intended to have in God's plan for reaching the lost. Calling on the Lord is meaningless apart from some assurance that he is worthy of confidence and trust, that he has something to offer that guilty sinners need. Calling on him and trust in him are two sides of the same coin. The verse suggests that calling on the Lord continues to be a mark of the believer, not simply the first step in the direction of establishing relationship to him (cf. 1 Cor 1:2). Paul proceeds to the second consideration in his closely reasoned argument, and it is this—that faith depends on knowledge. One must hear the gospel before he can be expected either to receive it or reject it. The choice of words is suggestive. To "hear" the message was the one vehicle open to people in that day. The NT had not yet been written so as to be available to the reader, though a few churches had received letters from Paul. There was no visual depiction of the Savior and his mission. The message had to be communicated by word of mouth to the hearing of others. This was as true in the days of the apostles as in the time of the prophets. A glance at the concordance reveals the consistent prevalence of hearing throughout Bible times.

The third step is the necessity that there be someone to proclaim the message. "How shall they hear without a preacher?" (v.14, KJV) is somewhat misleading as a translation, suggesting that the one who communicates the gospel must hold the office of clergyman. This is not the intent. "Someone preaching" (NIV) accurately reflects the original text. We are saved to serve, and the paramount element in that service is to bear witness to the saving power of Christ.

"And how can they preach except they be sent?" (v.15) rounds out this series of questions. No answers are given, for the logic is so airtight that no one could properly question the essential role of each step in the process. To be "sent" suggests at least two things: that one operates under a higher authority and that his message does not originate with himself but is given him by the sending authority. The prophets were men who were sent in these two respects. So was the Lord Jesus (John 3:34; 7:16). So is the Christian in his witness-bearing capacity. The apostles received their commission from the risen Lord as he in turn had been sent by the Father (John 20:21). In addressing the Roman church, Paul was careful to state at the very beginning that he was called and set apart for the ministering of the gospel (1:1).

Is the apostolate alone in view here as representing Christ and his gospel? This is unlikely, judging from what Paul says later about the widespread proclamation of the gospel to the Jews (vv.17, 18). The task was too big for a handful of men. In this connection, see Acts 8:4; 11:19. It is not clear from vv.14, 15 whether the sending that is in view here is intended to include the sending out of missionaries by a sponsoring group of believers, as in Acts 13:3. But even if this is not included, it is obviously an integral part of the entire process of the communication of the gospel. In the case of the church at Antioch, the divine and the human aspects of the sending were closely bound together (Acts 13:2, 3).

Once again (v.15) Paul corroborates his words by the sayings of the prophets, this time by the word of Isaiah (52:7) heralding the favor of the Lord to the city of Jerusalem that had lain desolate during the Babylonian captivity. The tidings are good; the proclamation is one of peace. Paul changes the wording somewhat—the single announcer in Isaiah becomes a company in line with the "they" in his own depiction of gospel messengers in the same verse. If the message to returning Israel in the former day was good news, how much more the promise of eternal salvation in God's Son!

16–18 But here an element of tragedy enters. The good news of physical restoration may have been welcome to Israel, but the spiritual salvation God promised to provide through his Servant and did provide in the fullness of time has met with unbelief. What a change of atmosphere from Paul's quotation of Isaiah 52:7 (v.15) to his quotation of 53:1 (v.16)! The prophet foresaw a repudiation of the message about salvation through a suffering Servant. History has sustained prophecy (1 Cor 1:23).

Paul sums up by saying (v.17) that faith depends on hearing the message, that is, hearing it with understanding and acceptance. "And the message is heard through the word of Christ" (v.17). This could mean either the word about Christ or the word proclaimed by Christ. The former sense is somewhat favored by the fact that in Isaiah 53, which may still be in Paul's thought, the Servant is not a proclaimer but a suffering Redeemer. On the other hand, the second possibility cannot be ruled out. Barrett, for example, says, "Christ must be heard either in his own person, or in the person of his preachers, through whom his own word (v.17) is spoken; otherwise faith in him is impossible" (in loc.).

18,19 In his indictment of Israel, Paul is prepared to investigate any possibility that would offer an excuse for the nation's failure. Could it be, he asks, that they did not hear (the gospel)? He is writing more than twenty-five years after Pentecost. Not only in Palestine but also out in the dispersion, where he himself has been especially active, the message has been heralded. But instead of appealing to this activity, of which the Book of Acts testifies, he is content to cite Scripture, that Israel may stand condemned by the testimony of God rather than by that of man. In making use of Psalm 19:4 (v.18), he does not say that this passage has been fulfilled, for he is aware that the heavens bear a different kind of testimony than the Word of God. But he sees a parallel between the diffusion of light and darkness every day and night, of which no one can be ignorant who has eyes to see, and the widespread proclamation of the gospel in the areas where Jews made their home. This was essentially the Mediterranean basin, where Paul and his helpers had been laboring for some years. His countrymen could not claim lack of opportunity to hear the gospel (cf. Acts 17:6; 21:28).

There remains the possibility, however, that in spite of hearing the message, Israel has not understood it (v.19). So in all fairness this should be considered, for if it were true, it would be a mitigating factor in their situation. But the very form of the question in the original contains an implicit denial that Israel's failure results from lack of understanding. At Pentecost Peter spoke of the ignorance of his countrymen as explaining the crucifixion. But as time went on, fewer and fewer Jews in proportion to the total population of the nation responded to the gospel. A hardened attitude set in. The precedent of the Jews who did respond to the gospel, instead of moving their fellow-Jews, only embittered them. Then, as the gospel spread abroad and was received by Gentiles in ever greater numbers, this served to antagonize them still further.

It is over against this situation that Paul quotes Deuteronomy 32:21b, a part of Moses' song to Israel in which he chides the congregation for perversity and (in Deut 32:21a, not quoted here) voices the complaint of God that the people had provoked him to jealousy by their idolatry. This in turn prompts God to resort to something that is calculated to make Israel jealous. It will be done through "a nation that has no understanding." This is to be understood of Gentile response to God and his Word in such a way as to surpass the response of Israel. Exactly such a situation had developed by the time Paul wrote, so the quotation is apt and telling in its effect. Those who lacked special revelation and the moral and religious training God provided for Israel have proved more responsive than the chosen people.

20,21 The quotation from Isaiah 65:1 is clearly intended to support what has been declared in the previous passage (Deut 32:21), as is evident from the "then" in v.20, which answers to "first" in v.19. Paul sees in the Isaiah passage an anticipation of what has come to pass in his day. The thought is somewhat similar to the implication in 9:30, that the pagan world, occupied with its own pursuits, was in the main, not seeking after God. If there was a religious interest, cults and superstitions abounded to which one could turn.

In the following quotation from Isaiah (65:2) the paradoxical situation regarding Israel is set forth. God is the one who is seeking, reaching out to his people continually with a plea that Israel return to him in loving obedience, only to be rebuffed. So we may draw the conclusion that the spiritual condition of Israel does not come from a lack of opportunity to hear the gospel or a lack of understanding of its content, but must be traced to a stubborn and rebellious spirit such as cropped up in the days of Moses and the days of the prophets. It is the more grievous now because God has spoken his final word in his Son and has been rebuffed by those who should have been the most ready to respond.

Notes

5 MSS vary considerably in the wording of the quotation from Lev 18:5. Those that read "shall live in [or by] them" (αὐτοῖς, *autois*) doubtless have been influenced by LXX and by Paul's wording in Gal 3:12, where he follows LXX because "in them" fits the context ("all things written in the book of the law"). But here in Rom 10:5 Paul substitutes "in it" (ἐν αὐτῇ, *en autē*) (i.e., "in the righteousness that is by the law") because this is his own expression at the beginning of the verse. This sort of liberty in handling OT quotations is not uncommon.

17 "The word of God" is the reading of TR, but "the word of Christ" clearly has superior attestation (א* B C D*, et al.)

E. *Israel Not Entirely Rejected; There Is a Remnant of Believers* (11:1–10)

Thus far, Paul has treated the problem of Israel from two standpoints. In chapter 9 he has emphasized the sovereignty of God in choosing this people for himself in a special sense. In chapter 10 he has dealt with Israel's failure to respond to God's righteousness, ending with the verdict that she is "a disobedient and obstinate people" (10:21). These two presentations involve a serious tension. Will Israel's sin and stubbornness defeat the purpose of God, or will God find a way to deal effectively with the situation so as to safeguard his purpose? To this question Paul now turns. His answer will dip into Israel's past, encompass her present, and reveal her future.

11:1–10

1I ask then, Did God reject his people? By no means! I am an Israelite myself,
a descendant of Abraham, from the tribe of Benjamin. 2God did not reject his
people, whom he foreknew. Don't you know what the Scripture says in the pas-
sage about Elijah—how he appealed to God against Israel: 3"Lord, they have killed
your prophets and torn down your altars; I am the only one left, and they are trying
to kill me"? 4And what was God's answer to him? "I have reserved for myself
seven thousand who have not bowed the knee to Baal." 5So too, at the present
time there is a remnant chosen by grace. 6And if by grace, then it is no longer by
works; if it were, grace would no longer be grace.

7What then? What Israel sought so earnestly it did not obtain, but the elect did.
The others became hardened, 8as it is written:

"God gave them a spirit of stupor,
eyes so that they could not see
and ears so that they could not hear,
to this very day."

9And David says:

"May their table become a snare and a trap,
a stumbling block and a retribution for them.
10"May their eyes be darkened so that they
cannot see,
and their backs be bent forever."

1–6 Preparation for this section has been made—especially in 9:27–29, where the teaching of the OT concerning the remnant is summarized by quotations from Isaiah. That teaching involved both judgment and mercy—judgment on the nation as a whole for its infidelity and wickedness, and mercy on those who are permitted to escape the judgment and form the nucleus for a fresh start under the blessing of God.

The opening question, "Did God reject his people?" (based on Ps 94:14) requires that we keep in mind what was made clear early in the discussion—that "not all who are descended from Israel are Israel" (9:6). The loss of the bulk of the nation that proved disobedient (both in OT days and at the opening of the gospel period) should not be interpreted as rejection of "his people." The remnant is in view, as the ensuing paragraph demonstrates.

Why is it that Paul, in repudiating the suggestion that God has rejected his people, injects himself into the discussion as an Israelite, descended from Abraham, and belonging to the tribe of Benjamin (cf. Phil 3:5)? Some understand this as intended not for proof but only as assurance that in view of his background Paul can be expected to handle the subject with fairness to Israel rather than with prejudice. Perhaps the position of this personal note, placed before the OT illustration, favors this view somewhat. But it is also possible to hold that Paul, sensing his prominence in the purpose of God, is willing to risk the charge of lack of modesty by citing himself as evidence sufficient to refute the charge that God had rejected Israel. Barrett gives the sense as follows: "I myself am both a Jew and a Christian; this proves that Christian Jews may exist" (in loc.).

For God to reject his people would require repudiation of his deliberate, unilateral choice of Israel (for the meaning of "foreknew," see commentary on 8:29). The inference is that God could not do such a thing (v.2). But instead of dealing in abstractions, Paul turns to the OT for confirmation, to the time of Elijah. If ever there was a period of flagrant apostasy, it was during the reign of Ahab, when his queen Jezebel promoted Baal worship in the court and throughout the land. The situation was so bad that Elijah, in his loneliness, cried to God against the killing of prophets and destruction of altars. He even went so far as to assert that he was the only one left and that he was being hunted down so as to complete the destruction of God's servants (1 Kings 19:10). He knew that other prophets had escaped through the action of Obadiah (1 Kings 18:13), but they were in hiding. Elijah had stood alone on Mt. Carmel and later fled alone to the desert—an object of pursuit. It is just possible that Paul, likewise persecuted by his own countrymen, felt a special kinship with Elijah, and this may help to account for his mention of himself in v.1.

The really important thing is the contrast between the assertion of Elijah—"I am the only one left"—and God's reply: "I have reserved for myself seven thousand who have not bowed the knee to Baal" (v.4). If in that dark hour such a goodly company of the faithful existed, this is sufficient evidence that God does not permit his own at any time to approach the vanishing point. The sparing of the remnant is inseparably related to the choice of the remnant. The very fact of God's choice excludes the possibility of his desertion of his own. In the Greek, God's "answer" is literally his "oracle" (*chrēmatismos*), indicating both its revelatory character and its intrinsic importance (it was given to Elijah at Horeb, the mount of God, the place where God had appeared to Moses to affirm his preservation of Israel in her affliction and his purpose to deliver her from bondage in Egypt; cf. Exod 3; 1 Kings 19).

Since Paul sees a parallel between the days of Elijah and his own time, the inference can be drawn that when he wrote, the vast majority of Israel had resisted the gospel, and that therefore, despite their claim of loyalty to God and the law, they had failed to move forward in terms of the climactic revelation in his Son. Those who had turned to Christ were only a remnant (v.5).

But the matter of numbers is not crucial. What is more important is the reminder that irrespective of its size, it is "chosen by grace." This means that the character of the remnant is also not important, as though the choosing depended on the quality of its constituency. "The remnant has its origin, not in the quality of those saved, but in the saving action of God" (Herntrich in TDNT 4:203). Notice how this is brought out in the quotation "I have reserved *for myself* seven thousand" (v.4). It is also evident, though not expressed, that the existence of the church, far from being contrary to the will of God, as the leaders of Judaism supposed, is actually the present channel of the operation of his grace. Having mentioned grace at the end of v.5, the apostle cannot pass by the opportunity to contrast grace with works (v.6). They are mutually exclusive as a means of establishing relationship to God (cf. Eph 2:8, 9).

7–10 Here is set forth in the case of Israel according to the flesh the tragic consequences of persisting in the pattern of "works." Once again Paul cannot overlook Israel's "earnestly" seeking to get from God what they prized. There is a clear connection with 10:3, which refers to the effort of Israel to attain righteousness in God's sight by their method rather than his. The elect obtained righteousness because they did not go about it the wrong way but depended on divine grace. While this was true in the past, Paul is apparently thinking mainly of the present situation (cf. v.5). In distinction from the elect, Israel as a whole has become hardened. The comparison between present and past, already made on the favorable side between the current remnant according to the election of grace and the 7,000 in Elijah's time, is now projected to cover the dark aspects of the situation.

The failure of the bulk of Israel to attain divine righteousness and their being hardened instead, is in line with OT history. By the device of quoting, Paul throws the weight of Scripture behind his presentation and by so doing avoids having to speak on his own as bluntly and severely as the Word of God has done. In the first quotation, he weaves together two passages (Deut 29:4 and Isa 29:10) so as to provide illustration from two periods. In Deuteronomy, it is the testimony of the eyes that is stressed; the people have seen the wonders of the Exodus time and the miracles of the nation's preservation in the wilderness, but from these experiences they did not derive a heart of loving trust in God. In Isaiah, the background is the faithful testimony of the prophets. Yet the people shut their ears to the voice of God through these spokesmen. As a consequence, God sent them a spirit of stupor. The verb (*katanussōmai*) from which the word "stupor" comes means "to prick." At first sight, this appears to give a wrong idea, but the thought is as follows: "The torpor seems the result of too much sensation, dulled by the incitement into apathy" (A.T. Robertson, *Word Pictures in the New Testament.* Richard R. Smith, Inc., 1931, 4:393). From our observation of the setting of the quotations, it is clear that God did not give his people deaf ears to mock them any more than he gave them blind eyes to taunt them. What was involved was a judicial punishment for failure to use God-given faculties to perceive his manifested power and to glorify him. See John 12:39, 40.

Before leaving v.7, something should be said on the word rendered "hardened," especially since it is not the same as the term used in 9:18. Liddon (in loc.) has a note on this distinction:

> The *pōrōsis* of v.7, though describing the same moral fact as the *to sklērynesthai* of 9:18, is perhaps stronger in its import. The metaphor implies not merely the stiffening of the existing soul and character, but the outgrowth of a new feature, which obscures while it hardens, by an outer coating of mental habit. *Pōrōsis* differs from *sklērynesthai* by the idea of a *new outgrowth* of mental obduracy. *Pōros,* the tufa-stone, is especially used of a callus or substance exuding from fractured bones and joining their extremities as it hardens: hence *pōroō* to petrify, form a bony substance, and so metaphorically, to harden. . . . This *pōrōsis* produced permanent bluntness and insensibility in the intelligence.

David's word of imprecation follows in vv.9, 10, taken from Psalm 69:22, 23. He suffers reproach and torment from his enemies, who are also viewed as the enemies of the Lord. Apparently their feasts are times for special outbreaks of blasphemy. David prays that the Lord will make their table their snare so as to entrap them. Then comes the prayer for the darkening of the eyes that have looked with complacency and even glee at the sufferings of the one whom God has permitted to be smitten. John 15:25 and other NT passages indicate that Psalm 69 was treated as messianic, so that its use here makes the application to Paul's own day the more obvious and meaningful.

One problem arises in connection with the final word of the quotation. "Forever" renders *dia pantos,* which in Greek usage may occasionally mean forever but which more commonly means "continually." This latter sense has the advantage of fitting in with the following context, where Israel's obduracy and rejection is not treated as lasting indefinitely, certainly not eternally, but as giving way to a great ingathering of repentant Israel (see article by C.E.B. Cranfield in SE 2:546–50). The bending of the back, as Paul would be likely to apply it, suggests bondage to the law (cf. Acts 15:10).

Notes

6 The additional words, "But if it be of works, then is it no more grace: otherwise work is no more work," made familiar by KJV, lack sufficient MS authority to be included in the text.

F. *Israel's Temporary Rejection and the Salvation of Gentiles*

11:11–24

[11]Again I ask, Did they stumble so as to fall beyond recovery? Not at all! Rather, because of their transgression, salvation has come to the Gentiles to make Israel envious. [12]But if their transgression means riches for the world, and their loss means riches for the Gentiles, how much greater riches will their fullness bring!

[13]I am talking to you Gentiles. Inasmuch as I am the apostle to the Gentiles, I make much of my ministry [14]in the hope that I may somehow arouse my own people to envy and save some of them. [15]For if their rejection is the reconciliation of the world, what will their acceptance be, but life from the dead? [16]If the part of the dough offered as firstfruits is holy, then the whole batch is holy; if the root is holy, so are the branches.

[17]If some of the branches have been broken off, and you, though a wild olive shoot, have been grafted in among the others and now share in the nourishing sap from the olive root, [18]do not boast over those branches. If you do, consider this: You do not support the root, but the root supports you. [19]You will say then, "Branches were broken off so that I could be grafted in." [20]Granted. But they were broken off because of unbelief, and you stand by faith. Do not be arrogant, but be afraid. [21]For if God did not spare the natural branches, he will not spare you either.

[22]Consider therefore the kindness and sternness of God: sternness to those who fell, but kindness to you, provided that you continue in his kindness. Otherwise, you also will be cut off. [23]And if they do not persist in unbelief, they will be grafted in, for God is able to graft them in again. [24]After all, if you were cut out of an olive tree that is wild by nature, and contrary to nature were grafted into a cultivated olive tree, how much more readily will these, the natural branches, be grafted into their own olive tree?

Having dealt with the remnant, Paul returns to a consideration of Israel as a whole, insisting that her rejection is not final and that during the period when the nation continues to resist the divine plan centered in the Messiah, God is active in bringing salvation to the Gentiles. The figure of the olive tree emphasizes that Gentile salvation is dependent on Israel's covenant relationship to God. Gentiles have to be grafted into the olive tree. The purpose of Gentile influx into the church is not merely to magnify the grace of God toward outsiders, but to evoke envy on the part of Israel as a factor in leading to her ultimate return to God as a people. This in turn prepares the way for the climax in 11:25–27.

11,12 A dark picture of Israel has been painted both from the OT and from present observation. This leads naturally to an inquiry. What is the result of this hardening? Is it a hopeless situation? Now that the people have eyes that do not see, are they doomed to stumble so as to fall and rise no more? "Not at all." The stumbling is admitted; an irreparable fall is not. This is a broad hint of the future salvation of Israel that Paul goes on to affirm. Those who stumbled are "the others" of v.7, not included in the believing remnant. The language recalls the indirect reference to the Messiah in 9:32, 33 as the stumbling stone.

God is bringing good out of apparent evil. Israel's stumbling has opened the way for Gentile salvation on such a scale as to make Israel envious (cf. Acts 13:42–47). That envy, though it may involve bitterness, will ultimately contribute to drawing the nation to her Messiah. The longer the process goes on, the more unbearable the pressure on Israel becomes. Her transgression "means riches for the world"; i.e., the nations in contrast to Israel, as the following statement—"means riches for the Gentiles" (v.12)—makes clear.

A word should be said about "loss." The Greek term *hēttēma* seems to involve the idea of defeat, both here and in 1 Corinthians 6:7. It is basically a military figure. An army loses the battle because of heavy casualties. The logic of the verse compels us to take it in this sense, that as surely as Israel's defeat (identified with her stumbling) has brought the riches of God's grace to the Gentiles on a large scale, the conversion of Israel to her Messiah (v.26) will bring even greater blessing to the world. The word "fullness" refers to the conversion, meaning the full complement in contrast to the remnant. It will mark an end to the state of hardening that now characterizes the nation.

13–16 This paragraph follows naturally from the preceding, because Paul now applies to his own position and ministry the truth he has stated. He wants the Gentiles in the Roman church to catch the full import of what he is saying. They have looked on him as "the apostle to the Gentiles" ("an apostle" is the strict rendering of the Gr.). Very well, but they must not suppose that he has lost sight of the need of witnessing to Israel. He is returning to the idea of emulation set forth in v.11, meaning that his work among Gentiles is regarded not simply as an end in itself but as a means of reaching his countrymen. "The Gentiles are not saved merely for their own sake, but for the sake of God's election of Israel. How unshakable is the faithfulness of God to the nation he has chosen!" (James Daane, *The Freedom of God* [Grand Rapids: Eerdmans, 1973], p. 145). "However strange it may sound, the way to the salvation of Israel is by the mission to the Gentiles" (Munck, *Paul and the Salvation of Mankind*, p. 301). This involves the envy/emulation idea already stated in v.11. Paul hopes thereby to "save some of them"—that is, fellow Israelites (cf. 1 Cor 9:22). He knows that only Christ can save, but he himself can be the instrument. The word "some" is important. It is a clear indication that he does not expect his efforts to bring about the eschatological turning of the nation to the crucified, risen Son of God, when "all Israel will be saved" (cf. v.26). This belongs to the indefinite future. There is warmth in Paul's reference to Israel as "my own people." If God could turn *him* around, this proud Jew who bitterly set himself against Jesus as the Christ, surely through him as God's instrument others can be won. These others are the firstfruits who contain in themselves the promise of the ultimate harvest of a nation of believers (cf. v.16).

There is some difficulty in ascertaining the meaning of "life from the dead" (v.15). In order to retain the balance of the sentence, it seems necessary to understand this expression as pertaining to the world (cf. the structure of v.12). Life from the dead could refer to literal resurrection, though it is strangely general for such an explicit event, but it is perhaps better to see in it the promise of a worldwide quickening and deepening of spiritual life when Israel is restored to divine fellowship. She becomes a tonic to the nations that are to be saved.

There is no great difficulty in understanding the relation between "the dough offered as firstfruits" and "the whole batch" (v.16). The word "firstfruits" is the key, referring to the remnant of Israel, whereas "the whole batch" has in view the nation as converted. Both are holy in the primary sense of the word—separated, consecrated to God. The grain taken from the fields as the firstfruits was prepared and worked into dough, then baked into a cake for an offering (Num 15:18–21). The difficulty in interpretation lies in the final statement: "if the root is holy, so are the branches." We have observed that the parallelism in vv.12, 15 points the way to proper assignment of the component parts used there. One would suppose that the same thing should apply here, meaning that the root is the remnant and the branches the rejuvenated Israelites of the future. There is, however, an obvious awkwardness in this interpretation, since presently Paul uses "root" in reference to the historic Israel, especially of its patriarchal foundation (vv.17ff.). So it is prudent to assume that the close of v.16 looks forward rather than backward. As to the meaning, it is sufficient to quote Godet: "Their [Israel's] future restoration is in conformity with the holy character impressed on them from the first; it is therefore not only possible, but morally necessary" (2:244).

17–24 Here Paul continues to use the figures of root and branches, enlarging on the theme so as to set forth the allegory of the olive tree. Actually, there are two trees, the cultivated olive and the wild olive. Israel is the cultivated olive, the Gentiles the wild olive. The breaking off of some of the branches of the former and the grafting in of the branches of the latter represent the present partial rejection of Israel and the corresponding reception of the Gentiles. From this presentation two lessons are drawn. The first is a warning to the Gentile Christians who may be in danger of repeating the sin of the Jew—boasting of their privileged position (vv.18–21). Even more important is the point that if God, by cutting off the branches of the natural olive, has made room for Gentile believers, how much easier will it be for him to restore the natural branches to their place in the cultivated olive (vv.23, 24)! So the groundwork is laid for the next stage in the argument. God is not only able to do this; he will do it (vv.25–27).

By stating that only some of the branches have been broken off (v.17), Paul inserts a reminder of the fact that Israel's rejection is not complete (cf. v.5). The "others" are the Jewish Christians who rub shoulders with Gentile believers in the church. Both depend on the "olive root," the patriarchal base established by God's covenant (cf. 4:11, 12). Here we may consider with profit what the apostle says in Ephesians 2:11–22. The Gentiles, once aliens and foreigners, are now fellow citizens with God's people and members of God's household. The two are made one in Christ.

"Do not boast over those branches" (v.18). They are the broken-off branches mentioned in vv.17, 19. The temptation to boast must have been considerable, a kind of anti-Semitism that magnified the sin of the nation Israel in rejecting the Lord Jesus and saw in Jewish persecution of the church a sure token of an irreparable rift between the nation and her God. But Israel's plight is not to be traced to a change of attitude on the part of God toward her. It is due simply to her unbelief, a condition noted earlier (3:3). The reason Gentile believers have a standing with God is that they have responded to the gospel in faith, the very thing that Israel has failed to do. Paul treats the Gentile element in the church as a unit, addressing it as "you" (singular—Gr. *su*). This should not be understood on an individual basis as though Paul were questioning their personal salvation. The matter in hand is the current Gentile prominence in the church made possible by the rejection of the gospel on the part of the nation of Israel as a whole. Let Gentile Christians beware. Their predominance in the Christian community may not last!

Kindness and sternness (v.22) are aspects of the divine nature, the latter experienced by Israel in her present condition, the former being the portion of Gentile believers. But the positions can be reversed, and if this occurs, it will not be due to any fickleness in God, but to the nature of the human response. Gentiles can become objects of God's sternness and Israel can just as easily become the object of his kindness. Once her unbelief is put away, God is prepared to graft her branches in again (v.23).

Paul's concluding observation (v.24) has a double value. It helps to explain the curious circumstance that his illustration of the olive tree does not follow the pattern of grafting ordinarily found in the ancient Mediterranean world but is in fact the reverse of it. Paul seems to be granting that his allegory is "contrary to nature." William M. Ramsay, making use of the research of Professor Theobald Fischer, observed:

> As regards Palestine, but no other Mediterranean country, he [Fischer] points out that the process which St. Paul had in view is still in use in exceptional circumstances at the present day. He mentions that it is customary to reinvigorate an olive-tree which is ceasing to bear fruit, by grafting it with a shoot of the Wild-Olive, so that the sap of the tree ennobles this wild shoot and the tree now again begins to bear fruit.... The cutting away of the old branches was required to admit air and light to the graft, as well as to prevent the vitality of the tree from being too widely diffused over a large number of branches (*Pauline and Other Studies* [London: Hodder and Stoughton, 1906], pp. 223–224).

A more specific matter in which the illustration runs counter to horticulture is the expectation that the natural branches, though broken off, will in fact be grafted in again. Paul's argument is that if the hard thing, the thing contrary to nature—i.e., the grafting of wild branches into the cultivated olive—has been accomplished, one should not find it difficult to believe that God will restore the broken-off branches of the cultivated olive to their former position. "The future restoration of the Jews is *in itself* a more probable event than had been the introduction of the Gentiles into the Church of God" (Liddon, in loc.). Since in tree culture this would be impossible because of the deadness of the branches after they were removed, Paul is indeed talking "contrary to nature." But he rests his case not on nature but on God's being "able" to do it. With God nothing is impossible. Inevitably, the branches that will be grafted in are not identical with those that were broken off, but they are the same in two respects, their Israelitish heritage and the attitude of unbelief they have maintained in the past. They represent a continuum with the Israel of Paul's day. It should also be noted that the grafting in again of Israel is not intended to suggest that this involves a supplanting of the Gentiles, but only that both Jew and Gentile share together the blessings of God's grace in Christ.

G. *Israel's Future Salvation* (11:25–32)

This is the crowning feature of the discussion, the outcome everything in the three chapters has been pointing to. The same mercy that has overtaken the Gentiles who were formerly disobedient will finally overtake the now disobedient Israel.

11:25–32

25I do not want you to be ignorant of this mystery, brothers, so that you may not be conceited: Israel has experienced a hardening in part until the full number of the Gentiles has come in. 26And so all Israel will be saved, as it is written:

> "The deliverer will come from Zion;
> he will turn godlessness away from Jacob.
> 27And this is my covenant with them
> when I take away their sins."

28As far as the gospel is concerned, they are enemies on your account; but as far as election is concerned, they are loved on account of the patriarchs, 29for God's gifts and his call are irrevocable. 30Just as you who were at one time disobedient to God have now received mercy as a result of their disobedience, 31so they too, as a result of God's mercy to you, have now become disobedient in order that they too may now receive mercy. 32For God has bound all men over to disobedience so that he may have mercy on them all.

25 Now Paul speaks of a mystery, lest his readers imagine that either he or they are capable of understanding the course of Israel's history simply by observation and insight. The term "mystery" (*mystērion*) as used in the NT does not mean "enigma," but the activity of God in salvation history made known to his people by revelation. Paul is not claiming revelation in the sense of those mentioned in 2 Corinthians 12:4, 7, but presumably in the sense of the guidance of the Spirit. The mystery relates to things hidden in the past (16:25), but now made known. In fact, the content of the mystery of Israel is stated immediately. It embraces Israel's hardening, which is "in part" in the sense that the believing remnant constitutes an exception and that the hardening is limited in duration, lasting only "until the full number of the Gentiles has come in." Therefore it also embraces what follows—the salvation of "all Israel."

26,27 The expression, "all Israel," when taken in the light of the context, must be understood of the nation Israel as a whole, in contrast to the present situation when only a remnant has trusted Christ for salvation. The language does not require us to hold that when this occurs every living Israelite will be included, but only that Israel as a nation will be saved.

Not all interpreters agree, however, on the meaning of "all Israel." It was the view of Calvin, for example, that the entire company of the redeemed, both Jew and Gentile, is intended. But "Israel" has not been used of Gentiles in these chapters, and it is doubtful that such is the case anywhere in Paul's writings, even in Galatians 6:16 (cf. Richardson, pp. 74–84). There may be grounds for speaking of the church as the new Israel, but so far as terminology is concerned, Israel means the nation or the godly portion of it (cf. 9:6). To be sure, Gentiles are included in the seed of Abraham (4:11, 12). Though this concept is applicable to the church at the present time, Paul is speaking of something definitely eschatological, actually to be fulfilled in the future, and he has not used the seed of Abraham concept in chapters 9 to 11 (it appears only in 11:1, where it has its literal, historical connotation). As Paul does not discuss the situation of those Jews who remain unbelievers during this age, so in v.26 he drops from view the Gentiles who have figured in vv.17–24.

Another suggested possibility is that "all Israel" refers to the total number of elect

Jews, the aggregate of the godly remnant that exists in each age of the church's history. This fails to come to grips with the climactic nature of Paul's argument, in particular the contrast between all Israel and the remnant as set forth, for example, in v.16a. It fails also to explain the use of the word "mystery" in v.25. "While it is true that all the elect of Israel, the true Israel, will be saved, this is so necessary and patent a truth that to assert the same here would have no particular relevance to what is the apostle's governing interest in this section of the epistle" (Murray, in loc.). Clearly "all Israel" stands over against "in part" by way of contrast.

It is tempting to the modern man to argue that since Israel has not acknowledged Jesus of Nazareth as the Messiah in great numbers, Paul's teaching here should be understood only as a hope, a hope that has not been realized. It is by a similar process of reasoning that some would rule out the related promise of the Lord's return. But a thousand years are as a day in the reckoning of God. The Christian period has not yet approached in length the time required for the fulfillment of the promise of Messiah's first coming.

Does our passage throw light on the time when Israel's national conversion is to be expected? Certainly not in terms of "that day or hour" (Matt 24:36), but rather in terms of the time when the full number of the Gentiles has come in (v.25). The "so" (v.26) is apparently intended to correlate with "until" (v.25), thereby acquiring temporal force (cf. 1 Cor 11:28 for a similar usage of *houtōs*). The NEB rendering in this passage is: "when that has happened"; and JB has "then after this."

The declaration concerning the future of Israel, made on apostolic authority, is now confirmed by citing Isaiah 59:20, 21 and 27:9. The interpretation is somewhat clouded by the fact that the Hebrew has "to Zion" and LXX "for" (on account of), whereas Paul has "out of." Liddon comments, "The change of preposition is probably an intentional variation from the [LXX and Heb.] text of Isaiah, suggested by Ps. xiv. 7, liii. 7, in order to bring into stronger relief the promises made to the Jewish people" (in loc.). The perplexity over the prepositions is largely cleared up by the supposition that Paul has chosen his own wording in order to hint that the conversion of Israel will occur at Messiah's return, when he will come out of Zion, i.e., from the heavenly Jerusalem (cf. Gal 4:26; Heb 12:22). It is hard to account for the wholesale conversion of Israel in any other way, since the activity of the Spirit of God has not produced any such mass movement of Israel during the course of this age. It is at least possible that Paul sensed a certain parallel between his own conversion and what he foresees for his people as a whole. Christ revealed himself to him directly, sweeping away his rationalizations and his self-righteousness.

The effect upon Israel is not couched in terms of material prosperity or martial invincibility, but purely in spiritual terms, in the forsaking of godlessness and the removal of sins by the Lord God. The reference to covenant suggests that Jeremiah 31:31–34 was in the mind of the apostle along with the passages from Isaiah.

28,29 Even though under the gospel economy Israelites as such are considered enemies (by God) for the sake of the Gentiles, yet all the time, when viewed from the standpoint of their national election, they are loved of God for the sake of the fathers (cf. v.16). God's promises are irrevocable and time will prove it. There is an evident parallel as well as contrast between "enemies" and "loved," so both must be referred to God. But as Leenhardt notes, the word "enemies" connotes "the condition of Israel before God rather than sentiments of animosity in God Himself" (in loc.). Likewise there is a parallel between "gospel" and "election," which forbids taking the latter word in the concrete sense of an elect people. Rather, it is the purpose or principle of election that is meant.

The gifts of God are doubtless the special privileges of Israel mentioned in 9:4, 5. These bear witness to the reality of the calling—the summons of Israel to a unique place in the purpose of God. By being first in the Greek sentence, the word "irrevocable" (v.29) is emphatic.

30–32 God's purpose must be implemented if it is to be effective. His mercy is the needed factor. Paul is addressing his Gentile readers here. In fact, the "you" is emphatic, as though to remind Gentile believers (who might be prone to think it strange that God has a glorious future in store for Israel) that they themselves were formerly disobedient toward God. It was Jewish disobedience in regard to the gospel that opened the gates of mercy for the Gentiles. It was the recurrence of a characteristic often displayed before. Israel had scarcely become a nation when the people rejected the good news about Canaan and as a result had to face years of wilderness wandering (Heb 4:6). The consequence of their disobedience to the gospel (Acts 14:2; 19:9) was still more tragic, for it meant shutting themselves out of the kingdom. This disobedience was stubborn unbelief, a confirmed negative attitude.

Again, to warn the Gentiles against being inflated over their present position in grace, Paul advances the reminder (v.31) that it was the very mercy received by the Gentiles that made the Jews more firm in their disobedience. This is graphically illustrated by the effect of the Jerusalem Council (Acts 15). While it gave marked encouragement to the Gentile mission by its decision, it deepened and strengthened Jewish opposition to the gospel. Yet God did not give up on his chosen people, but ever keeps in view his plan for their salvation and continues to extend his mercy. The second "now" in v.31 is somewhat perplexing in the light of the eschatological emphasis in vv.26, 27. It may refer to the present salvation of the remnant or it may even be intended to include the future along with the present and so anticipate the ultimate salvation of the nation. The conclusion of the whole matter is that God magnified his mercy by the very fact of disobedience, binding all men over to it (cf. 3:9) that he might have mercy on all. So disobedience does not have the last word (cf. Gal 3:22).

H. *Praise to God for His Wisdom and His Ways*

11:33–36

33 Oh, the depth of the riches, the wisdom and
the knowledge of God!
How unsearchable his judgments,
and his paths beyond tracing out!
34 "Who has known the mind of the Lord?
Or who has been his adviser?"
35 "Who has ever given to God,
that God should repay him?"
36 For from him and through him and to him
are all things.
To him be the glory forever! Amen.

In view of the assurance generated by v.32, it is no wonder that Paul, despite his burden for the Israel of his day, is able to lift his heart in adoring praise to God. We are reminded of Isaiah 55, where the ungodly and sinful man is urged to return to the Lord and find mercy, for God's thoughts and ways are not those of men but are infinitely higher and better. Instead of being vindictive, God is gracious. His plans defy the penetration of the human mind and his ways surpass the ability of man to trace them out. The Lord has not been obliged to lean upon another for advice (v.34). He has not had to depend on human assistance that would make him indebted to men (v.35). He is the source, the means, and the goal of all things (v.36).

While this exalted and moving ascription of praise has in view God's plans and operations in the history of salvation affecting the great segments of mankind, Jew and Gentile, the closing verse applies also to the individual life that pleases God. For that life has its source in God, lives by his resources, and returns to him when its course has been run. To God be the glory!

VII. Our Spiritual Service: The Practice of Righteousness (12:1–15:13)

Every reader of Romans is conscious of a distinct break in the train of thought as he moves from 11:36 to 12:1. The theological exposition (or argument) centering around the problem as to how sinful man can be put into right relationship with God is over. But there is more to be said, because when man is made right with his Maker, he needs to know what difference this makes in his relations with his fellowmen. He needs to know what is expected of him and how to apply his new resources to all the situations confronting him. This last main section of the Epistle is designed to meet these needs (cf. Eph 4:1).

Students of Scripture in recent years have begun to employ two terms that serve as convenient labels for the two broad types of instruction just noted. It will be recognized at once that these designations are borrowed from the sphere of grammar. They are "the indicative" and "the imperative." The one expression covers what God has done in terms of the gospel; it deals with divine provision. The other deals with what the Christian is expected to do by way of working out the salvation that has been given him (cf. Phil 2:12, 13), and consequently majors in exhortation. It is notable that the key word "righteousness," which has so dominated the book up to this point, occurs only once in the closing chapters (14:17) and then not in the forensic sense denoting right relationship with God but rather in the practical meaning of right relations with one's fellows. The hortatory element includes both commands and prohibitions and is spread over various areas of application, including Christian conduct toward fellow believers, toward society (especially in meeting hostile reactions), and toward the state.

A. *The Appeal for Dedication of the Believer*

12:1, 2

1Therefore, I urge you, brothers, in view of God's mercy, to offer yourselves as living sacrifices, holy and pleasing to God—which is your spiritual worship. 2Do not conform any longer to the pattern of this world, but be transformed by the renewing of your mind. Then you will be able to test and approve what God's will is—his good, pleasing and perfect will.

This introductory portion is a prelude to the discussion of specific duties of the believer. It sets forth the fundamental obligations one must meet before he is prepared to face the challenge of living as a believer in this world. Only an intelligent commitment of life in the light of God's gift of salvation will suffice.

1 "Therefore" establishes a connection with the entire foregoing presentation rather than with chapters 9 to 11 alone. The connection is particularly close with 6:13, 19, as a comparison of the terminology will show. The apostle begins now to "urge" his readers instead of simply instructing them. His choice of this word "urge" (*parakaleō*) is discriminating, seeing that its force lies between commanding and beseeching. It possesses something of the element of authority that is more forcefully expressed by "command," and has in it something of the element of appeal that attaches to "beseech."

"Mercy," rather than the familiar "mercies" of the KJV, is justified on the ground that the word used here (*oiktirmos;* cf. *eleos* in 11:30–32, also translated "mercy"), though plural in form, reflects the Hebrew *rahamîm,* which is a so-called intensive plural, meaning "great mercy" or "compassion." Sometimes it is used in LXX together with the more common *eleos,* as in Isaiah 63:15 and Hosea 2:19 (2:21 in LXX). It denotes that quality in God that moves him to deliver man from his state of sin and misery and therefore underlies his saving activity in Christ. Here "mercy" is the leverage for the appeal that follows. Whereas the heathen are prone to sacrifice in order to obtain mercy, biblical faith teaches that the divine mercy provides the basis for sacrifice as the fitting response.

Other problems of translation are somewhat more difficult. "Yourselves" is literally "your bodies" (*sōmata hymōn*). In the closely related discussion in 6:13 the original text does not have the word "body," but instead has "your members" (*melē hymōn*) and "yourselves" (*heautous*). Both are what the believer is to present to God for his service. Since the milieu of thought is so similar in 12:1, it is natural to conclude that "body" is intended to include both the person (the volition of the one making the dedication) and the bodily powers that are thus set apart for God's use. Though Greek thought was prone to consider the body the receptacle containing the soul, this was not the Hebraic concept, which viewed man as a unit. So it should be clear that Paul is not urging the dedication of the body as an entity distinct from the inner man. Rather, he views the body as the vehicle that implements the desires and choices of the redeemed spirit. It is essential for making contact with the society in which the believer lives. Through the body we serve.

One is reminded by "offer" and "sacrifices" that the apostle is using cultic language here (cf. 15:16). Before a priest in Israel could minister on behalf of others, he was obliged to present himself in a consecrated condition and the sacrifices he offered were to be without blemish (Mal 1:8–13). "Holy" is a reminder of that necessity for the Christian, not in terms of rite or ritual but as renouncing the sins of the old life and being committed to a life of obedience to the divine will (cf. 6:19). The body is not evil in itself; if it were, God would not ask that it be offered to him. As an instrument, it is capable of expressing either sin or righteousness. If the latter, then it is an offering "pleasing to God." The word "living" may glance by way of contrast to the animal sacrifices of the OT, which, when offered, no longer possessed life. But it is also a reminder that spiritual life, received from God in the new birth, is the presupposition of a sacrifice acceptable to him. Christian sacrifice, though made decisively and once-for-all (this is the force of "offer"), has in view a *life* of service to God. In Israel the whole burnt offering ascended to God and could never be reclaimed. It belonged to God.

Next the living sacrifice is equated with "spiritual worship." The exact sense is difficult to determine. "Spiritual" (NIV, RSV) may be an improvement on "reasonable" (KJV), since the latter term could be understood in the sense of adequate, seeing that no less a sacrifice could be offered in view of the sacrifice God has made in Christ for our salvation. The idea is rather that the sacrifice we render is intelligent and deliberate, perhaps to be understood in contrast to the sacrifices of the Jewish cultus in which the animals had no part in determining what was to be done with them.

"Worship" translates *latreia,* which Paul has already used for the entire Jewish cultus (9:4). Here he gives it a metaphorical turn. The problem to be faced is whether "worship" may not be too restricted a rendering, for worship in the strict sense is adoration of God, which does not fit well with the concept of "bodies" ("your bodies" is rendered "yourselves" in NIV). It is just at this point that the term "service" (KJV) has an advantage, since it covers the entire range of the Christian's life and activity (cf. Deut 10:12). Service is the proper sequel to worship.

2 The dedicated life is also the transformed life. Whereas v.1 has called for a decisive commitment, v.2 deals with the maintenance of that commitment. We need to "bind the sacrifice with cords . . . unto the horns of the altar" (Ps 118:27 KJV). Significantly, there is a shift in the tense of the verbs (from the aorist "offer") to the present tense, pointing up the necessity of continual vigilance lest the original decision be vitiated or weakened. The threat comes from "this world," whose ways and thoughts can so easily impinge on the child of God. Paul has used *aiōn,* essentially a time word, meaning "age," but it has much common ground with *kosmos,* the more usual term for "world." The believer has been delivered from this present evil age (Gal 1:4), which has Satan for its god (2 Cor 4:4). He lives by the powers of the age to come (Heb 6:5), but his heavenly calling includes residence in this world, among sinful men, where he is to show forth the praises of him who called him out of darkness into God's marvelous light. He is in the world for witness, but not for conformity to that which is a passing phenomenon (1 Cor 7:31).

Complementary to the refusal to be conformed to the pattern of this world is the command to be "transformed." The two processes are viewed as going on all the time, a continual renunciation and renewal. Our pattern here is Christ, who refused Satan's solicitations in the temptation and was transfigured (*metamorphoō*—the same word as that translated "transformed") in his acceptance of the path that led to Calvary (Mark 9:2, 3). As his mission could be summarized in the affirmation that he had come to do the Father's will (John 6:38), the Christian's service can be reduced to this simple description also. But he must "test and approve," refusing the norms of conduct employed by the sinful world and reaffirming for himself the spiritual norms befitting the redeemed. Aiding this process is "the renewing of your mind," which seems to mean that the believer is to keep going back in his thought to the original commitment, reaffirming its necessity and legitimacy in the light of the grace of God extended to him. In this activity the working of the Holy Spirit should no doubt be recognized (cf. Titus 3:5). It appears from the context that the believer is not viewed as ignorant of the will of God, but as needing to avoid blurring its outline by failure to renew the mind continually (cf. Eph 5:8–10). Dedication leads to discernment and discernment to delight in God's will. That there is an intimate connection between certifying the will of God and making oneself a living sacrifice is indicated by the use of "pleasing" in each case (cf. Phil 4:18; Heb 13:16).

B. *Varied Ministries in the Church, the Body of Christ*

12:3–8

[3]For by the grace given to me I say to every one of you: Do not think of yourself more highly than you ought, but rather think of yourself with sober judgment, in accordance with the measure of faith God has given you. [4]Just as each of us has

one body with many members, and these members do not all have the same function, [5]so in Christ we who are many form one body, and each member belongs to all the others. [6]We have different gifts, according to the grace given us. If a man's gift is prophesying, let him use it in proportion to his faith. [7]If it is serving, let him serve; if it is teaching, let him teach; [8]if it is encouraging, let him encourage; if it is contributing to the needs of others, let him give generously; if it is leadership, let him govern diligently; if it is showing mercy, let him do it cheerfully.

3 The will of God, concerning which Paul has just spoken, is identical for all believers in respect to holiness of life and completeness of dedication. But what that will involves for each one with respect to special service in the church may be considerably diverse. Since individual application is called for in appropriating the teaching, the apostle finds it expedient to remind his readers of his authority to expound this subject even though he is unknown to most of them and their gifts are unknown to him (cf. 1:5; Gal 2:9; Eph 3:7). But this reminder is not intended to erect a barrier between himself and them, because what he has by way of authority and teaching ability is traced to divine grace, the same grace that has bestowed spiritual gifts on them.

In addressing himself deliberately to "every one of you," Paul seems to be granting that every believer has some spiritual gift (cf. v.6; 1 Peter 4:10). But the primary purpose in getting the attention of each one is to drive home the necessity of appropriating and using his gift with the utmost humility. After all, God was not obligated to spread his gifts around so lavishly. Paul recognizes the danger that the possession of a gift could easily result in a self-esteem that was nothing more or less than wretched pride (v.3). His experience with the Corinthian church (1 Cor 12:14–31; 13:4; 14:12, 20) had alerted him to this problem. He virtually equates humility with "sober judgment," as opposed to thinking of oneself more highly than one should. In v.16 Paul comes back to this fundamental matter. Obviously, there is less danger of a person's depreciating himself than of exaggerating his own importance.

Is there some gauge that will enable a person to estimate his position with respect to spiritual gifts? Paul answers in the affirmative, pointing to "the measure of faith." Though this is intimately related to sober judgment, its precise meaning is not easy to determine. We may at once exclude the possibility that "faith" in this context means "the faith" in the sense of a body of truth that is believed. Such a usage is familiar to us from Jude 3, but Paul seems to avoid it. To him faith is what the Christian exercises. It is subjective rather than objective. That this is so here is clear from the close of v.3. Faith is God's bestowal. C.E.B. Cranfield, understanding "measure" in the sense of standard, takes the phrase to mean that one's faith should provide the basis for a true estimation of himself, since it reveals that he, along with other believers, is dependent on the saving mercy of God in Christ (NTS 8 [July 1962] 345–351). To be sure, that ought to induce humility. Godet understands "measure" in the sense of degree. "This gift, the measure of the action to which we are called, is the divine limit which the Christian's renewed mind should discern, and by which he should regulate his aspirations in regard to the part he has to play in the church" (in loc.). This view brings "measure of faith" into close agreement with "in proportion to his faith" (v.6). It should be added that faith, as used in this passage, is hardly saving faith, but faith in the sense of grasping the nature of one's spiritual gift and having confidence to exercise it rightly.

4,5 To offset the danger of individualistic thinking with its resulting danger of pride, Paul refers to the human body—an illustration familiar from its earlier use in 1 Corinthians 12:12ff. Three truths are set forth: the *unity* of the body; the *diversity* of its members, with corresponding diversity in function; and the *mutuality* of the various members—"each member belongs to all the others."

The third item calls attention to the need of the various parts of the body for each other. They cannot work independently. Furthermore, each member profits from what the other members contribute to the whole. Reflection on these truths reduces preoccupation with one's own gift and makes room for appreciation of other people and the gifts they exercise.

6–8 "We have different gifts." Paul is not referring to gifts in the natural realm, but to those functions made possible by a specific enablement of the Holy Spirit granted to believers. The gift does not contradict what God has bestowed in the natural order and, though it may even build on the natural gift, it must not be confused with the latter.

Variety in the gifts should be understood from the standpoint of the needs of the Christian community, which are many, as well as from the desirability of giving every believer a share in ministry. With his eye still on the danger of pride, Paul reminds his readers that these new capacities for service are not native to those who exercise them but come from divine grace. Every time he delves into this subject he is careful to make this clear (1 Cor 12:6; Eph 4:7; cf. 1 Peter 4:10).

Although he has spoken of different gifts, Paul does not proceed to give anything like an exhaustive list (cf. 1 Cor 12:27, 28). He seems more intent on emphasizing the need for exercising the gifts and for exercising them in the right way—"in proportion to [one's] faith." He uses this expression only in connection with prophesying, but there is no reason to suppose it is not intended to apply to the other items as well.

What is meant by "in proportion to his faith" (v.6)? Theologians have tended to favor the translation "according to the analogy of the faith" (transliterating the Greek word *analogia* and stressing the definite article before "faith"). Upon this construction is built the Reformed principle that all parts of Scripture must be interpreted in conformity to the rest. This is a valid principle but hardly germane to this context. Another view of the matter, held by Godet (in loc.), for example, understands the phrase as referring to the hearers rather than to the prophets, so that, in framing the messages given them, those who speak should consider the stage of development attained by their audience. This view, too, may have merit, but against it is the fact that in this passage it is not spiritual gifts that are being treated for the edification of the hearers, as in 1 Corinthians 14, but the proprieties that should govern those who use the gifts.

The most satisfactory explanation is that "faith" retains the subjective force it has in v.3 and that the whole phrase has the same thrust as "measure of faith" there. A prophet is not to be governed by his emotions (1 Cor 14:32) or by his love of speaking (1 Cor 14:30) but by entire dependence on the Spirit of God.

Paul does not give a definition of prophecy here, but if we are to judge from the earlier reference to it in 1 Corinthians 14:3, 31, the nature of the gift is not primarily prediction but the communication of revealed truth that will both convict and build up the hearers. This gift is prominent in the other listings of gifts (1 Cor 12:28; Eph 4:11), where prophets are second only to apostles in the enumeration. That Paul says nothing of apostles in the Romans passage may be a hint that no apostle, Peter included, had anything to do with the founding of the Roman church (see Introduction, background).

"Serving" (v.7) is such a broad term that some difficulty attaches to the effort to pin it down. The Greek *diakonia* is sometimes used of the ministry of the word to unbelievers (Acts 6:4; 2 Cor 5:18), but the gifts in this passage in Romans seem intentionally restricted in their exercise to the body of Christ (it may be significant that there is no mention of evangelists as there is in Eph 4:11). Despite its place between prophesying and teaching, the narrower meaning of service as ministration to the material needs of believers is probable here. NEB and JB translate the word as "administration," perhaps hinting that the term should be taken as referring to the supervision of the giving of aid to the needy, which was specifically the province of the deacons. Even so, it should be recognized that others also could engage in a variety of helpful ministries to the needs of the saints (1 Cor 16:15). In fact, Paul inserts in the midst of a catalog of restricted terms dealing with gifts this very broad designation, "those able to help others" (1 Cor 12:28).

The gift of teaching (v.7) is mentioned next. It differed from prophesying in that it was not characterized by ecstatic utterance as the vehicle for revelation given by the Spirit. In 1 Corinthians 14:6 teaching is paired with knowledge, whereas prophecy is coupled with revelation. Probably the aim in teaching was to give help in the area of Christian living rather than formal instruction in doctrine, even though it must be granted that the latter is needed as a foundation for the former. Indeed the very structure of Romans attests this. Paul himself gives a notable example of teaching in vv.9–21. In the latter part of this section his considerable use of the OT suggests that early Christian teachers were largely dependent on it for their instruction.

"Encouraging" (v.8) is the translation of the Greek *paraklēsis*, which has a variety of meanings. Only the context can indicate whether the most suitable rendering is "encouragement" or "exhortation" or "comfort." All are closely related. In Acts 15:31 encouragement is certainly the idea conveyed. But in 1 Timothy 4:13 exhortation is clearly involved, evidently the application of the OT as it was read in the assembly during worship (cf. Acts 13:15). Assuredly some encouragement could be included, but exhortation seems to be the dominant meaning.

"Contributing to the needs of others" (v.8) has to do with spontaneous private benevolence (cf. 1 John 3:17, 18). This is evidently not intended as a repetition of "serving" (v.7), and this favors the view that the latter activity belongs to the public distribution of aid by the church to its needy. The only doubt concerning this interpretation resides in the word "generously" (NIV), which is a possible translation but hardly as likely as "with simplicity" (KJV)—that is, with singleness of heart, free of mixed motives, without regret (over having given so much). That wrong motivation could enter into giving is shown by the account of the sin of Ananias and Sapphira in Acts 5.

"Leadership" (v.8) is the translation of a word that means to stand before others, so the idea of governing derives readily from it. The need is for one to carry out his ministry "diligently." Even in church life some people are tempted to enjoy the office rather than use it as an avenue for service. A few interpreters, doubtless influenced by the items immediately preceding and following, favor the meaning of "giving aid," "furnishing care," etc., and this is possible. However, the exercise of leadership is the more common in NT usage (1 Thess 5:12; 1 Tim 3:4, 5; 5:17). "Diligently" fits well in either case.

"Showing mercy" does not pertain to the area of forgiveness or sparing judgment. It has to do with ministering to the sick and needy. This is to be done in a cheerful, spontaneous manner that will convey blessing rather than engender self-pity. Way renders it freely, "If you come with sympathy to sorrow, bring God's sunlight in your face" (Arthur S. Way, *Letters of St. Paul and Hebrews*. 6th edit. [London: Macmillan, 1926]).

C. *Principles Governing Christian Conduct*

12:9–21

> [9]Love must be sincere. Hate what is evil; cling to what is good. [10]Be devoted to one another in brotherly love. Honor one another above yourselves. [11]Never be lacking in zeal, but keep your spiritual fervor, serving the Lord. [12]Be joyful in hope, patient in affliction, faithful in prayer. [13]Share with God's people who are in need. Practice hospitality.
>
> [14]Bless those who persecute you; bless and do not curse. [15]Rejoice with those who rejoice; mourn with those who mourn. [16]Live in harmony with one another. Don't be proud, but be willing to associate with people of low position. Don't be conceited.
>
> [17]Do not repay anyone evil for evil. Be careful to do what is right in the sight of everybody. [18]If it is possible, as far as it depends on you, live at peace with everyone. [19]Do not take revenge, my friends, but leave room for God's wrath, for it is written: "It is mine to avenge, I will repay," says the Lord. [20]On the contrary: "If your enemy is hungry, feed him; if he is thirsty, give him something to drink. In doing this, you will heap burning coals on his head." [21]Do not be overcome by evil, but overcome evil with good.

The presupposition here is the dedicated life, which enables one to discover and demonstrate the will of God. Relationship to fellow Christians is treated first (vv.9–13), then the stance to be assumed toward those who are without (vv.14–21).

9,10 Love is primary, but if it is not sincere, it is not real love but only pretense. When one recalls that Paul paused in his discussion of spiritual gifts to inject a chapter on love (1 Cor 13), it is altogether fitting that he should follow his presentation of spiritual gifts here in Romans with the same emphasis. The whole of the believer's conduct, in fact, should be bathed in love. If he fails to love his brother, doubt is cast on his professed love for God (1 John 4:19–21).

Love readily suggests purity. The two are found together in God, who is of too pure eyes to behold evil (Hab 1:13) and cannot be tempted by it (James 1:13). Hatred readily follows love—hatred, that is, of what is evil. The human attitude must follow the divine in this respect also, because it is the opposite of the command to love. The two belong together. To "cling to what is good" (v.9) is to be wedded to it. Total commitment leaves neither time nor inclination to court evil.

The apostle has called for love, but lest this be construed simply as an ideal, he now puts it in a living context (v.10). Love is to be shown to people, not lavished on a principle. He uses a special term denoting brotherly love (*philadelphia*). "Devoted" is appropriate, since it customarily denotes the family tie. Believers are members of the family of God.

"Honor one another above yourselves" (v.10). To honor is to accord recognition and show appreciation. Presumably, this is based not on some personal attractiveness that is perceived or usefulness that is known but rather on the fact that every Christian has Christ in his heart and is able to express him through his own individuality. Consequently, this recognition is based on the new creation (2 Cor 5:17) rather than on the old. One honors God when he recognizes his transforming work in human life. If the according of such honor seems to diminish the recognition of what God has done in one's own life, the problem is readily solved by the example of the Son's exalting of God the Father despite the Son's equality with him (John 10:30; Phil 2:4–6).

11,12 Paul now momentarily directs attention toward the Lord and his service before returning to horizontal relationship with the body of Christ (v.13). After converts have experienced the initial glow and ardor of Christian life there is often danger of their slipping back into a deadening spiritual inertia. To counter this, the apostle urges diligent endeavor fed by fervency of spirit. Such is the characterization of Apollos (Acts 18:25). On the other hand, it was the lack of such fire that brought down the rebuke of the Lord upon the Laodicean church (Rev 3:15, 16). In brief, the thrust here (v.11) is that the Lord's service calls for our best. Jesus is no ordinary master. Not the least element in his uniqueness is the confidence he instills in those who serve him that though he remains invisible, he is wonderfully real to the eye of faith, and this carries forward into the present the indelible influence of his life and ministry in the world during the days of his flesh. This in turn arouses the hope, tinged with joy, of seeing him in his glory and being united with him (1 Peter 1:7, 8). This hope sustains the servant of Christ, enabling him to be "patient in affliction" (tribulation), recalling what Paul had written in 5:3, 4. At this point, Paul's mention of prayer is natural, since it is the Christian's great resource when he is under stress and strain.

13 Even under persecution one should not allow himself to be so preoccupied with his own troubles that he becomes insensitive to the needs of other believers. Apparently, it is temporal need that is in view. To share with others is never more meaningful than when one is hard pressed to find a sufficient supply for himself. When this sharing takes place under one's own roof, it is labeled "hospitality." The Greek term (*philoxenos*) is more expressive than the English, for it means "love for strangers." Paul's word for "practice" (*diōkō*, "pursue") is strong (the same word is used in the sense of "persecute" in v.14), calling for an undiminished ardor in extending this courtesy to traveling believers. The Lord had encouraged his disciples to depend on such kindness during their missions (Matt 10:11). Without it, the spread of the gospel during the days of the early church would have been greatly impeded. With it, the "church in the house" became a reality (16:23; cf. 16:5). What sanctified this practice above all was the realization that in receiving and entertaining the traveler, those who opened their doors and their hearts were receiving and entertaining Christ (Matt 10:40; 25:40).

14–16 The material in these cases is not so easy to characterize as that in the foregoing and following paragraphs. It seems to describe the Christian's relations to their neighbors and friends (not excluding believers), as well as one reference to their opponents, whereas the next section definitely pictures the people of God bearing up under pressure from the unbelieving world. Perhaps the best thing is to view this portion in the light of Paul's word in Galatians 6:10 and consider it transitional.

Paul's injunction to bless persecutors rather than curse them undoubtedly goes back to the teaching of our Lord (Matt 5:44; Luke 6:28) through oral tradition. The teaching was incarnated in the Savior himself and became clearly manifested during his trial and his suffering on the cross. To persecute is literally "to pursue." Persecution could take various forms, running the gamut from verbal abuse and social ostracism to the use of violence resulting in death. A few years later, Roman Christians were to lose their lives in great numbers at the hands of Emperor Nero. Persecution in some form or another was so common in the experience of the early church that Paul is able to assume as a matter of course that it is a factor in the lives of his readers. If such treatment is not encountered in our society, we can at least cultivate the readiness to meet it and so fulfill the injunction in spirit. To bless one's persecutors involves praying for their forgiveness and for a change of outlook regarding the Christian faith. It can be done only by the grace of Christ.

One charge follows another without any apparent connection as Paul calls on his readers to share one another's joys and sorrows (v.15). It has often been noted that it is easier to fulfill the first half of this command than the second, because our natural inclination is to feel genuine sympathy for those in sorrow, but to share the joy of their rejoicing may present difficulty if the achievement or good fortune that prompts the joy is viewed with envy. This is one of the things that Philippians 4:13 is designed to cover. In general, however, people have less need for fellowship in times of joy than in times of grief, for if loneliness is added to sorrow, the trial is compounded. For an earlier statement of this teaching on sharing others' joys and sorrows under all circumstances see 1 Corinthians 12:26.

"Live in harmony with one another" (v.16) is not so literal a rendering as "have equal regard for one another" (NEB), but is warranted by the fact that the language closely resembles that of Philippians 2:2, which was written to dispel the discord in the church. As a means to attaining this harmony, Paul stresses the necessity of rejecting the temptation to think high thoughts about oneself, as though one were a superior breed of Christian, and of coming down off the perch of isolation and mingling with people "of low position" or of a humble frame of mind (the Gr. has simply "the lowly"). And lest one consent to do this while still retaining heady notions of his own superiority, Paul puts in a final thrust: "Don't be conceited" (v.16). Conceit has no place in the life ruled by love (1 Cor 13:4).

17–21 Here Paul takes his stand alongside the believer by giving him explicit counsel about how to face the hostile world. "Do not repay evil for evil" (v.17), for to do so would be to follow the inclination of the flesh. The remainder of the verse is open to more than one interpretation. It could mean that the Christian should be concerned to do what all persons understand to be right. But this presupposes no real difference between Christian and non-Christian in their evaluation. Consequently, the other explanation is preferable, namely, that believers are constantly under the scrutiny of unsaved persons as well as of fellow Christians, and they must be careful that their conduct does not betray the high standards of the gospel (cf. Col 4:5; 1 Tim 3:7). The verb "be careful" (*pronoeō*) is literally "to think of beforehand," which suggests that the conduct of believers ought not to be regulated by habit, but rather that each situation that holds prospect for a witness to the world be weighed so that the action taken will not bring unfavorable reflection on the gospel.

The charge to live at peace with everyone (v.18) is hedged about with two qualifying statements. "By this cumulation of conditions the difficulty of the precept is admirably brought out" (Field, in loc.). "If it be possible" suggests that there are instances in human relations when the strongest desire for concord will not avail. This, in turn, is explained by the statement "as far as it depends on you." In other words, if disharmony and conflict should come, let not the responsibility be laid at your feet. The believer may not be able to persuade the other party, but he can at least refuse to be the instigator of trouble. He can be a peacemaker (Matt 5:9) only if he is recognized as one who aims to live at peace with his fellows.

This peace-loving attitude may be costly, however, because some will want to take advantage of it, figuring that Christian principles will not permit the wronged party to retaliate. In such a case, what is to be done? The path of duty is clear. We are not to take vengeance. This would be to trespass on the province of God, the great Judge of all.

"Leave room for God's wrath" (v.19). Trust him to take care of the situation. He will not bungle. He will not be too lenient or too severe. Here Paul quotes Deuteronomy 32:35, whose context indicates that the Lord will intervene to vindicate his people when their enemies abuse them and gloat over them. God's action will rebuke not only the adversaries but also the false gods in which they have put their trust.

There is no suggestion that the wrath of God will be visited upon the wrongdoer immediately. On the contrary, that wrath is the last resort, for in the immediate future lies the possibility that the one who has perpetrated the wrong will have a change of heart and will be convicted of his sin and won over by the refusal of the Christian to retaliate (v.20). Here again Paul lets the OT (Prov 25:21, 22) speak for him. The course of action recommended is the positive aspect of what has been stated in v.17. "Burning coals" are best understood as "the burning pangs of shame and contrition" (Cranfield, in loc.). There is no definite promise at this point that the offender will be converted, but at least he will not be a threat in the future. Moreover, by going the second mile and showing unexpected and unmerited kindness, the believer may well have spared his companions from having the same experience he has endured. In that measure, society has benefited.

Guidance on the problem of coping with evil reaches its climax in the final admonition: "Do not be overcome by evil, but overcome evil with good" (v.21). In this context, "to be overcome by evil" means to give in to the temptation to meet evil with evil, to retaliate. To overcome evil with good has been illustrated in v.20. Many other illustrations could be given, such as David's sparing the life of Saul, who was pursuing him to snuff out his life. When Saul realized that David had spared his life, he said, "You have repaid me good, whereas I have repaid you evil" (1 Sam 24:17 RSV). The world's philosophy leads men to expect retaliation when they have wronged another. To receive kindness, to see love when it seems uncalled for, can melt the hardest heart.

Notes

11 It is reasonably certain that the variant reading **καιρῷ** (*kairō*), found principally in Western witnesses, arose by a misreading of **κυρίῳ** (*kyriō*, "Lord"), which was **κῶ** (*kō*), as **κρῶ** (*krō*), a contraction of **καιρῷ** (*kairo*, "opportunity").

D. *The Duty of Submission to Civil Authority*

13:1–7

[1]Everyone must submit himself to the governing authorities, for there is no authority except that which God has established. The authorities that exist have been established by God. [2]Consequently, he who rebels against the authority is rebelling against what God has instituted, and those who do so will bring judgment on themselves. [3]For rulers hold no terror for those who do right, but for those who do wrong. Do you want to be free from fear of the one in authority? Then do what is right and he will commend you. [4]For he is God's servant to do you good. But if you do wrong, be afraid, for he does not bear the sword for nothing. He is God's servant, an agent of justice to bring punishment on the wrongdoer. [5]Therefore, it is necessary to submit to the authorities, not only because of possible punishment but also because of conscience.

[6]This is also why you pay taxes, for the authorities are God's servants, who give

their full time to governing. 7Give everyone what you owe him: If you owe taxes, pay taxes; if revenue, then revenue; if respect, then respect; if honor, then honor.

This is the most notable passage in the NT on Christian civic responsibility. It probably reflects the famous word of Jesus: "Give to Caesar what is Caesar's, and to God what is God's" (Matt 22:21). That Paul lived in conformity with his own teaching is apparent from his relation to various rulers as recorded in the Book of Acts. Pride in his Roman citizenship and his readiness to appeal to it in critical situations are also reflected in Acts. Because Paul realized that this subject had a definite bearing on the spread of the gospel (1 Tim 2:1ff.), he saw its relevance in this Epistle on the theme of salvation.

Some, however, have found it difficult to relate this thirteenth chapter to the flow of thought in Romans. It seems to them detached and so isolated from the material on either side of it as to suggest that it might even have come from a later period when such concerns were more pressing for the church. Nevertheless, it is possible to see in 13:1–7 an expansion and special application of the teaching about good and evil (12:17, 21) and living "at peace with everyone" (12:18). Perhaps the reference to "wrath" (*orgē*, 12:19) is intended to anticipate the same word in 13:5, where it is translated "punishment."

More important, however, is the broader connection in terms of thought. Here there are two pertinent elements. One is the natural connection with 12:1, 2, where the foundation is laid for Christian service in its various ramifications. The believer's relation to the state is one of those areas. Another and more specific connection with the foregoing material is possible. Paul may be intent on warning the Roman church, which contained some Christian Jews as well as Gentile believers who sympathized with them over the plight of their nation, not to identify with any revolutionary movement advocating rebellion against Rome (Marcus Borg in NTS 19 [Jan. 1973] 205–218). If this need was in Paul's mind as he wrote, then 13:1–7 may be considered a kind of postscript to chapters 9 to 11. This would put the apostle solidly behind the stance taken by our Lord, who was faced with pressure from Zealot elements in Palestine but refused to endorse their use of violence. Borg inclines toward the view that the expulsion of Jews from Rome by Claudius (Acts 18:2; Suetonius, *Claudius*, 25:4) was not due to Christian proclamation of Jesus as the Messiah which excited and divided the Jewish community at Rome, but to messianic agitation involving the expressed hope that the deliverer would bring release from the grip of Rome. If this is indeed the background, then Paul was not simply giving counsel of a general or universal nature (although applicable elsewhere), but was speaking to a definite historical situation that could have proved explosive from the Christian as well as the Jewish standpoint. Adjustment to the state was especially difficult for the Jew because his people, from the days of the OT theocracy, looked to God as supreme and felt no tension in their own national life between the realms of politics and religion. There is also a possibility that the Jews who returned to Rome after the death of Claudius (including some Christian Jews) were hostile toward the state because of the way Claudius had treated them. These needed to be mollified.

1 The teaching that follows is addressed to "everyone." Presumably this means every believer rather than everyone in general, even though government is necessary for society as a whole. Paul could admonish only Christians. What he requires is submission, a term that calls for placing oneself under someone else. Here and in v.5 he seems to avoid using the stronger word "obey," and the reason is that the believer may find it impossible to comply with every demand of the government. A circumstance may arise

in which he must choose between obeying God and obeying men (Act 5:29). But even then he must be submissive to the extent that, if his Christian convictions do not permit his compliance, he will accept the consequences of his refusal.

Those to whom submission must be rendered are called "governing authorities" (v.1). The first word (*exousia*) is not a specific or technical term; it simply means those who are over others. With respect to the second word (*archōn* v.3), we find Josephus using it, as Paul does, with reference to Roman rulers, but specifically those who ruled in the name of Rome over the Jews in Palestine (*Jewish War* II, 350). (See note.)

Paul makes a sweeping statement when he says, "There is no authority except that which God has established" (v.1b). It is true even of Satan that what authority he exercises has been given him (cf. Luke 4:6). God has ordained this tension between authority and submission. "God has so arranged the world from the beginning—at the creation, by all means, if you like—as to make it possible to render him service within it; and this is why he created superiors and subordinates" (E. Käsemann, *New Testament Questions of Today* [Philadelphia: Fortress Press, 1961], p. 208).

It is probably significant that the name of Christ does not appear anywhere in the passage. The thought does not move in the sphere of redemption or the life of the church as such, but in the relation to the state that God in his wisdom has set up. While the Christian has his citizenship in heaven (Phil 3:20), he is not on that account excused from responsibility to acknowledge the state as possessing authority from God to govern him. He holds a dual citizenship.

2 Those who refuse submission are in rebellion against what God has ordained. To ground refusal on the fact that the believer is not of the world (John 17:14) is to confuse the issue, because the state cannot be identified with the world no matter how "worldly" its attitude may be. The world can be set over against God (1 John 2:16) but this is not true of the state as an institution, despite the fact that individual governments may at times be anti-God in their stance. Midway in v.2 Paul shifts from the singular ("he who rebels") to the plural ("those who do so"). If this is more than a stylistic variation, it may be intended to recognize that rebellion is not feasible at all unless it is instigated by collective action. Defiance of government is futile on an individual basis except as a demonstration of personal disagreement. Those who rebel "will bring judgment on themselves." By rendering judgment as "damnation," KJV suggests forfeiture of final salvation, which is wide of the mark. From the movement of thought, the judgment is to be conceived of as coming from God in the sense of bearing his approval, even though administered through human channels and in the sphere of human affairs. One may cite the words of Jesus, given in warning to one of his own: "All who draw the sword will die by the sword" (Matt 26:52). Sufficient illustration is provided by the Jewish war of revolt against Rome that was to begin within a decade of the time Paul wrote. This disastrous rebellion led to the sack of Jerusalem and the dispersion of the nation.

The question as to whether rebellion is ever justified (in the light of this passage) cannot profitably be examined till more of the paragraph has been reviewed.

3,4 Here we encounter the most difficult portion of the passage, for the presentation seems to take no account of the possibility that government may be tyrannical and may reward evil and suppress good. A few years after Paul wrote these words, Nero launched a persecution against the church at Rome; multitudes lost their lives, and not because of doing evil. Later on, other emperors would lash out against Christians in several waves of persecution stretching over more than two centuries. However, the empire did not persecute Christians for their good works, and not directly because of their faith, but rather, as Stifler observes, "because of . . . the mistaken notion that the peace and safety of the state were imperiled by the Christians' refusal to honor the gods" (in loc.).

One way to deal with the problem is to assume that Paul is presenting the norm, that is to say, the state as functioning in terms of fulfilling the ideal for government, which is certainly that of punishing evil and rewarding or encouraging good. If this is the correct interpretation, then we can understand why Paul warns against rebellion and makes no allowance for revolutionary activity. The way is then open to justify revolution in cases where rights are denied and liberties taken away, making life intolerable for freedom-loving men and women, since the state has ceased to fulfill its God-appointed function. However, Christians will not as a church lead in revolution, but only as citizens of the commonwealth. At the very least, under circumstances involving a collapse of justice, the Christian community is obliged to voice its criticism of the state's failure, pointing out the deviation from the divinely ordained pattern. Subjection to the state is not to be confused with unthinking, blind, docile conformity.

Another possibility is to introduce the principle of Romans 8:28 whereby God finds ways to bring good out of apparent evil, so that even in the event that the state should turn against the people of God in a way that could rightly be termed evil, he will bring good out of it in the long run. Käsemann remarks, "Sometimes the Lord of the world speaks more audibly out of prison cells and graves than out of the life of churches which congratulate themselves on their concordat with the State" (*New Testament Questions of Today,* p. 215).

The state is presented as "God's servant" to extend commendation to the one who does good and, conversely, to punish the wrongdoer. This certainly implies considerable knowledge on the part of the governing authority as to the nature of right and wrong, a knowledge not dependent on awareness of the teaching of Scripture but granted to men in general as rational creatures (cf. 2:14, 15). While "God's servant" is an honorable title, it contains a reminder that the state is *not* God and that its function is to administer justice for him in areas where it is competent to do so. Even as God's servant in the spiritual realm can err, so the state is not to be thought of as infallible in its decisions. Yet this does not entitle the individual to flout the state's authority when the decision is not to his liking.

The warning to the believer to avoid evil carries with it the admonition that if this warning is neglected, fear will be in order because the authority has the power to use the sword. This can hardly have to do with private misdoing that would rarely if ever come to the attention of those in power, but presumably refers to public acts that would threaten the well-being or security of the state. Consequently, even though traditionally the bearing of the sword is thought to signify the power of punishment, even to death, which the government rightly claims for itself in handling serious crimes, that understanding of the matter is somewhat questionable, because these words are addressed to Christians. Were Christians liable to descend to such things? Interpreters who have assumed that Paul's allusion to the sword refers to the *ius gladii* (the law of the sword) need to consider the new evidence to the effect that at the time of Paul this term had a very restricted application that would not fit our passage. A.N. Sherwin-White states, "For the first two centuries of the Empire the term referred only to the power given to provincial governors who had Roman citizen troops under their command, to enable them to maintain military discipline without being hampered by the provisions of the laws of *provocatio*" (*Roman Society and Roman Law in the New Testament* [Oxford: 1963], p. 10). *Provocatio* denotes right of appeal. So it is probable that Paul is warning believers against becoming involved in activity that could be construed by the Roman government as encouraging revolution or injury to the state. In that case he is not referring to crime in general. To engage in subversive activity would invite speedy retribution, as the word "sword" implies.

5 In bringing this portion of the discussion to a close, Paul advances two reasons why the Christian must be in submission to the state. One is the threat of punishment (the Gr. word is *orgē*, "wrath") if one does not put himself in subjection. This appeal is based on personal advantage, the instinct of self-preservation. To defy the state could mean death. The other reason is more difficult to determine. Pierce understands conscience (*syneidēsis*) to mean here, "the pain a man suffers when he has done wrong" (*Conscience in the New Testament* [London: SCM Press, 1955], p. 71). This is certainly what the word means in most other places, but it is questionable here, because the believer who goes so far as to defy the state could not be described as having a tender conscience; in fact, he has steeled his will and suppressed his conscience. More satisfactory is the statement of Christian Maurer: "*Syneidēsis* is responsible awareness that the ultimate foundations both of one's own being and also of the state are in God. Members of the community are to have neither a higher nor a lower estimation of the state than as a specific servant of God" (TDNT, 7:916). In other words, the Christian, by virtue of divine revelation, can have a clearer understanding of the position of the governing authority than an official of the government is likely to have. Let that knowledge guide him in his attitudes and decisions. This usage of the word "conscience" is found again in 1 Peter 2:19.

6,7 Building on his allusion to conscience, the apostle explains the payment of taxes on this very basis. The clearer the perception of the fact that the governing authority is God's servant, the greater appears the reasonableness of providing support by these payments. The man in authority may be unworthy, but the institution is not, since God wills it. Without financial undergirding, government cannot function. For the third time Paul speaks of rulers as God's servants, but this time he uses a different word, one that means workers for the people, public ministers. But the relationship to God is added in keeping with the emphasis made in v.4. Their work is carried on under God's scrutiny and to fulfill God's will. These public servants give their full time to governing; therefore they have no time to earn a living by other means. This is a reminder of the truth that "the worker deserves his wages" (Luke 10:7).

There is deliberate repetition in the sense that the paying of taxes is assumed (v.6), then enjoined (v.7). But in the repetition Paul adds an important ingredient, found in the word "give" (*apodote*). It is full of meaning, for literally it is "give back." When Jesus was interrogated on the subject of taxes, his questioners used the word "give," but in his reply he used "give back" (Mark 12:14, 17), suggesting that what is paid to the government in the form of taxes presupposes value received or to be received. It is quite possible that Paul, through familiarity with the tradition concerning Jesus' teaching, was aware of the language the Master had used and adopts it for himself. Some of the reluctance to pay taxes to the Romans that was associated with political unrest in Palestine may have infected Jewish believers at Rome, accounting for Paul's specific allusion to the subject. But on this point one cannot be sure, since the allusion comes in rather naturally during a discussion of the believer's relation to the state. Furthermore, the assumption is that the Roman Christians are already paying taxes (v.6).

The various items mentioned in v.7 are all classified as obligations. Since the Christian ethic demands the clearing of whatever one owes another (cf. v.8), no basis is left for debate. The very language that is used supports the imperative form of the communication.

The word for "taxes" means tribute paid to a foreign ruler (it appears in Luke 20:22 in the incident concerning paying tribute to Caesar). "Revenue" pertains to indirect taxation in the form of toll or customs duties. It forms a part of the word for tax gatherer (*telōnēs*, Matt 10:3). "Respect" is defined by Liddon as "the profound veneration due to the highest persons in the state." He characterizes "honor" as "respect due all who hold public offices" (in loc.). It is just possible, however, that Paul intends the former term to refer to God, in which case it should be translated "fear" (cf. 1 Peter 2:17, where it is used in relation to God and in contrast to honor paid the supreme earthly ruler).

Notes

1 This term ἐξουσίαι (*exousiai*, "authorities") has become the center of a keen debate in recent years. Does it denote earthly rulers alone, or is it intended to refer also to invisible powers, as in Ephesians 1:21; 6:12? Oscar Cullmann has advocated the latter position, arguing that the plural form calls for this meaning and that Christ by his death and exaltation has triumphed over these powers of darkness, so that they are subject to him even when they influence earthly rulers (*Christ and Time* [London: SCM Press, 1951], pp. 191–210; *The State in the New Testament* [New York: Scribners, 1956], pp. 95–114). Though we cannot go into the pros and cons of this debate, suffice it to say that victory over the powers of the invisible world does not necessarily mean that Christ has pressed them into his service. If Paul had meant to include them, it seems logical that he would have made this clear by a more specific description. Beyond v.1 he shifts from the plural to the singular, which suggests that the plural is meant to refer to the emperor and subordinate rulers, whereas the singular indicates any official of the government with whom a believer might become involved. It is difficult, furthermore, to believe that Paul could advocate submission to unseen powers even in indirect fashion, since in Ephesians 6:12ff. he calls for the most strenuous resistance to them.

E. *The Comprehensive Obligation of Love*

13:8–10

8Let no debt remain outstanding, except the continuing debt to love one another, for he who loves his fellow man has fulfilled the law. 9The commandments, "Do not commit adultery," "Do not murder," "Do not steal," "Do not covet," and whatever other commandment there may be, are summed up in this one rule: "Love your neighbor as yourself." 10Love does no harm to its neighbor. Therefore love is the fulfillment of the law.

Although Paul has previously put in an urgent call for love (12:9, 10), he now returns to this theme, knowing that he cannot stress too much this essential ingredient of all Christian service. The connection of the present paragraph with the foregoing section is indicated by the use of the word "debt," which has the same root as "owe" in v.7. There is a neat transition to the very highest demand on the child of God. He owes submission and honor to the civil authorities, but he owes all men much more.

8 "Let no debt remain outstanding." This translation has the advantage of avoiding the

danger of giving a wrong impression, such as might be conveyed by "Owe no man anything." If incurring any indebtedness whatever is contrary to God's will, the Lord would not have said, "Do not turn away from the one who wants to borrow from you" (Matt 5:42). On the other hand, to be perpetually in debt is not a good testimony for a believer, and to refuse to make good one's obligations is outrageous. Now comes the exception to the rule. There is a "continuing debt to love one another." One can never say that he has completely discharged it. Ordinarily, "one another" in the Epistles refers to relationship within the Christian community. But such is not the case here, for the expression is explained in terms of one's "fellow man" (literally, "the other person"). Since the passage goes on to refer to one's neighbor, we may be reasonably sure that the sweep of the obligation set forth here is intended to be universal. It is therefore a mistake to accuse the early church of turning its eyes inward upon itself and to a large extent neglecting the outside world. Granted that the usual emphasis is on one's duties to fellow believers, yet the wider reference is not lacking (Gal 6:10; 1 Thess 3:12). We may see something of a parallel in the fact that Jesus prayed for his own rather than for the world (John 17:9), since they were his one hope of reaching the world.

In saying that the one who loves has fulfilled the law, Paul presents a truth that parallels his statement in 8:4 about the righteous requirement of the law being fulfilled in those who live in accordance with the Spirit. The connecting link between these two passages is provided by Galatians 5:22, 23, where first place in the enumeration of the fruitage of the Spirit is given to love and the list is followed by the observation that against such fruit there is no law. So the Spirit produces in the believer a love to which the law can offer no objection, since love fulfills what the law requires, something the law itself cannot do.

9 When one seeks to know what the law requires, he is naturally referred to those precepts that pertain to human relationships, since love for one's neighbor is at issue, not love for God. Consequently, Paul lifts from the second table of the law certain precepts calling for the preservation of the sacredness of the family, the holding of human life inviolable, and the recognition of the right to ownership of property, concluding with the key item that is involved in the other three, viz., the control of one's desires (cf. 7:7).

One might object that these prohibitions belong to the sphere of justice rather than that of love, but this limited view is ruled out by the affirmation that these and other demands of the law are summed up in the positive command, "Love your neighbor as yourself." Incidentally, the original does not use "command" (NIV, "rule") here, but "word" (*logos*). However, this does not diminish the force of the term, since in the OT the Ten Commandments are sometimes called the "ten words" (e.g., Exod 34:28, Heb.).

Once again Paul follows the Lord Jesus in summarizing the horizontal bearing of the law by the use of Leviticus 19:18 (Matt 22:39). Jesus rebuked the narrow nationalistic interpretation of the word "neighbor" in the parable of the good Samaritan. The literal meaning of neighbor is "one who is near." Both the priest and the Levite found their nearness to the stricken man a source of embarrassment (Luke 10:31, 32), but the Samaritan saw in that same circumstance an opportunity to help his fellowman. In the light of human need, the barrier between Jew and Samaritan dissolved. Love provides its own imperative; it feels the compulsion of need.

10 "Love does no harm to its neighbor." This is an understatement, for love does positive good. But the negative form is suitable here, because it is intended to fit in with the prohibitions from the law (v.9). By concluding with the observation that love is the fulfillment of the law, Paul returns to the same thought he began with (v.8).

What, then, is the relationship between love and law? In Christ the two concepts, which seem to have so little in common, come together. To love others with the love that Christ exhibited is his new commandment (John 13:34). And if this love is present, it will make possible the keeping of all his other commandments (John 14:15). Love promotes obedience, and the two together constitute the law of Christ (Gal 6:2).

Notes

9 "You shall not bear false witness" (οὐ ψευδομαρτυρήσεις, *ou pseudomartyrēseis*) occurs in a few MSS, no doubt being added to conform to OT statements of the Decalogue.

F. *The Purifying Power of Hope*

13:11–14

[11]And do this, understanding the present time. The hour has come for you to wake up from your slumber, because our salvation is nearer now than when we first believed. [12]The night is nearly over; the day is almost here. So let us put aside the deeds of darkness and put on the armor of light. [13]Let us behave decently, as in the daytime, not in orgies and drunkenness, not in sexual immorality and debauchery, not in dissension and jealousy. [14]Rather, clothe yourselves with the Lord Jesus Christ, and do not think about how to gratify the desires of your sinful nature.

The passage contains no explicit mention of hope. The same is true of love. But both are surely involved. Even as Paul turns to a new subject, he is loath to let go of the theme of love. So, with a final word about it, "And do this," he is ready to plunge into a delineation of the critical nature of the time that intervenes before the Lord's return. It is as though he is saying, "Show love while you can, and meanwhile keep girded with hope and sobriety for the consummation." If love singles out the Christian because he seeks to identify with others in their need, hope puts a gulf between the Christian and the worldling. He refuses to be conformed to this age that is satisfied with earthly things (cf. Phil 3:18–21). His summons is to self-discipline rather than profligate living.

11 First, Paul sounds a call for alertness. The era between the advents is critical, because the promise of the return of Christ hovers over the believer. He must not be lulled to sleep by indulgence in pleasure or be influenced by the specious word of those who suggest that the Lord delays his coming or may not return at all. Paul does not say how near the day of the Lord's appearing is. As a matter of fact, he does not know. He is content to advance the reminder that "our salvation is nearer now than when we first believed" (v.11). To be sure, salvation is already an achieved fact for the believer (Eph 2:8) and a continuing fact as well (1 Cor 15:2, Gr.; 1 Peter 1:5). But it has also its future and final phase, as Paul here intimates (cf. 1 Peter 1:9). With this third aspect in mind, he says elsewhere that we "await a *Savior*" (Phil 3:20), for only then, at his return, will salvation be complete. The time of the appearing is subordinate to the fact of the appearing. "If primitive Christianity could note, without its faith being shaken thereby, that the 'end' did not come within the calculated times, that is just because the chrono-

logical framework of its hope was a secondary matter" (Leenhardt, in loc.). The believer is not like a child looking for a clock to strike the hour because something is due to happen then. He is content to know that with every passing moment the end is that much closer to realization.

12,13 The line of thought closely resembles the treatment in 1 Thessalonians 5:1–11. Even as darkness is symbolic of evil and sin, the light fittingly depicts those who have passed through the experience of salvation. Paul pictures the Christian as one who anticipates the day by rising early. His night clothes are the works of darkness, the deeds that belong to the old life. The garments to which he transfers, however, are unusual. They are likened to armor as in 1 Thessalonians 5:8. Evidently the purpose is to suggest that to walk through this world as children of light involves a warfare with the powers of darkness (cf. Eph 6:12, 13). Even though the day as an eschatological point has not yet arrived, the believer belongs to the day (1 Thess 5:8), anticipating by the very atmosphere of his transformed life the glory that will then be revealed (2 Cor 3:18; 4:4).

This is the basis for the plea, "Let us behave decently, as in the daytime." The Christian is to live as though that final day had actually arrived, bringing with it the personal presence of Christ. There should be no place, then, for the conduct that characterizes unsaved people, especially in the night seasons. Paul describes this manner of life (all too common in Corinth, where he was writing) in three couplets, the first emphasizing intemperance (which sets the stage for the other two), then sexual misconduct, followed by contention and quarreling. Here we learn the double lesson that one sin leads to another and that the committing of sin does not bring rest to the spirit but rather dissatisfaction that betrays itself by finding fault with others, as though they are responsible. The sinner tries hard to find a scapegoat.

14 In conclusion, the apostle returns to his figure of putting on clothing (cf. v.12), but now the garment is personalized. He urges his readers to put on the Lord Jesus Christ. This amounts to appropriation—the deliberate, conscious acceptance of the lordship of the Master—so that all is under his control—motives, desires, and deeds. A slight difficulty meets us at this point, since believers have already put on Christ, according to Galatians 3:27, at conversion and baptism. But there is always room for decisive renewal, for fresh advance. To be clothed with Christ should mean that when the believer comes under scrutiny from others, he enables them to see the Savior.

If, however, this putting on of Christ is done in a spirit of complacency, as though a life of godliness and uprightness will automatically follow, disappointment will result. The redeemed person must be attuned to the Savior. He must exercise ceaseless vigilance lest the flesh prevail. He must not give thought to how the desires of the old nature can be satisfied. Though the language differs from the teaching in chapter 6, the message is the same. If union with Christ is to be experientially successful, it must be accompanied by a constant reckoning of oneself as dead to sin and alive to God and his holy will.

G. *Questions of Conscience Wherein Christians Differ* (14:1–15:13)

It is uncertain to what extent Paul possessed definite information about the internal affairs of the Roman church. Consequently, it is difficult to know whether his approach to the problem of the "weak" and the "strong" is dictated by awareness of the precise nature of the problem in Rome or whether he is writing out of his own experience with other churches, especially the Corinthian congregation (1 Cor 8:1–11:1). His treatment in Romans is briefer and couched in more general terms, though there are obvious similarities, such as the danger that by his conduct the strong will cause the weak to stumble or fall, and the corresponding danger that the weak will sit in judgment on the strong. The differences are numerous: there is no mention in Romans of idols or food offered to idols; the word "conscience" does not appear; the strong are not described as those who have knowledge. On the other hand, we read in Romans of vegetarians and of those who insist on observing a certain day in contrast to others who look on all days as being alike. Neither of these features appears in 1 Corinthians.

Possibly the weaker brethren at Rome should be identified with the Jewish element in the church, because believing Jews might easily carry over their avoidance of certain foods from their former observance of the dietary laws of the OT. It is possible that information had reached Paul to the effect that with the return of Jewish Christians to Rome after the death of Emperor Claudius in A.D. 54 tension had developed in the church with the Gentile element that had been able for several years to enjoy without challenge its freedom in the matter of foods.

Judging from his discussion in 1 Corinthians, Paul would place himself among the strong. Yet he was careful not to become an occasion of stumbling to a weaker brother. He has words of warning and words of encouragement to both groups. His primary concern is to promote a spirit of unity in the church (15:5).

1. *Brethren must refrain from judging one another.*

14:1–12

1Accept him whose faith is weak, without passing judgment on disputable matters.
2One man's faith allows him to eat everything, but another man, whose faith
is weak, eats only vegetables. 3The man who eats everything must not look down
on him who does not, and the man who does not eat everything must not condemn
the man who does, for God has accepted him. 4Who are you to judge someone
else's servant? To his own master he stands or falls. And he will stand, for the Lord
is able to make him stand.

5One man considers one day more sacred than another; another man considers
every day alike. Each one should be fully convinced in his own mind. 6He who
regards one day as special, does so to the Lord. He who eats meat, eats to the
Lord, for he gives thanks to God; and he who abstains, does so to the Lord, and
gives thanks to God. 7For none of us lives to himself alone and none of us dies
to himself alone. If we live, we live to the Lord; and if we die, we die to the Lord.
So, whether we live or die, we belong to the Lord.

9For this very reason, Christ died and returned to life so that he might be the
Lord of both the dead and the living. 10You, then, why do you judge your brother?
Or why do you look down on your brother? For we will all stand before God's
judgment seat. 11It is written:

> " 'As I live,' says the Lord,
> 'Every knee will bow before me;
> every tongue will confess to God.' "

12So then, each of us will give an account of himself to God.

1–4 "Eat" is the recurring word that characterizes this section. Diet practices differ and the differences are bound to be observed; they become a topic of conversation and a basis of disagreement. Paul's designation for the overscrupulous believer is "weak in faith," meaning that this man's faith is not strong enough to enable him to perceive the full liberty he has in Christ to partake. He is not troubled by questions of doctrine but is plagued by doubt as to whether it is right for him to eat some foods (cf. v.23). The injunction to those who do not share this weakness is to "accept him" (v.1). That this word (*proslambanō*) is capable of conveying the sense of warm wholeheartedness is shown by its use in Acts 18:26; 28:2. Such acceptance is impossible as long as there is any disposition to pass judgment on disputable matters. "The weak man should be accepted as the Christian brother he claims to be. One should not judge the thoughts which underlie his conduct. This is for God alone to do" (F. Büchsel in TDNT, 3:950). The weak brother must not be made to feel inferior or unwanted or "odd."

The specialized use of "faith" becomes clearer when Paul gives it a definite context (v.2). One man, obviously strong in faith, feels he can "eat everything" ("anything" would be a more cautious translation). Paul would concur that the believer has this freedom (1 Tim 4:3, 4). Another, weak in his faith, confines his diet to vegetables. No reason is advanced for this self-limitation. It could have been due to ascetic zeal. Some modern vegetarians believe they are healthier for not eating meat. Others have scruples about eating anything that has been consciously alive (perhaps unaware of research tending to establish that plants also have sensation). But the motive is a personal matter, and for that reason Paul does not make it an issue. He is solely concerned with specific practice and the reaction of the strong to this practice. The omnivorous man is apt to "look down" on the weak brother, an attitude that is not conducive to full fellowship. The weak brother may retaliate by condemning the one who has no inhibitions about his food. If so, the latter needs to reflect on the fact that God has accepted (same word as in v.1) this man (v.3). And why should he himself not do so?

To enforce the rebuke, Paul cites the relationship of a servant to his master (v.4). In ordinary life, it would be unseemly for anyone to attempt to interfere in a case involving the servant's actions. One might go so far as to inform the master of what the servant was doing, but even that could be regarded as an unjustified intrusion. Perhaps the analogy might be pushed to this extent: though reporting to the master might be inappropriate, one might conceivably pray to the Master in heaven about the conduct of the strong brother, asking the Master to deal with the case, while refraining from criticism directed at the brother himself. But the closing statement discourages such a line of thought. Paul affirms that the strong does not necessarily stand on slippery ground when enjoying his freedom in Christ. This assurance is grounded not so much on the discretion of the strong as on the power of Christ to sustain him. "The Apostle . . . is confident that *Christian* liberty, through the grace and power of Christ, will prove a triumphant moral success" (Denney, in loc.).

5–8 Here the recurring phrase is "to the Lord," indicating that whether one be thought of as "weak" or "strong," the important thing is that he conduct his life in the consciousness of God's presence, because God's approval is more significant than the approval or disapproval of fellow Christians. Eating is still in view, but alongside it Paul places a fresh topic—the holding of certain days as sacred.

5,6 Whether the question of regarding one day as more sacred than another refers to Sabbath observance or to special days for feasting or fasting is not easily determined. Since the early church in Jerusalem almost certainly observed the Sabbath (as well as the first day of the week) because of its Jewish constituency and the danger of giving offense to non-Christian Jews, and since the Roman church presumably had a good-sized minority of Jews, it is not impossible that Paul has the Sabbath in mind. Perhaps because the observance of the day was not being pressed upon the Gentile believers in the church in the way that Jewish sects challenged such believers elsewhere (Col 2:16), it was not necessary to identify the day explicitly. Even so, if the day of worship is in view, it is strange that any believer could be said to consider "every day alike." The close contextual association with eating suggests that Paul has in mind a special day set apart for observance as a time for feasting or as a time for fasting. The important thing is that one should "be fully convinced in his own mind" as to the rightfulness of his observance. More important still is the certitude of the individual involved that his motivation is his desire to honor the Lord in what he is doing. It is possible for the observant and the nonobservant to do this, as illustrated by the giving of thanks at mealtime (cf. 1 Tim 4:5). The one partaking can give thanks for the meat before him, while the one abstaining from meat can give God thanks for his vegetables. The latter should be able to do this without resentment toward his brother who enjoys richer fare.

7,8 Here we should not understand Paul as expressing a maxim applicable to all people, as though he intended to suggest that everyone has some sort of influence with others, even though in some instances it is more limited than in others. He is speaking of believers, as v.8 shows. The reason the Christian does not live to himself is that he lives to the Lord. This attachment, which is also an obligation, does not cease with death but carries forward into the next life (Phil 1:20). Paul has already affirmed that death cannot separate Christians from the love of God in Christ (8:38, 39; cf. 2 Cor 5:9). Their death is not merely a transfer from the arena of struggle to the realm of rest. Rather, it is to be viewed as an enlarged opportunity to show forth the praises of the Lord. Relationship to him is the key to life on either side of the veil.

9–12 Here Paul makes the point that both groups will have to answer to God in the coming day. So it is premature to pass judgment on one another (cf. 1 Cor 4:5), seeing that an infallible judge will assume that responsibility.

9 The Savior gave his life, laying it down in obedience to the will of God, and thereby purchased the church by his blood (Acts 20:28). But only after his resurrection could he assume the active headship of his people. Though the title "Lord" was appropriate to him in the days of his flesh (e.g., Mark 5:19), the title came into more frequent and more meaningful use after the resurrection, since that event established his claim to deity, his claim to Saviorhood, and his claim to universal dominion. His triumph included victory over death, so that even though his people may be given over to death's power temporarily, they have not ceased to be his, as the future bodily resurrection of Christians will demonstrate. He is in fact the Lord of both the dead and the living. The order in which these two divisions appear reflects the order in the previous statement about Christ in his death and return to life.

10–12 Against this background the apostle returns to direct address, first to the weak brother, then to the strong. The former is prone to judge, the latter to depreciate or even scorn. Both attitudes are virtually the same, because they involve improper judgment. The true judge is God, and his time for judging is coming, making man's judgment not only premature but also a usurpation of God's role. Notable is the ease with which Paul passes from the Lord (v.9) to God (v.10) in the same milieu of thought. The two are inseparable in their operations. In fact, God's judgment seat (v.10) is to be identified with the judgment seat of Christ (2 Cor 5:10). We see the same phenomenon in the quotation introduced here (v.11), which is a combination of Isaiah 49:18 and 45:23. In Philippians 2:10, 11 the same passages from Isaiah are utilized and the relationship between God and the Lord is made clear. In the summary of the situation (v.12) the note of judgment is retained, but the emphasis falls on the fact that each person must give account of *himself* (not of his brother) to God (cf. Gal 6:5). The same word for "account" (*logos*) occurs in Hebrews 4:13.

Notes

4 Some MSS have "God" instead of "the Lord." This change apparently crept into the text as copyists carried the mention of "God" over from v.3.

10 At the end of the verse "of Christ" occurs instead of "of God" in many witnesses, some of them early, apparently because of the copyists' desire to conform the statement to 2 Cor 5:10.

2. *Brethren must avoid offending one another*

14:13–23

13Therefore, let us stop passing judgment on one another. Instead, make up
your mind not to put any stumbling block or obstacle in your brother's way. 14As
one who is in the Lord Jesus, I am fully convinced that no food is unclean in itself.
But if anyone regards something as unclean, then for him it is unclean. 15If your
brother is distressed because of what you eat, you are no longer acting in love.
Do not by your eating destroy your brother for whom Christ died. 16Do not allow
what you consider good to be spoken of as evil. 17For the kingdom of God is not
a matter of eating and drinking, but of righteousness, peace and joy in the Holy
Spirit, 18because anyone who serves Christ in this way is pleasing to God and
approved by men.

19Let us therefore make every effort to do what leads to peace and to mutual
edification. 20Do not destroy the work of God for the sake of food. All food is clean,
but it is wrong for a man to eat anything that causes someone else to stumble.
21It is better not to eat meat or drink wine or to do anything else that will cause
your brother to fall.

22So whatever you believe about these things keep between yourself and God.
Blessed is the man who does not condemn himself by what he approves. 23But
the man who has doubts is condemned if he eats, because his eating is not from
faith; and everything that does not come from faith is sin.

In this section, the appeal for the most part is directed to the strong brother, who is warned that his example may have a disastrous effect on the one who is weak by leading him to do what his spiritual development provides no ground of approval for. The discussion proceeds along the same line as before—what a Christian should include in his diet.

13–18 The opening statement gives the gist of what has been already said. Both parties have been guilty of passing judgment on one another. Then by a neat use of language, Paul employs the same verb "judge" (*krinō*) in a somewhat different sense ("make up your mind"). He is calling for a determination to adopt a course of action that will not hurt another brother, a decision once for all to avoid whatever might impede his progress in the faith or cause him to fall. Though Paul does not single out the strong brother, it appears that he must have him in mind in this admonition against putting a stumbling block in a brother's way. A stumbling block (*proskomma*) is literally something against which one may strike his foot, causing him to stumble or even fall. The second term (*skandalon*, rendered "obstacle" here) presents a different picture, that of a trap designed to ensnare a victim. It is used of something that constitutes a temptation to sin. Jesus applied this word to Peter when that disciple sought to deter him from going to the cross (Matt 16:23). In v.13 it could be taken as a stern warning against deliberately enticing a brother to do what for him would be sinful (cf. v.23). Even if such an act were motivated by the desire to get the brother out of the "weak" category, it would still be wrong.

Paul himself is convinced of something that the weak brother does not share, viz., that "no food is unclean in itself" (v.14). Elsewhere he affirms in a similar context that everything God created is good (1 Tim 4:4), an observation that rests on the record of creation (Gen 1:31). But in the passage before us the apostle seems to have reference to some utterance made by our Lord during his earthly ministry (note the human name "Jesus" here). We find it in Mark 7:15–23, where the Master declares that one is not rendered unclean by what goes into him but rather by what comes out of him, from his inner life. Mark adds the comment that in this pronouncement Jesus declared all foods "clean." But not everyone has been enlightened on this issue, and if one is convinced in his heart that some foods are unclean (e.g., in terms of the Levitical food laws), for him such foods remain unclean. Until he is convinced otherwise, it would violate his conscience to partake of them. Even the apostle Peter, who had been with Jesus and had heard his teaching, was in bondage on this point until some time after Pentecost (Acts 10:9–15).

Moreover, even if the strong brother does not try to convince the weak to change his habits, his own practice, since it is known, can be a stumbling block to the other, causing distress of soul. This distress may be viewed as reaction to the callous indifference of the strong brother. But it may contain a hint of something tragic, a sorrow of heart induced by following the example of the strong, only to find the conscience ablaze with rebuke and the whole life out of fellowship with the Lord. In such a situation, love is not operating.

Paul's basis of approach to the strong brother has changed from granting him his position on the grounds of his liberty to eat. Now the appeal is not to liberty but to love, which may call for a measure of sacrifice. If such sacrifice is refused, then the strong brother must face the responsibility for bringing spiritual ruin on the weak. Moule (in loc.) admirably sums up the situation. "The Lord may counteract your action and save your injured brother from himself—and you. But your action is, none the less, calculated for his perdition. And all the while this soul, for which, in comparison with your dull and narrow 'liberty,' you care so little, was so much cared for by the Lord that He died for it." A selfish insistence on liberty may tear down and destroy, but love, when it is exercised, will invariably build up (1 Cor 8:1).

"Do not allow what you consider good to be spoken of as evil" (v.16). Some understand this in terms of possible slander by the unsaved who find occasion to deride the Christian community for its squabbling over such minor matters. But the thought does not necessarily range beyond the circle of the redeemed. The good is naturally understood as the liberty to eat, since all foods are regarded as clean. This liberty, however, if resented because it has been flaunted in the face of the weak, can be regarded as an evil thing on account of its unloving misuse.

Then, with pastoral insight, Paul lifts the entire discussion to a higher level than mere eating and drinking (v.17). His readers, all of them, are the loyal subjects of Christ in the kingdom of God. In that sphere the real concerns are not externals such as diet but the spiritual realities motivating life and shaping conduct. Surely the strong will agree that if their insistence on Christian liberty endangers the spiritual development of the church as a whole, they should be willing to forgo that liberty. In this context "righteousness" (*dikaiosynē*) is not justification but the right conduct to which the believer is called in obedience to the will of God (cf. 6:13, 16, 18). This conclusion is supported by the fact that joy is an experiential term. Peace is sometimes peace *with* God (5:1), at other times the peace *of* God (Phil 4:7). The second meaning is appropriate to this passage (cf. v.19). Mention of the Spirit is understandable, because joy and peace are included in the fruit he produces in the believer's life. The list in Galatians 5:22 is not intended to be complete (see Gal 5:23), so we may legitimately claim practical righteousness as effected by his indwelling. Further confirmation of this interpretation is furnished by v.18, where Paul links these matters to the believer's service of Christ. The manifestation of the fruit of the Spirit is acceptable not only to God who provides it, but also to men who see it in operation and experience its blessings.

19–21 The entire church is urged to pursue peace (harmony between the two groups is the immediate application), which alone can provide the atmosphere in which "mutual edification" can take place. It will be recalled that "edification" (*oikodomē*) was Paul's key word in dealing with the problems created by the manifestation of spiritual gifts in the Corinthian situation (1 Cor 14:5, 12, 26). Mutual edification implies that the strong, despite their tendency to look down on the weak, may actually learn something from them. It may be that they will come to appreciate loyalty to a tender conscience and begin to search their own hearts to discover that they have cared more about maintaining their position than about loving the weaker brethren. Through the fresh manifestation of love by the strong the weak will be lifted in spirit and renewed in faith and life.

Having spoken of the edification (literally, the building up) of the saints, Paul reinforces his point by warning of the reverse process (v.20). To "destroy" the work of God is to tear it down, so that much time and painful labor will be required to restore the edifice to the point where it can function again as the instrument of the divine purpose. It is disheartening to realize that such colossal loss could be occasioned by a difference of opinion over food! Since all food can properly be regarded as clean, it is not wrong in itself for one to eat whatever he finds healthful or desirable. The wrong lies in his causing someone to stumble by his eating.

The "better" (literally, noble or praiseworthy) course is to do without meat under the circumstances and to refrain from drinking wine, if partaking would be a stumbling block to anyone. Paul extends the principle to include *anything* that might have this effect. For the first time in the discussion wine is mentioned, suggesting that a measure of asceticism may be in view here. The apostle may have anticipated this item by referring to drinking in v.17. In view of his strong stand taken in connection with a similar question involving the Corinthians (1 Cor 8:13), his counsel here (v.21) is not something new. He is simply commending to others what has for some time been the rule for himself.

22,23 Although the language of the opening statement of this section is general (cf. vv.1, 2), and could therefore apply to both groups, in all probability Paul is directing his counsel chiefly to the strong, since it is the strong person who is warned to act on his confidence privately, where God is his witness. The natural explanation is that the exercise of his freedom in public would grieve the weak brother and raise a barrier between them, and this is the very thing to be avoided if at all possible. The strong is "blessed" (*makarios*, which can mean "fortunate" or "happy") in this private enjoyment of his freedom, because he is free from doubt and because no one who might be scandalized is looking on. In this way he is not faced with the danger confronting the weak brother—viz., that of condemning himself by approving something his conscience will not endorse. It should be granted that the language of v.22b can with equal propriety refer to the weak brother. But since the next verse is so definitely applicable to the weak brother, Paul is probably following his practice of having a word of encouragement or admonition for each party. This seems to be confirmed by the way he introduces his remark about the weak brother in v.23: "But. . . ."

It is important to understand "faith" here (v.23) in the same way it was used at the beginning of the chapter. Again, there is no question of saving faith, but only of confidence that one is free to make use of what God has created and set apart for man's good. In keeping with this, "condemned" does not refer to a future action of God excluding one from salvation, but, as the tense indicates, means that the person stands condemned by his own act as being wrong. The case of Peter comes to mind. In his actions at Antioch, "he stood condemned" (Gal 2:11 RSV). When Paul pointed out his fault, Peter had no defense. He was in the wrong and he knew it. To act in contradiction to conscience or to the known will of God inevitably brings this result. Christian experience shows that when a believer refuses to move in a certain direction because he lacks confidence that the step is in line with the will of God, he receives strength by the refusal so that it is much easier on other occasions to move on the basis of faith, even when to do so may be difficult because of possible misunderstanding by fellow Christians.

Notes

19 Though the indicative διώκομεν (*diōkomen*, "we pursued") has strong support (א A B, et al.), the subjunctive διώκωμεν (*diōkōmen*, "let us pursue"), expressing exhortation, seems to be the better choice here.

22 An alternate reading calls for the tr. "Do you have faith?" at the beginning of the sentence. Either reading makes tolerably good sense.

23 See note on 16:25–27, p. 171.

3. *The unity of the strong and the weak in Christ*

15:1–13

1We who are strong ought to bear with the failings of the weak, and not to please
ourselves. 2Each of us should please his neighbor for his good, to build him up.
3For even Christ did not please himself but, as it is written: "The insults of those
who insult you have fallen on me." 4For everything that was written in the past was
written to teach us, so that through endurance and the encouragement of the
Scriptures we might have hope.

5May the God who gives endurance and encouragement give you a spirit of unity
among yourselves as you follow Christ Jesus, 6so that with one heart and mouth
you may glorify the God and Father of our Lord Jesus Christ.

[7]Accept one another, then, just as Christ accepted you, in order to bring praise
to God. [8]For I tell you that Christ has become a servant of the Jews on behalf of
God's truth, to confirm the promises made to the patriarchs [9]so that the Gentiles
may glorify God for his mercy, as it is written:

"For this reason I will praise you
among the Gentiles;
I will sing hymns to your name."

[10]Again, it says,

"Rejoice, O Gentiles, with his people."

[11]And again,

"Praise the Lord, all you Gentiles,
and sing praises to him, all you peoples."

[12]And again, Isaiah says,

"The root of Jesse will spring up,
one who will arise to rule over the nations;
the Gentiles will hope in him."

[13]May the God of hope fill you with great joy and peace as you trust in him, so
that you may overflow with hope by the power of the Holy Spirit.

Two fairly distinct motifs run through this portion. In vv.1–6 the appeal to both the strong and the weak is grounded on the example of Christ who did not please himself but gladly accepted whatever self-denial his mission required. In vv.7–13 Christ is again the key. He has graciously accepted both Jew and Gentile in accordance with the purpose of God. To refuse to accept each other is to resist that purpose in its practical outworking.

1–4 As Paul draws the discussion to a close, he openly aligns himself with the strong. They are the ones who hold the key to the solution of the problem. If they are interested simply in maintaining their own position, the gulf between the two groups will not be narrowed and the weak will continue to be critical and resentful. But if the strong will reach out the hand of fellowship and support, this will be a bridge. So to the strong belongs the responsibility of taking the initiative. "Ought" is not to be watered down as though it means the same thing as "should." It speaks not of something recommended but of obligation. The word "bear" was used earlier when the apostle enjoined the Galatian believers to "carry [bear] each other's burdens, and in this way . . . fulfill the law of Christ" (Gal 6:2). Let the strong, then, bear the burden of the scrupulousness of the weaker brethren. But if they do this in a spirit of mere resignation or with the notion that this condescension marks them as superior Christians, it will fail. When the strong bear with the weak, they must do it in love—the key to fulfilling the law of Christ. The temptation to be resisted by the strong is the inclination to please themselves, to minister to self-interest. This is the very antithesis of love. For example, were a strong brother to indulge his liberty openly in the presence of a weak brother, this would be labeled self-pleasing, for it would do nothing for the other but grieve or irritate him.

2 Indeed, the refusal to live a life of self-pleasing should characterize every believer, whether strong or weak, and should extend beyond the narrow circle of like-minded people to all with whom we come in contact—in short, to our neighbor, whoever he is.

As Hodge remarks, what is called for here is not "a weak compliance with the wishes of others" (in loc.). It is rather a determined adjustment to whatever will contribute to the spiritual good of the other person. The present injunction is akin to Paul's own principle of making himself all things to all men in order to win as many as possible to the Lord (1 Cor 9:19–23). There is no conflict between such a principle and his refusal to "please men" (Gal 1:19), since in the latter context he is merely setting himself against any trimming of the gospel message designed to avoid giving offense to those resisting revealed truth. The goal to be achieved here is the good of the other person, his edification (cf. 14:19). This leaves no room for anything like mere ingratiation.

3 For the first time in this letter Paul holds Christ before his readers as an example. Christ was faced with the same problem that continues to confront his followers. Should they please themselves, go their own way, speak what people want to hear; or should they resolve to be guided by their commitment to do the will of God? Christ's own affirmation is recorded for us: "I always do what pleases him" (John 8:29). The cost was heavy. "The insults of those who insult you [God] have fallen on me" (quoting Ps 69:9). Even in Israel, through the years, God's servants had suffered reproach and insult when they attempted to warn their countrymen that their sin and rebellion were inviting the judgment of God. The first half of Psalm 69:9 is quoted in John 2:17 in connection with the cleansing of the temple—"Zeal for your house will consume me." This is generally interpreted to mean that the opposition stirred up by Jesus would lead eventually to his death. To espouse the cause of God fervently is to arouse the passions of sinful men. See John 15:25, quoted from the same psalm (69:4), where Jesus acknowledged that human hatred had dogged his steps, but unjustly. Our Lord did not on this account discontinue his faithful ministrations that were designed to help those about him. Paul would have his readers realize that similarly they are to seek the good of others even if they are misunderstood or maligned in doing so.

4 Having citated Psalm 69, a portion evidently regarded in the early church as messianic, the apostle is led to refer to the Scriptures in a more general way as useful for the instruction of NT believers—in fact, as deliberately planned for their edification. The very phenomenon of quoting from the OT speaks loudly of the dependence of the church on the course of redemption history reflected there. Things both new and old enter into Christian faith. The example of Christ was bound to influence the church to revere and use the OT, and this was made easier because at the beginning its constituency was largely Jewish-Christian. As for the Gentiles, in many cases at least, they had become familiar with the OT in the synagogue (Acts 13:44–48) before hearing the gospel and putting their trust in the Lord Jesus. The use of the Scriptures promotes "endurance" and supplies "encouragement." Both may be learned by precept and example from these records of the past. These two elements are intimately connected with hope, for the endurance is worthwhile if it takes place on a course that leads to a glorious future, and the encouragement provides exactly that assurance.

5,6 Endurance and encouragement are ultimately God's gift, though they are mediated through the Scriptures. They tend, however, to be individually appropriated, some realizing them to a greater degree than others. So Paul prays for a spirit of unity (like-mindedness) that will minimize individual differences as all fix their attention on Christ as the pattern for their own lives (cf. v.3). This does not mean that believers are intended to see eye-to-eye on everything, but that the more Christ fills the spiritual vision, the greater will be the cohesiveness of the church. The centripetal magnetism of the Lord can effectively counter the centrifugal force of individual judgment and opinion. Though this unity will help the church in its witness to the world, Paul is more interested here in its effect on the worship of the people of God—"with one heart and mouth" glorifying the God and Father whom Jesus so beautifully glorified on earth.

7 As he moves forward to the conclusion of his treatment of the strong and the weak, Paul, good teacher that he was, pauses to summarize what he has already stated. "Accept one another" picks up the emphasis of 14:1, where the same verb occurs, but here the charge is directed to both groups rather than to the strong alone. Then, in line with 15:3, 5, he brings in the example of Christ once more and states that bringing praise to God is the grand objective, in agreement with v.6. It is not fully clear whether this final phrase relates grammatically to the command to receive one another or to the fact that Christ has received them. As far as the sense of the passage is concerned, it could apply to both.

8–12 From the three elements that constitute v.7 Paul now singles out the second—Christ's acceptance of all who make up his body—and proceeds to enlarge on it, first in relation to the Jewish Christians (v.8) and then in relation to the Gentiles (vv.9–12). The central thrust is to show that in these two directions Christ has fulfilled the anticipations of the OT.

"Christ has become a servant of the Jews" (v.8). This simple, brief statement epitomizes the earthly ministry of our Lord, who announced that he was sent only to the lost sheep of the house of Israel (Matt 15:24) and restricted the activity of his disciples during those days to their own nation (Matt 10:5, 6). The word "servant" reminds us to what lengths Jesus was prepared to go to minister to the needs of Israel (cf. Mark 10:45). This dedicated limitation of ministry to his own people was in the interest of "God's truth" in the sense of God's fidelity to his word, more specifically his promises made to the patriarchs (cf. 9:4, 5). God pledged himself to provide for Abraham a progeny that would culminate in Christ himself as the Redeemer (Gal 3:16). This was a salutary reminder to the Gentile element in the church (the strong) that God had given priority to Israel, lest Jewish believers should be slighted or depreciated. As noted earlier, a similar motive underlies Paul's treatment of the Jewish question in chapters 9 to 11.

Once that point has been made, however, Paul brings out the truth that all the time God's purpose was not exclusively directed toward the nation of Israel (cf. Gen 12:3), since ever and again in the Scriptures the Gentiles are viewed as embraced in the saving mercy of God and responding to it. Consequently, the Jewish believer of Paul's time should not think it contradictory for God to lavish his grace on the nations through the gospel.

There is an element of progression in the marshaling of quotations from the OT. The first (from Ps 18:49) pictures David as rejoicing in God for his triumphs in the midst of the nations that have become subject to him. In the second (from Deut 32:43), the position of the Gentiles is elevated to participation with Israel in the praise of the Lord (according to LXX). In the third and fourth quotations the Gentiles, no longer pictured in relation to Israel, are seen in their own right, whether as praising the Lord (Ps 117:1) or as hoping in him whom God has raised up to rule over the nations (Isa 11:10).

13 As he had done at the close of the first section in this chapter (v.5), Paul again expresses his desire that God will meet the needs of his readers. Although eschatology in a formal, structured sense has little place in Romans, its subjective counterpart, hope, is mentioned more often than in any other of his letters, especially in this portion (vv.4, 12, 13).

The expression "the God of hope" (v.13) means the God who inspires hope and imparts it to his children. He can be counted on to fulfill what yet remains to be accomplished for them (5:2; 13:11). Likewise, in the more immediate future and with the help of Paul's letter, they can confidently look to God for the working out of their problems, including the one Paul has been discussing. Hope does not operate apart from trust; in fact, it is the forward-looking aspect of faith (Gal 5:5; 1 Peter 1:21). Paul in his pastoral zeal is not satisfied with anything less than a rich, abounding experience of hope, even as he expects from them an overflowing of love (Phil 1:9; 1 Thess 3:12; 4:10), of pleasing God (1 Thess 4:1), and of thanksgiving (Col 2:7). The reason for this is that the God who is supplicated here has so wonderfully abounded in the exercise of his grace (5:15) that he can be expected to enable his people to increase in the manifestation of Christian graces, especially as this is insured "by the power of the Holy Spirit" who indwells and fills the inner life.

VIII. Conclusion (15:14–16:27)

A. *Paul's Past Labors, Present Program, and Future Plans*

15:14–33

14I myself am convinced, my brothers, that you yourselves are full of goodness, complete in knowledge and competent to instruct one another. 15I have written you quite boldly on some points, as if to remind you of them again, because of the grace God gave me 16to be a minister of Christ Jesus to the Gentiles with the priestly duty of proclaiming the gospel of God, so that the Gentiles might become an offering acceptable to God, sanctified by the Holy Spirit.

17Therefore, I glory in Christ Jesus in my service to God. 18I will not venture to speak of anything except what Christ has accomplished through me in leading the Gentiles to obey God by what I have said and done—19by the power of signs and miracles, through the power of the Spirit. So from Jerusalem all the way around to Illyricum, I have fully proclaimed the gospel of Christ. 20It has always been my ambition to preach the gospel where Christ was not known, so that I would not be building on someone else's foundation. 21Rather, as it is written:

> "Those who were not told about him will see,
> and those who have not heard will understand."

22This is why I have often been hindered from coming to you.

23But now that there is no more place for me to work in these regions, and since I have been longing for many years to see you 24I plan to do so when I go to Spain. I hope to visit you while passing through and to have you assist me on my journey there, after I have enjoyed your company for a while. 25Now, however, I am on my way to Jerusalem in the service of the saints there. 26For Macedonia and Achaia were pleased to make a contribution for the poor among the saints in Jerusalem. 27They were pleased to do it, and indeed they owe it to them. For if the Gentiles have shared in the Jews' spiritual blessings, they owe it to the Jews to share with them their material blessings. 28So after I have completed this task and have made sure that they have received this fruit, I will go to Spain and visit you on the way. 29I know that when I come to you, I will come in the full measure of the blessing of Christ.

30I urge you, brothers, by our Lord Jesus Christ and by the love of the Spirit, to join me in my struggle by praying to God for me. 31Pray that I may be rescued from the unbelievers in Judea and that my service in Jerusalem may be acceptable to the saints there. 32Then by God's will I can come to you with joy and together with you be refreshed. 33The God of peace be with you all. Amen.

The remainder of this chapter can be regarded as complementary to the introduction of the letter, since there is a similar prominence of personal matters Paul feels will be of interest to the believers at Rome. In both portions, however, his own affairs are invariably regarded as important only as they relate to the gospel of Christ of which he is such a committed minister.

14–16 Paul now reflects on the character of his readers and what he can expect his letter to accomplish for them. If his assessment of them seems unexpectedly favorable after his admonition in the last chapter and a half, we need not conclude that he was beginning to chide himself for being too hard on the brethren. Study of his Epistles reveals that he had a sense of fairness that led him to strike a just balance between pointing out deficiencies and finding things he could honestly commend. Concerning the church at Rome, since he has acknowledged their strong faith (1:8), it is now in order to add some other things he has picked up from various sources of information, including people mentioned in the closing chapter. In reference to v.14, George Edmundson writes, "Such a declaration implies a conviction based upon trustworthy evidence, otherwise his readers would be the first to perceive that here was only high-flown language covering an empty compliment" (*The Church in Rome in the First Century* [London: Longman, Green and Co., 1913], p. 15).

The first item is goodness. Having just written of the Holy Spirit, Paul undoubtedly has in mind the goodness that is the fruit of the Spirit (Gal 5:22). So it is not a native disposition but the moral excellence wrought into the texture of life by the Spirit's indwelling. He may give it prominence as the quality needed to carry out the recommendations directed to both groups in the previous discussion. Desire to do the right thing by another is essential, but it must be coupled with knowledge of what is rightly expected of the believer. Paul goes so far as to call his readers "complete" in this area and therefore "competent to instruct one another" (v.14). Such language shows his confidence that the Roman church, which had been in existence for at least a decade, had been well taught (cf. 6:17). At the same time this relative maturity did not make his contribution superfluous, because it served to confirm what they knew, underscoring it with apostolic authority, making them the more capable of instructing each other. This word "instruct" (*noutheteō*) reflects more than the imparting of information. "Inculcate" comes close to expressing its force (cf. Col 3:16, "counsel," and 1 Thess 5:14, "warn"). In the absence of resident pastors, brethren were the more under obligation to exercise such a ministry among themselves. Paul's use of the term at this point reflects the admonition in the preceding chapter.

Though he was not the founder of the Roman church, Paul has been outspoken, and he proceeds to explain this lest he be thought immodest or tyrannical or simply tedious in going over things he now admits they were already aware of. He is simply doing his duty, fulfilling the commission God in his grace has granted him as a minister of Christ (vv.15, 16). Furthermore, his boldness has been in evidence "on some points" (v.15) but has not pervaded the letter as a whole. Since in this connection he emphasizes his call to go to the Gentiles, one may assume that most of his readers were Gentiles (cf. 1:13) and would be especially interested in this allusion. Redeemed Gentiles are his special offering, a sacrifice acceptable to God (cf. Isa 66:18–20). His own function as a priest pertains directly to the proclamation of the gospel and the winning of Gentiles to Christ.

It remains for them to make their own personal commitment to God (12:1). He is not claiming, of course, that he has won his readers to Christ, but is speaking generally. Directly, he will refer to his labors in the East that have involved precisely this sort of ministry. Before doing this, he pauses to note that the acceptability of Gentiles to God comes not only from their reception of the gospel of Christ but also from the ministry of the Holy Spirit that sets them apart to God as the people of his possession (cf. 1 Cor 6:11). This initial sanctification makes possible the progressive spiritual development that spans the two great foci of justification and final redemption (1 Cor 1:30). This setting apart by the Spirit is a natural consequence of the new birth by the Spirit and is closely connected with it.

17–22 Paul refuses to boast in his ministry to the Gentiles. He restricts his glorying to Christ Jesus (cf. Gal 6:13, 14), the one he serves as a minister (cf. v.16). This relationship means not only that the glory goes to the Savior, but also that as the minister of Christ Paul must depend on him for everything that is accomplished in connection with his mission. Paul is only the instrument by which God brings Gentiles to obey him in faith and life (cf. 1:5). Christ is the one ultimately responsible as he continues to work through his servant (cf. Acts 1:1). The ministry has consisted both of word and deed ("what I have said and done," v.18). As far as the ministry of the word is concerned, it is sufficient at this stage in the letter to express the content of it as the gospel of Christ, since he has been explaining the gospel from almost the first word he has written. So he enlarges on the other aspect of his ministry.

"Signs and miracles" (v.19) served to accredit the messenger of God and validate the message he brought. It was so in the ministry of Jesus (Acts 2:22) and in that of the original apostles (Acts 5:12). Paul is able to certify the same for himself (cf. 2 Cor 12:12). A "sign" is a visible token of an invisible reality that is spiritually significant. The same act may also be a "wonder," something that appeals to the senses and is recognized as a phenomenon that needs explanation. In the OT, God's presence and power were indicated through such means, especially at the time of the Exodus and during the wilderness sojourn. However, "the power of the Spirit" was required to persuade people to make the connection between the miracles and the message and so believe the gospel and be saved. Israel saw countless miracles, both in OT times and during the ministry of Jesus, but often without profit. Stephen supplied the explanation for this fruitlessness: They resisted the Spirit (Acts 7:51).

How well has Paul fulfilled his task in proclaiming the gospel as a minister of Christ? He now affords his readers a glimpse into his activity over many years (v.19b). There is no account of churches founded or the number of converts or the sufferings entailed in all this service. Paul is content to draw a great arc reaching from Jerusalem to Illyricum (a Roman province northwest of Macedonia) to mark the course of his labors. Years—perhaps as many as ten—were spent in Syria and Cilicia before his ministry in Antioch that led in turn to travels in Asia Minor and Greece and establishing congregations in those areas. Luke's account of Paul's final visit to Macedonia and Achaia before going up to Jerusalem for the last time is very brief (Acts 20:1, 2). Yet it is at least possible that a visit to Illyricum or its border was made before settling down at Corinth for the winter. The Egnatian Way would have made travel easy from Thessalonica to the Adriatic Sea. Paul mentions Illyricum probably because he was closer to Italy there than he had ever been before. We can picture him anticipating in Illyricum the day when he would be free to cross the water and set foot in Italy, making contact with the Roman church.

The statement "I have fully proclaimed the gospel of Christ" is not intended to mean that he had preached in every community between the two points mentioned but that he had faithfully preached the message in the major communities along the way, leaving to his converts the more intensified evangelizing of surrounding districts. His ministry in Jerusalem was brief and met with great resistance, for he was a marked and hated man for abandoning the persecution of the church that he had carried on with such vigor in Jerusalem (Acts 9:28, 29). But the very fact that it was attempted at all displayed his determination to fulfill that part of his commission that included Israel (Acts 9:15). His habit of visiting the synagogues wherever he went points in the same direction.

From this brief outline of his missionary activity, the apostle turns to the drive that kept him ceaselessly at his task (v.20). He had a godly "ambition" to preach the gospel where Christ was not known. Such an item was not contained in his call to service except by implication in connection with reaching the Gentiles, so it represents his desire to shoulder the responsibility for blazing a trail for the gospel no matter how great the cost to himself. He longed to preach "in the regions beyond" (2 Cor 10:16). This man could not be an ordinary witness for his Lord. Somewhat parallel is his insistence on preaching the gospel without charge, supporting himself by the labor of his hands (1 Cor 9:18). Verse 20 should be taken in close connection with vv.18, 19 as providing a reason for the passing of so many years without a visit to Rome: Paul had been fully occupied elsewhere. When conditions in the Corinthian church detained him so long, it burdened him that he was not free to pursue his ambition to move on to another area. His dislike of building on another's foundation did not come from an overweening sense of self-importance that could be satisfied only when he could claim the credit for what was accomplished. Actually, he preferred to work with companions, as the Book of Acts attests, and he was always appreciative of the service rendered by his helpers. His statement about "not . . . building on someone else's foundation" requires no more explanation than that he was impelled by the love of Christ to reach as many as possible. He felt deeply his obligation to confront all men with the good news (1:14). This is confirmed by the quotation (v.21) of Isaiah 52:15. Isaiah was a favorite source for Paul's quotations, especially the sections dealing with the Servant of the Lord and his mission, to which this citation belongs.

Concluding this section of the letter is the observation that Paul's delay in coming to Rome was the result of his constant preoccupation with preaching the gospel elsewhere (v.22). Now his readers will understand why he has not come from Jerusalem, the holy city, directly to Rome, the royal city, with the message of reconciliation and life in Christ.

23–29 Only as we take into account the restless pioneer spirit of Paul can we understand how he could claim to have "no more place . . . to work" in the regions where he had been laboring. Plenty of communities had been left unvisited and several groups of believers could have profited from a visit, but his eyes were on the western horizon to which they had been lifted during his stay at Ephesus (Acts 19:21). In view of his mention of "many years," perhaps we may believe that his desire to go to Rome had been born even earlier, though not crystallized into resolve till the successes at Ephesus showed him that a move to more needy fields was in order. Others could carry on after he had laid the foundation.

Now a still more remote objective than Rome comes into view. Spain (v.24) marked the frontier of the empire on the west. So the stay in Rome is seen as limited. Though Paul looks forward to fellowship with the believers there, in line with his earlier statement (1:11, 12), he hopes to go beyond. Openly, he announces his hope that the Roman church will assist him in making the Spanish campaign a reality. This sharing will naturally include their prayers on his behalf, their financial cooperation, and possibly some helpers to go with him to the limits of the West. If Paul were ever to reach Spain, he would no doubt feel that he had realized in his own ministry a measure of fulfillment of the Lord's Great Commission that bade his followers go to the ends of the earth (Acts 1:8).

Whether Paul actually reached Spain is not certain. The strongest positive evidence is found in First Clement V.7, a late first-century writing: "He [Paul] taught righteousness to all the world, and when he had reached the limits of the West he gave his testimony before the rulers, and thus passed from the world." Spain fits "the limits of the West." The remainder of the statement applies more naturally to Rome, but may be intended to refer to a later period in Paul's life.

The contemplated trip to Spain by way of Rome will have to be postponed until another mission is accomplished, namely, his impending visit to Jerusalem. So three geographical points lie commingled in the mind of the apostle: Rome as the goal of much praying, hoping, and planning; Jerusalem as the necessary stop on the way; and Spain as the ultimate objective. One can see how necessary the journey to Jerusalem was in his thinking, since otherwise the lure of the West might take precedence over everything else. So Paul explains just how important this trip to the mother church is, that his readers will understand that he is not dilatory about visiting them.

The principal reason, no doubt, for his having to remain in the East so long is the situation necessitating this final trip to Jerusalem. Paul's churches were made up mainly of Gentile converts. While the Hebrew-Christian element in the church, strongest in Jerusalem, had an interest in the growing work among the Gentiles (Acts 11:21, 22; 15:4), some were concerned that these Gentiles were not being required to accept circumcision in accordance with the OT provision for receiving proselytes into Israel (Exod 12:48) and were not keeping the various ordinances of the Levitical law, such as avoiding foods listed as unclean (Acts 15:1, 5). A further concern was the rapid growth of the Gentile churches, while growth in Jerusalem and Judea had diminished because of persecution and other factors. Jewish believers might be outnumbered before long.

As the leading apostle to the Gentiles, Paul found this situation troubling. What could be done to cement relations between the Jewish and Gentile elements in the church? He was led to conclude that the answer might well lie in a great demonstration of love and desire for unity on the part of his churches toward the mother church in Jerusalem. This could take the same form as the gift of assistance to the poor Christians there that Barnabas and Paul had brought years before on behalf of the Antioch church (Acts 11:27–30). The gratitude of the recipients was real and lived on in the memory of Paul. One cannot help surmising that the quick trip Paul himself made to Jerusalem as reported in Acts 18:22 was undertaken with the definite purpose of conferring with the leaders of the church there about the plan taking shape in his mind—namely, to enlist the cooperation of all his churches in raising a fund to help the mother church, which had a hard time caring for its poorer members. At an earlier period he had expressed eagerness to help the leaders at Jerusalem in ministering to their needy (Gal 2:10). Shortly thereafter he began to inform his congregations of the plan and their responsibility to participate in it (1 Cor 16:1; cf. 2 Cor 8–9). Soon after writing to the Romans, he made preparation for the trip to Jerusalem, in which he was accompanied by representatives of the various churches bearing the offerings that had been collected over a period of time (Acts 20:3, 4).

According to Paul's remarks (v.27), this contribution could be looked at from two standpoints: as a love-gift ("they were pleased to do it") and as an obligation ("they owe it to them"). The latter statement is then explained. Had it not been for the generosity of the Jerusalem church in sharing their spiritual blessings (the gospel as proclaimed by people from Jerusalem and Judea, as seen in Acts 10; 11:19–22; 15:40, 41), the Gentiles would still be in pagan darkness. So it was not such a great thing that they should reciprocate by sharing their "material blessings" (v.27). Some have seen another aspect of this element of obligation. Bruce, in loc., writes:

> Here indeed the question suggests itself whether the contribution was understood by Paul and by the Jerusalem leaders in the same sense. For Paul it was a spontaneous gesture of brotherly love, a token of grateful response on his converts' part to the grace of God which had brought them salvation. But in the eyes of the Jerusalem leaders it perhaps was a form of tribute, a duty owed by the daughter-churches to their mother, comparable to the half-shekel paid annually by Jews throughout the world for the maintenance of the Jerusalem temple and its services.

This must remain a conjecture, though it gains somewhat in plausibility by the fact that Luke's report of the arrival of Paul and his companions in Jerusalem says nothing about any word of thanks by James and the elders for the offering they brought (Acts 21:17ff.).

Paul mentions only those of Macedonia and Achaia as taking part in the contribution (he calls it a *koinōnia,* a participation, v.26) perhaps because he was in Achaia at the time of writing and had recently passed through Macedonia (2 Cor 8–9 reflects the last stages of preparation by these churches). From 1 Corinthians 16:1 and Acts 20:4, it is clear that believers in Asia Minor participated also.

Evidently Paul looks forward to a great feeling of relief when he will be able to convey the monetary offering into the custody of the Jerusalem church. It will mark the completion of an enterprise that has taken several years. He speaks of the gift as "this fruit" (v.29), probably meaning that the generosity of the Jerusalem church in dispersing the seed of the gospel to the Gentiles will now be rewarded, the offering being the fruit of their willingness to share their spiritual blessings.

The completion of the service to be performed at Jerusalem will free Paul to make good on his announced purpose to visit the saints at Rome. He looks forward to it as a time when the blessing of Christ will be poured out upon all. It will be a time of mutual enrichment in the Lord. KJV has "the fulness of the blessing of the gospel of Christ," but the added words are not sufficiently attested to warrant inclusion in the text. Paul's expectations were somewhat shadowed, as it turned out, by the emergence of a group in the Roman church that he characterizes in Philippians 1:15 as motivated by envy and rivalry, but his initial welcome was hearty, despite his coming as a prisoner (Acts 28:15).

30–33 At the time of writing, Paul was aware of stubborn Jewish opposition to him and his work. The attempt on his life when he was about to leave for Jerusalem (Acts 20:3) clearly shows that his apprehension was justified. He had experienced deadly peril before and knew that prayer was the great resource in such hazardous times (2 Cor 1:10, 11). So he requests prayer now (v.30), the kind involving wrestling before the throne of grace that the evil designs of man may be thwarted (cf. Eph 6:18–20). In doing so, he enforces his request by presenting it in the name of Him whom all believers adore—the Lord Jesus Christ—and adding, "by the love of the Spirit." This could mean the love for one another that the Spirit inspires in believers (Gal 5:22). But since the phrase is coupled apparently equally with that of the person of Christ, it is probably better to understand it as the love that the Spirit has (cf. 5:5). The warmth of the expression is enough to warn us against thinking of the Spirit rather impersonally as signifying the power of God. Paul had already affirmed the Spirit's deity and equality with Father and Son (2 Cor 13:14).

The request for prayer includes two immediate objectives. One was deliverance from nonbelieving Jews in Judea. This group had forced his departure from the city at an earlier date (Acts 9:29, 30) and there was no reason to think they had mellowed. The other objective concerned the attitude of the Jerusalem church to the mission that was taking him and his companions to the Jewish metropolis. Evidently the opposition of the Pharisaic party in the church (Acts 15:5) had not ceased, despite the decision of the council (Acts 15:19–29). This opposition, as it related to Paul, was nourished by false rumors concerning his activities (Acts 21:20, 21). So there was reason for concern. It would be a terrible blow to the unity of the church universal if the love-gift of the Gentile congregations were to be spurned or accepted with only casual thanks. The body of Christ could be torn apart.

These two items are intimately related to the successful realization of his hope of reaching Rome safely, coming with joy because of the goodness of God in prospering his way and finding refreshment in the fellowship of the saints (v.32). Yet he knew that all this had to be conditioned on God's will (cf. 1:10). As it turned out, that meant that he would reach Rome, but not as a free man. Yet that very circumstance enabled him to demonstrate the all-sufficient grace and power of Christ (Phil 1:12–14; cf. 2 Tim 4:17). However strife-torn may be his lot in the immediate future, he wishes for his friends the benediction of the God of peace (v.33; cf. v.13).

Notes

19 "Of the Spirit" (*πνεύματος*, *pneumatos*) has the support of B. The other principal reading, *πνεύματος θεοῦ* (*pneumatos theou*), is found in P[46] א, et al., but *θεοῦ* (*theou*) may well be a scribal addition.

29 "The blessing of Christ" has the support of the leading MSS. Later witnesses have "the blessing of the gospel of Christ," an apparent expansion.

B. *Warning Concerning Schismatics, Personal Greetings, and Doxology* 16:1–27

16:1, 2

> I commend to you our sister Phoebe, a servant of the church in Cenchrea. [2]I ask you to receive her in the Lord in a way worthy of the saints and to give her any help she may need from you, for she has been a great help to many people, including me.

Paul has referred to his hope of coming to the believers at Rome (15:32) but he has also mentioned a circumstance that prevented his immediate departure (15:25). Another person, however, is about to leave for the imperial city, so Paul takes this opportunity to commend her to the church. It was customary for believers who traveled from place to place to carry with them letters of commendation (2 Cor 3:1) roughly similar in function to letters of transfer used today when Christians move from one church to another. Here "sister" refers to a woman who is a believer rather than to a blood relative.

"Phoebe" means "bright" or "radiant," a well-known epithet of the Greek god Apollo. She belonged to the church at Cenchrea, located some seven miles from Corinth and serving as the seaport of the city for commerce to the East. Paul had sailed from this port when he went from Corinth to Ephesus several years before (Acts 18:18). It was one of the communities to which the gospel spread from Corinth during and after Paul's original ministry in that city (2 Cor 1:1).

Phoebe is called a "servant" of this church. The same word can be rendered "deaconess" (RSV, JB). Men were serving as deacons about this time (Phil 1:1), and before long women were being referred to in a way that suggests they held such an office in the church (1 Tim 3:11), though the word "deaconess" is not used in that passage. In any event, Paul is not stressing office but service, as we gather from v.2.

Phoebe, it seems, had stopped at Corinth on her way from Cenchrea to Rome. A logical inference from what is said about her is that Paul is sending his letter in her care. She is accustomed to serve, so this will be in character for her. Many had reason to thank God for her assistance in the past, Paul among them. Possibly, like Lydia, she was a businesswoman as well as being active in Christian work and would need help in connection with her visit to the great metropolis.

Notes

2 The word "help" (προστάτις, *prostatis*) as applied in the last clause of v.2 to the service of Phoebe is not the same as that used for assistance to be given her; it is a somewhat rare term used nowhere else in the NT, conveying the idea of affording care and protection (for papyri examples, see MM). One may conclude that she was outstanding in her ministry of aiding and befriending others.

16:3–16

3Greet Priscilla and Aquila, my fellow workers in Christ Jesus. 4They risked their lives for me. Not only I but all the churches of the Gentiles are grateful to them.
5Greet also the church that meets at their house.
Greet my dear friend Epaenetus, who was the first convert to Christ in the province of Asia.
6Greet Mary, who worked very hard for you.
7Greet Andronicus and Junias, my relatives who have been in prison with me. They are outstanding among the apostles, and they were in Christ before I was.
8Greet Ampliatus, whom I love in the Lord.
9Greet Urbanus, our fellow worker in Christ, and my dear friend Stachys.
10Greet Apelles, tested and approved in Christ.
Greet those who belong to the household of Aristobulus.
11Greet Herodion, my relative.
Greet those in the household of Narcissus who are in the Lord.
12Greet Tryphaena and Tryphosa, those women who work hard in the Lord.
Greet my dear friend Persis, another woman who has worked very hard in the Lord.
13Greet Rufus, chosen in the Lord, and his mother, who has been a mother to me, too.
14Greet Asyncritus, Phlegon, Hermes, Patrobas, Hermas and the brothers with them.

15Greet Philologus, Julia, Nereus and his sister, and Olympas and all the saints with them.
16Greet one another with a holy kiss.
All the churches of Christ send greetings.

Certain preliminary observations are in order before plunging into these greetings to individuals. It has seemed strange to some Pauline scholars that he would know so many people in the imperial city, seeing that he had never been there. Clearly, he must have met them or at least heard of them elsewhere. Travel, however, was facilitated by peaceful conditions in the empire, by the fine network of Roman roads connecting the principal centers, and by available shipping in sailing season. With regard to references to travel in early Christian documents, Sir William Ramsay comments, "Probably the feature in those Christian writings which causes most surprise at first to the traveller familiar with those countries in modern times, is the easy confidence with which extensive plans of travel were formed and announced and executed by the early Christians" (HDB, extra volume, pp. 396, 397).

But on the assumption that many if not most of those mentioned in chapter 16 were obliged to leave Rome because of the edict of Claudius expelling the Jews (Acts 18:2) and that they crossed Paul's pathway, returning to Rome after the death of the emperor, a problem is created by the almost complete lack of Semitic names (Mary in v.6 is an exception). However, this is not an insuperable difficulty. "We have sufficient evidence from papyri and inscriptions which indicates that both in the diaspora as well as in Palestine, the changing of personal names was a common practice. The Jews acquired not only Greek, but Latin and Egyptian appellations as well" (K.P. Donfried in JBL 89:445). Paul's relatives (vv.7, 11) were Jews, but do not bear Jewish names.

An element of doubt may remain, however, because most of Paul's letters lack personal greetings. How are we to account for so many here? A clue is provided by his letter to the Colossians, which also contains greetings and is written to a church he did not personally establish. In his letter to the Romans Paul is taking advantage of all the ties he has with this congregation that he hopes to visit in the near future. To send greetings to individuals in churches where he knew virtually the entire congregation would expose Paul to the charge of favoritism. But the congregation at Rome was not such a church.

Since his letter to the Philippians was in all probability written from Rome, the greetings he sends from those of Caesar's household (Phil 4:22) to the believers at Philippi may well have been from slaves and freedmen serving in the imperial establishment, people who had been converted before Paul wrote to the Roman church. That this is so seems evident from the fact that many of the names in Romans 16 appear also in the burial inscription of households (establishments) of emperors of that period, notably those of Claudius and Nero (the reigning emperor when Paul wrote). J.B. Lightfoot made a study of the inscriptions available in his time (*Saint Paul's Epistle to the Philippians* [London: Macmillan, 1879], pp. 171–178) and concluded that even though it is not demonstrable that the individuals mentioned in Romans 16 are identical with those whose names occur on the inscriptions, at least it can be said that "the names and allusions at the close of the Roman Epistle are in keeping with the circumstances of the metropolis in St. Paul's day" (ibid. p. 177). So the appropriateness of this chapter as a close for the letter is confirmed.

3–5 First to be greeted are Priscilla and her husband, Aquila. Paul's friendship with them went back several years to his mission at Corinth, when they gave him hospitality, encouragement, and cooperation in the Lord's work (Acts 18:2). Their usefulness is confirmed by his taking them with him on leaving Corinth (Acts 18:18). When he left Ephesus for Jerusalem, they remained in Ephesus to lay the groundwork for his long ministry there (Acts 18:19) and were used of God in the life of Apollos (Acts 18:24–28). It was during the mission at Ephesus that these "fellow workers" proved their mettle and personal devotion to Paul. They "risked their lives for me" (v.4). Probably the reference is to the dangerous riot that broke out, endangering the apostle's life (Acts 19:28–31; cf. 1 Cor 16:9, 2 Cor 1:8–10). Their presence with him at Ephesus just prior to this incident is confirmed by 1 Corinthians 16:19; cf. v.8). At that time they had a church in their house, so it is not surprising to find that the same is true of their situation in Rome. Their return to the imperial city fits in with their earlier residence there (Acts 18:2), even though Aquila came originally from Pontus. He had a Roman name meaning "eagle." It is quite likely that their return to Rome was encouraged by Paul, so that they could prepare for his arrival by acquainting the church with his work in some detail and with his plans for the future (cf. Acts 19:21). It may have been their business interests that dictated the return of this couple to Ephesus at a later time (2 Tim 4:19), but the work of the Lord must have engrossed them along with their occupation. It has been observed that Priscilla and Aquila represent a splendid image of Christian married life. "Neither Luke nor Paul ever thinks of either of these apart from the other; their names are as truly wedded as their lives" (Herbert S. Seekings, *Men of the Pauline Circle* [London: Chas. H. Kelly, 1914], p. 99). Since several women are mentioned in this chapter, it is well to note that in addition to single women who served Christ, there was a married woman whom Paul encouraged to labor in the gospel along with her husband. Paul's habit of naming Priscilla first seems to testify to her great gifts and usefulness in the kingdom of God.

Epaenetus ("praiseworthy") is the next to be greeted (v.5). It is understandable that Paul should speak of him as "my dear friend" (literally, "my beloved"), since this man was the first convert to Christ in connection with the mission to the province of Asia, of which Ephesus was the leading city. Actually Paul calls him the firstfruits of that area, which hints that many more were expected to follow as the full harvest, and this indeed came to pass. This individual, however, naturally held a special place in the heart of the missionary. If the statement is somewhat differently rendered as "the first of Asia's gifts to Christ" (JB), then the emphasis falls more on what Epaenetus meant to the believers who came after him. His dedication to the work of the Lord as well as his faith may be implied. The presence of Epaenetus in Rome, in view of travel conditions, creates no more difficulty than that of Priscilla and Aquila.

6–16 Mary (Miriam) is a Semitic name borne by several women in the NT. Paul indicates his precise knowledge of her, testifying to her hard work for the saints, but without any hint as to the nature of the work. Emphasis falls rather on her willingness to grow weary in serving them. If Paul had been writing to Ephesus, as some assert, it is doubtful that he would have made this precise observation; it would have exposed him to the criticism of playing favorites. He could safely make the comment, however, in writing to a church where he knew a limited number of people.

Andronicus and Junias (v.7) are Latin and Greek names respectively. Three things out of the four said about them create difficulty for the interpreter. What is the meaning of "relatives"? The identical word (*sungeneis*) is found in 9:3, but there it is qualified by the addition, "according to the flesh," indicating that the meaning is fellow Israelite. Here in Romans 16 other Jewish people are named (e.g., Aquila and Mary) who are not described in this way. Yet even so this may be the best conclusion if one adds mentally—"who are also Christians." To take the word in the ordinary sense of "relative" is difficult, since Paul gives the impression that he suffered the loss of all things for Christ's sake (Phil 3:7), which should embrace kindred. Added to this is the improbability of his having three kinfolk in Rome (cf. v.11) and three more in Corinth (v.21). Sir William Ramsay suggests that all these were fellow tribesmen in the sense that the Jews at Tarsus were organized into a "tribe" by the civil authorities, as in other leading communities where Jews were prominent (*The Cities of St. Paul* [New York: A.C. Armstrong and Son, 1908], pp. 175–178). A possible objection to this solution is that Greek has a word for fellow tribesmen—and it is not used here.

Paul adds that these have been in prison with him. Since such an experience befell him many times (2 Cor 11:23), the expression in this case is doubtless intended to be taken literally, even though we are left uninformed as to the circumstances.

The pair are further described as "outstanding among the apostles." We cannot well reduce the word "apostle" to "messenger" in this instance, however suitable it may be in Philippians 2:25, and it goes without saying that Andronicus and Junias do not belong in the circle of the Twelve. What is left is the recognition that occasionally the word is used somewhat broadly to include leaders in Christian work (cf. 1 Thess 2:7). To interpret the statement as meaning that these men were outstanding in the estimation of the apostles scarcely does justice to the construction in the Greek. Evidently their conversion to the faith occurred in the early years of the history of the church, so they have had ample time to distinguish themselves as leaders.

Ampliatus (v.8) is a Latin name. Again, as in the mention of Epaenetus (v.5), Paul confesses to a very warm personal attachment, demonstrating the reality and depth of Christian friendship that developed between him and others who remain rather obscure to us. Paul was a man who gave himself to the people among whom he served and to those who worked alongside him.

Urbanus (v.9), another Latin name, means "refined" or "elegant." Paul seems to indicate that this man helped him at some time in the past and that he assisted others also in the work of the Lord ("*our* fellow worker").

Regarding Stachys (v.9), Paul contents himself with indicating, as with Ampliatus, a very close bond of affection.

Apelles (v.10) was a fairly common name, but this man has an uncommon pedigree, for he is one who is "tested and approved in Christ." This was Paul's desire for Timothy (2 Tim 2:15) and for himself (1 Cor 9:27).

Something of an enigma confronts us in trying to identify those who belong to the household of Aristobulus (v.10). Lightfoot identified Aristobulus as the grandson of Herod the Great, who lived in Rome and apparently died there (*Philippians,* pp. 174, 175). If this is correct, Aristobulus was either not a believer or had died before Paul wrote, since he is not personally greeted. Those addressed would then be his slaves and employees who had become Christians. On the other hand, if this identification is incorrect, we must think of an otherwise unknown figure whose family is mentioned here. The former alternative is somewhat favored by the fact that the next person to be greeted (v.11) is Herodion, a name suggestive of association with, or admiration for, the family of Herod. Even though no actual relationship may have existed, the placing of the two names with Herodian association so close together may support Lightfoot's thesis. That Herodion was a Hebrew Christian is evident from the use of the word "relative."

Regarding the household of Narcissus (v.11), Lightfoot judges that again contemporary history furnishes a clue.

> Here, as in the case of Aristobulus, the expression seems to point to some famous person of the name. And the powerful freedman Narcissus, whose wealth was proverbial ... whose influence with Claudius was unbounded, and who bore a chief part in the intrigues of this reign, alone satisfies this condition.... As was usual in such cases, his household would most probably pass into the hands of the emperor, still however retaining the name of Narcissus. (ibid., p. 175)

Similar in name, Tryphaena and Tryphosa (v.12) were likely sisters. It was not uncommon then, as now, to give daughters names with a certain resemblance (cf. Jean and Joan). Possibly they belonged to an aristocratic family, since "dainty" and "delicate" (or "luxuriating"), as their names mean, would seem to fit this category. If so, their Christian convictions led them to put aside any tendency to live a life of ease. They are given an accolade for being hard workers in the Lord's cause.

To these two Paul adds another, probably a single woman. Persis (v.12) means simply "a Persian lady." She was close to Paul—a "dear friend." Possibly from their correspondence he was able to know enough about her efforts to commend her as having worked "very hard" in the Lord.

A person bearing the name of Rufus (Latin for "red," v.13) is mentioned in Mark 15:21, where it is indicated that he was one of the sons of Simon, the man who was compelled to bear the cross of Jesus. On the supposition that Mark's Gospel was composed at Rome, all is clear: Rufus is referred to in Mark because of being well known to local readers, being a member of the Roman church. He is designated here as "chosen in the Lord," which is awkward if the usual meaning "elect" is intended, since the whole Roman church would qualify also. Possibly the word is here intended to connote the idea of "choice," "noble," or "eminent." There may also be a hint that the incident involving his father brought him a certain fame among believers at Rome. This possibility is heightened if he was a tried and true Christian workman.

Paul cannot think of Rufus without turning his thought to the mother. Though she remains unnamed, she was special in the eyes of the apostle, because she evidently perceived his loneliness after the loss of his family when he became a Christian (Phil 3:8) and resolved to mother him. This required great understanding and tact, but Paul sensed her loving purpose and did not resent her ministrations. Where this occurred remains unknown (Syrian Antioch is a possibility), but her presence in Rome made him look forward with special anticipation to his visit. Incidentally, the Mark 15:21 reference serves as a confirmation that chapter 16 is genuinely a part of the Roman Epistle rather than being intended for the church at Ephesus, as some scholars contend.

In vv.14, 15 two groups of believers are mentioned without accompanying descriptions or commendations. Apparently Paul's ties with them were less strong than his ties with those previously mentioned. Lightfoot notes that the name of Hermes (v.14), famous as the messenger of the gods, was often borne by slaves. (Hermas is a variation.) In connection with both groups, a greeting is extended to the believers associated with them. This appears to indicate a church in the house in both cases. Rome was a large place, making it probable that there were circles of believers in several sections of the city. They would certainly maintain communication and, when necessity dictated, could arrange to meet together.

The admonition to share a holy kiss (v.16) may well be intended in this case to seal the fellowship of the saints when the letter has been read to them (cf. 1 Cor 16:20; 2 Cor 13:12; 1 Thess 5:26). The reminder that it is a "holy" kiss guards it against erotic associations. It was a token of the love of Christ mutually shared and of the peace and harmony he had brought into their lives.

Desiring to encourage warm relations among churches as well as among individuals within them, Paul takes the liberty of extending the greeting of the churches he has founded in the East.

In summary, two observations concerning the greetings should be made, since the church at Rome was destined to become the strongest in all Christendom. First, as Lightfoot has pointed out, several of these names appear in inscriptions of the period at Rome in reference to slaves of the imperial household. If many of Paul's friends were actually slaves, this may seem a rather inauspicious beginning for an influential church. But slaves in the Hellenistic age were often people of education and outstanding ability. Frequently they were able to gain their freedom and play a larger role in society. The very fact that at Rome believers were found in the service of the emperor (Phil 4:22) augured well for the growth of the church in subsequent days. Yet it should be remembered that God's grace, not man's nobility, is the important thing. See 1 Corinthians 1:26–31.

Another feature of this list of names is the prominence of women in the life of the church. They occupied various stations—one a wife, another a single woman, another a mother—and all are represented as performing a valuable service for the Lord. Evidently Paul esteemed them highly for their work's sake. His relation to them and appreciation for them makes suspect the verdict of those who would label him a misogynist on the basis of such passages as 1 Corinthians 14:34 and 1 Timothy 2:11–15.

16:17–20

17I urge you, brothers, to watch out for those who cause divisions and put obstacles in your way, contrary to the teaching you have learned. Keep away from them. 18For such people are not serving our Lord Christ, but their own appetites. By smooth talk and flattery they deceive the minds of naive people. 19Everyone has heard about your obedience, so I am full of joy over you; but I want you to be wise about what is good, and innocent about what is evil.

20The God of peace will soon crush Satan under your feet.

The grace of our Lord Jesus be with you.

17,18 This warning concerning schismatics raises questions that cannot be answered with certainty. How can we account for its position between greetings from Paul to members of the Roman church and greetings from those who are with him? Could it be an insertion from a later time? This is improbable, for if both groups of greetings were originally one unit, it is doubtful that anyone would destroy this unity by placing something between them. The language and style are certainly Pauline. Is it not simply that at this point the danger Paul speaks of gripped him so powerfully that he felt urged to mention it at once? Dodd (in loc.) may be right in thinking that here Paul took the pen from his secretary and wrote this final admonition himself. That v.20b contains the usual benediction found in his letters is somewhat favorable to this conclusion.

Is it possible to identify the troublemakers? Could this passage be intended to glance back at the problem of the strong and the weak already discussed in 14:1–15:13? One conceivable link is the word "obstacles" (v.17), found also in 14:13. However, the general tone of vv.17–20 is so much sharper than the earlier one that any relationship is dubious. If the church read it as related to the foregoing discussion, it could well have been offensive and could have undone the good Paul's irenic approach had already accomplished.

What sort of people were those the apostle singles out here? Were they already in the church at Rome, or were they simply in the offing? Dealing first with the latter question, one gets the impression that they had not yet come on the scene but posed a threat of doing so. If they had already been active in Rome, those who corresponded with Paul, such as the spiritually discerning Priscilla and Aquila, would surely have given information to enable him to point out specifically the nature of the danger the false teaching of these schismatics presented. Observe that Paul does not specify the particular content of the doctrine of these interlopers. Apparently he is counting on the instruction given the Roman church by others (6:17), buttressed by his own teaching in this letter, to enable his readers to recognize the propaganda as spurious when they hear it, even though it may be sufficiently attractive to some to cause division in the church.

By contrast, Paul is much more pointed in identifying the motives and tactics of these people, which suggests that his warning is based on his missionary experience that had brought him into contact with false teachers who tried to build their own work on the foundation he had laid (Phil 3:18, 19; Acts 20:29, 30). Some of them may even have kept track of Paul's movements and, being aware of his plan to visit Rome, were hoping to arrive there before him. If they could gain a foothold in this influential church, it would be a notable success.

17,18 "Watch out." Alertness to the danger is the main consideration, because failure to be on guard could result in being deceived. "Obstacles" (*skandala*) is too general a term to yield anything specific for our knowledge of the propagandists. Whatever they did, their activity could affect the whole church; therefore they should not be identified with those in 14:13, where the singular "obstacle" (*skandalon*) occurs, seeing that these were a problem to only one segment of the congregation.

As an antidote to the corrupting influence that may threaten the Roman believers, the apostle points them to "the teaching you have learned" (v.17). This is hardly to be identified solely with the contents of this letter, but is more particularly intended to refer to the instruction they have already received in the basics of the faith (cf. 6:17). This should serve as the touchstone enabling them to discern error. But such counsel is not enough. As a practical measure, it is necessary to "keep away from them," giving no opportunity for inroads into the congregation. Religious errorists covet opportunities for "friendly discussion."

Paul speaks of "such people" (v.18) rather than "these people," a slight distinction, perhaps, but nevertheless an important one, confirming the opinion already given that he does not have in mind a group he could name or identify precisely, but a class he has become all too familiar with in his travels. They may talk about the Lord but they do not serve him. Rather, they serve "their own appetites" (cf. Phil 3:18, 19; 1 Tim 6:3–5). With their smooth talk and flattery intended to deceive, they brand themselves as sophists and charlatans. Those they aim to reach are the "naive," the simpleminded folk so innocent of ulterior motive themselves that they imagine others are like them. Their gullibility can be their downfall (cf. "the simple" in the Psalms, a class distinguished both from "the wise" and "the foolish").

19 Here, despite the warning, the apostle affirms his confidence that his readers will be able to handle the situation (cf. a similar expression in 15:14 after dealing with the weak and the strong). This assurance is based chiefly on their "obedience" (cf. 1:5; 6:16), which is so well known in the church at large as to make it almost inconceivable that there will be a failure in the matter under discussion. An appeal to one's record always puts a person on his mettle. So Paul strikes a balance: on the one hand, he has joy as he thinks of the good name of this congregation; on the other hand, he wants to make sure that they are discerning, able to spot trouble and avoid falling into it.

20 Perhaps the mention of "what is evil" leads Paul to think of the instigator of it, namely, Satan, and of the One who blocks his efforts and will thwart his hoped-for triumph. God is the God of peace (cf. 15:33; Phil 4:9; 1 Thess 5:23), who is concerned to preserve harmony among his people and protect them from divisive influences. He is able to defeat the adversary who delights to sow discord among Christians. Though Paul's statement in v.20 has often been taken as a reference to the Second Advent, it is doubtful that this is the intent. "Paul means . . . not that the victory will be near, but that it will be speedily gained, once the conflict is begun. When the believer fights with the armour of God (Eph VI), the conflict is never long. Victory will result from two factors, the one divine (*God shall bruise*), the other human (*under your feet*). God communicates strength; but it passes through the man who accepts and uses it" (Godet, in loc.). The word "crush" suggests that Paul has in mind the "promise" of Genesis 3:15 as the background for his statement.

The benediction, as usual, magnifies the grace of our Lord. The odd feature, however, is that it does not conclude the letter. Did Paul intend to stop here, or did he as an afterthought decide to allow his companions to send greetings when they requested the privilege?

16:21–23

21 Timothy, my fellow worker, sends his greetings to you, as do Lucius, Jason and Sosipater, my relatives.

22 I, Tertius, who wrote down this letter, greet you in the Lord.

23 Gaius, whose hospitality I and the whole church here enjoy, sends you his greetings.

Erastus, who is the city's director of public works, and our brother Quartus send you their greetings.

Paul usually had co-workers and friends around him. This occasion is no exception, and they take this opportunity to send greetings. Timothy, named first, had been Paul's helper on the mission to Macedonia and Achaia (Acts 17–18) and his assistant in handling problems in the Corinthian church (1 Cor 4:17; 16:10).

The next three persons named (v.21) are called "relatives," raising the same problem of interpretation faced in vv.7, 11. Though Lucius could be an alternate form for Luke, this is not the spelling Paul uses for the beloved physician (Col 4:14). And if "relative" is the proper meaning of the word so rendered here, Luke is excluded from this group anyway, because he is distinguished from Paul's Jewish-Christian companions (Col 4:11). It seems likely that Luke *was* with Paul at Corinth (Acts 20:5), so the temptation is strong to identify him with Lucius. Yet it should probably be resisted. Jason could be the individual who entertained Paul and his two helpers at Thessalonica (Acts 17:5). But here, too, there is uncertainty because he is not named as a representative of the Thessalonian church traveling to Jerusalem (Acts 20:4). Sosipater, on the other hand, could be the Sopater mentioned in that passage, since these are forms of the same name (cf. Hermes-Hermas in v.14). His home was in Berea.

At this point (v.22) Paul's amanuensis, who by this time had become thoroughly wrapped up in the message and had developed a feeling of rapport with the Roman

Christians, asks for the privilege of adding his personal greeting. His name, Tertius, is Latin, meaning "third." Though it was Paul's habit to dictate his letters except for the close (2 Thess 3:17), we may be sure he was careful to use believers rather than public secretaries who would do their work without any spiritual concern. We also may be sure that people like Tertius would undertake the task as work for the Lord, so that it would cost the apostle nothing.

Resuming his closing remarks, Paul passes on the greeting of Gaius, with whom he had been staying while he wintered at Corinth (v.23). Evidently his man had a commodious house that he made available for the meetings of the congregation. He seems to have been one of the early converts in Paul's mission to the city (1 Cor 1:14), and the very fact that Paul made an exception in his case by personally baptizing him suggests that his conversion was a notable event due to his prominence. Because of Paul's remark that the whole church enjoyed Gaius's hospitality, it is tempting to suppose that he is the man (Titius Justus) who invited believers into his home after the break with the synagogue (Acts 18:7). This involves the supposition that Paul is giving only a part of his name and that Luke provides the rest (Romans had three names). At any rate, the mention of Gaius as Paul's host is strong evidence that the apostle was writing from Corinth rather than from Cenchrea or from some point in Macedonia.

Erastus (v.23) also, a notable figure because of his public office, sends a greeting. Oscar Broneer, who has done considerable excavating at the site of ancient Corinth, reports in *The Biblical Archaeologist* XIV (Dec. 1951) p. 94:

> A re-used paving block preserves an inscription, stating that the pavement was laid at the expense of Erastus, who was *aedile* (Commissioner of Public Works). He was probably the same Erastus who became a co-worker of St. Paul (Acts 19:22: Rom. 16:23, where he is called *oikonomos,* "chamberlain" of the city), a notable exception to the Apostle's characterization of the early Christians: "Not many wise men after the flesh, not many mighty, not many noble are called" (1 Cor 1:26).

One should add, however, that the correlation with the Erastus named in Acts 19:22 is uncertain.

Nothing more is known of Quartus than what is stated here. He was probably a member of the Corinthian church and may have had some contact with the congregation in Rome.

Notes

---

24 This verse is omitted by leading witnesses, including P^{46} ℵ A B C. It is included by Western witnesses (D G, et al.), which omit it at v.20.

16:25–27

> [25]Now to him who is able to establish you by my gospel and the proclamation of Jesus Christ, according to the revelation of the mystery hidden for long ages past, [26]but now revealed and made known through the prophetic writings by the command of the eternal God, so that all nations might believe and obey him—
> [27]to the only wise God be glory forever through Jesus Christ! Amen.

Since Paul has already given his usual benediction of grace (v.20) found at the close of all his letters, we must see some explanation for the doxology here. The greetings in vv.21–23 may have seemed to Paul a somewhat ill-fitting close, leading him to write this magnificent doxology that draws into itself words and concepts found in his earlier Epistles and gives special emphasis to the leading matters broached in the preceding chapters of the present letter. Whereas a benediction is the pronouncing of a blessing from God on his people, a doxology is an ascription of praise to him. This one is rather lengthy, so much so that the final verse is separated from the rest by a dash in order to indicate a resumption of the thought with which the passage begins and to bring it to a proper conclusion.

25 The opening words express confidence in God's ability to do what is needful for the readers. The same formula is found in Ephesians 3:20 (cf. Jude 24). In the introduction (1:11) Paul wrote that he was looking forward to his ministry at Rome as a means of strengthening the congregation. Now he acknowledges that in the ultimate sense only God can bring this result (*stērizō* the Greek word for "strengthen," tr. "establish" in NIV, is the same in both places). As an instrument for establishing the saints, nothing can compare with the gospel. Paul is not being egotistical or possessive in calling it "my gospel" (cf. 2:16; 2 Tim 2:8). Lagrange rightly raises the question whether he could ask God to confirm readers in his gospel if it were different from that preached by others. Doubtless the possessive pronoun points up the fact that in Paul's case it came by direct revelation (1:1; cf. Gal 1:12), though confirmed as to its actual historical content by leaders of the Jerusalem church (1 Cor 15:1–11). Another term for the gospel is the "proclamation of Jesus Christ," by which we should understand not the preaching done by the Lord Jesus while on earth and probably not his preaching through his servant Paul (2 Cor 13:3 uses this conception, but with emphasis on authority), but rather the preaching that has Jesus Christ as its message (cf. 1:2, 3). This is the only time the word "proclamation" (*kērygma*) occurs in Romans, but Paul had used it earlier (1 Cor 1:21; 2:4; 15:14).

"Proclamation" follows upon "revelation," and both stand in contrast to "mystery" and "hidden." There is a similar tension between mystery and revelation in 1 Corinthians 2:7–10. In fact, this is usual in the apostle's reference to mystery. What is hidden in the divine purpose ultimately becomes revealed and is then the property of all his people. The only other allusion to mystery in Romans (11:25) is more restricted in its scope than in the present passage. How long was the mystery hidden? "For long ages past" may possibly be intended to embrace the OT period (though the Scriptures contained data on the gospel, according to 1 Cor 15:3, 4). The most natural reference, however, is to "eternity past" (cf. 2 Tim 1:9; Titus 1:2), and this is confirmed by the matching description of the deity as "the eternal God" (v.26).

26 "Now revealed" recalls 3:21 (where the same root word is used in the Greek). "Made known through the prophetic writings" raises again the problem faced in v.25 concerning the meaning of the "long ages." This somewhat favors referring these ages to the precreation setting. Of course, it is true that the presence of prophetic material in the OT did not necessarily mean that people understood it as referring to Christ (Luke 24:44, 45). The OT prophets themselves were puzzled by the messianic element in their own predictions (1 Peter 1:10–12). Prophets were active in NT days, engaged not only in exhortation and comfort (1 Cor 14:3) but also in revelation (1 Cor 14:29, 30; Eph 3:5). But all this was on an oral basis; so it seems necessary to refer "prophetic writings" to the OT. No doubt Paul is taking a backward glance at what he had set down at the beginning of the letter concerning the gospel as promised by God through his prophets in the Holy Scriptures (1:2).

"The command of the eternal God" points to the Great Commission, which includes all the nations as embraced in the divine purpose (Matt 28:19). This emphasis recalls the language Paul used in speaking of his own commission (1:1, 5; cf. Titus 1:3). Colossians 1:25–27 is in the same vein. Paul had a special concern to reach the Gentiles (11:13).

27 God is described under two terms. "Only" (cf. 1 Tim 1:17) may well be intended to recall the line of thought in 3:29, 30. He is God of both Jew and Gentile, with a provision for both groups in the gospel of his Son. "Wise" invites the reader to recall the outburst of praise to God in his wisdom (11:33) that brings to a close the long review of his dealings with Israel in relation to his purpose for the Gentiles. Wisdom is also allied to the hidden/revealed tension noted in v.25, as we gather also from 1 Corinthians 2:6, 7. So the God whose eternal purpose has been described as hidden and then manifested in the gospel of his Son, draws to himself through his Son the praise that will engross the saints through all the ages to come. The silence that for so long held the divine mystery has given way to vocal and unending praise.

Notes

25–27 The doxology presents problems. One of these is the varying position it holds in the MSS. Although most of them have it at the end of the letter, a few place it after 14:23, one after 15:33, and a few others after 14:23 and also after 16:24. Marcion, the second-century heretic, refused to include the doxology as well as the two final chapters.

Another source of difficulty is the style and content of this portion. It has been said that nothing like it is to be found elsewhere in Paul's acknowledged writings (Eph 3:20, 21 and 1 Tim 1:17 are held by many scholars to be post-Pauline). It must be granted that a few terms do not occur elsewhere in the Pauline corpus: "eternal God," "prophetic," and "hidden" (lit. "kept in silence"), though a synonym for the latter is fairly frequent in Paul, used, as here, in contrast to "revealed" or "manifested."

On the other hand, most of the items in these three verses agree very well indeed with Paul's teaching in his letters, and especially with his teaching in Romans, as we have already seen. Hence, there is no insuperable difficulty in ascribing the doxology to him. For more detailed treatment, see Bruce pp. 26–29, 281, 182; Barrett pp. 10–13.

1 CORINTHIANS

W. Harold Mare

1 CORINTHIANS

Introduction

1. Background, Including General Historical and Archaeological Data
2. Unity
3. Authorship
4. Date and Place of Origin, and Destination
5. Occasion
6. Purpose
7. Literary Form
8. Theological Values
9. Canonicity
10. Text
11. Bibliography
12. Outline
13. Maps: Corinth, Corinthia

1. Background, Including General Historical and Archaeological Data

The ancient city of Corinth was located on the isthmus between Attica to the northeast and the Greek Peloponnesus to the south and had controlling access to two seas—the Aegean, about five miles to the east and the Ionian on the west. Its eastern port was Cenchrea, located on the Saronic Gulf (Acts 18:18; Rom 16:1), its western harbor was at Lechaeum on the Corinthian Gulf. This proximity to the seas and its nearness to Athens, only forty-five miles to the northeast, gave Corinth a position of strategic commercial importance and military defense. It lay below the steep north side of the 1,800-foot high fortress rock, the Acrocorinth with its temple of Aphrodite (Strabo, *Geography*, 8.6.21). Thus located, the city received shipping from Italy, Sicily, and Spain, as well as from Asia Minor, Syria, Phoenicia, and Egypt. Instead of going "round the horn" at Cape Malea at the south end of the Peloponnesus, ships either docked at the Isthmus and transported their cargoes by land vehicles from one sea to another, or if the ships were small, they were dragged the five miles across the isthmus. Today there is a canal running through the narrowest part of the isthmus near Corinth.

Corinth was called "the bridge of the sea" (Pind. *Nem* VI. 40) and "the gate of the Peloponnesus" (Xen. *Ages.* 2.17). It was considered a "prosperous" (Pind. *Olym.* 13.4.; Herodotus 3.52) and "rich" (Thucydides, *Hist.* 1, 13, 5) city. For Strabo (8.6.23) Corinth was "always great and wealthy." At the peak of its power and influence the city probably had a free population of 200,000 in addition to half a million slaves in its navy and in its many colonies (HDAC, p. 249).

About the end of the third millennium B.C. Corinth and the rest of Greece were invaded in the Bronze Age by an alien people who may have been forerunners of the Greeks. From that time the site of Corinth itself was abandoned until about 1350 B.C., when a new settlement came into being. But for the next three hundred years material evidences for the city are scarce. It would seem that this resettled Corinth had by the time of the Trojan War (c. 1200 B.C.) prospered so greatly that Homer could speak of it as "wealthy Corinth" (Il. 2.570).

During the Iron Age, the city grew in size and wealth. By about 800 B.C. it had acquired considerable importance as a commercial and military center. The importance of Corinth continued with fluctuations that were due to the struggles among the Greek states and their subjugation under Philip II of Macedon and his son, Alexander the Great.

Still later, when the Greeks attempted to break the yoke of Macedon, the Romans became involved and so Corinth was destroyed by the Romans under Lucius Mummius in 146 B.C., only to be reestablished in 46 B.C. by Julius Caesar and called Colonia Laus Julia Corinthus. Caesar populated it with Roman war veterans and freedmen. In the reign of Augustus (27 B.C.–A.D. 14) and his successors, Corinth was built on the pattern of a Roman city, with all remaining buildings reclaimed and new ones added in and around the old market place (the *agora*), the place in which the *bema* (the judgment tribunal platform) stood, where Paul appeared before Gallio (Acts 18:12).[1] In this period Corinth became the capital of the Roman province of Achaia (cf. Acts 18:1, 2), which included all the Peloponnesus and most of the rest of Greece and Macedonia.

During the Roman period and in its position as a political center, Corinth again became prosperous, with vast income coming from its sea trade and from the development of its arts and industries. Its pottery and Corinthian brass (a mixture of gold, silver, and copper) were world famous (cf. Ovid [43 B.C.–17 A.D.] *Met.* 6:416).

The celebration of the Isthmian games at the temple of Poseidon (Strabo 8.6.22) made a considerable contribution to Hellenic life. This temple was located about seven miles east of Corinth, not far from the eastern end of the isthmus. But with the games there came an emphasis on luxury and profligacy, because the sanctuary of Poseidon was given over to the worship of the Corinthian Aphrodite, (probably a counterpart of the Syrian Astarte) whose temple on the Acrocorinth had more than 1,000 *hierodouloi* (female prostitutes). Strabo says (8.6.20) that many people came to Corinth on account of these priestesses, and the city grew rich. *Korinthiazomai* (meaning "to live like a Corinthian in the practice of sexual immorality") was the expression used at an earlier time by Aristophanes (*Fragmenta* 354) to describe a person of loose life.

Paul probably came to this important but immoral city in the fall of A.D. 50, after having preached the gospel to the highly intellectual Athenians. That this is the time of Paul's stay at the city is established by comparing the reference in Acts 18:12 to Gallio, the Roman procounsul (*anthupatos*) with that to a Gallio, procounsul of Achaia, mentioned on an inscription of the Emperor Claudius at Delphi to be dated between January and August, A.D. 52.

Now since the Gallio of the inscription is already mentioned as in office in the first half of A.D. 52, he must have begun his proconsulship July 1, A.D. 51, July 1 being the time each year when Roman proconsuls took office. Paul ministered a year and a half in Corinth (Acts 18:11) before he was brought by the Jews into court before Gallio (v.12). No mention is made of Gallio being in office as proconsul of Achaia when Paul first came to Corinth to work as a tentmaker and to preach (Acts 18:1–5). But some time later, after opposition to the gospel had had time to grow (vv.6–10), Gallio is mentioned as having a case against Paul brought before him (vv.12–17). So the conclusion is that Paul arrived

[1] *Cf.* Oscar Broneer, "Corinth," *Biblical Archaeologist*, vol. 14 (Dec., 1951), no. 4, 80–82.

in Corinth some time before Gallio, probably by the fall of A.D. 50, a period of about nine months before the proconsul took office on July 1, A.D. 51. Sometime after this official opposition Paul left Corinth for Syria, sailing from Cenchrea (v.18).

In the Corinthian church were both Jews and Gentiles, as inferred from Paul's reference to them in chapter 1. This is also attested by Latin names, such as Gaius, Fortunatus, Crispus, Justus, and Achaicus (1 Cor 1:14; 16:17) and by the mention of the Jews, Aquila and Priscilla (Acts 18:1–4) and of Crispus, the ruler of the synagogue (v.8). Sosthenes, another synagogue ruler there (v.17)—if he is the Sosthenes of 1 Corinthians 1:1—also became a member of the congregation. But no doubt the greater part of the church was composed of native Greeks; cf. Paul's reference to the Greeks who seek after wisdom (1 Cor 1:20–24) and also his reference to the congregation's being Gentiles (12:2).

The existence of a synagogue in Corinth (Acts 18:4–8) is pointed to by an inscribed lintel block with enough of the words remaining to make out the reading "Synagogue of the Hewbrews."[2] From the way the letters are formed, Broneer thinks that the inscription is of the fourth or fifth centuries A.D.[3] However, others think the inscription is to be dated between 100 B.C. and A.D. 200. Deissmann (quoted with approval by Finegan) says that "as extreme limits within which the inscription must have been made, the dates of 100 B.C. and 200 A.D. might with some reservation" be assumed. Deissmann also comments that the miserable nature of the inscription, which has no ornamentation, fits the social position of the Jewish people at Corinth with whom Paul was dealing.[4] This agrees with Paul's remarks to the Corinthians: "Not many of you were wise by human standards; not many were influential; not many were of noble birth" (1 Cor 1:26). But even if it is argued that the inscription is later than the time the Corinthian Church was founded, it is natural to assume, because of the Jews tenacity in remaining settled in religious communities where they were dispersed, as at Rome[5] and Alexandria, that the Jewish community in Corinth had an earlier synagogue building when Paul established the church there. Pausanias in his *Descriptions of Greece* describes the city following his visit to Corinth at about A.D. 170, but his interest is more in heathen cults.

Though it is not possible to identify the building in Corinth to which the synagogue inscription belonged, archaeological work can identify other buildings of the ancient city. An ornamented triumphal gateway, located at the south end of the Lechaeum Road, led into the marketplace (*i.e.,* the Greek *agora,* or Roman forum)—c. 600 feet long and c. 300 feet wide. Around the market were a good many shops, numbers of which had individual wells, suggesting that much wine was made and drunk in the city. (Cf. Paul's warning in 1 Cor 6:10 that drunkards will not "inherit" the kingdom of God.)

Located near the center of the marketplace was the *bema* (Gr.) or *rostra* (Latin), the judicial bench or tribunal platform (cf. 2 Cor 5:10, "the judgment seat of Christ"). This was a speakers' platform; officials addressed audiences assembled there. Originally, the *bema* was covered with carved marble, as extant fragments bear testimony. On either side of it were waiting rooms with mosaic floors and marble benches, and in these rooms

---

[2][ΣΥΝ] ΑΓΩΓΗΕΒΡ[ΑΙΩΝ], [*Sun*] *agōgē Ebr* [*aiōn*]. Cf. Merrill C. Tenney, *New Testament Times* (Grand Rapids: Eerdmans, 1965), p. 275.

[3]Broneer, "Corinth," p. 88, footnote.

[4]A. Deissmann, *Light from the Ancient East,* revised (New York: George H. Doran Co., 1927), p. 16. Cf. J. Finegan, *Light from the Ancient Past* (Princeton, N.J.: Princeton University Press, 1959), pp. 361, 362.

[5]Inscriptions indicate that at Rome there were a large number of synagogue communities as early as the Emperor Augustus's time, (cf. Philo, *The Embassy to Gaius,* 155, 156; cf. also Emil Schürer, *A History of the Jewish People in the Time of Jesus Christ,* 2nd rev. ed., DW 2, vol. 2 (New York: Charles Scribner's Sons, 1890, 1891) pp. 247, 283.

cases were heard by the magistrate. It was not, however, in one of these side rooms, but outside in front of the *bema* proper, that the antagonistic Jews brought Paul before the Roman proconsul Gallio (Acts 18:12–17), for such a mob action would not have been allowed in a Roman court room.

To the south of the *bema* toward the Acrocorinth (the rocky butte behind the city) at the south stoa (a colonnaded building) there came into the marketplace a paved road that probably connected with the road leading east to Cenchrea, the port from which Paul sailed to Ephesus and then to Syria (Acts 18:18–22).

Besides its many temples and shrines, including the temple of Apollo, the remains of which stand out on the landscape today, the city had two theaters to the north and west, one of which could seat 18,000 people. In a paved street at the east side of this theater was found a re-used paving block with this inscription: "Erastus, the aedile [commissioner of public works] bore the expense of this pavement" (Latin: ERASTUS PRO. AED. S. P. STRAVIT. Cf. Tenney, *New Testament Times,* p. 274). This Erastus may well have been the one who became Paul's fellow worker. See Acts 19:22 and Romans 16:23 (where he is called "the city's director of public works"). Erastus was evidently one of the few "influential" and "noble" persons Paul refers to in 1 Corinthians 1:26.[6]

Later on, by the tenth century A.D., a church existed on the ruins of the *bema,* but the superstructure of the *bema* had by this time fallen. Also in the Julian Basilica on the east side of the market a ninth-to-tenth-century A.D. inscription on a fragment of a white marble slab has been found. It includes the letters, "The —— Church of Saint Paul" and is probably from the church built on top of the *bema.*[7]

Besides his initial stay in Corinth as recorded in Acts 18, Paul's contact with the Corinthians can be outlined as follows: At Ephesus (Acts 19) he apparently wrote the "previous letter" (1 Cor 5:9—now lost to us). Besides hearing of the Corinthians' seeming misunderstanding of his "previous letter," Paul had reports from Chloe's household of disorders in the church there (1 Cor 1:11). He then may have received a delegation from Corinth (16:17) who presented him with questions from the congregation (cf. 7:1). As a result, he wrote 1 Corinthians. Paul may have heard other unfavorable reports from the church and paid them a "painful visit" (2 Cor 2:1), which evidently occurred following the writing of 1 Corinthians and its reception by the church. The painful visit was no doubt necessary because the church had failed to act on Paul's advice given in 1 Corinthians. Upon his return to Ephesus, he sent the church a "sorrowful letter" (2 Cor 2:4; 7:8, 9), probably carried by Titus.

Some have taken this letter to be 1 Corinthians but others feel that 1 Corinthians does not express the feeling of Paul's shedding "many tears" (2 Cor 2:4). That he repented of having written this "sorrowful letter" (2 Cor 7:8) is thought to be inappropriate for an inspired letter like 1 Corinthians. However, if this "sorrowful letter" is simply a lost epistle of Paul, the question is whether it, too, was inspired and, if so, how are we to understand his repenting of writing it? The question is answered, in part at least, by realizing that the word "repent" in 2 Corinthians 7:8 is not *metanoeō,* for repenting of sin, but *metamelomai,* "to be sorry," "to regret." Further, Paul means he regretted that they had been made sad, not that he regretted writing the letter under the guidance of

---

[6]Cf. Finegan, *Light from the Ancient Past,* pp. 359–362; and Broneer, "Corinth," pp. 90–94.

[7]R.L. Scranton, *Corinth: Results of Excavations,* vol. 1, part 3, *Monuments in the Lower Agora and North of the Archaic Temple* (Princeton: American School of Classical Studies at Athens, 1951), p. 132; and J.H. Kent, *Corinth: Results of Excavations,* vol. 8, part III, *The Inscriptions 1926–1950* (Princeton: The American School of Classical Studies at Athens, 1966), pp. 211, 212.

the Holy Spirit.[8] From Ephesus Paul went to Macedonia, where he received from Titus an encouraging report (2 Cor 7:5–7). So he wrote 2 Corinthians expressing his gratitude for the improvement. Later he spent the winter in Corinth (Acts 20:2, 3) before departing for Jerusalem with the contribution for the poor among the Christians of Palestine. On the basis of this analysis of the events, we may conclude that Paul wrote the Corinthians four letters (two of which have been lost) and that he paid the church three visits, including the one referred to in Acts 18. (See also Guthrie, pp. 424–438.)

2. Unity

1 Corinthians gives all indications of being a unity. The thought progresses in orderly fashion from the greetings and thanksgiving to the discussion about the rival cliques in the church and its internal problems of incest and lawsuits. Members of Chloe's household seem to have reported to Paul on all these matters. Next Paul discusses the questions brought by the Corinthian delegation (1 Cor 16:17)—questions of marriage, eating meat offered to heathen idols, disorderly public worship, spiritual gifts, and the resurrection. Then Paul naturally goes on to remark about the Corinthians' offering for the poor and his travel plans; he closes with greetings. Obviously the letter is a connected whole. Because of supposed contradictions, some scholars have thought 1 and 2 Corinthians to be a mixture of different sections of Pauline writing pieced together in their present form. But such theories do not afford Paul a natural latitude for developing his material in accord with the particular church problem or problems coming to his attention over a period of time (Guthrie, pp. 439–441).

3. Authorship

It is generally acknowledged that, whether the material we have in 1 Corinthians is as it came from Paul, he was the author. Early external evidence from the following confirms this conclusion: Clement of Rome, *To the Corinthians* (ch. 47), Polycarp, *To the Philippians* (ch. 11), Irenaeus, *Against Heresies,* 4, 27 (45), Clement of Alexandria (e.g., *Paedag.* 1, 6 [33]), and Tertullian, *de Praescript. adv. Haer.*, (Ch. 33, 11:46).[9]

4. Date and Place of Origin, and Destination

Quite obviously, the letter was written some time subsequent to Paul's first visit to Corinth. Following his departure from the city, he sailed from Cenchrea for Syria by way of Ephesus. Landing at the Palestinian port of Caesarea, he then visited the Jerusalem churches and journeyed on north to his home church at Antioch in Syria (Acts 18:18–23).

After some time in Antioch, Paul left on his third missionary journey and visited the churches of Galatia and Phrygia (Acts 18:23). He finally came to Ephesus (19:1), preaching and teaching there for almost three years (19:10; 20:31). According to Bruce, the two

---

[8]Cf. H.A.W. Meyer, *The Epistles to the Corinthians* (New York: Funk and Wagnalls, 1884), pp. 566, 567.
[9]Henry Alford, *Greek Testament,* vol. 2, 5th ed. (London: Revingtons, 1865), p. 46.

years was probably that and a few months more. With the three months of 19:8, this would make up the three years of 20:31; i.e., three years less a few months.[10]

While at Ephesus, Paul heard of the Corinthians' troubles and questions through reports from Chloe's house (1 Cor 1:11) and possibly through a delegation from Corinth (16:17). At this point he wrote the Epistle.

That 1 Corinthians was written on the third missionary journey and from Ephesus and in the spring of A.D. 55/56 is evident from the following reasons: (1) Paul says he is writing from Ephesus (1 Cor 16:8, 9, 19). (2) He wrote the letter several years after his initial departure from Corinth in the fall of A.D. 51, because it was written subsequent to Apollos's stay at the city (Acts 18:26, 27; 1 Cor 1:12) and after Timothy and Erastus had been sent by Paul from Ephesus to Macedonia (Acts 19:22) and Timothy had been sent on to Corinth (1 Cor 4:17). Further, it took some time for the Corinthian problems to develop and for news of them to reach Paul. (3) The letter was written before the beginning of summer, because in 1 Corinthians 16:8 Paul intimates that it is a relatively short time to Pentecost (i.e., late spring) after which he intends to leave Ephesus. The time of writing is certainly before winter, for Paul states that he wants to come and winter with them (1 Cor 16:6, cf. Acts 20:3). This all adds up to some four or five years after his initial departure from Corinth in the fall of A.D. 51, counting his journey to Jerusalem and extended stay in Syrian Antioch (Acts 18:18, 23) and his almost three-year ministry in Ephesus (19:8, 10; 20:31).

It is not fully clear who carried the letter to Corinth. But it seems likely that its bearers were Stephanas, Fortunatus, and Achaicus who according to 1 Corinthians 16:17 had arrived from Corinth and were with Paul. Since in 1 Corinthians 16:18 the apostle says that the Corinthian Christians should show respect for these men, it is logical to conclude that they were returning to Corinth and so it would have been natural for Paul to send the Epistle with them.

5. Occasion

First Corinthians is a source book of answers to church problems in the past and today. Findlay calls it "the doctrine of the cross in its social application."[11] After the introductory material, Paul begins to answer the theological and practical problems raised through a report (either oral or written) from members of the household of Chloe (1 Cor 1:11). Following this, a letter came from the church (7:1), possibly brought by a delegation (16:17) and posing a number of questions. These things, together with Paul's desire to send greetings to Corinth, was sufficient occasion for him to write the letter.

6. Purpose

In responding to the reports and answering the questions, it was Paul's purpose to rectify certain serious doctrinal and moral sins and irregularities of Christian living, including disorderly conduct in worship. These aberrations included false views of the resurrection of Christ and the resurrection of the body (1 Cor 15), incest, adultery, and

---

[10]F.F. Bruce, The Acts of the Apostles: *The Greek Text with Introduction and Commentary* (Grand Rapids: Eerdmans, 1965), p. 356.

[11]*Expositor's Greek Testament,* vol. 2 (Grand Rapids: Eerdmans, n.d.), p. 739.

other sexual immorality (1 Cor 5). They also included unchristian actions in taking fellow Christians to court (1 Cor 6), misuse of Christian liberty (1 Cor 8 and 10), disorders in observing the Lord's Supper (1 Cor 11:17–34), and other disorders in the worship service (1 Cor 14).

7. Literary Form

Modern critics have tried to divide up the Corinthian Epistles in an attempt to show how they were compiled. Among recent partition theories are those of J. Weiss, J. Hering, M. Goguel, and J.T. Dean (Guthrie, p. 439). For example, Weiss saw 1 Corinthians as composed of three parts representing a development in Paul's relationship with the Corinthians. Hering found the Epistle composed of two parts. Goguel, taking 1 and 2 Corinthians together, saw six parts. But such complex theories do not sufficiently account for the psychological factors and different subjects involved. These factors argue for the unity of 1 Corinthians, as Paul in writing it deliberately changed the subject matter and tone as he proceeded from section to section of the letter. Moreover, it may well be that he did not compose the whole letter at one time. He may have written the first part in response to reports that came through Chloe; then later, after receiving the letter from the Corinthians (1 Cor 7:1) he may have written the rest.

So though the expression and tone change in various parts of 1 Corinthians, we may take it that the letter is from Paul who wrote it within a relatively short period of time. The Greek is characteristically that of the apostle.

8. Theological Values

Several theological emphases stand out in 1 Corinthians and are related to the daily living of Christians as well as to the corporate testimony of the worshiping church. For example, in chapter 15 Paul sets forth valid reasons for believing in the bodily resurrection of Christ and relates this to Christ's second coming. And in chapter 11 the doctrine of the Lord's Supper is effectively taught, along with the admonition for Christians to take it seriously.

In chapters 5 and 6 Paul speaks forcefully against the incident of incest and adultery in the church and condemns all sexual immorality. The practical problem of whether a Christian should marry and how he should conduct himself in a married or unmarried state is adequately discussed in chapter 7. In the sixth chapter the thorny problem of believers' taking other believers into secular court is faced and Christian arbitration suggested. The believer's Christian liberty versus his responsibility to his Christian brother is clearly delineated and explained in chapters 8 and 10. In the area of ecclesiology, the subjects of Christian gifts and their use for the church, as well as orderly conduct in church services, are fully expounded in chapters 12 to 14.

9. Canonicity

There is no question of the canonicity of 1 Corinthians. Since the book was clearly written by Paul, an apostle, it was to be accepted immediately by the church as God's

Word.[12] Paul makes the strong statement: In 1 Corinthians 14:37 "If anybody thinks he is a prophet or spiritually gifted, let him acknowledge that what I am writing to you is the Lord's command."

Second, the early church bore witness that 1 Corinthians was considered authoritative and a part of the NT canon. Marcion ascribes (c. A.D. 140–150) to this corpus the term *apostolikon,* and undoubtedly 1 Corinthians was a part of that corpus.[13] Guthrie has noted that "of great significance is the fact that the earliest Canon of the New Testament writings of which we have any evidence consisted almost exclusively of Pauline writings" (Guthrie, p. 643). Some thirty to forty years after the period of Marcion's major activity as noted above, the Muratorian canon (c. A.D. 170) appeared and included 1 Corinthians as one of the thirteen Epistles of Paul, so implying its equal authority with the others.

Obviously, 1 Corinthians was considered from the beginning one of the NT canonical books.

10. Text

The Greek text of 1 Corinthians is in good order, with relatively few crucial problems. In one place (1 Cor 15:47–55), the textual variants suggest some changes in the emphases of these verses. The basic Greek ms text of 1 Corinthians is good; it is the same as that of other of the Pauline Epistles and includes early uncials such as א A B C D (Paris, Claromontanus) and early papyri including P^{46} (Chester Beatty, c. 200), P^{51} (P Oxy 2157; c. 400) and P^{65} (Florence, 3rd cent.).[14]

11. Bibliography

Alford, Henry. *Greek Testament,* vol. II, 5th ed. London: Revingtons, 1865.

Barrett, C.K. *The First Epistle to Corinthians* in "Black's New Testament Commentary." New York: Harper, 1968.

Calvin, John. *New Testament Commentaries.* Philadelphia: Westminster Press, 1958.

Craig, C.T. and Short, J. *1 Corinthians* in IB, vol. 10. New York: Abingdon-Cokesbury, 1953.

Dean, J.T. *St. Paul and Corinth.* London: Lutterworth, 1947.

Evans, Ernest. *The Epistles of Paul the Apostle to the Corinthians.* Oxford: Clarendon Press, 1944.

Glen, John Stanley. *Pastoral Problems in First Corinthians.* Philadelphia: Westminster Press, 1964.

Godet, F. *Commentary on St. Paul's First Epistle to the Corinthians,* n.d. Reprint, tr. A. Cusin, Grand Rapids: Zondervan, 1971.

Grosheide, F.W. *Commentary on the First Epistle to the Corinthians* in NIC. Grand Rapids, Eerdmans, 1968.

Guthrie, Donald. *New Testament Introduction,* 3rd ed. revised. Downers Grove, Ill.: Inter-Varsity Press, 1970, 421–449.

---

[12]Cf. R.L. Harris, *Inspiration and Canonicity* (Grand Rapids: Zondervan, 1957), pp. 234, 235.

[13]P. Schaff, *History of the Christian Church,* vol. 2 (New York: Charles Scribner's Sons, 1891), pp. 484–486; *The Cambridge History of the Bible,* vol. 1, ed. P.R. Ackroyd and C.F. Evans (Cambridge: Cambridge University Press, 1970), pp. 239, 240, 294.

[14]For more details, see Kurt Aland, et al., *The Greek New Testament,* 2nd ed. (New York: United Bible Societies, 1968), Introduction; Bruce M. Metzger, *A Textual Commentary on the Greek New Testament* (New York: United Bible Societies, 1971), Introduction.

Hering, J. *The First Epistle of St. Paul to the Corinthians* from the second French ed. by A.W. Heathcote and P.J. Allcock. London: Epworth Press, 1962.

Hodge, Charles. *I Corinthians.* New York: A.C. Armstrong, 1891.

Howard, W.F. *1 and 2 Corinthians* in "Abingdon Bible Commentary," Nashville: Abingdon, 1929.

Lenski, C.H. *The Interpretation of St. Paul's First and Second Epistles to the Corinthians.* Columbus, Ohio: Wartburg Press, 1946.

Metzger, Bruce M. *A Textual Commentary on the Greek New Testament,* A Companion Volume to the United Bible Societies' *Greek New Testament.* 3rd ed. New York: United Bible Societies, 1971.

Moffatt, J. *The First Epistle of Paul to the Corinthians* in "Moffatt's New Testament Commentary." New York: Harper, 1938.

Morris, Leon. *The First Epistle of Paul to the Corinthians* in "The Tyndale New Testament Commentary." Grand Rapids: Eerdmans, 1958.

Parry, John. *The First Epistle of Paul the Apostle to the Corinthians in the Revised Version* in "The Cambridge Bible for Schools and Colleges." Cambridge: Cambridge University Press, 1957.

Parry, R. St. John, ed. *The First Epistle of Paul the Apostle to the Corinthians,* in "Cambridge Greek Testament for Schools and Colleges." Cambridge: Cambridge University Press, 1916.

Reuf, J.S. *Paul's First Epistle to Corinth* in "Pelican's New Testament Commentaries." Baltimore: Hammondsworth, 1971.

Robertson, A. and Plummer, A. *A Critical and Exegetical Commentary on the First Epistle of St. Paul to the Corinthians,* 2nd ed., in ICC. Edinburgh: T. & T. Clark, 1929.

______. *I Corinthians* in ICC. New York: Charles Scribner's Sons, 1916.

Scharlemann, Martin Henry. *Qumran and Corinth.* New York: Bookman Associates, 1962.

Schmidt, John. *Letters to Corinth.* Philadelphia: Muhlenberg Press, 1947.

Walter, Eugene. *The First Epistle to the Corinthians,* tr. Simon and Erika Young. New York: Herder and Herder, 1971.

Williams, C.S.C. *I and II Corinthians,* in "Peake's Commentary on the Bible." Edited by Matthew Black. London: Thomas Nelson, 1967.

12. Outline

I. Greetings (1:1–3)

II. Paul's Thanksgiving for God's Work in the Lives of the Saints (1:4–9)

III. The Problem of Divisions in the Church (1:10–17)

IV. The Wisdom of God—the Preaching of Christ Crucified (1:18–2:16)
- A. Christ, the Power and Wisdom of God (1:18–31)
- B. Paul Preaches Christ in the Power of God (2:1–5)
- C. Wisdom of Christ Revealed by the Holy Spirit (2:6–16)

V. Servants of Christ (3:1–4:21)
- A. Workers With God—False Estimate Corrected (3:1–23)
  1. Spiritual immaturity and divisiveness (3:1–9)
  2. Building on Christ, the foundation (3:10–17)
  3. Complete dependence on God, not men (3:18–23)
- B. Servants of Christ: The Ministry of the Apostles (4:1–21)
  1. Faithful servants (4:1–5)
  2. The proud Corinthians and the despised servants (4:6–13)
  3. The challenge to be God's humble servants also (4:14–21)

VI. Paul's Answer to Further Reported Problems in the Church (5:1–6:20)
- A. Paul's Condemnation of Sexual Immorality—Incest (5:1–13)
- B. Christian Morality Applied to Legal and Sexual Matters (6:1–20)
  1. Christian morality in legal matters (6:1–11)
  2. Christian morality in sexual matters (6:12–20)

VII. Paul's Answers to Questions Raised by the Church (7:1–14:40)
- A. Instructions Concerning Marriage (7:1–40)
  1. Christian obligations in marriage (7:1–16)
  2. Christian obligation to live according to God's call (7:17–24)
  3. Instructions concerning virgins (7:25–40)
- B. Instructions Concerning Christian Freedom: Its Privileges and Responsibilities (8:1–11:1)
  1. Eating meat sacrificed to idols (8:1–13)
     - a. Knowledge and love contrasted (8:1–3)
     - b. The meaning of eating meat sacrificed to idols (8:4–6)
     - c. Freedom to be used with care (8:7–13)
  2. Paul: on giving up his rights as an apostle (9:1–18)
     - a. Rights of an apostle (9:1–12a)
     - b. Rights not used (9:12b–18)
  3. Paul: subjection of self for others and to meet God's approval (9:19–27)
  4. Warning: Israel's lack of self-restraint (10:1–13)
  5. Warning: attendance at pagan sacrifices means fellowship with idolatry (10:14–22)

6. Freedom, but within limits: do all to the glory of God (10:23–11:1)

C. Worship in the Church (11:2–14:40)
1. Propriety in worship: covering of women's heads (11:2–16)
2. The Lord's Supper (11:17–34)
3. The use of spiritual gifts (12:1–14:40)
a. The Holy Spirit, the source of spiritual gifts (12:1–11)
b. Unity in the diversity of gifts in the body of Christ (12:12–26)
c. Offices and gifts in the one body of Christ, his church (12:27–31)
d. The supreme position of love in the ministry of the church (12:31b–13:13)
e. The priority of prophecy over tongues, and rules for the exercise of both (14:1–25)
f. Orderly conduct in Christian worship (14:26–40)

VIII. The Resurrection of Christ and of the Christian (15:1–58)
A. The Resurrection of Christ (15:1–11)
B. The Validity of the Resurrection of the Dead (15:12–19)
C. Christ the Guarantee of the Resurrection From the Dead (15:20–28)
D. Implications of Denying the Resurrection From the Dead (15:29–34)
E. The Resurrection Body: Its Nature and Change (15:35–58)

IX. The Collection for God's People, Requests, and Final Greetings (16:1–24)
A. The Collection for God's People (16:1–4)
B. Personal Requests (16:5–18)
C. Final Greetings (16:19–24)

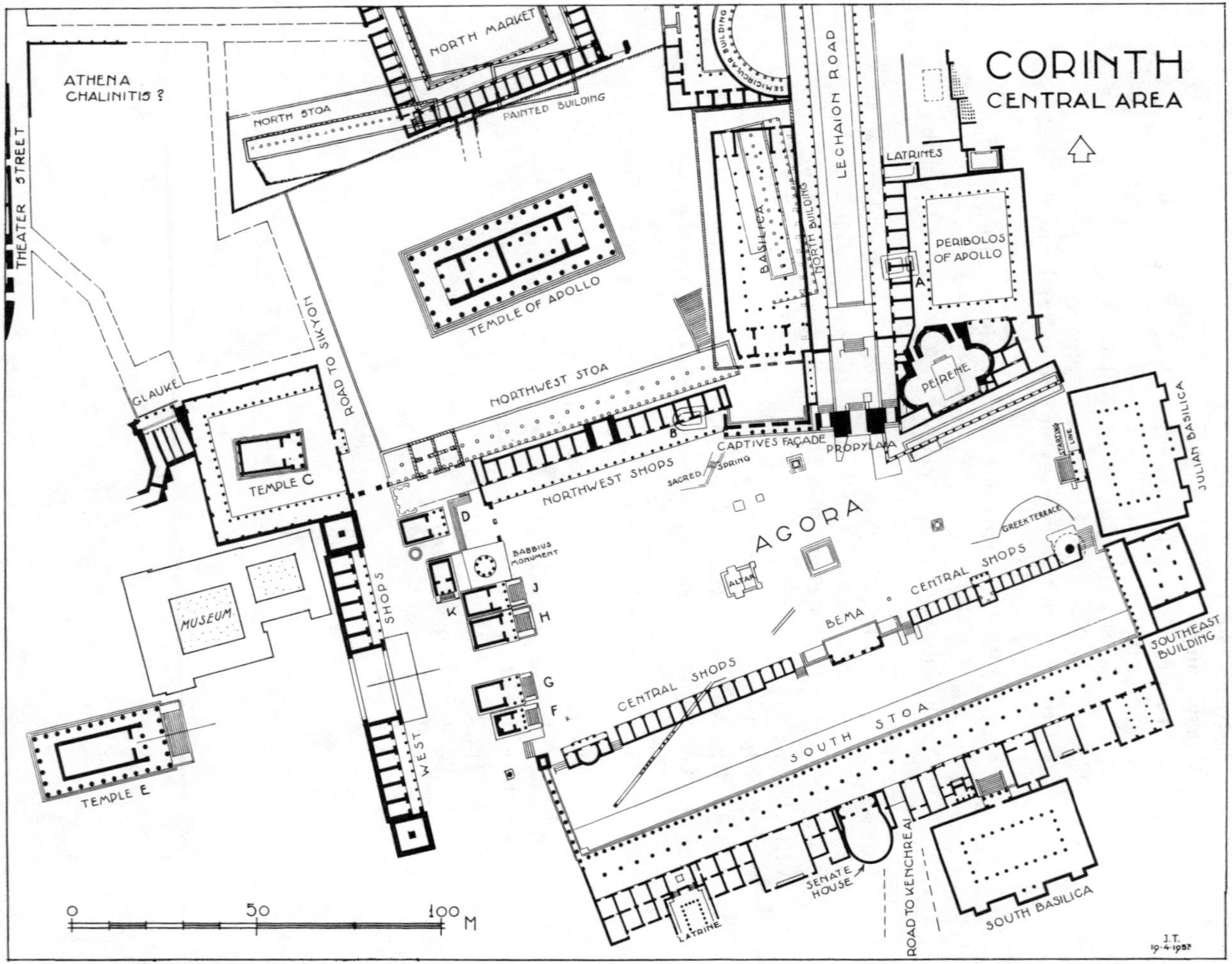

PLAN OF THE CENTRAL AREA OF CORINTH

Courtesy of the American School of Classical Studies at Athens

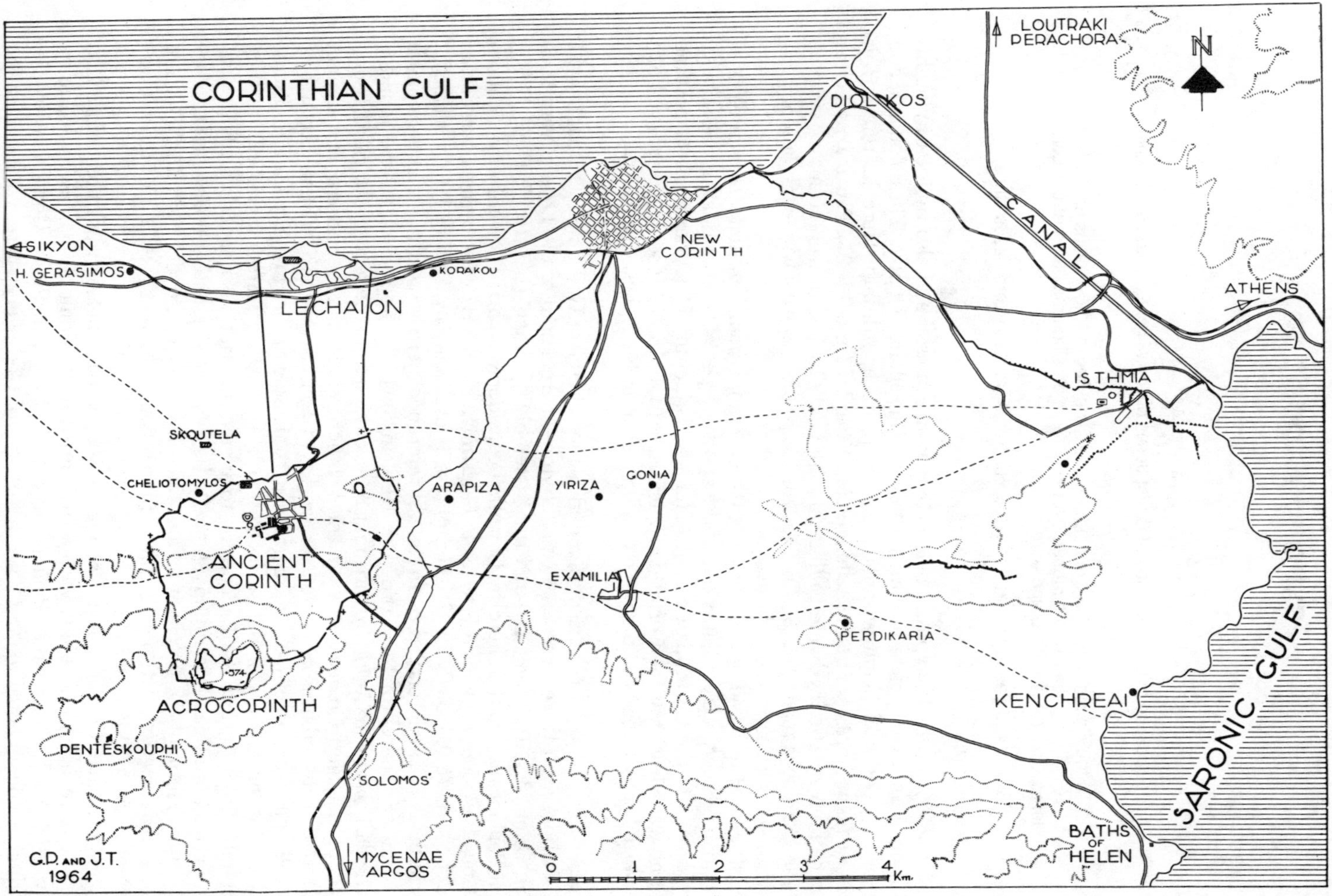

PLAN OF THE CORINTHIA

Courtesy of the American School of Classical Studies at Athens

Text and Exposition

I. Greetings

1:1–3

[1]Paul, called to be an apostle of Christ Jesus by the will of God, and our brother Sosthenes,

[2]To the church of God in Corinth, to those sanctified in Christ Jesus and called to be holy, together with all those everywhere who call on the name of our Lord Jesus Christ—their Lord and ours:

[3]Grace and peace to you from God our Father and the Lord Jesus Christ.

1 Characteristically, the apostle begins by naming himself and also by identifying his position as an apostle of Jesus Christ. Only in Philippians, 1 and 2 Thessalonians, and Philemon does Paul begin without mentioning his apostleship. Here he refers to it because his authority has been challenged (cf. 1 Cor 1:12 and 9:1–27). Paul makes it clear that he is an apostle by divine calling through God's sovereign will (cf. his experience on the Damascus road, Acts 9:15). The word "apostle" (*apostolos*) means "a sent one" and connotes a commissioned envoy.

Sosthenes (the name was a common Greek one), whom Paul links to himself as a Christian brother, was evidently one of the apostle's special helpers and was presumably well known to the Corinthian church. Though his identity is not certain, it is possible that he was a leader of the Corinthian synagogue (Acts 18:17). If so, he must have been converted subsequently and gone off to help Paul in his Ephesian ministry.

2 The believers in Corinth are designated as the "church of God," a phrase that has OT associations as in the expression "assembly [or congregation] of the Lord" (Num 16:3; 20:4; Deut 23:1; 1 Chron 28:8) and the "assembly of Israel" (Lev 16:17; Deut 31:30). That Paul means that this church at Corinth is considered a part of the universal "church of God" is evident from his reference to Palestinian churches as also being a part of that body (1 Cor 15:9; cf. 10:31, 32). The phrase is used only by Paul in 1 Corinthians, 2 Corinthians 1:1, and Acts 20:28. (In the last reference there is a textual variant—"church of God" or "church of the Lord"; cf. UBS, in loc.) The apostle may have found it particularly useful in Corinth to distinguish the church from the secular *ekklēsiai* (assemblies) of mainland Greece and from the heathen religious organizations. The ancient *ekklēsiai* or assemblies of the secular world, in contrast to the Christian *ekklēsia* or church in its worship of God, were gatherings of the citizenry in a city-state to discuss and decide on matters of public interest (cf. Acts 19:39; Herodotus 3.142), as they certainly did in Corinth itself according to ancient inscriptions found there. For example, in two Corinthian inscriptions shown to be near the first half of the second century B.C., by the form of the letters, it is said, "The assembly decreed." (*Corinth: Results of the Excavations*, Vol. VIII, Part I, *Greek Inscriptions, 1896–1927*, ed. B.D. Meritt [Cambridge: Harvard University Press, 1931], numbers 2, 3.)

The Corinthian Christians are described as set apart and in a holy position before God because of their spiritual union with Jesus Christ. In speaking of them as "called to be holy"—i.e., set apart for God—Paul means that they are called to be God's holy people. So they are on an equal footing with the people of God everywhere, who also call on the name of Jesus Christ as Savior and Lord (cf. Acts 9:14, 21). The unity of believers in Christ is shown by Paul's emphatic words in v.2, "their Lord and ours."

3 This verse is identical to Romans 1:7b; 2 Corinthians 1:2; Galatians 1:3; Ephesians 1:2; and Philemon 1:3. Though carrying a sense of greeting, "grace and peace" also refer to the truth of redemption purchased by Christ. It was of God's grace that the Corinthian believers were saved (2 Cor 8:9; Eph 2:8, 9), just as all Christians are saved, and through this redemption Jesus Christ purchased peace with God for the sinner (Eph 2:14; cf. Rom 5:1).

Paul emphasizes that this grace and peace are of divine origin; they are from (*apo*) God our Father who planned redemption and from Christ who purchased it on the cross for the justification of his people and for blessing in their daily lives (cf. Rom 15:13, 33; Phil 4:6, 7).

Notes

1 Notice Paul's emphasis on κλητός (*klētos*, "called") in the phrase "called to be holy." Cf. v.9, "God through whom you were called into fellowship with His Son" (NASB). It was "through" (διά, *dia* with the genitive) the instrumentality of God's sovereign will that Paul was called. God is the efficient cause.

2 Ἐκκλησία (*ekklēsia*), is frequently LXX tr. for קָהָל (*kahal*, "assembly," "congregation," as in Deuteronomy 4:10; 9:10. Compare Acts 7:38, ἐν τῇ ἐκκλησίᾳ ἐν τῇ ἐρήμῳ (*en te ekklēsia en te erēmō*, "in the congregation in the desert"). The church of God is one church of which the church at Corinth was a part.

The participial form ἡγιασμένοις (*hēgiasmenois*) is in the perfect tense, indicating a position of holiness accomplished by God and continuing in force. The expression ἐν Χριστῷ Ἰησοῦ (*en Christō Iēsou*, "in Christ Jesus") speaks of the believer's spiritual location in Christ and so has the meaning "union with Christ." The term ὄνομα (*onoma*, "name") used here as in a number of other places (cf. Acts 4:12), signifies the person and the inherent character of the person designated by the name. Here the name, that is, the person Jesus Christ, is called on. The verb ἐπικαλέω (*epikaleō*, "called upon") is in the present middle participial form, indicating a continual earnest appeal and dependence on Christ, who alone can save.

II. Paul's Thanksgiving for God's Work in the Lives of the Saints

1:4–9

4 I always thank God for you because of his grace given you in Christ Jesus. 5 For in him you have been enriched in every way—in all your speaking and in all your knowledge—6 because our testimony about Christ was confirmed in you. 7 Therefore you do not lack any spiritual gift as you eagerly wait for our Lord Jesus Christ to be revealed. 8 He will keep you strong to the end, so that you will be blameless on the day of our Lord Jesus Christ. 9 God, who has called you into fellowship with his Son Jesus Christ our Lord, is faithful.

4–6 As is characteristic of Paul in other letters (cf. Rom 1:8; Phil 1:3–7; Col 1:3–8, et al.), he begins with thanksgiving to God for those he is addressing. He realizes that God has given them his grace through their union with Christ, enriching their lives by their ability to speak about God and by their knowledge of him (v.5). Paul is thankful that the testimony he gave them was confirmed or established in their lives.

The verb *eucharisteō,* in its present form here (a customary present) with the adverb *pantote,* ("I at all times give thanks"), indicates Paul's habitual prayer life in which he regularly interceded for the believers at Corinth as well as those at every place he preached the gospel (cf. Eph 1:16; Phil 1:3, et al.). Elsewhere Paul uses the concept of the grace of God to express his own call into the ministry as an apostle (Rom 12:3; 1 Cor 3:10; Gal 2:9; Eph 3:2, 3). But here he uses the expression to indicate aspects of God's work in the daily lives of the Christians at Corinth.

Greeks naturally put emphasis on knowledge and wisdom (cf. 1 Cor 1:18–25) and they certainly were good at expressing their thoughts. However, God had so enriched the lives of these people in spiritual perception and expression that they had been given increased ability in speaking. The extent of their enrichment is seen in the use of the adjective "all" with both concepts—"speaking" ("word," *logos*) and "knowledge" (v.5). Paul is convinced that this was a real work of God's grace because he saw his witness about Christ established in their lives at the time of their conversion and had heard about it since then.

The phrase "in every way" (*en panti*) is obviously limited to the qualities and experiences that were relevant to the Corinthians as exemplified by their ability in speaking and by their abundance of knowledge. "You have been enriched" (*eploutisthete*) certainly does not refer here to conversion or to baptism, but rather to God's blessing in knowing and speaking Christian things. The aorist tense of this verb here in a constative sense (*i.e.,* emphasizing a total definitive action), sums up God's work in the lives of the Corinthians—God did it, he made them rich! That their "speaking" and "knowledge" were interrelated is evidenced by the use in the Greek text of a single Greek preposition *en* ("in") to unite these two terms. Perhaps eloquent speaking was uppermost in their minds (cf. Apollos the orator, Acts 18:24–28). Or they may have tried to display vainly their wisdom, which Greeks were apt to do (cf. 1 Cor 1:22).

The reference to "knowledge" (*gnosis*) in v.5 should not be construed to mean that the Corinthians possessed some hidden mystical knowledge by which in itself and without the cross of Christ they could somehow reach God and be saved. As the heresy known as Gnosticism developed in later centuries, some thought they could do this. They were called Gnostics, from the Greek word *gnosis* (the word used in 1 Cor 1:5), which in Paul's day simply meant "knowledge." Cf. "*knowing* Christ Jesus my Lord" (Phil 3:8) and "I want to *know* Christ and the power of his resurrection and the fellowship in his sufferings, becoming like him in his death" (Phil 3:10). Paul is speaking of concrete knowledge based on the reality of Christ's person and his death on the cross. This is not Gnosticism's secret, mystical, and symbolic knowledge supposedly leading through self-effort to higher levels toward God.

7,8 Now Paul addresses himself to their needs for present and future Christian living. He introduces the thought by "therefore" followed by a present-tense verbal form: "Therefore you do not lack any spiritual gift." The verb *hystereō* has the basic meaning of "fail" or "lack." This potential lack does not necessarily refer to the lack of special gifts mentioned in 1 Corinthians 12–14, because there Paul indicates that each Christian is not to exercise every gift (1 Cor 12:27–31). Rather, he seems to be referring more generally to God's grace actively counteracting the sins and faults so prevalent in the Corinthian congregation. Paul expresses confidence that God will keep them strong and will present his people blameless before him at Christ's return, which they are eagerly waiting for (vv.7, 8).

The circumstantial participle *apekdechomenous*—translated "eagerly wait for" in NIV—is one of attendant circumstance. The word *apokalupsis* ("an unveiling," "a disclosure") can mean a revealing of truth, but here refers to the unveiling of Christ, his appearance at his second coming. Cf. "the day of our Lord Jesus Christ" in v.8. See also 1 Peter 1:7, 13.

It is not clear in v.8 who "he" refers to—the Father or Christ. Christ is the nearer antecedent (v.7), but in the light of the reference to God's faithfulness in v.9, it is best taken as referring to the Father. Through God's power and strengthening, Christians will certainly be blameless when Christ comes again.

9 Before concluding this section of thanksgiving, Paul assures the Corinthians of God's faithfulness. As God called them initially into fellowship with Christ, so he is faithful in completing the work, granting them every grace and gift for daily life (cf. Phil 1:6).

Observe the apostle's fivefold repetition of the name of Jesus Christ in this brief section. All of salvation—past, present, and future—is based on Christ's redemptive work. And he is coming again!

Some scholars, such as Schmiedels, have claimed that Paul's opponents were Jewish Christian Gnostics, on the theory that gnosticism was already fully developed in Paul's day or had been developed in pre-Christian times. (Cf. W. Schmithals, *Gnosticism in Corinth* [Nashville: Abingdon, 1971] and *Paul and the Gnostics* [Nashville: Abingdon, 1972].) Paul seems to have had foes with gnostic tendencies in mind when he wrote about "hollow and deceptive philosophy, which depends on human tradition and the basic principles of this world rather than on Christ" (Col. 2:8), calling them to depend on Christ himself "in whom are hidden all the treasures of wisdom and knowledge" (2:3). But this is far removed from a developed gnosticism of the second to the fifth centuries A.D., which depended on knowledge and wisdom themselves for rising higher to God. R.M. Wilson has shown that the parallels between NT terminology and thought, on the one hand, and that of later fully developed gnosticism and later Gnostic treatises of the second to fifth century A.D., on the other, are not sufficient to show a fully developed first-century gnosticism. (R.M. Wilson, *Gnosis and the New Testament* [Philadelphia: Fortress Press, 1968], pp.51ff. See also Donald Guthrie, *New Testament Introduction* [Downers Grove, Ill.: Inter-Varsity Press, 1970], pp.422, 423.)

III. The Problem of Divisions in the Church

1:10–17

[10]I appeal to you, brothers, in the name of our Lord Jesus Christ, that all of you agree with one another so that there may be no divisions among you and that you may be perfectly united in mind and thought. [11]My brothers, some from Chloe's household have informed me that there are quarrels among you. [12]What I mean is this: One of you says, "I follow Paul"; another, "I follow Apollos"; another, "I follow Cephas"; still another, "I follow Christ."

[13]Is Christ divided? Was Paul crucified for you? Were you baptized into the name of Paul? [14]I am thankful that I did not baptize any of you except Crispus and Gaius, [15]so no one can say that you were baptized into my name. [16](Yes, I also baptized the household of Stephanas; beyond that, I don't remember if I baptized anyone else.) [17]For Christ did not send me to baptize, but to preach the gospel—not with words of human wisdom, lest the cross of Christ be emptied of its power.

10 In the light of information given him about divisions in the church, Paul exhorts the Christians both positively and negatively. "I appeal" (*parakalo*) can have the note of appeal as in "exhort" or "encourage," or the stronger emphasis of "implore" or "entreat." It is this latter idea that best fits the context here. First he charges them to have a united testimony ("speak the same thing," KJV; "agree with one another," NIV, v.10). Then he adds his plea for inward harmony in mind and confession about Christ. Between these two positive exhortations Paul introduces the solemn purpose: "that there may be no divisions" in the Christian community. The word "divisions" (*schismata*, literally "tears" or "cracks") graphically conveys the idea of the dissensions that were rending the church. He makes this exhortation through (*dia*) the authority of Jesus Christ (10a), whose name they revere.

11 Paul, as this verse indicates, had received word about the divisions in the Corinthian church from members of a certain Chloe's house. Presumably, all of them were Christians and obviously had some vital connection with the church, doubtless being among its members. The genitive expression *tōn Chloēs* ("some from Chloe's household," literally "those of Chloe," does not make clear what the exact relationship was, whether relatives, slaves, or friends. Paul speaks very specifically. He says that "those of Chloe" reported that there were "quarrels" in the church, quarrels of such a nature as to call for his reprimand.

12 The Corinthian church was divided into at least four factions, each having its own emphasis, following its own leader, and acting in antagonism to the other three. How frequently local church congregations today are likewise divided into cliques! At Corinth the four groups centered around four prominent leaders. First, there were those who claimed to be special adherents of Paul, possibly because of his emphasis on the ministry to the Gentiles, a ministry with which many of them were connected. Then there were those following Apollos, enamored of that learned and eloquent preacher from Alexandria (Acts 18:24; 19:1, Titus 3:13). The followers of Cephas (Peter's Aramaic name John 1:42) were no doubt impressed by this apostle's emphasis on the Jews. Possibly they connected him with the Judaizers. The mention of the "Christ" party suggests that some Corinthians claimed special relationship to Christ (2 Cor 10:7), or placed a special emphasis on him—an emphasis they felt the followers of Paul, Apollos, and Cephas had neglected or did not have.

13 Paul quickly destroys the validity of such distinctions. Christians are all one in Christ. He teaches this by asking, "Is Christ divided?" He shows the foolishness of even raising the question. This he does by asking two other questions by which he denies that Paul was crucified for them and that they were baptized in his name. The same could be said also of Apollos and Peter.

14–16 The mention of baptism leads Paul to comment that the Corinthian believers had no reason to depend on the efficacy of baptism by him as a sanctifying grace, because he had baptized so few—Crispus, Gaius, and the house of Stephanus, these being the only ones he could remember for the moment as having been baptized by him. Crispus probably was at one time the head of the Corinthian synagogue (Acts 18:8) and Gaius was probably the Gaius mentioned as Paul's host in Romans 16:23. Stephanas we know as the one Paul calls the "first fruits of Achaia" and he, with Fortunatus and Achaicus, was with Paul at Ephesus (1 Cor 16:15, 17). The whole house or household of this prominent man was baptized by Paul.

Oikos basically means "house." In some places (e.g., Luke 12:39) it means the dwelling itself, the physical building, but here it means the people who make up the household, the family. Presumably this included both his blood relations and their servants—an example of a household baptism.

17 Why Paul did not baptize more during his stay at Corinth we are not told. It could be that he counted the new Corinthian believers to be in a catechetical-instruction stage under his teaching and that he would depend on Apollos his successor at Corinth (Acts 19:1) to take care of this sacrament of Christian witness at the proper time. At any rate, in order to balance his rather prominent reference to baptism, the apostle now states that his essential work was preaching the gospel (Acts 26:17, 18). His baptizing people was, he teaches (v.17), an accompaniment of his preaching, and his mention of this gives him an opportunity to talk about the thrust of his preaching ministry. His method was to preach not "with words of human wisdom," by which he means, not with the cleverness of human argumentation. He states this lest, in dependence on human argument, the heart of the message of the cross should be emptied of its essential meaning.

The present tense of the verb *euangelizesthai* stresses the priority of Paul's continuing task of preaching the gospel; baptizing was a consequence of preaching and was of secondary importance.

The phrase *en sophia logou* can be translated "in cleverness of speaking," with dependence on philosophical arguments such as those of Plato and Aristotle and the clever sophistries of current Greek life.

Notes

13 The perfect tense verb form *μεμέρισται* (*memeristai*) conveys the thought "Has Christ already been divided and continues so in the congregation?" In this kind of a situation, each leader with his group could have claimed to have a special source through Christ for salvation. By bringing up himself as an example (second negative; see the *μή* [*mē*] negative that expects a "no" response to a question), Paul shows that no one of the human leaders has any vicarious power for salvation but that Christ is the savior who unites all.

R. St. John Parry (in loc.) suggests that *memeristai* can be taken passively (as we have done) and tr., "Has Christ been divided?" or in the middle voice: "Has Christ shared [you] with others?" But he notes that for this latter there is no expressed object (you) for the verb. He correctly favors the passive.

IV. The Wisdom of God—the Preaching of Christ Crucified (1:18–2:16)

A. *Christ, the Power and Wisdom of God*

1:18–25

18For the message of the cross is foolishness to those who are perishing, but to us who are being saved it is the power of God. 19For it is written:

"I will destroy the wisdom of the wise;
the intelligence of the intelligent I will frustrate."

> 20Where is the wise man? Where is the scholar? Where is the philosopher of this age? Has not God made foolish the wisdom of the world? 21For since in the wisdom of God the world through its wisdom did not know him, God was pleased through the foolishness of what was preached to save those who believe. 22Jews demand miraculous signs and Greeks look for wisdom, 23but we preach Christ crucified: a stumbling block to Jews and foolishness to Gentiles, 24but to those whom God has called, both Jews and Greeks, Christ the power of God and the wisdom of God. 25For the foolishness of God is wiser than man's wisdom, and the weakness of God is stronger than man's strength.

In this section Paul emphasizes that salvation is in Christ and not in the wisdom of men. Because Christ, the power and wisdom of God, is the source of men's salvation, men have no basis for boasting.

18–25 These verses flow logically from the proposition of v.17 that Paul did not come preaching with human wisdom. As he avoids this human ostentation, he realizes that the straightforward presentation of the message of the cross produces two effects. It is foolishness to those who are lost, but the power of God to those who are being saved (Rom 1:16). In his emphasis that God's power for salvation is in the cross, Paul in v.19 introduces an OT quotation from Isaiah 29:14 to show that God dismisses the wisdom of men as a means of salvation. In the Isaiah context, the Lord deplores the man-made precepts and mouthing of words for salvation (Isa 29:13) and declares that he will set aside men's wisdom and understanding as a means of finding favor with him. This thought Paul now adapts to his argument.

Having established God's rejection of man's striving for salvation through wisdom, the apostle now asks just where in fact "the wise man" (v.20) can be found who is able to do what the message of the cross of Christ has done. By "wise man" Paul may already be alluding to the Greeks (v.22b). The "scholar" (*grammateus*, "scribe"—"teacher of the law," NIV elsewhere) was the Jewish professional who was skilled in the law and often emphasized its technicalities. "The philosopher of this age" (v.20) was the man who wanted to dispute every issue and solve it by human reason. The designation could fit both Greek and Jew.

The term *grammateus* (v.20), related to the verb "write," sometimes means merely "secretary" or "clerk" (Acts 19:13), but in first-century A.D. Jewish circles it was a technical term to indicate "a teacher of the law," "an expert in the Jewish law." For the saved Jews in the Corinthian congregation this idea would be relevant. *Suzētēs* ("philosopher," "disputer," "debater") is a more general term used here to cover any other human attempt by intellectual endeavor to insure salvation. The negative *ouchi*, the strengthened form of *ouk*, ("not") used at the beginning of a question anticipates a positive response whether obtained or not: "Has not God made foolish . . . ?"

Paul goes on to explain in v.21 that in God's all-wise purpose men with all their philosophical and religious wisdom and searching "did not come to know God" as the definite aoristic effect of the verb shows. This is not to deny the truth that, as Paul says in Romans 1:18–20, men have had a certain knowledge of God through the natural creation. Rather, Paul says, it was God's good purpose (*eudokēsen*) to save those who believe by the seemingly foolish process of preaching the cross. The *kerygma* is the preached message, "the message of the cross" (v.18).

In explanation of the world's seeking God through wisdom, Paul states that the Jews seek for "miraculous signs," and the Greeks seek wisdom (v.22), and through these means they hope to find the answers to the questions about God and life. The Jews were seeking signs to identify the Messiah and the apocalyptic deliverance they hoped God would bring them (cf. Mark 8:11; John 6:30). But Jesus had said that the Jews would be given only "the sign of the prophet Jonah" (Matt. 12:39, 40) to point to his death as Messiah. Thinking of an eschatological Messiah, the disciples of Jesus also wondered about the restoration of the kingdom to Israel, which the Lord said would come later in God's time (Acts 1:6, 7). By the word Hellēnes ("Greeks") the apostle referred primarily to the native Greeks of Corinth, though in a broader sense that word also refers here to the whole non-Jewish world (cf. Col. 3:11). See in v.23 Paul's use of "Gentiles" instead of "Greeks."

Paul now says (v.23) that his task is to preach Christ crucified. The perfect-tense form of the participle (*estaurōmenon*) conveys the thought that Christ's death has a continuous vicarious effect (cf. Gal. 2:20). To the unsaved Jews, however, this message of a crucified Christ was a "stumbling block," an offense, (Gr. *skandalon;* cf. English "scandal") for they expected a political deliverer. To the non-Jewish world (ethnē) the cross was "foolishness"—criminals died on crosses, and they could not see how the cross provided any moral philosophical standard to help them toward salvation. Furthermore, the Greeks and Romans looked on one crucified as the lowest of criminals, so how could such a one be considered a savior? (Lucian, *De morte Peregrini,* 13, mocks at those who worship a crucified sophist.) From their viewpoint, the Greeks would have had difficulty in conceiving of how a god, being spirit, could become incarnate and thus provide a god-man atonement for sin. This was a philosophical problem for them, though they conceived of the Olympian gods—Zeus, Hera, Athena, etc.—as having human characteristics, including sin, and as somehow having the ability of begetting and of being begotten by humankind.

In contrast, Paul states that God has his chosen ones, "the called" (*klētous*) from both the Jews and Gentiles (v.24). Paul has preached to such people about God's effective power to save them and of his wise plan through Christ to bring this about. He next uses a kind of paradoxical hyperbole (v.25) to present the greatness of God's wisdom: God has foolishness, God has weakness! What Paul means is that God's smallest, least significant thought is more worthwhile than the wisest plans of mankind. And God's seemingly insignificant expression of his creative and providential power, as the coming of the dew or the unfolding of a leaf, is greater and more effective than the mightiest thoughts and acts of men. He has complete control and fully accomplishes his purposes, while the power, acts, and thoughts of men are in comparison as nothing.

Notes

---

18 The present tense used in both the participles **τοῖς ἀπολλυμένοις** (*tois apollymenois,* "those who are perishing") and **τοῖς σωζομένοις** (*tois sōzomenois,* "those who are being saved,") emphasizes the progressive state of those concerned: those who think the message foolish are now on the way to a final lostness in hell; those who respond are in the process of being saved by God's power—they are declared righteous by God and are in the process of being made holy, a process to be completed when Christ comes again. (Compare the use of these words in Luke 13:23; Acts 2:47; 2 Cor 2:15; 4:3; and 2 Thess 2:10). By **μωρία** (*mōria,* "foolishness") Paul means that the message does not make any sense to those who are perishing.

19 The meaning of the perfect tense form **γέγραπται** (*gegraptai,* "it is written") conveys the idea that the effect of what God promised in Isa 29:14 continues to be true. The passage as Paul cites it is practically identical with LXX. It differs from LXX only in the use of the verb **ἀθετήσω**

(*athetēsō*, "I will set aside, "thwart") in the place of κρύψω (*krypsō*, "I will hide, conceal"). The idea, however, is the same: God will make ineffective the insight or understanding of man as a means of attaining salvation. The Heb. term סתר (*satar*) in Isa 29:14, in the Hithpael stem, carries a passive connotation with its intensive reciprocal meaning; "shall be hid completely from themselves." This idea Paul may have sought to convey from the Heb. by his use of *athetēsō*.

24 In the Gr. text, before the word χριστόν (*Christon*) a verb is understood. The verb "preach" can be supplied from v.23 with the meaning "We preach Christ as the power of God and the wisdom of God."

25 The expression τῶν ἀνθρώπων (*tōn anthrōpōn*, "of the men") is inclusive of all mankind: God's "insignificant" thought and smallest act are greater than those of "the men"; i.e., the totality of men.

1:26–31

26Brothers, think of what you were when you were called. Not many of you were wise by human standards; not many were influential; not many were of noble birth.
27But God chose the foolish things of the world to shame the wise; God chose the weak things of the world to shame the strong. 28He chose the lowly things of this world and the despised things—and the things that are not—to nullify the things that are, 29so that no man may boast before him. 30It is because of him that you are in Christ Jesus, who has become for us wisdom from God—that is, our righteousness, holiness and redemption. 31Therefore, as it is written: "Let him who boasts boast in the Lord."

26 Having contrasted God's strength and man's weakness, Paul now speaks about the circumstances under which God has called his people. Not many of them were of the intellectual-philosopher class, nor of the politically powerful, nor of the upper level of society.

The present tense of the verb *blepete* (NIV, "think of") emphasizes the current attention to be paid to God's calling of his people. *Klēsis* ("calling"; NIV, "called") is a noun with an action ending (*-sis*) and stresses God's dynamic drawing of his people to himself (Rom 11:29; Eph 1:18). In the light of its use in 1:22, *sophoi* ("wise") here places the emphasis on the Greek intellectual or philosopher class, those wise "according to human standards" (*kata sarka*). By *dunatoi* ("influential") Paul means to include the politically powerful. *Eugeneis* ("those of noble birth") includes all the upper classes—the aristocracy. By these three terms, then, Paul has given the sweep of all that men count socially, politically, and intellectually important.

27 God has chosen from the world those who seem foolish and those who seem weak and helpless so that he might put to shame the wise and powerful by showing how temporary and insignificant as to salvation their achievements are. And in his grace he has showered his mercy on the foolish and weak of this world and made them strong and wise in Christ.

28 Paul continues by stating that God has chosen those of the lower levels of society. First he mentions the slave class (the *agenē*, "low born") and the despised (*ta exouthenēmena*). These terms were particularly appropriate for the situation at Corinth because there were so many slaves there. Also among those God has called, Paul lists the *ta mē onta*, "the things that are not"—i.e., "the nonexistent," those who seem to the world to be nonentities. God has done this, Paul says, that he might show those who seem to be important (*ta onta,* "the things that are") that they can accomplish nothing for their own salvation because their wisdom, power, and importance are ineffective for this.

29 God has worked this way—chosen men according to his grace and not according to their merits—to show that no man may boast in God's presence that he has gained his salvation by his own effort.

30,31 Instead of boasting, redeemed men must realize that salvation is all of God's grace: it is because of God's effective plan that they are in Christ Jesus, (i.e., in saving union with Christ; cf. John 15:1–7; Rom 5:12–21). This saving relationship is a true one because Christ has become or been made for us wisdom from God so that through him we have come to know God (John 1:18; 14:6–9) and are made "wise for salvation" (2 Tim 3:14–17). Paul shifts from "you" to "we" to make certain the readers understand that all Christians, including himself, have this vital union with Christ.

Paul adds other effects or results of our union with Christ: he is righteousness, sanctification, and redemption for us. These concepts may be taken (1) as separate truths in addition to God's wisdom in sending Christ to die or (2) as explanatory of the wise plan effective in the substitutionary atonement. The second interpretation is to be preferred because of the particles *te kai . . . kai.* The sentence, then, should read: "He has become for us wisdom from God, that is, righteousness and sanctification and redemption." Christ in God's wise plan has become our righteousness and has taken our sin on himself (2 Cor 5:21). Christ has become our sanctification and has made possible our growth in grace in the Christian life (Rom 8:9, 10; Eph 2:8–10; 2 Pet 3:18). He is our redemption (*apolutrōsis*)—the person by whom we have been delivered from sin (Rom 3:24), the devil, hell, and the grave (1 Cor 15:55–57).

Because of God's gracious provision of salvation in this way, all praise must go to the Lord. To strengthen this conclusion, he appeals (v.31) to the authority of an OT quotation (Jer 9:24), using it in a condensed form. In OT times as in NT times, it was the duty of saved persons to glory in the Lord for his great salvation.

So it is not through human wisdom, strength, or worldly position that one is saved, but only through God's wise plan and power accomplished through the cross.

Notes

---

27 By using the neuter pl. forms with μῶρα (*mōra,* "foolish things"), ἀσθενῆ *asthenē* ("weak things"), and ἀγενη (*agenē,* "lowly things"), Paul indicates that his emphasis is not on individuals as such but on the qualities and characteristics that make up those individuals. The present tense subjunctive form καταισχύνῃ (*kataischynē*) shows that God continually brings to shame all those who think themselves strong in these respects. The aorist form καταργήσῃ (*katargēsē*) emphasizes that God will totally nullify the efforts of those who make their influence felt in this world.

29 The term πᾶσα σὰρξ (*pasa sarx,* lit. "all flesh") is a figure of speech (synecdoche, a part of a whole) meaning "all people"—they will have no right ever to "boast"—aorist, καυχήσηται (*kauchēsētai*)—in God's presence.

30 The ἐξ αὐτοῦ (*ex autou,* "of him") is Paul's way of expressing, like Aristotle, the efficient cause—God is the ultimate efficient cause, through this sovereign plan, of his people being "in Christ Jesus" (cf. John 15:1–10).

31 The *hina* clause would naturally expect a subjunctive form of the verb, but the apostle does not complete the thought in this normal way because of the imperative καυχάσθω (*kauchasthō*), which he gets from the OT quotation of Jer 9:23, 24.

B. *Paul Preaches Christ in the Power of God*

2:1–5

> [1]When I came to you, brothers, I did not come with eloquence or superior wisdom as I proclaimed to you the testimony about God. [2]For I resolved to know nothing while I was with you except Jesus Christ and him crucified. [3]I came to you in weakness and fear, and with much trembling. [4]My message and my preaching were not with wise and persuasive words, but with a demonstration of the Spirit's power, [5]so that your faith might not rest on men's wisdom, but on God's power.

Paul now returns to the manner of his own preaching introduced in 1:17. He argues that since salvation is attained not through human wisdom or might but only through the cross, he came to Corinth in dependence on the Holy Spirit as he simply preached Christ and the efficacy of his death.

1 In alluding to his visit to Corinth, he is thinking of the initial trip recorded in Acts 18:1–18, when the Corinthians first heard the message and believed. He did not depend on overpowering oratory (*hyperochēn logou*) or philosophical argument (*sophia*). He rather came preaching the "mystery" (*mystērion*) of God—the message not fully understood by them before, but now explained by him and illuminated by the Holy Spirit (2:10–14). In this verse, however, NIV has "testimony" (*martyrion*). See note on v.1.

2 Paul says he came with the sole purpose of centering his attention on the truth concerning Jesus Christ—on the fact and meaning of his crucifixion. The "for" (*gar*) introducing this verse confirms the statement of v.1 about his simple proclamation of the cross. It was not sufficient for Paul to tell about Jesus and his life; he had also to tell about his death for sinners (Acts 10:37–43). Christ died on a Roman cross at Jerusalem and his death was effective then and is effective now to bring forgiveness to sinners (Gal 2:16).

3 Now Paul adds, in effect, "I came preaching, simply as a frail insufficient human being; I came with fear and a great deal of trembling as I realized the importance of preaching the eternal gospel." In writing somewhat later to the Christians at Philippi, he encourages them to live their lives in a similar humble attitude, but at the same time with complete reliance on God (Phil 2:12, 13).

4 So his message and preaching conform to his personal attitude—he does not present his message in a way that depends on overpowering them with wise and persuasive arguments. Though he came in this unostentatious way, yet (*alla*) he came in a display of spiritual power because of the work of the Spirit. In this Epistle it is here that Paul first mentions the Holy Spirit's ministry.

5 Paul's purpose (*hina*), accompanying his humble presentation, is that their Christian faith might not be a superficial, misdirected belief coming from human wisdom, but a real Christian faith generated by the power of God, who also worked in Paul as he preached (v.4). "The faith" (*hē pistis*) spoken of here with the definite article is not to be taken just as the act of believing but as the substance of their belief based on the person and work of Christ. It might be paraphrased, "their Christian faith." We must have the word of God as well as the power of God through the Spirit.

Notes

1 The better combination of MSS favor the word μυστήριον (*mystērion*), though some good MSS have μαρτύριον (*martyrion*, "testimony," "witness"), the tr. given by KJV. In the Bible, *mystērion* does not mean something necessarily unknown, but something not as fully understood at one time as it was at another (See Dan 2:18ff.; 4:9; and Rom 16:25, 26; also see W.H. Mare, "Paul's Mystery in Ephesians 3," *ETS Bulletin*, vol. 8, no. 2 [Spring, 1965], pp. 77ff.)

By the phrase καθ ὑπεροχήν (*kath' hyperochēn*), Paul implies that he did not come depending on any superiority of speech. This term is used elsewhere in the NT only in 1 Tim 2:2 of rulers in a superior or prominent position. The verb καταγγέλλω (*katangellō*, "proclaim"), like its synonym κηρύσσω (*kērysso*), is sometimes used, as in 1 Cor 9:14, with εὐαγγέλιον (*euangelion*, "gospel," the "good news"; cf. also the use of *kēryssō* with *euangelion* in Matt 4:23; Mark 1:14; Gal 2:2).

2 By the use of the aorist form ἔκρινα (*ekrina*, "I resolved" or "decided"), Paul sets forth the total objective of his Corinthian ministry to preach the crucified Christ. The negative οὐ (*ou*) may be taken more properly with *ekrina* in nearer antecedent than with the infinitive εἰδέναι (*eidenai*), thus: "I did not resolve to know." In smoother English this may be tr., "I resolved not to know" or, "I resolved to know nothing" (NIV).

The perfect passive participal ἐσταυρωμένον (*estaurōmenon*) carries with it the definiteness of the past factualness of Christ's crucifixion, but also carries its effects into the present.

4 The words πειθοῖς σοφίας λόγοις (*peithois sophias logois*, "wise and persuasive words") have somewhat shaky MS support; almost of equal value is the reading πειθοῖ ... (*peithoi* ..., "with persuasiveness of wisdom expressed in words"). The basic meaning is the same. The insertion of the word ἀνθρωπίνης (*anthrōpinēs*, "human") found in some MSS seems to be an explanatory gloss inserted by copyists and is plainly secondary (Metzger, p.564).

5 The twin prepositional phrases ἐν σοφίᾳ ... ἐν δυνάμει (*en sophia* ... *en dynamei*) are both causal in force here and are in absolute contrast (ἀλλ,' *all'*, "but")—i.e., not men but God.

C. *Wisdom of Christ Revealed by the Holy Spirit* (2:1–16)

2:6–9

6We do, however, speak a message of wisdom among the mature, but not the wisdom of this age or of the rulers of this age, who are coming to nothing. 7No, we speak of God's secret wisdom, a wisdom that has been hidden and that God destined for our glory before time began. 8None of the rulers of this age understood it, for if they had, they would not have crucified the Lord of glory. 9However, as it is written:

"No eye has seen,
  no ear has heard,
no mind has conceived
  what God has prepared for those who love him"—

Paul now makes clear that his presentation of God's eternal plan of salvation (v.7) is based, through the Holy Spirit, on the wisdom of God revealed to Paul and to others, a wisdom to be understood by those who are God's people.

6 In case some think that the gospel is devoid of wisdom, Paul states that it involves a higher wisdom discernible by those who are mature (*teleioi*)—those who have attained the goal and are spiritually mature. Though some understand "the mature" as referring to those far advanced in spiritual understanding compared with infants in Christ (cf. 1 Cor 3:1), the context favors the conclusion that these spiritually mature were the saved—those enlightened by the Holy Spirit—in contrast to the unsaved. This latter view is supported by Paul's argument that it is the unsaved who think the gospel is foolish (1:21–23) and that the unsaved person does not receive the things of the Spirit of God (2:14). This wisdom, Paul says, does not come from this age of time and space and certainly not from the rulers of this age (those who are of highest importance in the world), because such people crucified the Lord of glory (v.8). Paul says these rulers with their wisdom will end up in futility (v.6b).

7 Describing God's wisdom further, Paul states that it is a wisdom that is contained in a mystery ("God's secret wisdom") not fully revealed, but which God had planned before the beginning of the ages. This plan originated in God's mind, and though outlined in the OT, is not as fully explained and understood there as it is in the NT. Moreover, God conceived of this plan of redemption in relation to the final glory of the Christian when he shares with Christ the glory of God (Rom 8:17, 18).

8 None of the earthly rulers understood such redemption relating to wisdom, Paul explains. Otherwise, they would not have crucified "the Lord of glory." (Compare elsewhere the titles "King of glory" [Ps. 24:7–10] and "God of glory" [Ps. 29:3; Acts 7:2].) Christ's divinity ("Lord of glory") and his human nature (he was crucified in a real body on a hard, real cross) are now brought together by the apostle, leading to the conclusion that God the Son as incarnate in man died on the cross (Acts 20:28, ". . . the church of God, which he bought with his own blood"). By "rulers" Paul means the leaders of the Sadducees, Pharisees, teachers of the Law, and Herod Antipas, as well as the Romans represented by Pilate and his soldiers (Acts 4:25–28).

9 However, Paul says, the "hidden" wisdom he has been preaching is the wisdom referred to in the OT. It was set forth in the promises God had prepared and laid up for his people—for those who love him. It is these promises that people like the rulers of this world do not see and have not obeyed. The thought of them has not even entered the natural man's mind. That God has prepared these things for us Christians implies that sometime we will know and share in these promised blessings (Rom 8:18–25), which, Paul hastens to say, have been revealed to God's people by the Spirit (v.10).

The expression "it is written" (*gegraptai*) (v.9), though often used to cite OT Scripture (cf. Matt 4:4; Mark 11:17; Rom 1:17, et al.), might merely mean "to use the language of Scripture," or "to speak generally from Scripture" (cf. John 1:45), without meaning that the passage is formally cited. The first two lines of the quotation and the last line are a loose reference to Isaiah 64:4, whereas the third line may be merely a thought from the OT generally as summarized by Paul. Verse 9 does not make a complete sentence in Greek (see the dash at the end of the verse in NIV), but Paul, in giving more than one OT thought, is not attempting strictly to weave them into his sentence structure.

Notes

6 The term τέλειοι (*teleioi*, "mature") can possibly be taken to mean "adults" in comparison with the νήπιοι ἐν Χριστῷ (*nēpioi en Christō*, "immature Christians") of 1 Cor 3:1. But the contrasting term in 3:1 is πνευματικοί (*pneumatikoi*, "spiritual"), not *teleioi*. Rather, the meaning of *teleioi* as "mature" here is more likely an expression for those with the "mature insight" of the saved in distinction from the unsaved, contrasting with the technical use of this term for the "initiates" inducted into the mystery religions (cf. *Hermetic Writings* 4, 4; BAG).

The present tense of the participle καταργουμένων (*katargoumenōn*), stresses the continual passing away of the stream of rulers of this age.

7 Δόξα (*doxa*, "glory," "splendor,") implies reminiscences of the glorious God dwelling with his people in the OT (Exod 24:17; 40:34; Num 14:10) and a foretaste of the future glory the Lord's people will share with the triune God (Rev 21:10, 11, 22, 23).

8 The ἣν (*hen*—fem. accusative relative pronoun) beginning this v. does not refer to the immediately preceding δόξαν (*doxan*, "glory"—also fem.) because it is not glory that the rulers did not understand. Rather, they did not grasp the ςοφία (sophia, "wisdom") of the plan of God. Also this *hen* clause is parallel to the similiar type of clause in v.7, which obviously refers to an expressed σοφίαν (*sophian*) at the beginning of that v.

The perfect form ἔγνωκεν (*egnōken*, "they did not understand"; NIV—"None . . . understood it") conveys the totality of their ignorance of God's wisdom continued from the past.

9 It is not certain whether even the first two (and fourth) lines are to be taken as a formal quotation from the OT. If they are, Isa 64:4 is loosely quoted by Paul here from LXX. That Paul's use of the v. in this place does not fit with the context of the v. in Isa is no difficulty, because the apostle shows he is not trying to prove his argument about God's wisdom by Isa 64:4, or he would have begun with ὅτι (*hoti*, "because"). But he uses "as," in the sense of citing general truth from this Isa passage. The third line of the quote may possibly echo Isa 65:17, "come into mind."

2:10–16

10but God has revealed it to us by his Spirit.

The Spirit searches all things, even the deep things of God. 11For who among men knows the thoughts of a man except the man's spirit within him? In the same way no one knows the thoughts of God except the Spirit of God. 12We have not received the spirit of the world but the Spirit who is from God, that we may understand what God has freely given us. 13This is what we speak, not in words taught us by human wisdom but in words taught by the Spirit, expressing spiritual truths in spiritual words. 14The man without the Spirit does not accept the things that come from the Spirit of God, for they are foolishness to him, and he cannot understand them, because they are spiritually discerned. 15The spiritual man makes judgments about all things, but he himself is not subject to any man's judgment:

> 16"For who has known the mind of the Lord
> that he may instruct him?"

But we have the mind of Christ.

These verses stress the work of the Holy Spirit in revealing the wisdom of God.

10 "But" (*de*), Paul says, God has revealed "to us"; that is, to Paul, to the other apostles, and their associates, the spiritual wisdom that the unsaved rulers of this world did not understand. The verb Paul uses (*apokaluptō*, "reveal") is a strong term, usually used in the NT to indicate divine revelation of certain supernatural secrets (Matt 16:17; Luke

10:22) or used in an eschatological sense of the revelation connected with certain persons and events (Rom 8:18; 1 Cor 3:13). Note also that throughout vv.10–16 Paul speaks mostly in the first person plural, "we" (not "you"), strengthening the interpretation that he is referring primarily to divine revelation given to apostles. Later in 1 Corinthians 3:1–3 Paul returns to addressing the Corinthians as "you." But what is true primarily of Paul and the other apostles, is true secondarily for all Christians—the Spirit helps them to interpret Scripture. The phrase "by [or through] the Spirit" certainly refers to the Holy Spirit, as is shown by the presence of the definite article (*tou*) with Spirit—*the* Spirit. The interpretation "through the human spirit" would not make any sense here because the rulers of this age did not (through human spirit) understand the wisdom of God.

The latter part of v.10 amplifies the first part by showing the *extent* ("all things") and *depth* ("the deep things of God") of the Holy Spirit's revelation of God's wisdom and truth. The present tense of the verb (*eraunaō*, "searches") indicates the continual and effective ministry of the Spirit in his all-pervading infallible guidance of the writers of Scripture (2 Peter 1:21) and in his effective work in the lives of believers (Eph 1:17–19; 3:16–19).

11 The *gar* ("for") here points to an illustration that will show that the spiritual wisdom and truths of God can be understood only through the Holy Spirit, just as human wisdom needs the human spirit to understand it. The conclusion is that only the Holy Spirit can reveal God's wisdom and truth to man. The concept of "spirit" in this verse involves a real personality who thinks and acts—not a force. The expression "the man's spirit within him"—i.e., his human personality being in him—is not to be taken as suggesting that the Holy Spirit of God is in God in the same way—the grammar of v.11b does not suggest this. The only analogy made is that as the human spirit knows or understands human wisdom, so (*houtōs*), the Spirit of God, being God himself, understands the wisdom of God.

12 By way of application, Paul states that it is the Spirit of God they have received. This is in contrast to some other kind of spirit through which some might try to know God's wisdom and truth—whether the spirit of the wisdom of this world (1 Cor 1:20; 2:6; 3:19) or another kind of spirit (cf. 1 John 4:2–6). The purpose of the Holy Spirit's special work of revelation (v.10), Paul says, is that "we may understand what [i.e., the truths] God has freely given us" (v.12).

13 Here Paul reverts to the nature of his own ministry (cf. vv.4, 5). He wants it known that he speaks "not in words taught . . . by human wisdom but in words taught by the Spirit," as he and other associates express spiritual truths in words conveying the real spiritual truth. Again, the contrast is between human wisdom and wisdom from God.

14 In using the generic term "man" (*anthrōpos*), the apostle now shows he is speaking of unsaved man in general, governed as he is only by his "soulish-human" (*psychikos*) nature, not accepting the enlightenment and truths from the spirit of God. Therefore such a person considers those truths to be foolish. Paul makes it even stronger when he says that "the man without the Spirit" cannot understand because these truths can be discerned and understood only with the guidance of the Spirit.

Psychikos (the Greek word that begins this verse) basically means "that which pertains to the soul or life," a word used in NT and patristic literature to refer to the life of the natural world and so contrasted with the supernatural world and the Spirit. So from this comes the translation "man without the Spirit."

It is possible that the words "of God," with the words "the Spirit," are a copyist's addition—a number of MSS omit the words. However, the vast majority of MSS favors their inclusion. Note that the sense is clear either way, that the Spirit of God is in view.

It is to be observed that the verb *anakrino,* translated "discern" in v.14, is the same verb translated "make judgments" and "subject to man's judgments" in v.15. The idea in each case is to make intelligent spiritual decisions. *Anakrino,* though meaning "examine," here includes the decision following the examination (cf. 4:3).

15 In contrast, the person who is guided by the Spirit draws discerning conclusions about all things, that is, about all kinds of spiritual things, but such a spiritual man is not subject to spiritual judgments by any man, i.e., by any man without the Spirit (v.14). This is undoubtedly what Paul means by v.15b, for he elsewhere teaches Christians to make judgments concerning the spiritual condition and actions of other Christians. (See 1 Cor 5:9–12; 12:3; Gal 1:8.)

16 This verse is confirmatory of v.15. In quoting the LXX of Isaiah 40:13, Paul establishes further that the Christian is not subject to man's judgment in spiritual things. The quotation in the form of a question casts doubt on man's knowing God's wisdom, but the statement (v.16b) gives reassurance that the Christian does know it. This explains v.15b—the person who has God's Spirit is not subject to judgments by one who does not have the Spirit.

Paul introduces the "mind of Christ" terminology in order to relate it to the OT expression he has just quoted—"the mind of the Lord." The verse implies that we and *all* God's people can understand spiritual truths and spiritual wisdom in a way similar to the way the Lord knows them. Verse 16 climaxes Paul's argument about his preaching God's "foolishness" (the cross of Christ) without ostentation. Let the philosophers of Greece (cf. Acts 17:18, 32) and the Jews in their sign-seeking jeer and mock. They cannot really judge the message of Paul, who has the mind of Christ, because they do not have the Spirit of God and cannot judge spiritual truths.

Notes

10 Some MSS represented by TR (and KJV) add the pronoun αὐτοῦ (*autou,* "his") to πνεύματος (*pneumatos,* "spirit") but this is clearly an explanatory addition not supported by the better MSS.

11 In v.11b there is no corresponding ἐν αυτῷ (*en autō,* "in him") and the clause simply states that only the Spirit of God (an OT and NT designation of the third person of the Trinity; cf. 1 Sam 10:10; 2 Chron 15:1; Rom 8:9; 1 John 4:2) can understand the things of God.

12 A few MSS have added the demonstrative pronoun τούτου (*toutou*) after κόσμου (*kosmou,* "of this world") a copyist's addition probably to parallel the expression with the phrase "of this age" in 2:6. The shorter text without *toutou* is to be preferred and is supported by the best and the most MSS.

13 The phrase πνευματικοῖς . . . συγκρίνοντες (*pneumatikois . . . synkrinontes*) has evoked at least four different interpretations, depending on how the participle *synkrinontes* is tr.: (1) "bring together" or "give," (2) "compare," or (3) "explain" or "interpret," and depending also on how

the gender of the adjectives is taken. *Pneumatikois* can be either masc. or neuter dative pl.; *pneumatika* can in this context be only neuter accusative pl. The phrase can mean (1) "giving spiritual truth a spiritual form," (2) "comparing spiritual truths with spiritual truths," (3) "interpreting spiritual truths to spiritual men," and (4) "explaining or expressing spiritual truths in spiritual words." Though any of the four interpretations can be argued, view 4 best fits the context of the v. in which Paul has said that he speaks in spiritual words (i.e., words taught by the Spirit, who gives to Paul spiritual truths in spiritual words)—words filled with concrete but spiritual meaning.

15 The τα (*ta*, "the") before (*panta*, "all things") has some good MS evidence, though copyists could have added it, fearing that *panta* could otherwise be taken as masc. accusative sing., "every man."

16 Paul is evidently quoting from the LXX of Isa 40:13; he varies from Rahlfs' LXX text by adding a γάρ (*gar*) and using the verb ὅυμβιβάσει (*symbibasei*) instead of its cognate noun. The meaning is the same.

V. Servants of Christ (3:1–4:21)

A. *Workers With God—False Estimate Corrected (3:1–23)*

1. *Spiritual immaturity and divisiveness*

3:1–9

[1]Brothers, I could not address you as spiritual but as worldly—mere infants in Christ. [2]I gave you milk, not solid food, for you were not yet ready for it. Indeed, you are still not ready. [3]You are still worldly. For since there is jealousy and quarreling among you, are you not worldly? Are you not acting like mere men? [4]For when one says, "I follow Paul," and another, "I follow Apollos," are you not mere men?

[5]What, after all, is Apollos? And what is Paul? Only servants, through whom you came to believe—as the Lord has assigned to each his task. [6]I planted the seed, Apollos watered it, but God made it grow. [7]So neither he who plants nor he who waters is anything, but only God, who makes things grow. [8]The man who plants and the man who waters have one purpose, and each will be rewarded according to his own labor. [9]For we are God's fellow workers; you are God's field, God's building.

In this passage Paul speaks to the Corinthians about the lack of spiritual discernment he has been discussing in chapter 2. This lack is seen in their misconceptions about those who are co-laborers with God. The corrective is given in his later statements about the importance of working correctly for the Lord (3:10–17) and not depending on man or on human wisdom (3:18–23).

1 As in 2:1, Paul calls the Corinthians "brothers" before reprimanding them for their spiritual immaturity. Not only had he not preached to them with persuasive words (2:1–5), but here he states he could not even speak to them as to those with spiritual maturity. They were acting immaturely as those motivated by the world's thoughts and actions. Part of what he means is shown by his reference in vv.4, 5 to the party contentions he had discussed in 1:10–17. The word *pneumatikos* ("pertaining to the spirit," "spiritual") must be interpreted differently in 3:1 from its meaning in 2:14, 15, where Paul uses it to denote the saved person in contrast to the unsaved (one who is without the Spirit). Here in combination with *sarkinos* ("fleshly") and *nēpios* ("infant;" cf. 1 Cor

2:6, *teleios*, "mature"), the adjective *pneumatikos* applies to believers who are spiritually mature Christians—i.e., those led into maturity by the Spirit in contrast with the immature ones still controlled by the fleshly prejudices and viewpoints dominating the unsaved of the world.

2 Paul now amplifies the reference in v.1 to infants, by explaining that when he first came, he fed the Corinthian Christians spiritual milk—i.e., the elementary salvation truths of the gospel. He could not teach them deeper doctrines (*brōma*, "solid food") because as infants in Christ they could not spiritually digest them. The *alla oude eti nyn*, ("Indeed you are still not ready," v.2), emphasizes their continuing immaturity.

3 The descriptive term *sarkikos* ("fleshly") further indicates that these Christians showed characteristics of spiritual immaturity. The *gar* ("for") prepares for Paul's illustrations of this worldliness—"jealousy" (*zēlos*) and quarreling (*eris*), which plague the Christian community. Also implied is allusion to their divisions (v.4).

The question in v.3 is stated in Greek in a way that expects a positive answer. This suggests that the Corinthians, if honest with themselves, should admit their failing here. To walk *kata anthrōpon* ("according to man"—NIV, "acting like mere men") means to live only the way the ordinary sinful man lives—in selfishness, pride, and envy.

4 Paul's example of himself and Apollos who shared in the ministry at Corinth (Acts 18:1–28) was needed to show the Corinthians that they had a distorted view of the Lord's work. Whenever they thought of God's work in terms of belonging to or following a particular Christian worker, they were simply acting on the human level and taking sides just as the world does.

5 In using *oun* ("then"; "after all," NIV), Paul shows he is answering the question "How should Paul and Apollos be viewed?" Observe how, because Paul wants to impress the Christians with the fact that he and Apollos are simply servants, he avoids using the first person plural, "we are servants" but leaves out the verb, so that the implication is that he and Apollos and whatever other workers there might be are no more than servants. The point is that no Christian worker is ever to be idolized. Indeed, those who are idolized can become instruments for fragmenting the work of God. Believers are to realize that Christian workers are simply God's servants (*diakonoi*)—agents through whom people believe in Christ. By "believe" in v.5 Paul does not mean just the initial trust in Christ (Rom 3:22–24) but, as v.6 shows, the planting, watering, and God-given increase—the whole process of growth in the Christian life to maturity (2 Pet 3:18).

6–9 Paul bluntly states, "I planted the seed" and quickly adds, "Apollos watered it, but God made it grow." In vv.7–9 he draws some conclusions from his basic premise: First, since we are merely God's servants, we are really nothing in that we cannot ourselves produce any spiritual results. Rather (again *alla*, "but," is used), it is only God who can do that (v.7).

Second, Paul teaches that the servants with their various functions are really one, being united in God's work (v.8a). Third, though they are one in the work, yet (*de*) they are individually subordinate to God and responsible to him who will reward them according to their faithful labor (v.8b).

Finally, Paul concludes (v.9) that all is of God and that the church ("God's building") is his work. Yet he uses men of different talents and temperaments to help him cause the church to grow. They are, Paul says, the spiritual "field" (*georgion*) in which God's servants are working. In speaking of their being God's *georgion* (God's cultivated field) and of Paul and Apollos and others as God's workers in the field (1 Cor 3:6–9), the apostle brings to the minds of the Corinthians the farming going on in the plain below the city. There the land was plowed, the crops reaped, the grapevines tended, and the grapes gathered—a crop "for which Corinth has for centuries been famous (our word 'currant' is a medieval corruption for Corinth)" (Broneer, "Corinth," B A, Vol SIV 1951, p. 96). Note also the familiar figure of the church in Ephesians 2:20–22 and 1 Peter 2:5. And now, in what Paul has said in vv.6–9 there is a transition to his discussion that is to follow in vv.10–17.

Notes

1 Actually, **πνευματικοῖς** (*pneumatikois*), taken as masc., can be tr. "spirit-filled people" in contrast to **σαρκίνοις** (*sarkinois*, "fleshly," "those controlled by the flesh").

3 The word **διχοστασία** (*dichostasia*, "dissensions," "quarreling"—not in the Gr. text used as the basis for NIV), following **ἔρις** (*eris*), is early and has diversified MS witness (P^{46} D, et al.). Yet its absence in such MSS as $P^{11\ vid}$ ℵ B, et al., speaks against it and favors the possibility of the additional word being a western gloss, possibly derived from the list of vices in Galatians 5:22 (cf. Rom 16:17). The phrase **κατὰ ἄνθρωπον** (*kata anthrōpon*) is an adverbial phrase: "humanly," "in a human way," in contrast to "in a godly way."

Whereas in v.1 **σαρκίνοις** (*sarkinois*) means "belonging to the flesh," "having the characteristics of the flesh," **σαρκικοί** (*sarkikoi*), used in v.3, means "composed of flesh" and stresses that the Corinthian Christians were full of fleshly activities.

The **οὐχί** (*ouchi*, "not"), a strengthened form of **οὐκ** (*ouk*), expects an affirmative response when beginning a question.

5 Here **διάκονοι** (*diakonoi*) is not used in a technical sense of those who serve as church officers (as in Phil 1:1; 1 Tim 3:8), but in the general sense of "servants," whether of a king (Matt 22:13) or otherwise.

The aorist form, **ἐπιστεύσατε** (*episteusate*, "you believed"), is to be taken as punctiliar action in the broadest circle of their Christian experience. They believed initially in Paul's ministry when they were born again, but that trust in the Savior deepened and broadened in their sanctification through the continued ministry of Paul and then of Apollos.

6 The three aorist verb forms in this verse **ἐφύτευσα, ἐπότισεν, ηὔξανεν** (*ephyteusa, epotisen, ēuxanen*, "planted, watered, gave the increase"), coming in quick succession, stress the accomplishment of work for Christ and the finality of God's blessing in spiritual fruit following upon it.

7 Though the participle **αὐξάνων** (*auxanōn*) means here "cause to grow," yet in the figure of the grain field it must include that spiritual germinating principle God alone initiates (cf. John 3:5), just as he does for the physical seed the farmer plants and waters.

8 **Κόπον** (*kopon*, "labor, toil") suggests that the Christian is to serve God intently and intensely to the best of his ability—i.e., to "toil" for the Lord. For this he will receive a reward.

2. *Building on Christ the foundation*

3:10–17

[10]By the grace God has given me, I laid a foundation as an expert builder, and others are building on it. But each one should be careful how he builds. [11]For no

one can lay any foundation other than the one already laid, which is Jesus Christ.
12If any man builds on this foundation using gold, silver, costly stones, wood, hay
or straw, 13his work will be shown for what it is, because the Day will bring it to
light. It will be revealed with fire, and the fire will test the quality of each man's work.
14If what he has built survives, he will receive his reward. 15If it is burned up, he
will suffer loss; he himself will be saved, but only as one escaping through the
flames.

16Don't you know that you yourselves are God's temple and that God's Spirit
lives in you? 17If anyone destroys God's temple, God will destroy him; for God's
temple is sacred, and you are that temple.

Paul now discusses how God's servants can build the church of Christ. The foundation laid down through the preaching of the cross of Christ (1:18) is always the same—Jesus Christ. The Christian workers bring to it their labor and the spiritual materials they use to build the church upon Jesus Christ. At the end is the payday, at the second coming of Christ, when the right kind of work will be rewarded and the wrong kind will be destroyed. The section ends with a declaration that Christians are the temple of God, and a warning that no man is to destroy this temple, for he will then be destroyed.

10,11 Paul views his skill as an expert builder as being possible only through the grace of God. As an expert builder (cf. Prov 8:30), one who knew God's plan for the building of his church (Eph 3:7–10), he had laid the doctrinal foundation of "Jesus Christ and him crucified" (2:2; cf. Isa 28:16; Acts 4:11; Eph 2:20; 1 Peter 2:6). He acknowledges that others, such as Apollos, also build on this foundation of Christ. Then he gives a warning: Every builder—Paul, Apollos, and whoever works for God—must be careful how he builds. The shift in thought is now from the worker to his work.

Verse 11 implies the reason for the warning: though the workers cannot lay a foundation other than Christ, they had better be careful how they build on him. Any defects in their work will be their own fault. Christ cannot be blamed for it.

12–15 Instead of talking about the details of the building itself, Paul turns his attention to the kind of materials Christian workers are using: the materials of preaching the cross for the salvation, building up believers (cf. 1:18), and living a Christian life that is commensurate with that preaching (2:2–4). The purity and depth of such Christian teaching and a life corresponding to it are crucial, for that kind of building material will stand the test of fire on the day of the Lord's judgment.

Since valuable metals and precious stones (cf. Rev 21:18–21) were used to adorn ancient temples, Paul could have taken his imagery from Herod's temple in Jerusalem (Matt 24:1, 2) or from the beautiful public and religious buildings in Athens (Acts 17:23) and Corinth (where the remains of the sixth century B.C. temple of Apollo still stands today). Such imagery would be sufficient to convey the thought of pure doctrine. The frames of ordinary houses and buildings were built of wood; hay or dried-grass, mixed with mud, was used for the walls; and roofs were thatched with straw or stalks. So the kind of insipid teaching and life represented by these lesser things will also have to face the test of the pure fire of God's justice and judgment, when it will be consumed.

The "day" is not a day of calamity or hardship brought by man, but rather "the day of the Lord" (1 Thess 5:2–9), the day of the second coming of Christ (cf. 2 Thess 2:2). The "quality" (v.13) is to be equated with the kinds of materials of doctrine and life that are used. The fire is the fire of God's judgment. Fire in the Scripture is used figuratively in two ways: as a purifying agent (Matt 3:11; Mark 9:49); and as that which consumes

(Matt 3:12; 2 Thess 1:7, 8; Heb 12:29). So it is a fitting symbol here for God's judgment, as he tests the quality of the Christian's work.

Those Christians whose works stand the test of fire (v.14; cf. 1 Peter 1:7) will be rewarded (cf. Matt 25:14–30; Luke 19:11–27). Those whose works are consumed by the fire will themselves escape the flames (as if they were to jump out of the burning wooden structure they had built) and will be saved alone, without any works of praise to present to Christ.

16,17 The temple is reminiscent of the OT tabernacle and temple as well as the holy sanctuary built by Herod. It is to be distinguished from *hieron,* the "temple area." As Jesus speaks of his earthly body as the "temple" (John 2:19–21), so his redeemed people, indwelt by the Spirit of God (1 Cor 6:19), can be called individually and collectively God's temple.

Paul challenges the church with the fact that they together (note the plural constructions) are the spiritual temple of God, because the Spirit of God dwells in them (Eph 2:22; 1 Peter 2:5). Therefore anyone who builds this temple in a shoddy way deserves the destruction of his doctrine and false testimony described in v.15. Implicit in this is a warning against any false teachers coming in among the believers.

More pointedly, Paul states (v.17) that anyone who actually destroys or tends to destroy (i.e., defile or damage) God's temple will be destroyed by God (cf. Lev 15:31). The reason is clear: God's temple is holy, sacred, set apart (Isa 28:16; Rev 3:12). God in his justice and holiness cannot allow part of his holy work to be damaged without bringing retribution. Here is a fitting warning to every Christian minister and worker.

Notes

10 The **ἀρχιτέκτων** (*architectōn,* "expert builder"; cf. "architect") in Gr. practice was the one who supervised the other workers. In a sense, this broad meaning applies here, for though Paul performed his task skillfully, leaving Apollos and others to do their own work, yet he felt responsible for the total work of the church (cf. 2 Cor 11:28). The present tense of the verb **ἐποικοδομεῖ** (*epoikodomei,* "[others are] building on it") allows for the inclusion of other Christian workers besides Apollos.

13 The article **ἡ** (*ē,* "the") with **ἡμέρα** (*hēmera,* "day") shows that Paul is talking about the specific time when judgment will come for Christians—that time referred to in 2 Cor 5:10, when all Christians will appear before Christ's judgment bench to give account of Christian service. NIV rightly capitalizes "Day."

The intensive pronoun **αὐτό** (*auto*) used with the word "fire," meaning "the fire itself," is supported by some of the best early MSS but omitted by others. NIV leaves it out.

14–17 The **εἰ** (*ei*) conditional sentences (first class, assumed as true), posit that some in fact will be faithful workers and some will not.

3. *Complete dependence on God, not men*

3:18–23

[18]Do not deceive yourselves. If any one of you thinks he is wise by the standards of this age, he should become a "fool" so that he may become wise. [19]For the wisdom of this world is foolishness in God's sight. As it is written: "He catches the

wise in their craftiness" 20and again, "The Lord knows that the thoughts of the wise are futile." 21So then, no more boasting about men! All things are yours, 22whether Paul or Apollos or Cephas or the world or life or death or the present or the future—all are yours, 23and you are of Christ, and Christ is of God.

18–20 Paul now returns to the subject of wisdom and warns the believers not to be deceived into thinking that the wisdom of this human age is sufficient for obtaining salvation and for building up the church of God. Rather, if some Christian thinks himself to be wise by this world's standards, he must renounce dependence on this wisdom so that he may really receive God's wisdom (v.18).

In proof of this, Paul again mentions the truth of 1:18–25—the seeming foolishness of the preaching of the cross is really God's true wisdom for salvation. Directly and forcefully he declares that the wisdom of this world is foolishness in God's sight (v.19). He uses two OT Scriptures to support this. The first, is a somewhat free rendering of Job 5:12, 13, which he applies in a special sense to God. The graphic word "catches" vividly portrays the idea that men in their craftiness are no match for God—they set up their schemes of salvation against God's but he catches them up short.

20 Here Paul's quotation of the LXX of Psalm 94:11 shows that the Lord knows all the futile thoughts of the so-called wise men—nothing that enters their minds is beyond his understanding. All that is not in tune with God's thoughts is vain.

21,22 The conclusion of the matter is that no Christian is to boast or glory in the wisdom and attainments of men—not even Paul or Apollos. We are not to put our trust in anything human. The reason is that all things—yes, all the blessings of God in the whole universe—belong to the redeemed church. So the ministry of Paul, Apollos, Cephas (Peter), and any other Christian worker belongs to God's people. Also the *kosmos* (the world itself), the processes of living and dying, the present and the future—all are to be viewed in relationship to God's purposes and plans for his redeemed people. So Paul can say, "All things are yours." Everything is for the believers' benefit, everything belongs to them.

23 "And you are of Christ, and Christ is of God." Though all things belong to the Christian, they are not centered in him, for all things actually and finally belong to God. They belong to the Christian, then, as he himself belongs to God through the mediatorship of Jesus Christ, the Son of God. Christ and the Father are one (John 1:1; 10:30), yet Christ was sent by the Father into the world (John 10:36; 17:18) to effect our redemption so that we may "inherit the kingdom" (James 2:5).

Notes

18 The present imperative ἐξαπατάτω (*exepatatō*) suggests that some in the congregation were already deceiving themselves and must stop doing so.

The first class conditional sentence with εἴ (*ei*) and the indicative suggests that a factual condition existed in that some were actually thinking they were wise according to the world's standards.

20 In the LXX quotation of Ps 94:11 Paul leaves out the broader term, ἀνθρώπων (*anthrōpōn*,

"men") so that he may apply the passage to the narrower thought of "wise men." The rest of the statement is identical with LXX. The term διαλογισμούς (*dialogismous*) may include the reasoning processes of men's minds (cf. Matt 16:7; Luke 12:17).

21 The ὥστε (*hōste*, "so then") clause with the imperative introduces the climax of the argument: Since God knows the so-called wisdom of the world and makes it ineffectual and worthless in the light of his great plan of salvation, the Christian has no right to boast about men and their wisdom.

22 The perfect participle ἐνεστῶτα (*enestōta*) means that which exists in the present, "the present age," (cf. Gal 1:4) in contrast to the coming age, the second coming of Christ and beyond (cf. Eph 1:21).

B. *Servants of Christ: the Ministry of the Apostles* (4:1–21)

1. *Faithful servants*

4:1–5

> [1]So then, men ought to regard us as servants of Christ and as those entrusted with the secret things of God. [2]Now it is required that those who have been given a trust must prove faithful. [3]I care very little if I am judged by you or by any human court; indeed, I do not even judge myself. [4]My conscience is clear, but that does not make me innocent. It is the Lord who judges me. [5]Therefore, judge nothing before the appointed time; wait till the Lord comes. He will bring to light what is hidden in darkness and will expose the motives of men's hearts. At that time each will receive his praise from God.

The beginning of this chapter follows up the preceding discussion about Christian workers. Here Paul adds that these who are counted as servants of Christ are also to be considered stewards of God—those to whom a trust has been committed, a trust they are to prove faithful to.

1 The impersonal *anthrōpos* simply makes the command general: Let man after man count Paul and other Christian workers servants of Christ. The genitive, "of Christ," can be taken in the sense of possession—"servants belonging to Christ." Though *hyperetas* ("servants") may once have had a more etymological meaning relating to "a rower" on board ship, its more general meaning was "servant" or "attendant." Here it means a subordinate servant functioning as a free man, not as a slave (*doulos*). Thus, Paul and Apollos were free servants of Christ, fully responsible to him, and not to the Corinthians.

"Those entrusted with" (*oikonomous*, "house stewards") refers to a position often held by a slave (Joseph, Gen 39:2–19), who managed the affairs of the household entrusted to him. "The secret things of God" indicates those mysteries of salvation God has revealed in his Word (Rom 16:25; Eph 1:9; 3:3, 4; 1 Tim 3:16)—the things man cannot discover by his human wisdom. (See note on "mystery" under 1 Cor 2:1.) These truths of the cross have been entrusted to Christian workers to be carefully used and guarded. As subordinate servants of Christ, they have no right of authority over those truths, but minister them in Christ's name to God's people.

2 Here Paul turns to examine the character of those who are handling God's truth: they, including himself, must first of all show themselves faithful.

3,4 In these verses, the apostle expresses the truth that since he is the Lord's servant and steward, it is to the Lord that he owes responsibility and it is the Lord who judges him for the quality of his service. Human judgment has little value. Even self-evaluation is unreliable, Paul says. Christ is the Lord of the conscience and is the one who can evaluate it properly.

5 Now the apostle leaps forward to the return of Christ when all Christians will have their works examined at the judgment seat of Christ (2 Cor 5:10). Because of this, he charges the Corinthians not to judge his faithfulness. This can be done truthfully only by the Lord when he comes. The present tense of *krinō* ("judge") is graphic and implies that the Corinthians were already judging. Paul is saying to them, "Curb your habit of judging." *Kairos* ("time") is strictly the appointed or definite time when the Lord will come back.

Ta krypta tou skotous ("what is hidden in darkness") are the acts and motives concealed in the inner recesses of a person's mind and heart. In Hebrew poetic style (cf. Pss 18:10; 22:1), Paul says the Lord will "expose the motives of men's hearts" in explanation of his statement "He will bring to light what is hidden in darkness."

Thus, at the second coming of Christ those who have been faithful in their work for the Lord will receive praise from him. Paul has already spoken about the servant receiving "wages" from the Lord (3:8). Compare the parables of the talents and the pounds, in which there is praise and pay for faithful work (Matt 25:14–23; Luke 19:12–19). As the final judging must be done by God, so the final praise will come from him.

Notes

2 The aorist subjunctive form εὑρεθῇ (*heurethē*, with punctiliar action—"that he be found, be proved") looks at the person's ministry as a whole. The Lord looks at it as one picture, expecting to find the servant faithful in all his ministry.

3 The verb ἀνακρίνω (*anakrinō*) definitely conveys the idea of "examine" (Acts 12:19; 17:11), but it can also include, as here, the additional concept of the decision made following the examination (cf. 1 Cor 2:15).

Strictly speaking, the phrase ὑπὸ ἀθρωπίνης ἡμέρας (*hypo anthrōpinēs hēmeras*) means "by a human day." But just as the term "day of the Lord" (1 Cor 1:8; 5:5) involves God's judgment in that eschatological day, so in this context a "human day" means man's judgment in the day when his (man's) courts are in session. NIV well tr. the phrase "by any human court."

4 Paul's use of the δικαιόω (*dikaioō*), "justify" for "judges" does not involve the teaching of justification, which he presents elsewhere (Rom 3:24; 5:1; cf. also *Westminster Shorter Catechism*, Question 38). What he is now saying is that his conscience cannot declare his ministry to be perfectly faithful and therefore make him innocent of any wrongdoing in his service. Rather, God must make that judgment. The perfect tense form, δεδικαίωμαι (*dedikaiōmai*), gives this meaning: "I do not stand in a perfect state of justification or innocence just because my conscience is clear."

5 Paul uses here the simple form κρίνω (*krinō*, "judge") rather than the compound ανακρίνω (*anakrinō*, "examine and then judge"). In using *krinō*, Paul is saying that the Corinthians were actually making a final judgment regarding his faithfulness. If he had used *anakrinō*, he would have been stating that they were judging him in accordance with a full and proper investigation. At any rate, in using *krinō* and the accompanying phrase, "till the Lord comes," the apostle assumes a hasty and inappropriate judgment on their part.

Καιρός (*kairos*), which can indicate a point of time (Matt 24:45) as well as a period of time (Rom 3:26), is to be taken here in the context of the Lord's day of judgment as "an appointed time." At times *kairos* is to be contrasted with **χρόνος** (*chronos*), extended time (cf. Acts 1:7: **χρόνους**, "times"; **καιρούς**, "dates").

---

2. *The proud Corinthians and the despised servants*

4:6–13

6Now, brothers, I have applied these things to myself and Apollos for your benefit, so that you may learn from us the meaning of the saying, "Do not go beyond what is written." Then you will not take pride in one man over against another. 7For who makes you different from anyone else? What do you have that you did not receive? And if you did receive it, why do you boast as though you did not?

8Already you have all you want! Already you have become rich! You have become kings—and that without us! How I wish that you really had become kings so that we might be kings with you! 9For it seems to me that God has put us apostles on display at the end of the procession, like men condemned to die in the arena. We have been made a spectacle to the whole universe, to angels as well as to men. 10We are fools for Christ, but you are so wise in Christ! We are weak, but you are strong! You are honored, we are dishonored! 11To this very hour we go hungry and thirsty, we are in rags, we are brutally treated, we are homeless. 12We work hard with our own hands. When we are cursed, we bless; when we are persecuted, we endure it; 13when we are slandered, we answer kindly. Up to this moment we have become the scum of the earth, the refuse of the world.

Paul describes the difference between himself and Apollos and some of the other Christian leaders. The Corinthians, he says, were proud and claimed to be spiritually rich. On the other hand, Paul and Apollos were considered weak and were despised and persecuted.

6 What Paul has said about not judging or misjudging Apollos or himself he wants understood as applying to the Corinthians' attitude toward all of God's people; they should not take pride in some and despise others. In referring to this tension and misconception on their part, the apostle could be alluding to the real leaders of the factious parties for whom the other names—Paul, Apollos, Peter, and Christ—had been substituted. But then it seems strange that he does not name them. Or he may be simply referring to some who were responsible for stirring up this misconception about how God's ministers should be viewed.

In using the expression "I have applied these things to myself and Apollos" (v.6), Paul is saying that he is teaching them by personal illustration that ministers are only examples, and not merely teaching them abstract principles.

The saying "Do not go beyond what is written"—since it contains in it the familiar *gegraptai*, "it is written," used often to introduce OT quotations—seems to be a general statement advising the Corinthians not to go beyond any written doctrine in the OT. The last clause in v.6, like the preceding clause, is one of result and fits into the context as follows: If they learn not to go beyond the teaching of the Scripture about how they should treat God's teachers and all of God's people, then the result will be that they will not be conceited in taking a stand for one teacher or person over against another.

7 Some Christians evidently were boasting because of their talents and because of their positions and parties. So Paul puts the rhetorical question to them: "What do you have that you did not receive?" The obvious answer is that they received all from God and had no right to boast.

8 Paul derides their conceit. He does this with irony by a series of dramatic boasts of theirs: they, so they think, have all they need; they are rich and are reigning like kings, even without any help from Paul. The Corinthians evidently thought they had reached full maturity and were ruling and reigning rather than walking humbly with God.

9 Continuing the irony, Paul replies that in his opinion—he speaks mildly, using the expression "it seems to me"—God has not placed the apostles in a reigning position such as the Corinthians think they themselves are in. The irony is that the Corinthians were trying to "reign," while their spiritual fathers and examples were far from "reigning." Actually, Paul goes on to explain that God has publicly displayed the apostles as humble, despised men—men worthy of death. He seems to be using the term "us apostles" in the widest sense to include not only Peter and himself but also Apollos (1:12) and perhaps other prominent Christian workers who were associated with the apostles—e.g., Barnabas (Acts 14:14), Andronicus and Junius (Rom 16:7), and James, the Lord's half brother (Gal 1:19). He pictures those of the apostolic band as condemned to death and led forth by a conqueror. By his use of *theatron* ("spectacle") he seems to be alluding to the figure of condemned men tortured and exposed to the wild animals in the colosseum. They are also pictured as despised before the whole world (*kosmos*) and the angelic hosts.

10 Paul makes a series of contrasts between the proud Corinthians and the "dishonored" apostles—all from the warped viewpoint of the Corinthians. What a contrast: the apostles—foolish, weak, and dishonored; the Corinthians—wise, strong, and honored!

11–13 To set the record straight, Paul goes on to describe in detail the hardships he and his fellow Christian workers have suffered throughout their ministry (cf. the expressions "to this very hour" [v.11] and "up to this moment" [v.13]). He first emphasizes the physical deprivations they were suffering: hunger, thirst, lack of clothing, rough treatment, and homelessness. To remind the Corinthians again that he has no desire to be a physical burden to them, he injects the statement "We work hard with our own hands" (v.12).

Then he continues the list of his sufferings. This time he mentions mainly the verbal abuse Paul and his friends took and their response to it. They were frequently reviled, but they called on God to bless their revilers! He interjects, "When we are persecuted, we endure it." Then he goes back to the theme of verbal abuse (v.13a): "When we are slandered, we answer kindly." Climaxing this moving passage, Paul states that he and his fellow workers have become the scum of the earth, and the refuse of all men.

Notes

---

6 The word μετασχηματίζω (*metaschēmatizō*) literally means "to change the form of something,"

and as used here means "to say something in a different form," or "speak in a figure of speech or practical illustration."

7 The γάρ (*gar*, "for," "indeed") makes a vital connection with v.6: Why, Paul is asking, should you take pride in some men over others, for who really makes you different from others? The conclusion follows that all men receive what they have from God. The εἰ (*ei*, "if") is a condition assumed to be true—i.e., "if you received it, as in fact you did."

8 The perfect tense of the verb construction **κεκορεσμένοι ἐστέ** (*kekoresmenoi este*) stresses the present continuance of a fact that is already true as they view it: "You are already living in a state of having all the spiritual food you need." The next verbs in this sentence are in the aorist tense, indicating point of fact: "You have become rich! You have become kings. . . ."

9 **Κόσμος** (*kosmos*) is used here in the enlarged sense of "universe," introducing the dual concept of angels who inhabit the universe and men who live on earth.

10 The use of ἀσθενεῖς (*astheneis*, "weak") and ἰσχυροί (*ischyroi*, "strong") may be a reference to 1 Cor 1:27, to the weak and strong things of this world.

11,12 The tenses of these verbs are all present, emphasizing that these activities were experienced day by day by Paul and his companions. The verb γυμνιτεύω (*gymniteuō*), tr. "naked" in KJV actually means to be "poorly clothed." (Cf. "in rags," NIV.)

13 The term περικαθάρματα (*perikatharmata*), denotes the dirt or filth removed by thorough cleansing; περίψημα (*peripsēma*) also indicates dirt removed by scraping. The use of both terms strongly emphasizes how the world has despised and rejected Paul and his friends. Both words can be used ritually of filth that has been removed, and so some have tr. the words as "scapegoats" (BAG, s.v.).

---

3. *The challenge to be God's humble servants also*

4:14–21

14 I am not writing this to shame you, but to warn you, as my dear children. 15 Even though you have ten thousand guardians in Christ, you do not have many fathers, for in Christ Jesus I became your father through the gospel. 16 Therefore I urge you to imitate me. 17 For this reason I am sending to you Timothy, my son whom I love, who is faithful in the Lord. He will remind you of my way of life in Christ Jesus, which agrees with what I teach everywhere in every church.

18 Some of you have become arrogant, as if I were not coming to you. 19 But I will come to you very soon, if the Lord is willing, and then I will find out not only how these arrogant people are talking, but what power they have. 20 For the kingdom of God is not a matter of talk but of power. 21 What do you prefer? Shall I come to you with punishment, or in love and with a gentle spirit?

Paul concludes this section (4:1–21) with a challenge for the Corinthian Christians to be spiritually humble, and to this end he says that he has sent Timothy to help them and that he himself will come, too.

14–17 Paul now explains that his seeming harshness in writing this to the Corinthians was not to shame them but to warn them of the seriousness and perverseness of their actions and their pride. He grants that they have countless guides or guardians but denies that they have spiritual fathers to advise them. But since he has begotten (*egennēsa*) them in Christ (i.e., by Christ's atoning work) through the gospel and is therefore their spiritual father, he feels he has a right to advise them. In speaking of the leaders of the Corinthians as *paidagōgoi* ("guardians"), the apostle is calling attention to the distinction between himself, their spiritual father, and those leaders, many of whom could be called "guardians," or "guides." In the ancient Roman Empire, *paidagōgoi* indicated "slave-guides," who escorted the boys to and from school and were in charge of their general conduct. So, in a sense, they could be called instructors (cf. Gal 3:24). Hodge has well said that there are three agencies used by God for the conversion of men: "The efficiency is in Christ by his Spirit; the administrative agency is in preachers; the instrumental agency is in the word" (in loc.).

Since Paul could rightfully claim to be their spiritual father, he feels he can ask them to become imitators of him (cf. 1 Cor 11:1; Gal 4:12; Phil 3:17; 1 Thess 1:6; 2 Thess 3:9). In the light of this request, he says he has sent Timothy to them to help them in their progress. Timothy, too, was Paul's beloved child, "begotten" through the gospel, and faithful in the Lord—i.e., in his service for Christ.

Though Paul mentions having sent Timothy, the latter was evidently not the messenger who brought the 1 Corinthians letter. It is true that *epempsa* ("I have sent") can well be taken to mean, "I have sent [him and he has just arrived with 1 Corinthians]" (an epistolary aorist). But *epempsa* could just as well be interpreted, "I sent [him before I sent this letter to you]" (a common definitive past-tense use of the aorist). Supporting this latter interpretation is the fact that Timothy is not mentioned in the greetings either at the beginning or at the end of this letter, indicating he was not with Paul in Ephesus at the time Paul wrote 1 Corinthians. Further, Acts 19:22 states that Paul had sent Timothy from Ephesus to Macedonia, also the implication from 1 Corinthians 16:10 is that he was to continue on to Corinth and was still on his way there when this first letter to the Corinthians had reached the city. It is more likely that Stephanus, Fortunatus, and Achaicus, who are indicated as being from Corinth and who are said to be with Paul (1 Cor 16:17), were the bearers of the letter. In 1 Corinthians 16:18 they are commended and respect is asked for them. So Paul implies that these three were to return to Corinth. Paul expects that when Timothy arrives at Corinth he will cause the saints there to reflect on all Paul's work and actions, which correspond to his teaching in all the churches. As should be true of every Christian, Paul practiced what he preached.

18–21 Now concerning his own proposed trip to Corinth, Paul addresses some in the church who had acted arrogantly as though he were not going to come and did not dare to do so. These were the false teachers who were trying to undermine his authority (cf. 1 Cor 9:1–3; 2 Cor 12:12) by saying he was unstable (2 Cor 1:17) and weak and that his message was of no importance (2 Cor 10:10).

Paul replies that, the Lord willing, he will come without delay, and then will find out the real power of the arrogant persons who are doing all the talking against him (v.19). *Alla* ("but") emphasizes the contrast: Talk is cheap! What real power do these people have to promote their unscriptural and derogatory ideas? Paul uses the expression "kingdom of God" in v.20, not in its future eschatological sense, but, as the reference to the arrogant Corinthians here shows, in a present spiritual sense of God reigning over his people and demonstrating his power in their lives. The apostle is talking about the life that comes from Christ (2 Cor 5:17), the new birth and its power (cf. John 3:3–8).

Paul climaxes his thought with the question, "What do you prefer?" (v.21). He poses two alternatives: Do you want me to come "with punishment or in love and with a gentle spirit?" So Paul has answered their charge that he is afraid.

The expression "a spirit of gentleness" is certainly not to be taken as referring to the Holy Spirit, but to Paul's own spirit. Coupled as it is with "in love," it means that Paul wants to come in a manner expressing gentleness.

Notes

14 With ἀλλά (*alla*, "but"), the position of the participles ἐντρέπων (entrepōn, "shame") and νουθετῶν (nouthetōn, "warn") at opposite ends of the sentence emphasizes the contrast by putting stress on the second participle ("warn") as the result the apostle really desires.

15 The ἐάν (*ean*, "if") condition is to be taken here with ἀλλά (*alla*, "but") in the conclusion: "If you should have . . . " to mean, "Even though you have . . . you certainly do not have many fathers." The contrast is strong between πατέρας (*pateras*, "the many fathers") and ἐγέννησα (*egennēsa*, "I have fathered [you]").

16 Μιμηταί (*mimētai*), from which we get our word "mimic" simply means "imitators," a fitting description of the role of little children who naturally imitate the actions and attitudes of their fathers and mothers. The present form of the dynamic verb γίνεσθε (*ginesthe*, "become") here is graphic: "continue to become in practice [imitators]."

17 Grammatically, the expression "in the Lord" can go with both "beloved" and "faithful": "my child beloved and faithful in the Lord."

18 The relative adverb ὡς (*hōs*) here denotes the idea of "on the assumption that," the entire statement then reading, "some have been arrogant on the assumption that I am not going to visit you."

19 The verb γινώσκω (*ginōskō*) here conveys more than simply to know a fact. It means "ascertain, find out" the inner working of the arrogant Corinthians. The perfect participle πεφυσιωμένων (*pephysiōmenōn*) indicates that those who had become arrogant are still in that state.

VI. Paul's Answer to Further Reported Problems in the Church (5:1–6:20)

A. *Paul's Condemnation of Sexual Immorality—Incest* (5:1–13)

5:1–8

1It is actually reported that there is sexual immorality among you, and of a kind that does not occur even among pagans: A man has his father's wife. 2And you are proud! Shouldn't you rather have been filled with grief and have put out of your fellowship the man who did this? 3Even though I am not physically present, I am with you in spirit. And I have already passed judgment on the one who did this, just as if I were present. 4When you are assembled in the name of our Lord Jesus and I am with you in spirit, and the power of our Lord Jesus is present, 5hand this man over to Satan, so that his sinful nature may be destroyed and his spirit saved on the day of the Lord.

6Your boasting is not good. Don't you know that a little yeast works through the whole batch of dough? 7Get rid of the old yeast that you may be a new batch without yeast—as you really are. For Christ, our Passover lamb, has been sacrificed. 8Therefore, let us keep the Festival, not with the old yeast, the yeast of malice and wickedness, but with bread without yeast, the bread of sincerity and truth.

The sin of sexual immorality and the church's indifference to it is the second major evil in the Corinthian congregation that Paul mentions. Corinth was noted for its loose and licentious living (cf. introduction, p. 180), a situation duplicated in the prevailing lack of moral standards in these latter years of the twentieth century.

In this chapter Paul condemns the sin of incest, which he calls *porneia* ("sexual immorality"). He rebukes the church for its arrogance in the matter and its failure to excommunicate the violator—something Paul insists on (vv.1–5). The purity he describes is symbolized in the removal of leaven in the celebration of the OT Passover, which is fulfilled in Christ, "our Passover lamb" (vv.6–8).

Later (vv.9–13) he gives instruction that the church should guard its own membership against sexually immoral persons, but that it should not try to Christianize unbelievers by forcing biblical standards on them.

1 "Fornication," used in KJV for *porneia,* does not communicate today. *Porneia* conveys the idea of extramarital sexual relations of any kind, so the NIV translation, "sexual immorality," is accurate. The word *holōs,* translated "commonly" in KJV, is better rendered "actually." This may mean, "generally speaking it is reported," or "it is really reported"; the present tense of the verb *akouetai* helps convey the idea that the report is continually spreading. The use of *gunaika,* literally "woman," graphically shows that it was the man's stepmother he had married. The NT expression "to have a woman" means to marry her (cf. Matt 14:4; 22:28 [Greek]; 1 Cor 7:2, 29). The sin of incest, Paul says, is not even practiced among the non-Christians. Cicero (*pro Cluent* 5, 6) states it was an incredible crime and practically unheard of. Such a marriage was strictly forbidden according to Leviticus 18:8 and Deuteronomy 22:30 and carried with it a curse (Deut 27:20). Rabbinic law in the main seems to have allowed such a marriage when a proselyte married his stepmother, since his becoming a proselyte broke all bonds of relationship. (See Strack-Billerbeck, *Kommentar zum N.T. aus Talmud und Midrasch* [Munich: Beck, 1922–1961], 3:343–358.) It is possible that some in the Corinthian church who may have come from the synagogue there could have known of this allowance. Part of an inscription indicating the presence of such a synagogue has been found. (See J. Finegan, *Light From the Ancient Past* [Princeton, N.J., Princeton University Press, 1959], pp. 361, 362; see also page 177 above in this commentary.) Though as a Pharisee (cf. Phil 3:5), Paul knew the system of Jewish law with its varying interpretations, he applies the OT law and the teaching on marriage quite strictly.

2,3 Paul again alludes to the pride of the Corinthians. This time it was a pride that, rather than cause them to mourn over the shocking sin, allowed them to tolerate such a sinner in the congregation. Paul presses his judgment of the case by saying that he is with them in spirit and has already passed judgment on the offending person.

4,5 Though the local congregation itself is to gather and discipline the offender, Paul reminds them of his apostolic authority over them by saying, "I am with you in spirit." However, he does not overassert his authority, because he recognizes that the decision is to be made "in the name of our Lord Jesus" (i.e., by the authority of the Lord Jesus; because of his person, his name carries authority—see also Acts 4:12) and that it is to be done with "the power of our Lord Jesus." These two expressions amplify each other: church discipline is to be exercised carefully on the authority of Jesus' name and the verdict given is accompanied by the spiritual power of the Lord Jesus. By saying, "Hand this man over to Satan, so that his sinful nature [or body] may be destroyed," Paul means to include the man's excommunication (at least by implication; cf. v.2) and his suffering physically in some way, even as far as death (cf. 1 Tim 1:20). The word *sarx* (flesh, v.5) can mean the "sinful nature" (NIV), but since "flesh" in this verse is in contrast to "spirit," the reference seems to be to the body. That Satan had power to afflict the body is evident from frequent NT references to the effects of demon possession (cf. Matt 9:32, 33; Luke 9:39–42) and to satanic activity in causing affliction or limitation (2 Cor 12:7; 1 Thess 2:18). This bodily punishment by Satan, Paul hoped, would have the effect of causing the man to repent so that his spirit (his person) might be saved in the day of the Lord—i.e., at the second coming of Christ. Though Paul teaches church excommunication here and a deliverance to Satan for physical punishment with a view to repentance, he does not say that the man should divorce his stepmother. This would be in accord with the scriptural teaching that marriage is an indissoluble bond (Gen 2:24). He does imply that the man should repent so that his spirit would be saved. Some have held the interpretation that 2 Corinthians 2:6, 7 and 7:9–12 refer to this man and that he repented. If true, such an interpretation implies that the man was to be allowed to come back into fellowship in spite of his incestuous marriage.

6–8 Paul illustrates Christian holiness and discipline by the OT teaching that no leaven was allowed in the bread eaten at the Passover feast. "Leaven," or "yeast," in Scripture generally conveys the idea of evil or sin (cf. Matt 16:6). That the church should allow such sin as that in the Corinthian church to go undisciplined would affect the attitude of the entire Christian community toward sin—"a little yeast works through the whole batch of dough." The church is to get rid of the old yeast—"the sin that so easily entangles" (Heb 12:1). So the command is to get rid of such sin individually and in the church, for the believing community is an unleavened batch of dough, a new creation in Christ, who has been sacrificed as our Passover lamb.

Christ, "our Passover lamb," died at the time of the Jewish Passover celebration. Actually he died on the next day following the sacrifice of the Passover lambs. This Passover day, which began the evening before when the lambs were sacrificed, is called rather generally the first day of the Feast of Unleavened Bread (Mark 14:12). This was the day of Preparation of Passover Week (John 19:14, NIV; cf. Matt 27:62; Mark 15:42; Luke 23:54), the "day of Preparation" being understood in the early Christian church to be Friday (cf. *Martyrdom of Polycarp* 7:1; it also means this in modern Greek).

So Paul concludes in v.8, "Let us keep the Festival"—that is, let us live the Christian life in holy consecration to God (cf. Rom 12:2; 1 Pet 2:5). This means, he says, that we are to live not with the old yeast of malice and wickedness, but on the basis of the unleavened principles of sincerity and truth. Therefore, such sins as incestuous marriage and the like cannot be tolerated or left undisciplined in the church.

Notes

---

1 Ολως (*holōs*) may go either with ἀκούεται (*akouetai*), meaning "it is actually reported," or with πορνεία (*porneia*), meaning "[it is reported that there is] actually sexual immorality. . . ." The former interpretation (as in NIV) is better because, by grammatical position and as an adverb, *holōs* fits better with the verb *akouetai.* Probably because of Lev 18:8 ("father's wife") Paul uses the expression γυναῖκα . . . ἔχειν (*gunaika . . . echein,* "to have [his father's] wife") rather than the Gr. designation μητρυία (*mētryia* "stepmother").

2 The verb in the perfect passive form—i.e., "you exist in your arrogant pride," emphasizes again the general attitude Paul referred to in 4:18, 19. Οὐχὶ μᾶλλον (*ouchi mallon,* "not rather") strongly emphasizes the contrast between their arrogance and the grief they should have had. The expression ἀρθῇ ἐκ μέσου ὑμῶν, (*arthē ek mesou humōn,* literally, "he should be expelled from your company") is to be compared with ἀποσυνάγωγος γένηται (*aposynagōgos genētai,* "he should be put out of the synagogue," John 9:22). Both mean "to be excommunicated." The implication is that the church will perform this act (5:4, 7).

5 Ancient NT Gr. MSS favor somewhat the reading "the day of the Lord" (as in NIV) over the variants, "the day of the Lord Jesus," or ". . . of our Lord Jesus Christ." The meaning is the same.

7 The aorist verb ἐκκαθάρατε (*ekkatharate*, "get rid of completely") is very expressive here: "clear out of the house, get rid of any evidence of the old yeast." Cf. the first Passover with its unleavened bread (Exod 13:3–7). Generally in the NT and other related literature the verb θύω (*thyō*) indicates the sacrifice of animals. Christ is here clearly identified with the sacrificial lamb—Christ the Lamb of God (cf. John 1:29).

5:9–13

[9]I have written you in my letter not to associate with sexually immoral people—[10]not at all meaning the people of this world who are immoral, or the greedy and swindlers, or idolaters. In that case you would have to leave this world. [11]But now I am writing you that you must not associate with anyone who calls himself a brother but is sexually immoral or greedy, an idolater or a slanderer, a drunkard or a swindler. With such a man do not even eat.

[12]What business is it of mine to judge those outside the church? Are you not to judge those inside? [13]God will judge those outside. "Expel the wicked man from your number."

9 Though the letter here referred to could possibly be a reference to the preceding part of the present letter and the verb *egrapsa* could be taken to mean, "I write" (an epistolary aorist, taken from the reader's viewpoint; cf. Rom 16:22), it is more natural to conclude that this is a reference to a former letter that we do not possess. (That not all of an apostle's writings have been preserved presents no problem regarding the completeness of the canon. The church has all of the inspired writing God intended his people to have. [See Hodge, in loc.])

Paul now comments further on a subject referred to in the former letter—that of not associating with sexually immoral people (*pornoi*), a point the Corinthians had not fully understood. The social milieu in Corinth was notoriously immoral (cf. Introduction) and if the Corinthians took the command in the previous letter too literally, as they seem to have done, they would have had no contact with even some family members, business associates and social acquaintances. The word *pornos* ("the sexually immoral person") has reference to all types of sexual sins, including the sin of incest. The verb *sunanamignysthai* ("to associate with") could refer to church fellowship or more widely, as here, to any social contact.

10 Paul now proceeds to correct their misunderstanding. By referring to other categories of sinners besides the sexually immoral, he shows that in having referred to the *pornoi* in the previous letter, he meant only that they should not be a part of the church community. If Paul had meant that contact or even acquaintance with all sinners was to cease, then Christians could not live at all in human society.

By the words *ou pantos* ("not at all") Paul limits the extent of his command. The *pornoi* are the sexually immoral persons of all kinds. That they are called the sexually immoral "of this world" (the secular world system) establishes that they are not to be included as a part of the church community. The greedy persons here are literally the ones "who must have more." Compare the sin of greed (*pleonexia*) listed in Romans 1:29; Ephesians 4:19; Colossians 3:5. Greed is a serious sin and Paul touches on aspects of it in 6:7, 8. The *harpax* is one who steals by violence. "Extortioner" (KJV) does not convey this today and "swindler" (NIV) seems too weak.

11 The verb form *egrapsa* taken with *de nun* ("but now") is certainly here to be understood as an epistolary aorist and translated, "But now I am writing." Having explained that he did not mean Christians are to be totally dissociated from the world, Paul hastens to add that the church community is not to include such as the flagrant sinners he now enumerates, even if they carry the name "brother," a term that would identify them as part of the Christian fellowship. The kind of association not permitted with such false brothers is explained by the command "With such a man do not even eat." In sharing in a common meal Christians show their union with one another. This "eating" is not to be understood as the Lord's Supper, and probably indicates any meal, including the Christian *agape* (love) feast. The application then and now is that Christians are not to have this kind of association, for if a believer does so, he may raise a question concerning the validity of his own Christian profession. To the list of sinners in v.10 Paul now adds the slanderer (*loidoros*—probably referring to those who denigrated Paul) and the drunkard (*methusos*; cf. 1 Cor 6:10; 11:21; Eph 5:18; 1 Thess 5:7).

12,13 Here Paul teaches that though it is logical for the church to exercise spiritual discipline over members in its fellowship, it is not for the church to judge the present unsaved society.

By the Greek expression *tous exō* ("those without") the apostle means those outside the church's communion or fellowship. The words *tous esō* ("those within") means those within the church's fellowship. Paul now concludes (v.13) on the basis of the preceding argument that the wicked man who had married his stepmother must be put out of the church. This he commands by quoting somewhat loosely from Deuteronomy 22:24 (a context of adultery) and from Deuteronomy 24:7 (a context of stealing).

The strengthened form of the negative (*ouchi*, "not") used with the indicative verb in a question expects a positive response: "Are you not to judge those inside [the church]?" "Yes" is the expected reply.

Notes

13 There is a variation in the MSS as to whether κρινεῖ (*krinei*, "judge") is present or future (it is only a matter of the accent), and since the present tense of the verb can be interpreted as a futuristic present, there is no difference in meaning. The sense is "God will judge" as in NIV. The quotation from Deut 22:24 and 24:7 is exactly like the wording of LXX in those two passages, except that Paul has changed the LXX verb form ἐξαρεῖς (*exareis*) to the pl. ἐξάρατε (*exarate*) to fit his application to the Corinthians.

B. *Christian Morality Applied to Legal and Sexual Matters* (6:1–20)

1. *Christian morality in legal matters*

6:1–11

[1]If any of you has a dispute with another, dare he take it before the ungodly for judgment instead of before the saints? [2]Do you not know that God's people will judge the world? And if you are to judge the world, are you not competent to judge trivial cases? [3]Do you not know that we will judge angels? How much more the things of this life! [4]Therefore, if you have disputes about such matters, appoint as judges even men of little account in the church! [5]I say this to shame you. Is it

possible that there is nobody among you wise enough to judge a dispute between believers? 6But instead, one brother goes to law against another—and this in front of unbelievers!

7The very fact that you have lawsuits among you means you have been completely defeated already. Why not rather be wronged? Why not rather be cheated? 8Instead, you yourselves cheat and do wrong, and you do this to your brothers.

9Don't you know that the wicked will not inherit the kingdom of God? Do not be deceived: Neither the sexually immoral nor idolaters nor adulterers nor male prostitutes nor homosexual offenders 10nor thieves nor the greedy nor drunkards nor slanderers nor swindlers will inherit the kingdom of God. 11And that is what some of you were. But you were washed, you were sanctified, you were justified in the name of the Lord Jesus Christ and by the Spirit of our God.

Continuing in the area of moral and ethical practice, Paul now discusses the apparently common practice of the Corinthians of settling noncriminal property cases before non-Christian judges or arbitrators. He refers to the Roman law courts, such as those on either side of the *bema* (tribunal platform) where Roman law was strictly administered in accordance with Roman standards. "What about God's standards?" Paul asks. They as a Christian community should have been deciding such cases among themselves. In Christian love they should have "turned the other cheek" (Matt 5:39) and suffered wrong and loss of material goods (v.7) rather than go to court over such matters.

1,2 In speaking of Christians taking other Christians to court, Paul does not specify any criminal cases because he teaches elsewhere that these must be handled by the state (Rom 13:3, 4).

In the expression *pragma echōn* ("having a lawsuit or dispute"), Paul means to include different kinds of property cases (v.7). By "dare" (*tolmā*), he strongly admonishes rather than commands Christians to take their legal grievances for settlement before qualified Christians. In this way, he allows for the possibility that under some circumstances Christians might take cases to the secular civil court. Paul writes in the light of Roman law, which allowed Jews, for instance, to apply their own law in property matters; and Christians, who were not yet distinguished as a separate class, must have had the same privilege (Hodge, in loc.). According to rabbinic interpretation, it was unlawful to take cases before Gentile judges. Customarily, three judges were to handle cases among the Jews. (C.T. Craig, *The First Epistle to the Corinthians,* IB, vol.10 [New York: Abington-Cokesbury Press, 1953], p. 69; Strack and Billerbeck, *Kommentar zum N.T. aus Talmud und Midrasch,* 3:364, 365; Jean Juster, *Les Juifs dans l'Empire Romain,* 2 [Paris: P. Geuthner, 1914], pp. 93–126.) If appeal was made to Roman law for the right of Jewish and Christian communities to try their own property cases, certainly it would be right to take some cases before the civil court. By analogy, Paul who had received his Roman citizenship according to Roman law, appealed to the civil courts—to the Roman commander (Acts 22:25–29), to the governor (Acts 23:27; 24:10–21), and to the emperor (Acts 25:4–12)—to establish his right to a proper trial and proper treatment as a Roman citizen (Acts 16:37–39). In modern life this biblical principle allows for church cases to be brought into civil courts to determine the extent of the rights of the congregation, as for example, their right to own and retain their own church property. What concerned Paul was that the Corinthians were failing to exercise their prerogative in settling such cases themselves, a prerogative they would exercise at the Second Coming and in the eternal state (vv.2, 3).

The saints (*hoi hagioi*) are those who are holy—consecrated and set apart for God; thus the translation, "God's people" (v.2). They are in sharp contrast with the "ungodly" (*adikoi*, those who practice injustice—the unsaved). In saying that God's people will judge the world, Paul is writing eschatologically. At the second coming of Christ, God's people, who are joint heirs with Christ (Rom 8:17) will reign and judge the world with him in his millennial kingdom (2 Tim 2:12; Rev 20:4; cf. Dan 7:22 and Matt 19:28).

In cases now to be judged by Christians, decisions would be ministerial and declarative (Matt 16:18, 19; 18:18–20; John 20:19–23), and not punitive, penalties being reserved for the state (Rom 13:1–7).

3 To make his argument even stronger for the validity and competence of Christians to settle cases at Corinth, Paul teaches that Christians will even judge angels, but he does not specify any details (v.3). By using *angelous* without the article, Paul is not necessarily including all the angels. He must mean that Christians, when ruling in the future with Christ, will have a part in judging the devil and the fallen angels at the Second Coming (cf. Rev. 19:19, 20; 20:10). Or, the statement could mean, as Hodge suggests, that Christians will judge angels, even the good ones, in the sense of presiding with Christ over the angelic host (in loc.). Compare the statement of Matthew 19:28 about sitting "on twelve thrones, judging the twelve tribes," i.e., presiding over them.

4 It is uncertain whether the main verb *kathizete* ("appoint") should be taken as imperative with a sarcastic tone or as an indicative in a rhetorical question. In the first instance, the thought is this: "If you must have disputes about these mundane matters when you are destined to judge men and angels, well then go ahead and set the least esteemed members of the congregation to take care of these little matters!" On the second interpretation, the emphasis is on the apostle's surprise: "If you have such a case, do you set the least esteemed in the church in charge of it?" The answer then is "No," with the assumed concluding question as to why then they would turn these affairs over to the unsaved who know less about Christian affairs. The first option (cf. NIV) seems better, since it fits in with Paul's other ironic remarks to the Corinthians, such as in 4:8. For the second interpretation, the material is too elliptical and demands too much to be supplied. Some have tried to take the phrase "men of little account" as referring to the unsaved judges, but there is no evidence in the context that the Corinthians despised these judges.

5,6 Paul argues that if it is really necessary for such disputes to be handled, they should find a Christian wise enough to take care of them, rather than have Christian brothers opposed to each other in secular litigation. The apostle says they should be ashamed of themselves.

7,8 In climaxing his argument that though legal cases may have to be handled, Paul feels that their very existence among the Corinthians shows a malicious attitude and spiritual failure. Instead of being involved in all these disputes, they should be willing to suffer wrong rather than harm and cheat their fellow Christians.

9,10 Paul concludes that in practicing such acts of wickedness (*adikeo*) toward others they must realize that the wicked (*adikoi*) will not inherit the kingdom of God (cf. John 3:3–5). They are in a dangerous frame of mind—they need to clear their heads and realize that if they act wickedly in this way, they are no better than the wicked idolaters and others who will not inherit heaven. To the list of sinners already mentioned in 5:10,

11 Paul points out specific kinds of sexually immoral people: the adulterers (*moichoi*), the male prostitutes (*malakoi*) and homosexuals (*arsenokoitai*). (In Romans 1:26 Paul also mentions lesbians.) Also added to his list here are those who are thieves (*kleptai*). In the light of this comparison, the Corinthians should have seen how unchristian and sinful their actions were toward one another.

11 In describing their conversion, the apostle lists three transactions that occurred at the time when the Lord saved them: they were washed (*apolousasthe*), that is, they were spiritually cleansed by God, an act symbolized by baptism (cf. Matt 28:19); they were sanctified (*hēgiasthēte*), an expression either to be interpreted as an amplification of the concept "washed" (cf. Titus 3:5, 6) or meaning that they had been set apart as God's people (cf. 1 Pet 2:9); and they were justified (*edikaiōthēte*), showing God's act as judge in declaring the sinner righteous because of Christ (Rom 3:23–26; 5:1). This expression gives the legal basis for the cleansing mentioned above.

All this, Paul says, was done by God for them on the authority (in the name) of the Lord Jesus Christ and by the Spirit of our God—the regenerating power of the Holy Spirit.

Notes

2 Κριτηρίων (*kritēriōn*) is strictly the "law court," but is to be taken here as "the cases" that are tried in such courts.

4 The perfect passive participle ἐξουθενημένους (*exouthenēmenous*) means "those that stand despised or disdained" and so the tr. "men of little account." Καθίζω (*kathizō*, "cause to sit," or "seat") in this context means "install" or "appoint" judges for court (see Jos. *Ant* 13, 75).

7,8 The μὲν οὖν (*men oun*, "so," "then") denotes a continuation of the argument and so heightens the effect of the conclusion Paul is drawing from his previous discussion. There is a vivid contrast between the passive and the active uses of the two verbs ἀδικέω (*adikeō*, "suffer wrong" "do wrong") and ἀποστερέω (*apostereō*, "be cheated" "cheat"). The present tense in each case suggests that these injustices are currently in practice.

9 Μὴ πλανᾶσθε (*mē planasthe*), the present prohibition construction with the verb in the middle voice may be tr., "Stop deceiving yourselves."

11 The use of ταῦτα (*tauta*—neuter, "these things") with people is startling: "Some of you were these things." This expression points up the horrible condition they were in. The three aorist verb forms in v.11b emphasize the definiteness (point action) of the work of the Lord in their salvation. The verb ἀπελούσασθε (*apelousasthe*) is in the middle voice, meaning, "you washed yourselves" or "you got yourselves washed"; that is, they submitted themselves to the baptism sacrament (or ordinance) as the identifying sign for Christians and their covenant children (Acts 2:38, 39), indicating their belonging to Christ and his church. Others take this aorist middle as a passive, "you were washed," because the two following verbs are passive. This looser tr. is permissible under this interpretation: "You permitted yourselves to be washed." That baptism is likely referred to here as a sign of their spiritual cleansing and justification by God (cf. the sign of circumcision in Rom 4:9–12) is shown by the phrase "in the name [or 'authority' connected with the person] of the Lord Jesus Christ and by the Spirit of our God." Paul may well have in mind the words of Jesus in Matt 28:19.

2. *Christian morality in sexual matters*

6:12–20

12"Everything is permissible for me"—but not everything is beneficial. "Every-
thing is permissible for me"—but I will not be mastered by anything. 13"Food for
the stomach and the stomach for food"—but God will destroy them both. The body
is not meant for sexual immorality, but for the Lord, and the Lord for the body. 14By
his power God raised the Lord from the dead, and he will raise us also. 15Do you
not know that your bodies are members of Christ himself? Shall I then take the
members of Christ and unite them with a prostitute? Never! 16Do you not know that
he who unites himself with a prostitute is one with her in body? For it is said, "The
two will become one flesh." 17But he who unites himself with the Lord is one with
him in spirit.

18Flee from sexual immorality. All other sins a man commits are outside his
body, but he who sins sexually sins against his own body. 19Do you not know that
your body is a temple of the Holy Spirit, who is in you, whom you have received
from God? You are not your own; 20you were bought at a price. Therefore honor
God with your body.

Every action we contemplate should be tested by two questions: "Is it beneficial?" and "Will it overpower and enslave me and so have a detrimental effect on the church and my testimony for Christ?" Hodge (in loc.) entitles this section "Abuses of the Principle of Christian Liberty" but the passage includes far more than that. The main thrust of these verses argues against sexual immorality and for the glorifying of God in the Christian's body.

12,13 Undoubtedly there were some professing Christians in Corinth who, without examining the Scriptures and its implications, claimed that it was permissible for them to do anything they desired. In making such claims to unrestricted freedom, some evidently used the argument that since the physical activity of eating and digesting food ("food for the stomach and the stomach for food") did not have any bearing on Christian morals and one's inner spiritual life, so other physical activities such as promiscuous sex did not touch either on morals or spiritual life.

Paul grants that food and the stomach are temporal and transitory and, in God's providence, will disappear—but he denies that what affects the body is unimportant and this denial especially includes the undisciplined and unscriptural use of the body in sexual practices (v.13b). So he denies the argument of a parallel between eating and digesting food as a natural process and practicing sexual immorality as a natural process. Of course, he is not denying that sex in wedlock is natural and wholesome (7:3–5; cf. also Heb 13:4).

The apostle sets the stage for his discussion of the horrors of sexual immorality and in contrast the holy use of the Christian's body by stating that as the Christian evaluates his right to do "all things," he should face four questions: (1) Is the thing contemplated beneficial (*sumpherei*)? (2) Will the practice in question overpower and dominate (*exousiasthesomai*) him and will the result affect others? (3) Will the practice support the truth that the body is "for the Lord" who created it and intended it to be used for his glory? Also, (4) will it support the truth that "the Lord is for the body"—that is, the Lord has redeemed the body (vv.19, 20)? So the Christian must have no part with sexual immorality, because the body is not meant for sexual license (v.13b, cf. Gen 2:24) but for the Lord.

14 Now Paul states God's interest in the Christian's body. As God raised the body of Jesus from the tomb, so he will raise the bodies of his people from the grave through his power. Of interest is the difference in the verbs used: *ēgeiren,* "he raised" (the Lord); and *exegerei,* "he will raise [us] out of" (the grave)—the implication being that we, in contrast to the Lord, will be raised from corruption and from the group of corrupt sinners. The phrase "through the power of God" is probably to be taken with both parts of the sentence: the power of God that was used to raise the Lord is the same that will be used to raise his people.

15–17 A further argument that the Christian's body is for the Lord is that God's people are members of his mystical body (cf. 1 Cor 12:27). So Christians may not unite their bodies with that of a prostitute. For they should understand that sexual relations involve more than a physical act—they join the two persons together (v.16; quoting from Gen 2:24; cf. Matt 19:5). Since Christians have been joined in union to the Lord, they dare not form another union with a prostitute. Verse 17 states the case even more strongly: the one who cleaves (*kollōmenos*) to a prostitute is one body with her, but the one who cleaves (*kollōmenos*) to the Lord is united to him spiritually. In saying this, Paul is not making the union of normal marriage mutually exclusive of the union of God with his people. In Ephesians 5:21–32 Paul teaches that the human marriage union is valid and is to be viewed in the light of the Christian's higher union with the Lord—the wife to be subject to her husband "as to the Lord" (v.22) and the husband to love his wife "as Christ loved the church" (v.25). What Paul argues against in 1 Corinthians 6:15–17 is that the unholy union with a prostitute is a wicked perversion of the divinely established marriage union.

18 Paul goes on to say that the one who commits sexual immorality sins against his own body—that is, by weakening and perverting the very life process, as well as human character. In contrast, other sins are "outside the body."

19,20 Now Paul talks positively about how the Christian should view his body. First, he should consider that his body, including his whole personality, is the temple—the sacred dwelling place—of God, the Holy Spirit (cf. the Shekinah glory in the tabernacle, Exod 40:34). Second, the Christian has received the Spirit from God to help him against sin. Third, the Christian has no right to pervert and misuse his body, for he is not his own master but has been purchased by God for a price (v.20). That price, though not mentioned here, is the blood of Jesus Christ (Eph 1:7; 1 Pet 1:18, 19 et al.). The picture is of a slave of sin (Rom 6:17; cf. 1 Cor 7:23) being purchased from the horrible system of slavery.

The conclusion of the matter is that the Christian is to glorify God in his body. Because "body" and "temple" are both singular, some understand the teaching to be that not only each believer's body is a temple, but the whole body of believers is a temple (Grosheide, in loc.). However, since in the context Paul is writing about individuals and since the individual Christian is indwelt by the Holy Spirit, it is best to understand v.19 to mean that each individual Christian's body is a temple of the Holy Spirit. (*Naos* is the temple itself [cf. John 2:20, 21] in distinction from *hieron,* the entire temple area.)

"You were bought" is in the aorist tense, pointing back to Christ's redemptive work on the cross (Matt 20:28). There may be implications of the Christian's having been freed from becoming overpowered by sin (Rom 6:17, 18) and Satan (Col 1:13) and being benevolently enslaved to Christ (Rom 1:1) and to righteousness (Rom 6:18) in reflection of the Corinthian situation in which the "slave was from the time of his manumission the slave of the god" (Craig, in loc.)

Notes

12 There is a contrast between πάντα (*panta*, "all things") and τινός (*tinos*, "any one thing"). The emphasis is not on the "all things" that are permissible but on the "one thing" that may overpower.

13 Καταργέω (*katargeō*) is vivid. Literally, it means "make ineffective or powerless"; so here it indicates that God will do away with food and the need for the digestive processes of the stomach, evidently referring to the changed status of the resurrection body after the second coming of Christ.

15 The negative optative μὴ γένοιτο (*mē genoito*) indicates a strong wish—literally tr. "may it not be," more freely rendered, "Never!" "By no means!" "Perish the thought!" Robertson calls this use of the optative the volitive, which stresses the wish, the will (A.T. Robertson, *A Grammar of the Greek New Testament in the Light of Historical Research,* 5th ed. [New York: Harper and Brothers, 1923], pp. 936, 937).

16 The οἴδατε (*oidate*, "know") in vv.16, 19 goes beyond just knowing a fact. It implies recognition and understanding. The negative οὐκ (*ouk*) with a question implies in the argument a positive reply. The verb κολλάω (*kollaō*, "cleave") in this participial form, which can be taken as a middle as the context suggests, stresses the sexual offender's personal initiative and responsibility: "he joins himself to" the prostitute.

Whereas the Gen 2:24 quotation uses σαρξ (*sarx*, "flesh") in LXX, Paul uses the word σῶμα (*sōma*, "body"), but the same idea is in mind: the physico-spiritual life of the individuals is involved.

18 The present tense (durative action) of φεύγετε (*pheugete*), meaning "be fleeing from," suggests that constant vigilance against sexual immorality is called for.

20 The words "and in your spirit, which are God's," found in KJV, are not supported by many of the best ancient MSS and are not necessary nor central to Paul's argument regarding the Christian's use of his body. The words may have been added by scribes in later MSS, first in the margin and then in the text, to complete the thought on the nature of man as body and spirit and "to soften Paul's abruptness" (B.M. Metzger, *A Textual Commentary on the Greek New Testament* [New York: United Bible Societies, 1971], p. 553).

VII. Paul's Answers to Questions Raised by the Church (7:1–14:40)

In this section Paul begins to answer questions raised by the Corinthians in a letter they had written him (7:1). The material from 7:1 to 14:40 is devoted in a large part to answering questions raised in this communication. In his introductory expression "Now for the matters you wrote about," Paul shows he is answering this letter.

He uses the same introductory phrase (*peri de*) in other parts of 1 Corinthians in discussing other questions they had brought up: the unmarried (7:25), food sacrificed to idols (8:1), and spiritual gifts (12:1). It is not certain whether his instruction regarding giving for the need of the saints (16:1–4) was in answer to their written question, since it is separated by chapter 15 from the main section (7:1–14:40) dealing with these questions. But since the same introductory phrase occurs in 16:1, it is reasonable to conclude that 16:1–4 is a postscript answer to another of their questions. The subject of this "collection" (16:1) certainly was a matter on which the Corinthians needed enlightenment.

A. *Instructions Concerning Marriage* (7:1–40)

The Corinthians had written, asking at least two questions concerning this subject that is the topic of the entire chapter. The first was whether a Christian should get married at all (7:1) and the second was whether virgins should get married (7:25). Evidently there were those in Corinth who, as Jewish believers relying on Genesis 2:24, were advocating marriage. Others were no doubt arguing for the unmarried state.

Besides answering these questions, Paul deals with an additional point, that a Christian should live according to God's calling, whether married or single (7:17–24).

1. *Christian obligations in marriage*

7:1–16

> [1]Now for the matters you wrote about: It is good for a man not to marry. [2]But since there is so much immorality, each man should have his own wife, and each woman her own husband. [3]The husband should fulfill his marital duty to his wife, and likewise the wife to her husband. [4]The wife's body does not belong to her alone but also to her husband. In the same way, the husband's body does not belong to him alone but also to his wife. [5]Do not deprive each other except by mutual consent and for a time, so that you may devote yourselves to prayer. Then come together again so that Satan will not tempt you because of your lack of self-control. [6]I say this as a concession, not as a command. [7]I wish that all men were as I am. But each man has his own gift from God; one has this gift, another has that.
>
> [8]Now to the unmarried and the widows I say: It is good for them to stay unmarried, as I am. [9]But if they cannot control themselves, they should marry, for it is better to marry than to burn with passion.
>
> [10]To the married I give this command (not I, but the Lord): A wife must not separate from her husband. [11]But if she does, she must remain unmarried or else be reconciled to her husband. And a husband must not divorce his wife.
>
> [12]To the rest I say this (I, not the Lord): If any brother has a wife who is not a believer and she is willing to live with him, he must not divorce her. [13]And if a woman has a husband who is not a believer and he is willing to live with her, she must not divorce him. [14]For the unbelieving husband has been sanctified through his wife, and the unbelieving wife has been sanctified through her believing husband. Otherwise your children would be "unclean," but as it is, they are holy.
>
> [15]But if the unbeliever leaves, let him do so. A believing man or woman is not bound in such circumstances; God has called us to live in peace. [16]How do you know, wife, whether you will save your husband? Or, how do you know, husband, whether you will save your wife?

1 As to the question of the church on the pros and cons of being married, Paul may seem to agree completely with those who argued for a celibate life, and this in contrast to Genesis 2:18, "It is not good that the man should be alone" (RSV) and the usual Jewish view in favor of the married state. (The rabbis considered that marriage was an "unqualified duty for a man" [Craig, in loc.].) But Paul's statement of 7:1 is not to be taken absolutely; it is his suggestion specifically for Corinth because of some present crisis there that he refers to in 7:26 (cf. 7:29, 35). Part of this crisis may have been connected with possible times of persecution they might have to suffer for the Lord.

It is difficult to hold, as some do, that Paul here is teaching against marriage because he felt the second coming of Christ was necessarily near (Craig, in loc., and Parry, in loc.). If that were his position, he would naturally have argued against marriage in his other letters also. In Ephesians 5 and 1 Timothy 3 he speaks in favor of marriage. Further, in 1 Timothy 4:1–3 Paul states that "forbidding to marry" is one of the signs of the approaching end-time apostasy, and in Hebrews 13:4 it is said that "marriage should be honored." As Hodge has remarked, distresses and crises are connected with both the first and second comings of Christ and, we could add, in the time in between (*1 Corinthians*, in loc.; cf. Matt 24:3–14; 1 Peter 1:10–12). However, reference to "crises" (7:26) need not be pressed to mean that the Corinthian Christians should not get married because the Lord was to come shortly.

2–7 Having said that it would be good under the present circumstances not to get married, Paul hastens to add that the general rule for marriage should apply. The reason, especially true at Corinth, is the prevalence of sexual immorality—*porneias* is plural—and they also might be tempted to fall into this sin. Since the temptation might affect either sex, Paul specifies that each man is to have his own wife and each woman her own husband.

So that there will not be abnormal situations in the Christian marital status that may lead to sexual immorality (v.5), the apostle gives instruction as to the normal sexual behavior and attitude that the Christian man and wife should have (vv.3–6), and in doing so he argues against a forced asceticism. He argues that they should have normal sexual relations and he strengthens his argument by stating that the bodies of the marriage partners belong to each other. The verb *exousiazō* literally means "has rights over"; that is, "has exclusive claim to," which has already been shown in the teaching of 1 Corinthians 6:16, "the two will become one flesh." Having stated the principle in v.4, Paul adds the command that husbands and wives are not to withhold these normal marital rights from each other, except by mutual consent and agreement, and that only for a specified purpose and a specified period of time (v.5). This he says is so that they may spend time in prayer—i.e., that as those who are also united to Christ (6:17), they may exercise their rights and privileges in communing with God. But when this separate time of prayer is over, the married pair are to come together again, lest Satan tempt one or the other partner with sexual immorality because of their possible lack of sexual self-control. Paul recognizes the strong but normal sexual drive in the human being (cf. Gen 1:28, "be fruitful . . . fill the earth").

The present tense of the verb *apostereite* ("deprive") in the prohibition in v.5 indicates that some at Corinth were practicing a kind of celibacy within marriage. The construction may be translated, "Do not deprive one another (as you are doing)," or "Stop depriving one another." Through the word *kairon*, "time"—i.e., a specific period of time—the apostle impresses on Christians the limitation of time to apply for marriage partners to agree to be parted from one another.

Paul is quick to point out that Satan, the enemy of Christians (1 Peter 5:8), is present to motivate the people of God to use even good and normal human processes wrongly and so to displease God.

When Paul states (in v.6) that he says "this" not by direct command (from the Lord) but by permission or concession (*syngnōmēn*), it is not clear what the "this" refers to (cf. Hodge, in loc.). Some refer it to v.5, "come together again," but this thought is in a subordinate clause and does not fit the context that husband and wife were to be separated only for a limited time. Others refer it to the whole of v.5, with the inference that they could separate for other reasons than that given in v.5 and for unlimited periods, but this is against the commands of vv.3, 4. So it is better to understand "this" to refer to v.2, indicating that though marriage is desirable and is according to God's creation plan, it is not mandatory. That this is Paul's meaning is evident from v.7 where he says he really wishes all men were single like him. However, he recognizes that God gives each man his own gracious gift (v.7). Some are given the desire or the inclination to be married, and some have the power to refrain from marriage. *Charisma* ("gift of grace") seems to mean the wholesome inclination given by God either to pursue marriage or to refrain from it.

8,9 Paul gives advice to the single, whom he now classifies as the unmarried and the widows. It is, he states, good or advisable (*kalon;* cf. v.1) for them to remain in their single state for the reasons spelled out in 7:26, 32–35. (Observe that in another situation Paul counsels the younger widows to marry [1 Tim 5:14].) But now he hastens to add a postscript. If the situation is such that these persons cannot control their sexual desires, they should marry. The explanation (*gar,* "for") Paul gives is that it is better to get married than be inflamed with sexual desire, which is hard to control outside of marriage. *Pyrousthai,* related to *pyr* ("fire"), means "burn" or "be enflamed," and is here used figuratively of sexual desire.

10–16 Paul's next major concern relates to Christians and divorce. What he states in v.10 "to the married" (*gegamēkosin*) is by "command" (*parangellō*)—not his own, but the command of the Lord. For he has stated above that for the unmarried to remain so was a "good" thing if a person could control his sexual desires. But for a married couple to stay together is not just "good"—it is commanded by the Lord. How specifically Paul is citing the words of Jesus depends on whether at this time he had access to the notes of one of the gospel writers or to one of the Gospels themselves.

Paul could have had access to notes on the Gospels or to a Gospel itself, acquired from the apostles when Paul visited the Jerusalem area in the earlier part of his ministry (cf. Acts 9:26–28; 11:30; 15:1, 2). That such material, as well as any accurate oral tradition regarding Jesus, was available is seen from the statement given by Luke, Paul's close companion, that there were gospel accounts being drawn up and that he, Luke, had obtained accurate information from the eyewitnesses of the gospel events (Luke 1:1–4). Furthermore, the formula for the Lord's Supper in 1 Corinthians 11:23ff. certainly gives evidence that Paul acquired accurate information from an oral or written source concerning Jesus' teaching.

The burden of Christ's command was that the married were not to be divorced (Matt 5:32; 19:3–9; Luke 16:18)—a principle Paul summarizes from both sides of the marriage partnership—the woman is not to be separated from (or, possibly, separate herself from; cf. note on v.10) her husband, and the husband must not divorce his wife (v.11). There seems to have occurred at Corinth such a separation of a wife from her husband, for Paul says, "If she does [separate], she must remain unmarried, or else be reconciled to her husband." The change of verb tenses emphasizes the direction of Paul's thinking. She is to remain unmarried (present tense continuous action) like the other unmarried (v.8), or, better, she is to be "reconciled" to her husband (aorist, accomplished action). The stress of the passage on maintaining the marriage bond unbroken definitely strengthens the injunction for separated marriage partners to become reconciled.

In vv.12–16 Paul adds instructions beyond those given by the Lord Jesus—instructions having to do with mixed marriages, where one partner has, since marriage, become a Christian. Paul addresses himself to this problem and later to the subject of virgins marrying (7:25–40) when he says, "To the rest [to the others with marital questions] I say this. . . ."

The factual indicative condition in v.12 (as in v.13), "If any brother has a wife who is not a believer [as some do] . . . ," shows that there were mixed marriages in the Christian community in this pagan city. Since Paul preached in Corinth for over a year and a half (Acts 18:11, 18), with many turning to the Lord, we may conclude that while he was still with them many marriages became mixed marriages. Had he at that time given them advice about this? Doubtless, he had. But the problem then was probably not so acute for the unbelieving partner when the other partner was a new Christian. The unbelieving one may have thought this stand for Christ was a passing fad or a superstition. As time went on, however, the condition in many Corinthian homes became more serious. In spite of Paul's teaching about Christian living and the sanctity of the home (cf. Eph 4–6), the unbelieving partners in some instances were threatening to leave their Christian husbands or wives. So Paul was confronted with the question, "What should the Christian marriage partners do?" We should note first, in the light of 2 Corinthians 6:14–7:1 (cf. Ezra 10:10), that Paul would not have allowed an already-professing Christian to marry an unbeliever. But on the question of what should be done by a husband or wife who has turned to the Lord after marriage, Paul is decisive (vv.12, 13). If the unbelieving partner is content or willing to live with the Christian, then the Christian must not divorce the partner—for the sake, Paul implies, of the marriage bond God has ordained. The present tense prohibition, *mē aphieto,* stresses that the marriage relationship is not to be broken at any time. The literal meaning is "He [she] is not to be attempting at one point or another to divorce her [him]."

Rather (v.14), the Christian partner should think of the truth that the Lord can use him as a godly, holy influence in such a mixed family relationship and in helping that family to be consecrated (set apart) to God. The word *hagiazō* ("to sanctify") does not refer to moral purity—Paul is certainly not teaching that the unbelieving partner is made morally pure. What the word emphasizes is a relationship to God, a claim of God on the person and family to be set apart for him (cf. Acts 20:32; 26:18). The perfect tense of the verb *hēgiastai* stresses that, being in a Christian family, the unbeliever has already become and continues to be a part of a family unit upon which God has his claim and which he will use for his service. The same is true of children born in such a family. That God has laid his hand on the Christian means that God has laid his hand on the children, and set them apart for himself. They are holy (*hagia,* "set apart for God") and not "unclean"—that is, not spiritually separated from God, as was and is the case in unbelieving families. The Bible's teaching elsewhere about the Christian parent and his covenant children set apart for God is also relevant to this passage. Consider Genesis 17:1–14, where the children of God's people of the OT are included among God's covenant people, and Acts 2:38, 39, where it is emphasized that God's promise applies to the children of believers, whether of those who are "near," the Jews, or those "afar off," the Gentiles (cf. Eph 2:12, 13). Covenant children are to be counted a part of God's people and should be nurtured in the Christian faith and in the fear of the Lord (Eph 6:4).

Dealing with the actual situation at Corinth, Paul realizes that in some instances the unbelieving marriage partner will not stay. So he teaches that in such an event (v.15) the believer must let the unbelieving partner go—"If [in fact—an actual condition] the unbeliever leaves, let him do so." At this point, Paul adds two reasons: First, in this case the believer is not "bound," for the unbeliever by willful desertion (the other legitimate reason for divorce besides sexual immorality [Matt 19:9]) has broken the marriage contract. The Greek perfect form of the verb is graphic—i.e., "the Christian brother or sister is not in a bound condition as a slave." A second reason for allowing an unwilling partner to leave is that God has called his people to live in peace, which would not be possible if the unbelieving partner were forced to live with the believer. Try to live with the unbelieving partner in the peace that God gives (Phil 4:6, 7), but do not attempt to force the unbeliever to stay.

The force of v.16 tempers any tendency to foster or encourage a rupture in the marriage. For Paul is teaching that the believer is to try to keep the mixed marriage together in the hope that the testimony of the believer will be used by God to bring the unbeliever to Christ. The factual condition of v.16 suggests there is a good hope that God in his providence will do just that.

Notes

1 Though the verb ἅπτομαι (*haptomai*), in the middle voice, literally means "to touch, take a hold of," in this context it means "to have sexual relations with." Since Paul has been arguing against illicit sexual relations in chapter 5, he obviously is referring here to legitimate marriage relations. This verbal expression is a euphemism for such relations (cf. Jos. *Ant* 1, 163; Gen 20:6; Prov 6:29).

3,4 The present tense imperative ἀποδιδότω (*apodidotō*) and present tense indicative, ἐξουσιάζει (*exousiazei*) are to be taken as gnomic presents, indicating that a general practice is advocated. Paul is not addressing a particular individual, but Christian men and women concerning the normal practice expected of them. Normal sexual relations are considered by Paul ὀφειλή (*opheilē*, an "obligation," a "duty,") to meet the normal emotional, spiritual, and physical needs of the human being.

5 The μήτι (*mēti*) "seems to add an element of uncertainty to the exception: 'unless perhaps;' ἂν (*an*) if genuine='in a particular case', further limiting the exception" (Parry, in loc.). Paul, as Findlay notes, considerably limits the exception of man and wife being separated from one another. First he adds τι (*ti*, "in some measure," "somehow"), then ἄν (*an*, "if the case should arise"), then ἐκ συμφώνου (*ek symphōnou*, "of consent"), assuring that the temporary separation is voluntary), and finally he adds πρὸς καιρόν (*pros kairon*, "for a time"). To safeguard any voluntary separation further from abuse, he adds the purpose for it: that they might spend time separately in prayer (G.G. Findlay, EGT [Grand Rapids: Eerdmans, n.d.], in loc.). Some later MSS have "and fasting," but this was no doubt added later by scribes because of the emphasis on asceticism. (Cf. Metzger, *A Textual Commentary*, p. 554.) Ἀκρασία (*akrasia*) means "lack of power," "indulgence," and certainly fits the thought of an overpowering sex drive to which Paul is alluding.

9 The condition here is a factual one ("If, as is sometimes true, . . .") and the change in the verb tenses is important—"For it is better to marry (γαμῆσαι, *gamēsai*, aorist) than to burn with passion" (πυροῦσθαι, *purousthai*, present).

10 The perfect tense γεγαμηκόσιν (*gegamēkosin*) means that "they have been married and are continuing in that state." The condition with the subjunctive (probability, possibility) in v.10 suggests that such separations were very possibly to happen.

Alford (in loc.) tr. Χωρισθῆναι (*chōristhēnai*) as passive: "be separated," adding, ". . . whether by formal divorce or otherwise; the χωρισθῇ below is, like this, an absolute passive; undefined whether by her own or her husband's doing." The succeeding ἀφιέναι (*aphienai*, "divorce," v.11), "the husband must not divorce his wife" seems to influence the passive form in v.10 to mean that the wife in v.10 is the offending party: "She must not separate herself."

14 Though the majority of ancient MSS have ἀδελφῷ (*adelphō*, "brother"), a few inferior witnesses, which TR follows, read "believing husband," evidently a scribal attempt to parallel the language to v.14a, "an unbelieving husband." (Cf. Metzger, *A Textual Commentary*, p. 555.)

15 The perfect tense form κέκληκεν (*keklēken*, "God has called") stresses the initial divine call of the believer with its continuing effect in daily living.

---

2. *Christian obligation to live according to God's call*

7:17–24

17Nevertheless, each one should retain the place in life that the Lord assigned
to him and to which God has called him. This is the rule I lay down in all the
churches. 18Was a man already circumcised when he was called? He should not
become uncircumcised. Was a man uncircumcised when he was called? He
should not be circumcised. 19Circumcision is nothing and uncircumcision is nothing.
Keeping God's commands is what counts. 20Each one should remain in the situa-
tion which he was in when God called him. 21Were you a slave when you were
called? Don't let it trouble you—although if you can gain your freedom, do so. 22For
he who was a slave when he was called by the Lord is the Lord's freedman;
similarly, he who was a free man when he was called is Christ's slave. 23You were
bought at a price; do not become slaves of men. 24Brothers, each man, as respon-
sible to God, should remain in the situation God called him to.

In extension of the principle that God has called his people to live in peace (v.15), Paul teaches that the Christian should live contentedly in any station of life in which God places him. The example is that of living obediently to God with full confidence in his sovereign purpose, whether one is a Jew or Gentile, slave or freedman. It is not that Paul is for the subjugation or elevation of certain segments of society, but he wants individual Christians to realize and accept God's sovereign purpose in saving and keeping them regardless of the level of society they are in. Paul is more afraid of the spirit of anarchy and rebellion, personal and national (cf. Rom 12:3; 13:1–7; 1 Cor 12:4–11; 2 Cor 10:13) than of social inequality.

It may well be that Paul's teaching that all Christians are equal (Gal 3:28), that all things material should be viewed as relatively insignificant in the light of eternal spiritual realities (2 Cor 4:18), and that the second coming of Christ will bring in a complete and new order of divine rule (1 Cor 15:23–28) had made the Christians restless and somewhat discontented with their lot in life. This place in life is what God has "assigned" and called (*keklēken* and *memeriken*) them to. God's people can and must live as Christians, whatever the social, economic, and religious level of society they are in. Their conditions do not affect their relationship and service to Jesus Christ,—whether they are married to a believer or, after having been saved, to an unbeliever; whether they are saved as Jews or Gentiles; or whether they are saved as slaves or freedmen.

17 The expression *ei me* ("nevertheless") at the beginning of this verse presents problems of interpretation. To take it as "unless," "except that," makes it difficult to relating the verse to what Paul has just said about the Christian who is married to an unbeliever, that he may possibly lead his partner to the Lord. It is best to translate the *ei mē* as "but" (KJV) or "nevertheless" (NIV), meaning that Paul is expanding his thought of the Christian's call to other areas besides that of marital status. The Christian should live for the Lord wherever he is. This, Paul says, is the principle that he orders to be followed in all the churches (cf. Eph 5:21–6:9; Col 3:18–4:1)—a principle that transcends all boundaries.

18,19 The apostle's first application of this principle is to the religio-national distinctions related to being Jews or Gentiles, being circumcised or uncircumcised. In a Gentile situation like that in Corinth, some Christian Jews may have tried to obliterate the OT covenant mark of circumcision (cf. 1 Macc 1:15). On the other hand, Judaizers tried to force circumcision on the Gentile Christians (cf. Acts 15:1–5; Gal 3:1–3; 5:1). Paul argues that this outward sign of circumcision with its stress on the Jew versus the non-Jew now has no significance. If a person was a circumcised Jew when he was saved, he should not become uncircumcised. If he was an uncircumcised Gentile, he should not be circumcised in order to become Jewish. Circumcision and uncircumcision now make no difference (Rom 2:25, 29; Gal 5:6), but keeping God's command is essential (v.19; cf. John 14:15).

20 By repetition, this verse emphasizes the principle in v.17. In the NT, *klēsis* is used of God's effectual call of his people to salvation (cf. Rom 11:29; Heb 3:1), but here it must be taken to include one's station in life.

21–23 Paul's other illustration relates to slavery. The key phrase in this passage is "Don't let it trouble you" (v.21). Paul is not speaking against human betterment or social service, but he is stressing that the Christian in Corinth is to live for the Lord *without anxiety* in his present situation. If he was a slave when he became a Christian, he should live on as a Christian even though he remains a slave. Some have interpreted Paul's use of *all' ei kai* (literally, "but if even") to mean that even if a slave had an opportunity to gain freedom, he should not follow it, in the light of his emphasis that the Christian is to remain in the social status in which he is called. (So H.A.W. Meyer in *The Epistles to the Corinthians* [New York: Funk and Wagnalls, 1884], pp. 166, 167.) But Paul's stress is on one's not being "troubled" as a Christian in his social situation, and the *all' ei kai* can just as well be translated "but if also" or "although also." So then the meaning would be "But if also you can gain your freedom, you had better take that opportunity," or, as NIV has it, "although if you can gain your freedom, do so." Observe, however, that the Bible teaches that Christianity does not guarantee material or social betterment but makes it a matter of individual responsibility (cf. Ps 73; Acts 11:29; 20:35).

Verse 22 refers to v.21a. Paul is saying, "If you were a slave when God called you, don't let it trouble you—you are the Lord's freedman. If you were free when called, remember you are Christ's slave." The spiritual antithesis is striking. The Lord has freed the Christian from the penalty of sin (2 Cor 5:21) and from Satan and his kingdom (Col 1:13) and bound us as "slaves" to himself (Rom 1:1).

Verse 23 points up the priority of Christ's authority over the Christian. In all earthly service he is to realize that his obedience and service is to Christ, not men. The reason is that God bought us with the price of Christ's blood (1 Cor 5:7; 1 Pet 1:18, 19). So because on this higher level we are slaves to Christ, we are not to become mere slaves of men. We serve faithfully in our earthly position, but we serve as slaves of Christ (cf. Eph 6:5–9, Col 3:24; 1 Tim 6:2).

In verse 24 Paul repeats the command of vv.17, 20 but adds the phrase *para theō* ("before God"), as though he is saying, "God is looking on and is there with you to help you."

Notes

17 The εἰ μή (*ei mē*) here is best taken with Blass-Debrunner as equivalent to ἀλλά (*alla*) or πλήν (*plēn*) and tr. "nevertheless" or "but." They observe that in the Gospels, at any rate, both *ei mē* and *alla* are a tr. for the Aramaic אלא (*illa*). The present tense (durative) imperative περιπατείτω (*peripateito*) here indicates literally that the person is to go on walking, and so stresses the continuous walk of the believer under God's sovereign direction.

23 The expression μὴ γίνεσθε (*mē ginesthe,* the present imperative of the verb "become") stresses the continual danger of becoming mere slaves of men. It might be tr. "Stop becoming. . . ."

3. *Instructions concerning virgins* (7:25–40)

7:25–35

[25]Now about virgins: I have no command from the Lord, but I give a judgment as one who by the Lord's mercy is trustworthy. [26]Because of the present crisis, I think that it is good for you to remain as you are. [27]Are you married? Do not seek a divorce. Are you unmarried? Do not look for a wife. [28]But if you do marry, you have not sinned; and if a virgin marries, she has not sinned. But those who marry will face many troubles in this life, and I want to spare you this.

[29]What I mean, brothers, is that the time is short. From now on those who have wives should live as if they had none; [30]those who mourn, as if they did not; those who are happy, as if they were not; those who buy something, as if it were not theirs to keep; [31]those who use the things of the world, as if not engrossed in them. For this world in its present form is passing away.

[32]I would like you to be free from concern. An unmarried man is concerned about the Lord's affairs—how he can please the Lord. [33]But a married man is concerned about the affairs of this world—how he can please his wife— [34]and his interests are divided. An unmarried woman or virgin is concerned about the Lord's affairs; Her aim is to be devoted to the Lord in both body and spirit. But a married woman is concerned about the affairs of this world—how she can please her husband. [35]I am saying this for your own good, not to restrict you. I want you to live in a right way in undivided devotion to the Lord.

Now Paul answers the second main question: What about virgins and marriage? In this section he discusses the advisability in the present situation of remaining in an unmarried (virgin) state (vv.25–35). Then he advises that they do what they think is right for the virgin who is unmarried, whether it is by initiating marriage or by remaining single (vv.36–38). He concludes with a statement regarding the married woman's responsibilities to her husband and regarding her freedom to be married again in the Lord if her husband dies. However, Paul thinks she would be happier if she remained unmarried (vv.39, 40).

25–35 Paul argues that "because of the present crisis" it is better for a man or woman to remain in their present state, whether married or single (v.26). He advises this because there is such a short time to do the work of the Lord (v.29); and anyway the material conditions of this world are changing and disappearing—"this world in its present form is passing away" (v.31). Paul introduces certain corrective statements lest the Corinthians draw false conclusions from the main principle. In saying that they should stay married, he insists that marriage itself is not a matter of right or wrong (v.28). Paul also argues that the real problem they face in their present world situation is the proper expenditure of their time and energies. He is desirous that they devote their energies to the service of the Lord, and this they can do better if they are unmarried (vv.32–34). But he hastens to add that he does not mean to hamper them in such a way as to keep them from marrying—he only wants to help them. His advice, he implies, is not an argument for the superiority of celibacy or the obligatory nature of it (v.35).

25 Here the apostle makes it clear that he is not relying directly on a command from the Lord—i.e., from Jesus—as he was, for example, in Acts 20:35. Rather, he says that he is giving his own opinion on the matter, but that his opinion is to be taken seriously because by the Lord's mercy he is trustworthy and they should therefore listen to him. So he is not suggesting that his command is any less inspired but is only calling attention to the fact that what he is presenting is not derived from a direct teaching of Jesus himself.

26,27 Each person should remain as he now is "because of the present crisis." What this is he describes in v.27. In other words, remain married if you are married; single if you are single.

28 Here Paul hastens to make it plain that there is nothing sinful in marriage, whether entered into by a widow, a widower, or by a virgin. His main motive in dissuading the unmarried from marriage is to spare them the hardship and suffering in physical life ("in the flesh") that accompanies times of trouble and persecution.

29–31 The apostle explains that the time for doing the Lord's work is short and is coming to an end. This does not necessarily mean that he is speaking of the second coming of Christ, for Paul may have been anticipating severe persecutions and a resulting curtailment of freedom to witness. So for the time remaining Paul admonishes them not to be overwhelmed by the social and material problems of the world but to live as for the Lord. By "those who have wives should live as if they had none" (v.29) he means, "Live for the Lord in marriage." If life brings sadness, live beyond it, do not be bound by it. If things are joyous, do not be engrossed in them. Those who are blessed with material possessions are not to cling to them, as though they were to have them always. The reason for this challenge is that the *material things* (this is the meaning of *schēma*, v.31, "the present form") of this world are changing and disappearing (cf. Col 3:12–14).

32–35 Paul goes on to argue that if they want marriage, they must realize that it brings extra cares. And he wants them to be free from concern. They must observe that married persons, whether men or women, have their attentions centered on the desires and needs of their spouses (vv.33, 34). In saying that the unmarried woman or virgin is concerned with how she may please the Lord (v.34), Paul implies that the married person is apt to neglect this Christian duty. Since the apostle upholds the right and privilege of marriage even for himself (1 Cor 9:3–5), he must here be advising against marriage because of particular abuses and tensions at Corinth. He gives the advice, he says, for their own profit or benefit (*symphoron*), not to restrain them or put them in a noose (*brochos*). Rather, he wants them to live properly in complete and undivided devotion to the Lord (v.35).

Notes

---

25 It is possible that the gen. pl. τῶν παρθένων (*tōn parthenōn*) is to be taken as masc. (cf. Rev 14:4) including both masc. and fem. virgins, but the masc. form is used only infrequently in the literature of the early church period.

26 Ἄνθρωπος (*anthrōpos*) without the article means man generically—i.e., both men and women, as the illustrations of vv.27, 28 show.

27 The perfect tense of δέω (*deō*, "bind") and λύω (*luo*, "loose") stresses the permanent nature of the conditions described, whether of the married or the single.

29 The ἵνα (*hina*) with the subjunctive, expressed here and implied in succeeding vv., is to be taken as an imperative or volitive idea—they are to live this way (cf. Mark 5:23; Eph 5:33).

34 The MS witness is weak for v.34a: "and his interests . . . the Lord's affairs." But it is better than a few MS witnesses that say, "the woman and the unmarried virgin are divided. . . ." (See B.M. Metzger, *A Textual Commentary on the Greek New Testament* [New York: United Bible Societies, 1971], pp. 555, 556.)

35 The figure βρόχον ὑμῖν ἐπιβάλω (*brochon hymin epibalō*, "I may put a noose on you") is appropriate in the light of Paul's contention that in the special circumstances at Corinth marriage may be an encumbrance.

7:36–40

36 If anyone thinks he is acting improperly toward the virgin he is engaged to, and if she is getting along in years and he feels he ought to marry, he should do as he wants. He is not sinning. They should get married.
37 But the man who has settled the matter in his own mind, who is under no compulsion but has control over his own will, and who has made up his mind not to marry the virgin—this man also does the right thing.
38 So then, he who marries the virgin does right, but he who does not marry her does even better.

39 A woman is bound to her husband as long as he lives. But if her husband dies, she is free to marry anyone she wishes, but he must belong to the Lord.
40 In my judgment, she is happier if she stays as she is—and I think that I have the Spirit of God.

36–40 Paul teaches that a virgin of marriageable age must be treated honorably, whether she becomes married or not. It may be right for her either to marry or remain single.

36 But who is meant by "he" is in v.36, the father of the virgin or the man who is engaged to her? Some have even interpreted the second view to mean that the virgin was a "spiritual" bride who lived with the man as a virgin. This latter view presents problems in the light of the Scriptures that teach that a man is to cleave to his wife and they are to be one flesh (Gen 2:24) and to "be fruitful" (Gen 1:28). The decision as to whether the "he" is father or fiancé turns on the meaning of *gamizō* ("marry") in v.36. Frequently, verbs ending in *—izō* are causative. If this is so here, then the translation "he who causes or gives his virgin to be married" would mean that "he" indicates the father, who in ancient times arranged for his daughter's marriage. But another viable view is that *gamizō* is not causative here, but is equivalent to *gameō* ("to marry"). If so, then "he" refers to the man who is considering the possibility of marrying his fiancée. Two arguments speak in favor of the second interpretation. First, v.38b has no object expressed for the verb *gamizō* and so the verb can better be translated "marry," not "cause to marry." Second, *gameō* ("marry") is used in the plural in v.36, "They should get married," where one might expect the singular form of *gamizō* if Paul meant to say, "Let *him* give her in marriage."

So the teaching is that if the situation in Corinth seems to be unfair to a particular virgin and especially if (*ean* with the subjunctive) she is passing her prime marriageable years, then the fiancé should go ahead and marry her. The word *hyperakmos* literally means "beyond the peak" of life, and so can be translated "if she should be getting along in years." Paul adds that there is no sin in their getting married (v.36).

37,38 In contrast, the man who feels no need to get married has done the right thing too. (The words "who is under no compulsion" refer to outward pressure to marry, such as some prior engagement contract or the pressure of a master on a slave.) However, Paul favors the man who does not marry (v.38).

39,40 In climaxing the discussion, Paul states that marriage is a life-long contract. If a woman marries, she is to cleave to her husband (Gen 2:24) till he dies. But when he dies, she is free to marry anyone she chooses, so long as he is a Christian. But, Paul says, the woman will be happier—freer from hardship and care—if she remains unmarried. This is his judgment for the Corinthian situation. When he says, rather modestly, "And I think that I have the Spirit of God," he means that in writing this also he is inspired by the Holy Spirit as were the other writers of Scripture. It is possible that some in Corinth were claiming inspiration; if so, Paul is contrasting himself with them in a veiled way.

"A woman is bound" (v.39, *dedetai,* perfect tense) is a strong expression for the unbroken ties of marriage. The passive *gamethēnai* ("to be married"; NIV, "to marry") indicates the women's consent to the new marriage relationship. The phrase *monon en kuriō* ("only in the Lord") means that the woman should marry only a Christian. The NIV translation "but he must belong to the Lord" brings this out.

Notes

36 The indicative condition of fact (v.36a) assumes that such a situation really exists. Ἀσχημονεῖν (*aschēmonein,* "to act improperly") in the light of what is implied by the clause "if she is getting past her prime of life" is best interpreted as meaning that the man could be treating his fiancée dishonorably by depriving her of the privilege of the marriage she desires. Paul seems to be making a play on words in using *aschēmonein,* "to act improperly" when he has just used εὐσχημον (*euschēmon,* "live in a right way," v.35).

B. *Instructions Concerning Christian Freedom: Its Privileges and Responsibilities* (8:1–11:1)

This section focuses on the next question the delegation from Corinth put to Paul: "What about eating food offered in heathen sacrifices to idols?" Paul's answer leads to a discussion of the larger question of how a believer should use his Christian liberty. Paul lays down the principle that love for one's brother in Christ should be the motivating factor in contemplating one's Christian liberty (8:1–13). Then he gives a personal example of how he was ready to forego the exercise of his own rights as an apostle for the sake of God's people (9:1–18). He argues that though he was under obligation to no man, he showed his self-restraint and love by placing himself on the cultural and social level of all men so that he might reach some for Christ (9:19–27). By way of warning, he speaks of the lack of self-restraint of the OT Israelites, who actually embraced the idolatry they toyed with (10:1–13). So God's people must avoid participation in idol feasts and "flee from idolatry," because they belong to the Lord and have their own feast with him, the Lord's Supper (10:14–22). So Paul's conclusion is this: Live your testimony with loving concern for your brother, but, do not make an issue of meat sold in the market. Eat it as a gift from God. Do this, except when the point is explicitly made that the meat was offered in sacrifice to an idol. For you would in such a case seem to be participating in this religious heathen practice. Refrain, then, for your weaker brother's sake and for your own peace of mind. Above all, do everything for the glory of God (10:23–11:1).

1. *Eating meat sacrified to idols* (8:1–13)

a. *Knowledge and love contrasted*

8:1–3

> [1]Now about meat sacrificed to idols: We know that we all possess knowledge. Knowledge puffs up, but love builds up. [2]The man who thinks he knows something does not yet know as he ought to know. [3]But the man who loves God is known by God.

1 By the *peri de* ("now about") Paul shows he is referring to another question asked by the Corinthian delegation (cf. 7:1, 25). The importance of the question of "foods offered in sacrifice to idols" (*eidōlothutōn*) becomes evident when one realizes how thoroughly idolatry and pagan sacrifices permeated all levels of Greek and Roman society. Indeed, people could hardly escape contact with the pagan practices and their influence. The meat offered on the pagan altars was usually divided into three portions: one portion was burned up, a second given to the priest, and the third given to the offerer. If the priest did not use his portion, it was taken to the meat market. Thus a considerable amount of sacrificed meat ended up in the public market, on the tables of pagan neighbors and friends, or at the pagan festivals. The problems Christians faced are obvious. Was the meat spiritually contaminated? Did the pagan god actually have an effect on the meat? Even if one did not think so, what would his participation do to his Christian brother who might have scruples about this? Though Christians today do not have to deal with this particular problem, they too must face questions of how to conduct themselves in a non-Christian society.

In v.1 Paul concedes that all Christians know—at least theoretically—the real meaning about the meat sacrificed to idols. But, he implies, there is something more—some may really feel that there is something wrong with that meat (v.7). So he adds that the mere knowledge that there is nothing wrong with it inflates one to a level of false security and indifference. Thus, love (*agapē*) is necessary. Love takes one beyond himself to aid another; it builds up. (It is possible to take v.1a, as some do, as a quotation from the Corinthians themselves: "We know that you say we all have knowledge.")

2 Paul now warns against dependence on simply knowing something, since a person never knows all he ought to know about a subject. Such an attitude exhibits a complete dependence on one's own self-sufficient knowledge and illustrates what Paul means by saying, "Knowledge puffs up."

3 With the essential ingredient of love, knowledge is tempered and made the right kind of discerning and compassionate knowledge exhibited when one loves God. In loving God, a person shows that he is known by God—that God recognizes him as his own and as having the right kind of knowledge, because he is exercising it in love to his fellow-Christians and to God.

b. *The meaning of eating meat sacrificed to idols*

8:4–6

> 4So then, about eating meat sacrificed to idols: We know that an idol is nothing at all in the world, and that there is no God but one. 5For even if there are so-called gods, whether in heaven or on earth (as indeed there are many "gods" and many "lords"), 6yet for us there is but one God, the Father, from whom all things came and for whom we live; and there is but one Lord, Jesus Christ, through whom all things came and through whom we live.

4 The word translated "meat" is really the broader word "food" (*brōsis*), but since the subject involves altar sacrifices and the meat market (*makellon,* 1 Cor 10:25; see commentary on this verse), the translation "meat" is proper. The main thing to remember in connection with such meat, Paul says, is that the idol before which it was sacrificed and the god it represents are actually nothing—that is, nothing as to personal reality and power. That he means this is clear from his statement "There is no God but one" (cf. Deut 6:4–9; 1 Kings 18:39; Isa 45:5). The phrase "in the world" means "in the universe."

5,6 Paul grants that there are "so-called gods" in heaven and earth such as those the pagans recognized in Greek and Roman mythology. In addition, he mentions the many "gods" and "lords" who are called such in Scripture (cf. Deut 10:17; Ps 136:2, 3) and who in the widest sense represent rulers in the universe who are subordinate to God (Col 1:16). So Paul is teaching that the "so-called gods" of the pagans are unreal and that the real "gods" and "lords," whatever they may be, are all subordinate to the only one supreme God whom alone we recognize. Actually, Paul declares the Christian's "one God, the Father . . . one Lord, Jesus Christ, to be the source of all things and the One for whom Christians live" (v.6). Concerning the world, the Father is the source (*ex hou*) of all creation, and Jesus Christ is the dynamic One through whom (*di' hou*) creation came into existence. As for the Christian, he lives for God, the source of all, and has the power for so living through Jesus Christ. So why, implies Paul, should we be concerned with idols or meat sacrificed to idols?

c. *Freedom to be exercised with care*

8:7–13

> 7But not everyone knows this. Some people are still so accustomed to idols that when they eat such meat, they think of it as having been sacrificed to an idol, and since their conscience is weak, it is defiled. 8But food does not bring us near to God; we are no worse if we do not eat, and no better if we do.
>
> 9Be careful, however, that the exercise of your freedom does not become a stumbling block to the weak. 10For if anyone with a weak conscience sees you who

have this knowledge eating in an idol's temple, won't he be emboldened to eat what has been sacrificed to idols? [11]So this weak brother, for whom Christ died, is destroyed by your knowledge. [12]When you sin against your brothers in this way and wound their weak conscience, you sin against Christ. [13]Therefore, if what I eat causes my brother to fall into sin, I will never eat meat again, so that I will not cause him to fall.

7 The knowledge Paul now speaks of is the perceptive knowledge regarding an idol and the existence and position of the "so-called gods." But some may not fully realize the significance of these truths, because in their former unsaved state they had become so accustomed to idols and to the sacrificed meat that now when they eat such meat, they think of it only as something sacrificed to the idol, rather than as food provided by God. Their moral awareness—their conscience (*syneidēsis*)—is weak, being unable to discriminate in these matters and so is defiled. The verb *molunō* can mean "defile" as in Revelation 14:4, or can be used, as here, of being brought into a sense of guilt.

8 Paul's next statement can have a twofold thrust. First, as in 8:1, we should know that there is nothing inherently wrong with sacrificial meat and that in itself food neither enhances nor minimizes our standing before God. Second, since the eating of meat is of no spiritual importance and so is a matter of indifference, the Corinthians should realize that to eat sacrificial meat is not a practice to be insisted on for maintaining Christian liberty (Hodge, in loc.).

9–12 Though Christians have the *exousia* (the "authority") to act in such cases as the one mentioned, they must "be careful" (*blepete*), lest through the exercise of this authority to act in freedom they somehow cause the weak (in conscience) to stumble in living their Christian lives. By "stumbling block" is meant causing the weak brother not only to have a sense of guilt (v.7), but to go beyond this into sin (v.13) by compromising with pagan idolatry.

So Paul depicts for the Corinthians what may well have been an actual scene (v.10): Suppose, a brother who is weak in conscience sees you, who understand that an idol is nothing, reclining at table to eat (*katakeimenon*) in an idol temple; won't he also be encouraged to eat and so do what his conscience forbids him to do? When you do such a thing, he continues (v.11), you are using your freedom and knowledge to bring your weak brother down the path (*apollutai*, present tense of *apollumi*, "destroy") toward spiritual weakness and destruction. Paul does not mean ultimate spiritual destruction, for he calls this man a "brother, for whom Christ died." The stress is on weakening the faith and ruining the Christian life of the brother.

Speaking to the "strong" brother (v.12), Paul is saying, "If you cause the weak brother to stumble into sin, you yourselves are sinning in a twofold way: (1) against your brothers and (2) against Christ in that you are wounding the conscience of those who belong to Christ. The plurals in this verse imply that Paul has in mind a sizeable group at Corinth who were both the offenders and the offended.

13 In closing the discussion, the apostle includes himself. He may be indicating that when he was in Corinth, he had had to face this question and had, for the sake of the Christians there, refrained from eating meat that had been sacrificed to idols. So he ends with the personal declaration: Therefore, if what I eat causes my brother to fall into sin,

I will never eat meat again, so that I will not cause him to fall" (v.13)—a noble resolve that stands as an enduring principle for Christian living.

Notes

1 The article ἡ (*hē*, "the") used with γνῶσις (*gnōsis*, "knowledge") is demonstrative: "*This* kind of knowledge puffs up."

3 The perfect form here, ἔγνωσται (*egnōstai*) goes beyond the idea of "know" to that of "acknowledge," or "recognize," almost with the idea of "elect"—recognized by God as his own, (cf. Amos 3:2).

7 The textual problem in v.7a is whether the reading should be συνείδησις (*suneidēsis*, "conscience") instead of συνήθεια (*sunētheia*, "become accustomed to"). The latter, followed by NIV, is the witness of the better Gr. texts. If *suneidēsis* should be read as in KJV, then the idea is that their thought has been permeated with the consciousness or awareness that the idol is real.

11 The verb ἀπόλλυμι (*apollumi*) carries not only the meaning "destroy," in the sense of eternal destruction, but also the more qualified meaning of temporal "ruin" or "loss" (cf. Matt 9:17, of wineskins that are ruined; and James 1:11, of a blossom as it withers and its beauty fades, and in that sense is thought of as destroyed).

13 Here again Paul uses the first-class condition with εἰ (*ei*) and the indicative verb. By this construction he stresses the reality of the situation: "If food actually causes my brother to stumble. . . ."

2. *Paul: on giving up his rights as an apostle* (9:1–18)

a. *Rights of an apostle*

9:1–12a

1 Am I not free? Am I not an apostle? Have I not seen Jesus our Lord? Are you not the result of my work in the Lord? 2 Even though I may not be an apostle to others, surely I am to you! For you are the seal of my apostleship in the Lord.

3 This is my defense to those who sit in judgment on me. 4 Don't we have the right to food and drink? 5 Don't we have the right to take a believing wife along with us, as do the other apostles and the Lord's brothers and Cephas? 6 Or is it only I and Barnabas who must work for a living?

7 Who serves as a soldier at his own expense? Who plants a vineyard and does not eat of its grapes? Who tends a flock and does not drink of the milk? 8 Do I say this merely from a human point of view? Doesn't the Law say the same thing? 9 For it is written in the Law of Moses: "Do not muzzle an ox when it is treading out the grain." Is it about oxen that God is concerned? 10 Surely he says this for us, doesn't he? Yes, this was written for us, because when the plowman plows and the thresher threshes, they ought to do so in the hope of sharing in the harvest. 11 If we have sown spiritual seed among you, is it too much if we reap a material harvest from you? 12 If others have this right of support from you, shouldn't we have it all the more?

1,2 Paul's reference to the spiritual freedom we have in Christ, together with his claim of apostleship, leads him to expand the theme of Christian freedom and apply it in a wider context than that of sacrificial meat. The illustration is particularly pertinent because it involves himself and relates to his important rights as an apostle and Christian worker. The four rhetorical questions in v.1 relate to two themes: freedom and apostleship, the last three specifically relating to his apostleship. Paul contends that he is an apostle and then states one of the criteria for an apostle: he had seen the Lord (Acts 1:21, 22; 9:3–9). Another evidence of apostleship, as Hodge has pointed out (in loc.), is the working of signs and wonders (2 Cor 12:12), which Paul no doubt did in Corinth. This is followed by the contention that his apostleship had produced spiritual work "in the Lord"—the Corinthians were the fruit of his work. As v.2 shows, he expected them to accept him as an apostle—though others did not—because they were really the seal that stamped his apostleship in the Lord as genuine.

All four questions in v.1 are introduced by the Greek negative *ou*, which implies that the answer expected to each is yes. The "if" condition in v.2 is a factual one; he assumes the condition that some did not accept him as an apostle, but the Corinthians certainly (*ge*) did. *Sphragis* ("seal," "sign," or "stamp of approval") is used here in a figurative sense of that which authenticates: "You certify my apostleship."

3 Paul now begins to answer those who have criticized his apostleship on the ground that he had not exercised all the rights one might expect an apostle to use.

The word *apologia* is to be taken in the sense of a "defense" against a charge, a charge concerning which some men were judging him as it were in court. The verb *anakrinō* ("question, examine") has legal connotations, used in connection with judicial hearings. Here it is best taken figuratively of those who sat in judgment on Paul.

4–6 In these verses Paul brings up certain rights he and others, such as Barnabas, had the authority (*exousia*) to exercise. The first one, "the right to food and drink," must mean, in the context, at the expense of the church (cf. 1 Cor 9:9–11). Next he claims the right to have a wife join him in his missionary travels. To take this only spiritually, as some have done, and refer to rich women accompanying the apostles to meet their financial needs, is certainly out of keeping with the context—observe that Cephas (Peter) had a wife (Mark 1:30). In referring to the "rest of the apostles" (v.5), Paul is not saying that all were necessarily married, but that at least a larger part were. The phrase "brothers of the Lord" should be taken at face value—physical brothers, that is, half-brothers, children of both Joseph and Mary after Jesus was born (Matt 1:18–25; 12:46; 13:55; Acts 1:14; Gal 1:19). In v.6 Paul raises the practical question of his and Barnabas's right to be supported financially in the ministry. It was Paul's practice to support himself materially by tentmaking (Acts 18:2, 3; 1 Cor 4:12) in order not to be a burden to the church. Some apparently misunderstood this to mean that he was not on a par with other apostles and Christian workers who depended on the church to support them. In not denying that principle, Paul asserts, by way of a question, that he has a right to be supported.

7–10 These verses present illustrations supporting the proposition that God's servants have the right to be supported with food and drink and other necessities of life as they labor in the work. Verse 7 gives illustrations from common experiences in ancient life: the soldier supported at public or royal expense; the vineyard keeper, who eats of the grapes he gathers; the shepherd, who drinks milk from his flock. These illustrations are all obvious and might be added to from modern life. But as an additional argument (v.8), Paul adds the authority of Scripture, citing Deuteronomy 25:4, "Do not muzzle an ox when it is treading out the grain." This merciful command covered the practice in ancient times of oxen pulling the threshing sledge over the grain or treading it out with their feet (Isa 28:28; 41:15; Hos 10:11). The reason for the command, Paul says, is not just God's care for the cattle (cf. Matt 6:26–29), but because by it he wants to teach us a lesson about God's care for us (v.10). This is evident, too, in the provision for the farmer: When a plowman and thresher do their work, they do so expecting that through God's blessing they will share in the crop.

11,12 In these verses the same principles of the worker's sharing in the results of his crop are applied to God's spiritual work. Those who have sown the spiritual seed at Corinth with its resultant harvest can expect to have their material needs supplied from that harvest. Then Paul argues in v.12 that if the Corinthians have supported other Christian workers, should they not also support Paul and his companions, who have sown spiritual seed among them?

This basic principle is true today. The Christian worker who sows the spiritual seed of the gospel has a right to be supported materially by those who benefit from the gospel.

Notes

4,5 The double negative in this order, μὴ οὐ (*mē ou*), introduces the question with *mē,* here used as an interrogative indicator only, and negates the verb with *ou,* implying a qualified affirmative response, which can be translated here, "Do we fail to have the right to eat and drink?" This anticipates the answer "Of course not" (cf. Robertson, *A Grammar of the Greek New Testament,* pp. 1173, 1174; and Blass and Debrunner, *A Greek Grammar of the New Testament,* para. 427).

8 The question with μή (*mē*) gives the same negative turn: "I don't speak these things from a human viewpoint, do I?" The answer is "Of course not."

11 Σαρκικός (*sarkikos,* "fleshly") can refer to what is weak and sinful (1 Peter 2:11), but here it is to be taken as that which pertains to or satisfies the needs of the flesh, that is, "material things" (cf. also Rom 15:27).

b. *Rights not used*

9:12b–18

> But we did not use this right. On the contrary, we put up with anything rather than hinder the gospel of Christ. [13]Don't you know that those who work in the temple get their food from the temple, and those who serve at the altar share in what is offered on the altar? [14]In the same way, the Lord has commanded that those who preach the gospel should receive their living from the gospel.
>
> [15]But I have not used any of these rights. And I am not writing this in the hope that you will do such things for me. I would rather die than have anyone deprive me of this boast. [16]Yet when I preach the gospel, I cannot boast, for I am compelled to preach. Woe to me if I do not preach the gospel! [17]If I preach voluntarily, I have a reward; if not voluntarily, I am simply discharging the trust committed to me. [18]What then is my reward? Just this: that in preaching the gospel I may offer it free of charge, and so not make use of my rights in preaching it.

12b The apostle goes on to announce that he will not exercise these rights that are his and says that he and his companions do so that they may not hinder the advance of the gospel. The word *enkopē,* here with the more general meaning of "hindrance," has a basic idea of a "cutting" of some sort, such as that made in a road to hinder an enemy (Liddell-Scott).

13 To emphasize further the reason and importance for his self-restraint in exercising this right of support, Paul now turns to a religious illustration, applicable in biblical worship as well as in pagan temples. Observe that Paul does not quote Scripture here. His illustration is much broader. This argument has a particularly telling relation to the Corinthians with their former connections with pagan worship. Paul's language is pointed: When people serve in the temple, they are working (*ergazomai*), and this is true, too, of those who serve in performing sacrifices at the altar. Both eat of the temple offerings. Although Paul includes in his illustration worship-practices in general, it is noteworthy that he does not use the pagan word *bōmos* for altar, but *thysiastērion. Bōmos* does not occur anywhere in the NT except in Acts 17:23, where an Athenian altar is referred to, and carries too many heathen connotations to be used. (See W. Harold Mare, "The Greek Altar in The New Testament and Inter-Testamental Periods," *Grace Journal,* Vol. 10, No. 1, Winter, 1969.)

14 Now Paul applies the general religious principle (also practiced in the OT) to the NT, to the ministers of the gospel. The adverb "thus" shows that the principle of giving material support for those who serve in the temple is to be applied also to ministers of the gospel. That the Lord Jesus commanded (*diatassō*) that those who preach the gospel are to live (be supported) by the gospel—that is, by those who believe the gospel—is shown by Matthew 10:10 and Luke 10:8.

15,16 In spite of all this evidence, Paul again states that he has not used these privileges. He adds that he is not writing this to get them to give to his support, because he wants to be able to face those opposing him at Corinth with the boast that he is unselfishly serving them and the Lord in the gospel. For, he says, if it should be a matter only of his preaching, that gives him no cause to boast, because the Lord has laid on him the necessity of preaching (Acts 26:16–18). In further explanation, he cries out that woe would descend on him through God's judgment if he did not preach.

17,18 Now he explains that there is reward or pay (*misthos*) in preaching. He states the alternatives. If he preaches freely, voluntarily, he has a reward. If not, he is merely fulfilling the commission entrusted to him (Acts 26:16). His reward is the boasting he can make before them that he is preaching to them without charge and not making use of his rights as a gospel minister. Paul wants to prove to the Corinthians the genuineness of his ministry.

Notes

13 The question stated in this v. begins with the negative οὐκ (*ouk*) by which Paul expects an affirmative reply. The participle ἐργαζόμενοι (*ergazomenoi,* "working") is a general term used here to express temple service, but in the phrase παρεδρεύοντες τῷ θυσιαστηρίῳ (*paredreuontes tō thysiastēriō*) Paul emphasizes the heart of that service—serving at the altar.

14 The teaching then is that gospel ministers are also (οὕτως, *houtōs*) serving at the altar (cf. Rev. 1:6) in telling of Christ's sacrifice on the cross.

15 The perfect tense of χράομαι (*chraomai*, "to use") here conveys the idea that Paul had determined in the past not to use these rights and his resolve continues in the present. The aorist form ἔγραψα (*egrapsa*) could be taken as simple past—"I wrote" (that is, in some previous letter). It is better to take it as an epistolary aorist—present in idea as Paul writes it but past when it was read. So the tr. "I am not writing."

There is a grammatical break in v.15, a figure of speech called aposiopesis. Paul says, "I would rather die than—," a reading favored by the better MSS. If he had completed his statement in normal construction, it would have been something like the copyists' attempt at smoothing it out with ἵνα τις (*hina tis*); "I would rather die than have anyone deprive me of this boast" (NIV). But Paul's shortened expression is more dramatic.

16 The present tense form of εὐαγγελίζομαι (*euangelizomai*) suggests Paul's continual preaching all over (v.16a), but the aorist looks at his entire preaching activity as one total calling from God (v.16b).

17 The perfect passive form πεπίστευμαι (*pepisteumai*) carries with it the idea of a trust committed and carried on in the present.

---

3. *Paul: subjection of self for others and to meet God's approval*

9:19–27

[19]Though I am free and belong to no man, I make myself a slave to everyone, to win as many as possible. [20]To the Jews I became like a Jew, to win the Jews. To those under the law I became like one under the law (though I myself am not under the law), so as to win those under the law. [21]To those not having the law I became like one not having the law (though I am not free from God's law but am under Christ's law), so as to win those not having the law. [22]To the weak I became weak, to win the weak. I have become all things to all men so that by all possible means I might save some. [23]I do all this for the sake of the gospel that I may share in its blessings.

[24]Do you not know that in a race all the runners run, but only one gets the prize? Run in such a way as to get the prize. [25]Everyone who competes in the games goes into strict training. They do it to get a crown of laurel that will not last; but we do it to get a crown that will last forever. [26]Therefore, I do not run like a man running aimlessly; I do not fight like a man shadow boxing. [27]No, I beat my body and make it my slave so that after I have preached to others, I myself will not be disqualified for the prize.

19 Going beyond his right to financial support, the apostle now discusses other areas of life in which he had forfeited his right to freedom in order to win more to Christ. His statement is a strong one: "I am free from all men, but I have enslaved (*edoulōsa*, aorist) myself to all."

20 In discussing his self-sacrificing concern in vv.20–23, Paul mentions three groups—the Jews, the Gentiles, and those whose consciences are weak. For the Jews' sake Paul became like a Jew. That is, when necessary and regarding indifferent matters, he conformed to the practice of Jewish law (Acts 16:3; 18:18; 21:20–26) to win the Jews. "Those under the law" need not be taken as a separate group such as proselytes to Judaism, but as reference again to Jews—those to whom Paul accommodated himself. In the parenthetical phrase "though I myself am not under the law," Paul means that in his freedom he was not obligated to practice such Jewish laws as their rigorous ceremonial washings.

21 For the Gentiles "without the law," those who did not have any written revelation from God (Rom 2:12), Paul says he became like one not having the law and took his place in their culture in order to reach them (cf. Gal 2:11–21). But he hastens to correct any misunderstanding: he counts himself still under God's law, and even more, under Christ's law.

22 Those with a weak conscience (1 Cor 8:9–12) he also wants to be sure to win (v.22). He becomes "weak"—that is, he refrains from exercising his Christian freedom, and acts as they do respecting these indifferent things. He has forfeited his freedom for the sake of all, that by all these means some may be saved.

23 Paul does all this for the sake of the gospel that he might be a co-sharer (*synkoinōnos*, "communion," "fellowship") with the gospel, sharing in its blessings personally and in seeing others come to Christ.

24–27 By way of practical application, Paul now gives a strong exhortation for Christian self-denial, using himself as an example and employing athletic figures familiar to the Corinthians at their own Isthmian athletic games, which were hosted every other year by the people of Corinth. The particular events he refers to are running and boxing.

24,25 Paul assumes their common knowledge (*ouk oidate*, "don't you know") of the foot race in the stadium. Every one of them should run as these runners do, with all-out effort to get the prize. By the words "strict training," Paul refers to the athlete's self-control in diet and his rigorous bodily discipline. He observes that the athletes train vigorously for a "corruptible crown"—a laurel or celery wreath that would soon wither away. But the Christian's crown, eternal life and fellowship with God, will last forever (Rev 2:10).

26,27 Paul says of himself that he does not contend like an undisciplined runner or boxer. He states that he aims his blows against his own body, beating it black and blue (*hypōpiazō;* see the same word in Luke 18:5). The picture is graphic: the ancient boxers devastatingly punishing one another with knuckles bound with leather thongs. And so by pummeling his body, Paul enslaves it in order to gain the Christian prize. The ancient *kēryx* was the herald in the Greek games who announced the rules of the contest, but the Christian herald—*i.e.*, preacher—not only announces the rules but "plays" in the game as well. Paul had not only to preach the gospel but also to live the gospel. As Hodge has said (in loc.), Paul here acts on the principle that the righteous can scarcely be saved, though he also stresses that nothing can separate the Christian from God's love (Rom 8:38, 39). The Christian, confident of God's sovereign grace, is nevertheless conscious of his battle against sin.

Notes

---

20 The circumstantial participle ὢν (*ōn*) stresses Paul's present existent state; the phrase may be tr. "though I am not existing under the control of the law"; i.e., the Jewish ceremonies. The phrase μὴ . . . νόμον (*mē . . . nomon*) was not in TR and so was omitted from KJV. However, it is decisively supported by the best ancient MSS. It probably was accidentally omitted by some scribe(s) who overlooked one of the four occurrences of ὑπὸ νόμον in this verse.

21 There seems to be a play on the words ἄνομος (*anomos*, "without law"; i.e., outside the rules of Jewish ceremonies) and ἔννομος (*ennomos*, "within the law"; i.e., within the rules and control of Christ).

Excursus

In Paul's time many of the structures dedicated to the ancient gods had been restored and were in use again in worship of the gods and were no doubt evident to the visitor to Corinth. These included the archaic temple of Apollo, built about 550 B.C., seven of whose columns are still to be seen today. Nearby, on the north slope of the hill, was the shrine to Athena, the Bridler. It had been built to commemorate Bellerophon's harnessing of the winged horse, Pegasus, who was caught with Athena's help, when he was drinking at the fountain of Peirene at Corinth. Bellerophon (a local mythical hero) then used Pegasus in slaying the Chimaera (a she-monster with a lion's head, a goat's body, and a serpent's tail). This well-known story led to the winged horse's becoming the emblem used for hundreds of years on Corinthian coins. Poseidon, the sea-god, also had his shrine and fountain at Corinth, though his chief cultic place in this area was at Isthmia about seven miles to the east. (For location of places mentioned, see map, p. 187).

A short distance west of the archaic Apollo temple stands a stone-cut fountain house. Here, according to Greek myth, the Corinthian princess, Glauke, the bride of Jason, threw herself into the fountain waters at a time when her body was being destroyed by the poisoned robe given to her by Medea, the sorceress from the Black Sea area. In vengeance, Medea killed her own sons born of Jason. Close by was a statue of Terror, in the form of a woman, which was in existence in Paul's day, when images of baked clay were evidently thrown into the Fountain House of Glauke. This ceremony is believed to be a development from earlier human sacrifices made there by the Corinthians. The goddess Hera was worshiped in connection with this festival and a small temple of Roman times with colonnaded court near the Fountain of Glauke is identified as that of Hera.

Apollo was also worshiped at another place besides the archaic temple of Apollo. This shrine, located near the Fountain of Peirene in the northeast section of the excavated area of Corinth, was the Peribolos sanctuary of Apollo with its large paved court and colossal statue of the god in the center.

Other remains of the Roman period found in the Corinthian excavations include those of the temple of Aphrodite-Tyche (Venus-Fortune); a Pantheon, or "temple of all the gods"; a temple of Heracles (the Greek mythical hero famous for achieving "The Twelve Labors"); and a temple of Hermes (Mercury, the messenger of the gods). Besides these, there were the temple to Octavia, (the deified sister of the Emperor Augustus) and the temple of Jupiter Capitolinus (Zeus Koryphaios). Some distance from the marketplace, to the north, was the temple of Asklepios, the god of healing, to whom terra cotta likenesses of the diseased parts of the body were offered by those who were afflicted with these sicknesses. Some of these terra cotta likenesses are on display today in the Antiquities Museum at Ancient Corinth. Paul may have had in mind such sicknesses affecting the perishable human body as represented by the clay likenesses of these diseased parts when he declared to the Corinthians the truth of God's triumph over decay and death when at the resurrection the Christian dead "will be raised imperishable, and we shall be changed" (1 Cor 15:52; cf. also vv.53–55).

On the top of the Acrocorinth (the rocky pinnacle) behind ancient Corinth was the famous temple of Aphrodite (Venus) in whose service were one thousand prostitute slave priestesses. On the Acrocorinth's north slopes facing the city were other temples, such as that in honor of the Egyptian gods, Isis and Serapis. The worship of these gods probably started at Corinth either in the Hellenistic period (c.330 to 63 B.C.) or in the Roman period, after the city was founded as a Roman Colony in Caesar's time. (See Broneer, "Corinth," pp. 83–88.) On the Acrocorinth's north slopes was the temple of the goddess Demeter that had been in use from c.600 B.C. to A.D. 350. This structure contained a number of dining rooms, which may account for Paul's warning about not being a stumbling block by "eating in an idol's temple" (1 Cor 8:10; see Henry S. Robinson, "Excavations at Corinth, 1961–1962," in AJA, 67, [1963], pp. 216, 217; Miriam Ervin, "Newsletter from Greece," AJA, 74 [1970], pp. 267, 268; and Nancy Bookidis, *Hesperia,* 28 [1969], No. 3, pp. 297–310).

With such idolatry and other pagan practices dominating the life and culture of Corinth, no wonder Paul was so concerned for Christians not to be reckless in exercising their freedom to eat meat sold in butcher shops after it had been offered to some idol and consecrated in pagan worship in the city. Also, that is why Paul disciplined himself (1 Cor 9:19–27) in refraining from eating meat sacrificed to idols or in doing any other thing by which he would disappoint the Lord or offend his brothers in Christ.

4. *Warning: Israel's lack of self-restraint*

10:1–13

> [1]For I do not want you to be ignorant of the fact brothers, that our forefathers were all under the cloud and that they all passed through the sea. [2]They were all baptized into Moses in the cloud and in the sea. [3]They all ate the same spiritual food [4]and drank the same spiritual drink; for they drank from the spiritual rock that accompanied them, and that rock was Christ. [5]Nevertheless, God was not pleased with most of them, so their bodies were scattered over the desert.
>
> [6]Now these things occurred as examples, to keep us from setting our hearts on evil things as they did. [7]Do not be idolaters, as some of them were; as it is written: "The people sat down to eat and drink and got up to indulge in pagan revelry." [8]We should not commit sexual immorality, as some of them did—and in one day twenty-three thousand of them died. [9]We should not test the Lord, as some of them did—and were killed by snakes. [10]And do not grumble, as some of them did—and were killed by the destroying angel.
>
> [11]These things happened to them as examples and were written down as warnings for us, on whom the fulfillment of the ages has come. [12]So, if you think you are standing firm, be careful that you don't fall! [13]No temptation has seized you except what is common to man. And God is faithful; he will not let you be tempted beyond what you can bear. But when you are tempted, he will also provide a way out so that you can stand up under it.

In this passage Paul takes the sins of Israel during the time of Moses as a basis for warning the Corinthians. Though the people of Israel had the covenant blessings and were miraculously delivered and sustained, yet most of them died in the wilderness because of disobedience and unbelief. Paul uses their experiences as examples, which he exhorts the Corinthians to heed.

1–5 The Greek word *gar* ("for") connects these verses with the argument in chapters 8 and 9. Having challenged the Christians in Corinth to self-discipline, Paul now looks back to Israel. First, he stresses their miraculous passage through the Red Sea. All the fathers shared in God's grace and all were in the race described in 9:24–27, but only

Caleb and Joshua entered Canaan and won the prize. Five times in vv.1–4 Paul says that all Israel shared in the blessings and the privileges of God's grace. But (*alla,* strong negative) God was not pleased with most of them, so he scattered their corpses over the desert (v.5).

"I do not want you to be ignorant," meaning "I want you to know," is elsewhere used by Paul in presenting important truth (Rom 1:13; 1 Thess 4:13). "Under the cloud" indicates that they were under God's guidance (Exod 13:21, 22; Num 9:15–23; 14:14; Deut 1:33; Ps 78:14)—a guidance that was sure, since they all passed through the Red Sea.

That "they were all baptized into Moses in the cloud and in the sea" simply means they were initiated and inaugurated under God into union with him and also with Moses and his leadership. Compare the expression "baptized into Christ" (Rom 6:3, 4; cf. Gal 3:27; and see Heb 3:1–6). The aorist middle form *ebaptisanto,* or the alternate passive MS reading *ebaptisthēsan,* means "they received baptism." Some have taken the expression to specify either sprinkling or immersion, but these ideas need not be pressed. The thought is a spiritual one (v.3). They were united to God and to his servant Moses. The cloud is a representation of God in his shekinah glory; the sea, of God's redemption and leadership.

That the food and drink in the wilderness are called spiritual (vv.3, 4) means that these physical objects were to be a means of grace to God's people. They were typical of Christ the true bread and drink to come (cf. John 6:30–65). That the terms are to be taken as typical is seen in the statement "that rock was Christ" (cf. 1 Cor 5:7), who was with them to save them.

But though they all shared these blessings, most of them were not pleasing to God (v.5; Heb 3:17–19). He saw in them a heart of unbelief (vv.6–10) and scattered their corpses in the desert.

6–10 Paul explains here that all these things were examples (*typoi*) for us to think about, lest we who also have received the covenant blessings should become displeasing to God by lusting after evil things as Israel did.

Then he describes (vv.7–10) what that lusting involved and warns against following their example. Many of Israel became idolaters. The illustration is that of Exodus 32:1–6, where it is said that Israel had Aaron make the golden calf. Exodus 32:6, quoted here, tells how Israel ate a sacrificial meal in dedication to the calf and then got up "to play" (KJV), that is, to dance in ceremonial revelry as the pagans danced before their gods. This may look back to Paul's discussion in 1 Corinthians 8 about meat sacrificed to idols.

As he continues his warning, he alludes to Israel's joining herself to Baalpeor (Num 25:1–9), an act involving both spiritual and sexual unfaithfulness. Hodge notes (in loc.), "This Baal-peor was the god of the Moabites who was worshiped by the prostitution of virgins. Idolatry and fornication were in that case inseparable." In v.8 Paul uses *porneuō,* the common NT word for "committing sexual immorality" that is a cognate of the words used in chapter 5. He softens its force, however, by including himself in the exhortation. The Greek text says 23,000 died, whereas the Hebrew and LXX texts of Numbers 25:9 says 24,000. Paul is speaking about how many died in that one day; he does not include others who were killed subsequently, among them being the leaders in the rebellion, whom God ordered Moses to hang (Num 25:4).

Verse 9 relates to the murmuring of Israel against the Lord for bringing them out of Egypt and tells of their drastic punishment (Num 21:6). Observe the plural pronoun "we," with which Paul includes himself in cautioning the Corinthians against complaining as Israel did. The verb *ekpeirazō* means "to put to the test—i.e., testing the Lord to see what he will do.

The next example (v.10) relates to Israel's grumbling against the Lord at Kadesh-barnea (Num 14:2) and their wishing they had died in Egypt or in the wilderness. The "destroyer" was the angel of God (cf. Exod 12:23), whom Paul indicates was sent to bring the plague spoken of in Numbers 14:37. The incident referred to may also be taken to be the destruction of Korah, Dathan, and Abiram (Num 16:30).

11–13 Paul now makes an application for the Corinthians. Paul sets forth the examples he uses as actually having occurred in history (notice the imperfect verb *sunebainen,* "they were happening") and as having been written down to warn us. The KJV translation "ends of the world" (v.11b) seems to suggest too much, as though Paul thought he and the Corinthians were in the time of the Second Coming. Actually, he is speaking of the stretch of time called "the fulfillment [or 'end'] of the ages," which was to continue from Paul's time into the indefinite future. The warning amounts to this: Do not be smug in your firm stand for Christ. Keep alert lest you fall.

Verse 13 is one of the most helpful verses in the NT and presents the great antidote to falling into sin through temptation. *Peirasmos,* "trial" or "temptation" is not itself sinful. God allows it as a way of purifying us (James 1:12), but the devil uses it to entice us into sin (cf. Matt 4:1). The temptations that come to the Christian are those all human beings face—they are unavoidable. But, says Paul, God is right there with us to keep us from being overwhelmed by the temptation. The words "with the temptation" could perhaps be taken to mean that God brings the temptation, but this is contrary to James 1:13. So it means, rather, that when we are tempted, God will help. He will provide a way out, not to avoid the temptation, but to meet it successfully and to stand firm under it.

Notes

---

2 Some MSS have the aorist middle of βαπτίζω (*baptizō*)—"they got themselves baptized." Other MSS have the passive—"they were baptized." The meaning is the same.

4 The article ἡ (*hē*) with both πέτρα (*petra,* "the rock") and Χριστός (*Christos,* "the Christ") shows that the rock typifies *the* Christ.

5 The verb κατεστρώθησαν (*katestrōthēsan*) is passive and vividly describes the scattering of the corpses (by the hand of God) all over the desert.

6 The term ἐπιθυμία (*epithymia,* "strong desire, longing") can be used in a good sense (Phil 1:23), but more often, as here, in a bad sense of lusting after what is forbidden (cf. 2 Tim 2:22).

10 The ὀλοθρευτής (*olothreutēs*) is the destroyer (cf. Exod 12:23; הַמַּשְׁחִית, *hammašḥit;* and Heb 11:28)—the angel of God designed to bring divine judgment.

---

5. *Warning: attendance at pagan sacrifices means fellowship with idolatry*

10:14–22

14Therefore, my dear friends, flee from idolatry. 15I speak to sensible people;
judge for yourselves what I say. 16Is not the cup of thanksgiving for which we give
thanks a participation in the blood of Christ? And is not the bread that we break

> a participation in the body of Christ? 17Because there is one loaf, we, who are many, are one body, for we all partake of the one loaf.
>
> 18Consider the people of Israel: Do not those who eat the sacrifices participate in the altar? 19Do I mean then that a sacrifice offered to an idol is anything, or that an idol is anything? 20No, but the sacrifices of pagans are offered to demons, not to God, and I do not want you to be participants with demons. 21You cannot drink the cup of the Lord and the cup of demons too; you cannot have a part in both the Lord's table and the table of demons. 22Are we trying to arouse the Lord's jealousy? Are we stronger than he?

Here Paul applies the example of Israel's idolatry to the problem of 1 Corinthians 8—eating meat sacrificed to idols. There is the danger of going a step beyond just eating sacrificed meat to that of joining the pagans in the sacrificial feasts in their pagan temples. To do this would be wrong and sinful. Paul illustrates this by showing that participation in the Lord's Supper signifies that the believer is in communion—in a sharing relationship (*koinonia*)—with the Savior. So participation in idol feasts in pagan temples means sharing in the pagan worship. Such participation is forbidden. This is the mistake Israel made. Christians today must discern how the illustration applies to their own lives.

14,15 The apostle's terse injunction, "Flee [present tense] from idolatry," applies not only to the weak who through eating might be led into idolatry but also to those with a strong conscience who in leading the weak into sin were guilty. Paul asks the Corinthians to use good sense and determine the truth of what he says.

16,17 Paul teaches that the cup of blessing or thanksgiving (*eulogia*) brings us spiritually into participation in the blood of Christ and into fellowship with him. The same is true of the bread. The "cup of blessing" was a technical term for the third cup drunk at the Jewish Passover, the time when the Lord's Supper was instituted (Matt 26:17–30 and parallel passages: Mark 14:12–26; Luke 22:7–23; John 13:21–30). That "participation in Christ's blood" is meant to be a memorial symbol of fellowship with Christ, and not a literal drinking of his blood, is clear from the fact that Christ had not yet died when he instituted this supper and that this participation is in remembering him, not in drinking him (1 Cor 11:25). So also we are one body because we partake of one bread.

18–20 Here Paul compares the OT sacrifices with pagan offerings. When the people of Israel sacrificed at the altar and ate part of the sacrifice (Lev 7:15; 8:31; Deut 12:17, 18), they participated in and became a part of the sacrificial system and worship of God. Paul says he does not mean that the meat sacrificed to an idol or the idol itself is anything, but he does mean that when the pagans sacrifice, they do so to demons and he doesn't want the Corinthians to share in worship having to do with demons. For one cannot be both—a participant in Christ and in demons also.

21 To make it clearer, Paul speaks of "The Lord's table"—a term that the Corinthian converts from paganism would readily associate with "tables" used for pagan idol meals. In the Oxyrhynchus Papyrus CX there is a revealing sentence that says, "*Chairemon invites you to a meal at the table of the lord Serapis* in the Serapeum, tomorrow the fifteenth from nine o'clock onwards." So Paul is teaching that a Christian cannot at the same time participate in the meal at the table of the pagan god and the table of the Lord.

22 The conclusion is that if we as Christians share in pagan idolatry, we will "arouse" (i.e., "stir up") the Lord's jealousy and thus incite him to action in his hatred of sin and for mixed allegiance (Deut 32:21; Ps 78:58). And surely, Paul says, we are not stronger than God and cannot overcome or subdue his jealousy and anger against sin if we share in pagan practices.

Notes

18 Κατὰ σάρκα (*kata sarka*, "according to the flesh") refers to Israel "physically, in the flesh"; hence the tr. "the people of Israel."

19 Φημί (*phēmi*, "I say") has the force of "I mean" (NIV, "Do I mean then . . . ?").

21 Note that μετέχω (*metechō*, "share, participate") is used here, rather than κοινωνία (*koinōnia* —used of a Christian's fellowship with Christ) because the same mutual fellowship could not exist in sharing both the table of the Lord and the table of demons.

6. *Freedom, but within limits: do all to the glory of God*

10:23–11:1

23"Everything is permissible"—but not everything is beneficial. "Everything is permissible"—but not everything is constructive. 24Nobody should seek his own good, but the good of others.

25Eat anything sold in the meat market without raising questions of conscience, 26for, "The earth is the Lord's, and everything in it."

27If some unbeliever invites you to a meal and you want to go, eat whatever is put before you without raising questions of conscience. 28But if anyone says to you, "This has been offered in sacrifice," then do not eat it, both for the sake of the man who told you and for conscience' sake—29the other man's conscience, I mean, not yours. For why should my freedom be judged by another's conscience? 30If I take part in the meal with thankfulness, why am I denounced because of something I thank God for?

31So whether you eat or drink or whatever you do, do it all for the glory of God. 32Do not cause anyone to stumble, whether Jews, Greeks or the church of God—33even as I try to please everybody in every way. For I am not seeking my own good but the good of many, so that they may be saved. 11:1Follow my example, as I follow the example of Christ.

Returning to the thought of 1 Corinthians 8 that eating meat sacrificed to idols is essentially a matter of indifference, Paul now adds that it can be harmful. He lays down three principles: First, though the Christian has the right to do all things, such as eating sacrificial meat, it may not be beneficial to themselves. Second, such practices of liberty may not in fact build up a fellow Christian. Third, in summary Paul teaches that Christians are not merely to seek their own good but to promote the good of their fellow Christians.

25–30 Specifically, Paul says, meat eaten at an idol feast is associated with pagan worship and is contaminated. Meat sold in the public meat market has lost its religious significance and is all right to eat.

The word *makellon* ("meat market," v.25) has interesting connections in Corinth. Near the Lechaeum Road, the paved footroad leading north from Corinth toward the western part of Lechaeum (see map of Corinthia, p. 187), a commercial building has been excavated. It has a paved court, which was surrounded by colonnades and small shops. Broneer ("Corinth," p. 89), relates that in the pavement of one shop a marble slab has been found, and claims it is inscribed with the Latin word for market and that this word has been transliterated in the Greek text of v.25. But J. Schneider, in TDNT, 4:370–372, says that the word *makellon* is of Greek origin, occurring on a building inscription in Epidauros about 400 B.C., though it appears in Roman inscriptions in Italy and in Latin-speaking colonies more than in Greek on Greek inscriptions. The word means "food market" as well as "meat market," which was a part of the *makellon.* Excavations have revealed the plan of such markets: a rectangular, columned court with a central fountain and a dome-shaped roof supported by columns and with booths on the sides and porticoes in front of them. According to Schneider (ibid.), the food market at Pompeii had on the east side an imperial cult area, embellished with statues, and in the southeast area there seems to have been a room for sacrificial meals.

Cadbury argues (in JBL, 53:134–141) that the *makellon*–meat market mentioned on the inscription found in Corinth was in existence in Paul's day, and so this establishment could be the very one Paul is referring to, where meat previously offered in sacrifice to idols was being sold. As has been said, this meat no longer retained its religious significance and was really all right to eat.

So, Paul teaches, eat this meat without raising questions, remembering that meat and all things come from the Lord (v.26). The OT quotation from Psalm 24:1 (cf. Pss 50:12; 89:11) was used as a Jewish blessing at mealtimes.

In approving of a believer joining an unbeliever at the latter's house for dinner (v.27), the apostle is thinking of the believer's giving the unbeliever a quiet, appreciative testimony. If, however, at the dinner someone (probably a fellow Christian; cf. v.29a) points out that the meat was offered to an idol, then the believer is to refrain from eating the meat. The reason for this is that he does not want his Christian freedom condemned through another man's conscience (v.29). Paul asks why he should be condemned for partaking of something in the meal he could really thank God for. The verb *blasphemeō* (v.30) means "to injure the reputation of," or actually "to revile" or "denounce" someone who has presumably done wrong. So the strong brother has the power to protect his "right" to eat by not eating meat in such a case.

31–33 These verses introduce a positive and more ultimate perspective. It is not just the other brother who should be in view, but God the creator and giver of all things. The *oun* ("therefore," "so") relates this ultimate concept to one's attitude toward the weak brother. The glory of God must be the Christian's objective in everything (1 Pet 4:11; Col 3:17; cf. *Westminster Shorter Catechism,* Question 1). But Paul says that doing all for the glory of God means thinking of the good of others, both Christians and non-Christians (v.32). The mention of Jews and Greeks may refer to the unsaved groups talked about in 1 Corinthians 1. By "the church of God" Paul means to include the brother with the weak conscience (cf. Rom 14:13, 21). So we find encompassed by these verses the two great commandments—love God and love your neighbor (Matt 22:37–39). Paul seeks to benefit others, not himself. His ultimate objective in all his conduct is that people might be saved—not superficially but fully and to the glory of God.

11:1 This verse really belongs to the previous discussion. The dynamic present imperative of *ginomai* gives the command a continual relevance then and now. "Ever become imitators (*mimētai;* cf. English "mimic") of me" is the literal translation. Paul is calling the Corinthians to the unity that had been disrupted (ch. 1). He can do this because he himself is an imitator of Christ (Gal 2:20)—the same Christ who had dealt gently with Paul in all his prejudices (Acts 26:12–18).

Notes

23 Συμφερεῖ (*sympherei,* "be useful," "beneficial") deals more with the basic principle, whereas οἰκοδομεῖ (*oikodomei,* "to build up," "edify") deals with the causative effect of Christian actions—they actually affect the spiritual growth of believers.

30 Χάρις (*charis,* "grace")—the grace of God (cf. Titus 2:13)—also often has the idea "be grateful for," and so means "thanks," "thankfulness" (e.g., 2 Cor 9:15).

32–11:1 Observe the occurrences of γινεσθε (*ginesthe*): "become blameless" (v.32), "become imitators" (11:1). Christianity always presents the challenge of responsible Christian living.

33 The aorist (constative) subjunctive σωθῶσιν, (*sōthōsin* "that they might be saved") has the total view in mind—that they be shown to be totally saved with all the divine means of grace and through human agency, by God's plan to accomplish that salvation, which includes justification and sanctification (growth in grace) and finally glorification, when the believer gets to heaven (cf. 2 Tim 4:6–8).

C. *Worship in the Church* (11:2–14:40)

This entire section deals with problems connected with church worship—matters concerning the veiling of women (11:2–16), observing the Lord's Supper (11:17–34), and the granting and use of spiritual gifts (12:1–14:40).

1. *Propriety in worship: covering of women's heads* 11:2–16

2I praise you for remembering me in everything and for holding to the teachings, just as I passed them on to you.

3Now I want you to realize that the head of every man is Christ, and the head of the woman is man, and the head of Christ is God. 4Every man who prays or prophesies with his head covered dishonors his head. 5And every woman who prays or prophesies with her head uncovered dishonors her head—it is just as though her head were shaved. 6If a woman does not cover her head, she should have her hair cut off; and if it is a disgrace for a woman to have her hair cut or shaved off, she should cover her head. 7A man ought not to cover his head, since he is the image and glory of God; but the woman is the glory of man. 8For man did not come from woman, but woman from man; 9neither was man created for woman, but woman for man. 10For this reason, and because of the angels, the woman ought to have a sign of authority on her head.

11In the Lord, however, woman is not independent of man, nor is man independent of woman. 12For as woman came from man, so also man is born of woman. But everything comes from God. 13Judge for yourselves: Is it proper for a woman to pray to God with her head uncovered? 14Does not the very nature of things teach you that if a man has long hair, it is a disgrace to him, 15but that if a woman has long hair, it is her glory? For long hair is given to her as a covering. 16If anyone wants to be contentious about this, we have no other practice—nor do the churches of God.

2,3 By his use of *de* ("now"; not *peri de*, "now about," as in 7:1 and 12:1) to begin this section, Paul shows he is taking up the subject on his own, not necessarily answering one of their questions.

3–16 These verses have evoked considerable difference of opinion about the nature of the head covering and the place of woman both in public worship and in her relationship to the man. The head covering has been taken to be either a veil or shawl, or else hair—either long or short. As to the use of veils, women in the ancient Orient were veiled in public, or when among strangers, but otherwise they were unveiled. Note that Rebecca was unveiled till she met Isaac (Gen 24:65). James B. Hurley notes that in contrast, ancient pottery shows Greek women in public without head coverings. ("Did Paul Require Veils or the Silence of Women? A Consideration of 1 Cor 11:2–16 and 1 Cor 14:33b–36," WTJ vol.35 [Winter, 1973], no. 2, p. 194). In Corinth the women may well have gone to public meetings without veils. But the question is whether Paul is talking about the use of veils in public worship (as Hodge, St. John Parry, and others hold) or about women letting their long hair hang loose (a sign of mourning or of the shame of an accused adultress [Hurley, ibid.; cf. Grosheide, in loc.]) rather than having their hair "put up."

4–6 Whichever view is held as to the nature of the head covering, the same basic principles emerge from the passage. In vv.3–10 Paul emphasizes the order of authority and administration in the divine structure of things. As every man is to be under Christ's authority and Christ is under God's authority, so the woman is under her husband's authority. (Paul does not mean by his analogy that subordination in each case is of the same completeness.) Therefore, the woman should not demonstrate her authority by having her head uncovered, as the man did when he was praying and prophesying. Evidently at Corinth women were coming to church with their heads improperly covered, thus causing disorder and disrespect in the services. Paul is not necessarily giving his opinion on the propriety of women praying or prophesying in the church, which he observes was being done, though he does so in 1 Corinthians 14:34 (Hodge). Some feel that since he mentions women praying and prophesying here, he approves of the practice (so Hurley). Paul does state here, however, that if a woman is in the public worship with her head uncovered, it is as if she had her head shaved (v.5). He concludes the argument by saying that if the woman in fact does have her head uncovered, she should have her hair cut; on the other hand, if it is shameful (and it is—note the condition of fact) for a woman to have her hair cut or her head shaved, then, of course, she should have her head properly covered (v.6).

7–9 In stating that a man should not have his head covered in church, Paul argues that this follows from the principle that man was prior to woman and is the image and glory of God—that, is he is to be subject to and represent God in authority. The woman, however, is the glory of the man—i.e., she is to be subject to man and to represent him in authority. Although God created Adam and Eve and gave them dominion over the creation (Gen 1:26), Paul argues for man's exercise of authority above woman's on the basis of man's prior creation to woman. The argument goes like this: Woman came from (*ex*) man (i.e., she was made from his body) and she was made for man's sake (*dia* with the accusative) and not the reverse (Gen 2:7).

Although it was not proper for a first-century Jewish man to cover his head for prayer (a custom, originally meant to indicate sorrow, that evidently really developed as a practice in the fourth century A.D.), yet the act seems to have been innovatively tried in the Jewish synagogues of Paul's time. (See Strack and Billerbeck, *Kommentar Zum N.T.*, 3:423–426; Craig, in loc.)

10 The woman has a certain authority (*exousia*) in that in having her head properly covered in worship, she shows respect to the (good) angels who were in attendance. That these angels might be evil angels over whom women would have power certainly does not agree with the scriptural teaching that God's ministering angels (the good angels) serve God's people (Heb 1:14).

Perhaps angels are mentioned in this discussion about the place of women in the church to remind Christians that angels are present at the time of worship and that they are interested in the salvation of God's people (1 Peter 1:10–12; cf. Gal 3:10) and sensitive to the conduct of Christians at worship. So the angels would recognize the breach of decorum were Christian women not to have proper head coverings and the long hair distinguishing them as women—the "sign of authority on her head" (v.10), which symbolized her husband's authority over her.

11,12 But lest he be misunderstood as wanting to demote women, Paul now argues that man and woman are equal in the Lord and mutually dependent.

13–15 The final point in the passage is that man is to be distinguished from woman. Thus the Corinthians are to see that the woman should not pray with her head uncovered as the man does. They are reminded that in ordinary life man with his short hair is distinguished from woman with her long hair. If a man has long hair like a woman's, he is disgraced, but with long hair the woman gains glory in her position of subjection to man. Also long hair is actually given to her as a natural veil.

16 Finally, Paul states that the churches and he himself follow this principle that in worship men come with short hair and women with long, and that the man exercises the position of authority (v.16). This, he implies, should deter those who would want to be contentious about the matter. In using "we" (meaning the apostles), Paul teaches that the Corinthians are to take his statements given in the preceding verses (1 Cor 11:2–16) as having apostolic authority, and not as pious advice.

Summary

2–16 The instructions given by Paul relating to the place of women in the church were addressed to the cultural milieu of the Corinthian believers in the first century A.D. Corinth was a pagan Greek city out of which God was calling a church of his redeemed. That Greek women did appear in public without a head covering is evident from ancient Greek vase paintings, and women in the Corinthian church may have come to worship services in this way. Also some Christian women who were Greeks or Jews may have been going to church with hair disheveled and hanging loose. This might have given the impression that they were mourning or it might even imply that they had been accused of adultery. So disorder and unrest might have begun to mar the services.

The apostle Paul, of course, wanted to correct any such improprieties. But his teaching in 1 Corinthians 11:2–16 goes far beyond the cultural conditions affecting the Corinthian church. Indeed, it was applicable also to other first-century churches (1 Cor 11:16b) and to God's people at any time. The principles Paul presents here that are to govern the church and individual Christians in their life and conduct are as follows:

1. Christians should live as individuals and in corporate worship in the light of the perfect unity and interrelatedness of the persons of the Godhead. The Father and the Son are perfectly united (John 10:30) and yet there is a difference administratively: God is the head of Christ (1 Cor 11:3). So Christians are one, but they too have to be administratively subordinate to one another.

2. Christians are to remember that God first created man, then woman (Gen 2:21–23) and placed the man as administrative head over the woman and the woman as his helper-companion (Gen 2:18). So in the Christian community, the man is to conduct himself as a man (1 Cor 11:4) and as the head of the woman (v.3), while the woman is to conduct herself as woman with dignity without doing anything that would bring dishonor to her (v.5).

3. Since Christians live in the Christian community of the home and that of the church, they are to remember that God has established the man and the woman as equal human beings: "As woman came from man, so also man is born of woman" (v.12). So in the Christian community believers should treat one another with mutual respect and admiration as they realize each other's God-given special functions and positions.

4. Christian men and women should remember that, though God has made them equal human beings, yet he has made them distinct sexes. That distinction is not to be blurred in their realization that they are mutually dependent (v.11)—the man on the woman and the woman on the man. It is also to be observed in their physical appearance (vv.13–15), so that in worship the woman can be recognized as woman and the man as man.

5. God is a God of order. This means order in worship and peaceful decorum in the church (v.16). Therefore Christian men and women should conduct themselves in a respectful, orderly way not only in worship but also in daily life.

Notes

4 The phrase κατὰ κεφαλῆς ἔχων (*kata kephalēs echōn*) is to be interpreted as meaning "having something on the head" (literally, "having [something] down from [or over] one's head"), such as a veil (BAG, κατά, I, 1a).

5,6 Ξυράω (*xyraō*) in the middle voice means "to have oneself shaved" and is used here of the head, whereas κειρῶ (*keirō*) in the middle voice means "to have one's hair cut."

10 The use of ἐξουσία (*exousia*) in this context has been taken as pointing to "a means of exercising power or authority." Some have interpreted this to mean that by the veil the woman could avoid amorous glances of angels. But since angels do not marry (Matt 22:30), this view is unacceptable. On the contrary, by covering her head, a woman reverently shows her position as the angels look on.

15 Ἀντί (anti) here is to be taken to mean "as" or "for" in the sense that the Christian woman's hair is to be considered a *proper* substitute for a head covering for worship. This is perhaps preferable to the tr. "instead of," which might lead to the conclusion that the apostle is suggesting that the hair is a replacement for any kind of head covering, even that worn by the pagan women.

2. *The Lord's Supper*

11:17–34

[17]In the following directives I have no praise for you, for your meetings do more
harm than good. [18]In the first place, I hear that when you come together as a
church, there are divisions among you, and to some extent I believe it. [19]No doubt
there have to be differences among you to show which of you have God's approv-
al. [20]When you come together, it is not the Lord's Supper you eat, [21]for as you
eat, each of you goes ahead without waiting for anybody else. One remains
hungry, another gets drunk. [22]Don't you have homes to eat and drink in? Or do
you despise the church of God and humiliate those who have nothing? What shall
I say to you? Shall I praise you for this? Certainly not!

[23]For I received from the Lord what I also passed on to you: The Lord Jesus,
on the night he was betrayed, took bread, [24]and when he had given thanks, he
broke it and said, "This is my body, which is for you; do this in remembrance of
me." [25]In the same way, after supper he took the cup, saying, "This cup is the new
covenant in my blood; do this, whenever you drink it, in remembrance of me." [26]For
whenever you eat this bread and drink this cup, you proclaim the Lord's death until
he comes.

[27]Therefore, whoever eats the bread or drinks the cup of the Lord in an unworthy
manner will be guilty of sinning against the body and blood of the Lord. [28]A man
ought to examine himself before he eats of the bread and drinks of the cup. [29]For
anyone who eats and drinks without recognizing the body of the Lord eats and
drinks judgment on himself. [30]That is why many among you are weak and sick,
and a number of you have fallen asleep. [31]But if we judged ourselves, we would
not come under judgment. [32]When we are judged by the Lord, we are being
disciplined so that we will not be condemned with the world.

[33]So then, my brothers, when you come together to eat, wait for each other. [34]If
anyone is hungry, he should eat at home, so that when you meet together it may
not result in judgment.

And when I come I will give further directions.

In dealing with the Lord's Supper, Paul discusses three matters: first, the problem of believers making a mockery of the Supper because of abuses practiced at the *agape*—the love feast or dinner accompanying the Supper (vv.17–22); second, the necessity of taking the Lord's Supper seriously through rehearsing its institution as given by the Lord (vv.23–26); and third, the warning about partaking of the Supper unworthily (vv.27–34).

17–19 Regarding the meal that evidently preceded the communion service, the apostle condemns the conduct of the believers as harmful (v.17) and degrading to the communion (see v.20). Their actions at the common *agape* meal were betraying the divisions, including class distinctions between the rich and the poor. Though he might discount part of what he heard, Paul felt he had to believe some of it (v.18). Knowing human nature, he assumes some such divisions are inevitable even among Christians, so that those who act worthy of God's approval might be evident (v.19). The word *haireseis* must mean "factions" here, not "heresies" or "heretical sects" as the word can also mean.

20 "It is not the Lord's Supper you eat" may be interpreted in two ways—either by supplying the word "it" as in NIV, or by taking the verb *estin* ("to be") followed by the infinitive to mean "can." Thus the rendering may be, "You cannot eat [or celebrate] the Lord's Supper" (Hodge). Either translation fits the context. What Paul means is that in acting the way he is about to describe, they were not approaching the Lord's Supper in the right manner but were nullifying its spiritual meaning.

21,22 The Christian common meal or *agape* feast apparently followed the pattern of public sacred feasting among the Jews and Greeks. Following Greek custom, the food was brought together for all to share (cf. the modern church's "potluck" or "bring-and-share" supper), with the rich bringing more and the poor less. As Paul described it, however, cliques were established and the food was divided inequitably. The rich took their "lion's" share and became gluttons and the poor remained empty. So they were despising or bringing contempt on the church of God and humiliating the poor.

23,24 The chief reason why Paul cannot commend their actions is that they do not agree with the spirit of the Lord's Supper as he had received it. Using technical words relating to "receiving" and "passing on" the tradition, he says he "received" (*parelabon*) the ceremony of the Lord's Supper from (*apo*) the Lord. Some (e.g., Hodge) have felt that he received it from Christ directly. But the preposition *apo* ("from") does not prove that Paul means he received the message directly from the Lord; in that case the preposition *para* ("from," "from beside") would have been appropriate (G.G. Findlay, EGT, in loc.). Yet some have thought that when Jesus appeared to Paul (Acts 9:4–6 et al.), he could have given him this message also. The preferred interpretation, however, is probably that Paul received (*parelabon*) the words of the institution of the Supper through its being passed on through others just as he then passed them on (*paredōka*) to the Corinthians—i.e., through a process of repetition. (Observe the similarity of Paul's words about the Supper with Matt 26:26–29; Mark 14:22–25; Luke 22:14–20.)

Since the Supper was celebrated in connection with the Passover (according to Matt 26:17–29; Luke 22:7–20), we assume that the bread that was available was unleavened. Jesus gave thanks (*eucharistēsas*—cf. Eucharist). This was the Jewish practice at a meal. The breaking of the bread (also in the Synoptics) was symbolic of Christ's bruised and broken body (Isa 53:5). The better MSS, reflected in NIV and other newer versions, read, "This is my body which is for you" without the addition "broken" (KJV), which, however, is implied from the context. The word "this" most naturally means in the context "this bread" that Christ held in his hand as a symbol to represent his body, not Christ's body itself, as some hold (cf. somewhat similar figures in John 10:7; 1 Cor 10:4). The command (cf. Luke 22:19) "Do this in remembrance of me," which, along with Luke 22:20, some versions omit (RSV, NEB) or print in brackets (TEV, BV), though others (NIV, JB) retain them (cf. note on 1 Cor 11:24), is implied in the words "Take, eat."

25,26 That the Lord's Supper was connected with the Passover meal is clear in the phrase "after the supper," meaning, as the synoptic Gospels show, "after the Passover Supper." This cup was the third of the Passover cups, as C.E.B. Cranfield, shows in "St. Mark" in *The Cambridge Greek Testament Commentary,* C.F.D. Moule, ed. (Cambridge: Cambridge University Press, 1966), p. 426. The word "cup," used metonymously for its contents, symbolizes the covenant in Jesus' blood (Luke 22:20). The covenant (*diathekē*) idea is that of God's sealing his agreement of salvation with his people through Christ's blood. It is a new covenant in being the fulfillment of the covenant promises of God in the OT exemplified in the sacrificial system (cf. Eph 2:12). In the ceremony Jesus does not say how often the communion was to be held but indicates that it is to be periodic—"whenever you eat . . . and drink"—and it is to be continued to the Second Advent—"until he comes" (v.26). The statement "you proclaim" involves the personal application of the meaning of the Lord's death in the believer's testimony.

27 Participating "in an unworthy manner" entails coming to the table in an irreverent and sinful way and so sinning against the body and blood of Christ. This is what some of the Corinthians had been doing (vv.20–22). (Of course, any other sinful approach to the table would be unworthy also.) The apostle does not teach that in eating and drinking the elements Christians are physically eating of Christ. The supper is a memorial feast (v.24) and a means of grace.

28–30 Now Paul shows how to guard against unworthy partaking of the Lord's Supper. "To examine [oneself]" is to put oneself to the test as to the attitude of his heart, his outward conduct, and his understanding of the true nature and purpose of the Supper. This is making the Supper a means of spiritual grace. By self-examination the believer guards against eating and drinking to his own judgment through not recognizing the importance of this Supper that commemorates the death of Christ. That Paul is not speaking about God's eternal judgment is seen by the lack of the article with *krima.* It is "judgment," not "the judgment." Examples of such judgment are in sickness and death.

31,32 The purpose of self-examination is to come to the table prepared in heart. Paul's teaching justifies the wholesome practice of some churches in having a communion preparatory service that affords opportunity for such self-examination. Here he quickly adds that even when a Christian is judged by the Lord, this judgment is not punitive to destruction, but a form of fatherly discipline (Heb 12:5) to bring God's child to repentance, so that he will not be finally and totally judged with the unsaved world (Rev 20:12–15).

33,34 Paul now deals positively with the *agape* meal. In eating it, the Corinthians should show respect for their brothers' physical as well as spiritual needs by waiting for each other and eating together. If they come only to satisfy their physical craving and not for communion with the Lord and his people, then they should eat their meal at home, for otherwise God will judge them in some way.

Verse 34b suggests that there were other irregularities regarding worship and the Lord's Supper but they were not sufficiently urgent for the apostle to deal with them here.

Notes

---

20 Κυριακός (*kyriakos*) strictly meaning "belonging to the Lord," is here used of the Lord's Supper. Compare Rev 1:10, ἐν τῇ κυριακῇ ἡμέρᾳ (*en tē kyriakē hēmera,* "on the Lord's day"); i.e., the day belonging to Jesus and his resurrection—the first day of the week.

23 The impf. verb form παρεδίδετο (*paredideto*) stresses that the betraying process was in motion when Jesus instituted the Supper. There is no evidence that the Supper was derived from Hellenistic pagan cult meals as some have argued (see Craig, in loc.).

24 Some MSS, mostly koine-Byzantine, add the word "broken." But the best reading (P^{46} ℵ A B C, et al.) does not have it. This statement of Jesus in v.24 is practically equivalent to Jesus' words given in Luke 22:19, as tr. in NIV. Some scholars have suggested that most of the statement in Luke was originally not in this Lucan passage because a few MSS witnesses (the Western-type texts) omit it. But the vast majority of the ancient MS evidence favors its inclusion in Luke 22:19

and so points to its authenticity there. And that Paul cites these words suggests that it was an original saying of Jesus currently available for Luke also to put into his Gospel.

30 The verb κοιμάω (*koimaō*, only passive in NT) means "fall asleep," sometimes of physical sleep (Luke 22:45), but often is a euphemistic figure for dying (cf. John 11:11–14; Acts 7:60).

31 Διακρίνω (*diakrinō*, "judge [correctly]") adds a legal aspect to the thought that δοκιμάζω (*dokimazō*, "examine [v.28]," "test" [as of gold, 1 Peter 1:7]) does not include.

32 The tenses of the verbs παιδευόμεθα (*paideuometha*, present) and κατακριθῶμεν (*katakrithōmen*, aorist) contrast the present continuing experience of discipline with the final reality of the future judgment.

---

3. *The use of spiritual gifts*

12:1–14:40

This long section on spiritual gifts may be divided into several sections. The first emphasizes the source of the gifts, the Holy Spirit (12:1–11); the second the diversity of the gifts in their unity (12:12–31a); the third, the necessary ingredient of love in the exercise of all gifts (12:31b–13:13); the fourth, a discussion of the priority of prophecy over tongues with rules for the exercise of each (14:1–25); and finally, Paul teaches that all church worship must be done decently and in order (14:26–40).

a. *The Holy Spirit, the source of spiritual gifts*

12:1–11

1 Now about spiritual gifts, brothers, I do not want you to be ignorant. 2 You know that when you were pagans, somehow or other you were influenced and led astray to dumb idols. 3 Therefore I tell you that no one who is speaking by the Spirit of God says, "Jesus be cursed," and no one can say, "Jesus is Lord," except by the Holy Spirit.

4 There are different kinds of spiritual gifts, but the same Spirit. 5 There are different kinds of service, but the same Lord. 6 There are different kinds of working, but the same God works all of them in all men.

7 Now to each man the manifestation of the Spirit is given for the common good. 8 To one there is given through the Spirit the ability to speak with wisdom, to another the ability to speak with knowledge by means of the same Spirit, 9 to another faith by the same Spirit, to another gifts of healing by that one Spirit, 10 to another miraculous powers, to another prophecy, to another the ability to distinguish between spirits, to another the ability to speak in different kinds of tongues, and to still another the interpretation of tongues. 11 All these are the work of one and the same Spirit, and he gives them to each man, just as he determines.

1 This section presents a new subject and an answer to another question asked by the Corinthian delegation (cf. *peri de*, "now about," 1 Cor 7:1, 25; 8:1; 16:1).

2–6 In saying that they had been "led astray to dumb idols," Paul implies that the Corinthians had experienced the effects of evil spirits in their former pagan worship. In contrast, he now stresses the twofold test of the presence of the Holy Spirit in a believer's life. Negatively, no person by the Spirit can curse Jesus; and positively, only by the Spirit can a person openly testify that Jesus is Lord (v.3). The term *kyrios* ("Lord") is used by LXX to translate Jehovah in the OT (cf. Matt 16:16; John 4:2, 3, 15). In this context Paul recognizes the deity of Jesus and of the Holy Spirit in the use of the phrases "Jesus is Lord" and "Spirit of God." *Anathema* (translated "be cursed") was, strictly speaking, something that was devoted to God and that could be thought of as given over to him with a view to its destruction. So it could be thought of as being "accursed" (cf. Josh 6:17, 18)—the meaning consistently used in the NT. (See Hodge and Grosheide, in loc.).

By using the words *diakoniai* ("servings") and *energemata* ("workings"), Paul indicates that such gifts were useful in serving the Christian community (vv.5, 6). In vv.4–6 he teaches that the Trinity is involved in administration of these gifts: the Spirit; the Lord; God (cf. 2 Cor 13:13 and Eph 4:3–6).

For a full discussion of the Holy Spirit in the NT see Frederick Dale Bruner, *A Theology of the Holy Spirit* (Grand Rapids: Eerdmans, 1970).

7–11 Paul goes on to declare that many spiritual gifts are given by the spirit for the total good or profit (*sympheron*) of his church. Different gifts are given different people—not all have the same gift (cf. 12:29, 30). The gifts given to each person are clearly intended to be used for the common good.

The gifts listed begin with the most important one—the ability to express the message of God's wisdom in the gospel of Christ. The second is the ability to communicate with knowledge by the Spirit. "Knowledge" (*gnōsis*) in the biblical sense is to be taken as the knowledge of God's way of salvation through the cross, not the secret heretical gnostic teaching about working one's way to heaven. Compare the esoteric use of "know" in the Gnostic *Gospel According to Thomas*, tr. A. Guillaumont et al. (Leiden: E.J. Brill, 1959).

The gift of "faith" does not refer to the initial trust in Christ for salvation but to deeper expressions of faith, such as undergoing hardships, martyrdom, etc., and so *pistis* ("faith") can in this case be rendered "faithfulness." Others view faith here as exemplified in gifts of healing, tongues, etc. But this does not seem to be in view, since Paul speaks of these gifts in vv.9, 10.

The next two gifts—the outwardly demonstrable ones of healings and miracles—belong together and were particularly applicable to the ministry of Paul and the other apostles (Acts 19:11, 12; 28:7–9; 2 Cor 12:12). *Dynameis* means literally "acts of power" (cf. Acts 1:8), which here and in 12:28, 29 specifically means miracles. The mention of the gift of prophecy anticipates 1 Corinthians 14 and seems to include an ability to give insights into, and to convey the deeper meanings of, God's redemptive program in his Word. It is to be distinguished from the inspiration of the Holy Spirit (2 Tim 3:16) given the apostles and their associates to prophesy in setting forth God's truth. Paul separates the apostles' office from that of prophets in 12:28, where the prophetic office is listed between that of the apostles and the teachers and did not include in it, in this period of church development, the miracle-working function listed separately in 12:29. The latter function was often included in the earlier practice of the prophetic office (cf. John the Baptist, Christ, and his apostles). See a specific treatment of this point in W. Harold Mare, "Prophet and Teacher in the New Testament Period," JETS, vol.9, no.3 (Summer 1966), pp. 146–148.

By the gift of distinguishing between spirits (v.10b), Paul must be indicating a distinct ability beyond that which the apostle John calls on Christians in general to exercise (1 John 4:1). The ability to speak in different kinds of tongues has been taken to mean speaking in ecstatic, humanly unintelligible utterances, possibly similar to the ecstatic speech exhibited in pagan Greek Dionysiac expressions. In the light of Acts 2:4ff., where it is said that the Holy Spirit gave them ability to speak with different kinds of language, i.e., known foreign languages (Acts 2:7-11), we are safe to say that the ability mentioned here in 1 Cor 12:10 is the ability to speak unlearned languages. LSJ does not list under *glōssa* any meaning under the category of ecstatic speech. Rather, the emphasis of the word is "language," "dialect," "foreign" language.

There have been differences adduced, differences that can be shown not to be basic, between the tongues-speaking at Pentecost in Acts 2 and that in 1 Corinthians 12–14. The following supposed differences were proposed by J. Oswald Sanders (quoted by David M. Howard in *By the Power of the Holy Spirit* [Downers Grove, Illinois: Inter-Varsity Press, 1973], pp 115, 116):

1. At Pentecost the disciples spoke to men (Acts 2:6) but at Corinth the speaking was to God (1 Cor. 14:2, 9). Reply: In Corinth, though the speaking in tongues was to God, it was also a speaking to men when there was speaking in the church service with someone to interpret (1 Cor 14:26, 27).

2. At Pentecost tongues were a sign or credential to believers but at Corinth to unbelievers (1 Cor 14:22). Reply: At Pentecost at the time when the people heard the tongues they were unbelievers (Acts 2:12, 13); it was only when they heard the message in Peter's sermon that many of them believed (Acts 2:41).

3. At Pentecost the unbelievers were filled with awe and marvelled (Acts 2:7, 8), but at Corinth the unbelievers thought the Christians were mad (1 Cor 14:23). Reply: In Acts 2 the unbelievers also were bewildered (v.6); they were amazed and *perplexed* (v.12), and some even thought the believers were intoxicated and they made fun of them (v.13).

4. At Pentecost there was harmony (Acts 2:1), at Corinth confusion (1 Cor 14:23). Reply: This contrast must not be pressed to imply a difference in the nature of the tongues spoken; it only reveals the generally disorderly conduct of the Corinthian congregation seen in their party spirit (1:10–17) and in their reprehensible conduct at the Lord's Supper (11:17–34).

The foregoing points of Sanders do not prove a genuine difference in the nature of tongues between Acts 2 and 1 Corinthians 12–14. The only concrete evidence we have as to the nature of the tongues-speaking in the early church is to be found in the only clear scriptural example we have—that given in Acts 2 where the speaking is a speaking in foreign languages that were to be understood, and were understood. Since in this initial instance in Acts 2 the speaking in foreign tongues was done by the apostles and their close companions, it is logical to conclude that as the apostles were involved in the subsequent scriptural examples of tongues-speaking (Acts 10:44–46; 19:1–7; 1 Cor. 12–14), in these situations also speaking in tongues is to be understood as speaking in a foreign language.

In 1 Cor 12:10d Paul hastens to add that such speaking in tongues should be accompanied by interpretation or translation by someone with that ability. This subject is expanded in 1 Corinthians 14. (Also see my article "Guiding Principles for Historical Grammatical Exegesis," in *Grace Journal,* vol.14, no. 3 [Fall, 1973], p. 14.) That Paul is simply giving a sampling of gifts is evident from his expansion of the list in 12:27–30 and Romans 12:3–8.

Paul concludes that regardless of what spiritual gift each person has, the Holy Spirit has sovereignly distributed them to produce his own spiritual results (v.11). Therefore, no one should despise another person's gift, a gift given by the Spirit for the good of all (v.7). This theme the apostle develops in vv.12–26. The Spirit mentioned here is set forth as one who is sovereignly God (he wills to give the gifts) and personally active (he "works" all these gifts in the lives of his people).

Notes

8–10 Some have tried to classify the gifts by using ἕτερος (*heteros*) to indicate main divisions in the enumeration and ἄλλος (*allos*) to show subordinate divisions (Hodge; cf. also Meyer). However, such a classification does not always put similar gifts together. Compare v.10, where miracles and tongues go together, but one has *allos* and the other *heteros*. Here the words are to be taken as synonyms. Compare also the variety of prepositions used to indicate the same vital working of the Spirit: διά (*dia*, "through") and κατά (*kata*, "according to") in v.8, and ἐν (*en*, "by") in v.9.

10 Ἐνέργημα (*energema*; cf. the English word "energy") is an action word: "activities" that bring forth miracles.

---

b. *Unity in the diversity of gifts in the body of Christ*

12:12–26

12The body is a unit, though it is made up of many parts; and though all its parts
are many, they form one body. So it is with Christ. 13For we were all baptized by
one Spirit into one body—whether Jews or Greeks, slave or free—and we were
all given the one Spirit to drink.

14Now the body is not made up of one part but of many. 15If the foot should say,
"Because I am not a hand, I do not belong to the body," it would not for that reason
cease to be part of the body. 16And if the ear should say, "Because I am not an
eye, I do not belong to the body," it would not for that reason cease to be part
of the body. 17If the whole body were an eye, where would the sense of hearing
be? If the whole body were an ear, where would the sense of smell be? 18But in
fact, God has arranged the parts in the body, every one of them, just as he wanted
them to be. 19If they were all one part, where would the body be? 20As it is, there
are many parts, but one body.

21The eye cannot say to the hand, "I don't need you!" And the head cannot say
to the feet, "I don't need you!" 22On the contrary, those parts of the body that seem
to be weaker are indispensable, 23and the parts that we think are less honorable
we treat with special honor. And the parts that are unpresentable are treated with
special modesty, 24while our presentable parts need no special treatment. But
God has combined the members of the body and has given greater honor to the
parts that lacked it, 25so that there should be no division in the body, but that its
parts should have equal concern for each other. 26If one part suffers, every part
suffers with it; if one part is honored, every part rejoices with it.

12,13 Paul now illustrates the diversity and unity of the spiritual gifts by the example of the human body. It is made up of many parts, all of them of importance, and yet the whole body functions as a unit. By the words "So it is with Christ," he means so it is with Christ's body, the church. That the church, the invisible church, is an organic whole is seen in that every believer, regardless of racial and religious connection (Jew or Greek) or social standing (slave or freeman), has been united by the one Spirit into one spiritual body in baptism. The figure is now reversed—all the believers have drunk one Spirit; that is, each one has received the same Holy Spirit (cf. 1 Cor 6:19; Eph 5:18–20). Some have taken these thoughts as references to the Christian sacraments—water baptism and Holy Communion. But since there is no imagery of the cup, as in 1 Corinthians 11:25, it is doubtful that this is Paul's primary intent. Rather, he is emphasizing spiritual baptism, and the communion of spiritual food and drink (cf. Rom 6:4; 1 Cor 10:3, 4). It is not the local church alone Paul is speaking of here, but the church universal. This drinking of the Spirit is seen in Jesus' invitation in John 7:37–39.

14–20 Paul now emphasizes the necessity of having diversity in a body for it to operate as one. Each part (such as the eye or the ear) must be willing to perform its own function and not seek to function in a role for which it was not made. The whole body cannot be a single part, or it would not be a functioning body. So it is with the church. Members with one gift should not repudiate that gift and complain that they do not have some other gift. The apostles were to function as apostles, the elders as elders (1 Pet 5:5), the deacons as deacons (Acts 6:1–6), etc.

The logic of v.17 is compelling: no body can function as all eye, all hearing, or all smelling. So for the church to function properly, it must have different gifts and offices.

In vv.18–20 Paul brings the believers back to the sovereign purposes of God. It is God who has organized the body in the way he wants it. The implication is that it is the same with the church; according to God's will, it is composed of many parts, so that it may function as one body—the body of Christ.

21–26 Here the emphasis is on the mutual dependence and concern of the various members of the body. As the organs of the human body—such as the eye, hand, head, and feet—need each other, so the members of the church with their various functions need each other. Moreover, the least attractive and inconspicuous parts of the body are important and should be treated with respect (vv.22, 23). So also the inconspicuous members of the church are essential—those who pray, those who work with their hands and bring their meager tithes into the church, etc. As the humbler parts of the body are given special attention by covering them with appropriate clothing and, as in the case of the digestive organs, providing them with food, so the inconspicuous members of the church—the poor, the despised, the less prominent—are to be cherished and nurtured.

The *alla* ("but") in the middle of v.24 brings the argument back to God's sovereign purposes. He has brought the members of the body together in perfect harmony. By saying that God "has given greater honor to the parts that lacked it," Paul means that through implanting modesty and self-respect in our hearts, God has caused us to protect our unpresentable parts (as the sex organs) from exploitation by properly covering them. All this concern for the body is for the purpose of enabling it to operate in unity, so all its parts will mutually respond to each other's needs—e.g., the brain sending nerve signals to the hand. In using the word *schisma* ("schism," "division") in v.25 Paul reminds the Corinthians of the discussion in 1:10–17. As it is with the body, so with the church (v.26). What happens to one part affects the well-being of the whole.

Notes

---

13 The aorist forms ἐβαπτίσθημεν (*ebaptisthēmen*) and ἐποτίσθημεν (*epotisthēmen*) argue against the view that this verse refers to the ongoing practice of water baptism and Communion, as though the physical acts would somehow make the Christians one body. If the physical rites were in view, present tense verbs would be expected, giving the meaning "Members of your church are being baptized and you are sharing in the elements of Communion." Rather, the aorist tense of both verbs helps place the emphasis on the spiritual nature of baptism and regeneration: the total group, the church, was viewed collectively by Paul and seen by him in

a spiritual way as one body in Christ partaking of regeneration through the Holy Spirit (cf. Titus 3:5).

23 Εὐσχημοσύνη (*euschēmosynē*) meaning "presentability" as with clothing, in this context becomes related to "modesty." (So NIV; cf. BAG.)

24 Συγκεράννυμι (*synkerannymi*, "mix together" or "unite") means that God has united or blended the members effectively into one body.

---

c. *Offices and gifts in the one body of Christ, his church*

12:27–31

> [27]Now you are the body of Christ, and each one of you is a part of it. [28]And in the church God has appointed first of all apostles, second prophets, third teachers, then workers of miracles, also those having gifts of healing, those able to help others, those with gifts of administration, and finally those speaking in different kinds of tongues. [29]Are all apostles? Are all prophets? Are all teachers? Do all work miracles? [30]Do all have gifts of healing? Do all speak in tongues? Do all interpret? [31]But eagerly desire the greater gifts.
>
> And now I will show you the most excellent way.

As he speaks about that spiritual unity of the body of Christ, Paul declares that each Christian has his function as a part of that body. He illustrates this by a selective list of church offices and spiritual gifts (cf. Rom 12:3–8; Eph 4:11).

27 Some have thought that *sōma* without the article *to* ("the") refers to the local congregation and is to be translated "a body [of Christ]" (Grosheide). But the genitive form "of Christ" (without the article) used with the word "body" (also without the article) makes the whole phrase specific: "the body of Christ." Therefore, the entire Christian church is in mind. Observe also the plural "apostles," indicating a wider reference than to Corinth alone.

28 Paul is saying that it is the sovereign God who dispenses (*etheto;* cf. Acts 20:28; 1 Tim 1:12; 2:7; 2 Tim 1:11) offices and gifts to his church. The order of the gifts is instructive. The first three—apostles, prophets, and teachers—are in the same order as in Ephesians 4:11 (cf. Rom 12:6, 7) and, as placed first, are to be considered of greatest importance. The next gifts are set off from the first three by *epeita* ("then") and range in order from miracles to the ability to speak in different kinds of tongues, which, being mentioned last, seem to be of least importance. The office of apostle was all-encompassing, including the gifts of prophecy, teaching, miracles, and the rest. But the prophetic gift (cf. Acts 11:24; 13:1; 15:32; 21:10) did not include apostolicity, though it did include teaching. The teacher class did not compare, per se, with that of apostles or prophets. Paul speaks of the first three—apostles, prophets, and teachers—as classes of persons ruling in the church. The rest of the list includes gifts given various members of the church—gifts that, while of lesser significance, are yet of importance.

Those having the gift of *antilēmpsis* ("those able to help others," NIV) are persons gifted in helping the church officers deal with the poor and sick. Those with *kybernēsis* ("administration") have ability to govern and manage affairs in the church.

29,30 By these rhetorical questions, all of which imply "no" for an answer, Paul stresses the principle of divine selectivity. He is saying that not all believers function in each of the ways listed. God selects individuals and gives them their specific gifts (v.28). Paul ends v.30 with the gift of interpretation of tongues, because he is to comment on this in chapter 14. As in v.28, so in v.30, "tongues" comes last in his list.

31 Having mentioned tongues and their interpretation, Paul urges Christians to seek the better gifts—not that of speaking in tongues, which the Corinthians apparently wanted to have more fully. The possession of specific gifts, says Paul, is not so important as the way in which the gifts are exercised. Verse 31b serves to introduce chapter 13.

Notes

---

28 The aorist form ἔθετο (*etheto*, "he placed" or "appointed") emphasizes the sovereign act of God in determining who will exercise which gifts in his church.

---

d. *The supreme position of love in the ministry of the church*

12:31b–13:13

12:31b And now I will show you the most excellent way. 13:1 If I speak in the tongues
of men and of angels, but have not love, I am only a resounding gong or a clanging
cymbal. 2 If I have the gift of prophecy, and can fathom all mysteries and all
knowledge, and if I have a faith that can move mountains, but have not love, I am
nothing. 3 If I give all I possess to the poor and surrender my body to the flames,
but have not love, I gain nothing.
4 Love is patient, love is kind. It does not envy, it does not boast, it is not proud.
5 It is not rude, it is not self-seeking, it is not easily angered, it keeps no record of
wrongs. 6 Love does not delight in evil but rejoices in the truth. 7 It always protects,
always trusts, always hopes, always perseveres.
8 Love never fails. But where there are prophecies, they will cease; where there
are tongues, they will be stilled; where there is knowledge, it will pass away. 9 For
we know in part and we prophesy in part, 10 but when perfection comes, the
imperfect disappears. 11 When I was a child, I talked like a child, I thought like a
child, I reasoned like a child. When I became a man, I put childish ways behind me.
12 Now we see but a poor reflection; then we shall see face to face. Now I know
in part; then I shall know fully, even as I am fully known.
13 And now these three remain: faith, hope and love. But the greatest of these
is love.

This supremely beautiful chapter speaks first of the superiority and necessity of love—gifts are nothing without love (12:31b–13:1–3). It then describes the essential character of Christian love (4–7) and tells of the enduring nature of love (8–12). Finally, it proclaims love to be greater even than faith and hope (v.13).

12:31b–13:1–3 Love is the most excellent way for a Christian to use his spiritual gifts. (12:31b is repeated here, since it is an important transition.) The word *agapē* ("love") is used in the NT of the deep and abiding affection of God and Christ for each other (John 15:10; 17:26) and for us (1 John 4:9). It is also used of Christians in their relationship with one another (e.g., John 13:34, 35). Often more intense and deeper in meaning than *philos* ("having affection for," Matt 10:37; Luke 7:5, et al.), it is quite distinct from *eros*, sensual or sexual love. Christians are to love, because they belong to God, and "God is love" (1 John 4:8).

In referring to tongues and prophecy (vv.1–3), Paul is apparently trying to counteract the excessive emphasis the Corinthians were evidently placing on these gifts to the detriment of love for Christ and to their fellowmen. Tongues of men and angels are obviously the languages men and angels use. (On occasion, angels spoke to men in human language; e.g., Luke 1:13–20, 26–38). The mention of tongues in v.1 shows that Paul is referring in these chapters to human foreign languages as well as intelligent angelic communication. It was in the temple worship that the "resounding gong" and "clanging cymbal" were struck (2 Sam 6:5; 1 Chron 13:8; Ps 150:5). Also prophecy, understanding mysteries and knowledge, and possessing dynamic faith are all nothing apart from love. Both "mysteries" (*mysteria*) and "knowledge" (*gnōsis*) are governed by the same verb *eido* ("know," "fathom") and must mean the deep, secret things to be discovered about God's redemptive works. "Faith" (*pistis*) is not saving faith (as in Rom 5:1), but special acts of faith as in performing miracles, as the reference to the moving of mountains shows (cf. Matt 21:21). Moreover, Paul says that giving all one's material wealth to the poor can be done without love and that one can even be martyred or submit voluntarily to torture without a sense of love for others. To take "surrender my body to the flames" as referring to an extreme form of martyrdom is preferable to taking it as some form of branding connected with slavery (cf. Hodge, in loc.).

4–7 Christian love is now described positively and negatively. Its positive characteristics are patience and kindness (v.4a), delight in the truth, and a protective, trusting, hopeful, and persevering attitude (vv.6b, 7). That love is patient (v.4) means that it is slow to become resentful (Hodge, in loc.). Verses 4b–6a state love's characteristics negatively. To be "rude" or "behave disgracefully" (v.5) may refer obliquely to the disorderly conduct at worship referred to in 11:2–16 and in chapter 14). KJV's "thinks no evil" (v.5b) gives an incorrect idea. The verb *logizomai* means "to reckon or take account of." So NIV says, "It keeps no record of wrongs." Indeed, for love to keep a record of wrongs would violate its nature. In v.6 the verbs *chairō* and *syngchairō* are basically the same; yet there is a difference. Love does not "delight" or "rejoice" (*chairō*) in evil in which it has no part; but it does "rejoice in" (*syngchairō*) the truth with which it does have a part.

Furthermore, love covers the faults of others rather than delighting in them (v.7). It is trusting, optimistic, and willing to endure persecution (cf. Rom 5:3, 4). In short, it "perseveres."

8–12 Love is permanent, in contrast with prophecies, tongues, and knowledge—all of which will cease to exist because they will cease to be needed. In v.8, Paul uses the verb (*katargeō,* "abolish"; hence "cease," "pass away") to describe the cessation of prophecies and of knowledge; of tongues, he says "they will be stilled" (NIV). Here the verb is *pauō,* which also means "cease." The reason these three will cease is that they are imperfect and partial (vv.9, 10) compared to perfect knowledge and prophetic understanding in heaven. He does not say when they will cease. Some think he meant that the need for miraculous gifts would cease to exist at the end of the apostolic period. This view is based in part on the implications of the meaning of the term *teleion* ("perfection") v.10, which is taken to refer here to the completion of the canon at the end of the first century A.D. With this view, the term "prophecies" in v.8 is taken narrowly as referring to direct, inspired revelatory communication from the Holy Spirit or possibly to some special aid given by the Spirit to understand and present truth already revealed, as given in the written Scriptures (cf. Hodge, in loc.). All this, then, was done away when the canon was completed about A.D.100. This cessation would apply also to tongues and to the special gift of knowledge (vv.8, 9)—the "gift correctly to understand and properly exhibit the truths revealed by the apostles and prophets" (Hodge, in loc.).

There is something to commend this view as an argument against the position that the gifts mentioned in vv. 8–10 continued, beyond the apostolic period, especially prophetic revelation. For if such revelation is held to continue, then might not the Koran, *The Book of Mormon,* and *Science and Health* be considered inspired revelations from God?

Nevertheless, it is difficult to prove the cessation of these gifts at the end of the first century A.D. by taking *teleion* to refer to a completion of the canon at that time, since that idea is completely extraneous to the context. While *teleion* can and does refer to something completed at some time in the future, the time of that future completion is not suggested in v.10 as being close.

On the other hand, in a number of contexts the related words *telos* ("end," "termination," "last part") and *teleō* ("bring to an end") are used in relation to the second coming of Christ. This is true in both non-Pauline writing (cf. James 5:11; Rev 20:5, 7; 21:6; 22:13) and 1 Corinthians 1:8; 15:24. Since in the contexts of the Second Coming these related words are used and since Paul himself used *telos* in talking about the Second Coming elsewhere in 1 Corinthians, it seems more normal to understand *teleion* in v.10 to mean that "perfection" is to come about at the Second Coming, or, if before, when the Christian dies and is taken to be with the Lord (2 Cor 5:1–10).

There are other problems regarding the completion-of-the-canon view of *teleion* here. The conditional temporal *hotan* with the subjunctive form of the verb, "[whenever the end] should come" (v.10), suggests that Paul felt an indefiniteness about when the end he has in mind would come. But he shows no such indefiniteness in regard to the written Scriptures or the special position of the apostles (9:1, 2), whose work would be assumed to be coming to an end shortly upon their death. Similarly, the *hotan* with the subjunctive clauses and *telos* used of the Second Coming in 15:24, are also indefinite and open-ended: "then . . . when [or, whenever] he hands over the kingdom. . . ." Here again, Paul does not know exactly when this will occur. In contrast, the *hote* with the indicative clauses in 13:11 are quite definite as to the time of their occurrences: "When I was a child . . . when I became a man."

One more problem with taking *teleion* to refer to the completion of the canon is found in the *tote,* ("then," "at that time") clauses in v.12. Did Paul really expect to live to the time of the completion of the canon and then expect to "know" or "know completely," when other apostles (e.g., John) might (and actually did) live longer than he and it would be they who at that time would "know completely"?

All things considered, it is better to argue for the cessation of the gifts of prophecy, tongues, and the special gift of knowledge on the basis of the larger context of Paul's writings and on the basis of the grammar of vv.9, 13: prophecies, tongues, and knowledge will pass away soon. Paul's viewpoint seems to be that it would be when the important office of apostle with its requirement of men having seen the Lord and having been a witness to his resurrection (Gal 1:14–24) is no longer exercised. But "now" (*nyni*) faith, hope, and love continue to remain (*menei,* present continuous sense).

Paul's illustration of a child's thoughts and speech, real but inadequately conceived and expressed in comparison with those of a mature person (v. 11) aptly conveys the difference between the Christian's present understanding and expression of spiritual things and the perfect understanding and expression he will have in heaven (v.12). The metaphor is that of the imperfect reflection seen in one of the polished metal mirrors (cf. James 1:23) of the ancient world in contrast with seeing the Lord face to face (cf. Gen 32:30; Num 12:8; 2 Cor 3:18). Paul's thought in 12b may be expanded as follows: Now through the Word of God, I know in part; then, in the presence of the Lord I will know fully, to the full extent that a redeemed finite human being can know and in a way similar in kind to the way the Lord in his infinite wisdom fully and infinitely knows me. The Corinthians, Paul implies, must not boast now of their gifts (cf. 13:4), for those gifts are nothing compared to what is in store for the Christians in heaven.

13 In a temporal sense, the words "and now" can mean that faith, hope, and love continue "now, at this moment," to be succeeded later by something else. This, however, is out of context with the preceding verses. Rather, "and now" introduces a conclusion; namely, "and now, there are faith, hope, and love—they, to be sure, remain now and forever." By faith and hope remaining in eternity Paul means that trust (*pistis*) in the Lord begun in this life will continue forever and that hope in the Lord begun now (Rom 8:24, 25) will expand and issue into an eternal expectation of his perfect plan for our eternal existence with him (cf. Rev 22:3–5). Paul has alluded to a special faith in v.2; now he expands it into an ongoing eternal faith and hope in an eternal God. Love is the greatest of these three graces because through faith love unites the Christian personally to God (1 John 4:10, 19) and through God's love (Rom 5:5) we are enabled to love one another (John 13:34, 35). Love is communicating grace and identifies us as children of God (John 13:34, 35; 1 John 4:8, et al.).

Notes

3 The textual reading **καυθήσομαι** or **καυθήσωμαι** (*kauthēsomai, kauthēsōmai,* "burn") is supported by somewhat inferior MS evidence, but agrees with the OT events of Dan 3:15ff. The better-supported **καυχήσωμαι** (*kauchēsōmai,* "that I may glory" or "boast") does fit Paul's usage of the word elsewhere (9:15; 2 Cor 12:1; see Metzger, *A Textual Commentary,* pp. 563, 564) but does not fit well with Paul's other illustrations of good deeds. The concept of "boasting" in this list of good works is awkward. Therefore, the first reading is better. Later scribes must have changed the verb "burn" to "boast" to avoid any suggestion of ridiculing martyrdom by fire. (Cf. C. T. Craig, IB, 10:171.)

4–7 All the verbs are in the present tense and should be taken as gnomic presents, expressing characteristics of love that are true in all times.

12 It is better to take **δι᾿ ἐσόπτρου** (*di' esoptrou*) as instrumental, giving the reading "by means of a mirror" (cf. James 1:23) rather than "through a window," referring to opaque mica used for windows in ancient times (cf. Hodge, in loc.). The repeated verb **ἐπιγνώσκω** (*epignōskō*), tr. "know fully" in NIV, refers in its first occurrence in 12b to the limited horizon of a perfect but finite human being; in its second occurrence it shifts to the boundless horizon of the infinite Lord, the difference being accentuated by the aorist passive form **ἐπεγνώσθην** (*epegnōsthēn,* "I am known"); i.e., "I am known [by a greater one—the Lord]."

e. *The priority of prophecy over tongues and rules for the exercise of both*

14:1–25

Follow the way of love and eagerly desire spiritual gifts, especially the gift of prophecy. [2]For anyone who speaks in a tongue does not speak to men but to God. Indeed, no one understands him; he utters mysteries with his spirit. [3]But everyone who prophesies speaks to men for their strengthening, encouragement and comfort. [4]He who speaks in a tongue edifies himself, but he who prophesies edifies the church. [5]I would like every one of you to speak in tongues, but I would rather have you prophesy. He who prophesies is greater than one who speaks in tongues, unless he interprets, so that the church may be edified.

[6]Now, brothers, if I come to you and speak in tongues, what good will I be to you, unless I bring you some revelation or knowledge or prophecy or teaching? Even in the case of lifeless things that make sounds, such as the flute or harp, how will anyone know what tune is being played unless there is a distinction in the notes? [8]Again, if the trumpet does not sound a clear call, who will get ready for battle? [9]So it is with you. Unless you speak intelligible words with your tongue, how will anyone know what you are saying? You will just be speaking into the air. [10]Undoubtedly there are all sorts of languages in the world, yet none of them is without meaning. [11]If then I do not grasp the meaning of what someone is saying, I am a foreigner to the speaker, and he is a foreigner to me. [12]So it is with you. Since you are eager to have spiritual gifts, try to excel in gifts that build up the church.

[13]For this reason the man who speaks in a tongue should pray that he may interpret what he says. [14]For if I pray in a tongue, my spirit prays, but my mind is unfruitful. [15]So what shall I do? I will pray with my spirit, but I will also pray with my mind; I will sing with my spirit, but I will also sing with my mind. [16]If you are praising God with your spirit, how can one who finds himself among those who do not understand say "Amen" to your thanksgiving, since he does not know what you are saying? [17]You may be giving thanks well enough, but the other man is not edified.

[18]I thank God that I speak in tongues more than all of you. [19]But in the church I would rather speak five intelligible words to instruct others than ten thousand words in a tongue.

[20]Brothers, stop thinking like children. In regard to evil be infants, but in your thinking be adults. [21]In the Law it is written:

"Through men of strange tongues
  and through the lips of foreigners
I will speak to this people,
  but even then they will not listen to me,"
says the Lord.

[22]Tongues, then, are a sign, not for believers but for unbelievers; prophecy, however, is for believers, not for unbelievers. [23]So if the whole church comes together and everyone speaks in tongues, and some who do not understand or some unbelievers come in, will they not say that you are out of your mind? [24]But if an unbeliever or someone who does not understand comes in while everybody is prophesying, he will be convinced by all that he is a sinner and will be judged by all, [25]and the secrets of his heart will be laid bare. So he will fall down and worship God, exclaiming, "God is really among you!"

This significant chapter deals with two important subjects: (1) the relative value and use of prophecy and speaking in tongues (vv.1–25) and (2) orderly conduct in public worship (vv.26–40).

1–15 Having established in 1 Corinthians 13 that prophecy, tongues, and all spiritual gifts must be exercised in love, Paul now argues that prophesying is to be preferred over speaking in tongues because the former, since it is understood, edifies the church; whereas, without an interpreter, the latter does not. Because of Paul's stress on the need for interpretation (vv.5, 13), the implication is that the Corinthians, in their desire to speak in tongues and their pride in it alone, had neglected this essential matter.

1 In making the transition from the beautiful thirteenth chapter (14:1a), Paul uses a strong verb—"pursue" ("follow the way of," NIV; cf. Phil 3:12, 14)—as he charges them to seek love. This is a stronger verb than the following one—"eagerly desire"—which he applies to seeking spiritual gifts. So love must have the priority, and after that the gift of prophecy must particularly be sought.

2 Paul shows why tongues are not to be preferred. In speaking in tongues, the speaker is talking only to God (cf. Rom 8:26) in *a* "tongue" (note the singular noun)—i.e., in a language unknown to other people, who cannot understand what is said. "Mysteries" refers to the deep truths of God's salvation (cf. Acts 2:11). "By [or, with] the spirit" (*pneumati*) is not to be understood as referring to the Holy Spirit, who is not mentioned in the context, but to the person's own spirit (vv.14, 15; cf. John 4:24).

3,4 Paul now describes the advantage of prophesying. In prophesying, one edifies the church, whereas in speaking in tongues, he builds himself up in his seeking spiritual fellowship with God. There is no mention here that the speaker understood the tongues; not till later does Paul discuss the problem of understanding and insist that the gift of interpretation should be sought by speakers in tongues (vv.13–15). The verb *oikodomeō* ("edify") used in v.4 has the primary meaning of "build." Here Paul uses it in the nonliteral sense of "edify" or "strengthen." The related noun *oikodomē* ("the process of building," "a building" or "edifice") has, as in Paul's thought, the figurative meaning of "edifying" or "building up." "Encouragement" (*parakelēsis*) and "comfort" (*paramythia*) are aspects of that edifying.

5 Here is an emphatic restatement of v.1b. Speak in tongues, you Corinthians, yes; but more than that, I want you to prophesy, because this gift brings understanding and strengthening to the church. However, if there is an interpretation of the tongue, then speaking in tongues can strengthen the church.

6 At this point Paul draws a conclusion (*nyni de,* "but now"). Since tongues without interpretation do not edify, what good would it do the Corinthians if Paul came speaking in tongues unless the message he brought were understandable? The four kinds of messages he lists may be put into two categories: (1) supernatural revelation (cf. Gal 2:2) and prophecy and (2) natural tools of communication—knowledge and teaching (cf. 1 Cor 12: 8–10). It is possible, however, to take "prophecy" in this verse as nonsupernatural, in the sense of the ability to search out the deep things of God. Note also that the conditions are stated as possible, not factual. Paul is not saying that he will come to them speaking in tongues, but only that if he were to do so, it would be futile unless he brought an understandable message.

7–9 Paul now gives some vivid illustrations. The flute and the harp were well-known and valued musical instruments in Greece (cf. Apollo and his harp), and the Jews there would be acquainted with the music of temple worship. But music is nothing more than senseless sounds without systematic differences in pitch, tone, and time. All, both Greeks and Jews, would understand the necessity of the trumpet's call to battle. Compare the use of the *salpinx* (the "war trumpet") in Homer's *Iliad* (18.219) and the ram's horn trumpet of the OT (Num 10:9; Josh 6:4, 9). Applying the illustrations, Paul says that it is not the mere sound of speaking that is important, but whether the sounds can be understood by the hearers.

10–12 Paul's speaking of the languages of the world along with his reference to the "foreigner" (*barbaros,* "barbarian"; see note on v.11) substantiates the conclusion that in his discussion of tongues he has in mind known foreign languages. *Phōnai* ("languages") can at times mean "voices," "sounds" (cf. v.7; Rev. 5:2), but here in connection with *aphōnos* ("without meaning"), it indicates languages that can convey meaning by their systematic distinction of sounds. The "meaning" (*dynamin,* literally "power") of the language refers to its "power" to convey meaning. In v.12 Paul applies these things to the Corinthians—"so it is with you." They are, in short, to major in gifts that will strengthen the church.

13,14 With the possibility of a non-understood tongue before them, Paul now argues that its interpretation be sought. He urges this not only so that those who hear but do not understand may know the meaning, but also that the speaker himself may be benefited by getting an intellectual as well as a spiritual blessing from the exercise. The expression "my mind is unfruitful" means that the mind does not intelligently share in the blessing of the man's spirit. The mind (the *nous*) is that faculty involved in conscious, meaningful reasoning and understanding of a thinking, reasoning person (cf. Grosheide, in loc.). Paul desires the Corinthians to have a complete blessing here, both in their spirits *and* in their minds.

15–17 Praying and singing in the spirit and mind (v.15) are involved in praising and giving thanks to God (v.16), all of which are to be a coherent part of Christian worship (Eph 5:18, 19). The *idiōtēs* (the "unlearned") the one who does not understand, is the Christian who is a church member but does not understand the tongue without an interpretation, or, the "inquirer" about Christianity who does not understand the language. He, too, is important, Paul implies, for he also was to be able to say "amen" to the thanksgiving conveyed in the strange language. But how can he say "amen" and mean it, when he does not understand what he has heard? Paul grants that the tongue may in itself be conveying thanksgiving to God, but it was important for the Christian without that gift to understand it (v.17). (The "Amen," meaning "it is true," comes out of OT worship as in 1 Chronicles 16:36 and Nehemiah 5:13; 8:6, where it is connected with praise to the Lord. It was also used in the synagogue and then in the early church; cf. Galatians 1:5; Ephesians 3:21.)

18,19 Having said that he has the ability to speak in foreign tongues more than all of them (an ability he could properly use), Paul hastens to add he would rather speak a few words in a language the church knows so that they might grow spiritually (*katēcheō,* the word for catechize, Luke 1:4), than to speak volumes in a tongue that does not communicate.

20–25 In this section Paul implies that prophecy is superior to speaking in tongues because though tongues, as in Acts 2, can be impressive to the unbelievers in showing that God is present and can lead them to face the claims of Christ, yet prophecy can be more effectively used to bring the unbeliever to the place of conviction of sin. This was true of Peter's sermon following the speaking in tongues at Pentecost (Acts 2:14–37).

First Paul calls on the Corinthians to think maturely, as "adults" in Christ, and not to be controlled by evil dispositions and motives in their appraisal of tongues (v.20). To illustrate his point that tongues can impress the unbeliever, but that there is no special mark of divine blessing to have people in the congregation who can speak in a language not understood, Paul cites a prophecy from Isaiah 28:11, 12 (cf. Deut 28:49). The point of the quotation is that if Israel would not hear the Lord through the prophets, they would not hear even when he spoke in foreign languages to them through foreign people. So, Paul is saying, why put so much stress on tongues?

He concludes (*hōste,* "then," v.22) that tongues can be and really are a sign of something miraculous (*sēmeion*), an indication of God's presence to the unbeliever (cf. Acts 2). The believer does not need that sign. He already has the indwelling Holy Spirit (Rom 8:9–11; 1 Cor 6:19). But this is not all. Too much emphasis should not be placed on tongues even for unbelievers, for excessive use of this gift will have an adverse effect on them and they will think that the Christians are out of their minds (v.23). Furthermore, all—the whole church as well as the unbelievers—need the blessing of prophecy that can bring unbelievers who come into the church meeting under conviction of sin (vv.24, 25). The one who "does not understand," the *idiōtēs,* seems to be an unbeliever who has already begun to show interest in the Gospel—an inquirer. The effect of Christian prophecy on the unbeliever is threefold: He will be convicted of sin (cf. John 16:8); he will be called to take account of his sins and examine his sinful condition; and will have his sinful heart and past laid open to inspection (cf. John 4:16–19). The triple use of "all" in the Greek (v.24) emphasizes that all the church through its prophetic message has, in God's providence, a part in bringing the unbeliever to this place of conviction. For the unbeliever in the church service will recognize that God really is present and dealing with him.

Notes

1 The present-tense verbs are graphically descriptive: **διώκετε** (*diōkete,* "be pursuing"), **ζηλοῦτε** (*zēloute,* "be desiring"), and **προφητεύητε** (*prophēteuēte,* "that you may be practicing the gift of prophecy").

11 The **βάρβαρος** (*barbaros,* the "barbarian") was one who was not a Gr. and did not speak Gr. (Aeschylus, *Persians* 255; Herodotus 1:58, et al.).

19 The better-attested **τῷ νοΐ μου** (*tō noi mou,* "with my mind") was later changed, probably as an attempt at clarification, to **διὰ τοῦ νοός μου** (*dia tou noos mou,* "through my mind"), which was then mistaken by a few MSS to be **διὰ τοῦ νόμου** (*dia tou nomou*) "through the law," or **δια τôν νόμον** (*dia ton nomon*), "on account of the law."

22 The interpretation of this v. is difficult in the light of vv.23, 24, where unbelievers are repelled by tongues and blessed by prophecy. We reject, however, the view expressed by R. St. John Parry (in loc.) that v.22, therefore, possibly be considered a gloss. Rather, we feel an answer is to be found in seeing a difference in emphasis in the vv., as suggested in the commentary. Verse 22 suggests that tongues were an initial blessing for unbelievers as a miraculous sign of God's presence. Verses 23, 24 argue against too heavy an emphasis on "tongues" even with unbelievers, for they too need the meaningful instruction of prophecy. Compare the tongues and prophesying in Acts 2:1–37.

24 The ἄπιστος (*apistos,* "unbeliever") and ἰδιώτης (*idiōtēs,* "one without understanding," the "inquirer") are both in the unbeliever class in contrast to the saved of the Christian church.

---

f. *Orderly conduct in Christian worship*

14:26–40

[26]What then shall we say, brothers? When you come together, everyone has a hymn, or a word of instruction, a revelation, a tongue, or an interpretation. All of these must be done for the strengthening of the church. [27]If anyone speaks in a tongue, two—or at the most three—should speak, one at a time, and someone must interpret. [28]If there is no interpreter, the speaker should keep quiet in the church and speak to himself and God.

[29]Two or three prophets should speak, and the others should weigh carefully what is said. [30]And if a revelation comes to someone who is sitting down, the first speaker should stop. [31]For you can all prophesy in turn so that everyone may be instructed and encouraged. [32]The spirits of prophets are subject to the control of prophets. [33]For God is not a God of disorder but of peace.

As in all the congregations of the saints, [34]women should remain silent in the churches. They are not allowed to speak, but must be in submission, as the Law says. [35]If they want to inquire about something, they should ask their own husbands at home; for it is disgraceful for a woman to speak in the church. [36]Did the word of God originate with you? Or are you the only people it has reached?

[37]If anybody thinks he is a prophet or spiritually gifted, let him acknowledge that what I am writing to you is the Lord's command. [38]If he ignores this, he himself will be ignored.

[39]Therefore, my brothers, be eager to prophesy, and do not forbid speaking in tongues. [40]But everything should be done in a fitting and orderly way.

In this section on conduct in church worship, Paul insists that all the parts of worship should be conducive to instruction and edification. Tongues, prophecy, and other gifts were to be practiced under strict regulation (26–33a). Also, for the sake of decorum in the churches, women were not to speak in public worship (33b–36). Paul declares that what he is writing is the Lord's instruction (37, 38). He concludes by encouraging the Corinthian Christians to seek to prophesy and not to prohibit people from speaking in tongues, provided that the whole of the worship service is decorous and orderly (39, 40).

26–30 The third person imperatives "it must be done" in these verses show that Paul is not so much addressing his remarks to particular individuals as to the corporate entity, the church, which itself should maintain this decorum. All these imperatives are in the present tense, indicating that the church was to keep a constant supervision over all these aspects of its service.

26–28 Verse 26 gives us a short outline of the elements of worship in Corinth: a hymn, instruction, revelation, a tongue, an interpretation. Some of this is reminiscent of Jewish worship (cf. Matt 26:30; Luke 4:16–30). All is for strengthening the church. The one occurrence of *hekastos* used with each of the following five occurrences of the verb form *echei* ("each one has . . . each one has . . .") suggests again the unity and diversification of gifts in the church. One peron has this ability, another that one; but all (*panta*) together are to be used to build up the church. As for tongues, they must be regulated, with only two or three speaking, one at a time and with someone interpreting (v.27). The phrase *ana meros* ("in turn"), though used elsewhere in Greek literature, occurs only here in the NT. Though v.13 suggests that the speaker in tongues might do the interpreting himself, the inference here is that it would probably be someone else. Without an interpreter, there was to be no public tongues-speaking in the church. This apparently placed on the one speaking in tongues the responsibility of finding out first if an interpreter was present. If there were none, the speaker must be silent in the church service and speak only to himself and God (v.28). Perhaps this means that if no interpreter was on hand, one should do his tongues-speaking at home.

29–33a As for regulations for prophesying in church, only a limited number—not over three—should speak, lest so much be said as to cause confusion. The mention of revelation (v.30) suggests that the prophecy in mind involved a revelation, a special deep teaching, which, however, was distinct from the kind of revelation that Scripture is (2 Tim 3:14–17). Such teaching should be heard even from one who had not been on his feet to speak. In some way the person with this revelation was a spokesman for God in giving some edifying message to the church. The "spirits of the prophets" (v.32) are the spirits of the prophets themselves who were guided by the Holy Spirit in using this special gift. And these prophetic utterances are subject to being checked (*hypotassō*) by other prophets for accuracy and orthodoxy. All this leads to the peace and order of which God is the author (v.33). The word *akatastasia* is a strong one, indicating great disturbance, disorder, or even insurrection or revolution (Luke 21:9). Paul is afraid of unregulated worship that might lead to disorderly conduct and belie the God of peace who has called them to be orderly.

33b–36 Paul now turns to the role of women in public worship, the implication being that men were to lead in worship. Paul's instruction for Corinth is that followed in all the churches. The phrase *tais ekklesiais tōn hagiōn* ("the congregations [or, the churches] of the saints") is distinctive, occurring only here in the NT. The expression emphasizes the universality of the Christian community. All the churches are composed of saints (those set apart for God), and should be governed by the same principle of orderly conduct.

The command seems absolute: Women are not to do any public speaking in the church. This restriction is not to be construed as demoting woman, since the expressions "be in submission" (*hypotassō,* cf. v.32) and "their own husbands" are to be interpreted as simply consistent with God's order of administration (cf. 1 Cor 11:7, 8; Eph 5:21–33). "The law says" must refer to the law as set forth in such places as Genesis 3:16; 1 Corinthians 11:3; Ephesians 5:22; 1 Timothy 1:12, and Titus 2:5. Some have explained the apostle's use of the word "speaking" (v.34) as connoting only general speaking and not forbidding a public address. But this is incompatible with Paul's other uses of "speaking" in the chapter (vv.5, 6, 9, et al.), which imply public utterances as in prophesying (v.5). A woman's request for knowledge is not to be denied, since she is a human being equal to the man. Her questions can be answered at home, and not by asking her husband in the public service and so possibly interrupting the sermon.

The word *gyne* used in vv.34, 35 has the general meaning of "woman," an adult female (cf. Matt 13:33; 27:55). But the same word is used to indicate a married woman (cf. Matt 14:3; Luke 1:5). Here in vv.34, 35 Paul uses the word in the general sense when he declares as a broad principle that "women should remain silent in the churches." That he assumes there were many married women in the congregation is evident from his reference to "their husbands" (v.35). He does not address himself to the question of where the unmarried women, such as those mentioned in 7:8, 36ff., were to get their questions answered. We may assume, however, that they were to talk in private (just as the married women were to inquire at home) with other qualified persons, such as Christian widows (7:8), their pastor (cf. Timothy as a pastor counselor, 1 Tim 5:1, 2), or with elders who were "able to teach" (1 Tim. 3:2). At any rate, a woman's femininity must not be disgraced by her trying to take a man's role in the church.

But what about the seeming contradiction between these verses and 11:5ff., where Paul speaks of women praying and prophesying? The explanation may be that in chapter 11 Paul does not say that women were doing these things in public worship as discussed in chapter 14. (See B.B. Warfield, "Women Speaking in the Church" in *The Presbyterian*, Oct. 30, 1919, pp. 8, 9.)

Paul's rhetorical questions (v.36) are ironical and suggest that the Corinthians had their own separate customs regarding the role of women in public worship and were tending to act independently of the other churches who also had received these commands. They were presuming to act as though they had originated the Word of God (i.e., the gospel) and as if they could depart from Paul's commands and do as they pleased in these matters of church order.

37–40 Now, Paul steps delicately. He had given strict commands but wants to soften their impact. He asks for those who have the gift of prophecy and are spiritually gifted to authenticate the fact that his commands are from the Lord (v.37). But immediately Paul returns to his strict injunction (v.38). The tone is abrupt, the meaning is clear: anyone who ignores it will be ignored by Paul and the churches, or possibly even the Lord, and so be considered an unbeliever (1:18). (So Grosheide, in loc.)

The closing verses of the chapter (39, 40) revert to prophecy and tongues. Paul urges the Corinthians to keep on desiring to prophecy and not to prohibit people from speaking in tongues. But Christian worship must be marked by good order.

Notes

34,35 The Bezan codex (D) and related Western MSS put these vv. at the end of the chapter. Some suggest that this evidences a marginal gloss that got into the text at various places (Craig, in loc.) but there is no good evidence for this. The better MSS have the vv. as we read them.

37 Some MSS read the pl. ἐντολαί (*entolai* "commands"), obviously a scribe's assimilation to the previous plural relative pronoun ἅ (*ha*). The singular ἐντολή (*entolē*), is supported by a sufficiently widespread number of witnesses, including several early ones, as P[46] ℵ [c] A and B (cf. Metzger, *A Textual Commentary*).

38 Important representatives from the Alexandrian, Western, and Palestinian texts support the reading of the indicative passive form (probably futuristic in force) ἀγνοεῖται (*agnoeitai*, "he will be ignored"). This is against the imperative, active ἀγνοείτω (*agnoeitō*, "let him ignore it," as followed by KJV. It is better to take the reading *agnoeitai*, as NIV does, and observe that the alternative in the two occurrences of the word in this verse, one active and other passive, agrees with Paul's usage in 1 Corinthians 8:2, 3 (cf. Metzger, *A Textual Commentary*).

Summary

At this point a summary of the place of speaking in tongues in the apostolic community of the first century A.D. and also a discussion of tongues in the post-apostolic period and the relevance of tongues in the twentieth-century church is in order. First, in Paul's discussion of this and other gifts in chapters 12 to 14, he emphasizes priority of love over "tongues" and the other gifts (1 Cor 13).

Second, in the list of offices (those of apostles, prophets and teachers) and gifts for the church 12:27–31a), the office-gifts are listed first, with other gifts following, the last being "tongues." This implies that Paul gives priority to office-gifts over "tongues." Furthermore, among the office-gifts, that of apostles, who were unique in having seen the Lord, ceased to exist in the first century A.D.

Third, in his treatment of tongues and prophecy in chapter 14, Paul again shows his preference for prophecy over tongues, since the former was the gift that brought edification to the church (vv.1–5). He minimizes the importance of the gift of tongues when he says, "In the church I would rather speak five intelligible words to instruct others than ten thousands words in a tongue" (v.19).

Fourth, in his discussion in chapter 12 regarding the diversity of gifts and their functions in the church, the body of Christ, Paul uses the analogy of the human body with its various parts functioning in unique and distinct ways without each one trying to usurp the function of another part. So he shows that the gifts, including tongues, were not to be sought for the sake of the gifts nor was everyone to seek to have the same gift, such as tongues.

Fifth, God does not have to work by miraculous means to accomplish his purposes; he usually uses ordinary natural means—e.g., in the production of crops, he uses the sun, the rain, and the nutrients of the ground, as well as the hard work of men in farming the land. In connection with *charismata* (the Greek word from which we get the current term "charismatic"), which is translated "spiritual gifts" in NIV (1 Cor 12:4), it is significant that in 1 Corinthians 12:5–11 not all of the *charismata* mentioned are miraculous, as, e.g., the gifts of wisdom and knowledge (v.8), which are mentioned before the miraculous ones, including tongues. It is not essential that everyone have a miraculous gift; see 12:29, 30, where Paul uses rhetorical questions to show that not all Christians had, or were to have, one particular gift in common. The questions in the Greek sentences that comprise 12:29, 30 begin with *mē* negative, which expects a negative response.

Sixth, on the basis of the phenomenon of foreign languages spoken of in Acts 2:5–12, we have argued that the tongues referred to in 1 Corinthians 14:13–15, 20–25 were also foreign-language tongues—not ecstatic utterances, gibberish, or nonunderstandable erratic variations of consonants and vowels with indiscriminate modulation of pitch, speed, and volume.

Seventh, the essential offices for building up the body of Christ, the church, are, according to Paul (Eph 4:11–16), those of apostles, prophets, evangelists, and pastors-teachers (the one Greek article unites the pastor-teacher gift and office). He says nothing there about the necessity of miraculous gifts either in evangelism (Eph 4:11) or in the teaching-edifying ministry of the church (vv.12–16).

Eighth, the other NT passages in which Christian worship patterns are set forth do not include, or as in the exceptional case of the Corinthian church, do not emphasize, miraculous gifts and functions. This is true not only for worship in the developing church under Paul's ministry as portrayed in the last half of Acts and in the epistles, but also in the worship of the OT and early NT periods involving predominantly Jewish Christians—worship patterns taken over largely by the developing Jewish-Gentile Church. These important elements of worship were: the reading of Scripture and expounding it with understanding (Neh 8:1–8; Luke 4:16–30; Acts 2 and other sermons in Acts); prayer (1 Kings 8:10–61; Acts 14:23; 16:25); singing (1 Chron 25; Acts 16:25; Eph 5:19); Christian *koinonia* or fellowship (2 Kings 23:1–3; Acts 2:42); Christian ceremonies or sacraments (as the Passover [Exod 12] and the Lord's Supper [Acts 2:42; 20:7; 1 Cor 11:17–32]); and fasting (Acts 14:23). Miraculous gifts, including tongues, are (apart from the unique situation at Corinth—1 Cor 14:26), absent from these contexts, the conclusion being that they were not to be a necessary part of the general worship patterns of the church.

Ninth, miraculous activity, including speaking in a tongue, did come in biblical times from other sources than the Lord. Witness such activity induced by evil spirits and satanic forces—the Gerasene demon-possessed man (Luke 8:26–39), the spirit-possessed girl (Acts 16:16–18), the image of the evil beast that is given the power to speak by the other satanic beast (Rev 13:15). Psychological factors were involved in the superhuman strength and tongue-speaking activity of the Gerasene demon-possessed man, for upon his deliverance from the demons, he was found to be in his "right mind" (Luke 8:35). Therefore caution and balance are needed in relation to such miraculous activities as speaking in tongues.

Having pointed this out, we must also recognize that the Bible shows that other gifts were also perverted by Satan. The OT speaks more than once of false prophets, as does the NT. The Bible speaks of false pastors (e.g., "worthless shepherd," Zech. 11:17; "hirelings," John 10:12, 13) and frequently warns against false teachers. Yet no one would insist that either prophecy in its valid sense of speaking out for God to the people or the pastoral-teaching ministry is no longer valid. Misuse of a gift does not invalidate the gift itself. However, because of their intimate psychological nature, "tongues" must be viewed with special caution and not be overstressed.

Tenth, it is to be noted that directly after the first-century-A.D. apostolic period legitimate miraculous gifts, such as tongues, practically ceased. According to Warfield,

> There is little or no evidence at all for miracle-working during the first fifty years of the post-Apostolic Church; it is slight and unimportant for the next fifty years; it grows more abundant during the next century (the third); and it becomes abundant and precise only in the fourth century, to increase still further in the fifth and beyond. (*Miracles: Yesterday and Today* [Grand Rapids: Eerdmans, 1953], p. 10.)

In discussing the witness of the apostolic fathers (the early Christian writers of the late first century A.D. and the first half of the second century) Warfield goes on to say,

> The writings of the so-called Apostolic Fathers contain no clear and certain allusions to miracle-working or to the exercise of the charismatic gifts, contemporaneous with themselves. (Ibid.)

In the place of these authentic apostolic miraculous gifts, including tongues, there arose in later centuries reports of many preposterous miracles. One such story is told in *Los Evangelios Apocrifos* (ed. Aurelio de Santos Otero, 2nd ed. [Madrid, 1963], p. 219). According to the story, the infant Jesus, on the trip to Egypt, caused a palm tree "to bow down" so that a coconut might be picked for his mother. Such so-called miracles occur in the writings of the NT Apocrypha, both in the apocryphal gospels and the apocryphal apostolic and early church writings (E. Hennecke, *New Testament Apocrypha*, ed. W. Schneemelcher, Engl. trans. R.McL. Wilson, vols. 1, 2 [London: Lutterworth Press, 1963, 1965]). The questions to be asked are these: Why did the authentic miraculous gifts cease? Are such miraculous gifts to be sought today?

The first question leads us to ask why there was a preponderance of miraculous gifts, including tongues, at the time of the ministries of Jesus Christ and his apostles. Certainly, miraculous gifts do not appear as a part of God's working among the believers in all parts of the biblical record. Abraham, Isaac, Jacob, and the twelve patriarchs did not possess or use miraculous gifts (apart from receiving the Word of God in visions and dreams in a day when the Scriptures were being given). The same is true of David, Isaiah, Jeremiah, and others. However, when certain prophets of God needed particular support and verification, then God performed great miracles through them, as with Moses and Joshua (Exod 12–40; Joshua 1–7, et al.) and Elijah and Elisha (1 Kings 17–2 Kings 13).

Likewise, in the time of Jesus' ministry and that of his apostles, God verified the message and work of Jesus and the apostles, who had witnessed to God's work in Jesus' life, death, and resurrection, by performing mighty miracles through the apostles, including speaking in tongues. Then miracles ceased when the need for the particular witness was ended and the writing of the Scriptures was complete. Thus Warfield argues when, in speaking about the charismatic gifts, he says,

> It is required of all of them [the gifts, such as tongues] that they be exercised for the edification of the church; and a distinction is drawn between them in value, in proportion as they were for edification. But the immediate end for which they were given is not left doubtful, and that proves to be not directly the extension of the church, but the authentication of the Apostles as messengers from God. This does not mean, of course, that only the Apostles appear in the New Testament as working miracles, or that they alone are represented as recipients of the charismata. But it does mean that the charismata belonged in a true sense, to the Apostles, and constituted one of the signs of an Apostle. (*Miracles,* p. 21.)

Now as to the relevance of tongues-speaking in the church today, we may observe, in addition to the foregoing discussion, first, that the requirements Paul gives for the important offices of elder and deacon (1 Tim 3:1–13; Titus 1:5–9) say nothing about the necessity that the bearers of these offices have such gifts (cf. also Eph 4:11–13).

Second, the instructions given Christians as to how they are to live together in the various units of society (Eph 5:21–6:9; Col 3:18–4:1; 1 Peter 2:13–3:7; 5:1–7, et al.) say nothing about the exercise of these kinds of gifts.

In conclusion, the writer believes that the best answer to the question of the relevance of the gift of tongues today is found in the principle that God used this and other miraculous gifts in OT and apostolic times to authenticate the messengers of his Word, and that the present-day Christian is not to seek such gifts. This is not to say, however, that the churches collectively and individually should not pray that if it is God's will, the sick may be healed by his power, or that the church should not pray for deeper illumination in understanding God's inerrant written Word.

Having said this, the writer realizes that there are many Christians of orthodox and evangelical commitment who hold that the gift of tongues as set forth in Acts and 1 Corinthians 12–14 is relevant today. Some of them would no doubt recognize that speaking in tongues is the least of the gifts, as suggested in 1 Corinthians 12:28–30, where Paul placed it last in the list, or in 14:5, 18–20, 22–24, where he subordinates it to prophecy. But they would insist that the gift is not completely ruled out for this modern era, since Paul declares, "Do not forbid speaking in tongues" (14:39).

Moreover, some Christians who accept the present validity of tongues would doubtless say that contemporary conditions seem to point to the end time and are the reason for a resurgence of tongues. For corroboration, they point to actual instances of tongues-speaking, especially on the mission field. (For examples of the latter, see David Howard,

By the Power of the Holy Spirit [Downers Grove, Illinois: Inter-Varsity Press, 1973], pp. 29, 30, 107–110.) Also, they would emphasize that any practice of tongues-speaking today must be done in accordance with the guidelines laid down by Paul (14:26–40). Perhaps most would say that tongues-speaking may best be practiced in private (especially when there is no interpreter) where one can speak in a tongue to God alone (14:2, 8).

These present-day advocates of tongues would undoubtedly agree that this gift, as well as any of the other gifts, is not to be considered an end in itself but must be exercised in love (1 Cor 13:1–3)—not as a spiritual ornament to be seen or as a test of spiritual attainment. Rather, they would say, it is to be used as an instrument for the service and glorification of God.

VIII. The Resurrection of Christ and of the Christian (15:1–58)

This is the classic chapter on the resurrection. In it Paul argues the whole subject of the resurrection from the dead—a teaching that some in the church at Corinth had been questioning (see v.12).

How he had heard about this denial he does not say. But the question gives him an opportunity to bring again before the church the doctrine of the bodily resurrection of Christ, which, along with the death of Christ, he had faithfully communicated to them (vv.1–3). He validates the historical reality of Christ's resurrection by citing eyewitnesses, including himself (vv.4–11). He argues the validity of the resurrection of believers from the fact of the resurrection of Christ (vv.12–19) and then shows that Christ's having been raised and being the first-fruits of the believing dead, guarantees the sequence of events at the second coming of Christ (vv.20–28). He refers to the futility of certain practices of baptism for the dead (vv.29, 30) if the dead are not actually raised. He also asks why Christians should suffer for Christ if there is no resurrection and calls on the Corinthians to give up these doubts and witness to their faith in a risen Christ (vv.29–34). Finally, in a passage of great eloquence, Paul discusses the nature of the resurrection body and the victory over death that God will give us through our Lord Jesus Christ (vv.35–58).

A. *The Resurrection of Christ*

15:1–11

1Now, brothers, I want to remind you of the gospel I preached to you, which you
received and on which you have taken your stand.
2By this gospel you are saved,
if you hold firmly to the word I preached to you. Otherwise, you have believed in
vain.

3For what I received I passed on to you as of first importance: that Christ died
for our sins according to the Scriptures,
4that he was buried, that he was raised
on the third day according to the Scriptures,
5and that he appeared to Peter, and
then to the Twelve.
6After that, he appeared to more than five hundred of the
brothers at the same time, most of whom are still living, though some have fallen
asleep.
7Then he appeared to James, then to all the apostles,
8and last of all he
appeared to me also, as to one abnormally born.

9For I am the least of the apostles and do not even deserve to be called an
apostle, because I persecuted the church of God.
10But by the grace of God I am
what I am, and his grace to me was not without effect. No, I worked harder than
all of them—yet not I, but the grace of God that was with me.
11Whether, then, it
was I or they, this is what we preach, and this is what you believed.

1,2 In the beginning of his masterly discussion of the resurrection, Paul reminds the Corinthian Christians that it is an integral part of the gospel he had preached and they had received and believed. The "if" clause in v.2 implies that Paul believes they are really holding firmly to the Word of God and are therefore saved. So the sentence "Otherwise you have believed in vain" means that the gospel assures salvation unless the supposed faith they had was actually empty and worthless and therefore unenduring.

3–8 Some have understood the words translated "of first importance" in the temporal sense of "at the first." But that seems redundant because at all times Paul's preaching identified the death and resurrection of Christ with the gospel. The stress is on the centrality of these doctrines to the gospel message.

Paul cites two kinds of witness to the historic events of Christ's death and resurrection (vv.3–8): the OT Scriptures and the testimony of eyewitnesses. He does not quote specific OT passages but must have had in mind such texts as Isaiah 53:5, 6 and Psalm 16:8–11. He mentions Christ's burial to show the genuineness of his death and resurrection; he actually died and actually was raised. Paul feels no compulsion to cite any eyewitnesses of Christ's death, because its factuality was commonly accepted. The resurrection was a different matter. If supernatural Christianity was to be believed, valid eyewitnesses must be cited to attest this historical event and set to rest doubt about the resurrection of the dead.

That "Christ died for our sins" (v.3) implies that Christ was sinless. That he was raised forever (the perfect tense is used here) agrees with the Scripture in Psalm 16:10; so also does Paul's statement about the third day, which may be based on Jesus' words in Matthew 12:40 that relate his three days in the tomb to Jonah's three days inside the fish (Jonah 1:17). According to Jewish reckoning, "three days" would include parts of Friday afternoon, all of Saturday, and Sunday morning. Compare the parts of two Sundays implied in the phrase "after eight days" (John 20:26).

Part of the gospel message Paul passed on to the Corinthians was eyewitness reports of the resurrection of Christ. Observe the close-knit series of "that" clauses in vv.3–6, extending from, "that Christ died" (v.3) through "that he appeared" (v.6) to eyewitnesses, some of whom Paul names. It is natural for him to include Cephas (Peter) and the apostles (possibly referring to the meeting recorded in Luke 24:36ff. and John 20:19ff.). "The Twelve" is a designation of the apostles as a group and is not to be pressed numerically, since Judas was no longer there and on one occasion Thomas (John 20:24) was not with them. The apostolic witness was of vital importance for the Corinthians and Paul doubtless included the witness of the 500 especially to impress doubting believers with the sheer number of eyewitnesses of the event. Some of the 500 may have been known to the Corinthians. This appearance of Christ to so many at once may have taken place in Galilee, where the eleven and possibly many more, went to meet the risen Lord (Matt 28:10, 16). "Fall asleep" is an early Christian expression for dying (cf. Acts 7:60).

The James mentioned in v.7 certainly is not one of the two apostles of that name—James the son of Zebedee and James the son of Alphaeus (Matt 10:2–4), since the whole group of apostles is mentioned next and would include these two. Instead, it must be the Lord's half-brother (Matt 13:55), who had, with his brothers, joined the apostolic band (Acts 1:14) and had become prominent in the Jerusalem church (Acts 15:13). We do not know when this appearance took place. Since Paul had mentioned "the Twelve" in v.5, "all the apostles" (v.7) must be used more loosely to include others who met with the apostolic band (cf. Acts 1:13–15). All this evidence (vv.5–8) was received by Paul from eyewitnesses (cf. Gal. 1:18, 19) and very possibly from some of the gospel writers. Paul includes himself as the last witness (v.8). He describes himself as one born of a miscarriage, thus he conveys his feeling that he was not a "normal" member of the apostolic group, but one who had been "snatched" out of his sin and rebellion by the glorified Christ (Acts 9:3–6).

9–11 In these verses Paul reflects on his own unworthiness and on God's matchless redeeming grace. Though he taught that all are unworthy before God (Rom 3:10–18)—a fact to which the Twelve were no exception—he felt himself particularly unworthy because he had persecuted the church. He calls it the church of God; therefore, in persecuting it, he felt he had persecuted God. With true humility, he attributes all his hard work for the cause of Christ solely to God's grace (v.10)—grace that had saved him and enabled him to serve. Then with great emphasis he declares that all—both he and the other apostles—preached the same gospel with the same stress on the resurrection, and this is the message the Corinthians believed.

B. *The Validity of the Resurrection of the Dead*

15:12–19

> 12But if it is preached that Christ has been raised from the dead, how can some of you say that there is no resurrection of the dead? 13If there is no resurrection of the dead, then not even Christ has been raised. 14And if Christ has not been raised, our preaching is useless and so is your faith. 15More than that, we are then found to be false witnesses about God, for we have testified about God that he raised Christ from the dead. But he did not raise him if in fact the dead are not raised. 16For if the dead are not raised, then Christ has not been raised either. 17And if Christ has not been raised, your faith is futile; you are still in your sins. 18Then those also who have fallen asleep in Christ are lost. 19If only for this life we have hope in Christ, we are to be pitied more than all men.

12–16 Here Paul presents his major proposition. Some at Corinth had argued that there was no resurrection of the dead. He replies that this is absolutely contrary to the proclamation that Christ has been raised. The perfect tense *egēgertai* ("has been raised"), with its emphasis on the present reality of the historic fact is important to Paul (cf. Gal 2:20). In the present context he uses the same verb form seven times, in each case in reference to Christ (vv.4, 12, 13, 14, 16, 17, 20). When speaking of "the resurrection of the dead," he uses the present tense of the same verb (vv.15, 16). The conditional sentences throughout this section begin with *ei de,* the condition being an assumed fact: "If it is preached [as it is] that Christ has been raised . . ." (v.12). The same is true of vv.13, 14, 16, 17, and 19.

Having questioned the contention of some that the dead do not rise (v.12), the apostle states a series of conclusions flowing from the contention that the dead do not rise: (1) There is no resurrection of Christ (v.13); (2) preaching that he has been raised is then empty and meaningless (v.14a); (3) their resultant faith (in Christ who was supposed to have risen from the dead) is also meaningless (v.14b); and (4) his own testimony about Christ's resurrection is false, because it claims God did something he really did not do (v.15). Verse 16 closes this set of conclusions by reiterating the statement in v.13.

17–19 Once more Paul begins with *ei de* as he draws additional conclusions from the hypothesis that Christ has not risen from the dead: (1) Faith is not only vain or meaningless (*kenos*) (v.14), it is also fruitless (*mataios,* v.17); (2) believers still carry the guilt of their sins and are not justified (v.17b; cf. the converse in Rom 5:1); (3) there is no hope for those who have died in Christ—they have perished (v.18); and (4) therefore putting up with persecutions and hardships is futile; we are most to be pitied among men (v.19). The perfect tense of the verb *elpizō* ("we have hope") implies a continual hope in Christ throughout life.

Notes

1–3 That the gospel was a corpus of doctrine including the resurrection of Christ is clear from the neuter pronoun ὅ (*ho,* "that which"), the pronoun being repeated throughout vv.1–3. This "*ho* corpus" of the gospel is referred to in several ways: the Corinthians had received it (accusative case, vv.1b, 3b); they had taken their stand on it (dative case, v.1c); and they had been saved through it (genitive case, v.2a).

3 The phrase **ὑπὲρ τῶν ἁμαρτιῶν ἡμῶν** (*hyper tōn hamartiōn hēmōn*) is theologically strong, referring to the substitutionary atonement: Christ died *on behalf of our sins* or *in order to atone for* (or, *remove*) *our sins* (cf. Gal 1:4).

3,4 Γραφή (*graphē*), generally meaning "writing" of various sorts, has only a sacred significance in the NT, referring to the holy Scriptures.

5 The passive form ὤφθη (*ōphthē*), from ὁράω (*horaō*) is used deponently as "appeared" (cf. Luke 24:34; Heb 9:28) rather than passively, "was seen."

15 The phrase **κατὰ θεοῦ** (*kata theou*) strictly means "against God"; that is, accusing God of doing what he did not do (cf. St. John Parry, in loc.).

17 There is a shade of difference between **μάταιος** (*mataios*) and **κενός** (*kenos*) in v.14, the former meaning "fruitless," which augments the latter meaning of "empty."

18 The aorist (past-punctiliar) form **ἀπωλόντο** (*apōlonto,* "they have perished," "they are lost forever") is quite final. **κοιμάω** (*koimaō*) used for natural sleep (Luke 22:45), is used of the death of the body in such contexts as this one.

The comparative form **ἐλεεινότεροι** (*eleeinoteroi*) need not be taken as equivalent to a superlative, "most miserable," as in KJV. This is possible, but it makes best sense taken as a true comparative in meaning—"more pitied" or, as in NIV, "pitied more than all men." This agrees better with the order of the Gr. words, in which the comparative for *eleeinoteroi* is followed immediately by the genitive of comparison: **τῶν πάντων** (*tōn pantōn*). (Cf. 1 Cor 13:13, where μείζων [*meizōn*] is used to compare three things: "the greatest of these." But in 1 Cor 12:23, the comparative form ἀτιμότερα [*atimotera*] is to be taken with its usual comparative force: "less honorable." See Robertson, *A Grammar,* pp. 667, 668.)

19 The adverb **μόνον** (*monon,* "only"), though placed after the perfect periphrastic construction (i.e., a participle with the verb "to be") **ἠλπικότες ἐσμέν** (*ēlpikotes esmen*), is best taken with the entire clause to mean, "If all our hopes in Christ are confined to this life . . ." (Hodge).

C. *Christ the Guarantee of the Resurrection From the Dead*

15:20–28

20But Christ has indeed been raised from the dead, the firstfruits of those who have fallen asleep. 21For since death came through a man, the resurrection of the dead comes also through a man. 22For as in Adam all die, so in Christ all will be made alive. 23But each in his own turn: Christ, the firstfruits; then, when he comes, those who belong to him. 24Then the end will come, when he hands over the kingdom to God the Father after he has destroyed all dominion, authority and power. 25For he must reign until God has put all his enemies under his feet. 26The last enemy to be destroyed is death. [27]For God "has put everything under his feet." Now when it says that "everything" has been put under him, it is clear that this does not include God himself, who put everything under Christ. [28]When he has done this, then the Son himself will be made subject to him who put everything under him, so that God may be all in all.

The "but . . . indeed" (*nyni de*) is Paul's emphatic and conclusive way of introducing some vitally important affirmations (cf. *nyni de* in 13:13; Rom 3:21; 6:22; 7:6; Col 1:22, et al.). Certainly, Paul implies, none of the Corinthian believers would deny that an integral part of the gospel message is the resurrection of Christ (15:1–4). Therefore, they must now accept the sequel—Christ guarantees the resurrection of the Christian dead, as the word "firstfruits" teaches. By "firstfruits" Paul brings to bear the rich imagery of the OT. The "firstfruits"—the first sheaf of the harvest offered to the Lord (Lev 23:10–11, 17, 20)—was not only prior to the main harvest but was also an assurance that the rest of the harvest was coming. So with Christ. He preceded his people in his bodily resurrection and he is also the guarantee of their resurrection at his second coming.

21,22 These verses sound like Paul's two-category contrast in Rom 5:12–21. The man who brought death is Adam, and the one who will bring about the resurrection of the dead is Christ (cf. also 1 Cor 15:45). All who are represented in Adam—i.e., the whole human race—died. All who are in Christ—i.e., God's redeemed people—will be made alive at the resurrection (cf. John 5:25).

23 The expression, *hekastos en toi idioi tagmati* ("each in his own group") stresses the different times involved: Christ the "firstfruits" was made alive three days after his death; the other group, those who belong to Christ, will be made alive at the Parousia—his second coming. The term Parousia can simply mean a person's presence (Phil. 2:12), but when used of Christ, it refers especially to his second coming (cf. Matt 24:27).

Having recognized that Paul has time-sequences in mind (v.23), we assume that in vv.24ff. he continues with further time-sequences, as shown by the particle *eita* ("then"). That is, at the time of Christ's second coming and the resurrection of the blessed dead (cf. Rev 20:4–6), next ("then") in order will come the process of his handing over (*paradidoi* is *present* subjunctive) the kingdom to God. This will include his conquest of all earthly and all spiritual powers and enemies (cf. "things in heaven and on earth, visible and invisible . . . thrones . . . powers . . . rulers . . . authorities," Col 1:16). The picture is total, including the physical kingdoms of this world. This future total conquest of the rulers of this world is further suggested in the sentence beginning with "for" (*gar*, v.25). Christ must at that time (*eita*, "then," v.24) continue his reign—i.e., his millennial reign (Rev 20:4–6) till all his enemies are conquered. The expression "under his feet" is an OT figure for total conquest. Verse 25 is an allusion to Psalm 110:1 (cf. Matt 22:44). The mention of Zion in Psalm 110:2 suggests further that his enemies include those who attack Palestine (Rev 16:12–16) and Jerusalem (Rev 20:7–10) at the time of the millennial reign of Christ (Rev 20:4–6). Finally, the last enemy to be destroyed is death (v.26) at the close of the second-coming events at the great judgment (Rev 20:2–15). This will bring the consummation of Christ's conquest of his enemies and all other things, as implied by the prophetic statement about man and particularly about the incarnate Christ in Psalm 8:6, quoted in v.27.

Some think the reference to "the end" in vv.24–27 refers to the absolute end of this world, at which time believers will be raised. They hold that what follows "then" in v.24

is different from what follows "then" in v.23. According to this view, "There it [the 'then' of v.23] was the resurrection, but after 'the end' [v.24] there is no resurrection" (Grosheide, in loc.) preceded by a literal thousand-year reign in which Christ puts his enemies under his feet. But this interpretation changes quite radically Paul's idea of events following each other in temporal sequence, to an abrupt "then comes the end" where there is no more sequence. This seems arbitrary. Furthermore, it does not take adequate account of the fuller teaching on this subject in Rev 20:4–10—a passage that posits a reign of Christ and a time when this earth will have peace and rejuvenation before its final destruction (Rev 21:1). In Romans 8:18–25 it is stated that the whole creation (including the earth) will be delivered from "its bondage to decay" [NIV] and will be "brought into the glorious freedom" (that is, deliverance from decay) at the time of the "glorious freedom" of the children of God. All of this occurs, according to Revelation 20 and 21 *before* the destruction of the present heavens and earth. God's dealings with this present heaven and earth are described in Revelation 21:1, not as a rejuvenation, but as a total destruction of what is called the "first" heaven and earth; a "new" heaven and a "new" earth, an earth in which there is "no longer any sea," take the place of the old ones, we are told (cf. 2 Peter 3:10–13).

Verse 27 makes clear that in the "all things" God the Father is not made subject to Christ. On the other hand, v.28 suggests that the Son in a certain sense will be made subject to God the Father. That this does not mean inferiority of person or nature is shown by the future tense of the verb: "the Son himself will be made subject." If there were inherent inferiority, the present tense would be expected—i.e., "he is ever subjected to the Father." But the future aspect of Christ's subjection to the Father must rather be viewed in the light of the administrative process in which the world is brought from its sin and disorder into order by the power of the Son, who died and was raised and who then, in the economy of the Godhead, turns it all over to God the Father, the supreme administrative head. All this is to be done so that God will be recognized by all as sovereign, and he—the triune God—will be supreme (cf. Rev 22:3–5).

Notes

23 Ἔπειτα (*epeita,* "then" or "next") denotes succession in enumerations often with indications of chronological sequence (cf. 1 Thess 4:17) as well as here. Εἶτα (*eita,* "then" or "next") when following closely, indicates further chronological sequence (John 13:5; 19:27; 1 Tim 2:13, et al.), though sometimes, as in logical argumentation, it may not entail time sequence (Heb 12:9).

25 Though *βασιλεύειν* (*basileuein*) is a present infinitive with continuous action, it does not at this point in 1 Cor mean that Christ is reigning now. The context is "the end" (v.24) and the infinitive (a futuristic use of the present tense) is governed by the impersonal verb *dei,* meaning "It is necessary that he is to be reigning"—NIV, "For he must reign . . . ."

26 The present form *καταργεῖται* (*katargeitai*) is to be read as a futuristic present—"is going to be destroyed." Present spiritual death is not in view, for Paul speaks of death in an eschatological sense as the last enemy to be destroyed (see also vv.50–56).

D. *Implications of Denying the Resurrection From the Dead*

15:29–34

> 29Now if there is no resurrection, what will those do who are baptized for the dead? If the dead are not raised at all, why are people baptized for them? 30And as for us, why do we endanger ourselves every hour? 31I die every day—I mean that, brothers—just as surely as I glory over you in Christ Jesus our Lord. 32If I fought wild beasts in Ephesus for merely human reasons, what have I gained? If the dead are not raised,
>
> "Let us eat and drink,
> for tomorrow we die."
>
> 33Do not be misled: "Bad company corrupts good character." 34Come back to your senses as you ought, and stop sinning; for there are some who are ignorant of God—I say this to your shame.

29 Here Paul returns to his argument for the resurrection of the dead. There is a special difficulty in understanding v.29 because we do not know the background of the words "baptized for the dead." There are many interpretations, but it is difficult to find a satisfactory one. The present tense of "baptize" suggests that the practice of baptizing for the dead was current and evidently well known to the Corinthians.

Among the numerous explanations of the custom is that of Epiphanius (*Haer.* 28) who understood it to be a baptism of catechumens (i.e., those being instructed in Christian doctrine) on their death beds. But there is no evidence that this was practiced in Paul's day.

Other views center around the idea that Paul is referring to the practice of living believers being baptized for deceased believers. The reasons given for such a supposed practice are manifold. Chrysostom and others understood Paul to be referring to the statement in the baptismal creed "I believe in the resurrection of the dead," meaning that there was a baptism for the bodies of the dead in the hope of the resurrection. But the text does not support this complex thought, and such a creed came later than Paul's time. Craig (IB, in loc.) suggests that the custom may have been a reference to a superstitious baptism being practiced for those who had died as "outsiders" to the church. Or that believers may have baptized the graves above relatives who had died in Christ (Grosheide). But such a locative meaning as "above" or "over" for the preposition *hyper* with the genitive is not found elsewhere in the NT, and there is no historical evidence for any such custom. (H.A.W. Meyer, *The Epistles to the Corinthians* [New York: Funk and Wagnalls, 1884], p. 366.)

In another strange and complex view, Olshausen takes the passage to mean that the living believers had themselves baptized in place of the deceased believers, who thus had ceased to be members of the church, this custom being practiced so that the church membership would not be depleted. But new converts would fill up the ranks of the church, so that there would be no need for such a practice. Koster sees the practice as referring to living Christians who had got themselves baptized for the sake of deceased believers, to show their yearning for them and assuring their connection with them and participation with them in the resurrection. But not all this is implied in the text. (Ibid. pp. 364–368.)

In still another view, the concept of "baptize" in v.29 is interpreted not in relation to the actual sacrament or ordinance of baptism but is understood metaphorically and spiritually as meaning "identify." Thus, the idea would be "If there is no resurrection of the dead, why are believers identified as dead men? Why should they be crucified with Christ?" According to this view, Paul is saying, "I die daily," meaning "I am identified daily with Christ in his death." But a major problem with this interpretation is that it makes the preposition *hyper* mean "as," whereas its basic meaning with the genitive is "for," "in behalf of," or "in the place of." (See further D.G. Barnhouse, *God's Freedom: Exposition on Romans* [Grand Rapids: Eerdmans 1958], 6:32–35.)

According to Meyer, this verse means that believers already baptized were rebaptized for the benefit of believers who had died unbaptized. This was done on the assumption that it would count for the unbaptized dead and thereby assure their resurrection along with the baptized, living believers. As Meyer put it, "This custom propagated and maintained itself afterwards only among heretical sects, in particular among the Corinthians (Epiphanius, *Haer.* 28:7) and among the Marcionites (Chrysostom; cf. moreover, generally Tertullian, *de resurr. 48; Adv. Marc.* v.10)" (*The Epistles to the Corinthians*, pp. 364, 365).

At any rate, Paul simply mentions the superstitious custom without approving it and uses it to fortify his argument that there is a resurrection from the dead.

30–32 Another argument for the resurrection is that if it is not true, then suffering and hardship for the sake of Christ are useless. By "endangering ourselves every hour," Paul seems to be alluding to peril looming up in his ministry in Ephesus (cf. Acts 19), where he was when he wrote 1 Corinthians. He is in danger of death every day (v.31). He seals this assertion with the oath (Greek, *nē*, "I mean that, brothers") that this is as true as the fact that he glories over them and over their union with Christ. Paul's reference to fighting with wild beasts in Ephesus (v.32) may be taken literally or figuratively. But since from Acts 19 we see no evidence of such punishment and since it was questionable whether a Roman citizen would be subjected to such treatment, it is best to take the words metaphorically—the human enemies he fought with at Ephesus were like wild beasts. But, Paul says, why go through all this suffering if there is no hope of resurrection? To prove his point, he first quotes Isaiah 22:13, (possibly for the benefit of the Jewish believers at Corinth) from a context of reckless living that the Lord condemns. So without eternal hope through the resurrection, men have nothing to turn to but gratification of their appetites.

33 Turning now to Greek literature, Paul supports his position by quoting a piece of practical worldly wisdom from Menander's comedy, *Thais*, relevant to the situation in the Corinthian church. The "bad company" points to those who were teaching that there is no resurrection and so were a threat to the testimony of the church.

34 The call in v.34 is for the Corinthians to stop sinning in denying the resurrection of the dead and, so by implication, the resurrection of Christ—a denial leading to loose living. There were some in the church who did not know God or the precious doctrine of the resurrection. They were in a shameful condition, Paul says, because they had espoused such a denial of the truth.

Notes

31 The particle νή (*nē*) is one of strong affirmation and is used with an accusative of person or thing by which one swears or affirms.

32 The first-class Gr. condition of fact εἰ (*ei*) with the indicative, assumes the reality of Paul's encounter with danger in Ephesus—it had occurred. The second *ei* indicative condition assumes, for the sake of argument, that if it is in fact granted that the dead do not rise, then the pragmatic consequences are that one might as well live recklessly now. The aorist subjunctive forms Φάγωμεν (*phagōmen*) and πίωμεν (*piōmen*) relate to the total decision regarding living as if there were no resurrection: "Let us give ourselves over completely to eat and drink"—i.e., to total materialism.

34 The contrast in the kind of action in the two imperative verbs ἐκνήψατε (*eknēpsate,* aorist) and μὴ ἁμαρτάνετε (*mē harmartanete,* present) is graphic: "Come to your senses, fully and completely; and do not continue to sin."

E. *The Resurrection Body: Its Nature and Change*

15:35–58

35But someone may ask, "How are the dead raised? With what kind of body will
they come?" 36How foolish! What you sow does not come to life unless it dies.
37When you sow, you do not plant the body that will be, but just a seed, perhaps
of wheat or of something else. 38But God gives it a body as he has determined,
and to each kind of seed he gives its own body. 39All flesh is not the same: Men
have one kind of flesh, animals have another, birds another and fish another.
40There are also heavenly bodies and there are earthly bodies; but the splendor
of the heavenly bodies is one kind, and the splendor of the earthly bodies is
another. 41The sun has one kind of splendor, the moon another and the stars
another; and star differs from star in splendor.

42So it will be with the resurrection of the dead. The body that is sown is
perishable, it is raised imperishable; 43it is sown in dishonor, it is raised in glory;
it is sown in weakness, it is raised in power; 44it is sown a natural body, it is raised
a spiritual body.

If there is a natural body, there is also a spiritual body. 45So it is written: "The
first man Adam became a living being"; the last Adam, a life-giving spirit. 46The
spiritual did not come first, but the natural, and after that the spiritual. 47The first
man was of the dust of the earth, the second man from heaven. 48As was the
earthly man, so are those who are of the earth; and as is the man from heaven,
so also are those who are of heaven. 49And just as we have borne the likeness
of the earthly man, so we shall bear the likeness of the man from heaven.

50I declare to you, brothers, that flesh and blood cannot inherit the kingdom of
God, nor does the perishable inherit the imperishable. 51Listen, I tell you a mystery:
We shall not all sleep, but we shall all be changed—52in a flash, in the twinkling
of an eye, at the last trumpet. For the trumpet will sound, the dead will be raised
imperishable, and we shall be changed. 53For the perishable must clothe itself with
the imperishable, and the mortal with immortality. 54When the perishable has been
clothed with the imperishable, and the mortal with immortality, then the saying that
is written will come true: "Death has been swallowed up in victory."

> 55"Where, O death, is your victory?
> Where, O death, is your sting?"

56The sting of death is sin, and the power of sin is the law. 57But thanks be to
God! He gives us the victory through our Lord Jesus Christ.

58Therefore, my dear brothers, stand firm. Let nothing move you. Always give yourselves fully to the work of the Lord, because you know that your labor in the Lord is not in vain.

With imcomparable logic, Paul's argument mounts toward its magnificent climax. First, he discusses the nature of the resurrection body (vv.35–49). Then he describes the transformation the body must undergo before death is conquered and the believer lives with God eternally (vv.50–58).

35–49 Paul answers the question some believers were asking—viz., since a resurrection body was like the sinful mortal body we now have (Hodge, Craig), how could the resurrection of such a body occur? (Grosheide). Paul raises questions as a means of answering some of the proposed objections. He calls the questions foolish and in replying to them uses an analogy to the organizational structure of the physical life and world. Different beings, while organized alike in their own order, differ from other orders. The seed analogy (v.37—cf. John 12:24) teaches that through "dying" (decaying in the ground) the seed gives birth by God's power to a new and different "body," yet one related to the seed it came from (vv.36b–38).

A second analogy involves the body of flesh various forms of animal life have—the differing kinds of flesh for men, animals, birds, and fish (v.39). A third analogy relates to inanimate objects of creation (vv.40, 41), in connection with which Paul again uses *sōma* ("body"). These, too, differ. The "heavenly bodies"—sun, moon, and stars—differ from "the earthly bodies," and their "splendor" differs from "the splendor of the earthly bodies." (Paul does not specify what he means by the latter—perhaps he had in mind the great mountains, canyons, and the like.) Moreover, he adds that the heavenly bodies themselves differ from one another in splendor and brilliance. So, Paul is arguing, God is able to take similar physical material and organize it differently to accomplish his purposes.

In vv.42–44a the apostle applies this to the truth of the resurrection of the body. God can take the mortal body, perishable (Gal. 6:8), dishonored, humiliated because of sin (Phil 3:20, 21), and weak (Mark 14:38)—a natural body like those of the animal world—and bring that body that "is sown" in death (cf. John 12:24) into a different order of life in a spiritual body. Such a body will indeed have immortality (2 Tim 1:10), glory (Phil 3:21), and power. It will have a spiritual way of functioning similar to the way heavenly bodies function in contradistinction to earthly bodies (St. John Parry). That by "spiritual" here (v.44) Paul means completely nonmaterial is incompatible with the whole context, which discusses the differing organizations of material substance. The spiritual body is an imperishable yet utterly real body—one of a different order and having different functions from the earthly body; it is a body given by God himself—a body glorified with eternal life.

Verses 44b–49 develop the distinction between the natural body and the spiritual body, by bringing in two categories—one of Adam and his descendants and the other of Christ, the last Adam, and his redeemed ones. By "natural body" Paul means one such as Adam had (v.45) when he was made of the dust of the ground and given the breath of life (cf. Gen 2:7). By "spiritual body" the apostle means that an imperishable body that has received eternal life from Christ, the life-giving Spirit (cf. John 5:26), including a metamorphosis of the physical body to adapt it spiritually (without either corruption or mortality) for living with God (Phil 3:21), just as Christ in his resurrected and glorified human body (Luke 24:36–43) went to heaven to be with the Father (cf. Acts 1:11, 2:33). There is, indeed, a real sense in which the accounts of the post-resurrection appearances of Christ in Luke 24; John 20 and 21; and Acts 1:1–9 shed light on the nature of the resurrection body. (See also 2 Cor 5:1–10.)

Paul asserts that the natural life came first and then the spiritual life was added to it, v.46. He illustrates this in vv.47–49 from Adam, who was made of the dust of the earth, and whose descendants (the whole human race) have natural, earthly bodies. In contrast, "the last Adam," Christ, came from heaven into a human body (the incarnation), a body that was glorified following his resurrection (Phil 3:21). He is the God-Man (John 3:13). Those who belong to him, Paul says, are also "of heaven" and will ultimately be like him (cf. 1 John 3:2).

50–58 Paul now comes to the conclusion of his argument for the resurrection. God's people must have more than the natural body to inherit the eternal kingdom of God. "Flesh and blood" refers to the mortal body—our present humanity, which Christ fully shared through his incarnation (Heb 2:14). This mortal body is perishable and cannot inherit that which is imperishable. So the unsaved cannot be in heaven at all, and the saved must have their bodies changed.

By using "mystery" in reference to the resurrection body, Paul implies that there are things about that body that the Corinthians did not understand, and about which he wants to inform them. First, not all Christians will "fall asleep." Some will be alive when Christ returns (1 Thess 4:15). Second, all Christians will receive changed bodies when Christ comes back and summons his people at the sound of the last trumpet (cf. Rev 11:15). This is called "the rapture" (1 Thess 4:13–17). Third, the change will occur instantaneously and completely for all Christians, whether living or dead. Fourth, the change will occur from one kind of body to another. Paul does not use the term "imperishable" in speaking of those living when Jesus comes, but the word "changed" (v.52). The meaning is clarified by v.53: The "perishable," those in Christ whose bodies are decaying in the grave, must be given "imperishable" bodies. The mortal, those in Christ living in mortal bodies at the time of Christ's return, must be given "changed" immortal bodies—bodies that will not die. When all this occurs (v.54), the triumphant words in Isaiah 25:8 and Hosea 13:14 will become a reality for God's people. With powerful effect, Paul quotes Hosea's striking rhetorical questions.

Then, with strong emphasis on the words "victory" and "sting," Paul reaches the climax of this song of triumph in vv.56, 57. If it were not for sin, death would have no sting. It is the law of God with its stringent moral demands that strengthens the power of sin by showing us how sinful we are, and thus condemns us. But death does not have the final victory! Hear the glorious closing exclamation (v.57): "Thanks be to God! He gives us the victory through our Lord Jesus Christ." Yes, victory, even over death and the grave, has been won through our Lord, who died and rose and is coming again.

Following this glorious outburst of eloquence, Paul concludes with a practical, down-to-earth exhortation. It is almost as if he is saying to the Corinthian Christians and indeed to all of us: "Now, my brothers and sisters, in the light of these sublime truths, be steadfast in doing the Lord's work, knowing that he will reward you at his coming."

Notes

40,41 The use of *ἕτερος* (*heteros*) suggests a difference in kind between heavenly and earthly bodies. The ἄλλος (*allos*) indicates a comparison of things of like kind—the sun, moon, etc. The same is true of its use in v.39.

44–46 The ψυχικός (*psychikos*) body is the physical body in contrast to the πνευματικός (*pneumatikos*) body, that body imbued with additional life from the Spirit of God.

47 Some ancient MSS read ἄνθρωπος ὁ κύριος (*anthrōpos ho kurios*) "the man, the Lord" (which KJV follows). But the best MSS omit *ho kurios.*

49 Though the MS evidence somewhat favors the subjunctive φορέσωμεν (*phoresōmen,* "let us bear"—a form that has some good MS evidence), the context favors the future indicative φορέσομεν (*phoresomen,* "we shall bear"—a form that also has some good MS evidence). Εἰκον (*eikon*) is an "image," like that of an emperor's head on a coin, an exact likeness of someone.

51 The best MS witnesses read ἀλλαγησόμεθα (*allagēsometha,* "we shall be changed"). Other readings, such as "we shall not all be changed" or "we shall sleep, but not all of us shall be changed," suggest muddled theological thinking and must be scribal interpolations. The first and best reading agrees with the like statement in v.52.

54 There is a shortened reading of this v. that leaves out the words "this mortal shall be clothed with immortality" (NIV, "the mortal with immortality"). This omission, though supported by several important MSS, probably arose through an oversight in copying, especially since these words appeared before in v.53.

55 Two sets of variants developed in this v., because the LXX of Hos 13:14 differs in part from the Heb. The variant in which νῖκος (*nikos,* "victory") appears before κέντρον (*kentron,* "sting") is to be preferred to the reverse (which KJV has) because of the word order in LXX, which has *kentron* last. The repetition of θάνατε (*thanate,* "death") is to be preferred as Paul's synonym for ᾅδη (*hadē,* "Hades" or "the grave"), which he never uses. (Cf. Metzger, *A Textual Commentary,* p. 570.) Paul adapts LXX δίκη (*dikē,* "judgment") for Heb. "plagues" to his word νῖκος (*nikos,* "victory")—i.e., victory over plagues.

58 The present imperative γίνεσθε (*ginesthe*) stresses constant Christian stability, as does πάντοτε (*pantote*) also: "Continue to stand firm . . . always abound." The addition of the word κόπος (*kopos,* "toil") to ἔργον (*ergon*), the ordinary word for work, suggests that work for the Lord is to be hard work and that it involves hardship and suffering.

IX. The Collection for God's People, Requests, and Final Greetings (16:1–24)

A. *The Collection for God's People*

16:1–4

> [1]Now about the collection for God's people: Do what I told the Galatian churches to do. [2]On the first day of every week, each one of you should set aside a sum of money in keeping with his income, saving it up, so that when I come no collections will have to be made. [3]Then, when I arrive, I will give letters of introduction to the men you approve and send them with your gift to Jerusalem. [4]If it seems advisable for me to go also, they will accompany me.

1–4 This section begins with the same formula, "Now about . . ." (*peri de*), that was used in 7:1 and 12:1. The Corinthians had evidently asked about the collection to be taken up for God's people at Jerusalem (v.3). Paul must have spoken to them earlier about it, as he also did later (cf. 2 Cor 8–9). This offering for these poor in Jerusalem was much on his mind during his third missionary journey (cf. Rom 15:26). That he mentions the Galatian churches here, though not in 2 Corinthians 8–9 or Romans 15:26, implies that this collection was to be a widespread and extensive effort with the Corinthian Christians contributing along with those from other lands. Why some of the Christians in Jerusalem were poor (Rom 15:26) at this time (c. A.D. 55, 56) he does not say. It may have been in part because of the famine referred to in Acts 11:29 (c. A.D. 49). Some have thought that the poverty resulted from the Jerusalem Christians' being overgenerous in giving away their property and goods (cf. Acts 2:44, 45; 4:34, 35).

Verse 2 teaches that the collection was to be set aside by each individual (and family) on the first day of the week ("the first day from the Sabbath"—i.e., Sunday), but we are not told specifically that it was to be collected at church. Some have interpreted the words *par heautō* (literally "by himself") to mean "at home." But then why mention doing it on Sunday, when they could just as well do it regularly at home at other times? The meaning must rather be that the Christians were to bring their offerings to church on Sunday, since that was the day they assembled for worship (Acts 20:7; cf. Rev 1:10). It is significant that the early church father, Justin Martyr (second century A.D.) testified that contributions to the church were received on that day (Apology I, 67.6). Giving is to be proportionate; all were to participate, whether rich or poor; and the money was to be regularly set aside ("every week"). The offering was to be planned for and saved up ahead of time instead of being hurriedly and ineffectively collected when Paul visited them. It was to be properly handled by messengers approved by the Corinthians themselves (v.3)—i.e., those who, bearing letters of recommendation to the church at Jerusalem, carried the gift. Paul makes provision for approved messengers to avoid any suspicion of wrongdoing in connection with the funds (cf. 2 Cor 8:16–21).

In v.4 Paul does not explain why he is going to Jerusalem, but he probably is thinking that the pressure of missionary business to be conducted there (cf. Acts 21:17–19) might compel him to do so. Or, he may be thinking that it would be best for him to be in Jerusalem when the gift is delivered. At any rate, he says that if he should go, the approved messengers would go along with him.

Notes

---

2 Μίαν σαββάτου (*mian sabbatou*), literally "the first day of the sabbath," means first day from (i.e., after) the sabbath. The genitive *sabbatou* is ablatival in function here.

B. *Personal Requests*

16:5–18

[5]After I go through Macedonia, I will come to you—for I will be going through Macedonia. Perhaps I will stay with you awhile, or even spend the winter, so that you can help me on my journey, wherever I go. [7]I do not want to see you now and make only a passing visit; I hope to spend some time with you, if the Lord permits. [8]But I will stay on at Ephesus until Pentecost, [9]because a great door for effective work has opened to me, and there are many who oppose me.

[10]If Timothy comes, see to it that he has nothing to fear while he is with you, for he is carrying on the work of the Lord, just as I am. [11]No one, then, should refuse to accept him. Send him on his way in peace so that he may return to me. I am expecting him along with the brothers.

[12]Now about our brother Apollos: I strongly urged him to go to you with the brothers. He was quite unwilling to go now, but he will go when he has the opportunity.

[13]Be on your guard; stand firm in the faith; be men of courage; be strong. [14]Do everything in love.

> [15]You know that the household of Stephanas were the first converts in Achaia, and they have devoted themselves to the service of the saints. I urge you brothers, [16]to submit to such as these and to everyone who joins in the work and labors at it. [17]I was glad when Stephanas, Fortunatus and Achaicus arrived, because they have supplied what was lacking from you. [18]For they refreshed my spirit and yours also. Such men deserve recognition.

These requests revolve around Paul's travel plans (as he expects to leave Ephesus) and around his friends—Timothy, Apollos and others who have helped the apostle, and the Corinthians.

5–9 The projected journey through Macedonia fits the record of Paul's travel in Acts 19:21 and 20:1, 2, which shows how in following that route he ended by spending three months in Greece—a period evidently involving his stay at Corinth. This intention of spending the winter with them (v.6) apparently relates to the "three months" mentioned in Acts 20:3. "To help him on his journey" must mean endorsing Paul's intended trip and encouraging him perhaps with fresh supplies and equipment. Paul did not seem to want to burden them by asking directly for money (cf. 1 Cor 9:7–12).

His work, Paul feels, is not yet finished at Ephesus (vv.8, 9), because there is a great door (cf. "door" in Acts 14:27; 2 Cor. 2:12; Col 4:3) of opportunity open there for him. The perfect tense *aneogen,* sets forth a completed state: "A great door for effective work *stands open*"—the Lord had opened it and the Lord in his providence was keeping it open. We are not told just who the opponents at Ephesus were, but according to Acts 19:23–27 they must have included the pagan craftsmen engaged in making miniature silver shrines of Artemis. The reference to Pentecost (the Jewish festival held on the fiftieth day after Passover) means that Paul expected to stay at Ephesus till well on into spring, then go during the summer to Macedonia (including Philippi), and finally spend the winter in Corinth. The following spring, by Pentecost time, the apostle was at Jerusalem. Compare Acts 20:6, which says they sailed from Philippi after the Feast of Unleavened Bread. This would mean that they left at least a week after Passover, which began the celebration of the week of the Feast of Unleavened Bread. Thus, Paul would have had time to reach Jerusalem by Pentecost (Acts 20:16), which occurred fifty days after Passover.

10,11 The reference to Timothy's coming is to be connected with Acts 19:22, where Paul sent Timothy (and Erastus) into Macedonia. Therefore, at the time Paul wrote this, Timothy was traveling and was expected to arrive in Corinth (1 Cor 4:17). Because Paul remembered that the Corinthians had acted so harshly toward himself (4:1, 8–13), he was afraid they would treat the timid Timothy (1 Tim 4:12) coldly (v.10).

Paul's young helper, Timothy, had been with him for several years (Acts 16:1–3) and (as the Corinthians must have known) was doing effective work. When Timothy's work for the Lord was finished at Corinth, Paul expected the Corinthians to send him back with all his needs supplied and with their blessing—"Send him on his way in peace," he wrote (v.11). The brothers coming back with Timothy may have included Erastus (Acts 19:22), who was a Corinthian believer (Rom. 16:23).

12 The way Paul brings up the matter of Apollos—"now about" (*peri de,* cf. 7:1; 12:1; 16:1)—suggests that the Corinthians had asked about him and had perhaps suggested that he visit them. The text implies that Apollos was working independently of Paul, for

Paul could only strongly urge him to go. Apollos was apparently with Paul when the Corinthians made their inquiry, but because of the past tense of the verb ("he was quite unwilling to go"), we gather that when Paul actually wrote 1 Corinthians Apollos probably was no longer with him.

13,14 Now Paul includes several apt exhortations, as he generally does at the end of his letters (Rom 16:17–19; 1 Thess 5:12–22, et al.). His reference to "the faith" reminds one of the discussion of the faith in 15:14, 17. *Andrizesthe* (v.13) is a dramatic verb, stressing masculinity. NIV renders it, "Be men of courage," or it might be translated, "Be men and women of courage."

15–18 The reference to "the household of Stephanas" was evidently prompted by the Corinthians lack of respect for them; by personal experience the apostle knew full well that the Corinthians were capable of disrespect. There is no conflict with Acts 17:34 in the statement in v.15 that those "in the household of Stephanas" were the first converts in Achaia, for in Acts 17:34 only individuals like Dionysius, Damaris, and "a number of others" at Athens are mentioned; here, however, a whole household (including the family and slaves; cf. Latin *familia*) is in view. He urges the Corinthians to submit to the household of Stephanas and others like them because they were totally committed to serving God's people. That the service performed (*diakonia*, from which we get our word "deacon") was not an official one is evidenced by the plural subject of the verb: "they have devoted themselves to the service" (v.15). It was the entire family that did this.

Fortunatus and Achaicus—mentioned here for the first time (v.17)—were, along with Stephanas, probably the ones who brought the letter referred to in 1 Corinthians 7:1 to the apostle. That this delegation had "supplied what was lacking" may be taken to mean that their coming had encouraged Paul by showing him that the Corinthians were at least willing to ask his advice. So they "refreshed his spirit" and the spirit of the Corinthians also (v.18) in that they were willing to go to Paul. Or perhaps Paul means that the Corinthians will be refreshed when the three men get back home and tell of their visit to him.

Notes

7 The ἐάν (*ean*) subjunctive condition here, "If the Lord should permit," emphasizes Paul's complete dependence on God's will for his life. The apostle's plan for a future stay with the Corinthians is completely in the Lord's hands.

10 The ἐάν (*ean*) subjunctive condition of possibility does not deny that Timothy would come, for Paul had sent him (4:17). Timothy is on the way, but when or if he actually gets there is in God's providence.

14 The third person present imperative γινέσθω (*ginesthō*) is important here in contrast to the second person imperatives in v.13. It is as if Paul is writing to the Christian community as a whole, saying that their society should be seen to be permeated with love: "Let all you do continue to be done in love."

18 The verb ἐπιγνώσκετε (*epignōskete*, with its prefexed preposition ἐπί [*epi*], indicating thoroughness, as in 1 Cor 13:12 and Luke 1:4: "know through and through") is here (and possibly also in Matt 17:12) used in a distinctive sense of "acknowledge," "give recognition to." It should be noted, however, that in some contexts the preposition prefixed to this verb carries no emphasis and the verb is equivalent in meaning to the simple γινώσκω (*ginōskō*, "know"), as in Acts 27:39.

C. *Final Greetings*

16:19–24

19The churches in the province of Asia send you greetings. Aquila and Priscilla greet you warmly in the Lord, and so does the church that meets at their house.
20All the brothers here send you greetings. Greet one another with a holy kiss.
21I, Paul, write this greeting in my own hand.
22If anyone does not love the Lord—a curse be on him. Come, O Lord!
23The grace of the Lord Jesus be with you.
24My love to all of you in Christ Jesus.

Characteristically Paul concludes with a series of final greetings.

19,20 First, he wants the Corinthians to know that the churches of Asia are interested in them and send greetings. The term "Asia" is used by Paul for the Roman province of Asia located in what is now western Turkey. By "churches" Paul may be implying the existence of more than one church group in Ephesus and the existence of other churches in the area, such as at Colossae, Laodicea, and Hierapolis (Col. 4:13–16; also Rev 2, 3). The Word of the Lord had spread all over the province (Acts 19:10). It was natural for Aquila and Priscilla (Greek: "Prisca") to send greetings, since they had been of such help in founding the Corinthian church (Acts 18:2). They had left Corinth with Paul (Acts 18:18) and evidently were with him at Ephesus. While they were there, a church met in their house, which was also true at Rome (v.19; cf. Rom 16:3–5). To greet one "in the Lord" was to greet him as a professed believer. The holy kiss, mentioned also in Romans 16:16; 2 Corinthians 13:12; and 1 Thessalonians 5:26, was apparently a public practice among early believers to show their Christian affection and unity in the faith. The kiss of respect and friendship was customary in the ancient East. When the Corinthians receive this letter and read it in church, Paul encourages them to give one another this kiss of affection as a pledge of their spirit of unity and forgiveness. Such a greeting may have been practiced in the synagogue by first-century A.D. Jews—a practice in which men would have kissed men and women would have kissed women. (Cf. Archibald Robertson and Alfred Plummer, "The First Epistle of St. Paul to the Corinthians" in ICC [New York: Charles Scribner's Sons, 1916], p. 399.) If this custom was taken over by the early Christian church (which would be expected, since the church was at first composed basically of Christian Jews), it is unlikely that in the worship services the church would have practiced kissing between the sexes. Later, Tertullian seems to indicate that such kissing could be mixed (Ad Uxor II.4), but, in contrast, the Apostolic Constitutions (II.57.12) and the Clementine Liturgy, in instructions for Christian worship (cf. also Justine Martyr's Apology I.65) give the injunction that laymen should kiss laymen and the women should kiss women. (See H.L. Goudge, "The First Epistle to the Corinthians," in the *Westminster Commentaries*, 4th ed. [London: Methuen, 1915], p. 171.)

21–24 Paul is now ready to take the pen to append a greeting and sign the letter, as was his practice (Col 4:18; Philem 19). This was a mark of the letter's authenticity (2 Thess 3:17). Up to this point he had dictated the letter to an amanuensis (secretary).

Then, in view of the problems existing at Corinth, Paul felt the need of adding a strong warning: "a curse be on him" (v.22). A curse (Gr. *anathema*; cf. 12:3; Rom 9:3; Gal 1:8) meant that the person involved was to be delivered over or "devoted to the divine displeasure"; he was under the wrath and curse of God (cf. John 3:36).

Paul's use of this curse is not at variance with Jesus' words in Matthew 5:34, because there Jesus qualifies what he means, by saying in effect: "Do not take oaths on the basis of any of God's created things—the heavens, the earth, or Jerusalem." But here Paul is bringing God himself to witness and is saying he who does not love and obey God is under God's wrath. Having spoken so strongly, Paul then turns to the future hope and cries out, "Marana tha"—Aramaic words that came to be used in the early church (Grosheide) and that can best be translated "Our Lord, Come." This is better than translating it as Chrysostom does: "The Lord has come" (cf. Craig, in loc.).

Paul ends with his usual shorter benediction (Gal 6:18; Eph 6:24; Phil 4:23, et al.; cf. 2 Cor 13:14 for its enlarged trinitarian form). In concluding with an expression of his own love for all the believers (v.24), Paul wants the whole Corinthian church to know that, in spite of the stern way in which he has had to rebuke them, he really loves them.

Notes

19 Πολλά (*polla*, "many") is used here adverbially to intensify the verb "greet." So the meaning is "greet warmly."

20 Φίλημα (*philema*, "kiss") is related in word formation to φιλέω (*phileo*, "love," "regard with affection"). So the meaning could be "show affection outwardly, especially kiss."

22 The εἴ (*ei*) condition with the indicative is assumed to be true: "If in fact someone does not love the Lord." The use here of the verb φιλέω (*phileō*, "show affection for") helps this idea of the factual condition along. Real Christians would show in the Christian community and in society some outward indications of their affection for and commitment to, the Lord. If some, as seemed to be the case, did not, they were showing by that that they did not belong to the Lord. In this v. Paul did not use the word ἀγαπάω (*agapaō*), which is used in the NT many times more than *phileō* and which frequently expresses the idea "love deeply with purpose and understanding" (cf. John 3:16; 17:23, 24; Eph 5:2). The word *agapaō* would not have brought out so well for Paul an additional emphasis on the necessity of the outward affectionate expression of an inward love for the Lord which he could stress by using *phileō*. True as the above distinction between *phileō* and *agapaō* may frequently be, observe that in some cases there seems to be an overlapping of meaning between the two words (cf. John 3:35 and 5:20; but see Godet's comment, in his *Commentary on the Gospel of John*, 3rd. ed., vol. 2, p. 165).

The Aramaic words Μαρανα θα (*Marana tha*) have been thought to mean (1) "The Lord has come"; (2) "Our Lord is a sign"; (3) "Thou art Lord"; and (4) "Come, O Lord," as in NIV. The last is to be preferred because of the parallel prayer in Gr. in Rev 22:20.

2 CORINTHIANS

Murray J. Harris

2 CORINTHIANS

Introduction

1. Historical Background
    a. Paul's Ephesian ministry
    b. Events between 1 and 2 Corinthians
2. Unity
    a. 2 Corinthians 2:14–7:4
    b. 2 Corinthians 6:14–7:1
    c. 2 Corinthians 8–9
    d. 2 Corinthians 10–13
3. Authorship
4. Date
5. Place of Composition
6. Occasion and Purpose
7. Special Problems
    a. The "painful (or intermediate) visit"
        1) Its historicity
        2) Its time
        3) Its occasion, purpose, and outcome
    b. The "severe letter"
        1) Its purpose
        2) Its effect
        3) Its identification
    c. The collection for the poor at Jerusalem
        1) The contributors
        2) The recipients
        3) Its significance for Paul
        4) Its acceptance
    d. Paul's opponents at Corinth
        1) Their identity
        2) Their relation to Jerusalem
        3) Their teaching
8. Theological Values
9. Structure and Themes
    a. Structure
    b. Themes
10. Bibliography
11. Outline

1. Historical Background[1]

a. *Paul's Ephesian ministry*

There is probably no part of Paul's life more difficult to reconstruct accurately than the period of thirty or so months he spent in and around Ephesus (perhaps from the fall of A.D. 53 to the spring of A.D. 56). It was a stormy period, particularly toward its close. There were plentiful evangelistic opportunities (Acts 19:8–10; 20:20, 21, 31; 1 Cor 16:9) and many healings and conversions (Acts 19:11, 18–20). There was also widespread opposition owing to Paul's conspicuous success (Acts 19:9, 13–16; 1 Cor 4:9–13; 15:30–32; 2 Cor 4:8, 9; 6:4, 5, 8–10). Whether or not the Demetrius riot (Acts 19:23–41) actually precipitated his withdrawal from Ephesus, it must have climaxed the hostility directed against him by the devotees of Artemis, not to speak of the Jewish opposition he encountered in the city (Acts 20:19).

b. *Events between 1 and 2 Corinthians*

A chronological list of the events that took place between the writing of the two Corinthian Epistles will be helpful. Many of the details will be more fully discussed in the commentary or below under "Special problems" (7.). No such reconstruction of events, however, would command universal agreement.

1. After they received 1 Corinthians, the Christians at Corinth probably rectified most of the practical abuses for which Paul had censured them in his letter. For example, he says nothing further in 2 Corinthians about abuse of the Lord's Supper (1 Cor 11:17–34) or about litigation among Christians (1 Cor 6:1–8).
2. In spite of this and because of the arrival of Judaizing intruders from Palestine (2 Cor 11:4, 22), conditions in the church at Corinth deteriorated, necessitating Paul's "painful visit" (Ephesus–Corinth–Ephesus; see 7.a. below) (see 2 Cor 2:1; 12:14, 21; 13:1, 2).
3. At some time after this visit, Paul (or his representative) was openly insulted at Corinth by a spokesman of the anti-Pauline clique (2 Cor 2:5–8, 10; 7:12).
4. Titus was sent from Ephesus to Corinth with the "severe letter" (see 7.b. below), in which Paul called for the punishment of the wrongdoer (2 Cor 2:3, 4, 6, 9; 7:8, 12). In addition, Paul instructed Titus to organize the collection for the saints at Jerusalem (2 Cor 8:6a), which had gone by default since the Palestinian interlopers had arrived and had begun to derive their support from the church (cf. 2 Cor 11:7–12, 20; 12:14). Titus was to meet Paul in Troas, or, failing that, in Macedonia (= Philippi ?) (2 Cor 2:12, 13; 7:5, 6).
5. Paul left Ephesus shortly after the Demetrius riot (Acts 19:23–20:1), began evangelism in Troas (or the Troad) (2 Cor 2:12, 13), and then suffered his "affliction in Asia" (2 Cor 1:8–11).
6. Paul crossed to Macedonia (2 Cor 2:13; 7:5) and engaged in pastoral activity (Acts 20:1, 2) while organizing the collection in the Macedonian churches (2 Cor 8:1–4; 9:2).
7. Titus arrived in Macedonia with his welcome report of the Corinthians' responsiveness to the "severe letter" (2 Cor 7:5–16).

---

[1]For information about the city of Corinth and Paul's founding of the church there, see the Introduction to 1 Corinthians.

8. Paul wrote 2 Corinthians 1–9 during further pastoral work in Macedonia and/or during poineer evangelism along the Egnatian Road and probably in Illyricum (Rom 15:19–21).

9. On returning to Macedonia and hearing of fresh problems at Corinth, Paul wrote 2 Corinthians 10–13 and sent the whole letter to Corinth.

10. Paul spent three months in Greece (= primarily Corinth) (Acts 20:2, 3), during which time he wrote Romans.

2. Unity

In any consideration of the integrity of 2 Corinthians, four problem areas call for discussion.

a. *2 Corinthians 2:14–7:4*

Some scholars (e.g., W. Schmithals, G. Bornkamm, W. Marxsen) find in these chapters (without 6:14–7:1) a separate letter Paul wrote to Corinth before his "severe letter" (2 Cor 10–13). Now it is true that 7:5 naturally follows 2:13 in that it resumes the narrative of Paul's movements after leaving Troas. But it is not necessary to conclude that what intervenes forms a distinct letter. Indeed, 7:5 ("For when we came into Macedonia . . .") repeats what was said in 2:13 ("I . . . went on to Macedonia"), as though Paul recognized that he had digressed. And certain terms used in 7:4 (*paraklēsis,* "comfort"; *chara,* "joy"; *thlipsis,* "affliction") reappear in comparable forms in 7:5–7.

b. *2 Corinthians 6:14–7:1*

Within "the great digression" (2:14–7:4) there is found this pericope of six verses whose authenticity has been questioned on several grounds: (1) The passage forms a self-contained unit and lacks any specific references to the Corinthian situation. (2) It seems to interrupt the flow of thought from 6:13 to 7:2. (3) It contains six NT *hapax legomena* (words that occur only once in the specified text; i.e., here, the entire NT) and the allegedly un-Pauline expression "everything that contaminates body and spirit" (7:1, NIV). (4) It is said to betray a pharisaic exclusivism inappropriate to the apostle of liberty. (5) It contains striking affinities with the theology of the Qumran sect.

To accommodate these data, some have suggested that the passage is a non-Pauline interpolation (J.A. Fitzmyer, D. Georgi, J. Gnilka) or even an anti-Pauline fragment reflecting a viewpoint similar to that of Paul's Galatian opponents (H.D. Betz). Others believe it is Pauline, but an interpolation, perhaps a fragment of the "previous letter" (1 Cor 5:9) misplaced within the Corinthian correspondence (J.C. Hurd) or a fragment fortuitously inserted at this point in 2 Corinthians (R.P.C. Hanson). K.G. Kuhn suggests that Paul has remodeled an Essene text in a Christian mold.

All these proposals seem less convincing than the suggestion that Paul may be quoting an existing ethical homily of his own composition or simply digressing in typically Pauline fashion, possibly after a dictation pause at 6:13. At least, "make room for us in your hearts" in 7:2 seems to be intentionally resumptive of "open wide your hearts" in 6:13. Whether a Pauline quotation or a brief digression, these six verses may point to the reason for that element of uneasiness and embarrassed restraint (2 Cor 6:12, 13; 7:2) that marred the Corinthians' reconciliation with Paul, viz., an unwillingness to renounce all compromise with pagan idolatry.

c. *2 Corinthians 8–9*

Two hundred years ago J.S. Semler proposed that 2 Corinthians 9 was a separate epistle addressed to Christian communities in Achaia other than Corinth. In this way Semler sought to account for the apparent repetition of material in the two chapters; the seemingly independent self-contained character of each chapter; the introductory statement in 9:1, which seems to imply no earlier discussion; and Paul's appeal to the Macedonian example in 8:1–7 and to the Corinthian example in 9:1–5.

A few scholars (e.g., E. Dinkler, J. Héring, H.D. Wendland, K.F. Nickle) still argue for the separation of these two chapters, but the majority of commentators rightly claim that they belong together to the same letter as 2 Corinthians 1–7. The marked change of tone between chapters 7 and 8 is explicable by Paul's transition from relieved and almost excessive exuberance over the recent past to somewhat embarrassed and diffident admonition concerning the immediate future. Other alleged problems will be discussed during the exegesis of the text.

d. *2 Corinthians 10–13*

The relationship between 2 Corinthians 10–13 and 2 Corinthians 1–9 is the principal critical problem in this Epistle. Three major positions have been taken, the first two being called "the four-chapter hypothesis": (1) 2 Corinthians 10–13 was written earlier than 2 Corinthians 1–9 and forms part of the "severe letter"; (2) 2 Corinthians 10–13 was penned later than 2 Corinthians 1–9 and forms a separate fifth letter Paul wrote to Corinth (thus "previous letter" [1 Cor 5:9], 1 Corinthians "severe letter," 2 Cor 1–9; 2 Cor 10–13); and (3) 2 Corinthians is a unity; the first nine chapters and the last four belong to the same period of Paul's ministry.

Views (1) and (2) share a common foundation, though each builds a different super structure on it. They have in common the conviction that the change of tone a 2 Corinthians 10:1, which is unannounced, unexpected, pronounced, and sustained, supports the dissection of the Epistle. Patent relief, unbridled joy, and gentle appeal are succeeded, it is said, by scathing remonstrance, biting irony, and impetuous self-defense. Such a sudden change to what is almost unalleviated remonstrance would merely have served (it is thought) to renew Paul's earlier suspense concerning the Corinthians' response to harsh words and to jeopardize both his cordial relations with the Corinthians and the progress of the collection. Again, proponents of both these views observe that 2 Corinthians 1–9 gives no intimation of an imminent visit such as that promised or threatened in 2 Corinthians 12:14; 13:1.

1. *2 Corinthians 10–13 earlier than 2 Corinthians 1–9.* On this first view, the superstructure consists of two basic claims. First, several passages in 2 Corinthians 1–9, it is alleged, contain intentional allusions to previous statements in 2 Corinthians 10–13. For example, 2 Corinthians 7:16 ("I . . . have complete confidence in you") is said to allude to 2 Corinthians 10:1 ("I have confidence against you"); 2:3 to 13:10; 1:23 to 13:2; 2:9 to 10:6; 1:15 and 8:22 to 10:2; 4:2 to 12:16; 7:2 to 12:17; 1:12 to 11:10. But C.H. Buck has argued that 2 Corinthians 1:23; 2:3; 2:9 might just as appropriately allude to 1 Corinthians 4:18, 19; 4:21; 4:14 respectively. And R. Batey believes that in several passages in 2 Corinthians 10–13 Paul is intentionally retracting or modifying earlier expressions of confidence (cf. 2 Cor 10:8; 11:16–18, 30 with 2 Cor 1:12; 7:4, 16; and 2 Cor 10:1, 2 with 2 Cor 1:15; 7:16). The second claim relates to the phrase "the regions beyond you" in 2 Corinthians 10:16, that refers to Italy and Spain (see Rom 15:22–32). This expression is said to be geographically accurate only if Paul is writing from Ephesus

—the city where the "severe letter" was composed! But against this we may observe that, should a third point of reference in addition to Corinth and Italy-Spain actually be required by the phrase "the regions beyond you," Paul's missionary work began in Damascus—which would give an even straighter geographical line.

This version of "the four-chapter hypothesis" was first set forth systematically by A. Hausrath in 1870. It is probably still the dominant view, claiming such proponents as P.W. Schmiedel (1892), J.H. Kennedy (1897, the classic defense), A. Plummer (1903), K. Lake (1911), M. Goguel (1926), R.H. Strachan (1935), and R.P.C. Hanson (1954).

2. *2 Corinthians 10–13 later than 2 Corinthians 1–9.* This rival form of "the four-chapter hypothesis" was first proposed in a modified form by J.S. Semler in 1776, and as the twentieth century proceeds, it seems to be gaining increasing recognition among scholars as a viable alternative to Hausrath's theory. Its supporters in this century include C. Bruston (1917), H. Windisch (1924, the classic defense), L.P. Pherigo (1949), C.H. Buck (1950), J. Munck (1954), E. Osty (1959), C.K. Barrett (1964), R. Batey (1965), and F.F. Bruce (1968).

To continue the metaphor used above, the framework of this superstructure consists of two major arguments. First, 2 Corinthians 1–9 appears to bear testimony to a less critical stage of anti-Paulinism than that reflected in 2 Corinthians 10–13, and the opposition to Paul portrayed in 2 Corinthians 1–9 is more naturally interpreted as a foreshadowing rather than as the aftermath of the anti-Paulinism that led to 2 Corinthians 10–13. Second, what may be an identical visit of Titus to Corinth is mentioned in 2 Corinthians 8:17, 18, 22 as a future event but in 2 Corinthians 12:18 as a past event.

3. *2 Corinthians a unity.* The defenders of the integrity of 2 Corinthians have not been slow in highlighting the difficulties of the two hypotheses discussed above. Concerning Hausrath's theory they ask, Why is 2 Corinthians 10–13 silent about Paul's demand for the punishment of the offender (cf. 2 Cor 2:5, 6; 7:12) when this is the one incontestable feature of the "severe letter"? Would Paul have described the irony and invective of 2 Corinthians 10–13 as stemming from "great distress and anguish of heart" and as written "with many tears" (2 Cor 2:4)? Why does 2 Corinthians 10–13 promise an imminent visit (12:14; 13:1) when the "severe letter" replaced a painful visit (2 Cor 1:23; 2:1)? Why does 2 Corinthians 1–9 not describe the church's reaction to the invective of 2 Corinthians 10–13? And why does 2 Corinthians 1–9 betray no knowledge of a previous encounter between Paul and the group of intruders at Corinth, but refer only to a single erring member of the church? How could Paul have boasted to Titus about the Corinthians (2 Cor 7:14) if he had just composed 2 Corinthians 10–13?

Semler's theory raises the following questions, among others: What accounts for the relapse of the Corinthians into a state worse than that they had recently repented of? Why does 2 Corinthians 10–13 give no indication of Paul's having received news of the deterioration of conditions at Corinth?

Regarding both theories, some ask, What historical circumstances gave rise to the combination of two originally separate letters? How may the unambiguous textual tradition witnessing to the integrity of the Epistle be explained?

In further defense of the unity of 2 Corinthians, scholars have proposed numerous explanations of the sudden change of tone at 2 Corinthians 10:1. (See the commentary at the beginning of chapter 10.) Those who have defended the unity of the Epistle include J.H. Bernard (1903), H. Lietzmann (1909), A. Menzies (1912), H.L. Goudge (1927), E.B. Allo (1936, the classic defense), R.V.G. Tasker (1945), D. Guthrie (1961), P.E. Hughes (1961), W.G. Kümmel (1963), A.M.G. Stephenson (1964), and W.H. Bates (1965).

The choice seems to lie between views 2 and 3. In this commentary the unity of 2 Corinthians is tentatively assumed.

3. Authorship

Unlike some other Pauline Epistles, 2 Corinthians has rarely been called into question with regard to its authenticity. Even the founder of the so-called "Tübingen school," F.C. Baur, acknowledged it as genuinely Pauline, along with 1 Corinthians, Galatians, and Romans. As far as internal evidence is concerned, the author twice identifies himself as Paul (2 Cor 1:1; 10:1). A pious imitator would be unlikely to portray Paul as an apostle in danger of losing his authority at Corinth or an apostle struggling to preserve the Corinthians from apostasy.

With regard to the external evidence, the Epistle was unknown to Clement of Rome (c. A.D. 96), but is quoted by Polycarp (c. A.D. 105), Irenaeus (c. A.D. 185), Clement of Alexandria (c. A.D. 210), and Tertullian (c. A.D. 210). Also it is listed in Marcion's *Apostolicon* (c. A.D. 140) and in the Muratorian canon (late second century A.D.).

4. Date

By a brief examination of the data, we may reach a tentative conclusion regarding this complex question.

1. 1 Corinthians was probably written and sent in the spring, perhaps shortly before Passover. There may be allusions to an imminent paschal celebration in 1 Corinthians 5:7, 8 and to the presentation of the firstfruits in 1 Corinthians 15:20. And in 1 Corinthians 16:8 Paul indicates his intention to "stay on at Ephesus until Pentecost." This Pentecost must have been at least one or two months away, to allow time for Paul to take advantage of the opportunities for evangelism (1 Cor 16:9).

2. 2 Corinthians was probably written in the fall (autumn). Acts 20:6 relates that Paul left Philippi for Jerusalem in the spring ("after the Feast of Unleavened Bread"). Previously, three winter months had been spent in Corinth (Acts 20:3) where Paul arrived from Macedonia. Intimations of a forthcoming visit to Corinth found in 2 Corinthians 12:14; 13:1 suggest the Epistle was written shortly before that winter.

3. Possibly as much as eighteen or more months intervened between the writing of the two Epistles. Of course, if they were written in the spring and the fall, they could be dated in the same year, but the "winter" mentioned in 1 Corinthians 16:6 need not correspond to the winter alluded to in Acts 20:3, since Paul is simply stating tentative plans that were in fact superseded by those recorded in 2 Corinthians 1:15, 16. Nor does the phrase "last year" in 2 Corinthians 8:10; 9:2 necessarily point to a six-month interval. Which calendar Paul was using is uncertain. Thus the new year may have arrived on January 1 (Roman year), in the spring (Jewish ecclesiastical year), in midsummer (Athenian Olympiads), or in the fall (Jewish civil and Macedonian year). There are two positive pointers to a possible eighteen-month interval. In the first place, adequate time must be allowed for Paul to engage in pioneer evangelism along the Egnatian Way and in Illyricum of which he speaks in Romans 15:19. All agree that if Paul did evangelize the Roman province of Illyricum ("all the way around to Illyricum" may be inclusive or exclusive), it must have occurred between his Ephesian residence (Acts 19) and his arrival in Greece (Acts 20:2). Again, it is difficult, though not impossible, to fit into a

six-month period all the travel between Ephesus and Corinth and all the events at Corinth that took place between the writing of 1 Corinthians and 2 Corinthians (see 1.b. above).

4. The suggestion may therefore be made that 1 Corinthians was sent in the spring of A.D. 55 (Passover probably fell on April 2 and Pentecost on May 22 that year—so F.J. Badcock), while the sending of 2 Corinthians (assuming its unity) may be placed in the fall of A.D. 56. On the other hand, if 2 Corinthians 10–13 belongs to a later period than 2 Corinthians 1–9 (see 2.d.2 above), these last four chapters will date from the fall of A.D. 56, while the first nine chapters may have been sent at any time between the fall of A.D. 55 and early fall A.D. 56.

5. A tentative chronology of the major events occurring between 1 and 2 Corinthians (see 1.b. above) may now be suggested.

1 Corinthians	Spring A.D. 55
Painful visit	Summer or Fall 55
Severe letter	Spring 56
Paul leaves Ephesus	Spring 56
Paul in Macedonia	Summer 56
Titus arrives in Macedonia	Summer 56
2 Corinthians	Fall 56

5. Place of Composition

Several references within 2 Corinthians suggest that Paul was in the province of Macedonia when writing (see 7:5; 8:1; 9:2–4). Of special significance is the present tense (*kauchōmai*) in 9:2, "I have been boasting about it [viz., your eagerness to help] to the Macedonians" (NIV).

This is confirmed by those MSS (e.g., B[c] K L P) that note in the subscription to the Epistle that it was written "from Philippi." Also, in 2 Corinthians 11:9 "Macedonia" means Philippi (see Phil 4:15). But of course it is not impossible that Paul was at Thessalonica or Berea (also Macedonian cities), since 2 Corinthians 8:1 and 9:2 speak of the churches and people of Macedonia and not simply of the Philippians.

6. Occasion and Purpose

The outline of events given above (1.b.) suggests that the circumstances prompting Paul to send 2 Corinthians were twofold: the arrival of his pastoral assistant Titus, who brought welcome news of the favorable response of the majority of the Corinthians to the "severe letter" (see 2 Cor 7:6–16), and the arrival of fresh, disturbing news concerning Corinth. An interval between the arrival of Titus and the sending of 2 Corinthians seems indicated by 2 Corinthians 7:8 (see the commentary).

Paul had several overriding purposes in writing. He wished (1) to express his great relief and delight at the Corinthians' positive response to his "severe letter" that had been delivered and reinforced by Titus (2 Cor 2:6, 9, 12–14; 7:5–16); (2) to exhort the Corinthians to complete their promised collection for the saints at Jerusalem before his arrival on the next visit (2 Cor 8:6, 7, 10, 11; 9:3–5); (3) to prepare them for his forthcoming visit by having them engage in self-examination and self-judgment (12:14; 13:1, 5,

11), so that they could discover the proper criteria for distinguishing between rival apostles (chapters 10 to 13); and so that Paul could be spared the pain of having to exercise discipline (2 Cor 10:2, 5, 6, 11; 11:3; 12:19–21; 13:10).

There were, of course, other subsidiary aims, such as his desire to inform them of the intensity of his trouble in Asia and solicit their prayer for future deliverance (1:8–11), to explain his changes of itinerary (1:12–2:4), to encourage the reaffirmation of their love for the penitent wrongdoer (2:5–11), to insist on their separation from all idolatrous associations (6:14–7:1), and to describe the true nature and high calling of the Christian ministry (2:14–7:4).

Was 2 Corinthians successful where 1 Corinthians had been only partially so? Apparently it was, because Paul made the promised visit (Acts 20:2, 3) and during this three-month stay in "Greece" (primarily Corinth, in the winter of A.D. 56–57) he wrote or completed his letter to the Romans, which gives no hint of trouble at Corinth. Also Romans 15:26 shows that the Corinthians did complete their collection for their fellow-believers at Jerusalem.

On the other hand, when Clement of Rome wrote to the church at Corinth in A.D. 96 he had to rebuke the same internal strife and rebellion against authority that had plagued the church forty years earlier.

7. Special Problems

a. *The "painful (or intermediate) visit"*

1) *Its historicity*

Although Luke makes no reference to the visit in Acts, there are several passages in 2 Corinthians showing that Paul had already visited Corinth twice, the second visit being "painful." First, 2 Corinthians 12:14 and 13:1, 2 refer to two prior actual visits. Second, 2 Corinthians 2:1 and 12:21 indicate that one of the two earlier visits was painful (*en lypē*, 2 Cor 2:1). It is inconceivable that Paul would describe his founding visit as "painful," in spite of the opposition he encountered at that time (Acts 18:6, 9, 10, 12–17).

2) *Its time*

Some scholars have argued that the visit occurred either before or after the "previous letter" (1 Cor 5:9) was written, i.e., before 1 Corinthians. But the silence of 1 Corinthians about a painful visit damages this hypothesis. Only one previous visit is presupposed in 1 Corinthians (2:1–5; 3:1–3, 6, 10; 11:2, 23), though a second visit is announced (1 Cor 4:18, 19, 21; 11:34; 16:2, 3, 5–7). And why would painful memories be revived in 2 Corinthians after being ignored or forgotten in 1 Corinthians?

The silence of 1 Corinthians and the allusions in 2 Corinthians concerning this distressing visit point to the same conclusion—the visit took place between 1 and 2 Corinthians. More precisely, it occurred after 1 Corinthians and before the "severe letter," because in writing 2 Corinthians Paul is dependent on Titus for his information about the outcome of the "severe letter"; he had not himself visited the church after the sending of the "severe letter."

3) *Its occasion, purpose, and outcome*

At some stage after the receipt of 1 Corinthians at Corinth, conditions within the church there deteriorated. Possibly there was a cleavage over the implementing of Paul's injunction of 1 Corinthians 5:2, 5, 13 about the incestuous man. Perhaps an ultra-loyal group of Paulinists (cf. 1 Cor 1:12; 2 Cor 2:6, 7) confronted the influential anti-Pauline clique of intruders from Palestine and their Corinthian adherents in a bid for control of the uncommitted and vacillating majority who were acquiescing in the *status quo* and were unwilling to follow either minority in making an issue of a matter of private morals. In any case, Paul received adverse news, perhaps from Timothy, that induced him to hurry to Corinth to reinforce the effect of 1 Corinthians and prevent any further undermining of his authority at Corinth through the activities of the Judaizing pseudo-apostles.

Little is known about what happened during the visit. Certainly Paul would have explained the reasons for the change in his travel plans (see the commentary on 1:15–17), for the Corinthians were expecting him to arrive from Macedonia (cf. 1 Cor 16:5, 6), not from Ephesus. Apparently he rebuked those guilty of immorality ("those who sinned earlier," 2 Cor 12:21; 13:2), but refrained from exercising summary discipline, choosing rather to issue a warning: "If I come again, I will not spare you" (cf. 2 Cor 13:2). Also he seems to have been humiliated by the Corinthians' failure to champion his cause against the false apostles (cf. 2 Cor 12:21). It is unlikely that the visit became "painful" because Paul was affronted by an intruder or a native Corinthian (cf. 2 Cor 2:5–11; 7:12). He was not a man who would retreat before an enemy only to resort to a letter and the intervention of his delegate Titus to gain what he himself had failed to achieve.

The sequel of this brief visit was that Paul or his representative was personally insulted by some individual at Corinth in an open act of defiance by which all the Corinthians were to some extent pained—if not at the actual time, at least later on (2 Cor 2:5–11; 7:12). So Paul sent Titus to Corinth after considerable persuasion (2 Cor 7:14) as his personal envoy to deliver the "severe letter" and organize the collection (2 Cor 8:6a).

b. *The "severe letter"*

"I wrote you out of great distress and anguish of heart and with many tears, not to grieve you but to let you know the depth of my love for you" (2 Cor 2:4). Such is Paul's own description of what has come to be known as the "severe letter," the "sorrowful letter," or the "letter of tears." (The preceding account of the "painful visit" and its aftermath [7.a.] includes a sketch of the circumstances that led to Paul's writing this letter.)

1) *Its purpose*

Clearly the general aim of the "severe letter" was to arouse the church to discipline "the one who did the wrong" (2 Cor 2:6, 9; 7:12). But 2 Corinthians contains four additional statements of Paul's purpose in writing: (1) to spare the Corinthians and himself another painful visit (1:23–2:4), (2) to demonstrate his affection for the Corinthians (2:4), (3) to put to the test the Corinthians' obedience to apostolic authority (2:9), and (4) to make them aware before God of their genuine concern and affection for him as their spiritual father (7:12; cf. 1 Cor 4:15)—in retrospect, Paul states this last as his principal objective.

2) *Its effect*

It was Titus who related to Paul the outcome of this "sorrowful letter" (2 Cor 7:6–16). The Corinthians as a whole had felt concern, remorse, and even apprehension over their behavior during the "painful visit." They now longed to see Paul again to assure him of their change of attitude. They had been zealous to punish the offender whose scandalous action had now provoked their indignation. Some Corinthians were in danger of being merciless in their punishment; so Paul needed to stay their hand and encourage them to forgive the offender now that he had repented (2 Cor 2:6–8).

When Titus gave his report, Paul's initial reaction was to regret (*metemelomēn*) that he had caused such pain, though that pain had been only temporary (2 Cor 7:8). Upon reflection, however, his opinion had altered: *ou metamelomai,* "I do not regret it" (2 Cor 7:8). The infliction of pain, though unavoidable, had proved remedial; in fact, God had inspired their grief and had prevented the letter from causing them any permanent injury (2 Cor 7:9–11a).

3) *Its identification*

With respect to the identity of the "severe letter," we have three alternatives. It may be identified with (1) 1 Corinthians; (2) a letter, partially preserved in 2 Corinthians 10–13, that preceded 2 Corinthians 1–9; or (3) a letter, no longer extant, written between 1 and 2 Corinthians.

a) *1 Corinthians*

This time-honored identification rests chiefly on the similarity between 1 Corinthians 5 and 2 Corinthians 2:5–11; 7:12. The incestuous man is "the one who did the wrong"; this man's father is "the one who suffered the wrong." After being handed over to Satan (= excommunication?) "so that his sinful nature may be destroyed" (1 Cor 5:5), the wrongdoer repented. In 2 Corinthians 2:7, 8 Paul urges that he be received back into church fellowship.

In spite of the impressive array of scholars who endorse this view, there are several compelling reasons for questioning it. First, 2 Corinthians 2:6, 9 suggests that the "letter of tears" dealt primarily with the wrongdoer and the need for his punishment. This is not true of 1 Corinthians. Second, why would Paul personally offer to forgive a man guilty of incest (2 Cor 2:10)? Third, if these references in the two Corinthian Epistles are to be equated, the incestuous man was not simply living with his *widowed* stepmother, but with his stepmother while his father ("the injured party") was still living. Surely such an offense, more precisely described as adultery (*moicheia*) than as sexual immorality (*porneia,* 1 Cor 5:1), would have scandalized even the Corinthians and impelled them to seek some form of redress for the father, if not punishment for the son. Fourth, 1 Corinthians does not seem to have been written in the place of another painful visit (see 1 Cor 4:18, 19; 11:34; 16:2, 3, 5–7) as is demanded by 2 Corinthians 1:23; 2:1, 3.

b) *A letter embodying 2 Corinthians 10–13*

Many commentators who believe that 2 Corinthians combines two originally separate letters place 2 Corinthians 10–13 before 2 Corinthians 1–9 and affirm that these four chapters form the principal part of the "letter of tears" (A. Hausrath's theory). The difficulties of this proposal have been discussed above (2.d.3).

c) *A lost "intermediate letter"*

Scholars who reject the two identifications of the "sorrowful letter" mentioned above are compelled to assume that the letter is no longer extant. They believe that it was probably an intensely personal letter, quite brief, and addressed to a specific unedifying situation, so that its nonpreservation is not a matter of surprise (cf. the "previous letter" of 1 Cor 5:9, 11).

This is the view adopted in this commentary.

c. *The collection for the poor at Jerusalem*

From A.D. 52 to 57 a considerable proportion of Paul's time and energies was devoted to organizing a collection among his Gentile churches for "the poor among the saints in Jerusalem" (Rom 15:26).

1) *The contributors*

There is general agreement that Acts 20:4 contains a list of the appointed delegates from certain Gentile churches who were Paul's traveling companions on his final visit to Jerusalem when he was delivering the collection. Sopater, Aristarchus, and Secundus represented the Macedonian Christians (see Acts 19:22; 2 Cor 8:1–5; 9:2, 4); Gaius and perhaps Timothy were delegates from Galatia (see Acts 18:23; 1 Cor 16:1); Tychicus and Trophimus traveled on behalf of the churches of Asia (see Acts 20:35). It is not known who represented Achaia, though believers in that province contributed to the offering (see Rom 15:26; 1 Cor 16:1–4; 2 Cor 8–9).

2) *The recipients*

The offering was destined for the Hebrew Christians at Jerusalem, who may have referred to themselves as "the poor" (*hoi ptōchoi,* Rom 15:26; Gal 2:10; = Heb. *hā'eb̲yô-nîm,* cf. Ebionites)—those who were completely dependent on God's provision (cf. Matt 5:3). Several factors account for their continuing poverty: (1) After their conversion to Christianity many Jews in Jerusalem would have been ostracized socially and economically. (2) The "experiment in community sharing" described in Acts 2:44, 45 and 4:32, 34, 35 undoubtedly would have aggravated, though it did not cause, their poverty. (3) Persistent food shortages in Palestine because of overpopulation culminated in the famine of A.D. 46 in the time of Emperor Claudius (Acts 11:27–30). (4) As the mother-church of Christendom, the Jerusalem church was obliged to support a proportionately large number of teachers and probably to provide hospitality for frequent Christian visitors to the holy city. (5) Jews in Palestine were subject to a crippling twofold taxation —Jewish and Roman.

3) *Its significance for Paul*

Some of the many motives that impelled Paul to organize the offering may be mentioned here. First and foremost among them was brotherly love (Rom 12:13; 13:8; Gal 6:10), making the offering a tangible expression of the interdependence of the members of the body of Christ (1 Cor 12:25, 26) that would honor Christ (2 Cor 8:19) and help effect equality of provision (2 Cor 8:13–15). Moreover, it effectively symbolized the unity of Jew and Gentile in Christ (Eph 2:11–22) and may have been designed to win over those Jewish Christians who were still suspicious of Paul's Gentile mission (cf. Acts

11:2, 3). Also, the collection dramatized in material terms the spiritual indebtedness of Gentile believers to the church at Jerusalem (Rom 15:19, 27; cf. 1 Cor 9:11). Again, it marked the culmination of Paul's ministry in the eastern Mediterranean as he planned to turn westward after visiting Rome (Rom 15:24, 28). And finally, it was a visible sign of Paul's fulfillment of a promise (2 Cor 8:19; Gal 2:10) and perhaps a way of partially compensating for his earlier systematic persecution of the Jerusalem saints (Acts 8:3; 9:1; 26:10, 11; 1 Cor 15:9; Gal 1:13; 1 Tim 1:13).

4) *Its acceptance*

In spite of Paul's misgivings about the success of the enterprise (Rom 15:31), the offering was evidently gratefully received on his arrival in Jerusalem. Acts 21:17 suggests this. It is unlikely, however, that the collection accomplished all that Paul had hoped for regarding Jewish-Gentile relations within the Church. For example, Acts contains no record of Paul's receiving help from the Jerusalem church during his imprisonment in Jerusalem and Caesarea.

For an illuminating comparison between Paul's collection and the half-shekel temple tax paid annually by Jews, see K.F. Nickle, *The Collection* (Naperville: Allenson, 1966), pp. 87–93.

At the beginning of chapter 8 (p. 365 below) the progress of the collection at Corinth prior to the writing of 2 Corinthians is briefly summarized. For the outcome of the collection at Corinth, see the commentary at 9:15.

d. *Paul's opponents at Corinth*

Regarding the problem of Paul's opponents at Corinth, two basic questions clamor for solution: (1) their identity, and (2) their relation to the Twelve. Were they Jews or Judaizers or Gnostics? Were they in some sense delegates sent by the Jerusalem church, or were they wandering Hellenistic preachers with no relation to Judea?

In recent years these problems have prompted numerous articles, the more important being by E. Käsemann (1942), G. Friedrich (1963), and C.K. Barrett (1971) and several full-scale studies, including W. Schmithals, *Die Gnosis in Korinth* (1956, 1965[2])[2] (=*Gnosticism in Corinth*, 1971); D. Georgi, *Die Gegner des Paulus im 2. Korintherbrief* (1964); D.W. Oostendorp, *Another Jesus: A Gospel of Jewish-Christian Superiority* (1967).

1) *Their identity*

Although some scholars (e.g., F. Godet and W. Schmithals) have equated Paul's opponents in 2 Corinthians with those in 1 Corinthians, it is necessary to distinguish between certain native Corinthians who fostered the dissension described in 1 Corinthians and certain adversaries from outside Corinth (2 Cor 10:14; 11:4) who had a malevolent influence on the Corinthian believers. The link, if any, between these two groups may be found in the Christ "party" (thus E.B. Allo) or the Peter "party" (thus C.K. Barrett).

That Paul's adversaries were Jews is acknowledged on all hands (cf. 2 Cor 11:22). But were they Judaizers? If a Judaizer is defined as one who insists on circumcision as a prerequisite for salvation (cf. Acts 15:1), they were not Judaizers, for 2 Corinthians lacks

---

[2]The superscript number immediately following the date refers to the edition of the book; i.e., here, the second edition.

any trace of a dispute over circumcision. But if a Judaizer is a person who tries to impose Jewish practices upon Gentiles as conditions either for salvation or for the enjoyment of Christian fellowship, then the opposition to Paul may appropriately be labeled Judaizing. Evidently his opponents did not insist on circumcision, as occurred at Galatia (Gal 6:12, 13), or on calendrical observances, as did the opposition at Colossae (Col 2:16). Perhaps as part of their general strategy to reproduce Jerusalem in Corinth or to claim Corinth for Jerusalem, they sought to impose on the Corinthians the provisions of the codicil of the Apostolic Decree, especially its food regulations (Acts 15:20, 29).[3] This is the suggestion of F.F. Bruce and C.K. Barrett and the view adopted in this commentary.

The fact that in 2 Corinthians Paul is less concerned with wisdom, knowledge, and *charismata* than he was in 1 Corinthians makes it unlikely that his adversaries were simply gnostic, far less Gnostics, who, in any case, would not be likely to carry commendatory letters. Some scholars (notably D. Georgi and G. Friedrich) have therefore proposed that Paul's rivals in 2 Corinthians were Hellenistic-Jewish itinerant preachers who professed to be servants of Christ and *theioi andres* ("divine men"). But again, letters of commendation would hardly be necessary for such wonder-workers whose deeds were their credentials.

2) *Their relation to Jerusalem*

What was the relation between Paul's antagonists at Corinth and the church of Jerusalem, particularly the three "pillars" (Gal 2:9) or the Twelve? Three views are possible. His antagonists might have been (1) an official delegation; (2) a semi-official delegation that left Jerusalem with the cognizance and tacit approval of the Twelve but which misrepresented them; or (3) self-appointed agents from Judea who appealed to the authority of the Twelve, especially Peter, in defense of their Judaizing program. Each position has had its proponents.

In support of the third view, several points may be made. First of all, that these persons were from Palestine may be inferred from the term *Hebraioi* (2 Cor 11:22; cf. Phil 3:5), which refers to Jews of Palestinian descent, especially those whose linguistic and cultural heritage was Palestinian, and perhaps from a claim they may have made to have known Christ personally (cf. 2 Cor 5:16). Moreover, we should probably draw a distinction between the "super-apostles" of 2 Corinthians 11:5; 12:11 and the "false apostles" of 11:13. The former expression may be Paul's ironical description of the exalted view of the Twelve held by the "false apostles" who appealed to them. Paul uses the term "false apostles" (*pseudapostoloi*) to describe the Palestinian intruders who falsely laid claim to apostleship and preached "another gospel" (2 Cor 11:4). Again, some persons from Judea had already invoked the authority of the Twelve without their authorization (Acts 15:24; cf. Gal 2:4), while others (prophets) had left Jerusalem apparently without specific commission (Acts 11:27). Whether or not the "false apostles" carried letters of commendation from Jerusalem is discussed at 3:1. Finally, one clique at Corinth had already set a precedent for appealing to Jerusalem by using the name of Peter (1 Cor 1:12).

We now turn to the message of these Jewish missionaries.

---

[3]There is no evidence in the Corinthian Epistles of Paul's own effort to enforce at Corinth the supplementary addition to the Decree (cf. Acts 15:41; 16:4) or that he regarded it as permanently and universally binding on Christians.

3) *Their teaching*

There can be no doubt that the primary aim of Paul's adversaries was to undermine and so destroy Paul's apostolic authority. What they taught was calculated to bring about Paul's downfall, at least in Corinth, and to establish their own credentials as authentic servants of Christ.

Paul, they alleged, was a double-minded worldling who acted capriciously (2 Cor 1:17, 18; 10:2–4) and lorded it over his converts (1:24; 7:2), so restricting their spiritual development (6:12). He carried no letters of commendation (3:1; 10:13, 14) because he commended himself (4:2, 5; 5:12; 6:4; 10:12, 18; 12:11; cf. 1 Cor 9:1–3; 14:18; 15:10b) as would a madman (5:13; 11:1, 16–19; 12:6, 11) or imposter (6:8). Just as his gospel was obscure (4:3; 6:2, 3), so also the letters he wrote were unintelligible or devious (1:13) and written with the perverse aim of condemning and destroying (7:2, 3; 10:8; 13:10) and causing pain (2:2, 4, 5; 7:8). He was impressive at a distance but weak and contemptible when he deigned to make a personal appearance (10:1, 2, 9–11; 11:6; 13:3, 4, 9). His refusal to accept remuneration from the Corinthians proved that he cared little for them and that he was aware of being a counterfeit apostle, not the mouthpiece of Christ (11:5, 7–11, 15; 12:11–15; 13:3a, 6). Yet he exploited the willingness of a church to support him by having his agents organize a collection, ostensibly for the saints at Jerusalem but in reality for himself (12:16–18). Such were some of the charges made by Paul's calumniators.

They seem to have made many claims about themselves, as may be inferred from Paul's reply (4:5). Proof of their genuine apostolicity could be found, they claimed, in their polished eloquence and erudite knowledge (11:6), their visions and revelations (5:13; 12:1, 7), their healing miracles (12:12), their possession of commendatory letters (3:1), their willingness to accept remuneration (11:12; cf. 1 Cor 9:5–7, 11, 12), their pure Palestinian origin (11:22), their being disciples of Jesus (5:16; 10:7), their high estimate of Moses (3:7–16) and Abraham (11:22), and their preaching of the true gospel of Jesus (11:4). Little wonder that the impressionable Corinthians were swayed by the vaunted self-sufficiency (3:5) of these rival claimants to apostleship!

8. Theological Values

Traditionally, Paul's two letters to Timothy and one to Titus are called "the Pastorals." But 2 Corinthians has a strong claim to be recognized as the Pastoral Epistle *par excellence,* because it contains not "pure" but "applied" *pastoralia.* Paul the pastor has unconsciously penned a profound, though brief, autobiography. In this Epistle we can see beautiful examples of the tenderness of a spiritual shepherd sensitive to the needs of his flock (1:24; 2:6, 7; 6:1; 10:2; 13:5, 10) and also the pleading of a spiritual father jealous of his children's affection, purity, and unity (6:11–13; 11:2, 3; 13:11). To investigate Paul's pastoral techniques evident in both Corinthian Epistles is a rewarding study.

The Epistle also contains the classic discussions of the theology of Christian suffering (1:3–11; 4:7–18; 6:3–10; 12:1–10), the role of a minister of the new covenant (2:14–17; 4:1–5; 5:16–21; 11:28, 29; 12:14, 15), the relation between the old and new covenants (3:7–18), the theology of death and resurrection (4:7–5:10), and the principles and practice of Christian stewardship (2 Cor 8–9).

9. Structure and Themes

a. *Structure*

Second Corinthians falls into three clearly discernible sections: (1) chapters 1 to 7, which contain Paul's explanation of his conduct and apostolic ministry, are primarily apologetic; (2) chapters 8 and 9, which deal with the collection for the saints at Jerusalem, are hortatory; and (3) chapters 10 to 13, which form Paul's vindication of his apostolic authority, are polemical.

b. *Themes*

The distinctive tone of 2 Corinthians 1–7 (or 1–9) may be summed up in the phrase *chairein dei* ("I must rejoice"; see 2:3; 6:10; 7:4, 7, 9, 13, 16) while the expression *paraklēsis en thlipsei* ("comfort in the midst of affliction"; see 1:3–7; 7:4, 7, 13) epitomizes its major theme. On the other hand, *kauchasthai dei* (12:1, "I must boast") sums up the spirit of 2 Corinthians 10–13, and *dynamis en astheneia* (12:9, "strength in the midst of weakness") reveals its chief emphasis.

It is in establishing the principal themes of 2 Corinthians, rather than in illustrating its integrity or partition, that linguistic arguments are most potent. In 2 Corinthians 1–9 *paraklēsis* (as "comfort") occurs nine times and its verbal form (*parakaleō*, "comfort") eight times; *thlipsis* ("affliction") is found nine times and *thlibō* ("afflict") three times; *chara* ("joy") occurs twice and *chairō* ("rejoice") four times with reference to the joy of Paul or Titus at the Corinthian reconciliation. However, none of these words (except for two uses of *chairō* in 13:9, 11) is found in 2 Corinthians 10–13. Again, while *astheneia* ("weakness") is found six times and *astheneō* ("be weak") seven times in 2 Corinthians 10–13, neither word occurs in chapters 1 to 9. Finally, in chapters 10 to 13 the *kauchasthai* ("boast") concept appears nineteen times, always in an apologetic or vindicative sense, as opposed to the ten uses of the root in chapters 1 to 9 always in a complimentary sense.

10. Bibliography

Commentaries

Allo, E.B. *Saint Paul. Seconde Épître aux Corinthiens.* Paris: J. Gabalda, 1956, second edition.

Barrett, C.K. *A Commentary on the Second Epistle to the Corinthians.* London: A. and C. Black, 1973.

Bernard, J.H. "The Second Epistle to the Corinthians" in *The Expositor's Greek Testament.* Edited by W. Robertson Nicoll. Grand Rapids: Eerdmans, 1970 reprint of 1903 work, 3:1–119.

Bruce, F.F. *1 and 2 Corinthians.* London: Oliphants, 1971.

Denney, J. *The Second Epistle to the Corinthians.* London: Hodder and Stoughton, 1894.

Héring, J. *The Second Epistle of Saint Paul to the Corinthians.* London: Epworth, 1967.

Hodge, C. *A Commentary on the Second Epistle to the Corinthians.* London: Banner of Truth, 1959 reprint of 1857 work.

Hughes, P.E. *Paul's Second Epistle to the Corinthians.* Grand Rapids: Eerdmans, 1962.

Lietzmann, H. *An die Korinther. I. II.* Enlarged by W.G. Kümmel. Tübingen: J.C.B. Mohr, 1949, fourth edition.

Meyer, H.A.W. *Critical and Exegetical Handbook to the Epistles to the Corinthians.* New York: Funk and Wagnalls, 1884.

Plummer, A. *A Critical and Exegetical Commentary on the Second Epistle of St. Paul to the Corinthians.* Edinburgh: T. and T. Clark, 1915.

———. *The Second Epistle of Paul the Apostle to the Corinthians.* Cambridge: Cambridge University Press, 1903.

Tasker, R.V.G. *The Second Epistle of Paul to the Corinthians.* Grand Rapids: Eerdmans, 1958.

General Works

Barrett, C.K. *The Signs of an Apostle.* Philadelphia: Fortress, 1972.

Collange, J.F. *Énigmes de la Deuxième Épître de Paul aux Corinthiens.* Cambridge: Cambridge University Press, 1972.

Kennedy, J.H. *The Second and Third Epistles of St. Paul to the Corinthians.* London: Methuen, 1900.

Metzger, B.M. *A Textual Commentary on the Greek New Testament.* New York: United Bible Societies, 1971.

Nickle, K.F. *The Collection.* Naperville: Allenson, 1966.

Robertson, A.T. *The Glory of the Ministry.* New York: Revell, 1911.

Schmithals, W. *Gnosticism in Corinth.* New York: Abingdon, 1971.

Articles

Barrett, C.K. "Christianity at Corinth" in *Bulletin of the John Rylands Library,* XLVI (2, 1964), pp. 269–297.

———. "Paul's Opponents in II Corinthians" in *New Testament Studies,* XVII (3, 1971), pp. 233–254.

Bates, W.H. "The Integrity of II Corinthians" in *New Testament Studies,* XII (1, 1965), pp. 56–69.

Berry, R. "Death and Life in Christ. The Meaning of 2 Corinthians 5. 1–10" in *Scottish Journal of Theology,* XIV (1, 1961), pp. 60–76.

Bruce, F.F. "Paul and Jerusalem" in *Tyndale Bulletin,* XIX (1968), pp. 3–25.

Dunn, J.D.G. "2 Corinthians III. 17—'The Lord is the Spirit' " in *Journal of Theological Studies,* XXI (2, 1970), pp. 309–320.

Harris, M.J. "Paul's View of Death in 2 Corinthians 5:1–10" in *New Dimensions in New Testament Study.* Edited by R.N. Longenecker and M.C. Tenney. Grand Rapids: Zondervan, 1974, pp. 317–328.

Moule, C.F.D. "St. Paul and Dualism: The Pauline Concept of Resurrection" in *New Testament Studies,* XII (2, 1966), pp. 106–123.

Proudfoot, C.M. "Imitation of Realistic Participation? A Study of Paul's Concept of 'Suffering with Christ' " in *Interpretation,* XVII (2, 1963), pp. 140–160.

Stephenson, A.M.G. "A Defence of the Integrity of 2 Corinthians" in *The Authorship and Integrity of the New Testament.* London: SPCK, 1965, pp. 82–97.

11. Outline

I. Paul's Explanation of His Conduct and Apostolic Ministry (2 Corinthians 1–7)
- A. Introduction (1:1–11)
  1. Salutation (1:1, 2)
  2. Gratitude for divine comfort (1:3–7)
  3. Deliverance from a deadly peril (1:8–11)
- B. Paul's Conduct Explained (1:12–2:13)
  1. Characteristics of his conduct (1:12–14)
  2. Charge of fickleness answered (1:15–22)
  3. A cancelled painful visit (1:23–2:4)
  4. Forgiveness for the offender (2:5–11)
  5. Restlessness at Troas (2:12, 13)
- C. Major Digression—The Apostolic Ministry Described (2:14–7:4)
  1. Its grandeur and superiority (2:14–4:6)
     - a. The privilege of apostolic service (2:14–17)
     - b. The results of the ministry (3:1–3)
     - c. Competence for service (3:4–6)
     - d. The surpassing glory of the new covenant (3:7–11)
     - e. Veiling and unveiling (3:12–18)
     - f. The light brought by the gospel (4:1–6)
  2. Its suffering and glory (4:7–5:10)
     - a. The trials and rewards of apostolic service (4:7–15)
     - b. Glory through suffering (4:16–18)
     - c. Confidence in the face of death (5:1–10)
  3. Its function and exercise (5:11–6:10)
     - a. Motivation for service (5:11–15)
     - b. The message of reconciliation (5:16–6:2)
     - c. The hardships of apostolic service (6:3–10)
  4. Its openness and joy (6:11–7:4)
     - a. A plea for generous affection (6:11–13)
     - b. Minor digression—call to holiness (6:14–7:1)
     - c. Paul's pride and joy (7:2–4)
- D. Paul's Reconciliation With the Corinthians (7:5–16)
  1. Comfort in Macedonia (7:5–7)
  2. The severe letter and its effect (7:8–13a)
  3. The relief of Titus (7:13b–16)

II. The Collection for the Saints at Jerusalem (2 Corinthians 8–9)
- A. The Need for Generosity (8:1–15)
  1. The generosity of the Macedonians (8:1–5)
  2. A plea for liberal giving (8:6–12)
  3. The aim of equality (8:13–15)
- B. The Mission of Titus and His Companions (8:16–9:5)
  1. The delegates and their credentials (8:16–24)
  2. The need for readiness (9:1–5)
- C. The Results of Generosity (9:6–15)
  1. The enrichment of the giver (9:6–11)

2. The offering of thanks to God (9:12–15)

III. Paul's Vindication of His Apostolic Authority (2 Corinthians 10–13)
   A. The Exercise of Apostolic Rights and Authority (10:1–11:15)
      1. The potency of apostolic authority (10:1–11)
      2. Legitimate spheres of activity and boasting (10:12–18)
      3. Paul's jealousy for the Corinthians (11:1–6)
      4. Financial dependence and independence (11:7–12)
      5. False apostles (11:13–15)
   B. Boasting "As a Fool" (11:16–12:13)
      1. Justification for foolish boasting (11:16–21a)
      2. Paul's heritage and trials (11:21b–29)
      3. Escape from Damascus (11:30–33)
      4. A vision and its aftermath (12:1–10)
      5. Proof of apostleship (12:11–13)
   C. The Planned Third Visit (12:14–13:10)
      1. A promise not to be burdensome (12:14–18)
      2. Fears about the unrepentant (12:19–21)
      3. Warning of impending discipline (13:1–4)
      4. A plea for self-examination (13:5–10)
   D. Conclusion (13:11–13)

Text and Exposition

I. Paul's Explanation of His Conduct and Apostolic Ministry (2 Corinthians 1–7)

A. *Introduction* (1:1–11)

1. *Salutation*

1:1, 2

[1]Paul, an apostle of Christ Jesus by the will of God, and Timothy our brother,
To the church of God in Corinth, together with all the saints throughout Achaia:
[2]Grace and peace to you from God our Father and the Lord Jesus Christ.

1 In all his Epistles except 1 and 2 Thessalonians, Philippians, and Philemon, Paul begins with a reference to his being "an apostle" of Christ Jesus. Although he was not one of the twelve chosen by Christ (Mark 3:14–19), Paul claimed equality with them (see 11:5; 12:11; Gal 2:6) on the basis of the special revelation of Christ God gave him at the time of his conversion (1 Cor 9:1; Gal 1:15, 16). Like them, he had been commissioned "by the will of God" to be a "chosen instrument" (Acts 9:15).

Paul's delight in speaking of a fellow Christian as "our brother" (*ho adelphos*) may be traced to Ananias's generous and reassuring use of that term ("Brother Saul," Acts 9:17) at a time when Damascene believers had every reason to regard Saul as the archenemy of the church (Acts 9:1, 2, 13, 14). The mention of Timothy (not Sosthenes, cf. 1 Cor 1:1) as a cosender of the letter may be intended to reinstate this timid young man (1 Tim 4:12; 2 Tim 1:7; 2:1) in the eyes of the Corinthians, possibly after his failure or limited success as Paul's representative at Corinth (see 1 Cor 4:17; 16:10, 11). But it is not certain that Timothy reached Corinth from Macedonia (Acts 19:22). At any rate, Titus had replaced Timothy as Paul's chief envoy to Corinth by the time this letter was written.

Paul refers to the principal addressees not as "the church of Corinth" but as "the church of God in Corinth," the local representatives of God's universal church. Linked with the Corinthians are "the saints"—God's people (*hoi hagioi*)—at such places as Athens (cf. Acts 17:34) and Cenchrea (cf. Rom 16:1). Perhaps this joint address explains the absence of personal greetings at the end of chapter thirteen.

2 This characteristically Pauline (and also Petrine) salutation combines and elevates the traditional Greek and Hebrew greetings. *Chairein* ("greetings," Acts 15:23; 23:26; James 1:1) becomes *charis* ("grace," God's unsought and unmerited favor), to which Paul makes reference at the beginning and end of every Epistle. And the Hebrew *šālôm* ("peace") is replaced by *eirēnē* ("peace"), the latter term referring to the peace that comes to man from God (cf. Phil 4:7) as a result of his having peace with God (Rom 5:1).

2. *Gratitude for divine comfort*

1:3–7

[3]Praise be to the God and Father of our Lord Jesus Christ, the Father of compassion and the God of all comfort, [4]who comforts us in all our troubles, so that we can comfort those in any trouble with the comfort we ourselves have received from God. [5]For just as the sufferings of Christ flow over into our lives, so also through Christ our comfort overflows. [6]If we are distressed, it is for your

comfort and salvation; if we are comforted, it is for your comfort, which produces in you patient endurance of the same sufferings we suffer. 7And our hope for you is firm, because we know that just as you share in our sufferings, so also you share in our comfort.

The paragraph embodies the chief emphasis of chapters 1–7: "comfort in the midst of affliction" (see Introduction, 9). The *paraklēsis* ("comfort") root occurs no fewer than ten times in vv.3–7, the *thlipsis* ("trouble," "affliction") root three times, and the *pathēma* ("suffering") root four times.

3,4 Paul generally follows his salutation with thanksgiving for the divine grace evident in the lives of his converts (e.g., 1 Cor 1:4–9) and a summary of his prayer requests for them (e.g., Phil 1:3–11; Col 1:3–12). Here, however, he offers praise to God for consoling and encouraging him (see note), while later (v.11) he solicits his converts' prayer for himself. This untypical preoccupation with his own circumstances shows the distressing nature of the experience in Asia he had so recently been delivered from (vv.8–10). He highlights the aspects of God's character he had come to value in deeper measure as a result of personal need and divine response, viz., God's limitless compassion (cf. Ps 145:9; Mic 7:19) and never-failing comfort (cf. Isa 40:1; 51:3, 12; 66:13).

Paul sees his suffering (note Acts 9:15, 16; 20:22, 23) not merely as personally beneficial, driving him to trust God alone (v.9, and 12:7), but also as directly benefiting those he ministered to: "God . . . comforts us . . . so that we can comfort. . . ." To experience God's "comfort" (i.e., help, consolation, and encouragement) in the midst of all one's affliction is to become indebted and equipped to communicate the divine comfort and sympathy to others who are in any kind of affliction or distress.

5 This verse supplies the reason (*hoti,* "for") why suffering equips the Christian to mediate God's comfort. Whenever Christ's sufferings were multiplied in Paul's life, God's comfort was also multiplied through the ministry of Christ. The greater the suffering, the greater the comfort and the greater the ability to share with others the divine sympathy. "The sufferings of Christ" (cf. Gal 6:17) cannot refer to the atoning passion of Christ that Paul regarded as a historical fact, a completed event (Rom 5:8–10; 6:10). They probably included all the sufferings that befall the "man in Christ" (12:2) engaged in the service of Christ (cf. 4:11, 12). They are *Christ's* sufferings not simply because they are similar to his but because they contribute to the fulfillment of the suffering destined for the Body of Christ (Acts 14:22; Col 1:24) or because Christ continues to identify himself with his afflicted Church (cf. Acts 9:4, 5).

6,7 Verse 6a restates and applies v.4b. Paul's suffering of affliction and endurance of trial ultimately benefited the Corinthians in that he was thereby equipped to administer divine encouragement to them when they were afflicted and to ensure their preservation when they underwent trial (cf. Eph 3:13; 2 Tim 2:10). The apostle then makes explicit what he has assumed (in v.6a) in arguing from *his* experience of suffering to *their* experience of comfort and deliverance, viz., his own receipt of divine comfort in the midst of affliction ("if we are comforted"). Whether he suffered affliction or whether he received comfort, the advantage remained the same for the Corinthians (cf. 4:8–12, 15). They too would know an inner revitalization, an infusion of divine strength that would enable them to endure patiently the same type of trial that confronted Paul (cf. 1 Peter 5:9).

Since Paul realized that to share Christ's sufferings always involved the experience of God's comfort through that suffering, his hope that the Corinthians would be triumphant in their time of trial was securely grounded (v.7).

Notes

3 Whenever Paul uses a first-person plural pronoun or verb (e.g., ἡμῶν [*hēmōn,* "our"] in v.3; παρακαλούμεθα [*parakaloumetha,* "the comfort we . . . received"] in v.4), the referent(s) may be (1) a plural subject made clear in the context, (2) Paul himself ("epistolary plural"), (3) Paul and his co-workers mentioned in the salutation or his amanuensis (exclusive "we"), (4) Paul and his addressees (inclusive "we"), (5) Jews, (6) all Christians, or (7) men in general. That Paul can on occasion oscillate from singular to plural, apparently without intending a distinction to be drawn, is shown by the γράφομεν (*graphomen,* "we write"), ἐλπίζω (*elpizō,* "I hope"), and ἡμᾶς (*hēmas,* "us") of vv.13, 14 and the singulars of vv.15–17.

4 A distinction may be drawn between πᾶς (*pas*) with the articular θλίψις (*thlipsis*), "in all trouble" (v.4a; cf. 7:4) and πᾶς with the anarthrous θλίψις, "in any trouble" (v.4b)—see BDF, par. 275 (3); RHG, p. 772.

6,7 Textual variants arose here through the accidental omission of καὶ σωτηρίας. . .παρακλήσεως (*kai sōtērias. . .paraklēseōs,* "and salvation. . .comfort") due to homoeoteleuton (παρακλήσεως. . .παρακλήσεως) and subsequent efforts to reintroduce the words.

3. *Deliverance from a deadly peril*

1:8–11

8We do not want you to be uninformed, brothers, about the hardships we suffered in the province of Asia. We were under great pressure, far beyond our ability to endure, so that we despaired even of life. 9Indeed, in our hearts we felt the sentence of death. But this happened that we might not rely on ourselves but on God, who raises the dead. 10He has delivered us from such a deadly peril, and he will deliver us. On him we have set our hope that he will continue to deliver us, 11as you help us by your prayers. Then many will give thanks on our behalf for the gracious favor granted us in answer to the prayers of many.

8 Paul proceeds to describe the particular affliction (*thlipsis,* rendered "hardships" in NIV) in which he received divine comfort and empowering. It overtook Paul "in the province of Asia," which, as in Acts 19:22, probably refers to some part of the province other than the leading city, Ephesus. (Otherwise "in Ephesus" would have been used, as in 1 Cor 15:32; 16:8), possibly the Lycus valley (so G.S. Duncan), or Troas (2:12, 13). That it had occurred recently—certainly after 1 Corinthians was written—seems indicated by the vividness of Paul's description of the divine deliverance.

Evidently the Corinthians were already aware of Paul's trial—hence the vague reference to "the affliction. . .in Asia" (RSV). He now informs his converts of its overwhelming and unique character. He had been so "utterly, unbearably crushed" (RSV) that he was forced to renounce all hope of survival. The rare word *exaporēthēnai* ("despaired") implies the total unavailability of an exit (*poros,* "passage") from oppressive circumstances.

9 In his estimation Paul had received at that time a death sentence from which there was no reprieve (see notes). But in the wake of this trying experience that was tantamount to death there followed a further experience that was tantamount to resurrection. Only divine intervention enabled him to retreat from the portals of death to the realm of the living. All this undermined Paul's self-confidence (see 1 Cor 15:31; 2 Cor 12:9, 10) and compelled his utter dependence on a God who raises the dead (cf. Rom 4:17) and therefore can rescue the dying from the grip of death (cf. Phil 2:27, 30).

10,11 "The Father of compassion" had delivered Paul from a deadly peril (cf. vv.3, 4). But since such perils were likely to recur, continuing divine intervention on his behalf was necessary if death was to be robbed of its prey. Immediately Paul qualifies his bold assertion, "and he will deliver us" (cf. 2 Tim 4:18), by adding, ". . . on him we have set our hope that he will continue to deliver us." He could not presume on "the gracious favor" of protection or deliverance from danger and death. This came from "the God of all comfort" (v.3) "in answer to the prayers of many" and it would prompt still further thanksgiving.

Of the various proposed identifications of Paul's affliction in Asia, five deserve mention: (1) his "fighting with wild beasts in Ephesus" (1 Cor 15:32; so Tertullian); (2) his suffering the "thirty-nine stripes" (11:24) after being arraigned before a local Jewish ecclesiastical court (so G.S. Duncan); (3) the riot at Ephesus instigated by Demetrius, the silversmith (Acts 19:23–41; so W.M. Ramsay), or an unsuccessful attempt by the populace, after the Ephesian uproar, to lynch the apostle (so H. Windisch); (4) a particular persecution encountered in Ephesus or elsewhere (cf. Acts 20:19; 1 Cor 16:9) shortly before his departure for Troas (so A. Plummer); and (5) a prostrating attack of a recurrent malady (so E.B. Allo). The last-mentioned view seems favored by the allusion in v.10 to Job 33:30 (LXX); the fact that a Jew could regard sickness as death and healing or recovery as a return to life (see, e.g., Hos 6:1, 2); the present tenses of vv.4–6; the perfective implications of *eschēkamen* ("we feel we received") in v.9 (see note there); and the twice-repeated *rhysetai* ("he will deliver") in v.10.

Notes

9 Ἀπόκριμα (*apokrima*) could signify a judicial sentence (here, "the sentence of death") or an official verdict (here the divine reply to Paul's desperate appeal for deliverance; see MM, p. 64; Deiss BS, p. 257). Ἐσχήκαμεν (*eschēkamen,* cf. Rom 5:2) implies both ἔσχομεν (*eschomen,* "we received") and ἔχομεν (*echomen,* "we [still] possess"); thus "we feel we received"—the sentence or verdict had not been reversed. But in 2:13 and 7:5 this perfect is probably aoristic.

10 Καὶ ῥύσεται (*kai rhysetai,* "and he will deliver," future), which is to be preferred over καὶ ῥύεται (*kai rhyetai,* present) as the more difficult reading, implies that Paul expected comparable "deadly perils" in the future.

11 The genitive absolute συνυπουργούντων καὶ ὑμῶν (*synypourgountōn kai hymōn*) may be conditional in sense: "provided you too work together with us." The bestowal of divine favor is intimately related to the offering of human prayer (Phil 1:19; Philem 22). And the verb implies that prayer is cooperative work (Rom 15:30), expressive of the interdependence of the members of Christ's body (1 Cor 12:25, 26).

B. *Paul's Conduct Explained* (1:12–2:13)

1. *Characteristics of his conduct*

1:12–14

12Now this is our boast: Our conscience testifies that we have conducted ourselves in the world, and especially in our relations with you, in the holiness and sincerity that are from God. We have done so not according to worldly wisdom but according to God's grace. 13For we do not write you anything you cannot read or understand. And I hope that, 14as you have understood us in part, you will come to understand fully that you can boast of us just as we will boast of you in the day of the Lord Jesus.

12–14 Before defending himself against the specific charges of vacillation and domineering leveled against him by his opponents (1:15–2:4), Paul deals with two more general accusations: that he had acted shamelessly (or deviously, if *haplotēti*, "integrity," be the correct reading in v.12; see notes) and insincerely in his relations with the Corinthians (cf. v.12a), and that in his letters he had shown worldly shrewdness and had been evasive by writing one thing but meaning or intending another (cf. vv.12b, 13a).

These baseless charges Paul answers in the only way possible for him—by appealing to the testimony of his own conscience and the Corinthians' knowledge of his conduct. So, he claims that in both church and world his conduct had been characterized by God-given purity of intention and openness and had been governed by the grace of God (v.12). Then he asserts that in none of his correspondence—the Corinthians had already received at least three letters from him—did his meaning become apparent only by "reading between the lines." Rather, his meaning, which lay on the surface, could be understood simply by reading (v.13a). Paul concludes by reminding his converts at Corinth that they had already begun to appreciate his motives and intentions, especially through the recent visit of Titus (see 7:6–16). He expresses the hope that they would reach the full assurance that he could give them as much cause for pride now (cf. 5:12) as they would give him pride "in the day of the Lord Jesus" (cf. 1 Cor 15:31; Phil 4:1; 1 Thess 2:19, 20).

Notes

12 In all three editions of the UBS, ἁπλότητι, (*haplotēti*, "integrity"), a Western and Byzantine reading, is preferred over the Alexandrian reading ἁγιότητι (*hagiotēti*, "holiness," NIV), but the editors give their preference a "D" rating, showing that "there is a very high degree of doubt concerning the reading selected for the text."

2. *Charge of fickleness answered*

1:15–22

15Because I was confident of this, I planned to visit you first so that you might benefit twice. 16I planned to visit you on my way to Macedonia and to come back to you from Macedonia, and then to have you send me on my way to Judea.

[17]When I planned this, did I do it lightly? Or do I make my plans in a worldly manner so that in the same breath I say, "Yes, yes" and "No, no"?

[18]But as surely as God is faithful, our message to you is not "Yes" and "No." [19]For the Son of God, Jesus Christ, who was preached among you by me and Silas and Timothy, was not "Yes" and "No," but in him it has always been "Yes." [20]For no matter how many promises God has made, they are "Yes" in Christ. And so through him the "Amen" is spoken by us to the glory of God. [21]Now it is God who makes both us and you stand firm in Christ. He anointed us, [22]set his seal of ownership on us, and put his Spirit in our hearts as a deposit, guaranteeing what is to come.

15–17 In 1 Corinthians 16:2–8 and in these three verses are found the outlines of two different itineraries relating to Paul and Corinth. In the earlier Epistle, the plan (hereafter Plan A) was: Ephesus–Macedonia–Corinth–Jerusalem (possibly). But in 2 Corinthians 1, the route (Plan B) is: Ephesus–Corinth–Macedonia–Corinth–Judea (now definitely). If, as is probable, Plan A discloses Paul's original intention, Plan B, made after the writing of 1 Corinthians, introduces two modifications of that previous itinerary: Paul now planned to visit Corinth twice—before and after his activity in Macedonia; and his intention of traveling to Judea with the collection was now settled.

But not only did Paul have to explain these changes. His actual itinerary (see Introduction, 1.b) seems to have been: Ephesus–Corinth (= the "painful visit")–Ephesus (where the Demetrius riot occurred)–Troas (2:12, 13)–Macedonia (7:5—the place of writing). In other words, neither Plan A nor Plan B was carried out as intended. Plan A was nullified by Paul's crossing from Ephesus to Corinth on the "painful visit," and Plan B was annulled by his return to Ephesus after that visit. It may be said that after the "sorrowful visit" Paul reverted to Plan A (see Acts 20:1–3, 16). To Plan A Paul had seemed to say, "Yes–No–Yes"; to Plan B, "Yes–No." The apostle had apparently provided his opponents with a convenient handle for a charge of fickleness!

His detractors were shrewd enough to convert the charge into one of capricious vacillation, levity of character (*elaphria,* translated "lightly"). His arbitrary changing of travel plans, they urged, was motivated purely by self-interest, with no concern for broken promises or for needs at Corinth. He made his plans on mere impulse like a worldly man, according to the mood of the moment, so that he could say, "Yes, yes" one day and "No, no" the next day, or "Yes" at one moment and "No" immediately afterwards, with the result that he seemed to be saying both "Yes" and "No" in the same breath. That Paul is actually quoting the accusation of certain Corinthians seems indicated by his use of the definite article with *elaphria* ("fickleness") and with the twice-stated (cf. Matt 5:37) *nai* ("yes") and *ou* ("no") (v.17).

18 Paul is so distressed by this charge and so convinced of his innocence that he solemnly invokes the unquestionable trustworthiness of God (1 Cor 1:9; cf. 11:10) as guaranteeing and testifying to the consistency of his message to the Corinthians. Neither in proclaiming the good news to them nor in telling them of his travel plans was his language "an ambiguous blend of Yes and No" (NEB). How could the messenger of a faithful God vacillate between a reassuring "Yes" and a disconcerting "No" or deliver a message that was not an emphatic "Yes"?

19,20 Paul now elaborates this last point. The message originally proclaimed at Corinth (Acts 18:5) by the threefold testimony (cf. 13:1; Deut 19:15) of Paul, Silvanus, (= Silas) and Timothy centered in none other than God's Son in whom inconsistency and indecision had no place. So Paul draws a contrast between the humanity of the messengers and the divinity of the Person who was the essence of their message (the unusual position of *gar,* "for," emphasizes *tou theou,* "of God," v.19). Indeed, in and through him (*en autō*) the divine "Yes" has come into effect as a permanent reality (*gegonen,* perfect tense, v.19), because all God's promises (cf. 7:1; Rom 9:4; 15:8), whatever their number, find their fulfillment or affirmative in him (v.20a). "They are 'Yes' in Christ," since he forms the climax and summation of the divine self-revelation. That is why (*dio kai*), in their corporate worship offered to God through Christ, Christians joyfully utter the "Yes" or "Amen" of agreement and consecration (cf. Rev 1:7; 3:14; 22:20). Such a response enhances God's glory (v.20b).

The Corinthians' "Amen" to the gospel declaration itself validated the apostolic preaching (cf. 1 Cor 1:6; 2 Cor 3:2, 3; 13:5, 6). With his consistency confirmed here, was it likely that Paul would act in a worldly manner in relatively trivial affairs? How could they distrust the apostle who himself had taught them to affirm the trustworthiness of God by repeating the "Amen"? This is a potent *a fortiori* argument.

21,22 In defending himself against the charge of levity (v.17a), Paul has appealed to his making decisions as a man in Christ who acts *kata pneuma* ("by the Spirit" or "in a spiritual manner," a phrase implied in Paul's argument), not *kata sarka* ("in a worldly manner"—v.17b); the trustworthiness and faithfulness of God whose sure word he preaches (v.18); the unambiguous and positive nature of the message they proclaimed—Jesus Christ, the Son of God (v.19); and the validation of that sure proclamation in the Corinthian use of the liturgical response, "Amen" (v.20). Finally (vv.21, 22), Paul pointed to the constant activity of God in producing stability in Paul *and* the Corinthians!—those who have been brought into intimate and dynamic relation with Christ, who is God's secure and permanent "Yes."

Each of the four Greek participles in vv.21, 22 has God as its subject (*theos,* "God," being emphatic by position, v.21). The first (*bebaiōn,* present tense), a technical, legal term denoting a seller's guaranteeing of the validity of a purchase (see Deiss BS, 104–109), refers to God's continuous strengthening of believers in their faith in Christ and his progressive enriching of their knowledge of Christ. The other three participles are in the aorist tense, indicating what took place at the time of conversion and baptism. The phrase "he anointed (*chrisas*) us," which follows immediately after a reference to Christ (*Christos,* "the Anointed One"), shows that those to whom God now gives a firm standing, he once commissioned for his service by consecrating them as his "anointed ones" and imparting those gifts necessary for their task (see note). The last two participles are intimately related (see note). God "set his seal of ownership [*sphragisamenos*] on us" in that he "put [*dous*] his Spirit in our hearts as a deposit, guaranteeing what is to come." Associated with the idea of sealing are the ideas of ownership, authentication, and security; the believer is "branded" as God's property, the reality of his faith is attested, and his status is guaranteed "against the day of redemption" (Eph 4:30).

Notes

15 Since an apostolic visit might be both a means of spiritual benefit (χάρις, *charis;* Rom 1:11; 15:29) and a source of personal pleasure (χαρά, *chara;* Phil 1:25), the sense is not materially altered whether χάριν (*charin*) or χαράν (*charan*) be read. The latter variant may have arisen from 1:24 or 2:3.

18 It is noteworthy that several of the crucial Gr. terms in vv.15–24 represent various forms of the Sem. root אמן (*'-m-n*): **πιστός** (*pistos,* v. 18) = נאמן (*ne^{e}mān*), **ναί** (*nai,* vv.19, 20) or **ἀμήν** (*amēn,* v.20) = אמן (*'āmēn*), **βεβαιῶν** (*bebaiōn,* v.21) = מאמין (*ma^{a}mîn*), **πίστις** (*pistis,* v.24) = אמונה (*^{e}mûnāh*). It is possible that the train of Paul's thought was influenced by these word associations (a case of Sem. thoughts being clothed in Gr. words), though they would not have been recognized by the predominantly Gentile congregation at Corinth. See further W.C. van Unnik, "Reisepläne und Amen-sagen, Zusammenhang and Gedankenfolge in 2. Korinther 1:15–24," *Studia Paulina in honorem Johannis de Zwaan* (Haarlem: Bohn, 1953), pp. 215–234.

Ὁ λόγος ἡμῶν (*ho logos hēmōn,* "our message") probably refers to the preaching of the gospel as well as generally to Paul's written or spoken word. Thus "our message to you is (and was) not 'Yes' and 'No.' "

20 For the community use of "Amen" as a response indicating agreement and commitment, see Deut 27:15–26; 1 Chron 16:36; Neh 5:13; 8:6; Ps 106:48; 1 Cor 14:16; Rev 22:20.

21,22 Although σὺν ὑμῖν (*syn hymin,* lit. "with you") is not repeated with the last three participles, it is to be understood with each (Eph 1:13 and 4:30 use **σφραγίζειν** [*sphragizein*] in reference to all believers). Paul is not here thinking exclusively of the gift or office of apostleship.

The anarthrous participle **δούς** (*dous,* "having given"), which is linked to the articular participle **σφραγισάμενος** (*sphragisamenos,* "having sealed") by a virtually epexegetic **καί** (*kai,* "and"), is explicative. "Sealing" is God's giving of the Spirit as a "deposit" or "pledge" (**ἀρραβών**, *arrhabōn*) of inheritance (cf. Eph 1:14). For Paul the Spirit was thus the promise of fulfillment, as well as the fulfillment of promise (Gal 3:14; Eph 1:13).

---

3. *A cancelled painful visit*

1:23–2:4

> 23 I call God as my witness that it was in order to spare you that I did not return
> to Corinth. 24 Not that we lord it over your faith, but we work with you for your joy,
> because it is by faith you stand firm. 1 So I made up my mind that I would not make
> another painful visit to you. 2 For if I grieve you, who is left to make me glad but
> you whom I have grieved? 3 I wrote as I did so that when I came I should not be
> distressed by those who ought to make me rejoice. I had confidence in all of you,
> that you would all share my joy. 4 For I wrote you out of great distress and anguish
> of heart and with many tears, not to grieve you but to let you know the depth of
> my love for you.

Allied to the charge that Paul had arbitrarily altered his travel plans regarding Corinth according to the mood of the moment, there was in all probability the accusation that by doing so he had shown himself to be a spiritual dictator who tried to dominate his converts and their faith and did not hesitate to cause them pain.

1:23–2:1 In answering this charge, Paul solemnly invokes the God who is faithful (1:18) as Paul's own witness to the truth of statements like these: "The reason I postponed my intended visit to Corinth was to spare you a second painful visit (1:23b; 2:1). So far from being unstable in my desires, as some of you insist (cf. 1:17), I have the settled purpose of promoting your highest good and joy (1:24) and saving you unnecessary pain or sorrow."

The matter of Paul's planned and actual itinerary is complicated (see the discussion at 1:15–17, and Introduction, 1.b). It was to spare the Corinthians and himself further pain that he refrained from returning to Corinth from Ephesus after the so-called "painful visit." "I made up my mind" (2:1) refers to a decision Paul made at Ephesus after hearing of the insult hurled at him or one of his deputies at Corinth by "the wrongdoer" of 7:12 (see the commentary on 2:5–8). He resolved to pay the Corinthians an "epistolary visit" (2:3, 4; 7:8, 12) instead of another personal visit that might have proved mutually painful.

For Paul to speak of "sparing" the Corinthians (v.23) implied that he might have punished or pained them. He therefore proceeds in 1:24, which is parenthetical, to reject the inference—probably also an actual Corinthian charge—that he was some tyrannical overlord, seeking to intimidate and domineer in matters of faith and conduct. An apostle was obligated to serve his converts; he had no right to dominate them. It was his privilege to work with them to secure their "joy in the faith" (Phil 1:25), not to lord it over them by causing them unnecessary pain. Indeed, with regard to their faith, he could not be despotic nor had he any need to do so, because they had a firm standing of their own by their exercise of faith (or, "in the realm of faith," *tē. . .pistei,* 1:24).

2 Here Paul acknowledges that his decision not to revisit Corinth personally had been partially determined by his reflection that to inflict needless pain on the Corinthians at that time would have effectively dried up the only source of his own happiness. His joy was intimately connected with theirs (1:24). To cause them pain was to experience pain himself, a pain that could be relieved and then converted into gladness only by their repentance (see 7:8–10).

3,4 In place of a second painful visit to Corinth that would not have been advantageous in the situation, Paul wrote the Corinthians a letter that has come to be known as the "sorrowful [or, severe] letter" (see Introduction, 7.b). His aim in writing it was to avoid being pained by them when he finally did pay another personal visit (v.3a). It was incongruous to Paul that his converts, who ought to have been a constant source of joy to him (1 Thess 2:19, 20), could prove, and in fact had proved, to be a cause of distress to their spiritual father. Yet in writing the "severe letter" he had had the buoyant assurance that whatever made him glad would give all of them pleasure too, for they were all one in joy, as in sorrow (v.3b).

In v.4a Paul describes the origin (*ek,* "out of") and circumstances (*dia,* "with") of this sorrowful letter. It was born of anguish and produced with tears. While parts of 1 Corinthians may be said to have been written "out of deep affliction and spiritual anguish," this is hardly true of that Epistle regarded as a whole, especially if its beginning and ending are any indication of its general tone. Rather, the letter referred to here and in 7:8, 12 is to be identified with a letter, no longer extant, that Paul sent to Corinth after 1 Corinthians had been delivered and after his "painful visit" (see Introduction, 7.b. 3).

A second purpose (cf. v.3; 2:9; 7:12) behind the "tearful letter" is stated in v.4b. Although the letter arose from anguish and actually proved painful to its recipients (7:8), its aim was not vindictive or even vindicative. On the contrary, it sought to convince the Corinthians of the intensity of Paul's affectionate concern for them.

Notes

1:23 Ἐπὶ τὴν ἐμὴν ψυχήν (*epi tēn emēn psychēn* = Heb. עַל־נַפְשִׁי, *'al-napšî*), which is not represented in the tr., means "against myself" or "with my life as the forfeit." So sure is Paul of his own truthfulness at this point that he can say, "Let God destroy me if I am lying."

2:1 Since πάλιν (*palin*, "again," "another") precedes and qualifies ἐν λύπῃ (*en lypē*, "painful"), and not ἐλθεῖν (*elthein*, "visit"), there is the implication of an earlier painful visit (cf. 13:2). It is unlikely that this visit is to be equated either with 1 Corinthians, reckoned as a sorrowful visit (cf. 2:4), or with Paul's initial visit to Corinth (Acts 18:1–18), which, as far as the Corinthians were concerned, was anything but painful. The visit probably occurred between the sending of 1 Corinthians (where only the founding visit is referred to; see 1 Cor 2:1–3; 11:2; 15:3) and the dispatch of the "severe letter" (see the Introduction, 7.a).

2:2 There are eight uses of the λύπη (*lypē*) concept in vv.1–7 (cf. the eight uses in 7:8–11). This usage, which describes the feeling or creating of pain, can be consistently reflected in tr. by rendering λύπη (*lypē*) by "pain," λυπέω (*lypeō*) by "cause pain" or "pain," and ἐν λύπῃ (*en lypē*) by "painfully."

---

4. *Forgiveness for the offender*

2:5–11

5If anyone has caused grief, he has not so much grieved me as he has grieved all of you, to some extent—not to put it too severely. 6The punishment inflicted on him by the majority is sufficient for him. 7Now instead, you ought to forgive and comfort him, so that he will not be overwhelmed by excessive sorrow. 8I urge you, therefore, to reaffirm your love for him. 9The reason I wrote you was to see if you would stand the test and be obedient in everything. 10If you forgive anyone, I also forgive him. And what I have forgiven—if there was anything to forgive—I have forgiven in the sight of Christ for your sake, 11in order that Satan might not outwit us. For we are not unaware of his schemes.

In the preceding section (1:23–2:4) Paul has spoken about feeling pain, causing pain, and avoiding further pain. All three aspects recur in this paragraph with reference to a certain wrongdoer at Corinth. Particularly apparent here is Paul's sensitivity as a pastor: He avoids naming the culprit (vv.5–8); he recognizes that Christian discipline is not simply retributive but also remedial (vv.6, 7); he understands the feelings and psychological needs of the penitent wrongdoer (vv.6–8); he appeals to his own conduct as an example for the Corinthians to follow (v.10); and he is aware of the divisive operation of Satan within the Christian community (v.11).

5,6 Many older commentators found in vv.5–11 a further reference to the man guilty of incest (1 Cor 5). But most modern writers rightly reject this identification for a variety of reasons (see Introduction, 7.b.3]a; for a defense of the equation 1 Cor 5 = 2 Cor 2, see the commentary of P.E. Hughes, ad loc.).

Evidently, after Paul's painful visit an insult of some description had been directed against him or one of his representatives either by a visitor to Corinth (so C.K. Barrett) or by a Corinthian, who perhaps at that time headed the opposition to the apostle at Corinth and objected in particular to Paul's disciplinary methods such as those outlined in 1 Cor 5. Paul here discounts the sorrow caused him by the unfortunate episode. Verse 5 may be rendered, "If anyone has caused pain, he had caused pain not so much to me as to all of you—to some extent (*apo merous*), not to exaggerate the point" (see note).

On the basis of Titus's report about the Corinthian reaction to the "stern letter" (see 7:7–11), Paul counsels the church to terminate the discipline they had inflicted on "the individual in question" (*ho toioutos,* v.6; NIV, "him"). Whether a formal gathering of the church had been held and whether disciplinary measures (temporary suspension of church privileges?) had been decided on by general vote or consensus, it is impossible to say. The words rendered "the majority" (*hoi pleiones*) may simply mean "the main body," or "the whole group," referring generally to the membership (cf. the use of *hā-rabbîm,* "the many," by the Qumran community). But since "the majority" is certainly a possible rendering, the question remains: What was the view of the implied minority? In light of v.7a, it seems likely that they were a pro-Pauline clique, the "ultra-Paulinists," who regarded the penalty as insufficient.

7–9 Instead of continuing or increasing the punishment, the Corinthians ought to rescue the man from inordinate grief and complete his reformation by forgiving and encouraging him and by a public reaffirmation of their love for him. This would serve to assure the wrongdoer that God had, in fact, forgiven him. In this way, the community would in effect be remitting or loosing his sins (cf. Matt 16:19; 18:18; John 20:23) by declaring and confirming to him the reality of divine forgiveness.

A positive Corinthian response to this plea would afford Paul further evidence of the church's willingness to acknowledge his divinely given authority. By reproving the offender after hearing the "severe letter," they had stood the test and proved their obedience in all respects (cf. 7:11, 12). Now by ending the punishment, they would be doing the same. There was no inconsistency in first "binding" and then "loosing"; "if your brother sins, rebuke him, and if he repents, forgive him" (Luke 17:3). In each case they were proving their loyalty to the apostle.

10,11 Paul here aligns himself with the Corinthian decision to forgive the person in question—a decision he trusts they will make after receiving the present letter. "Your verdict of forgiveness is also mine," or as the NEB puts it: "Anyone who has your forgiveness has mine too." But he hastens to add that he has already forgiven the man—if, in fact, there was anything to forgive. Clearly it was Paul, not the Corinthians, who had taken the initiative in this matter of forgiveness.

Verse 10 affords perhaps the clearest evidence that the offense was basically a personal act of effrontery against Paul or possibly his acknowledged or delegated representative. There was need for Paul's personal forgiveness, although, in deference to the penitent offender's feelings, he discounts the personal pain he himself experienced (v.5) and deliberately understates the seriousness of the offense (v.10) lest anyone imagine that he considered himself virtuous in granting forgiveness so readily. All this would be inappropriate if he were describing a sin of incest (1 Cor 5).

The circumstances and purpose of Paul's forgiveness are then defined (vv.10b, 11). First, forgiveness was granted "in the sight of Christ," as Christ looked on as a witness and approved—Christ, who taught that willingness to forgive one's brother was a precondition for the receipt of divine forgiveness (Matt 5:12, 14, 15; 18:23–35). And in Colossians 3:13 (cf. Eph 4:32) Paul grounds the Christian obligation to forgive others on the Christian experience of God's forgiveness in Christ. Moreover, forgiveness was granted for the welfare of the Corinthians ("for your sake"), that is, to preserve unity and to relieve them of their patent embarrassment at not having acted against the offender before Paul wrote to them. They keenly felt their disloyalty to Paul (7:7, 11).

Verse 11 states an additional but related purpose. This was to avoid being outwitted by the master strategist, Satan, who was bent on creating discord within the church at Corinth, either between the church at large and a dissident minority or between the repentant wrongdoer and his fellow Christians. To withhold forgiveness when the man was repentant was to play into the hands of Satan, who already had gained one advantage when the man sinned. There is a point at which punishment can become purely vindictive (cf. v.6) and suffering a penalty can drive one to despair (v.7; Col 3:21). Christian discipline certainly includes punishment administered in love, but it is not simply retributive or punitive; it is also remedial or reformatory (cf. 1 Cor 5:5; 11:32; 2 Cor 7:9, 10; 13:10). It aims at reinstatement after repentance, through forgiveness and reconciliation.

Notes

5 Εἰ...τις (*ei...tis,* "if anyone") is conditional only in form; in sense it is equivalent to ὅς (*hos*, "the person who"; cf. 7:14, Gr.). Οὐκ ἐμέ (*ouk eme,* "not...me") should not be pressed to exclude Paul from the experience of pain. Sometimes he uses the negative, not with an absolute meaning ("not at all"), but in a relative sense ("not so much," NIV, or "not primarily" or "not only"; cf. 1 Cor 1:17; 2 Cor 7:12). If the verb ἐπιβαρέω (*epibareō*) is here used transitively, as it usually is, the meaning will be "not to be too severe [with him, or with anyone]"; if it is intransitive, "not to put it too severely" (NIV), or "not to labour the point" (NEB), or "not to exaggerate."

6 For a defense of the view that ἐπιτιμία (*epitimia*) should be rendered "reproof," not "punishment" or "penalty," see C.K. Barrett, in loc.

8 The verb κυρόω (*kuroō*) often means "ratify" or "validate," but here may carry the sense "decide in favor of (love for him)" (BAG, p. 462), perhaps implying a public reinstatement and readmission to fellowship following the earlier formal reproof or punishment. As a common legal term (see Gal 3:15 and MM, p. 366), its juxtaposition here with ἀγάπη (*agapē*, "love") is noteworthy.

11 Νοήματα (*noēmata*) here has the pejorative sense of "schemes," "designs," "plots," or "wiles" (= Gr. μεθοδείαι, *methodeiai,* Eph 6:11), but Paul uses it also with the neutral meaning of "minds" (3:14; 4:4; 11:3; Phil 4:7). His point in v.11 is that one of the Christian's defenses against the devil's stratagems is prior awareness of his purposes and methods, particularly his wish to turn good (the man's repentance) into evil (his downfall through excessive grief).

5. *Restlessness at Troas*

2:12,13

12Now when I went to Troas to preach the gospel of Christ and found that the
Lord had opened a door for me, 13I still had no peace of mind, because I did not
find my brother Titus there. So I said good-by and went on to Macedonia.

12,13 This is the final section in Paul's explanation of his recent conduct. For a reconstruction of the events leading up to the sending of the "severe letter," see the Introduction (7.a.3). Titus was dispatched to Corinth with this "letter of tears" while Paul continued work in and around Ephesus (cf. Acts 19:22b, "he stayed in the province of Asia a little longer"), the city to which he had returned after his brief "painful visit" to Corinth. Paul's departure for Troas, mentioned in v.12 (by a coasting vessel? cf. Acts

20:13–15), probably was precipitated by the Demetrius riot (Acts 19:23–41). Evidently he had already planned to leave the city, for when he sent Titus to Corinth, he arranged to meet him at Troas, or, failing that, probably at Philippi.

We may safely assume that Paul actually preached in Troas, though v.12 speaks only of his intent. He would recognize that the "door" of opportunity was "open" (note Acts 16:6–10) only after he had grasped the evangelistic opportunities initially afforded by the Lord. But evangelism was curtailed (remarkable, in the light of 1 Cor 9:16!) owing to Paul's restless spirit (perhaps seen as a device used by Satan, cf. v.11). This disquiet (7:5, 6) was caused by several factors: (1) the disheartening opposition at Ephesus, which had caused his premature departure; (2) persistent uncertainty and fears concerning the situation at Corinth (7:5b), because of Titus's nonarrival; and (3) concern for the safety of Titus in travel (note 7:6b, 7a), particularly if he was carrying the completed Corinthian collection.

Notes

12 Because Alexandria Troas was frequently the point where land travel became sea travel (or vice-versa) or where a change of ship occurred, it was a suitable center and base for missionary activity (W.M. Ramsay. "Roads and Travel [in NT]." HDB, 5:389, 400).

13 That Paul was somewhat embarrassed by his premature departure from Troas may be indicated by his particular mention of the reluctant and solemn farewell, the verb ἀποταξάμενος (*apotaxamenos*, "said good-by") never being used elsewhere by Paul. Αὐτοῖς (*autois*), "[I said good-by] to them" (not in NIV), indicates that some converts were won in Troas (cf. Acts 20:6–12).

C. *Major Digression—the Apostolic Ministry Described* (2:14–7:4)

1. *Its grandeur and superiority* (2:14–4:6)

a. *The privilege of apostolic service*

2:14–17

[14]But thanks be to God, who always leads us in triumphal procession in Christ and through us spreads everywhere the fragrance of the knowledge of him. [15]For we are to God the aroma of Christ among those who are being saved and those who are perishing. [16]To the one we are the stench of death; to the other, the fragrance of life. And who is equal to such a task? [17]Unlike so many, we do not peddle the word of God for profit. On the contrary, in Christ we speak before God with sincerity, like men sent from God.

14 Here begins the so-called "great digression," brought about by Paul's remembering his happy reunion with Titus in Macedonia, who brought encouraging news from Corinth that relieved Paul's fretful tension (7:5–16). In the favorable Corinthian reaction to the "letter of tears," reported by Titus, Paul saw God's vindication of his apostleship and a triumph of God's grace in the hearts of the Corinthians.

Paul likens the irresistible advance of the gospel, in spite of temporary frustration, to a Roman *triumphus* ("triumph") in which the victorious general, along with his proud soldiers, used to lead in triumphal procession the wretched prisoners of war who were thus exposed to public ridicule. Not all the details of this picture are to be pressed. The apostles, as well as Christians in general, may be either exultant soldiers who share in the benefits of Christ's victory (cf. Rom 8:37) or willing captives who count it a privilege to be part of God's "triumph" (cf. Rom 1:1; Col 4:10). The metaphor is certainly suggestive: Christ undertook a battle not rightly his; we share in a triumph not rightly ours.

In the following reference to the diffusion of fragrance, Paul may simply be developing the imagery, for sacrifices were offered when the procession reached the temple of Jupiter Capitolinus (Jos. *War* VII 5. 6) and perfumes may have been sprinkled or incense burned along the processional route. Through the apostles, God was spreading far and wide the fragrant knowledge of himself to be gained through knowing Christ (Col 2:2, 3).

15,16a Syntactically, v.15 is ambiguous so that several translations are possible: (1) "We are the sweet odor (of sacrifice) that ascends from Christ to God among those who are on the way to salvation and those who are on the way to destruction." (2) "I live for God as the fragrance of Christ breathed alike on those who are being saved and on those who are perishing" (Moffatt). (3) "We are to God the aroma of Christ among . . ." (NIV). This third option is to be preferred. As faithful preachers and followers of Christ, the apostles themselves formed a sweet savor of Christ rising up to God as a pleasing odor (cf. Lev 1:9, 13, 17; Num 15:7). To the extent that they diffused the fragrance of Christ, they were that fragrance or aroma. Irrespective of the human response to the gospel, its proclamation delights God's heart, because it centers on the Son whom he loves.

Behind Paul's thought in both these verses may be the rabbinic concept of the Law as simultaneously life-giving and death-dealing. "As the bee reserves her honey for her owner and her sting for others, so the words of the Torah are an elixir of life for Israel and a deadly poison to the nations of the world" (Deuteronomy Rabbah 1.5, cited by T.W. Manson; see notes). Just as the Torah had a beneficial effect upon those who received and obeyed it and a lethal effect upon those who rejected it, so the proclaimers of Christ are a "life-giving perfume" to those who believe the gospel and so are being saved and at the same time a "death-dealing drug" to those who repudiate it and so are perishing (vv.15b, 16a; cf. 1 Cor 1:18, 23, 24).

16b,17 To Paul's urgent question "Who is equal to such a task (of preaching the gospel of Christ or being the aroma of Christ)?" the answer may be either, "We apostles are, for we are not peddlers of an adulterated message," or "No one is, if he depends on his own resources." The latter reply is supported by 3:4–6; the former by 3:1.

By the phrase "unlike so many," Paul may be referring to the numerous wandering teachers and philosophers of the first century (see note on 11:8) who expected or demanded payment for what they claimed was "the word of God," or (and this is more likely; note the "some people" of 3:1) to the group of his Judaizing opponents at Corinth who converted preaching into a means of personal gain. In contrast, Paul appeals to the sincerity of his motives and the purity of the message. This was shown by his divine commission ("like men sent from God"; cf. Gal 1:1, 12, 15, 16), his sense of divine dependence and responsibility ("we speak before God") and his divine authority and power ("in Christ"). The principle is clear: As those who dispense the life-giving remedy for sin, preachers must avoid diluting or adulterating the medicine of life, the Word of God.

Notes

14 Θριαμβεύω (*thriambeuō*) means "lead [about] in triumphal procession," not "cause to triumph" (KJV). The only other NT use of the verb is in Col 2:15, where the despoiled powers and authorities are viewed as unwilling captives driven before the triumphal chariot of God or Christ. See further L. Williamson, Jr., "Led in Triumph. Paul's Use of *Thriambeuō*," INT, XXII (3, 1968), pp. 317–332.

Τὴν ὀσμὴν τῆς γνώσεως αὐτοῦ (*tēn osmēn tēs gnōseōs autou*) may mean "the fragrance that consists of [or results from] the knowledge of God" or "the fragrant knowledge of Christ [or God]."

16 Ὀσμή (*osmē*) may refer to either a pleasant odor ("fragrance"; John 12:3) or an unpleasant odor ("stench"; Tobit 8:3). Similarly, in Jewish literature סם (*ṣam*) is used of both a lethal drug ("poison") and a sweet-smelling perfume or spice. See the illuminating article by T.W. Manson, "2 Cor 2:14–17: Suggestions towards an Exegesis," in *Studia Paulina in honorem Johannis de Zwaan* (Haarlem: Bohn, 1953), pp. 155–162.

The twice-used ἐκ. . .εἰς (*ek. . .eis*, lit. "out of. . .into") combination defines nature or source (ἐκ) and effect (εἰς). Thus, "to the latter we are [or, the message is] an odor of death that brings death, to the former an odor of life that imparts life." C.K. Barrett renders the prepositional phrases as "issuing from. . .leading to. . . ," whereas A. Plummer paraphrases them in this way: "exhaled from. . .and breathing. . . ." Alternatively, the prepositions may point to a continual progression ("from. . .to") from bad to worse or from good to better, with death or life as the final outcome (M. Zerwick. *Analysis Philologica Novi Testamenti Graeci* [Rome: Pontifical Biblical Institute, 1966[3]], p. 395).

17 Some MSS (including the important p^{46}), versions, and Fathers read οἱ λοιποί (*hoi loipoi*, "the rest") in place of οἱ πολλοί (*hoi polloi*, "the many" or "the majority"). Either reading presents a remarkable accusation. On the term καπηλεύοντες (*kapēleuontes*, "hawking"; "peddle," NIV), see P.E. Hughes, in loc.

b. *The results of the ministry*

3:1–3

> [1]Are we beginning to commend ourselves again? Or do we need, like some people, letters of recommendation to you or from you? [2]You yourselves are our letter, written on our hearts, known and read by everybody. [3]You show that you are a letter from Christ, the result of our ministry, written not with ink but with the Spirit of the living God, not on tablets of stone but on tablets of human hearts.

1 Behind each of the two questions in this verse, both of which expect the answer "No!" stands an actual or expected charge against Paul. Since he had just spoken of the distinctive role of apostles (2:14–16) and of his divine commission and authority (2:17; note also 1:12 and 1 Cor 4:15, 16; 11:1; 14:18; 15:10), some might say, "Paul, once again you are indulging in your notorious habit of self-commendation." The second assertion, which Paul answers and which was made by some of "the many" who were making a profit out of preaching (2:17), might have run like this: "Since Jerusalem is the fount of Christianity, anyone working outside Jerusalem must be able to give proof of his commission by letters of recommendation. We brought you Corinthians commendatory letters from Jerusalem and you yourselves have supplied us with such when we have visited other places. Why should you regard Paul as an exception? Does not his unconcern about letters of recommendation prove he is an intruder and impostor?"

Paul is not here disparaging the use of letters of introduction. Their use had already become established within the Christian world (see Acts 18:27) and Paul himself had sought epistolary credentials from the high priest at Jerusalem before setting out for the synagogues of Damascus (Acts 9:2; 22:5). Also he himself gave what amounted to commendatory letters (Rom 16:1, 2; 1 Cor 16:3, 10, 11; 2 Cor 8:16–24).

His opponents apparently carried letters as their credentials, probably not from the three Jerusalem "pillars" (Gal 2:9) or the Twelve, but from the Pharisaic wing of the Jerusalem church, those Judaizers who regarded the scrupulous observance of the Mosaic law as essential for salvation (Acts 15:5) and were unable to distinguish between the law-abiding conduct of the Twelve and legalistic teaching.

2,3 The latter of the two questions posed in v.1 Paul now answers explicitly. He insists that for him to carry commendatory letters to Corinth would be completely superfluous. The most complimentary letter he could possibly possess had already been written (cf. 1 Cor 9:2). Their very lives as men and women "in Christ," the result of the grace of Christ operative in his ministry, were an eloquent letter all could read. To bring another letter would amount to a personal insult to the Corinthians; it certainly would ignore the past and present work of Christ in their hearts. They themselves were Paul's testimonial (see note), guaranteeing his apostolic status and authority.

It may have been Paul's immediate circumstances—dictating a letter to an amanuensis—that suggested the metaphor of letter writing. If Christ wrote the letter and the Spirit was the amanuensis who recorded it, Paul may have regarded himself either as the messenger who delivered it to its destination or as the person who published it. But the order of reference in v.3 (Christ–Paul–the Spirit) may suggest simply the twofold idea of author (Christ through the Spirit) and amanuensis (Paul).

Now the imagery is further developed and explained (v.3b). The letter was no human document recorded in ink on papyrus. Nor was it a divine composition, such as the Decalogue, engraved on inanimate tablets of stone (Exod 31:18; 32:15, 16). Rather the letter was of divine authorship, "written by the Spirit of the living God," and was indelibly inscribed on living tablets, sensitive human hearts (Jer 31:33; 32:38; Ezek 11:19; 36:26). Proof of Paul's genuineness was to be found not in written characters but in human characters.

So Paul delivers a powerful rebuttal to his opponents. His commendatory letter had been written before theirs; it was indelible; it was widely circulated, not confidential or unpublished; its author was Christ, not a partisan group within the Jerusalem church.

Notes

2 RSV prefers the reading ὑμῶν (*hymōn*, "your") (א 33) over ἡμῶν (*hēmōn*, "our"): "written on your hearts." This may be more in harmony with the context (7:3 could account for *hēmōn*), but the more difficult reading ("written on our hearts," NEB, NIV), which has the stronger MS support, is by no means impossible. Paul is saying, "Our own hearts [cf. 1:1, 19] testify that you are our credentials, and wherever we go and speak of your faith in Christ everyone else also can read your letter of recommendation about us."

c. *Competence for service*

3:4–6

> [4]Such confidence as this is ours through Christ before God. [5]Not that we are competent of ourselves to judge anything we do, but our competence comes from God. [6]He has enabled us to be ministers of a new covenant—not of the letter but of the Spirit; for the letter kills, but the Spirit gives life.

4,5 Paul's confidence before God in claiming that the Corinthians were a letter written by Christ validating his apostolic credentials came through Christ (v.4). It was not the product of a pious wish or imagination. Still speaking of this confidence before God, he disowns any ability to form a competent judgment on the results of his own ministry or any personal right to lay claim to the results of what was in reality God's work. His qualification and source of competence for the work of the ministry, including the assessment of its success, were not natural ability or personal initiative but divine enabling. Paul's confidence came through Christ, his competence from God, and he says all this against the background of his opponents' claim to be self-sufficient.

6 Paul realized that to be divinely commissioned was to be divinely equipped. His equipment to be a minister of a new covenant was given at his Damascus call when he was named a "chosen instrument" of God and filled with his Spirit (Acts 9:15, 17–19).

There follows a contrast between two basic characteristics of the old and new covenants. The basis of the old covenant between Yahweh (Jehovah) and Israel was a lifeless, written code, "the book of the covenant" (Exod 24:7). The basis of the new covenant between God and the church is a dynamic, pervasive Spirit. The written code (or "letter") pronounced a sentence of death (Rom 7:9–11; Gal 3:10), but the Spirit brings a transformation of life (Rom 7:6; 8:3). Though the new covenant was ratified by the shedding of Christ's blood (Heb 13:20) and is symbolized in the communion cup (Luke 22:20; 1 Cor 11:25), it becomes operative only through the indwelling Spirit who imparts new life. Where "the letter" was powerless, the Spirit is powerful in producing holiness of life, in enabling a person fully to meet the righteous requirements of the law (Rom 8:4). This is what makes the new covenant "new" (see note) and the old covenant (3:14) "old" (see Heb 8:6–13). In themselves words cannot produce righteousness, even though they be divine oracles. There has to be a vitalizing Spirit to charge the words with transforming power.

Notes

---

6 It is difficult, if not impossible, always to maintain a distinction in the NT between καινός (*kainos*) and νέος (*neos*) or cognate terms. Compare, e.g., the use of these terms and their cognate verbs in Eph 4:23, 24 and Col 3:10. Sometimes, however, *neos* implies recency (newness in time or origin) and *kainos*, superiority (newness in nature or quality). See further J. Behm, TDNT, 3:447–454; 4:896–901.

---

d. *The surpassing glory of the new covenant*

3:7–11

> [7]Now if the ministry that brought death, which was engraved in letters on stone, came with glory, so that the Israelites could not look steadily at the face of Moses because of its glory, fading though it was, [8]will not the ministry of the Spirit be even more glorious? [9]If the ministry that condemns men is glorious, how much more glorious is the ministry that brings righteousness! [10]For what was glorious has no glory now in comparison with the surpassing glory. [11]And if what was fading away came with glory, how much greater is the glory of that which lasts!

Thus far in chapter three, Paul's thought has progressed from the idea of commendatory letters written on hearts by the Spirit to reflection on the new covenant promised by God through Jeremiah under which the law would be written on men's hearts (Jer 31:31–34). This now prompts him to compare the old and new economies. Each involved a distinctive ministry that was accompanied by glory, but so superior was the glory of the new covenant that the glory of the old faded into insignificance by comparison.

7–9 Not only in these three verses but also in the remainder of the chapter Paul provides a commentary on selected points of the narrative in Exodus 34:29–35. When Moses descended from Mount Sinai with the two tablets on which were written the Ten Commandments, his face shone so brightly that "the Israelites could not look steadily" at him. Well then, argues Paul, if such glory attended the giving of the law under the ministry or administration that brought death and condemns men, how much more glorious will be the ministry of the Spirit that brings righteousness! What was a distinctive and positive feature of the old order must also characterize the new economy, but in greater measure. The new covenant has surpassing glory inasmuch as it is a more adequate revelation of God's character.

10,11 The comparison between the covenants advances one step further. The new covenant is not simply characterized by greater glory. So pronounced is the contrast between the two economies or dispensations that what once was rightly considered resplendent now appears scarcely resplendent at all (v.10). "If the sun is up, the brightness of the moon is no longer bright" (M. Zerwick), or as J.A. Bengel long ago expressed it, "The greater light obscures the lesser." The old covenant suffers immeasurably from a comparison with the new. It belonged in fact to a vanishing order, an economy that began to fade immediately after its inception, as was typified by the divine glory reflected on Moses's face—a glory that began to fade as soon as he left the divine presence. On the other hand, a covenant destined to be permanent (cf. Heb 13:20) must be invested with a far greater glory.

Notes

9 The third ed. of the UBS text, unlike the first and second, prefers the reading τῇ διακονίᾳ (*tē diakonia*) on the basis of the strong external evidence (p^{46} ℵ A C D* G), and explains the nominative reading ἡ διακονία (*hē diakonia*) as resulting from scribal assimilation to the *diakonia* that precedes (and follows). The tr. will then run: "If there was glory in the ministry that condemns men. . . ."

11 Τὸ καταργούμενον (*to katargoumenon;* cf. v.7) may mean "what was destined to pass away" or "what was in process of fading away."

---

e. *Veiling and unveiling*

3:12–18

> [12]Therefore, since we have such a hope, we are very bold. [13]We are not like Moses, who veiled his face to keep the Israelites from gazing at it while the radiance was fading away. [14]But their minds were made dull; for to this day the same veil remains when the old covenant is read. It has not been removed, because only in Christ is it taken away. [15]Even to this day when Moses is read, a veil covers their hearts. [16]But whenever anyone turns to the Lord, "the veil is taken away." [17]Now the Lord is the Spirit, and where the Spirit of the Lord is, there is freedom. [18]And we, who with unveiled faces all reflect the Lord's glory, are being transformed into his likeness with ever-increasing glory, which comes from the Lord, who is the Spirit.

12,13 As participants in the new covenant, Paul and his fellow apostles and fellow preachers had the sure hope that it was a permanent, irrevocable covenant, never to be superseded and never to be surpassed in splendor. This accounted for their boldness and confidence (see note on *parrhēsia*) in preaching. They had nothing to conceal but every reason for fearless candor (v.12).

This idea of openness prompts Paul to continue his *midrash* on Exodus 34:29–35. This OT passage suggested that after each encounter between Moses and Yahweh in the "tent of meeting," when Moses returned to the people of Israel to tell them what he had been commanded, they were dazzled by the radiance of his face. When he had finished speaking to them, he used to veil his face. "But whenever Moses went in before the Lord to speak with him, he took the veil off, until he came out"(Exod 34:34, RSV). Although the OT does not explicitly state that the radiance on the face of Moses gradually faded and then disappeared, Paul deduced that the reason for Moses's veiling or masking his face was not so much to prevent the Israelites from being dazzled by its brightness (cf. Exod 34:30, 31) as to prevent them from continuing to gaze in amazement till his face had totally lost the brilliance of the reflected glory (cf. v.7). He was attempting to teach them, Paul implies, that the newly established order was destined to be eclipsed and pass away.

P.E. Hughes (in loc.) argues that the purpose of Moses' veiling was to prevent the Israelites from looking "right on to the end" of what was transient. It was an acted parable condemning the people, showing them that their sins had made them unable and unworthy to behold even temporary glory without interruption. Others believe that Moses wished to avoid the personal embarrassment of having the people realize the splendor of his face was fading, or that he did not want to undermine their confidence in the present dispensation by letting them see it was transient (see note).

14,15 Moses' laudable attempt was however, unsuccessful; instead of recognizing the significance of his veiled face, the Israelites became dulled in their opwers of perception. Paul finds evidence of this spiritual insensitivity in the fact that down to his own day, when the old covenant (= the OT) was read in the synagogue or the Torah studied, the ability of the Jews to recognize the impermanence of the Mosaic order was impaired. A "veil" covered their hearts comparable to the veil that covered Moses's face. Paul could call it the "same" veil, because in both cases a veil prevented vision, whether physical or spiritual, or because it was identical to the veil of ignorance about the transitory nature of the Mosaic economy covering the hearts of the contemporaries of Moses. This veil remained unlifted (see note) in the case of the unbelieving Jew, because only as he came to be "in Christ" was the veil set aside.

16 In LXX Exodus 34:34 reads, "But whenever Moses went in before the Lord to speak to him, he used to take off the veil until he went out." Only three Greek words remain the same, as Paul here alludes to this verse (see note for the significance of the change of verb tenses). The subject of the verb *epistrepsē* ("turns") is unexpressed. It may be "the heart [of a Jew]," from v.15b; "the Jew" or "Israel"; or "a person," Jew or Gentile. The last option may be preferable, but in the context Paul is thinking particularly of the Jew.

The verse restates and amplifies what is stated at the end of v.14, viz., that only in Christ is the veil set aside. Whenever a person turns to the Lord and finds in him the end or fulfillment of the law (Rom 10:4), the Lord completely removes the veil from his heart. No longer is his spiritual perception impaired (v.14). He recognizes that the dispensation of grace has superseded the dispensation of the law (cf. John 1:17). He is a "new creation" in Christ (5:17).

17 Out of its context, this verse might suggest that Paul is identifying the risen Christ with the Spirit (as W. Bousset and others have held). But v.17 explains v.16. "The Lord" referred to in the quotation from Exodus 34:34, to whom the Jew must now turn for the removal of the veil, is none other than the life-giving Spirit of the living God (cf. vv.3, 6, 8). This is an affirmation about the Spirit, not about Christ; it describes his function, not his identity (as though the Spirit were the Lord [= Yahweh] of v.16).

Another view finds here a functional equivalence between Christ and the Spirit: in v.14 it is Christ who removes the veil; in v.16 it is the Spirit. Again, some believe Christ (*ho Kyrios*) is being identified as "life-giving Spirit" (1 Cor 15:45; cf. 2 Cor 3:6).

Paul's point in v.17b is that though the Spirit is Lord, who has the right to exercise authority, his presence brings liberation, not bondage (Rom 8:15). Not only does he remove the veil; he also sets a person free from bondage to sin, to death, and to the law as a means of acquiring righteousness.

18 In vv.4–6 Paul was speaking primarily of the apostolic ministry. Now, as he draws his conclusion concerning the superiority of the new covenant against the background of his commentary on Exodus 34, he refers to Christian experience in general. Under the new covenant, not one man alone, but all Christians behold and then reflect (see note) the glory of the Lord. Moreover, unlike the Jews, who still read the law with veiled hearts, Christians, with unveiled faces, behold in the mirror of the gospel the glory of Yahweh, which is Christ. Again, the glory is displayed not outwardly on the face but inwardly in the character. Finally, so far from losing its intensity or luster, the glory experienced under the new covenant progressively increases until the Christian finally acquires a "glorious body" like that of the risen Christ (Phil 3:21).

Paul concludes by noting that the progressive transformation of the Christian's character is the work of the Lord who is the Spirit (cf. v.17a). After conversion to the Spirit (v.16), there is liberation through the Spirit (v.17b) and transformation by the Spirit (v.18).

Notes

12 Παρρησία (*parrhēsia*) originally meant "frankness or freedom in speaking" or "fearless candor" but came to denote "barefacedness," "boldness," or "confidence" or "openness" in action as well as word. See further W.C. van Unnik, "The Christian's Freedom of Speech in the New Testament." *Bulletin of the John Rylands Library,* XLIV (2, 1962), pp. 466–488; and " 'With Unveiled Face,' an Exegesis of 2 Corinthians iii 12–18." Nov Test VI (2–3, 1963), pp. 153–169.

13 **Τοῦ καταργουμένου** (*tou katargoumenou,* neuter) seems to refer, not precisely to the **δόξα** (*doxa,* feminine) but to the fading brightness of the old order or dispensation (note the neuters of vv.10, 11). Thus "Moses used to place [**ἐτίθει**, *etithei*] a veil over his face to prevent the Israelites from gazing at the end of the fading brightness." Significantly, in rabbinic tradition the glory of Moses's face was undiminished right up to the day of his death when he was 120 years old.

14 H. Seesemann (TDNT, 5:720, n.13) suggests that Paul may have coined the phrase "old covenant" to match Jeremiah's "new covenant" (Jer 31:31) and the eucharistic tradition of the cup as the "new covenant" in Christ's blood (1 Cor 11:25).

The Gr. of v.14c may be punctuated in two basic ways: (1) with a comma after **μένει** (*menei,* "remains"), reflected in NIV (also NEB); (2) with a comma after **ἀνακαλυπτόμενον** (*anakalyptomenon,* lit. "being unveiled"), either (a) "that same veil remains unlifted, because [**ὅτι**, *hoti*] only through Christ is it taken away" (RSV), or (b) "the same veil remaineth unlifted; which *veil* [reading ὅ τι, *ho ti,* as = ὅ, *ho*] is done away in Christ" (RV; also KJV).

16 In Exod 34:34 LXX has **εἰσεπορεύετο** (*eiseporeueto*) and **περιῃρεῖτο** (*periēreito*), both imperfects, whereas Paul has an aorist (**ἐπιστρέψῃ**, *epistrepsē,* "turns" [single act]) and a present (**περιαιρεῖται**, *periaireitai,* "is removed"). The change accords with his omission of the subject "Moses." He is thinking not of the habitual practice of one man (viz., Moses' entering of the "tent of meeting"), but of a single "turning" and "removal" in the case of many men.

Περιαιρεῖται (*periaireitai*) may be (1) middle (like its LXX equivalent, where Moses is the subject): "whenever anyone turns to the Lord, he *removes* the veil," where "he" may be the "anyone" or the "Lord"; or preferably (2) passive: "whenever anyone [or the Jew, or Israel, or their heart] turns to the Lord, the veil *is removed*" (as in NIV).

17 In Pauline usage ὁ Κύριος (*ho Kyrios*) generally means "Christ," and Κύριος (*Kyrios*) signifies Yahweh. In this verse ὁ κύριος refers to Yahweh, for the article is anaphoric, pointing back to the anarthrous κύριον (*kyrion* = Yahweh) in v.16. See M. Zerwick, *Biblical Greek* (Rome: Pontifical Biblical Institute, 1963), p. 54, paragraph 169; and the article by J.D.G. Dunn, "2 Corinthians III. 17—'The Lord is the Spirit.' " *Journal of Theological Studies,* XXI (2, 1970), pp. 309–320.

18 Three related meanings of **κατοπτριζόμενοι** (*katoptrizomenoi*) are possible: (1) "beholding as in a mirror" (cf. 1 Cor 13:12); (2) "reflecting like a mirror"; (3) "beholding" (Vul. *speculantes*), with no necessary reference to a mirror. Some (e.g., K. Prümm, J. Jervell) believe Paul used this ambiguous verb intentionally. See further J.-F. Collange. *Énigmes de la deuxième Épître de Paul aux Corinthiens* (Cambridge: Cambridge University Press, 1972), pp. 116–118, and P.E. Hughes, in loc.

f. *The light brought by the gospel*

4:1–6

[1]Therefore, since through God's mercy we have this ministry, we do not lose heart. [2]Rather, we have renounced secret and shameful ways; we do not use deception, nor do we distort the word of God. On the contrary, by setting forth the truth plainly we commend ourselves to every man's conscience in the sight of God. [3]And even if our gospel is veiled, it is veiled to those who are perishing. [4]The god

of this age has blinded the minds of unbelievers, so that they cannot see the light of the gospel of the glory of Christ, who is the image of God. 5For we do not preach ourselves, but Jesus Christ as Lord, and ourselves as your servants for Jesus' sake. 6For God who said, "Let light shine out of darkness," made his light shine in our hearts to give us the light of the knowledge of the glory of God in the face of Christ.

1 At 4:1 Paul resumes the theme of 3:6—divine appointment and provision to be a minister of a new covenant. He had no reason to lose heart (cf. Gal 6:9), for God in his mercy had granted him a privilege exceeding that of Moses (cf. 1 Tim 1:12–16). He had been called not to communicate the law but to dispense grace. A minister of the gospel has a higher calling than even the mediator of the law. Paul regarded this divine commission to serve under the new covenant as more than compensating for all the trials he endured for being true to his calling (vv.7–12, 17; cf. Rom 8:18), including the malicious charges of his Corinthian opponents (note v.2).

2 To this thought of refusing to grow disheartened Paul will return presently (v.16). Now he expands his brief self-defense of 2:17. Evidently he had been accused of deceitful behavior (cf. 7:2; 12:16). This he emphatically rejects. The openness marking the new covenant had always been reflected in his conduct. His tactics had never been secretive or deceptive, nor had he ever dishonestly manipulated the message of God entrusted to him. His not insisting on Gentile compliance with the Mosaic law had probably given rise to the charge that he willfully adulterated the gospel (cf. 2:17).

In any self-defense, self-commendation must play some part. But Paul's self-commendation was distinctive. He commended himself, not by self-vindication at every point, but simply by the open declaration of the truth (in particular, the gospel and its implications). His appeal was not directed to a partisan spirit or the prejudices of men but "to every man's conscience." His self-commendation was undertaken with God as onlooker.

3,4 Paul's gospel, some had claimed, was designed only for a spiritually minded élite. What he said was obscure, just as what he did was underhanded (v.2). For the sake of argument, Paul concedes his critics' point. Even if his gospel is veiled in the case of some people, it is not his doing, because he sets forth the truth plainly (v.2). The veiling, where it exists (cf. 3:14, 15), comes from the unbelief of "those who are perishing" (cf. 1 Cor 1:18; 2 Cor 2:15), whose minds have been blinded by the god of "the present evil age" (Gal 1:4), who wishes to prevent them from seeing the gospel-light that focuses on Christ's glory as the image of God.

"The god of this age" refers, of course, not to God the Father, but to Satan regarded as "the prince of this world" (John 12:31) or as the one whom this age has made its god. If dualism is found in Paul, it is an ethical and temporal dualism, not a material or metaphysical one. Satan is *not* the god of "the age to come."

When Paul calls Christ "the image of God," he is asserting that Christ is the visible and perfect representation of the invisible God (Col 1:15; cf. John 1:18), the precise expression of the unseen God. When used of the relation of Christ to God, *eikōn* (image) implies both personality and distinctiveness.

5 Though Paul might have been forced to commend himself to every man's conscience (v.2; cf. 1:12; 6:4), he never advertised or preached himself. The essence of his gospel was the proclamation of "Jesus Christ as Lord" (Rom 10:9; 1 Cor 12:3; Col 2:6, NIV), a message faithfully delivered by him and eagerly embraced by the Corinthians (1:18–22). Paul saw himself related to his converts, not as a spiritual overlord (1:24) but as a willing servant as well as a concerned father (1 Cor 4:15). In this he followed in the footsteps of "the Lord of glory" (1 Cor 2:8), who himself had adopted the status and rôle of a servant (Phil 2:7; cf. Rom 15:8). Paul was both preacher (v.5a) and pastor (v.5b).

6 Paul now states the reason why he preached Christ and served the Corinthians. It was because God had dispelled his darkness by illuminating his heart and had given him a knowledge of Christ he wished to share (cf. Acts 9:15; 26:16, 18; Gal 1:15, 16). In the second creation, as in the first, darkness is dispersed and light is created by divine intervention, but in one case it was a personal word: "Let there be light" (Gen 1:3, which is expanded by Paul on the basis of Gen 1:2); in the other case it was a personal act: "God shone in our hearts" (cf. 1 Peter 2:9).

This is an unmistakable allusion to Paul's Damascus encounter with the risen Christ when God "saw fit to reveal his Son" to him (Gal 1:15, 16). Each of the three Lucan accounts of Paul's conversion mentions the noonday "light from heaven, brighter than the sun" (Acts 9:3, 8, 9; 22:6, 9, 11; 26:13) and emphasizes the personal and revelatory nature of the experience (Acts 9:4, 5; 22:7–10; 26:14–18). It was in the unveiled face (cf. 3:7, 13, 18) of Christ that Paul saw God's glory (see note).

Notes

2 Other possible meanings of *τὰ κρυπτὰ τῆς αἰσχύνης* (*ta krypta tēs aischynēs*) are (1) "the behaviour that shame hides" (C.K. Barrett) or "the things that one hides from a sense of shame" (BAG, p. 82), and (2) "the secrecy prompted by shame" (*Twentieth Century New Testament*).

4 The verb *αὐγάζειν* (*augazein*, lit. "to shine forth") is here used transitively: "so that they cannot [or, might not] *see* the light . . . ," not intransitively (as in many EV): "that the light . . . should not *dawn* [or, shine forth] upon them" (see ASV). This latter rendering requires *αὐτοῖς* (*autois*, "on them") (that is absent from the older MSS). See BAG, p. 120.

5 For a discussion of the significance of the early church's confession "Jesus is Lord," see the author's article on "Lord" in the revised ISBE.

6 The piling up of genitives is typical of Paul's Gr. style. Few studies are more rewarding for exegesis and theology than an examination of his use of the genitive. Here, "of the knowledge" may be an epexegetic genitive (the light consists of the knowledge), or better, a genitive of source (the illumination that springs from knowledge); "of the glory" is objective (Paul came to know the glory); "of God" and "of Christ" are possessive (the glory spoken of is God's, the countenance mentioned is Christ's).

Ἐν προσώπῳ (*en prosōpō*) here means "in the face of Christ" or "in the person of Christ," whereas in 2:10 it is not to be taken literally and means "in the presence of Christ" (the suggestion of C.F.D. Moule. *An Idiom Book of New Testament Greek* [Cambridge: Cambridge University Press, 1960[2]], p. 184).

2. *(The apostolic ministry) Its suffering and glory* (4:7–5:10)

a. *The trials and rewards of apostolic service*

4:7–15

[7]But we have this treasure in jars of clay to show that this all-surpassing power
is from God and not from us. [8]We are hard pressed on every side, but not crushed;
perplexed, but not in despair; [9]persecuted, but not abandoned; struck down, but
not destroyed. [10]We always carry around in our body the death of Jesus, so that
the life of Jesus may also be revealed in our body. [11]For we who are alive are
always being given over to death for Jesus' sake, so that his life may be revealed
in our mortal body. [12]So then, death is at work in us, but life is at work in you.
[13]It is written: "I believed; therefore I have spoken." With that same spirit of faith
we also believe and therefore speak, [14]because we know that the one who raised
the Lord Jesus from the dead will also raise us with Jesus and present us with you
in his presence. [15]All this is for your benefit, so that the grace that is reaching more
and more people may cause thanksgiving to overflow to the glory of God.

No person was ever more aware of the paradoxical nature of Christianity than Paul. And perhaps none of his Epistles contains more paradoxes than 2 Corinthians. With their numerous paradoxes, then, verses 7 to 12 are typical of this Epistle and of Paul's style.

7 Here is the first paradox—the difference between the indescribable value of the gospel treasure and the apparent worthlessness of the gospel's ministers. Verse 6 refers to the treasure in the "jars of clay" as "the illumination that comes from the knowledge of God's glory." In describing those to whom the gospel is entrusted (1 Thess 2:4) as "earthenware vessels," Paul is not disparaging the human body or implying that the body is simply the receptacle of the soul (see note). Rather, he is contrasting the relative insignificance and unattractiveness of the bearers of the light with the inestimable worth and beauty of the light itself. Behind this contrast Paul sees a divine purpose—that men may recognize that "this all-surpassing power" is God's alone. His power finds its full scope in human weakness (12:9).

8,9 There follows a series of four vivid antitheses that illustrate both the weakness of Paul in discharging his commission and the power of God in preserving his life and his spirit. Each metaphor may reflect gladiatorial or military combat. Paul was "hard pressed on every side," but not completely cornered or without room for movement, never driven to surrender. He was "bewildered . . . [but] never at . . . wits' end" (NEB), or (as an attempt to retain the word-play of the Greek) "at a loss, but never totally at a loss." He was hounded by the foe, but not left to his mercy. He was knocked to the ground, but not permanently "grounded."

10,11 Verse 10 summarizes the four preceding contrasts in the paradox: "always dying, yet never lifeless." In the phrase "the death [or, dying] of Jesus," Paul sums up the experience of being "hard pressed," "perplexed," "persecuted," and "struck down" during the course of his service for him. On the other hand, he uses the phrase "the life of Jesus" to express the Lord's saving him from being crushed, from despair, from abandonment, and from destruction, all of which prefigures the Christian's final deliverance from mortality at the resurrection. This idea of "life in the midst of death" is, of course, closely related to the theme of 2 Corinthians 1–7—"comfort in the midst of affliction" (see Introduction, 9).

But the meaning of the arresting phrase "the dying of Jesus" is also explained by what follows, since v.11a amplifies v.10a. "The dying of Jesus" that Paul "carried around" in his body (v.10a) was nothing other than his being always "given over to death for Jesus' sake" (v.11a). He faced perilous hazards every hour and death every day, as he says in 1 Corinthians 15:30, 31 (cf. 1 Cor 4:9). This contextual interpretation of the phrase seems preferable to understanding it as a reference to the Christian's once-for-all baptismal identification with Christ in his death (Rom 6:3–5), or his daily mortification of his sinful nature (Gal 5:24; cf. Luke 9:23), or the gradual weakening of his physical powers while serving Christ.

Both verses stress (through *hina kai*, "so that . . . also") the fact that the death and the life of Jesus were simultaneously evident in the apostle's experience (cf. 1:4, 5). It was not a matter of life after death, or even of life through death, but of life in the midst of death. Paul's repeated deliverances from death evidenced the resurrecting power of God (1:9, 10), just as his refusal to despair in the face of the danger of death and persistent opposition (4:1, 16; 5:6) displayed the resurrection-life of Jesus operative in his "mortal body" (cf. Phil 3:10).

12 With a bold stroke, Paul relates this theme of "life in death" to his earlier statements in chapter 1 about vicarious suffering (1:3–7). There he had said, "I suffer for Christ; God comforts me; I comfort you during your suffering." Here his thought seems to be "I suffer exposure to physical death for your sakes [cf. v.15a]; you enjoy more of the risen life of Christ as a consequence." He apparently saw not only a causal but also a proportional relation between his "death" and the "life" of the Corinthian believers. The deeper his experience of the trials and sufferings of the apostolic life, the richer their experience of the joys and privileges of Christian existence (cf. Col 1:24; 2 Tim 2:10). The "middle term" between his experience and theirs was the divine comfort that, having received, he could then dispense (cf. 1:4). This rich theology of suffering was forged on the anvil of his own experience of "the sufferings of Christ."

13,14 But what enabled Paul faithfully to discharge his ministry (3:6; 4:1, 5), even though it involved suffering? It was his sharing the psalmist's conviction that faith cannot remain silent and his own Christian conviction that Christ's resurrection guarantees the resurrection of believers.

The exact meaning of the Hebrew text of Psalm 116:10a is uncertain (see notes). In his quotation Paul follows the LXX (Ps 115:1) exactly: "I believed; therefore I have spoken," a translation of the Hebrew in accord with the spirit of the psalm, though not with its precise words. The psalmist recounts a divine deliverance from a desperate illness and its accompanying despondency (vv.1–11) and then considers how he might most fittingly render his devotion to the Lord (vv.12–19). In a real sense, then, the psalmist's expression of thanksgiving arose from his vindicated trust in God: "I held firm to my faith and was vindicated; therefore I have spoken." Paul, for his part, could not remain silent about the gospel he believed: "Woe to me if I do not preach the gospel" (1 Cor 9:16).

Another reason Paul proclaimed the good news with the utmost confidence (cf. 3:12) was his firm conviction of his personal resurrection and his being presented along with all believers before the presence of God or Christ (cf. 11:2; Eph 5:27; Col 1:22). Christians will be raised "with Jesus" (cf. 1 Thess 4:14) in the sense that the resurrected Christ forms the prototype and ground of their resurrection (1 Cor 15:23). In Christ's resurrection from the dead as the firstfruits of the Easter harvest, believers have the pledge of the full ingathering.

15 This verse concludes a section of Paul's thought, for in v.16 he repeats the phrase "we do not lose heart" from v.1. Rather movingly, the apostle reminds his converts that he endures all his afflictions with resilience, not to promote his own good but for their benefit (cf. 4:5), and ultimately for God's glory. As God's grace expanded in their hearts and through them reached ever-increasing numbers, so too, the volume of thanksgiving to God for the receipt of illumination (cf. 4:6) would increase and promote the glory of God.

Notes

---

7 For Paul the σκεῦος (*skeuos,* "jar") was no more the container in which was placed the "treasure" of a ψυχή (*psychē,* "life," "soul") than the "outer man" was a detachable outer garment clothing "the inner man." Σκεύη (*skeuē*) refers to whole persons, who, although insignificant and weak in themselves, become God's powerful instruments in communicating the treasure of the gospel. Paul's anthropology was basically monistic, not dualistic; see D.E.H. Whiteley, *The Theology of St. Paul* (Philadelphia: Fortress Press, 1964), pp. 31–44.

13 To facilitate understanding, the NIV breaks up one Gr. sentence into two and rearranges the word order. As it stands, v.13 reads, "But since we have the same spirit of faith as that reflected in the Scripture 'I believed and so I spoke,' we too believe and that is why we speak."

The Heb. of Ps 116:10a reads, האמנתי כי אדבר (*heᵉmantî, kî ʾᵃdabbēr*), which could be translated, (1) "I believed, for I will speak"; (2) "I kept my faith, even when I said, ('I am greatly afflicted')" (RSV; similarly JB); or (3) "I believed, therefore I spoke" (LXX, followed here by Paul; Vul.; similarly KJV). In the first case, speaking is the proof of belief; in the third, belief is the ground for speaking. Some (e.g., H.L. Goudge) have suggested that Paul viewed not the psalmist but Christ himself as speaking in the psalm (vv.3, 4 are thought to portray Gethsemane; and vv.5–9, Easter). Paul's spirit would then be "the spirit" of Christ.

15 Another possible tr. might be: "All this is for your benefit, so that the expansion of grace may cause thanksgiving to abound through [the winning of] increasing numbers [of converts], to the glory of God."

---

b. *Glory through suffering*

4:16–18

16Therefore we do not lose heart. Though outwardly we are wasting away, yet inwardly we are being renewed day by day. 17For our light and momentary troubles are achieving for us an eternal glory that far outweighs them all. 18So we fix our eyes not on what is seen, but on what is unseen. For what is seen is temporary, but what is unseen is eternal.

16 "Therefore we do not lose heart" looks back to vv.14, 15 and v.1. Paul has now supplied several reasons for his refusal to grow discouraged in spite of seemingly overwhelming odds: (1) his divine commission as a minister of a new and superior covenant (4:1), (2) the prospect of sharing Christ's triumphant resurrection from the dead (4:14), and (3) his immediate task of promoting the Corinthians' spiritual welfare and the glory of God (4:15).

But Paul was realistic enough to recognize that his toil and suffering had taken their toll physically. For this, however, there was splendid compensation. Matching the progressive weakening of his physical powers was the daily renewal of his spiritual powers (see note). It was as though the more he expended himself for the gospel's sake (cf. 12:15), the greater his spiritual resilience (cf. Eph 3:16).

17 Here Paul supplies a surprising definition of daily spiritual renewal. It is a constant production of solid, lasting glory (literally "an eternal weight of glory") out of all proportion to the slight, present affliction that causes physical weakness (v.16); or, as the NIV renders it, this eternal glory "far outweighs" any "light and momentary troubles" that are being presently experienced (cf. Rom 8:18). Quite naturally Paul seems to speak of glory as though it were a substantial entity that could be progressively added to. In a similar way in Colossians 1:5 Paul views Christian hope as an inheritance "stored up" in heaven.

Again, as in vv.12, 16, the idea of proportion seems to be present. Since it is actually the "troubles" that produce or achieve the glory, the greater the affliction Paul suffered, the greater the glory produced for him.

18 But this production of glory was by no means automatic. It was only as attention was focused on what was unseen that suffering led to glory. The participle with which the verse begins may be translated "provided [or, since] we keep our eyes fixed. . . ."

Behind the contrast between "what is seen" and "what is unseen" is the Pauline tension between the "already" and the "not yet" (cf. Rom 8:24, 25; 1 Cor 13:12), the contrast between what is now seen by mortals and what is as yet hidden from mortal gaze, rather than the Platonic antithesis of the real and the ideal or a philosophical distinction between the visible and the invisible (cf. Col 1:16). Paul is not repudiating any interest in the visible world. Rather, he is affirming that his affections are set "on things above" (Col 3:1, 2), on lasting realities as yet unseen, on the age to come that is present in promises and blessings still to be fully realized. The antithesis is temporal and eschatological, not essential and philosophical.

This preoccupation with the realm "where Christ is seated at the right hand of God" (Col 3:1) was not the result of an arbitrary choice; it was an informed decision. Paul was profoundly aware that the present age is transient (cf. 1 Cor 7:31), whereas the age to come is eternal in the sense of being "destined to last for ever," and that his afflictions were temporary but his reward eternal.

Notes

16 NIV appropriately renders the phrases "our outer man" and "our inner [man]" by "outwardly we . . ." and "inwardly we. . . ." Paul is not thinking of two distinct entities, "the body" and "the soul," but is considering his total existence from two different viewpoints. His "outer man" is his whole person in his "creaturely mortality" (J. Behm, TDNT, 2:699), the man of this age; his "inner man" is his whole person as a "new creation" (5:17) or a "new man" (Col 3:9, 10), the man of the age to come. Pauline anthropology is aspectival not partitive, synthetic not analytic. See W.D. Stacey, *The Pauline View of Man* (New York: St. Martin's, 1956), especially pp. 211–214.

17 Paul's unique phrase "an eternal weight of glory" was doubtless suggested to him by the Heb. כָּבוֹד (*kāḇôḏ*) which may mean both "weight" and "glory."

---

c. *Confidence in the face of death*

5:1–10

[1]Now we know that if the earthly tent we live in is destroyed, we have a building
from God, an eternal house in heaven, not built by human hands. [2]Meanwhile we
groan, longing to be clothed with our heavenly dwelling, [3]since when we are
clothed, we will not be found naked. [4]For while we are in this tent, we groan and
are burdened, because we do not wish to be unclothed but to be clothed with our
heavenly dwelling, so that what is mortal may be swallowed up by life. [5]Now it is
God who has made us for this very purpose and has given us the Spirit as a
deposit, guaranteeing what is to come.

[6]Therefore we are always confident and know that as long as we are at home
in the body we are away from the Lord. [7]We live by faith, not by sight. [8]We are
confident, I say, and would prefer to be away from the body and at home with the
Lord. [9]So we make it our goal to please him, whether we are at home in the body
or away from it. [10]For we must all appear before the judgment seat of Christ, that
each one may receive what is due him for the things done while in the body,
whether good or bad.

No passage in 2 Corinthians has prompted more discussion than this. As a consequence, the diversity of scholarly interpretation is rather bewildering.

What Paul says here is directly related to the latter part of chapter 4. There he pointed out that even in the midst of affliction, perplexity and persecution, there was, through divine consolation, the hope of glory (4:8, 9, 13, 14, 17). Even in the presence of the ravages of mortality and death, there was, through divine intervention, the operation of life (4:10–12, 16; cf. 6:9). This twofold theme—life in the midst of death, glory after and through suffering—is continued in 5:1–10. Paul now specifies the sources of divine comfort afforded the believer who faces the possibility of imminent death. Basically, they are three: (1) certainty of the future possession of a spiritual body (v.1), (2) the present possession of the Spirit as the pledge of ultimate transformation (vv.4b, 5), and (3) knowledge that death begins a walk "in the realm of sight" (v.7) and involves departure to Christ's immediate presence where personal fellowship with him is enjoyed (v.8).

1 Apparently for the first time in his apostolic career Paul reckons seriously with the possibility—now a probability—of his death before the return of Christ. Previously, to judge by 1 Thessalonians 4:15, 17 and 1 Corinthians 15:51, he had expected to be among those Christians living when Christ returned. But now, as a result of his recent devastating encounter with death in Asia (1:8–11), he realized that he was likely to die before the Parousia, though he always entertained the hope of survival until the Advent (note Phil 3:20, 21).

As a Cilician "leatherworker" whose duties would include tentmaking, Paul naturally likened his present body to an earthly tent (cf. vv.2, 4) that might at any moment be dismantled or destroyed. This would simply mark the termination of the process of weakness and decay already at work in his body (4:16). But this possibility did not daunt him, for he was the assured recipient of a permanent heavenly house—the spiritual body provided by God (see notes).

2–4 These verses belong together, since v.4 expands v.2, while v.3 is parenthetical (cf. the similar structure of vv.6–8). One reason for Paul's assurance of his future acquisition of a resurrection body was the raising up of the temple of Christ's body (Mark 14:58; John 2:19, 21, 22) alluded to by the phrase "not built by human hands" in v.1. An additional reason was the experience of Spirit-inspired groaning (vv.2, 4; cf. Rom 8:23). Paul's sighing did not stem from a desire to become permanently disembodied but from an intense longing to take up residence in his "heavenly dwelling" ("we sigh, because we long . . . ," v.2 Wey.).

The passage does not define the precise nature of the "sighing" or "groaning," but the immediate context and Paul's thought elsewhere (Rom 8:19–23; Phil 3:20, 21) suggest it was his sense of frustration with the limitations and disabilities of mortal existence, knowing as he did that he was destined to possess a spiritual body perfectly adapted to the ecology of heaven. Paul sought liberation only from the imperfection of present embodiment, from "bondage to decay," not from any and every form of corporeality. After all, it is to Paul that Christian theology owes the doctrine of the "spiritual body" (1 Cor 15:35–49).

But not all at Corinth shared Paul's view of the Christian's destiny. There were some who taught that resurrection lay in the past, acccomplished spiritually and corporately for all believers at the resurrection of Christ or else personally experienced at the moment of baptism (cf. 2 Tim 2:17, 18). Having in mind these "proto-Gnostics" who denied any future, bodily resurrection but envisaged a disembodied immortality, Paul asserts, "We do not wish to be *un*clothed but to be *over*clothed with our heavenly dwelling."

This background also affords a satisfying interpretation of v.3. Perhaps Paul's opponents (1 Cor 15:12) had fastened on the apostle's innocent statement in 1 Cor 15:53, 54 about "putting on immortality" (see RSV and most EV) as the epitome of their own view. If so, Paul could be now repudiating this aberrant conception of the future: ". . . since when we are clothed, we will not be found naked" (as some of you would like to believe).

Of the many other interpretations of vv.2–4a, one may be sketched. Not a few commentators believe that Paul is expressing his own eager desire to avoid the unpleasantness or pain of a disembodied intermediate state by being preserved alive till the coming of Christ. He shrinks from the denudation of death ("we do not wish to be unclothed") and longs to put on his heavenly dwelling *over* his preserved earthly tent (see notes), though he is uncertain whether this will happen ("if, in fact, we shall be found clothed and not naked").

Verse 4b states the purpose and actual result of the receipt of the heavenly dwelling—the swallowing up of the mortal body by the revivifying action of the indwelling Spirit of life (Rom 8:2, 11; 2 Cor 3:6, 18). This transformation forms the climax of the incessant process of inward renewal (4:16b). In other words, 5:4b is related to 4:16b as 5:1a is related to 4:16a. For Paul, resurrection consummates rather than inaugurates the process of spiritual re-creation. From one point of view, the spiritual body was a future gift that came by outward investiture; from another, it was a present creation that finally came by inward transformation.

5 "This very purpose," for which God had "made" (better, "prepared") the believer is defined by v.4b as the transformation of the mortal body. Verse 5b indicates how the preparation took place. God has prepared the Christian believer for the resurrection-transformation by giving him the Spirit as the pledge of it (or "as a deposit, guaranteeing what is to come").

Undoubtedly the crucial word in the verse is *arrhabōn,* which had two basic meanings in commercial usage. It was (1) a pledge or guarantee, differing in kind from the final payment but rendering it obligatory or (2) a partial payment (first installment, down-payment, deposit) that required further payments but gave the payee a legal claim to the goods in question (see BAG, p. 109, for this second use). Clearly not all these elements apply to Paul's use of the word, for redemption is no process of reciprocal bargaining ratified by some contractually binding agreement but is the result of the grace of God, who bestows on believers his Spirit as an unsolicited gift. Certainly Paul did not regard the Spirit as a pledge to be returned (cf. Gen 38:17–20) or as an inferior part of the Christian's inheritance. Significantly, in Modern Greek *arrhabōna* means "engagement ring."

But how can the Spirit be God's pledge of the Christian's inheritance (Eph 1:13, 14; cf. 4:30)? No doubt through his empowering the Christian's daily re-creation (3:18; 4:16; Eph 3:16) and his future effecting of the Christian's resurrection transformation (Rom 8:11). His present work prefigures and guarantees his future completion of that work (cf. Phil 1:6).

6–8 With the assured hope of his acquisition of a glorified body (v.1) and having a pledge of his transformation in the presence and activity of the Spirit within him (v.5), Paul was always confident, even in the face of death. "But," he continues, "because we realize that we are absent from the Lord's presence as long as this body forms our residence, it is our preference to leave our home in this body and take up residence in the presence of the Lord" (a paraphrase of vv.6, 8).

Just as the repeated verb "we groan" shows vv.2 and 4 to be related, so "we are confident" relates vv.6 and 8, vv.3 and 7 being parenthetical in each case. But v.8 does not simply repeat v.6; it stands in antithetical parallelism to it. The corollary of "residence in the body = absence from the Lord" (v.6) is "absence from the body = residence with the Lord" (v.8). That is, what is implied in v.6 is stated positively in v.8: as soon as departure from mortal corporeality occurs (v.8a), residence in the Lord's presence begins (v.8b). This then means that the same moment of death that marks the destruction of the transitory earthly tent-dwelling (v.1) also marks the taking up of permanent residence "with the Lord" (v.8).

What did Paul understand to be involved in being "at home with the Lord"? To be sure, the Greek preposition *pros* (here meaning "with") in itself simply denotes location. Yet when it describes the interrelation of two persons, it necessarily implies a fellowship both active and reciprocal (cf. *pros* in Mark 6:3: "Are not his sisters here *with* us?"). In any case, since the phrase "at home with the Lord" depicts the Christian's eternal destiny (cf. 1 Thess 4:17; Phil 1:23), what is thus signified must supersede earthly experience where the believer "knows" the Lord (Phil 3:10). So being "at home with the Lord" is a higher form of the intimate fellowship with Christ that the believer experiences on earth.

In v.7 Paul corrects a possible misinterpretation of v.6. If the clause "we are away from the Lord" (v.6) is interpreted in an absolute sense, present fellowship with Christ would appear illusory and mortal embodiment would seem a hindrance to spirituality. Since both deductions would be totally false, Paul qualifies his statement by observing that "we do in fact still walk in the realm of faith, not of sight." To the believer the Lord is present, not to sight but to faith. Any "spatial" separation is temporary, not final.

9,10 Verse 9 follows vv.1–8 in much the same way as an ethical imperative frequently follows a doctrinal indicative in Paul's Epistles ("You are; therefore be!"). After stating profound doctrinal facts (vv.1–8) Paul shows their implications for behavior (v.9). His constant ambition to please Christ (v.9) was the direct outcome (*dio kai,* "that is why"; "so" in NIV) of his awareness that death would terminate his relative exile from Christ and inaugurate his "walking in the realm of sight in the presence of the Lord" (vv.6–8). To entertain the hope of person-to-person communion with Christ after death (v.8) naturally prompts the aspiration of gaining acceptance in his eyes before and after death (cf. Gal 1:10; Phil 1:20; Col 1:10; 1 Thess 4:1).

We should not try to draw any implication from v.9 regarding the possibility of performing actions during the "intermediate state" that may be pleasing to Christ. The recompense spoken of in v.10 rests exclusively on the basis of "the things done while in the body." Accordingly, "away from it" (the body) in v.9 probably alludes to the judgment.

In v.10 we find a second and secondary reason for Paul's eager striving to win Christ's approval. Not only was there his destiny with Christ (v.8), but there was also his accountability to Christ (v.10) requiring his compulsory attendance before the tribunal of Christ. From 1 Corinthians 4:5 we see that this involves not merely an "appearance" in the court of heaven (cf. Rom 14:10) but the divine illumination of what has been hidden by darkness and the divine exposure of secret aims and motives. The person thus scrutinized will then receive an equitable and full recompense ("what is due him").

Of whom is this attendance required? It is true that all men are accountable to God their maker and judge (Rom 2:1–11). In this context, however, Paul is thinking primarily, if not exclusively, of the Christian's obligation to "give an account of himself" (Rom 14:12). Appearance before Christ's tribunal is the privilege of Christians. It is concerned with the assessment of works and, indirectly, of character, not with the determination of destiny; with reward, not status. Judgment on the basis of works is not opposed to justification on the basis of faith. Delivered from "the works of the law" (Rom 3:28), the Christian is presently committed to "the work of faith," "action stemming from faith" (1 Thess 1:3), that will be assessed and rewarded at the *bēma* ("tribunal"). Yet not all verdicts will be comforting. The believer may "suffer loss" (1 Cor 3:15) by forfeiting Christ's praise or losing a reward that might have been his.

Notes

1–10 On this passage, consult the articles (listed in full in the bibliography, Introduction, 10) by R. Berry, E.E. Ellis, C.F.D. Moule, and the present writer.

1 Not all agree that the οἰκοδομή (*oikodomē,* "building") refers to the believer's resurrection body. Other proposed identifications are: heaven or a house in heaven (C. Hodge), the heavenly temple (H. Odeberg, G. Wagner), a celestial dwelling place (cf. John 14:2) (R.V.G. Tasker), a vestment of celestial glory (F. Prat), the heavenly mode of existence (F.W. Grosheide), the church as the body of Christ or as the new temple (J.A.T. Robinson, E.E. Ellis). Against these proposals, it may be observed that (1) the parallel in v.1b to the "earthly tent" of v.1a (clearly the physical body; cf. 4:10, 11, 16) is likely to be another type of personal embodiment and (2) the fourfold description of the *oikodomē* in v.1 (from God, permanent, heavenly, spiritual) matches Paul's description of the "spiritual body" in 1 Cor 15:38–54.

The present tense ἔχομεν (*echomen,* "we have") of the apodosis could refer to a present possession (though this would convert the condition ["if . . ."] into a concession ["even if . . .]), but more probably it points to a future acquisition that is assured—viz., receipt of a spiritual body at the Parousia or at the moment of death.

2–4 Some commentators (e.g., H.A.W. Meyer, P.E. Hughes) emphasize the doubly compounded verb **ἐπ-εν-δύσασθαι** (*ep-en-dysasthai*) and translate it "to put [our heavenly dwelling] on *over* [the earthly tent we live in]," seeing here an allusion to Paul's desire to be alive at the Advent.

3 The UBS text (third ed.) expresses a slight preference ("D" rating) for **ἐκδυσάμενοι** (*ek-dysamenoi*, "being naked" over **ἐνδυσάμενοι** (*endysamenoi*, "being clothed") on the basis of internal evidence: "inasmuch as we, though unclothed, shall not be found naked." But B.M. Metzger rightly demurs (*A Textual Commentary on the Greek New Testament* [New York: United Bible Societies, 1971], pp. 579, 580). External evidence (p^{46} ℵ B C) supports *en-dysamenoi*, while *ekdysamenoi* (D F it) is an easier reading, an evident amendment to avoid the *prima facie* tautology of "clothed, not naked."

6–8 These verses are anacoluthic. Paul may have intended to write, "Therefore we are always confident, and because we know [**εἰδότες**, *eidotes*] that as long as we are at home in the body we are away from the Lord, we prefer to be away from the body and at home with the Lord." But the need to qualify his statement of v.6b prompted him to insert an explanatory parenthesis (v.7) that interrupted his flow of thought and caused him to recommence (with a resumptive **δέ**, *de*, "I say") in v.8 with his principal idea, "we are confident."

9 The NIV correctly supplies "in the body," where the Gr. has simply "whether at home or away." Others (e.g., E.B. Allo, J. Héring) supply "with the Lord" or its equivalent, producing the sense "whether at home with the Lord or absent from his presence."

---

3. (*The apostolic ministry*) *Its function and exercise* (5:11–6:10)

a. *Motivation for service*

5:11–15

[11]Since, then, we know what it is to fear the Lord, we try to convince men. What we are is plain to God, and I hope it is also plain to your conscience. [12]We are not trying to commend ourselves to you again, but are giving you an opportunity to take pride in us, so that you can answer those who take pride in what is seen rather than in what is in the heart. [13]If we are out of our mind, it is for the sake of God; if we are in our right mind, it is for you. [14]For Christ's love compels us, because we are convinced that one died for all, and therefore all died. [15]And he died for all that those who live should no longer live for themselves, but for him who died for them and was raised again.

11 "The fear of the Lord" here is not personal piety nor the terror that the omnipotent Lord arouses in the hearts of men (e.g., Gen 35:5), but the reverential awe Paul had for Christ as his divine assessor and future judge (v.10). Aware of his personal accountability, Paul strove to persuade men. Of what did he "try to convince" them? Of the truth of the gospel, and the truth concerning himself; viz., that his motives were pure and sincere (cf. 1:12) and that his apostolic credentials and conduct were sound (cf. 3:1–6; 4:1–6). Notice that the open statement and defense of "the truth of the gospel" includes both exposition of the Scriptures about Jesus and the kingdom of God (Acts 17:2–4; 18:4; 19:8; 28:23) and disputation concerning the practical implications of the gospel (Gal 2:14).

Whether or not the persons to whom Paul addressed his appeal recognized his claims about the gospel or himself, God recognized him for what he was. "What we are is plain to God." Yet Paul realized it was necessary for the Corinthians to come to a proper understanding of his apostolic status and conduct. "I hope it is also plain to your conscience."

12 Paul insists that these assertions about himself in relation to God and men should not be interpreted as a further attempt (cf. 3:1) at self-commendation. But he wished his converts to have the necessary ammunition with which to defend his apostleship. They ought, he implies, to have had sufficient pride in him to have undertaken this defense on their own initiative (cf. 12:11) with the weapons to hand—viz., their personal experience of his legitimate apostolic authority, their own knowledge of his devoted service. However, he reluctantly supplies them with additional weaponry by reminding them of the testimony of their individual consciences.

Paul describes the opposition as those who prided themselves on outward appearances. No doubt they made superficial claims to superiority over him—such as their relation to the Jesus of history (5:16) and to Palestinian orthodoxy (11:22) or their greater number of visions and revelations (cf. 12:1–7). Paul was content to take his stand on what was not outwardly evident or fully provable, i.e., what was "in the heart"—transparency before God and men and the testimony of the conscience.

13 Whatever the background to this difficult verse, its general import seems clear. Paul disowns self-interest as a motive for any of his action; all is for God's glory (1 Cor 10:31; 2 Cor 4:15). Of this the Corinthians can be justly proud (v.12). This interpretation accords well with his following appeal (v.14) to Christ as "the man for others," and his definition of the purpose of Christ's death (v.15)—that believers should lead a life that is not centered on self but on Christ.

Verse 13a has been explained in several ways: (1) Paul's critics had accused him of being "out of his mind" (cf. Mark 3:21), perhaps because of his allegedly esoteric teaching (cf. Acts 26:24) or his ecstatic experiences or his indefatigable zeal and tireless work. To this charge he replies, "That is for God to judge." (2) Paul is referring to his experience of glossolalia or visions (cf. Acts 22:17–21), when to some he seemed "beside himself." "It is for God" (cf. 1 Cor 14:2) or "it is a matter between God and me," he answers. (3) On occasion the Corinthians had viewed Paul as having been carried away by excessive emotion. "It led to the glory to God," he affirms. (4) Paul had been criticized for his self-commendation, which appeared to be sheer lunacy. "It is in defense of God's cause," Paul replies. (5) In Jewish eyes, Paul's conversion was evidence of his madness.

14,15 Why was a life of self-pleasing impossible for Paul? Because of the supreme example of his Lord in dying for all. "The love Christ showed for us [see note] compels us to love and serve him and you [cf. v.13b], because when he died, sin's penalty was paid and we died to the self-life, while through his resurrection we live to please him [cf. v.9] by serving you." This, it seems, is the force of these verses in the context of Paul's argument. He has now isolated two motives for Christian service: knowledge of accountability to Christ (v.11) and awareness of Christ's example of self-sacrificing devotion (v.14); in other words, Christ as Savior and as Judge.

Ever since his conversion, Paul had felt "hemmed in" or without an option (*synechei*); he must expend himself in the service of others for Christ's sake (4:11, 12; 12:15). Also dating from his conversion he had two convictions about the death of Christ. The first was that since one man died on behalf of and in the place of all men, all had undergone death (v.14b). Which death? Either the death deservedly theirs because of sin (R.V.G. Tasker) or the death to sin and self that is involved in Christian living (C.K. Barrett). In neither case was the death a physical death like Christ's (notice the subsequent phrase "those who live"). In each case it was a potential, not an actual, "death" of "all men." Paul is not suggesting that, irrespective of their response and attitude, all men know forgiveness of sins or experience selfless living. There is universalism in the scope of redemption, since no man is excluded from God's offer of salvation; but there is a particularity in the application of redemption, since not all men appropriate the benefits afforded by this universally offered salvation.

Paul's second conviction was this: "Dying" with Christ should lead to "living for Christ" (v.15). Paul is not speaking of all men without exception but of "those who live" in union with the resurrected Christ. While all men died potentially when the Man who represented them all died, not all were raised when he rose. But for those who rose with Christ to walk "in newness of life" (Rom 6:4; Col 3:1, 2), slavery to sin and self has ended while devotion to Christ and his church has begun (cf. Rom 6:6, 11). The outcome of Christian self-denial is a Christ-centered life filled with concern for others.

Notes

11 Here Paul twice uses in the perfect tense, with the meaning of "is plain," the same verb (φανερόω, *phaneroō*) employed in v.10, where it is translated "appear." What Paul must be before Christ's tribunal he now seeks to be before God—"transparently open" (F.F. Bruce, in loc.).

13 As an aorist, ἐξέστημεν (*exestēmen*, "we are out of our mind"; cf. the parallel present tense, σωφρονοῦμεν, *sōphronoumen*, "we are in our right mind") may refer either to a single specific occasion when Paul was thought to be "out of his mind," or to habitual or intermittent conduct regarded as a unit.

The two datives θεῷ (*theō*) and ὑμῖν (*hymin*) are probably datives of advantage or interest (thus BDF, 101 par. 188 (2); RHG, p. 539): "for the sake of God" and "for you" (NIV).

14 In the context the genitive in the phrase ἡ ἀγάπη τοῦ Χριστοῦ (*hē agapē tou Christou*, lit. "the love of Christ") is less likely to be objective ("our love for Christ") than subjective ("the love Christ showed"), though some commentators (e.g., H. Lietzmann) and grammarians (e.g., M. Zerwick) believe that both senses are intended. Zerwick comments (*Biblical Greek* [Rome: Pontifical Biblical Institute, 1963], p. 13): "In interpreting the sacred text . . . we must beware lest we sacrifice to clarity of meaning part of the fulness of the meaning." It is certainly true that the Christian's love for Christ motivates his action (i.e., love of Christ rather than love of money, love of position, etc.), but Paul here is concentrating on an earlier stage of motivation.

b. *The message of reconciliation*

5:16–6:2

16So from now on we regard no one from a worldly point of view. Though we once regarded Christ in this way, we do so no longer. 17Therefore, if anyone is in Christ, he is a new creation; the old has gone, the new has come! 18All this is from God, who reconciled us to himself through Christ and gave us the ministry of reconciliation: 19that God was reconciling the world to himself in Christ, not counting men's sins against them. And he has committed to us the message of reconciliation. 20We are therefore Christ's ambassadors, as though God were making his appeal through us. We implore you on Christ's behalf: Be reconciled to God.

21God made him who had no sin to be sin for us, so that in him we might become the righteousness of God.

1As God's fellow workers we urge you not to receive God's grace in vain. 2For he says,

"At the time of my favor I heard you,
and on the day of salvation I helped you."

I tell you, now is the time of God's favor, now is the day of salvation.

16 With the conjunction *hōste* ("so"; "therefore" in v.17a) Paul introduces the first of two (vv.16, 17) consequences of Christ's death and his own living for Christ. Since his conversion ("from now on"), when he gained the twofold conviction about his own "death" (v.14) and life (v.15), Paul had ceased to make superficial personal judgments (= regarding men "from a worldly point of view") based on external appearances (v.12). It was now his custom to view men, not primarily in terms of nationality but in terms of spiritual status. The Jew-Gentile division was less important for him than the Christian-unbeliever distinction (Rom 2:28, 29; 1 Cor 5:12, 13; Gal 3:28; 6:10; Eph 2:11–22; Col 3:11). Both men and events were seen in light of the new creation.

Similarly, his sincere yet superficial preconversion estimate of Jesus as a misguided messianic pretender whose followers must be extirpated (Acts 9:1, 2; 26:9–11) he now repudiated as being totally erroneous, for he had come to recognize him as the divinely appointed Messiah whose death had brought life (vv.14, 15). Paul's encounter with the risen Lord on the Damascus road effected the twofold change in attitude: Jesus was the Messiah and Lord; Gentile believers were his brothers "in Christ" while his unbelieving compatriots were "without Christ."

17 Paul next states the second outcome of the death and resurrection of Christ (vv. 14, 15). Whenever a person comes to be part of the body of Christ by faith, there is a new act of creation on God's part. One set of conditions or relationships has passed out of existence (*parēlthen*, aorist); another set has come to stay (*gegonen*, perfect). And v.16 indicates that the principal area of change is that of attitude toward Christ and other people. Knowledge "from a worldly point of view" has given place to knowledge in the light of the cross (cf. Gal 6:15). Clearly Paul emphasizes the discontinuity between the two orders and the "newness" of the person in Christ, but in other contexts he implies the coexistence of the present age and the age to come (e.g., 1 Cor 10:11; Gal 1:4) or speaks of the renewal or rebirth of the individual (Rom 12:2; Eph 4:23; Tit 3:5).

18,19 "All this is from God" looks back to the new attitudes of v.16 and the new creation of v.17. God is as surely the author of the second creation as he was of the first (cf. 4:6).

At this point Paul passes from the subjective to the objective aspects of the atonement as he states the fact of reconciliation. Elsewhere he shows that reconciliation is the divine act by which, on the basis of the death of Christ, God's holy displeasure against sinful man was appeased, the enmity between God and man was removed, and man was restored to proper relations with God. (See Rom 5:10, 11; Col 1:20–22, where the cosmic implications of reconciliation are expounded.) Reconciliation is not some polite ignoring or reduction of hostility but rather its total and objective removal.

These two verses make it clear that God was the reconciler, that it was mankind that God reconciled to himself (but cf. Col 1:20), although there is a sense in which this reconciliation was mutual; that Christ was God's agent in effecting reconciliation ("through Christ . . . in Christ"); that the reconciliation has been accomplished ("reconciled . . . was reconciling"); and that reconciliation involved the nonimputation of trespasses, i.e., forgiveness, which is complemented by the imputation of righteousness. In this passage those to whom God has committed the ministry or message of reconciliation (cf. 4:7) are primarily Paul and his fellow-ambassadors. Nevertheless, a reference to all believers cannot be excluded, particularly since not only apostles were reconciled to God (v.18a, "God . . . reconciled us").

20 As proclaimers of the "gospel of peace" (Eph 6:15), which was the good tidings about reconciliation, the apostles were acting on Christ's behalf as messengers and representatives duly appointed by him. Not only so. It was as if God were issuing a personal and direct invitation through them to their hearers to enter into the benefits of the reconciliation already achieved by Christ. "We implore you on Christ's behalf: Be reconciled to God" may be a summary of the "message of reconciliation" (there is no "you" in the Greek) or else specifically Paul's entreaty to the unregenerate at Corinth.

This appeal issued in Christ's name, this message of reconciliation, is the God-designed link between the objective work of reconciliation and its subjective appropriation by the sinner. From this viewpoint reconciliation is a continuing process as well as an accomplished fact. Yet there is a real sense in which reconciliation was effected before its results are subjectively felt. Paul speaks of *receiving* reconciliation (Rom 5:11), which would imply both an offer and something to offer.

21 Thus far Paul has been content to give the broadest outlines of the drama of reconciliation, stating merely the relationship between the principal actors, as it were. Now he explains, so far as human language and imagery permit, the "how" of reconciliation. The fifteen Greek words, carefully balanced, almost chiastic, defy final exegetical explanation, dealing as they do with the heart of the atonement.

There are three main ways of understanding the first section of the verse, particularly the second use of *hamartia,* "sin" (so L. Sabourin; see notes): (1) Treated as if he were a sinner, Christ became the object of God's wrath and bore the penalty and guilt of sin. (2) When Christ in his incarnation assumed human nature "in the likeness of sinful flesh" (Rom 8:3, RSV), God made him to be "sin." (3) In becoming a sacrifice for sin, Christ was made to be sin. The background to the first view is the idea of substitution; to the second, the notion of participation; to the third, the OT concept of sacrifice.

Although, as Sabourin observes, the Hebrew term *ḥaṭṭā'ṯ* (like *'āšām*) may mean both "sin" and "sacrifice for sin" (or "sin-offering"), it seems Paul's intent to say more than that Christ was made a sin-offering and yet less than that Christ became a sinner. So complete was the identification of the sinless Christ with the sin of the sinner, including its dire guilt and its dread consequence of separation from God, that Paul could say profoundly, "God made him . . . to be sin for us."

Paul's declaration of Christ's sinlessness may be compared with the statements of Peter (1 Peter 2:22, quoting Isa 53:9), John (1 John 3:5), and the author of Hebrews (Heb 4:15; 7:26). Just as "the righteousness of God" is extrinsic to us, so the sin with which Christ totally identified himself was extrinsic to him. He was without any acquaintance with sin that might have come through his ever having a sinful attitude or doing a sinful act. Both inwardly and outwardly he was inpeccable.

The glorious purpose of the Father's act in making Christ "to be sin" was that believers should "become the righteousness of God" in Christ. This is a bold restatement of the nature of justification. Not only does the believer receive from God a right standing before him on the basis of faith in Jesus (Phil 3:9), but here Paul says that "in Christ" the believer in some sense actually shares the righteousness that characterizes God himself (cf. 1 Cor 1:30).

6:1 If God made his appeal (*parakalountos*) to men through Paul (5:20), there was a sense in which Paul was a fellow worker with God (cf. 1 Cor 3:9, NIV). As such he was concerned to plead God's cause with unbeliever and believer alike. Hence this plea (*parakaloumen*), addressed to the whole body of Christians at Corinth, "not to receive God's grace in vain."

This latter phrase may mean one of two things: (1) The Corinthians were being exhorted not to show by their present lives that they had received God's grace to no purpose (cf. NEB: "You have received the grace of God; do not let it go for nothing"). Or (2) they were not now to spurn the grace of God, which was being perpetually offered to them (cf. Knox: "We entreat you not to offer God's grace an ineffectual welcome"). How would they fail, or show they had failed, to profit from that grace? By refusing to purify themselves from everything that contaminated body and spirit (7:1; 12:20, 21), or allowing a chasm to develop between faith and conduct, or embracing a different gospel (11:4)—one based on law keeping as the ground of acceptance before God.

2 To emphasize the seriousness and urgency of his appeal and to highlight the privilege of the present and the danger of procrastination, Paul quotes Isaiah 49:8 and then applies the passage to the age of grace.

In its original context the quotation belongs to a section of Isaiah 49 (vv.7–9) where Yahweh directly addresses his Servant who has been "deeply despised, abhorred by the nations" (Isa 49:7, RSV), promising him vindication before men in due time and calling on him to carry out the work of restoration after the return from exile. Paul uses the quotation to establish that the gospel era ("now") is "the day of salvation" when God's favor is shown to men. How unthinkable that such grace should be received in vain (v.1)!

Notes

16 Κατὰ σάρκα (*kata sarka*) in v.16b means "from a worldly point of view" (NIV, "in this way") and qualifies ἐγνώκαμεν (*egnōkamen*, "we regarded"), rather than meaning "after the flesh" (understood as = "physically") and qualifying Χριστόν (*Christon*). What Paul is rejecting is not knowledge of or interest in "Christ-after-the-flesh" (viz., the historical Jesus) but a κατὰ σάρκα outlook on Christ. His was a κατὰ πνεῦμα (*kata pneuma*, "after the spirit") or κατὰ σταυρόν (*kata stauron*, "after the cross") attitude. For a classification of views about this important verse, see J.W. Fraser, "Paul's Knowledge of Jesus: II Corinthians v.16 once more." NTS, XVII (3, 1971), pp. 293–313.

17 In the context the words καινὴ κτίσις (*kainē ktisis*) that form the verbless apodosis may mean either "he [the man in Christ] is a new creature [or creation, or being]" or "there is a new [act of] creation." Alternatively and with variant punctuation, it is possible to translate the verse: "So that if anyone is a new creature in Christ, the old order has passed . . ." (thus J. Héring).

On the meaning and significance of the "in Christ" formula in Pauline thought, see R.N. Longenecker. *Paul, Apostle of Liberty* (New York: Harper and Row, 1964), pp. 160–170.

19 The NIV, following a number of EV and commentators, regards ἦν . . . καταλλάσσων (*ēn . . . katallassōn*) as a periphrastic imperfect, "[God] was reconciling." This makes ἐν Χριστῷ (*en*

Christō, "in Christ") in v.19 parallel to διὰ Χριστοῦ (*dia Christou,* "through Christ") in v.18. But it is equally possible to take the *ēn* as absolute and the *katallassōn* as adjectival; "God was in Christ, reconciling the world to himself" (thus KJV, E.B. Allo, H. Windisch). Some EV (e.g., RV, RSV, NEB) appear to reproduce the ambiguity of the Gr.: "God was in Christ reconciling. . . ." On the doctrine of reconciliation, see L. Morris, *The Apostolic Preaching of the Cross* (London: Tyndale, 1955), pp. 186–223.

21 "God made him who had no sin to be sin for us" does not, of course, imply any reluctance or resistance on Christ's part that was finally overcome. Ἐποίησεν (*epoiēsen,* "he made") points to God's ordaining that Christ be "made sin" (cf. Acts 2:23). The Father's set purpose not to spare his own Son but to give him up for us all (Rom 8:32) was matched by the Son's firm resolution to go to Jerusalem to suffer (Mark 8:31; Luke 9:51).

For a discussion of the three interpretations of v.21a outlined in the commentary and a defense of the view that ἁμαρτία (*hamartia*) here means "sacrifice for sin," see L. Sabourin, "Note sur 2 Cor. 5, 21: Le Christ fait 'péché'." *Sciences Ecclésiastiques,* XI (3, 1959), pp. 419–424; or (with S. Lyonnet) his *Sin, Redemption, and Sacrifice* [Rome: Pontifical Biblical Institute, 1970], pp. 185–296 (which includes a history of the interpretation of this verse), especially 250–253.

6:1 For a treatment of NT passages dealing with the doctrines of perseverance and apostasy, see I.H. Marshall, *Kept by the Power of God* (London: Epworth Press, 1969).

---

c. *The hardships of apostolic service*

6:3–10

3We put no stumbling block in anyone's path, so that our ministry will not be
discredited. 4Rather, in every way we show ourselves to be servants of God: in
great endurance; in troubles, hardships and distresses; 5in beatings, imprison-
ments and riots; in hard work, sleepless nights and hunger; 6in purity, understand-
ing, patience and kindness; in the Holy Spirit and in sincere love; 7in truthful speech
and in the power of God; with weapons of righteousness in the right hand and in
the left; 8through glory and dishonor, praise and blame; genuine, yet regarded as
impostors; 9known, yet regarded as unknown; dying, and yet we live on; beaten,
and yet not killed; 10sorrowful, yet always rejoicing; poor, yet making many rich;
having nothing, and yet possessing everything.

3 Since v.2 is grammatically a parenthesis, v.3 is closely connected to v.1 and 5:20. As was fitting for a fellow worker with God who was acting as an ambassador for Christ, Paul tried to put "no stumbling block in anyone's path" lest the ministry should incur discredit. (This interpretation takes *didontes* as a conative present.) That various accusations should have been leveled against Paul was inevitable, given the success of his ministry and the jealousy of men. His concern was that such charges should be totally without foundation, that no "minister of reconciliation" should be guilty of inconsistent or dishonest conduct, and that no handle be given adversaries who wished to ridicule or malign the gospel. The life of the Christian minister is the most eloquent advertisement for the gospel.

4,5 Paul proceeds to itemize his hardships (cf. 1 Cor 4:9–13; 2 Cor 4:8, 9; 11:23–29) as he seeks to commend and defend his ministry as a servant of God and provide the Corinthians with further material they might use in his defense (cf. 5:12). Paul's commendation was a matter of actions, not words.

After a reference to the great endurance that marked all his service and suffering (cf.

12:12), Paul lists nine afflictions, which fall into three groups. First are general trials. "Troubles" are oppressive experiences. "Hardships" refer to unrelieved adverse circumstances, while "distresses" are frustrating "tight corners" (cf. 4:8). In the second group are sufferings directly inflicted by men—"beatings, imprisonments, and riots." To the third category belong self-inflicted hardships. "Hard work" includes the arduous task of incessant preaching and the toil of manual labor (cf. 1 Thess 2:9; 2 Thess 3:7, 8). *Nēsteiai* probably refers to voluntary hunger, i.e., fastings (cf. 11:27, where involuntary hunger (*limos*) and fastings (*nēsteiai*) seem to be distinguished), just as *agrypniai* (cf. 11:27) means voluntary abstention from sleep (e.g., Acts 20:7–11, 31).

6,7 From mention of outward circumstances (vv.4b,5) Paul moves on to specify the inward qualities he sought to display (v.6) and the spiritual equipment he relied on (v.7) during the discharging of his apostolic commission.

"Purity" refers to both moral uprightness and singleness of purpose." "Understanding" is not simply pastoral insight but also knowledge of the Christian faith and sensitivity to God's will (cf. 1 Peter 3:7). By "patience" Paul means the endurance of insult or injury without anger or retaliation. "Kindness" is the generous and sympathetic disposition that acts in love. Because a reference to the person of the Holy Spirit seems out of place in the midst of a catalog of moral virtues, some scholars (quite legitimately) have translated the phrase *en pneumati hagiō* by "in a spirit that is holy" (A. Plummer) or "in holiness of spirit" or "by gifts of the Holy Spirit" (NEB). This last rendering rightly emphasizes that Paul is thinking of the Spirit as the source of all spiritual graces. By metonymy, then, "the Holy Spirit" probably denotes the gifts or graces of the Holy Spirit (so J. Calvin).

After a reference to his proclamation of the truth in the power of God (v.7a; cf. 1 Cor 2:1–5), Paul introduces a military metaphor (cf. Wisd Sol 5:17–22) that he had used earlier (1 Thess 5:8) and would develop later (Rom 6:13; Eph 6:11–17). "Weapons of righteousness" means either "weapons supplied by God (Eph 6:10, 11) as a result of justification" or "weapons that consist of personal integrity" (or, of the gospel as "the word of truth," v.7a, RV). Weapons "in the right hand and in the left" could signify "for attack and for defense" or may allude to "the sword of the Spirit" and "the shield of faith" that form part of the Christian's armor (Eph 6:16, 17).

8–10 Behind these verses, which can all too easily be dismissed simply as evidence of Paul's oriental hyperbole or rhetorical style, there probably lie a number of actual allegations his calumniators made against him (cf. Rom 3:8; 1 Cor 4:13). Though we should not always try to find an opponent lurking behind Paul's statements, in some quarters, Paul had probably become an object of disrepute and slander (v.8). He was thought a "nobody" who relied on deceit to become a "somebody" (vv.8b, 9a), an irresponsible person who, needlessly courting danger and death, suffered for his trouble (vv.9b, c), a morose individual lacking the power that wealth affords (v.10). Precision in this reconstruction is impossible, since the charges of Paul's opponents are being inferred from his supposed reply to them.

"Glory and dishonor, praise and blame" (v.8) may epitomize the two types of response to Paul's preaching, or contrast the opinion of men (dishonor, blame) with the reward of God (glory, praise). In the contrasts that follow (vv.8c–10) the paradoxical character of Paul's apostolic ministry is emphasized. If in fact various charges had been made against him, he takes the accusation, lets it stand or invests it with his own meaning, and supplies an opposing complement to form a series of antitheses that point to the vicissitudes and tension of living as a persecuted "ambassador for Christ" (5:20). From another viewpoint, as F.F. Bruce (in loc.) observes, the pairs of contrasts give the divine and the worldly assessment of apostolic life.

Notes

3 An alternative rendering of ἐν μηδενί (*en mēdeni,* tr. "in anyone's path" in NIV) would be "[we give no opportunity for scandal] in anything," taking μηδενί as neuter rather than masculine and as parallel to ἐν παντί (*en panti,* "in everything"; "in every way," NIV—v.4).

4 Verse 4a might be rendered more accurately: "Rather, as servants of God [note nom. διάκονοι, *diakonoi,* not acc. διακόνους, *diakonous*] we commend ourselves in every way"; see RHG, 454.

6–10 Just as there are three triplets in vv.4b, 5 prefaced by a general phrase ("in great endurance"), which applies to each triplet, so in vv.6–10 there is a discernible pattern: after four single nouns, each introduced by ἐν (*en,* "in") (v.6a), four pairs of words follow, each introduced by *en* (vv.6b, 7a). Then comes a triad of antitheses expressed by διὰ . . . καί (*dia . . . kai,* "through . . . and") (vv.7b, 8), and finally seven anthitheses couched in a ὡς . . . καί (or δέ) (*hōs . . . kai* [or *de*], "as . . . and [or but]") contrast (vv.8c–10). This carefully balanced structure is well reflected in the fine paraphrase of A. Plummer, *A Critical and Exegetical Commentary on the Second Epistle of St. Paul to the Corinthians* (Edinburgh: T. and T. Clark, 1915), p. 166.

4. (*The apostolic ministry*) *Its openness and joy* (6:11–7:4)

a. *A plea for generous affection*

6:11–13

11 We have spoken freely to you, Corinthians, and opened wide our hearts to you. 12 We are not withholding our affection from you, but you are withholding yours from us. 13 As a fair exchange—I speak as to my children—open wide your hearts also.

11–13 It was not customary for Paul to address his readers by name. Only when his emotions had been deeply stirred—as at the bewitchment of the Galatians (Gal 3:1), at the generosity of the Philippians (Phil 4:15), or here, at the remarkable candor of his defense and the intensity of his affection for the Corinthians—did he depart from his custom. Behind his freedom of speech (cf. 3:12; 4:2) was a warmly receptive attitude of heart ("we have . . . opened wide our hearts to you," v.11). "If there are any feelings of constriction or restraint in our relationship," he continues, "they are on your side, not mine. I appeal to you as my spiritual children [cf. 1 Cor 4:14, 15]: in fair exchange for my unrestricted affection, give me yours, too" (vv.12, 13 paraphrased). Although Paul's desire was for complete reciprocity in family relationships, he was acutely aware that affection could only be given, not taken.

b. *Minor digression—call to holiness*

6:14–7:1

14 Do not be yoked together with unbelievers. For what do righteousness and wickedness have in common? Or what fellowship can light have with darkness?

15 What harmony is there between Christ and Belial? What does a believer have in common with an unbeliever? 16 What agreement is there between the temple of God and idols? For we are the temple of the living God. As God has said:

"I will live with them and walk among them,
and I will be their God,
and they will be my people."
17 "Therefore come out from them
and be separate,
says the Lord.
Touch no unclean thing,
and I will receive you."
18 "I will be a Father to you,
and you will be my sons and daughters,
says the Lord Almighty."

1 Since we have these promises, dear friends, let us purify ourselves from everything that contaminates body and spirit, and let us strive for perfection out of reverence for God.

For a brief discussion of the integrity of this section and for the suggestion that it forms a natural digression within Paul's argument, see the Introduction, 2.b.

14–16a Paul has just appealed to the Corinthians for mutual openness in affection as in speech. His own heart is open wide to them, but he knows and they know why they cannot reciprocate as fully as they ought. Some of them have an uneasy conscience about their continuing pagan associations they know Paul disapproves of. The apparent abruptness of v.14a after v.13 may be explained: (1) by this mutual knowledge; (2) by Paul's "coming to the point" immediately, as he sets forth the truth plainly (4:2) or speaks the truth in love (Eph 4:15); and (3) perhaps by a brief dictation pause.

Paul begins with a concise summary of his message in this brief digression (6:14–7:1), which repeats the main point of 1 Corinthians 10:1–22 where he warned the Corinthians of the danger of idolatry (note 1 Cor 10:14: "flee from idolatry").

"Do not be yoked together with unbelievers" (v.14a). Clearly this is not an injunction against all association with unbelievers (cf. 1 Cor 5:9, 10; 10:27). Paul actually encouraged the Christian partner in a mixed marriage to maintain the relationship as long as possible (1 Cor 7:12–16). Rather, this is a prohibition against forming close attachments with non-Christians. Paul's agricultural metaphor ("You must not get into double harness with unbelievers"—C.K. Barrett) is based on the command of Deuteronomy 22:10 that prohibited the yoking of an ox and an ass for ploughing, and also on Leviticus 19:19 where the crossbreeding of animals of different species is prohibited. Although precisely what might have constituted a "diverse yoke" or "double harness" for the Corinthians remains unstated, it clearly involved compromise with heathendom, such as contracting mixed marriages (cf. Deut 7:1–3) or initiating litigation before unbelievers in cases involving believers (1 Cor 6:1–8). Paul is content to state a general principle that needs specific application under the Spirit's guidance. In expanded form the principle might be expressed thus: "Do not form any relationship, whether temporary or permanent, with unbelievers that would lead to a compromise of Christian standards or jeopardize consistency of Christian witness. And why such separation? Because the unbeliever does not share the Christian's standards, sympathies, or goals."

Five rhetorical questions follow (vv.14b–16a), each of which presupposes a negative answer. They serve to stress the incompatibility of Christianity and heathenism, the incongruity of intimate relationships or fellowship between believers and unbelievers (cf. 1 Cor 10:21). After two comparisons of abstract nouns ("righteousness" and "light" with "wickedness" and "darkness"), there follow two personal comparisons—"Christ" and the "believer" with "Belial" (see note) and the "unbeliever." The final contrast (v.16a) climaxes the series and prompts what follows (vv.16b–18).

16b,c The chief reason why believers are not to enter any syncretistic or compromising relationship with unbelievers (v.14a) is that they belong exclusively to God. Corporately the Christian community forms "the temple [or sanctuary] of the living God" (cf. 1 Cor 3:16, 17; see also 6:19, which individualizes the truth); or, as Paul later expressed it, "a dwelling in which God lives by his Spirit" (Eph 2:22, NIV).

To establish this last point (v.16b) Paul quotes several OT passages. "I will live with them and walk among them" is based on Leviticus 26:11a, 12a, with possible allusions to Exodus 25:8; 29:45a; 1 Kings 6:13; Ezekiel 37:27a. God's promise to Israel in the wilderness, subsequently reiterated, becomes his promise to the church in the gospel era (cf. Rev 21:3). "I will be their God, and they will be my people" is a recurring promise of Yahweh to his covenant people (see Exod 6:7; Lev 26:12b; Jer 32:38; Ezek 37:27b).

17 In keeping with the promise of his presence and protection, God demands purity of life and separation from evil. " 'Therefore come out from them and be separate, says the Lord. Touch no unclean thing' " (v.17). Isaiah 52:11 is the source of Paul's citation; the differences may be explained by Paul's quoting from memory and applying the text to the Corinthian situation. In Isaiah, the call was for separation (= departure) from Babylon (*autēs*, "her," in LXX) with its pagan idolatry. In Paul, the call is for separation from unbelievers (*autōn*, "them," v.17 = *apistoi*, "unbelievers," v.14), with their pagan way of life. This verse, therefore, should not be used in defense of separation from believers on the ground of doctrinal differences.

"And [or then, *kai*] I will receive you" stems from Ezekiel 20:34, 41. God's acceptance and approval of his people is dependent on their obedience to his commands. Separation from the world leads to fellowship with God (cf. James 4:4).

18 The next mosaic of OT texts is composed of 2 Samuel 7:14a (with the necessary changes from singular to plural; cf. Hos 1:10) and 2 Samuel 7:27 (LXX, "Lord Almighty"), with the reference to "daughters" in 2 Corinthians 6:18 possibly coming from Isaiah 43:6. What God promised to Solomon through David and to Israel through Solomon (cf. Jer 31:9) finds its fulfillment in what God is to the community of believers through Christ (Gal 3:26; 4:6). If Christians corporately are the temple of the living God (v.16), individually they are the sons and daughters of the all-sovereign Lord (v.18).

7:1 In his chain of OT quotations Paul has stressed the privilege of being a dwelling place of God (v.16) and the benefits of compliance with the divine will (vv.17d, 18). So he continues, "Since we have promises such as these [*tautas* stands first for emphasis]. . ."—promises (vv.16, 17d, 18), not commands (v.17). As recipients of such promises of fellowship with God, all Christians ("let us," as in NIV; not "you must") are to avoid every source of possible defilement in any aspect of their lives. "Body and spirit" here denotes the Christian in his total personality, outwardly and inwardly, in his relations with other people and with God (cf. 1 Cor 7:34).

Paul is probably implying that the Corinthians had become defiled, perhaps by occasionally sharing meals at idol-shrines or by continuing to attend festivals or ceremonies in pagan temples (cf. 1 Cor 8:10; 10:14–22), or even by maintaining their membership in some local pagan cult. If they made a clean break (cf. *katharisōmen,* aorist) with pagan life in any and every form, they would be bringing their holiness nearer completion by this proof of their reverence for God. The Christian life involves separation (6:17), familial fellowship (6:18), and sanctification (7:1).

Notes

15 "Belial" (Heb. בְּלִיַּעַל, *b^eliyya'al*) may mean "worthlessness" or "the place from which there is no ascent" (= the abyss or Sheol); or, as here and in late Jewish literature, it may be used personally of the devil. See the full note of P.E. Hughes, in loc.

16 On the concept of the temple in biblical and extra-biblical literature, see R.J. McKelvey, *The New Temple: A Study of the Church* (New York: Oxford University Press, 1969).

17 On the Pauline formula λέγει κύριος (*legei kyrios,* "says the Lord") used in vv.17, 18, see E.E. Ellis, *Paul's Use of the Old Testament* (Edinburgh: Oliver and Boyd, 1957), pp. 107–113.

7:1 The end of the verse may be literally rendered: ". . . perfecting holiness (= becoming perfectly holy—BAG, p. 10) in the fear of God." The phrase ἐπιτελοῦντες ἁγιωσύνην (*epitelountes hagiōsynēn*) may indicate the result (". . . and thus make holiness perfect . . .") of the self-purification, viz., advance in holiness; if so, the emphasis on human responsibility in the process of sanctification is unmistakable. Or the phrase may denote the circumstances attendant on self-purification, being virtually a separate complementary injunction (so NIV). Ἐν φόβῳ θεοῦ (*en phobō theou*) may mean "in an atmosphere of reverential fear for God" (ἐν [*en,* "in"] denoting sphere or circumstances) or "by reverence for God" (instrumental ἐν).

c. *Paul's pride and joy*

7:2–4

[2]Make room for us in your hearts. We have wronged no one, we have corrupted no one, we have exploited no one. [3]I do not say this to condemn you; I have said before that you have such a place in our hearts that we would live or die with you. [4]I have great confidence in you; I take great pride in you. I am greatly encouraged; in all our troubles my joy knows no bounds.

2–4 After this brief digression (6:14–7:1) Paul renews his appeal (cf. 6:13) for the Corinthians' full affection. He knew of nothing in his past conduct or instruction that could cause them to doubt his sincerity or lose confidence in him. Paul had been accused of bringing about the moral and financial ruination of innocent victims at Corinth by callously exploiting them (v.2), and apparently some at Corinth were inclined, at least in part, to believe these charges. As before (cf. 1 Cor 4:4; 2 Cor 4:2; 5:11; 6:3), Paul can do no more in reply than appeal to his clear conscience and the Corinthians' knowledge of his conduct and insist that the charges are groundless.

But to mention the charges was not to imply that the Corinthians really believed them. "I do not say this to condemn you" (v.3a). Or Paul may mean that his effort to clear himself did not amount to blaming them. He reminds them (cf. 6:11) that they occupy a permanent and secure place in his love and concern. The leveling of charges, the arrival of death, the trials of life—none of these could divorce them from his affection (v.3b).

The situation at Corinth was not perfect and probably never would be. But Paul had grounds for great confidence and pride in his converts. In spite of all his frustrations and in the midst of all his affliction he was filled with comfort and overflowing with joy (v.4; cf. 6:10). The reason? The safe arrival of Titus in Macedonia with encouraging news about Corinth (vv.5–7). Quite naturally Paul has returned to his travel narrative that was suspended at 2:13.

Notes

4 Since παρρησία (*parrhēsia*) can mean "freedom of speech" as well as "confidence" (see note on 3:12), v.4a may also be rendered "I am perfectly frank with you" (NEB). And the following phrase can also be tr. thus: "I am always boasting about you" (*Twentieth Century New Testament*).

D. *Paul's Reconciliation With the Corinthians* (7:5–16)

1. *Comfort in Macedonia*

7:5–7

> [5]For when we came into Macedonia, this body of ours had no rest, but we were harassed at every turn—conflicts on the outside, fears within. [6]But God, who comforts the downcast, comforted us by the coming of Titus, [7]and not only by his coming but also by the comfort you had given him. He told us about your affection, your deep sorrow, your ardent concern for me, so that my joy was greater than ever.

5 At this point Paul resumes the account of his movements broken off at 2:13. Although he expected to meet Titus when he (Paul) arrived in Macedonia, his hopes were frustrated just as they had been at Troas (2:12, 13). His body (*sarx*, "flesh") had no rest (*anesis*). In 2:13 he had said that his spirit (*pneuma*, NIV "mind") had experienced no rest (*anesis*) at Troas. If a distinction is to be drawn between the *pneuma* of 2:13 and the *sarx* of 7:5, terms often contrasted in Paul's writing (e.g., Gal 5:16–24), the former denotes Paul in his spiritual sensitivity; the latter, Paul in his physical suffering. But it is quite possible that the terms are here virtually synonymous, being used loosely of the whole person under the influence of popular, nontechnical usage.

"Fears within" alludes to Paul's persistent apprehension about Titus's reception at Corinth, his safety in travel, and the Corinthian response to the "severe letter." "Conflicts on the outside" may point to violent quarrelling that focused on Paul or to persistent opposition or persecution that beset him after his arrival in Macedonia.

6,7 It probably seemed to Paul that from the human point of view his whole future as apostle to the Gentiles was related to the Corinthians' reaction to his assertion of authority in the letter delivered by Titus. And now the nonarrival of Titus tended to confirm his worst fears (see the commentary at 2:12, 13).

God used three means to dispense comfort to the depressed or downhearted (*tapeinos*—BAG, p. 811) apostle: the actual arrival of Titus, doubtless including his personal ministrations to Paul (note the twofold reference to Titus's *parousia*, "coming"); Titus's positive experience at Corinth ("the comfort you have given him"); and the reassuring news he brought concerning the Corinthians' attitude toward Paul—their "affection" for him or longing (*epipothēsis*) to see him and be reconciled to him, their "deep sorrow" over their disloyal behavior, and their "ardent concern" to defend Paul's cause and to follow his directions in disciplining the guilty party. Titus's safe arrival from Corinth and the encouragement he had received there had brought Paul a joy that was increased by the favorable news Titus brought.

2. *The severe letter and its effect*

7:8–13a

> [8]Even if I caused you sorrow by my letter, I do not regret it. Though I did regret it—I see that my letter hurt you, but only for a little while—[9]yet now I am happy, not because you were made sorry, but because your sorrow led you to repentance. For you became sorrowful as God intended and so were not harmed in any way by us. [10]Godly sorrow brings repentance that leads to salvation and leaves no regret, but worldly sorrow brings death. [11]See what this godly sorrow has produced in you: what earnestness, what eagerness to clear yourselves, what indignation, what alarm, what affection, what concern, what readiness to see justice done. At every point you have proved yourselves to be innocent in this matter. [12]So even though I wrote to you, it was not on account of the one who did the wrong or of the injured party, but rather that before God you could see for yourselves how devoted to us you are. [13a]By all this we are encouraged.

On the purpose and identification of the "severe letter," see the Introduction, 7.b.

8–10 "My letter" refers not to 1 Corinthians or a letter embodying 2 Corinthians 10–13 but to a letter no longer extant that was written after 1 Corinthians and Paul's "sorrowful visit" and was delivered by Titus. From the report of Titus Paul had learned for the first time that his letter had caused the Corinthians considerable distress, at least for a period (v.8). As a spiritual father who disliked causing pain for whatever reason, his first reaction was to regret (*metemelomēn*) that he had written so stern a letter that the recipients were pained by it: "I did regret it—[for, *gar,* read by some MSS] I see that my letter hurt you" (v.8b). But at some later time, possibly after Titus had completed his report or after Paul had had time to reflect on the whole episode, his initial regret caused by a natural, spontaneous reaction had altogether disappeared before the joyful realization that out of the temporary pain suffered by the Corinthians had come sincere repentance. So at the time of writing Paul could say, "I do not [now] regret it [*ou metamelomai*] ... now I am happy ... because your sorrow led you to repentance" (vv.8, 9). Of what had the Corinthians repented? Probably their failure to defend Paul before his detractor ("the one who did the wrong," v.12). Because their sorrow was "as God intended" (i.e., it produced repentance, v.10a), Paul's letter that had caused temporary pain caused no permanent harm (v.9b). The inference is clear: the imposition of discipline or the suffering of pain that does not, under God, lead to repentance, can cause irreparable harm.

Verse 10 describes two ways of reacting to pain or sorrow. God's way ("godly sorrow" or sorrow "as God intended," *kata theon,* vv.9, 10, 11) invariably produces a change of heart and this repentance "leads to salvation" and therefore gives no cause for regret. Sorrow borne in a worldly way (*tou kosmou*), on the other hand, does not lead to repentance but has the deadly effect of producing resentment or bitterness. What makes suffering remedial is not the actual experience of it but the reaction to it; a "godly" or positive reaction brings blessing, a "worldly" or negative reaction causes harm.

11 A splendid example of the beneficial outcome of "godly sorrow" was the positive response of the Corinthians to Paul's letter that had for a time pained them. It might have compounded trouble at Corinth and caused widespread resentment against Paul had it not been received in a spirit of humility and with a willingness to follow God's will. As it was, it produced in them "earnestness" or seriousness of purpose, "eagerness" to clear themselves from blame, "indignation" at the scandalous action of the person who denigrated Paul, "alarm" over their behavior and its effects, "affection" for Paul or longing (*epipothēsis*) to see him in person, "concern" lest he should visit them "rod in hand" (1 Cor 4:21; cf. 2 Cor 7:15; 13:2), and a "readiness to see justice done" by the punishment of the offender (cf. 2:6).

The second sentence in this verse has been interpreted in two ways. By their favorable response to the "severe letter" the Corinthians had proved themselves "to be innocent," i.e., they had now put themselves in the right after earlier complicity in the affair (thus A. Plummer). Alternatively, the meaning may be this: By their response the Corinthians showed Titus that they had always been guiltless in the matter (thus C.K. Barrett). The former view seems more probable in light of the term *odyrmos* ("mourning"; "deep sorrow," NIV) in v.7.

12,13a Paul's principal aim in writing the "severe letter" was that the Corinthians should come to recognize "before God" how devoted to their spiritual father they really were (cf. 2:9). Such recognition "before God" or "in the sight of God" would ensure future loyalty to Paul. Since this aim was achieved and God prevented the letter from making the Corinthians resentful (v.9b), Paul was encouraged (v.13a).

It is likely that this statement of Paul's chief aim in writing was influenced by his knowledge of the letter's outcome: Paul was unsure of Corinthian loyalty when he wrote the "severe letter"; hence his restlessness while waiting for Titus (2:12, 13; 7:5).

As it is stated, this Corinthian recognition was the sole purpose of the letter. However, what is expressed as a stark contrast ("not this, nor this, but that") is actually simply a comparison ("not so much this or this as that"). Another example of this Semitic thought pattern is found at 2:5 (where see note). Subsidiary objectives for the letter, then, were twofold: the punishment of the guilty party ("the one who did the wrong") (cf. 2:6, 9) and the vindication of "the injured party." Who the offender was is impossible to say (assuming he was not the man guilty of incest; see the commentary at 2:5, 6, 10, 11). C.K. Barrett (in loc.) argues strongly for his not being a Corinthian but an "anti-Pauline intruder." Commentators who believe that 1 Corinthians 5 and 2 Corinthians 2 are referring to the same matter (the case of the man guilty of incest) identify "the injured party" as the man's father (1 Cor 5:1). This is very unlikely (see Introduction, 7.b.3]a). More probably, Paul himself was the nameless "injured party."

3. *The relief of Titus*

7:13b–16

13b In addition to our own encouragement, we were especially delighted to see how happy Titus was, because all of you helped put his mind at ease. 14 I had boasted to him about you, and you have not embarrassed me. But just as everything we said to you was true, so our boasting about you to Titus has proved to be true as well. 15 And his affection for you is all the greater when he remembers that you were all obedient, receiving him with fear and trembling. 16 I am glad I can have complete confidence in you.

13b,14 Through the "godly sorrow" of the Corinthians, Titus was as relieved and encouraged as Paul (v.13a). Apparently Titus had had little or no occasion before his visit to Corinth as bearer of the "severe letter" to form an independent judgment about the Corinthians; so he was dependent on Paul's glowing recommendation. This would suggest that this visit, on which he also began to organize the collection (8:6a), was his first. But it is not impossible that he had already paid a very brief visit shortly after 1 Corinthians was received at Corinth to initiate the collection by carrying out the directions of 1 Corinthians 16:2.

Whether it was his first or second visit, he seems to have ventured on it with some trepidation that was possibly based on a previous encounter with the Corinthians. But all the believers had "helped put his mind at ease" (v.13b). However, the phrase (*anapepautai to pneuma autou*) may also mean "his spirit has been refreshed." Perhaps both refreshment and relief had come to Titus.

Paul's relief stemmed from the fact that his generous assurances to Titus about the Corinthians had not proved unfounded and therefore embarrassing (v.14). On the contrary (*alla*), just as his own truthfulness had been vindicated at Corinth (cf. 1:18–20), so also his boasting about them had now proved fully justified.

15,16 The reception of Titus at Corinth had been given "with fear and trembling"; i.e., the Corinthian Christians were anxious to the point of nervousness, fearing (cf. v.11) that corporately they would fail to meet all their obligations toward an envoy from Paul (cf. the same phrase *meta phobou kai tromou* in Eph 6:5; Phil 2:12; see also 1 Cor 2:3). Moreover, they had all readily complied with some demand Titus had made of them. Whenever he recalled their obedience and respectful deference to him, his affection grew all the warmer (v.15). This gave Paul good reason for complete confidence in the Corinthians (v.16) and a secure base from which to propose the completion of the collection (chs. 8, 9).

II. The Collection for the Saints at Jerusalem (2 Cor 8–9)

For a summary of the historical background and theological significance of the collection, see Introduction (7.c), where there is also a brief discussion of the integrity of these two chapters (2.c).

This was not the first time the Corinthians had heard of the collection for the poor at Jerusalem, for in 1 Corinthians 16:1–4 Paul gave them certain information and directions about the project they had probably requested in their earlier letter. (The *peri de*, "now about . . . ," in 1 Corinthians 16:1 points to a topic discussed in the Corinthians' letter to the apostle.) They may have been first informed about the collection by Paul's "previous letter" (referred to in 1 Cor 5:9, 11 and written perhaps in A.D. 53 or 54) or by news from the Galatian churches (cf. 1 Cor 16:1). Certainly 1 Corinthians 16:1 introduces the theme of "the collection for God's people" so abruptly and with such evident unconcern for the Corinthians' motivation or for their knowledge of the collection's purpose and destination that their previous acquaintance with the idea seems presupposed. Indeed, they had doubtless indicated to Paul their willingness to contribute.

Whether the Corinthians acted on Paul's instructions in 16:1, 2 is uncertain. But in all probability progress on the collection was soon halted in spite of Paul's "intermediate visit," particularly as the result of (1) the unfortunate incident alluded to in 2 Corinthians 2:5–11; 7:12 and its aftermath and (2) the malevolent influence of the intruders from Palestine who at least for a period gained their support from some Corinthian sympathizers (cf. 11:7–12, 20; 12:13–16). But when Paul sent Titus to deliver and reinforce the effect of the "letter of tears," he probably enjoined him to attempt to revive the flagging collection if the church responded favorably to the letter (cf. 8:6a). Now, with firm evidence from Titus of the Corinthians' loyalty to him (7:6–16), Paul can discuss the project again and press for its early completion.

A. *The Need for Generosity* (8:1–15)

1. *The generosity of the Macedonians*

8:1–5

> 1And now, brothers, we want you to know about the grace that God has given the Macedonian churches. 2Out of the most severe trial, their overflowing joy and their extreme poverty welled up in rich generosity. 3For I testify that they gave as much as they were able, and even beyond their ability. Entirely on their own, 4they urgently pleaded with us for the privilege of sharing in this service to the saints. 5And they did not do as we expected, but they gave themselves first to the Lord and then to us in keeping with God's will.

1,2 Tactfully, Paul begins with an example, not a plea. Although they were then facing a severe ordeal involving persecution (cf. 1 Thess 1:6; 2:14), the Macedonian churches, such as those at Philippi, Thessalonica, and Berea, had contributed generously. As Paul expresses it, their "rich generosity" was the overflow of "overflowing joy" and "extreme poverty" (v.2). Their proverty no more impeded their generosity than their tribulation diminished their joy. This liberal giving by destitute Christians to fellow believers not personally known to them Paul traces to the influence of God's grace (v.1; cf. 9:14). The apostle was not concerned about the actual size of the gift but about the attitude of the givers ("joy . . . generosity"; cf. Rom 12:8) and the relation between the size of the gift and the resources of the givers (cf. Mark 12:41–44).

3–5 In describing the nature of the Macedonians' "rich generosity," Paul makes several observations. First, they gave far more generously than their slender means and adverse circumstances really permitted them (v.3). Not that their judgment was unbalanced, but their eagerness to contribute led them to surpass all expectations.

Second, acting on their own initiative, they "urgently pleaded" with Paul for the privilege of fellowship (*koinōnia;* see note) in the collection (vv.3c, 4). Perhaps the request was conveyed by the Macedonians Gaius and Aristarchus, whom Luke describes as Paul's "traveling companions" (Acts 19:29) (cf. J. Weiss's suggestion in *Earliest Christianity* [New York: Harper, 1959], 1:354). Since 1 Corinthians 16:1 mentions only "the Galatian churches," not the Macedonian churches, and since 1 Corinthians 16:5 makes no reference to the collection, it seems likely that the collection in Macedonia began after the spring of A.D. 55 (the suggested date of 1 Corinthians). One reason for Paul's sending Timothy and Erastus into Macedonia (Acts 19:22) may have been to introduce the collection project there. Yet v.4a implies Paul's reluctance to encourage the Macedonians to contribute, since he knew of their desperate poverty (v.2).

Third, the reason the Macedonians exceeded Paul's expectations ("they did not do as we expected," v.5a) was that they did not restrict their contribution to financial aid. On the contrary (*alla*), "in keeping with God's will" they dedicated themselves first and foremost (*prōton*) to Christ but also to Paul for the performance of any service in connection with the collection (v.5). They recognized that dedication to Christ involved dedication to his servants and that dedication to them was in reality service for Christ. All was part of God's will.

Notes

1 The significant word χάρις (*charis*), found ten times in 2 Cor 8–9, has been appropriately rendered by the NIV in a variety of ways: (1) "grace," referring either to the divine generosity lavishly displayed (8:9) or to divine enablement, especially enablement to participate worthily in the collection (8:1; 9:8, 14); (2) "privilege," used of the honor and opportunity of participating in the offering (8:4); (3) "act of grace" or "offering," denoting the collection itself as an expression and proof of goodwill (8:6, 19); (4) "grace of giving," referring to grace as a virtuous act of sharing or as gracious help (8:7); and (5) "thanks" ("I thank . . .") (8:16; 9:15).

4 "The privilege of sharing [or fellowship]" (τὴν χάριν καὶ τὴν κοινωνίαν, *tēn charin kai tēn koinōnian*, an instance of hendiadys) alludes both to a brotherhood of contributors and to a fellowship between donors and recipients. As contributors to the collection, the Macedonian churches were giving tangible evidence of their oneness with other contributing Gentile churches and with the parent body in Jerusalem (with whom they had an affinity, see 1 Thess 2:14). On the concept of κοινωνία (*koinōnia*, "sharing"), see R.P. Martin. "Communion." NBD, pp. 245, 246.

2. *A plea for liberal giving*

8:6–12

6So we urged Titus, since he had earlier made a beginning, to bring also to completion this act of grace on your part. 7But just as you excel in everything—in faith, in speech, in knowledge, in complete earnestness and in your love for us—see that you also excel in this grace of giving.

8I am not commanding you, but I want to test the sincerity of your love by comparing it with the earnestness of others. 9For you know the grace of our Lord Jesus Christ, that though he was rich, yet for your sakes he became poor, so that you through his poverty might become rich.

10And here is my advice about what is best for you in this matter: Last year you were the first not only to give but also to have the desire to do so. 11Now finish the work, so that your eager willingness to do it may be matched by your completion of it, according to your means. 12For if the willingness is there, the gift is acceptable according to what one has, not according to what he does not have.

6,7 The sterling example of the Macedonians (vv.1–5) encouraged Paul to make arrangements for the completion of the Corinthian offering. "So we urged Titus . . . to bring . . . to completion this act of grace on your part" (v.6). None of the sophisticated and sensitive Corinthians would have missed the implication of the *eis to:* "The result was that [we urged Titus . . .]." Unlike the Macedonians, they were not facing persecution, nor were they in desperate financial straits. How willingly they ought to contribute!

Titus "had earlier made a beginning" (v.6). From the context it is clear that it was "a beginning" on the collection and also at Corinth. When it occurred is less clear. It may have been when he delivered the "severe letter," or at an earlier time either after or conceivably before Paul sent 1 Corinthians.

The earlier "act of grace" (NIV) or "gracious work" (RSV) that Titus had brought to a successful completion (implied by the "also," translating the first *kai*) was his task as Paul's special envoy to Corinth to deliver the "painful letter" and carry out its measures. In Paul's judgment something more than the dispatch of another letter was needed to make sure the Corinthians completed their offering. Titus should pay a second or third visit. Apart from his work at Corinth, he had probably already shown himself a man of considerable financial acumen (Gal 2:1 = Acts 11:29, 30).

A special visit from Titus, however, would not in itself guarantee the success of the collection. So Paul appeals to the Corinthians' desire to exhibit every sign of spirituality (cf. 1 Cor 1:5, 7; 12:31; 14:37). By using the word *charis* ("grace") of the virtue of giving (NIV, "grace of giving," v.7c), he makes it clear that generosity stands alongside faith, speech, knowledge, and love as an expression of divine grace in man (v.7). Already excelling in Christian virtues and gifts of the Spirit, the Corinthians were to make sure they exhibited the grace of liberality as well.

8 Although vested with full apostolic authority (10:8; 13:10), Paul declined to issue directives, preferring rather to request, suggest (cf. v.10), encourage, or appeal (cf. 1 Cor 7:6; 2 Cor 8:6, 10, 17). Spontaneity and warmth would be absent from the Corinthians' giving if coercion were present. But he did see in the enthusiastic generosity of the Macedonian churches a convenient standard for assessing the genuineness of the Corinthians' professed love for him and for all believers, as well as a compelling incentive to arouse them to action.

9 In encouraging the Corinthians to bring their contribution to a satisfactory completion (v.6), Paul has thus far appealed to the example of the Macedonians (vv.1–5), to their own promising beginning (v.6), to their desire for spiritual excellence (v.7), and again to the earnestness of the Macedonians (v.8). Now he turns to the supreme example of Christ. The transition from v.8 to v.9 (denoted by *gar,* "for") is illuminating, because it suggests that Paul saw in Christ the finest example of one who showed eagerness and generosity in giving as a demonstration of his love. If the sacrificial giving of the Macedonians did not stimulate emulation, the example of Christ's selflessness certainly would. Such doctrinal buttressing of ethical injunctions is typical of Paul (e.g., Rom 15:2, 3; Eph 5:2; Col 3:9, 10).

Christ "became poor" (*eptōcheusen,* an ingressive aorist) by the act of incarnation that followed his preincarnate renunciation of heavenly glory (cf. Phil 2:6–8). From wealth to "poverty"! Paul depicts the glory of heavenly existence as wealth, in comparison with which the lowliness of earthly existence amounts to "poverty." Thus it is not possible, from this verse alone, to deduce that Christ's life on earth was one of indigence. In the context the stress is on his voluntary surrender of glory contrasted with the spiritual wealth derived by others (Eph 1:3) through his gracious act of giving. Unlike the Macedonians, who gave when they were extremely poor (v.2), Christ gave when he was incalculably rich. In their present circumstances the Corinthians fitted somewhere between these extremes. Like the Macedonians (v.5), Christ gave himself. The Corinthians would do well to emulate these examples.

10,11 Again Paul emphasizes that he is not giving orders but offering advice (cf. v.8a), though an imperative follows in v.11! It is clear from 1 Corinthians 7:25, 40, however, that such a considered opinion came from one who regarded himself as worthy of trust.

The apostle hints at several reasons why it was "best" (or "expedient") for the Corinthians to bring their contribution to a completion quickly: (1) A considerable time (cf. "last year," v.10) had elapsed since they had expressed an "eager willingness" to help. (2) Since their enthusiastic intention had already been partially translated into action (v.10b), it was incumbent on them, having put their hands to the plough, not to look back but to bring the project to a successful completion. "Completion" needed to match intention (v.11; cf. Phil 1:6). (3) They enjoyed a twofold precedence over the Macedonians. In beginning a collection and even before that in deciding to contribute, they were earlier ("the first," v.10b). But now the Macedonians themselves had completed their offering! (4) The Macedonians had contributed "even beyond their ability" (v.3); now the Corinthians were being asked to contribute "according to . . . (their) means" (v.11).

12 The phrase "according to your means" at the end of v.11 is now explained. Provided a gift is willingly given, its acceptability is determined solely on the basis of what a person might possess, not on the basis of what he does not own. God assesses the "value" of a monetary gift not in terms of the actual amount given, but by comparing what is given with the total financial resources of the giver. This is the lesson of Mark 12:41–44 (the widow's offering). No one is expected to give "according to what he does not have."

Notes

7 The NIV translates the reading ἐξ ὑμῶν ἐν ἡμῖν (*ex hymōn en hēmin*, "your [love] for us"), which suits the context and has wide geographical support (Alexandrian, Western, and Byzantine families), but the three editions of the UBS give a slight preference (a "D" rating) to the alternative reading, ἐξ ἡμῶν ἐν ὑμῖν (*ex hēmōn en hymin*, "our [love] for you"), which is supported by important witnesses (such as p^{46} B 1739). However, the latter reading is awkward in the context unless it is taken to mean "[the love] that is in you which I inspired."

9 In the phrase τῇ ἐκείνου πτωχείᾳ (*tē ekeinou ptōcheia*, "through his poverty") the dative probably means "as a consequence of" rather than "by means of." Christians are enriched not exactly or solely by Christ's poverty (=incarnation) but by his death as the climax of his entire incarnate life of obedient service. Paul would have been the first to insist on the centrality of the cross (e.g., see Rom 5:8–10; Col 1:20, 22) and to observe that Calvary complements Bethlehem. The incarnation became a saving event through the crucifixion. However, if *ptōcheia* ("poverty") here sums up the total ministry and passion of Christ, the difficulty disappears.

10 The phrase ἀπὸ πέρυσι (*apo perusi*, 8:10, 9:2) is notoriously ambiguous, for it may mean "last year" (NIV, and see MM, p. 510) or "a year ago" (RSV), and it is uncertain which calendar Paul was following (see the possibilities mentioned in the Introduction, 4.3). Some period under two years is demanded. Moreover, the Corinthians' desire to contribute may date from their first hearing of the project in Paul's "previous letter" or from the Galatian believers, or from their written enquiry about the collection (answered in 1 Cor 16:1–4).

3. *The aim of equality*

8:13–15

[13]Our desire is not that others might be relieved while you are hard pressed, but that there might be equality. [14]At the present time your plenty will supply what they need, so that in turn their plenty will supply what you need. Then there will be equality, [15]as it is written:

> "He that gathered much did not have too much,
> and he that gathered little did not have
> too little."

13,14 Perhaps one reason the collection project had been languishing at Corinth was that there was some such objection as this to it: "As if we had no financial problems of our own, Paul is imposing fresh burdens on us so that others can become free of burdens." On the other hand, Paul may simply be anticipating an objection of this type. Christian giving, he insists, does not aim at an exchange of financial burdens but rather at an equal sharing of them and an equal supply of the necessities of life. The rich are not called upon to give so lavishly that they become poor and the poor become rich. That would simply prolong inequality. But those who enjoy a greater share of material benefits are called upon to make certain that those who have a smaller share through no fault of their own are not in want. Where the Christian poor give to the poor, as in the case of the extremely poor Macedonians, who gave "even beyond their ability" (8:2, 3), this is a notable demonstration of God's grace (8:1).

If v.13 alludes to an equal sharing of burdens that will lead to equality of supply, then v.14 speaks of mutual sacrifice that will maintain equality. Paul here is not predicting economic plenty in Jerusalem and an economic dearth in Corinth that would reverse present roles. But he saw that with the uncertainty of economic conditions in the first century it was not inconceivable for the Jerusalem Christians some day to become the donors of financial aid and the Corinthian Christians the recipients. Admittedly, the chronic poverty in Jerusalem would have made it appear unlikely that the Jerusalem church would ever come to have a surplus, even were the Corinthians to have a deficiency. This has led some scholars (e.g., E.B. Allo, K.F. Nickle) to suggest that Paul is not envisaging repayment in kind. What the Jerusalem believers would dispense was nothing other than what they had already supplied to Gentile churches—namely, the spiritual blessings of the gospel (cf. Rom 15:27).

15 Paul now illustrates this principle of equality of supply from the account of God's provision of manna to the Israelites in the wilderness (Exod 16:13–36). Although some gathered more than others and some less, the needs of all were met. Miraculously there was equal provision, with neither surplus nor deficiency. "He that gathered much had nothing over, and he that gathered little had no lack" (Exod 16:18 RSV). Any imbalance that might have been caused by hoarding was ruled out, for on the second day manna that had not been used putrefied (Exod 16:20). But Paul's illustration also points to a contrast. The equality the Israelites miraculously experienced in the wilderness was enforced; the equality Christians are themselves to create in the church and the world is voluntary.

Notes

13,14 A variant punctuation of the Gr. text (placing a stop after θλίψις [*thlipsis,* "distress"] and reading the following three words with v.14), favored by the UBS, produces this rendering: "Our desire is not that others might be relieved while you are hard pressed, but that, as a matter of equality [ἐξ ἰσότητος, *ex isotētos*], at the present time. . . ."

B. *The Mission of Titus and His Companions* (8:16–9:5)

1. *The delegates and their credentials*

8:16–24

16I thank God, who put into the heart of Titus the same concern I have for you. 17For Titus not only welcomed our appeal, but he is coming to you with much enthusiasm and on his own initiative. 18And we are sending along with him the brother who is praised by all the churches for his service to the gospel. 19What is more, he was chosen by the churches to accompany us as we carry the offering, which we administer in order to honor the Lord himself and to show our eagerness to help. 20We want to avoid any criticism of the way we administer this liberal gift. 21For we are taking pains to do what is right, not only in the eyes of the Lord but also in the eyes of men.

22In addition, we are sending with them our brother who has often proved to us in many ways that he is zealous, and now even more so because of his great confidence in you. 23As for Titus, he is my partner and fellow worker among you; as for our brothers, they are representatives of the churches and an honor to Christ. 24Therefore, show these men the proof of your love and the reason for our pride in you, so that all the churches can see it.

This section amounts to a "letter of commendation" (cf. 3:1) from Paul to the church at Corinth, giving the credentials of the three appointed delegates and encouraging the Corinthians to welcome them warmly.

16,17 Although Titus's affection for the Corinthians naturally developed as a result of his positive interaction with them (7:13–15), Paul could trace Titus's keen interest in their welfare to the providential working of God (v.16). Nothing could be more reassuring to the Corinthians than to know that the devotion and concern for them shared by Paul and Titus were simply a reflection of God's own affection for them. And it was concern for them, not for their money. As Paul later (12:14) comments, "What I want is not your possessions but you."

Paul proceeds (v.17) to describe the intensity of Titus's concern. It was true that Paul had "urged" him to arrange for the collection to be completed (v.6), but this invitation had merely confirmed Titus's eager willingness. Although technically he might be responding to an appeal he had "welcomed" (contrast with this 1 Corinthians 16:12), in reality he was going "on his own initiative" (*authairetos*). This word may contain a hint that Titus often worked independently of Paul's mission.

18,19 The unidentified Christian brother that Paul was sending with Titus had a double qualification. He was well known and highly praised in all the (Macedonian?) churches "for his service to the gospel" (v.18)—perhaps as an administrator (cf. 1 Cor 12:28) as well as an evangelist or teacher. Also, he had been selected and commissioned by an unspecified number of churches (in Macedonia?—see note on 8:23) to travel with Paul in administering the collection (v.19). Originally the verb *cheirotoneō* indicated election by "stretching out the hand" (i.e., voting), but this meaning cannot be pressed in NT usage where the term simply denotes appointment (e.g., Acts 14:23) with no implication of the "laying on of hands."

Paul adds a phrase explaining why he personally was supervising the administration of the collection. He sought to promote not his own glory but the Lord's and to prove his "eagerness to help" (v.19b; cf. Gal 2:10).

20,21 Experience had taught Paul that he must anticipate the suspicions or accusations of his detractors and take the necessary precautions (e.g., 11:9, 12). As the prime mover behind the Jerusalem collection that he expected to be sizable ("this liberal gift," v.20), he was particularly susceptible to malicious charges that the whole project was designed to bribe the Jerusalem church to fully support his ministry or that he was quietly retaining a commission for his services as administrator of the gift. This explains, for example, his original uncertainty as to whether he would accompany the churches' delegates to Jerusalem (1 Cor 16:3, 4; but cf. 2 Cor 1:16; Rom 15:25), his insistence that the Corinthians appoint their own accredited representatives (1 Cor 16:3), and his sending to Corinth (before he arrived!) two delegates along with his personal representative, Titus (vv.18, 19, 22, 23).

Paul was not one who sought the praise of men (Gal 1:10), but he recognized that the progress of the gospel was hindered if its ministers for any reason acquired a reputation for dishonest dealings (cf. 1 Cor 9:12; 2 Cor 4:2; 6:3). Verse 21 is virtually a quotation of Proverbs 3:4 in LXX: "And aim at what is honorable before the Lord and men."

22 The second anonymous representative who would travel to Corinth with Titus is identified simply as "our brother." As in v.18 ("the brother"), the relationship indicated is spiritual, not physical (see commentary on 1:1). On many occasions and "in many ways" Paul had proved his zeal, which in the present matter was all the greater "because of his great confidence" that this mission to Corinth would prove successful and that the Corinthians would fulfill his high hopes for a "liberal gift" (v.20).

Why are both the "brothers" who would accompany Titus mentioned without identification? Either because both would be personally introduced by Titus when the present letter was first read at Corinth, or because both delegates, as renowned appointees of the Macedonian churches, were already well known at Corinth, whether or not they had visited the city.

Why were three delegates chosen? Would not one have sufficed? Evidently Paul was more susceptible to misrepresentation at Corinth than in most of the other churches he had founded. Added precautions were necessary. To have sent one personal representative would have been to lay himself open to slanderous gossip (cf. 12:16–18). Two independent envoys would be able to testify to his honest intentions and conduct. Second, it is not impossible that Paul wished to exert some subtle yet legitimate pressure on the Corinthians (cf. 9:4), knowing as he did the somewhat erratic progress of the collection at Corinth thus far, the propensity of the Corinthians for disorderliness (cf. 1 Cor 14:33, 40), and the disturbing effect of the parasitical intruders from Palestine.

23 As he sums up the credentials of the three delegates, Paul draws a distinction between Titus, his "partner" or colleague and personally appointed representative, and the two "representatives of the churches." Titus, like Timothy (Rom 16:21), is described as Paul's "fellow worker," though the partnership seems to be restricted by the phrase "among you," another possible indication of Titus's relative independence of Paul before this association. If any one should raise questions about Titus's two companions, says Paul, three facts are relevant: they are "brothers" in Christ; they are the appointees and envoys (*apostoloi*) of the Macedonian churches; by life and service they are a credit (*doxa*) to Christ (though *doxa* here may indicate that they are a worthy reflection of the glory of Christ).

In light of the reference to "the Macedonian churches" in v.1, "[all] the churches" mentioned in vv.18, 19, 23, 24 are probably Macedonian and therefore the two delegates sent with Titus were probably from this province. Significantly, it was the Macedonians in general who had placed themselves at the disposal of Paul for service relating to the collection. But some writers (e.g., J.H. Bernard, P.E. Hughes, K.F. Nickle) object to this identification on the ground that Paul's appeal to the possible embarrassment of "any Macedonians" (9:4) at finding the Corinthians unprepared would have little point if Titus's companions were Macedonian. It should be observed, however, that the two colleagues of Titus did not expect to find the collection at Corinth complete.

24 Paul's short "letter of commendation" (vv.16–24) concludes with a warm appeal. The Corinthians were to give evidence of their love for Christ and for the members of his Body (cf. v.8) by extending to the three delegates warm hospitality and by cooperating with their efforts to supervise the final arrangements for the collection. Also, they were to show the reason for Paul's pride in them or to vindicate his proud, confident boasting about them (cf. 7:14) by contributing eagerly, promptly, and generously (cf. vv.7, 20). All was to be done "so that all the churches [of Macedonia, or, churches that are contributing to the collection] can see it"; or "[as though you were] in the presence and under the gaze of the churches from which the delegates have come."

Notes

17 The aorist ἐξῆλθεν (*exēlthen,* "he is coming"), like the aorists συνεπέμψαμεν (*synepempsamen,* "we are sending along," vv.18, 22) and ἔπεμψα (*epempsa,* "I am sending," 9:3), is probably epistolary (thus RSV, NEB, NIV, and most commentators). But it is not impossible that Titus and the two brothers had left after 2 Corinthians 1–7 was written and that all these aorists are preterite (thus E.B. Allo).

18 For a discussion of the possible identifications of the Christian brother mentioned in this verse, see the special note of P.E. Hughes, in loc.

23 Εἴτε ὑπὲρ. . .εἴτε . . . (*eite hyper. . .eite. . .*) is elliptical and means "if anyone enquires about. . .if anyone enquires about. . ." (cf. KJV, which rightly catches the sense).

2. *The need for readiness*

9:1–5

[1]There is no need for me to write to you about this service to the saints. [2]For I know your eagerness to help, and I have been boasting about it to the Macedonians, telling them that since last year you in Achaia were ready to give; and your enthusiasm has stirred most of them to action. [3]But I am sending the brothers in

order that our boasting about you in this matter should not prove hollow, but that you may be ready, as I said you would be. [4]For if any Macedonians come with me and find you unprepared, we—not to say anything about you—would be ashamed of having been so confident. [5]So I thought it necessary to urge the brothers to visit you in advance and finish the arrangements for the generous gift you had promised. Then it will be ready as a generous gift, not as one grudgingly given.

1 As rendered in some English versions, this verse suggests that Paul is introducing a new subject. An alternative translation, however, highlights the close connection between chapters eight and nine: "For to begin with [*men gar*], it is superfluous for me to be writing as I am [*to graphein*] about this [*tēs*] service to the saints, since I know your eagerness to help. . . ." Translated thus, vv.1, 2a are clearly resumptive and state the reason why Paul was convinced that his pride in the Corinthians and his boasting about them (8:24) would not prove to have been misguided.

2 In 8:10 (cf. 8:6) Paul dated the beginning of the collection at Corinth as "last year" (*apo perusi*). Here, using the same Greek phrase, he speaks of his current boast to the Macedonians—"since last year you in Achaia [certainly including the Corinthians] were ready to give" ("to give" has been rightly supplied from the context).

On the basis of this apparent discrepancy, some have concluded that chapters eight and nine cannot belong together within a single letter, chapter nine clearly being later than chapter eight. Others claim that Paul cannot be acquitted of duplicity: just as he exaggerated Macedonian poverty and generosity in exhorting the Corinthians to complete their offering (8:2–6), so here he unwittingly indicates that he was grossly overstating the extent of the Corinthians' "readiness" in his effort to have the Macedonians contribute quickly and liberally.

We must draw a careful distinction between the Corinthians' ready desire to give and the actual readiness of having completed the collection. In this verse, "eagerness to help," readiness "to give," and "enthusiasm" are all parallel expressions (cf. "eager willingness to do" the work, 8:11) and are virtually synonymous. From vv.3–5 it is clear that the Corinthians were not yet ready or prepared. The relation, then, between chapters eight and nine seems to be this: The Corinthian readiness of intention and eagerness in initiating the collection (cf. 8:10, 11) were appealed to by Paul as an example worthy of emulation when he was encouraging the Macedonians to make their contribution (9:2). Thus it was the Corinthians' "enthusiasm" to participate in the collection, not their "completion" of it (8:11), that had "stirred most of them [the Macedonians] to action" (9:2). On the other hand, because the Macedonians had successfully completed (8:1–5) what they had enthusiastically commenced under the stimulus of the Corinthian example, their exemplary action formed one ground of Paul's appeal to the Corinthians to complete their contribution (8:6, 10, 11).

3,4 Although Paul knew that the Corinthians were so eager to help that further written reminders about the collection were superfluous (vv.1, 2), he was sending (*epempsa*, epistolary aorist; see note on 8:17) a "personal" reminder in the form of the "brothers." This seems the sense of the *men. . .de* contrast between v.1 and v.3. Probably all three delegates mentioned in 8:16–24 are referred to. Without the discussion of chapter 8 immediately preceding, the allusive reference to "the brothers" in vv.3, 5 would be scarcely explicable; this argues for the unity of these two chapters.

There were two situations Paul wished to avoid. One was that his repeated and confident boast to the Macedonians about the Corinthians' "eagerness to help" (v.2) and their expected "readiness" on his arrival should turn out to be without foundation (v.3). The other was that when the delegates of the Macedonian churches (not to be confused with the two companions of Titus) arrived at Corinth with Paul on his forthcoming visit (12:14; 13:1, 2), the Corinthians would be still unprepared and this would lead to his acute embarrassment—not to mention that of the Corinthians themselves (v.4).

5 To make certain that neither of these predicaments arose, Paul "thought it necessary to urge the brothers" to prepare for his coming to Corinth by supervising final arrangements for the collection there. He reminds the Corinthians of their earlier commitment ("the generous gift you had promised"). By a prompt response when the brothers arrived, they would be fulfilling an obligation they had voluntarily assumed and would be ensuring that the gift was not "grudgingly given" (see note).

Twice in this verse the Corinthian contribution is called a *eulogia* ("generous gift"). In classical Greek the word was generally used of "fine speaking" (in a good or a bad sense) or of "praise" (cf. English "eulogy"). But in biblical Greek it commonly refers to the actual "act of blessing" or consecration whether by God or man, or to "a blessing" as some concrete benefit given by God or man (see BAG, p. 323). Here it may bear the latter sense, as "a benefit bestowed" by the Corinthian believers on the Jerusalem saints. But other ideas are suggested by the word. First, the Corinthian contribution would be "an act that produced blessing" (i.e., thanksgiving to God) (cf. vv.11–13). Second, Paul hoped that the collection (*logia,* 1 Cor 16:1) at Corinth would be a "first-rate collection" (*eu-logia*). Third, since blessing implies generosity, the word may denote "a generous (or bountiful) gift" (NIV).

Notes

1 Διακονία (*diakonia,* "service") here is virtually a technical term for the raising and administering of charitable financial relief (cf. Acts 6:1; 11:29; 12:25; Rom 15:31; 2 Cor 8:4; 9:12, 13).

2 The present tense καυχῶμαι (*kauchōmai,* "I have been boasting" [NIV]) indicates that 2 Cor was not written immediately after Paul's arrival in Macedonia. (See Introduction, 1.b. 6–9.)

5 The words μὴ ὡς πλεονεξίαν (*mē hōs pleonexian*) may mean (1) "not as a matter of avarice [or covetousness]," i.e., the Corinthians were not to give grudgingly as a result of a desire to get or keep rather than give; or (2) "not as a matter of extortion," i.e., neither Paul nor the envoys would forcibly or subtly extract a contribution from the Corinthians. The contrast with εὐλογίαν (*eulogian,* "generous gift") in v.5 and the use of φειδομένως (*pheidomenōs,* "sparingly") in antithesis to ἐπ' εὐλογίαις (*ep' eulogiais,* "generously") in v.6 support the former meaning (preferred by BAG, p. 673, and reflected in NIV). Two attitudes to giving (generously—grudgingly) are being contrasted, not two ways of securing a gift (by voluntary act—by extortion).

C. *The Results of Generosity* (9:6–15)

1. *The enrichment of the giver*

9:6–11

6Remember this: Whoever sows sparingly will also reap sparingly, and whoever sows generously will also reap generously. 7Each man should give what he has decided in his heart to give, not reluctantly or under compulsion, for God loves a cheerful giver. [8]And God is able to make all grace abound to you, so that in all things at all times, having all that you need, you will abound in every good work. [9]As it is written:

> "He has scattered abroad his gifts to the poor;
> his righteousness endures for ever."

[10]Now he who supplies seed to the sower and bread for food will also supply and increase your store of seed and will enlarge the harvest of your righteousness. [11]You will be made rich in every way so that you can be generous on every occasion, and through us your generosity will result in thanksgiving to God.

6,7 To emphasize the rewards of generous giving (v.5), Paul cites what appears to be a proverb (v.6): "scanty sowing, scanty harvest; plentiful sowing, plentiful harvest" (*Twentieth Century New Testament*). No exact parallel to this maxim is extant, but a similar sentiment is expressed in several places in Proverbs (e.g., 11:24, 25; 19:17; 22:8, 9), in Luke 6:38 (where Jesus says, "Give, and it will be given to you. . . . For with the measure you use, it will be measured to you," NIV), and in Galatians 6:7 ("A man reaps what he sows," NIV).

The image of the harvest naturally suggests the freedom of the sower to plant as much seed as he chooses—whether "sparingly" or "generously." Similarly, each man is responsible first to decide "in his heart" what he should give (cf. Acts 11:29; 1 Cor 16:2) and then to give what he has decided (v.7). Giving should result from inward resolve, not from impulsive or casual decision. Once the amount to be given has been determined, says Paul, the gift should be given cheerfully (since the cheerful giver always receives God's approval—*agapa*, gnomic present; cf. Prov 22:8, LXX), "not reluctantly [as though all giving were painful; cf. Tobit 4:7] or under compulsion" (because there seems to be no alternative or because pressure has been exerted).

8,9 One way God's approval of the cheerful giver (v.7b) finds expression is in the provision of both spiritual grace and material prosperity ("all grace") that will enable him constantly and generously to dispense spiritual and material benefits ("you will abound in every good work," v.8). As regularly as the resources of the cheerful giver are taxed by his generous giving, they are replenished by divine grace. This gives him a "complete self-sufficiency" (*pasan autarkeian;* "all that you need," NIV) born of dependence on an all-sufficient God. In the writings of the Cynics and Stoics, on the other hand, this same term (*autarkeia*) denoted an intrinsic self-sufficiency that made a man independent of external circumstance.

But *autarkeia* may also mean "contentment," as in 1 Timothy 6:6 ("godliness with contentment is great gain"). Some commentators therefore interpret v.8 to mean that God supplies the generous person with multiplied material blessings, so that, content as he himself is in every circumstance (cf. Phil 4:11), he may be able to shower multiplied benefits of every kind on the needy. But to restrict "all grace" to temporal benefits seems unnecessary.

At this point Paul quotes Psalm 112 to illustrate the generosity of "the man who fears the Lord" (112:1) and the positive results of his prodigal giving. From "the wealth and riches . . . in his house" (112:3a), the God-fearing man freely distributes his gifts to the poor (112:9a). As a result, his benevolent acts of piety ("his righteousness") will never be forgotten but rather will have permanent beneficial effects in this life, as well as gaining him an eternal reward in the life to come (112:9b).

10,11 In v.6 Paul observed that the person who sows sparingly will reap a meager harvest. Now he develops the imagery of sowing and reaping to reinforce the point that generosity pays handsome dividends. He argues from God's bounty in nature to his even greater liberality in grace. The crops of the generous person are always full and his harvests rich. If God supplies man with the seed needed to produce a harvest of grain, and thus food (cf. Isa 55:10), he certainly will supply and multiply all the resources ("your store of seed") needed to produce a full harvest of good deeds ("your righteousness"; cf. Hos 10:12, LXX).

Verse 11a restates v.8, though this is not to say, as some do, that vv.9, 10 are parenthetical. God continues to enrich the benevolent person so that he can go on enriching others by his generosity (cf. 1:4). The greater the giving, the greater the enrichment. The greater the enrichment, the greater the resources to give. Paul then adds a statement (v.11b) that he will develop in vv.12–15. The Jerusalem saints, as the grateful recipients of the Corinthians' liberal gift administered by Paul and his colleagues, would express their thanks to God, the source of all good gifts (cf. James 1:17). Liberality is thus seen to be truly a *eulogia* (v.8), a gracious act that prompts thanksgiving to God.

Notes

9 The two aorists (ἐσκόρπισεν, *eskorpisen,* and ἔδωκεν, *edōken*) in the quotation from Ps 112:9 are probably gnomic: "he distributes freely, he gives. . . ." For a discussion of the various possible meanings of "his righteousness endures for ever," see A. Plummer (ICC), in loc. Both the psalmist and Paul are speaking about a particular type of man, not about God.

11 The participle πλουτιζόμενοι (*ploutizomenoi,* "being made rich") has been construed as (1) in apposition to ἔχοντες (*echontes,* "having," v.8) and therefore dependent on ἵνα. . .περισσεύητε (*hina. . .perisseuēte,* "so that. . .you will abound"), vv.9, 10 being parenthetical; (2) standing for a finite verb, with either ἐστέ (*este,* "you are"), ἔστε (*este,* "be!") or ἔσεσθε (*esesthe,* "you will be") to be supplied with the participle; or (3) anacoluthic, being in agreement with the ὑμεῖς (*hymeis*) to be supplied from v.10.

2. *The offering of thanks to God*

9:12–15

[12]This service that you perform is not only supplying the needs of God's people but is also overflowing in many expressions of thanks to God. [13]Because of the service by which you have proved yourselves, men will praise God for the obedience that accompanies your confession of the gospel of Christ, and for your generosity in sharing with them and with everyone else. [14]And in their prayers for you their hearts will go out to you, because of the surpassing grace God has given you. [15]Thanks be to God for his indescribable gift!

12,13 The believers at Corinth are now reminded (vv.12–15) of the encouraging results that will stem from their generous gift. Not only does the service (*leitourgia;* see note) of giving enrich the donor (vv.6–11) and help supply the needs of the recipients (v.12a), but above all, it promotes the glory of God by prompting "many expressions of thanks" to him. The overflow of almsgiving is praise offered to God.

Having stated the bare fact that Corinthian liberality would prompt thanksgiving to God (vv.11b, 12b), Paul gives the reason for such thanksgiving (v.13a) and its content (v.13b,c).

The saints at Jerusalem, as well as other Christians who heard of the collection, would praise God because this act of Christian service had proved the reality and vigor of the Corinthians' faith (v.13a), which may have come under suspicion at Jerusalem through reports of certain irregularities in the Corinthian church. Then there would be two items for thanksgiving (vv.13b,c). One was the Corinthians' obedience to the dictates of the gospel that accompanied their "confession of the gospel of Christ," a gospel that called for "contributing to the needs of the saints" (Rom 12:13). The other was the Corinthians' sacrificial liberality (*haplotēs,* "generosity") demonstrated in sharing material benefits with the Jerusalem church and therefore in one sense with all Christians (cf. 1 Cor 12:26). Notice that praise is offered less for the gift itself than for the spiritual virtues of the donors expressed in the gift.

14 There are still other results of generosity. Paul is convinced the giving will be reciprocal. The Jerusalem believers will receive material benefits and in return will dispense the spiritual blessing of intercession for the Corinthians. (This, however, is not the clue to the interpretation of 8:14.) As they pray, they will recall "the surpassing grace" imparted to the Corinthians by God (cf. 8:1) and evident in their sacrificial liberality; as a result, their hearts will be warmed towards those at Corinth and they will long to see them and enjoy a closer relation with them.

15 This doxology is a final appeal to the lofty grandeur of divine giving (cf. 8:9; 9:8, 10, 11). Since the gift is said to be given by God ("his. . .gift") and beyond adequate human description ("indescribable"), it could hardly be the Corinthian contribution or even the boon of Jewish-Gentile reconciliation in Christ alluded to in v.14a, but must refer secondarily to the surpassing grace that God imparts (v.14b) and primarily to the Father's gift of the Son (cf. Rom 8:32).

Were Paul's appeals to the Corinthians in these two chapters successful? The apostle paid his third visit to Corinth as planned (12:14; 13:1), spending three months (the winter of A.D. 56–57) in Greece (Acts 20:2, 3), during which he wrote Romans (see Rom 16:23; 1 Cor 1:14). In Romans 15:26, 27 he writes, "For Macedonia and Achaia have been pleased to make some contribution (*koinōnian tina;* see note) for the poor among the saints at Jerusalem; they were pleased to do it. . ." (RSV). Evidently in the five or so months between the writing of 2 Corinthians and Romans, the believers at Corinth had responded to Paul's appeals. Why then does Acts 20:4 make no reference to a delegate or delegates from Achaia? It is unlikely that Paul himself was their appointed delegate, but it is possible that Titus was, and for some reason Titus is nowhere mentioned in Acts.

Notes

12 In extra-biblical usage λειτουργία (*leitourgia,* "service") denotes personal, civic, or priestly service often performed voluntarily (see MM, p. 373 and H. Strathmann, TDNT, 4:215–219).

Its use here may imply that Paul regarded the collection as a voluntary act of service to God as well as a means of promoting the welfare of the Christian community at Jerusalem.

13 The subject of δοξάζοντες (*doxazontes*, "praising") is unexpressed. The RSV (and UBS, by making v.12 a parenthesis) takes it to be the Corinthians ("you will glorify God"), while the NIV assumes an indefinite subject (doubtless with special reference to the Jerusalem Christians = οἱ ἅγιοι, *hoi hagioi*, "the saints"; NIV, "God's people," in v.12): "men will praise God" (similarly NEB). It is highly improbable that "unbelievers in Judea" (Rom 15:31) are included or that Paul envisaged that the conversion of Israel would result from the successful delivery of the collection and the witness of the Gentile delegates (for these views, see K.F. Nickle. *The Collection* [Naperville: Allenson, 1966], pp. 129–143). It is, however, fair to observe that Paul's optimism (reflected in vv.12–14) about the results of the collection did not blind him to the real uncertainties concerning the Jewish reaction to the project (see Rom 15:30, 31).

15 The indefinite adjective τινά (*tina*, "some") in Romans 15:26 should not be interpreted as a derogatory reference to the size of the contribution from Macedonia and Achaia. It simply refers to an indefinite yet not therefore insignificant quantity (see BAG, p. 828).

III. Paul's Vindication of His Apostolic Authority (2 Cor 10–13)

A. *The Exercise of Apostolic Rights and Authority* (10:1–11:15)

1. *The potency of apostolic authority*

10:1–11

[1]By the meekness and gentleness of Christ, I appeal to you—I, Paul, who am "timid" when face to face with you, but "bold" when away! [2]I beg you that when I come I may not have to be as bold as I expect to be toward some people who think that we live by the standards of this world. [3]For though we live in the world, we do not wage war as the world does. [4]The weapons we fight with are not the weapons of the world. On the contrary, they have divine power to tear down strongholds. [5]We demolish arguments and every pretension that sets itself up against the knowledge of God, and we take captive every thought to make it obedient to Christ. [6]And we will be ready to punish every act of disobedience, once your obedience is complete.

[7]You are looking only on the surface of things. If anyone is confident that he belongs to Christ, he should consider again that we belong to Christ just as much as he. [8]For even if I boast somewhat freely about the authority the Lord gave us for building you up rather than pulling you down, I will not be ashamed of it. [9]I do not want to seem to be trying to frighten you with my letters. [10]For some say, "His letters are weighty and forceful, but in person he is unimpressive and his speaking amounts to nothing." [11]Such people should realize that what we are in our letters when we are absent, we will be in our actions when we are present.

No commentator denies that there is an abrupt change of tone at this point in the letter. Defenders of the unity of the Epistle explain the change in various ways, some of which are more convincing than others: a pause in dictation (E. Stange, W. Michaelis), coupled with the arrival of disturbing news; like chapters 1–7, chapters 10–13 are tempered polemic, with not a few tender expressions of affection (e.g., 11:2, 3; 12:14, 15a); Paul intentionally reserves his criticism until after his commendation (A. Jülicher); after consolidating his apostolic authority (1–7), Paul then exercises it (10–13); the contrast between 1–9 and 10–13 has been overdrawn—all 2 Corinthians is polemical in tone, 10:1 marking an intensification of degree, not a variation of kind (W. Ellis); a change of audience—in 1–9 Paul addresses the whole church, in 10–13 the intruders and their partisans (A. Wikenhauser); uncertainty in Paul's mind concerning the sincerity of the Corinthians' repentance; the awkward transition at 10:1 reflects a previous suppression of deep feelings (A. Menzies, A. Robertson); the vagaries of Paul's temperament (W. Sanday, H.L. Goudge)—abrupt changes of mood are reflected elsewhere in Paul's letters (e.g., at 1 Cor 4:8). Some of these scholars give more than one of the above explanations.

1,2 There is no evidence that Paul now addresses only a sector of the Corinthian church—those favorably disposed toward his adversaries from Palestine. On the contrary, regularly throughout these next four chapters (as here in v.2) Paul identifies the views of certain unnamed people (e.g., 10:7, 10–12; 11:4, 12, 13, 15, 20–23; 13:2)—whether Paul's rivals or their partisans at Corinth—who formed a recognizable subversive element at Corinth. He does this in an effort to alert the entire church (cf. 12:19; 13:11–13) to the danger of becoming spiritually infected.

Paul had been accused of being courageous and bold at a distance, shooting his epistolary arrows, such as the "severe letter," but subservient and weak-kneed when personally present, feebly voicing his demands (cf. v.10 and 1 Cor 2:3). This charge Paul ironically repeats in v.1b as a prelude to an appeal ("I beg you") to all the Corinthians regarding a vocal minority ("some people") who persisted in thinking that worldly standards and motives governed all his conduct and that he relied on human powers and methods in his ministry (cf. 1:17; 2:17; 3:5; 4:2; 7:2).

What Paul wished to avoid on his forthcoming visit was a display of boldness—boldness when present not absent! Yet he indicates his total readiness to exercise his apostolic authority, whatever the outcome, if the Corinthians do not repudiate his calumniators and mend their ways (cf. 12:20, 21; 13:11). His "meekness and gentleness" as a true servant of Christ (cf. Matt 11:29) should not be confused with timidity (cf. 13:10). It was his preference to come to Corinth "with love in a spirit of gentleness" (also *prautēs*) but if necessary he was ready "to come rod in hand" (1 Cor 4:21).

3,4 A clear distinction is drawn between existence "in the world" and worldly conduct and techniques. Paul does not deny his human weakness, yet he affirms that a spiritual warfare demands spiritual weapons (vv.3, 4a; cf. Eph 6:11–17). A successful campaign can be waged in the spiritual realm only as worldly weapons are abandoned and total reliance is placed on the spiritual weaponry, which is divinely potent (see note) for demolishing apparently impregnable fortresses where evil is entrenched and from which the gospel is attacked (v.4b).

5 What are these fortified positions that crumble before the weapons of the Spirit? Fanciful human sophistry and intellectual pretensions, or as Paul expresses it in 1 Corinthians 3:19, "the wisdom of this world." The phrase *pan hypsōma* (translated "every pretension") refers to any human act or attitude that forms an obstacle to the emancipating knowledge of God contained in the gospel of Christ crucified and therefore keeps men in oppressive bondage to sin. Closely related is the expression *pan noēma* ("every thought"). By this Paul probably means every human machination or foul design that temporarily frustrates the divine plan (cf. "every act of disobedience," v.6) and so needs forcibly to be reduced to obedience to Christ. It is not a case of the Christian's effort to force all his thoughts to be pleasing to Christ. Rather the picture seems to be that of a military operation in enemy territory that seeks to thwart every single hostile plan of battle, so that there will be universal allegiance to Christ.

6 If circumstances forced Paul to turn from "meekness and gentleness" to a stern assertion of his authority, from appeal to discipline, his plan of action was in two stages. First, there was the need to bring the Corinthians' obedience to completion (cf. 2:9; 7:15). This would be achieved when they dissociated themselves from the interlopers, fully recognized Paul's apostolic authority, and made a total break with idolatry (6:14–7:1). Second, there was the punishment of "every act of disobedience" performed by his adversaries from Palestine or by any Corinthians who remained insubordinate. Precisely what form the punishment would take cannot be known.

Only after securing a firm base in the Corinthian church would Paul risk a face-to-face confrontation with those who still opposed him. Unless a church as a whole is willing to recognize and support spiritual discipline, that discipline will remain largely ineffective. Another important principle emerges when vv.5 and 6 are compared. Obedience to Christ entails submission to his appointed representatives.

7 Paul's opponents were not unaware that the most successful way to undermine his effectiveness was to cast doubt on the genuineness of his apostleship. If his converts could be persuaded that he lacked apostolic credentials, they would cease to believe his teaching.

In response, Paul does not discourage the testing of credentials (cf. 13:2, 3) but casts doubt on the adequacy of the criteria the Corinthians were using. They were impressed by externals or outward appearances (cf. 5:12). They were "looking only on the surface of things"—the confident claim to "belong to Christ" as his authorized apostle (see note), the commendatory letter (3:1), the authoritarian manner (11:20), the spectacular vision, the remarkable ecstatic experience (cf. 12:1–7), rhetorical skill (11:6), and "pure" Jewishness (11:22).

Here Paul argues that the right to make a subjective claim based on personal conviction cannot fairly be granted his opponents and yet denied him. Later he will mention more objective criteria for testing apostolic credentials (see 10:8; 11:23–28; 12:9, 10, 12–15; 13:5, 6). In all this, his motive was not personal vindication but the desire to defend the Corinthian church from the danger of apostasy (cf. 11:2, 3).

8 If the need for self-defense in the face of calumny compelled Paul to boast "somewhat freely" about his apostolic authority, he was confident that he would not be embarrassed by a charge of exaggeration or deception, for the facts themselves spoke eloquently in his favor. Everyone knew that the result of his service at Corinth had been the upbuilding of the Corinthian church in faith and in harmony, while the presence of the false apostles had produced friction and division ("pulling down") (cf. 1 Cor 3:17). In Galatians (1:1, 11, 12, 15, 16) Paul had emphasized against his opponents the divine origin of his call and gospel. Here he stresses the divine origin of his authority (cf. 3:5, 6; 13:10) and its employment for the common good (1 Cor 12:7).

9–11 However legitimately Paul may have boasted about his God-given authority, he decides to refrain from expanding his simple claim in v.8 lest he appear to be frightening the Corinthians into submission by "weighty and forceful" letters (vv.9, 10a). He had no desire to give substance to the charge that he was bold and impressive only when absent (cf. v.1). Those who compared unfavorably what they believed to be his epistolary boldness, "unimpressive" presence, or "contemptible" rhetoric (v.10) are reminded that when present with them he would act in precise accord with his letters (v.11; cf. 13:2, 10).

It is not difficult to understand the origin of the malicious accusation against Paul reported in v.10. His earlier letters to Corinth (the "previous letter," 1 Corinthians, and the "severe letter") had each been "forceful." In fact, to judge by their contents, actual or probable, they seemed to be growing more forceful each time! And 1 Corinthians was certainly a "weighty" or impressive letter (cf. 2 Peter 3:16). Moreover, unlike his opponents (11:20), Paul avoided self-assertiveness and admitted the inferiority of his rhetorical skills (1 Cor 1:17; 2:1–5; 2 Cor 11:6). What he firmly resists, however, is the inference drawn from the claim about his personal bearing and his manner of speaking—namely, that he was " 'timid' when face to face" (v.1).

Notes

---

4 The dative τῷ θεῷ (*tō theō*) after δυνατά (*dynata*) may be (1) instrumental, "made powerful by God" (cf. KJV); (2) a dative of respect or an ethic dative, "in the eyes of God" (cf. RV); (3) a dative of advantage or interest, "for God," "for God's service;" or (4) a Hebraism (cf. Jonah 3:3, LXX; Acts 7:20), with the sense of an elative superlative, "divinely [= extremely, supernaturally] powerful" (cf. Moff, NEB, NASB).

7 The form βλέπετε (*blepete*) may be (1) an indicative, thus NIV text ("You are looking"); (2) an imperative, thus NIV footnote ("Look at the obvious facts") and most EV; or (3) an indicative with an interrogative sense: "Do you see what is in front of you?" (similarly KJV).

In this context "belonging to Christ" does not mean being a Christian (cf. 1 Cor 15:23) or being a member of the Christ-party (1 Cor 1:12), but being a genuine apostle and servant of Christ (cf. 11:13, 23). Yet it is possible that, as a result of their denial of his claim to apostleship, Paul's rivals questioned his status as a Christian; a false apostle hardly "belonged tò Christ."

---

2. *Legitimate spheres of activity and boasting*

10:12–18

[12]We do not dare to classify or compare ourselves with some who commend themselves. When they measure themselves by themselves and compare themselves with themselves, they are not wise. [13]We, however, will not boast beyond proper limits, but will confine our boasting to the field God has assigned to us, a field that reaches even to you. [14]We are not going too far in our boasting, as would be the case if we had not come to you, for we did get as far as you with the gospel of Christ. [15]Neither do we go beyond our limits by boasting of work done by others. Our hope is that, as your faith continues to grow, our area of activity among you will greatly expand, [16]so that we can preach the gospel in the regions beyond you. For we do not want to boast about work already done in another man's territory. [17]But, "Let him who boasts, boast in the Lord." [18]For it is not the man who commends himself who is approved, but the man whom the Lord commends.

Behind Paul's continuing self-defense in this section lies an indirect attack on the intruders from Palestine. From his firm denials ("we do not," vv.12, 16; "we. . .will not," v.13; "we are not," v.14; "neither do we," v.15; "it is not," v.18) we may deduce the content of his charges against his rivals, not in this case, as so often elsewhere, the content of accusations made against him. Only in v.12b does Paul make a direct charge. It is twofold: First, the false apostles had trespassed on his legitimate "sphere of authority" or "province" at Corinth in defiance of the agreement of Galatians 2:1–10. Second, in their unrestrained self-commendation (v.12) his opponents were laying a false claim to credit for work he had done in his own "territory" in Corinth.

12 In one aspect of his conduct, Paul admits his "timidity" (cf. v.1). He lacked the boldness and temerity to align or compare himself with those who indulged in self-praise, "those who write their own testimonials" (Phillips)! Writing ironically, he asserts that in their folly his opponents were establishing their own conduct as normative and then finding great satisfaction in always measuring up to the standard. The implication is clear. If the Corinthians tried to assess Paul's credentials against the artificial and subjective criteria established by his detractors, they would be just as foolish.

13,14 Unlike his adversaries, Paul refused to boast of what had occurred beyond the limits of his own ministry as the apostle to the Gentiles (Acts 9:15; Gal 2:9). In boasting about his "field" at Corinth and appealing by implication to the very existence of the Corinthian church as a vindication of his apostleship (cf. 3:2, 3), he was "not going too far" or overstepping his limits, since historically his God-ordained field had included Corinth. In fact, he had been "the first to come all the way" (see note) to the Corinthians with the gospel of Christ (v.14b, RSV; cf. 1 Cor 3:6, 10). God's formation of a Christian community at Corinth as a result of Paul's pioneer evangelism established Corinth as his legitimate "province" or "sphere of influence" (*kanōn*). But in no sense was the territory of Achaia assigned exclusively to Paul before his actual ministry there.

The activity of the false apostles at Corinth encroached on Paul's legitimate "province" because it violated the concordat of Galatians 2:1–10. Whether or not this episode described in Galatians 2 is related to Acts 11:29, 30 (A.D. 46) or Acts 15:1–21 (A.D. 49), it predated the arrival at Corinth of these Palestinian intruders (perhaps late in A.D. 55). Even if these interlopers had no relationship with the Jerusalem church (see the Introduction, 7.d. 2), they must have been aware of the agreement of Galatians 2 and in particular the fact that the Jerusalem apostles recognized Paul as having been entrusted with special responsibility for the propagation of the gospel among the Gentiles or uncircumcised (Gal 2:7–9). True, their presence at Corinth was not technically an infringement on any precisely defined apostolic "treaty," but it amounted at least to a repudiation of the spirit of this agreement concerning apostolic "division of labor," for they were not in Corinth to aid Paul (as Apollos had been, 1 Cor 3:5, 6) but to supplant him.

This illegitimate invasion of Paul's rightful mission field may well have constituted one of those "acts of disobedience" (v.6) Paul planned to punish on his next visit.

15,16 Twice here (vv.15a, 16b) Paul indirectly chides his opponents for priding themselves on work already done by others. They probably boasted that the spiritual vitality of the Corinthians was directly attributable to them and had come in spite of Paul's influence. And not a few Corinthians were acknowledging their proud claim to spiritual jurisdiction (11:22). Paul, however, so far from "boasting of work done by others" (v.15), made it his policy to avoid preaching the gospel where Christ had already been named lest he build on another man's foundation (Rom 15:18–21), though he welcomed another's watering what he himself had planted (1 Cor 3:6, 10).

As their one spiritual father (1 Cor 4:15), Paul hoped that the enlargement of his influence among the Corinthians and the improvement of their estimation of him would accompany or even result from the growth of their faith. Then and only then would he contemplate fulfilling his eager desire to visit the Christians at Rome (Acts 19:21; Rom

1:11; 15:24) and to advance westward to Spain (Rom 15:24, 28). How could he prosecute pioneer evangelism in the western Mediterranean when his converts in the eastern Mediterranean were unsettled and in danger of apostasy (11:3)?

In one sense, Paul's future was in the Corinthians' hands. His evangelistic outreach would be the joyful outcome or the overflow (*eis perisseian*, "in overflowing measure;" NIV, "greatly") of his total acceptance at Corinth. The principle illustrated here is this: A task undertaken at the direction of God or in fulfillment of a divine commission should not be left unfulfilled simply for the sake of grasping new opportunities; consolidation precedes advance. The call to begin is the call to complete (cf. Phil 1:6).

17,18 As in 1 Corinthians 1:31, Paul cites Jeremiah 9:24. Boasting is illegitimate, whether it be of one's own accomplishments or status (1 Cor 1:31), or of another person's achievements as though they were one's own (v.16). For the Christian, only boasting "in the Lord" is legitimate—that is, boasting of what Jesus Christ has done for him (Gal 6:14) or through him (Rom 15:18; cf. Acts 14:27), or can do through him. (Here Paul is confident the Lord will make his work in Rome and Spain fruitful.)

So far from being an evidence or guarantee of divine approval, self-commendation (such as Paul's adversaries practiced) is a disqualification (v.18). Only the person who boasts in the Lord and so gives God his due glory enjoys the Lord's commendation, which is real approval. To gain Christ's approval during life and after death at Christ's tribunal was Paul's goal (5:9).

Notes

12,13 Some commentators (e.g., H. Windisch, J. Héring) prefer the shorter Western reading (D* G it) that omits the four words οὐ συνιᾶσιν. ἡμεῖς δέ (*ou syniasin. hēmeis de*, "they are not wise. We, however"). The sense will then be (reading the participles of v.12b as first person, not third person): "When we measure ourselves by ourselves and compare ourselves with ourselves (i.e., in terms of our God-given commission and self-imposed ideals), we will not be boasting beyond proper limits but in keeping with the limits determined by the sphere God has allotted to us." This Western text, however, probably arose through a transcriptional error (the scribe passing from οὐ [*ou*] to οὐκ [*ouk*]) or through an effort to remove the harsh οὐ συνιᾶσιν (*ou syniasin*, "they are senseless").

14 Although ἐφθάσαμεν (*ephthasamen*) could mean simply "we reached" (NIV, "we did get"), it may also be tr. "we were the first to reach" (NEB) (cf. 1 Thess 4:15), reflecting Paul's understanding of his apostolic commission as that of pioneer evangelism among the Gentiles.

15 If ἐν ὑμῖν (*en hymin*, v.15) here means "through you," "with your help" (BV), rather than "among you" (NIV), then the enlargement of Paul's sphere of activity is not at Corinth but "in the regions beyond" (v.16), viz., the western Mediterranean.

3. *Paul's jealousy for the Corinthians*

11:1–6

1I hope you will put up with a little of my foolishness; but you are already doing
that. 2I am jealous for you with a godly jealousy. I promised you to one husband,
to Christ, so that I might present you as a pure virgin to him. 3But I am afraid that
just as Eve was deceived by the serpent's cunning, your minds may somehow be

led astray from your sincere and pure devotion to Christ. [4]For if someone comes to you and preaches a Jesus other than the Jesus we preached, or if you receive a different spirit from the one you received, or a different gospel from the one you accepted, you put up with it easily enough. [5]But I do not think I am in the least inferior to those "super-apostles." [6]I may not be a trained speaker, but I do have knowledge. We have made this perfectly clear to you in every way.

1 Paul has firmly stated that self-praise is inadmissible and worthless (3:1; 5:12; 10:12), but he realizes that the present situation demands it if his converts at Corinth are to be preserved intact for Christ (v.2). His antagonists were indulging in self-praise (5:12; 10:7, 12–18) and the Corinthians were evidently to a large extent sympathetic. Consequently his hand was forced (12:11); he must indulge in foolish boasting in order to win the Corinthians' attention and gain a fair hearing. Reluctantly, he decides to employ his opponents' methods; unlike theirs, his motive is not personal gain but the Corinthians' welfare (v.2). He would be boasting "in the Lord" (10:17). So he ironically requests the Corinthians' indulgence, knowing they had already been humoring "a little of. . .[his] foolishness" (see 6:3–10; 10:13–17).

2 As R. Bultmann has rightly observed, Paul supplies three grounds (each introduced by *gar,* "for") for his appeal to the Corinthians to bear with him: (1) his divine jealousy for the Corinthians especially when they were endangered (vv.2, 3); (2) their willingness to put up with rivals who presented an adulterated message (v.4); and (3) his claim not to be in the least inferior to the "super-apostles" (v.5).

With a jealousy that sprang from God and was like God's own jealousy for his people (e.g., Hos 2:19, 20; 4:12; 6:4; 11:8), Paul was jealous for his converts' undivided loyalty to Christ in the interval between their conversion (=betrothal to Christ) and their glorification (=presentation to Christ). He pictures himself as the father of the bride (cf. 1 Cor 4:15; 2 Cor 12:14), whose ultimate purpose in betrothing "the church of God in Corinth" (1:1) to her heavenly bridegroom Jesus Christ, was to present her as a virgin to her husband at his appearance (cf. 4:14; Eph 5:27; 1 John 3:2, 3).

Human jealousy is a vice, but to share divine jealousy is a virtue. It is the motive and object of the jealousy that is all-important. There is a place for a spiritual father's passionate concern for the exclusive and pure devotion to Christ of his spiritual children, and also a place for anger at potential violators of that purity (11:29).

3 Prompting Paul's jealousy for Corinthian fidelity was his fear, based on disturbing evidence (v.4), that their minds and affections might be corrupted so that they would lose their single-minded faithfulness to Christ. He recognized the false apostles as Satan's agents (v.15), capable of repeating at Corinth what Satan had successfully achieved in the garden of Eden (Gen 3:13; 1 Tim 2:14)—complete deception (*exēpatēsen*) by cunning. The danger was not moral corruption but intellectual deception (see v.4) leading to spiritual apostasy.

4 Paul's fear had a foundation in fact. The "if" does not introduce some hypothetical condition ("if someone were to come") but an actual situation ("if, as has happened, someone comes"). In justification of his plea for the Corinthians' tolerance of his enforced boasting (v.1), Paul ironically appeals to the ready welcome they gave visitors who came proclaiming a message other than the gospel that they had embraced and that had

brought them salvation. Surely they ought to show their father in the faith the same degree of tolerance they showed a newcomer preaching a different faith!

It is impossible to reconstruct the precise content of the message of these false apostles, and it is uncertain whether Paul is here alluding to the Holy Spirit or to a spirit of fear and slavery (Rom 8:15; 2 Tim 1:7) as opposed to a spirit of peace and freedom (Rom 14:17; 2 Cor 3:17). What seems clear, however, is that the willingness of the Corinthian believers to entertain the eloquent preacher of an adulterated gospel (cf. Gal 1:6–9) that added human merit to divine grace and gave an interpretation of the earthly ministry of Jesus and the function of the Spirit radically different from Paul's illustrated their tendency to look "only on the surface of things" (10:7) and their preoccupation with manner rather than matter (1 Cor 1:17; 2:1, 4, 5; 13:1; 2 Cor 10:10; 11:6).

5 The third justification for the request of v.1a now appears (see commentary on v.2). Still engaging in his "senseless" but pardonable self-praise, Paul expresses his opinion that he is in no way inferior to the "super-apostles." It seems unlikely that he is referring to the false apostles themselves (alluded to in v.4 as visitors). Even writing ironically, Paul would scarcely claim to be on a par with those he describes in v.13 as "deceitful workmen" and in v.15 as servants of Satan. On the other hand, the "super-apostles" are not to be equated exactly with the Jerusalem apostles or the three "pillars" of the Jerusalem church (Gal 2:9). The expression is either the description of the Twelve used by Paul's opponents and here (as in 12:11, where see commentary) quoted by Paul, or, more probably, the apostle's ironical description of the exalted view of the Twelve held by the "false apostles" (see Introduction, 7.d.2). In this verse, then, Paul claims to be in no respect inferior to the original apostles (see 1 Cor 9:1; 15:5–8, 10) with whom he was being unfavorably compared and whose authority his adversaries illegitimately invoked in support of their Judaizing program at Corinth. If the Corinthians bore with intruders (v.4) and their exalted claims concerning the Twelve (v.5), they ought also to bear with Paul in his foolishness (v.1; cf. v.16).

6 This is not an explanation of the truth of v.5; to admit an exception ("I may not be a trained speaker") immediately after the bold assertion, "I am in no way inferior" (v.5), would be intolerable. Rather, Paul is rating himself by the criteria used by the Corinthians to assess the credentials of apostles or visiting missionaries (thus C.K. Barrett).

With regard to his lack of professional training and skill in rhetoric, Paul is quite willing to admit his deficiency (cf. 10:10) and perhaps even his inferiority to the "false apostles." But in his judgment his expertise in knowledge, which he had made perfectly clear to the Corinthians, more than compensated for this deficiency. Matter was more significant than manner (cf. v.4 and 1 Cor 2:13, NIV).

Notes

---

1 The NIV takes ἀνέχεσθε (*anechesthe*) in v.1b as an indicative. It may also be an imperative, giving v.1b the sense, "Yes, please do put up with me!" or "Please try... !" (PH).

3 In Jewish tradition Eve was thought to have been sexually seduced by the serpent (see C.K. Barrett, in loc.). Although the verb Paul uses (ἐξαπατάω, *exapataō,* "deceive") could refer to such seduction, here it probably simply denotes Satanic perversion of human intellectual or spiritual sensibilities (like the verb φθείρω, *phtheirō,* "lead astray," which follows). Paul here seems to view Christ as the last Adam and the Church as the last Eve in danger of infidelity.

6 On the theme "Paul's Boasting in Relation to Contemporary Professional Practice," see E.A. Judge, *Australian Biblical Review*, XVI (1–4, 1968), pp. 37–50.

---

4. *Financial dependence and independence*

11:7–12

[7]Was it a sin for me to lower myself in order to elevate you by preaching the gospel of God to you free of charge? [8]I robbed other churches by receiving support from them so as to serve you. [9]And when I was with you and needed something, I was not a burden to anyone, for the brothers who came from Macedonia supplied what I needed. I have kept myself from being a burden to you in any way, and will continue to do so. [10]As surely as the truth of Christ is in me, nobody in the regions of Achaia will stop this boasting of mine. [11]Why? Because I do not love you? God knows I do! [12]And I will keep on doing what I am doing in order to cut the ground from under those who want an opportunity to be considered equal with us in the things they boast about.

7,8 In spite of what Paul had written in 1 Corinthians 9:3–18 about the matter, the believers at Corinth had been influenced by the pseudo-apostles into thinking that the acceptance of remuneration for teaching was another criterion of true apostolicity. Their thought seemed to be: "If it is the apostles' right to refrain from working for a living and to get their living by the gospel [1 Cor 9:6, 14], why has Paul always refused to accept our gifts and yet receives support from other churches?" No doubt Paul's rivals interpreted his refusal as evidence of his being a false apostle.

In his defense, notable for its powerful irony, Paul makes two points. He committed no offense, surely, simply by waiving his apostolic right to support (1 Cor 9:12, 15, 18) so that no one could charge him with peddling God's word for profit (2:17). Second, his purpose in "humbling" himself in the Corinthians' eyes to undertake manual labor while ministering to them (see Acts 18:3) was to "elevate" them above their inherited idolatry and vicious past (v.7; cf. 4:12; 8:9), just as his "robbing" other churches of money they could not really spare was motivated solely by his desire to serve the Corinthians gratuitously and more effectively (v.8). It was Paul's policy not to accept financial support from churches in which he was currently ministering (see note).

9 During his initial visit to Corinth (Fall A.D. 50–Spring A.D. 52), Paul had at first supported himself by plying his trade as a "leather-worker" (*skēnopoios*, Acts 18:3), but on the arrival of Silas and Timothy from Macedonia, "he began to devote himself entirely to preaching" (*syneicheto tō logō*, Acts 18:5). It is a fair inference from the present verse that the reason for this alteration in Paul's daily schedule was that the "brothers who came from Macedonia" brought monetary gifts from Philippi (Phil 4:15) and possibly Thessalonica (cf. 1 Thess 3:6). Providentially the gift arrived just when his resources had failed and he had begun to feel need (*hysterētheis*). Even in this extremity he had not been a burden to anyone. Financial independence would continue to be his policy with regard to Corinth.

10–12 This policy, which enabled Paul to boast that he was preaching the gospel free of charge (v.7; cf. 1 Cor 9:18), he resolutely refused to abandon (cf. 1 Cor 9:15). It was Christ's truth he was speaking when he affirmed that he would not bow to pressure from his opponents anywhere in Achaia regarding this issue (v.10).

As to the motive for Paul's inflexible policy, two conflicting explanations are mentioned. Some had malevolently asserted that it was evidence of his lack of affection for the Corinthians. Paul dismisses this by appealing to God's knowledge of his heart (v.11). His own explanation is given in v.12.

Like the wandering preachers of the day (see note on v.8), the intruders at Corinth had apparently received some remuneration for their instruction. Regarding themselves as in some sense apostles, they probably felt fully within their rights in accepting or even demanding appropriate wages; this validated their apostleship. But Paul's stance was an acute embarrassment to them, for they could not boast as he did about preaching a message gratuitously. This, then, was Paul's motive for persisting in his longstanding policy—to deprive his opponents of the opportunity they longed for so they might boast that they were working at Corinth on precisely the same terms he had been. He hoped his financial independence would highlight his rivals' financial dependence and cause the Corinthians to rethink their attitude toward him.

Notes

8 The itinerant philosophers or teachers of the Hellenistic age commonly gained their financial support by charging a fee for their instruction, though the less scrupulous charlatans would rely on begging. Traveling teachers who were concerned about their reputation would often work at a trade. Under the influence of the example set by Jesus in the missions of the Twelve and the Seventy (Luke 9:3, 4; 10:4, 7), early Christianity came to recognize another legitimate method of support in addition to manual labor. An itinerant missionary might receive hospitality and even gifts from the community to which he was ministering (1 Cor 9:6, 11, 14; 3 John 5–8 and cf. Didache 11:4–6). In Christian usage the verb προπέμπω (*propempō*, "send forth," "escort") often had the technical sense of supplying a visitor with food, money, or companions for travel and so "helping him on his way" (see Acts 15:3; Rom 15:24; 1 Cor 16:6, 11; 2 Cor 1:16; Titus 3:13; 3 John 6).

12 "The things they [Paul's opponents] boast about" may refer to the legitimacy of their Corinthian ministry, their claimed apostleship, or, preferably, their acceptance of support as proof of their apostleship.

5. *False apostles*

11:13–15

13For such men are false apostles, deceitful workmen, masquerading as apostles of Christ. 14And no wonder, for Satan himself masquerades as an angel of light. 15It is not surprising, then, if his servants masquerade as servants of righteousness. Their end will be what their actions deserve.

13–15 Paul does not even contest the right of his adversaries to support but rather lays against them a single all-embracing charge. Those who vaunted their apostleship and vainly sought equality with him were in fact "false apostles," apostolic pretenders who passed themselves off as "righteous servants" of Christ (cf. 11:23) while in reality they were agents of Satan. Like their principal, the arch-deceiver (John 8:44) whose habit was to masquerade "as a shining angel," they relied on disguise and deceit in carrying out their nefarious schemes such as the corruption of the intellect and the diversion of the affections from Christ (vv.3, 4). What was false was not simply their claim to apostleship but also their message. Behind both were Satanic designs upon the Corinthians—designs Paul was well aware of (2:11). The destiny of these men would accord with the actual deeds they performed (cf. 5:10; Phil 3:19), not the outward appearance they adopted (cf. 5:12). As preachers of "a different gospel" (v.4), they stood under the anathema of Galatians 1:8, 9.

When referring to the "super-apostles" (11:5; 12:11), Paul shows remarkable restraint; he is not their inferior in any respect. But he does not hesitate to attack ruthlessly the Judaizing intruders from Jerusalem. In one case Paul is defensive and mildly ironical; in the other case he is polemical and intensely serious. The solution to the problem of the Palestinian interlopers was not excommunication, since it was not a case of professing believers whose conduct gave the lie to their profession. Part of the Pauline solution was outright condemnation, since the intruders were minions of Satan who sought to impose certain elements of Jewish teaching and practice on Gentile Christians as prerequisites for salvation (see Introduction, 7.d. 1, 3).

B. *Boasting "As a Fool"* (11:16–12:13)

1. *Justification for foolish boasting*

11:16–21a

16I repeat: Let no one take me for a fool. But if you do, then receive me just as you would a fool, so that I may do a little boasting. 17In this self-confident boasting I am not talking as the Lord would, but as a fool. 18Since many are boasting in the way the world does, I too will boast. 19You gladly put up with fools since you are so wise! 20In fact, you even put up with anyone who enslaves you or exploits you or takes advantage of you or pushes himself forward or slaps you in the face. 21aTo my shame I admit that we were too weak for that!

16 Paul now resumes from vv.1–6 the theme of foolish boasting, after he has digressed to defend his policy regarding financial support (vv.7–12) and to describe the true identity of his opponents (vv. 13–15). He has decided to boast as his opponents do, because he knows the Corinthians' determination to compare him with his rivals and their vulnerability to those who commend themselves. From 11:16 to 12:13 he engages in *ad hominem* argumentation, boasting about things that are not "boastworthy" and answering fools according to their folly (Prov 26:5). There was a danger, however, that some Corinthians might not see or wish to see that Paul was simply playing a part. But even if they thought he was actually a fool and not just a play-actor, he solicits their indulgence as he does "a little boasting."

17,18 The RSV is probably right in interpreting these two verses as a parenthesis, since "for [*gar*] you gladly bear with fools" (v.19a, RSV) looks back to "receive me just as you would a fool" (v.16). Under normal circumstances, Paul is saying (in vv.17, 18), his conduct and words as a servant of Christ and of the Corinthians (4:5; 11:23) would have been marked by "the meekness and gentleness of Christ" (10:1), not the "self-confident boasting" of the fool (v.17). It was not the example of Christ, but the need to follow the example of his opponents (note the *kagō*, "I too" in vv.16, 18) in order to win over the Corinthians, that had driven him to this desperate measure of self-exaltation.

As hesitant as Paul is to talk "as a fool," his reluctance is partially overcome when he recalls that his converts have grown accustomed to self-advertisement. Many (*polloi*, as in 2:17) at Corinth, as generally elsewhere, were bragging "in the way the world does," i.e., boasting of personal privileges and achievements (as Paul himself does, beginning at v.22).

19–21a Probably no verses in the epistle are more scathingly ironical than these. Not only do the Corinthians humor fools; they do so "gladly," because the folly of the fool serves to highlight the wisdom of "the wise" (*phronimoi*, as in 1 Cor 4:10).

Their tolerance apparently had no limits. They put up not only with the speech of fools but also with the despotism of tyrants. The intruding aliens had "reduced them to slavery" by robbing them of their liberty in Christ and seeking to reimpose the Mosaic law (cf. Gal 2:4; 5:1). They had exploited them by greedily devouring any and all maintenance offered them (cf. Mark 12:40). They had entrapped them with tantalizing bait (cf. Luke 5:5); they had put on airs of superiority and had gravely insulted and humiliated them.

None of Paul's readers or hearers would have failed to catch his message with its indictment of their inconsistency. Claiming to be followers of a meek, gentle Christ (10:1; cf. Matt 11:29), they were impressed by and willingly submitted to the aggressiveness and authoritarianism of teachers masquerading as apostles of Christ (v.13); yet they were unimpressed by Paul's "weak" considerateness as a genuine "apostle of Christ Jesus" (1:1; 10:1, 10). Paul has to confess with shame (but really with biting irony) that his character had been too weak and his disposition too mild to use the tactics of the opposition (v.21a)!

2. *Paul's heritage and trials*

11:21b–29

[21b]What anyone else dares to boast about—I am speaking as a fool—I also dare to boast about. [22]Are they Hebrews? So am I. Are they Israelites? So am I. Are they Abraham's descendants? So am I. [23]Are they servants of Christ? (I am out of my mind to talk like this.) I am more. I have worked much harder, been in prison more frequently, been flogged more severely, and been exposed to death again and again. [24]Five times I received from the Jews the forty lashes minus one. [25]Three times I was beaten with rods, once I was stoned, three times I was shipwrecked, I spent a night and a day in the open sea, [26]I have been constantly on the move. I have been in danger from rivers, in danger from bandits, in danger from my own countrymen, in danger from Gentiles; in danger in the city, in danger in the country, in danger at sea; and in danger from false brothers. [27]I have labored and toiled and have often gone without sleep; I have known hunger and thirst and have often gone without food; I have been cold and naked. [28]Besides everything else, I face daily the pressure of my concern for all the churches. [29]Who is weak, and I do not feel weak? Who is led into sin, and I do not inwardly burn?

21b,22 Already Paul has made several efforts to begin sustained boasting (see 10:8; 11:1, 6, 16). Now he finally brings himself to this distasteful task. No bold claim made by his rivals will go unmatched (v.21b). So to the first three claims mentioned, he responds with the simple, disarming word *kagō*, "so am I."

By "Hebrews" is meant Jews of Palestinian descent, especially those whose native tongue was Aramaic or Hebrew and whose intellectual and cultural heritage was within Palestinian rather than Diaspora Judaism. If this is an accurate description of "Hebrews," then "Hellenists" would be Jews living in Palestine (Acts 6:1) or the Diaspora for whom Greek was the first or only language and whose outlook owed more to Diaspora Judaism than to Palestinian Judaism, though this distinction within Judaism should not be pressed. Whether he was brought up in Tarsus or in Jerusalem (see note), Paul was a Hebrew of Hebrew parentage (Phil 3:5). As an "Israelite" Paul was a member of God's people and kingdom, Israel. As a descendant of Abraham who had been "circumcised on the eighth day" (Phil 3:5), Paul was an heir to the covenants based on God's promise (Eph 2:12). All in all, with regard to descent, citizenship, and heritage, he was the equal of his rivals.

23–25 When Paul turns from the matter of nationality (v.22) to that of achievement (vv.23–29), he lays claim to superiority over his rivals, not simply equality with them, and begins to speak as a madman (v.23), not simply as a fool (vv.16, 17, 21). Although he compares himself with both the "super-apostles" and the "false apostles," in the former case the comparison is negative ("I am not in the least inferior," 11:5; 12:11), in the latter case it is positive ("...more...much harder...more frequently...more severely," v.23).

In the light of v.13, where the false apostles are called "deceitful workmen, masquerading as apostles of Christ," it might seem unlikely that Paul, by implication, would here concede his opponents to be "servants of Christ." But note that "Are they...?" means "Do they claim to be...?" and that in v.13 is found Paul's estimate of them, in v.23 their estimate of themselves, which Paul concedes for the sake of the comparison that follows.

At v.23 Paul's list of "accomplishments" begins, but unlike the imperial *res gestae* Paul's list recounts not triumphs but apparent defeats and relates not to strengths but "weaknesses" (11:30; 12:5, 9, 10). This accords with his view that lowliness and weakness as seen in Christian service provide the only incontestable vindication of apostleship.

If we compare this list of Paul's sufferings (cf. 1 Cor 4:9–13; 2 Cor 4:8–12; 6:4, 5) with the account of his experiences given in Acts, it immediately becomes clear how fragmentary, but not how unreliable, Luke's record is. Since the writing of 2 Corinthians fits into Luke's account at Acts 20:2a, only the events recorded before this verse relate to the comparison. To be sure, Luke gives ample proof of Paul's hard work (v.23) and records his stoning at Lystra (v.25; Acts 14:19). But he mentions only one imprisonment (cf. v.23) before Acts 20—that at Philippi (Acts 16:23–40)—and only one of his three (Roman?) beatings with rods (v.25), also at Philippi (Acts 16:22, 23). From Acts we know nothing of other imprisonments (v.23; cf. 1 Clement 5:6). Those at Jerusalem, Caesarea, and Rome occurred later. Nor do we know about the five whippings in Jewish synagogical courts (v.24), about the other two beatings at the hands of Gentiles (v.25, but note 2 Tim 3:11), or about the three shipwrecks and the night and day in the open sea, probably clinging to wreckage while awaiting rescue (cf. the later shipwreck, Acts 27:13–44). (Verse 24 shows Paul's reluctance to surrender his Jewish status or associations—C.K. Barrett, in loc.) Paul's life was even more colorful than Acts would lead the reader to believe!

26,27 From specific hardships (vv.24, 25) Paul turns to the dangers he confronted (v.26) and the privations he endured (v.27; cf. 6:5). In speaking of "danger from rivers" and "danger from bandits" he would be thinking especially of crossing the Taurus range between Perga in Pamphylia and Antioch in Phrygia near Pisidia (Acts 13:14; 14:24), a journey made hazardous by the mountain torrents and the predatory Pisidian highlanders. Acts records several examples of Jewish plots against Paul's life before this time (e.g.,

Acts 9:23, 29; 14:19; 18:12) but only two incidents involving "danger from Gentiles" (at Philippi, Acts 16:16–40; and at Ephesus, Acts 19:23–41). "Danger from false brothers" may point to Paul's being betrayed to local authorities by counterfeit Christians and the resulting reprisals (similarly J. Héring).

Paul's "sleepless nights" (*agrypniai,* as in 6:5) could refer to insomnia because of physical discomfort or illness, but more probably the phrase alludes to voluntary sleeplessness from pressure of work. As C.K. Barrett (in loc.) suggests, Paul may have undertaken some of his voluntary fasts ("I. . .have often gone without food"; cf. 6:5) because of his determination not to accept support from the Corinthians (1 Cor 9:12, 15, 18; 2 Cor 11:7–12).

28,29 None of the afflictions mentioned in vv.23–27 was a continuous experience. Paul's crowning trial and privilege was, however, incessant—the daily pressure of his anxious concern (*merimna*) for all the churches (cf. Acts 20:18–21, 28–31). If his trials at Corinth were any indication, the total burden he always bore must have been well-nigh oppressive.

Yet Paul did not violate the teaching of Jesus about anxiety (cf. Matt 6:25–34, where the verbal form of *merimna* occurs frequently). His concern arose from seeking first the kingdom of God; he was grappling realistically with present, not future problems; and he had no anxiety about the relatively trivial matters of food and clothing (as v.27 shows). But as a faithful "under-shepherd," he shared the constant burden of the chief shepherd with regard to all the sheep.

This total identification of shepherd with sheep, or of spiritual father with children in the faith, is now illustrated (v.29). Paul was at one with all his converts (cf. 1 Cor 12:26), sympathizing with their weakness in faith, conduct or conscience (cf. 1 Cor 8:7–13; 9:22). It is difficult to know what Paul means when he says, "I inwardly burn" (29b). The following suggestions have been made: He was fired with indignation at the person who caused another to sin (cf. Matt 18:6; 1 Cor 8:10–13; Gal 5:12, and the present situation with the false apostles); his heart burned with shame when a Christian brother fell or when someone dishonored the name of Christ; or he was so ablaze with compassion for the person who was "led into sin" that he shared his remorse. Perhaps all three were involved, though the last view best suits the context.

Notes

22 On the terms "Hebrew" and 'Israelite" in NT usage, see W. Gutbrod, TDNT, 3:375–391. That Jerusalem was the city of Paul's boyhood and upbringing (cf. Acts 22:3; 26:4) has been argued by W.C. van Unnik in his book *Tarsus or Jerusalem: the City of Paul's Youth* (Epworth: London, 1962).

28 The phrase χωρὶς τῶν παρεκτός (*chōris tōn parektos*) means either "apart from external trials" (cf. KJV, RV, NEB; C.K. Barrett) or "apart from the things left unmentioned" (cf. RSV, Am. Trans., Wey, JB, NIV; A. Plummer, P.E. Hughes). Moff. takes the phrase with what precedes: ". . .and all the rest of it."

The noun ἐπίστασις (*epistasis*) probably means "pressure" (being defined by the phrase that follows), but other possibilities include "attention," "superintendence," "conspiring," "hindrance"; see BAG, p. 300, and the footnote in P.E. Hughes, in loc.

3. *Escape from Damascus*

11:30–33

30If I must boast, I will boast of the things that show my weakness. 31The God and Father of the Lord Jesus, who is to be praised forever, knows that I am not lying. 32In Damascus the governor under King Aretas had the city of the Damascenes guarded in order to arrest me. 33But I was lowered in a basket from a window in the wall and slipped through his hand.

30,31 For a moment Paul pauses and reflects on the paragraph he has just dictated to his stunned amanuensis. Both he and his opponents might boast, but *his* boasting was distinctive, since, paradoxically, he prided himself on evidences of his weakness that became evidences of God's surpassing power in supporting and delivering him (cf. 1:8–10; 3:5; 4:7, 10, 11; 12:5, 9, 10).

Because he had been so precise in describing his afflictions and perils (see especially vv.24, 25), he realized that the record sounded not only incredible but also out of keeping for an apostle and that his rivals might easily dismiss it as gross exaggeration. Hence his appeal to the divine omniscience (cf. 1:18; 11:10, 11 and Rom 9:1; Gal 1:20; 1 Tim 2:7). Such an invocation of God as a witness or testimony to his truthfulness (v.31) was not, of course, a repudiation of Christ's ban on unnecessary or frivolous swearing (Matt 5:33–37; James 5:12). The trustworthiness of Paul's word had been impugned (cf. 1:17, 18).

32,33 After the solemn invocation of v.31, the account of a nocturnal escape from Damascus might seem trivial and out of place. Perhaps Paul mentions the episode because it had shattered the residual pride of Saul the Pharisee (cf. Acts 9:1, 2) and had become the supreme example of the humiliation and weakness he was boasting about (v.30). Or he may be referring to it because his detractors had used it to ridicule him and prove his cowardice (cf. 10:1, 10). Or again, he may be speaking of it because it was probably the first attempt on his life and such a significant reversal of roles (Acts 9:1, 2!) that it had been indelibly impressed on his memory. Whatever the reason for its inclusion here, the episode forms a suitable backdrop for what follows: an embarrassing descent to escape the hands of men and then an exhilarating ascent into the presence of God (12:2–4).

Aretas IV, the father-in-law of Herod Antipas, ruled over the kingdom of the Nabataean Arabs from c. 9 B.C. to A.D. 40. Nabataea (=the "Arabia" of Gal 1:17) stretched east and south of the river Jordan. Why did Aretas or his governor (*ethnarchēs*) want to arrest Paul? Probably because the king had been offended by Paul's evangelistic activity in his kingdom (Gal 1:17). It is unlikely that Paul's sojourn in Arabia was simply a "spiritual retreat," for Luke is careful to note that *immediately* after his conversion Paul began to dispute in the synagogues of Damascus (Acts 9:20; see also Gal 1:22, 23).

Luke's account of Paul's escape (Acts 9:23–25) reveals that the Jews were watching the gates in order to kill Paul; here in 2 Corinthians 11 we are told that the governor under King Aretas had the city guarded in order to arrest Paul. What was the relation between the Jews and the governor? It is uncertain whether Damascus was under Nabataean rule, Roman rule, or joint sovereignty at the time (c. A.D. 35). From 63 B.C. until A.D. 34 Damascus was Roman. But since no Roman coins dating from A.D. 34–62 have been found in Damascus, some scholars hold that during that time (including the reigns of Caligula and Claudius, A.D. 37–41 and A.D. 41–54) the city was under Nabataean rule, the governor being a deputy of King Aretas who lived at Petra. P.E. Hughes (in loc.) proposes that the ethnarch himself was a Jew, responsible for Damascene Jews, so that the guard he appointed was composed entirely of Jews.

However, the gap in the numismatic record is negative and therefore indecisive as evidence. Damascus was probably still under Roman rule and the ethnarch may have been the head of a semi-autonomous colony of Nabataeans in Damascus (so F.F. Bruce, in loc., following E. Meyer). According to this view there was a coalition of Jews (thus Luke) and Nabataeans (thus Paul), acting through the Nabataean ethnarch to arrest and kill Paul. This is more probable than the suggestion that the Jews were watching for Paul inside the walls and the Nabataeans outside.

Whatever the solution to these historical questions, the fact of Paul's providential deliverance through the ingenuity of "his disciples" (Acts 9:25a) remains secure. He "slipped through the governor's hands."

4. *A vision and its aftermath*

12:1–10

1I must go on boasting. Although there is nothing to be gained, I will go on to
visions and revelations from the Lord. 2I know a man in Christ who fourteen years
ago was caught up to the third heaven. Whether it was in the body or out of the
body I do not know—God knows. 3And I know that this man—whether in the body
or apart from the body I do not know, but God knows—4was caught up to Paradise.
He heard inexpressible things, things that man is not permitted to tell. 5I will boast
about a man like that, but I will not boast about myself, except about my weak-
nesses. 6Even if I should choose to boast, I would not be a fool, because I would
be speaking the truth. But I refrain, so no one will think more of me than is
warranted by what I do or say.

7To keep me from becoming conceited because of these surpassingly great
revelations, there was given me a thorn in my flesh, a messenger of Satan, to
torment me. 8Three times I pleaded with the Lord to take it away from me. 9But
he said to me, "My grace is sufficient for you, for my power is made perfect in
weakness." Therefore, I will boast all the more gladly about my weaknesses, so
that Christ's power may rest on me. 10That is why, for Christ's sake, I delight in
weaknesses, in insults, in hardships, in persecutions, in difficulties. For when I am
weak, then I am strong.

1 Again Paul stresses that in this matter of boasting he has had no choice. By insisting that their teachers display their "credentials" ("one must boast," *kauchasthai dei* [v.1; 11:30], they said), the Corinthians were forcing him to break a fourteen-year silence (v.2) and boast about a vision the Lord gave him (see note) (cf. 1 Cor 4:7b). To do so would not edify the church or be a personal gain, though the Corinthians would see that he was not outmatched by his rivals in one important area of their boasting.

It should not be overlooked that Paul's mention of his ecstatic rapture was a necessary introduction to what he says about his "thorn in his flesh" (vv.7–10), another evidence of his weakness.

If Paul intended to distinguish between "visions" and "revelations," then the difference is that a vision is always seen, whereas a revelation may be either seen or perceived in some other way; all visions are also revelations, but not all revelations come through visions. From Acts it is clear that, apart from his Damascus vision of Christ (Acts 9:3–9; 26:19; Gal 1:16), Paul not infrequently had visions (Acts 9:12; 16:9, 10; 18:9, 10; 22:17–21; 23:11; 27:23, 24).

2–4 None of the visions recorded in Acts can be identified with the vision or revelation related here, since it occurred fourteen years before the time of writing (A.D. 56)—that is, c. A.D. 43 by inclusive reckoning, during the ten so-called "silent years" (A.D. 35–45) that Paul spent in Syria and Cilicia (Gal 1:21) and that Acts says nothing about. (But note Acts 9:30; 11:25.)

Is Paul recounting his own experience when he writes enigmatically, "I know a man in Christ ... he heard ..."? Undoubtedly so, for several reasons: (1) He knew the exact time the revelation took place (v.2) and that its content was beyond words even if it were permissible to try to communicate it (v.4). (2) The revelation was directly related to the receipt of a "thorn," which was given, says Paul, "to me" (v.7). (3) The reference to a lack of awareness whether he was in the body or not (vv.2, 3) points to a personal experience. (4) Paul would be unlikely to feel embarrassment (cf. v.1) about boasting on another person's behalf (cf. v.5a). (5) For Paul to relate a remarkable experience that happened to some Christian unknown to the Corinthians but known to Paul would scarcely fit the context.

The scene of the vision was the "hidden Paradise" of Jewish thought (see note), the abode of the righteous dead that is here located within the third heaven (literally, "... as far as [*heōs*] the third heaven ... into [*eis*] Paradise," vv.2b, 4a; cf. 2 Enoch 8:1). If Paul was quite certain of the location of the vision, he was equally *un*certain about whether the experience happened to him in his body or apart from it, (vv.2b, 3b). Consciousness of God totally eclipsed any awareness of the physical world of space and time, removing any consciousness of embodiment. The suddenness of Paul's loss of any sense of physical orientation is suggested by the verb *harpazein* (vv.2, 4), that denotes a sudden rapture, not a gradual ascent (cf. its use in Acts 8:39 of Philip, and in 1 Thess 4:17 of believers at the Parousia).

What Paul heard (and saw?), human words were inadequate to relate (v.4b). What is more, he was not permitted to try to share the content of the revelation, perhaps because it had been designed for him alone, to fortify him for future service and sufferings (Acts 9:16; Rom 8:18). Glimpses the NT does give of the coming glory are aimed at strengthening faith and promoting holiness (cf. 2 Peter 3:10–14; 1 John 3:2, 3), not at satisfying curiosity.

5,6 The remarkable distinction between Paul and the certain "man in Christ" (v.2) or "man involved" (*ho toioutos*, v.3) comes into even sharper relief in v.5 and naturally prompts the question, If Paul is speaking of himself in vv.2–4, why does he objectify his experience? There are several reasons. First, he was clearly embarrassed at needing to boast at all (v.1)—an activity that in itself did not contribute to the common good (cf. 1 Cor 12:7). Second, he wished to avoid suggesting that he was in any sense a special kind of Christian. The revelation was given him as "a man in Christ"; the initiative had been not his but God's. Verse 5 suggests a third reason: Although Paul recognized the honor involved in being the recipient of a vision ("I will boast about a man like that," v.5a), he wanted to dispel any idea that it added to his personal status or importance.

Concerning himself as a man in Christ who had received a special revelation, Paul was prepared to boast if circumstances demanded it. But concerning himself as a man of action and accomplishment, he refused to boast under any circumstances. Only experiences that showed his weakness were suitable material for any enforced boasting (v.5). But in case some should assert that he had done nothing worth boasting about anyway, he adds a word of defense (v.6). If he were to boast of his strengths or things that were not inexpressible, or if he chose to divulge further details about his vision or describe other visions the Lord had given him, he would not be shown up as some fool who had prided himself on imagined glories only to be exposed for his false claims. And why would he not be exposed? Because he would be speaking truth, not falsehood or fiction. He had good reason to boast if that was what he wished to do. But he refrains because he wanted the Corinthians' estimate of him to be based on their recollection of his personal credentials (cf. 5:11b; 12:12). All this suggests that his rivals may have been boasting about imaginary visions or about exploits they claimed to have done before their arrival at Corinth.

7 Others might be tempted, "because of these surpassingly great revelations" (v.7) accorded to Paul, to form an estimate of him that outstripped the evidence (v.6b). But he himself was in no such danger. To keep him from becoming conceited (see note) there was given him a thorn in his flesh. Two inferences are fair. (1) The agent implied by *edothē* ("there was given"; cf. the "theological passives" in vv.2, 4) is God. This is confirmed by the fact that the "thorn" (*skolops,* see note) was given to achieve a beneficial purpose—the prevention of spiritual conceit—and that Paul requested the Lord for the departure of the messenger (v.8). (2) The "thorn" was given immediately or shortly after the vision described in vv.2–4.

It is significant that in vv.7–10 Paul speaks of himself in the first person (cf. vv.2–5); his reputation was in no danger of being illegitimately enhanced (cf. v.6) by describing the outcome of the vision!

The efforts that have been made to identify Paul's "thorn" are legion. Among the recurring suggestions are Jewish persecution, carnal temptation, epilepsy, chronic ophthalmia, a speech impediment, and a recurrent malady (such as malaria or Malta fever). But paucity of information and the obscurity of Paul's language have frustrated all attempts to solve this enigmatic problem. In fact, had Paul revealed what his *skolops* was, Christians of succeeding generations who lacked his particular affliction or disability would have tended to find his experience (vv.8–10) irrelevant. As it is, countless believers have been helped by his reference to his "thorn."

It is remarkable that Paul could regard his affliction as given by God and yet as "a messenger of Satan." This may support the view that the affliction was some type of physical malady, because in 1 Corinthians 5:5 (cf. 1 Cor 11:30; 1 Tim 1:20) Satan appears as God's agent for the infliction of disciplinary illness (cf. Job 2:1–10). Certainly a recurrent and tormenting illness could be considered "a messenger of Satan," for it might bring Paul within the shadow of death (cf. 2 Cor 1:8, 9) or hinder the advance of the gospel either by arousing the contempt of his hearers (cf. Gal 4:13, 14) or by frustrating his travel plans. Be that as it may, behind any and every machination of Satan, Paul could discern the overarching providence of a God who perpetually created good out of evil.

8 The "thorn" proved so tormenting to Paul that on three separate occasions (*tris;* cf. Mark 14:32–42) he "pleaded with the Lord [*ton kyrion*] to take it away" from him. In Paul *ho kyrios* refers to Jesus and *kyrios* to Yahweh (Jehovah). His prayer, then, was addressed to Jesus. In the NT, formal or liturgical prayer was customarily offered through Christ to the Father in the Spirit (Eph 2:18), but on occasion an individual (Acts 7:59) or a group (Acts 1:24) seems to have invoked the Lord Jesus directly.

9,10 The answer to Paul's prayer did not take the form he had expected. The thorn remained, but so too did his recollection of the divine reply (*eirēken,* "he has said," v.9a). In the distressing weakness inflicted at various times by his ailment, he would never lack sufficient grace to be more than a conqueror (cf. Rom 8:35–37). This grace of Christ (13:14) was adequate for Paul, weak as he was, precisely because (*gar*, "for") divine power finds its full scope and strength only in human weakness—the greater the Christian's acknowledged weakness, the more evident Christ's enabling strength (cf. Eph 3:16; Phil 4:13). But it is not simply that weakness is a prerequisite for power. Both weakness and power existed simultaneously in Paul's life (note vv.9b, 10b), as they did in Christ's ministry and death. Indeed, the cross of Christ forms the supreme example of "power-in-weakness."

With this spiritual lesson well learned, Paul would gladly boast about things that exposed his weakness ("insults ... hardships ... persecutions ... difficulties," v.10) rather than pray for the removal of the "thorn" and its attendant weakness. It was not, however, in the weaknesses themselves that Paul took delight but in the opportunity sufferings endured "for Christ's sake" afforded him for Christ's power to reside and be effective in his life (v.9b).

Notes

---

1 NIV is right in taking κυρίου (*kyriou*) as a subjective genitive ("from the Lord") rather than an objective genitive ("of the Lord," in the sense that he was seen and revealed). This interpretation is confirmed by v.4 where Paul stresses what he heard rather than what he saw, and by the use of the "theological passives" ("was caught up," vv.2, 4; cf. "was given," v.7) where the unexpressed agent is clearly the Lord Jesus Christ or God the Father.

4 The eschatology of late Judaism drew a conceptual distinction among the first paradise (Gen 2 and 3), the last or eschatological paradise (cf. Rev 2:7), and the hidden paradise of the intervening period (cf. Luke 23:43; 2 Cor 12:4). See J. Jeremias, TDNT, 5:765–773.

7 In a wide variety of witnesses (including p^{46} B ψ 1739 syr cop) the words ἵνα μὴ ὑπεραίρωμαι (*hina mē hyperairōmai*) are repeated at the end of v.7 (in the 3rd. ed. of UBS this reading is given a "C" rating). The effect of this repeated telic clause is to emphasize the divine purpose in the bestowal of the "thorn."

In the punctuation of UBS, the words translated "[and] because of these surpassingly great revelations" are construed with v.6. This would produce the sense "But I refrain, so no one will think more of me than is warranted by what I do or say [and] because of. . . ."

In classical Greek σκόλοψ (*skolops*) commonly meant "stake" (Latin *sudis*), or, in the plural (σκόλοπες, *skolopes*), "stockade." In Septuagintal usage, however, as in the papyri (MM, pp. 578, 579), the word means "splinter" or "thorn" (e.g., Num 33:55; Ezek 28:24; Hos 2:6; Ecclus 43:19).

The dative τῇ σαρκί (*tē sarki*) may be either (1) locatival, "embedded in [or, driven into] my body," with σάρξ (*sarx*) being used in a neutral sense, or (2) a dative of "disadvantage," "to pierce my flesh" (*Twentieth Century New Testament*), with σάρξ referring either to the physical body or to the sensual nature.

8 Literally rendered, the verse runs: "With regard to this [messenger] I begged the Lord three times that he [the messanger] might depart from me. If τούτου (*toutou*, "this"; NIV, "it" is masculine, the antecedent could be either σκόλοψ (*skolopas*, "thorn") or ἄγγελος (*angelos*, "messenger"); if neuter, the meaning will be "about this matter" or "because of that."

5. *Proof of apostleship*

12:11–13

[11]I have made a fool of myself, but you drove me to it. I ought to have been

commended by you, for I am not in the least inferior to the "super-apostles," even though I am nothing. 12The things that mark an apostle—signs, wonders and miracles—were done among you with great perseverance. 13How were you inferior to the other churches, except that I was never a burden to you? Forgive me this wrong!

11 His "boasting as a fool" now virtually over, Paul reiterates that it had been by coercion. It was not really the foolish boasting of his opponents that had driven him to boast but the folly of the Corinthians in heeding it and their failure to rally to his defense. If any Christian community was qualified to write Paul's testimonial, it was the Corinthian church. They had remained silent, forcing Paul to speak up. His action had been excusable, but not theirs. Commendation was what he deserved and they owed.

Nor was it that they lacked good reason to commend him, for, as they well knew, he was "not in the least inferior to the 'super-apostles'" at Jerusalem whom his rivals invoked so readily in support of their claims (see comments on 11:5). "Even though I am nothing" may be an ironical citation of his opponents' opinion of him or a serious disavowal of any personal merit that might have made him worthy of apostleship (cf. 1 Cor 15:8–10).

12 Here Paul gently reminds his converts of certain characteristics of his ministry at Corinth that proved he was a genuine apostle worth commending and in no way inferior to the Twelve. "Signs, wonders and miracles" (*dynameis,* "mighty deeds") do not describe three types of miracles but miracles in general considered from three aspects—their ability to authenticate the message ("signs"), evoke awe ("wonders") and display divine power ("mighty deeds"). These, of course, were not the only marks of apostleship (see note). There was also faithfulness to the apostolic message (11:4) and conduct that was consonant with the example of Christ (10:1; 13:14). To the latter category belongs "great perseverance" in the face of opposition, such as that shown by Paul at Corinth (Acts 18:6, 9, 10, 12–16). It was this characteristic of fortitude that distinguished him from the false apostles, who also claimed to have worked "signs and wonders." Significant, too, is Paul's use of the passive voice in this verse ("the things that mark an apostle . . . were done among you"); he disowns any credit for the supernatural signs accompanying his ministry and marking it as apostolic.

13 Again indulging in gentle irony, Paul observes that the only respect in which the marks of a true apostle were not evident in the apostolic church of Corinth was that of support. He never was a financial burden to them—an injustice for which he playfully pleads forgiveness! As in 1 Corinthians 9:1–18 and 2 Corinthians 11:5–12 (see the discussion there), Paul has moved naturally from a consideration of apostleship (vv.11, 12) to the issue of apostolic rights. He is distinguishing between certain signs of apostleship (perseverance, signs, wonders, mighty deeds) and a particular right of apostleship—namely, support from the church or churches being served. A church in which the signs of apostleship were displayed was no less apostolic because this optional right of an apostle had been waived by him. Nor was insistence on every legitimate personal right a mark of a genuine apostle (as the Corinthians were inclined to believe).

Notes

12 An alternative tr. of this verse would be: "At least [μέν, *men*], the marks [σημεῖα, *sēmeia*] of an apostle were produced in your midst with great fortitude, and were accompanied by signs [σημείοις, *sēmeiois*], portents and mighty deeds." In this case the "marks" are distinguishable from the "signs, portents and mighty deeds" (contrast NIV) and may refer to the transformed lives of the Corinthians and the Christlike character of Paul (so P.E. Hughes, in loc.).

C. *The Planned Third Visit* (12:14–13:10)

1. *A promise not to be burdensome*

12:14–18

[14]Now I am ready to visit you for the third time, and I will not be a burden to you, because what I want is not your possessions but you. After all, children should not have to save up for their parents, but parents for their children. [15]So I will very gladly spend for you everything I have and expend myself as well. If I love you more, will you love me less? [16]Be that as it may, I have not been a burden to you. Yet, crafty fellow that I am, I caught you by trickery! [17]Did I exploit you through any of the men I sent you? [18]I urged Titus to go to you and I sent our brother with him. Titus did not exploit you, did he? Did we not act in the same spirit and follow the same course?

14,15 The apostle announces that his third visit to Corinth is imminent (see note) and that his policy regarding support will not be altered. He is determined always to be financially independent of the Corinthians (cf. 1 Cor 9:15; 2 Cor 11:9, 12). They will have to continue bearing the "injury" he is inflicting on them (cf. v.13)! His affections were set on the Corinthians themselves (cf. 6:11, 12; 7:2, 3), not on what they owned and could share with him. He craved their reciprocated love (6:13; 12:15b), their Christian maturity (cf. 1 Cor 3:1–4; Col 1:28, 29), and their exclusive devotion to Christ (11:2, 3).

In defense of this refusal to accept support, he appeals to the self-evident truth that it is no part of children's obligation to save up and provide for their parents, but only parents for children. The principle, however, is not universally applicable. Paul defended the right of apostles to be supported by their spiritual children (1 Cor 9:3–14) and later asserted, "If anyone does not provide for his relatives, and especially for his immediate family, he has denied the faith and is worse than an unbeliever" (1 Tim 5:8, NIV).

Far from coveting the Corinthians' property, Paul planned to use all his own resources to achieve their highest good; neither property nor energies would be spared in his efforts to win their affection for Christ (cf. Acts 20:24). Yet he looked for "a fair exchange" (cf. 6:13): "Am I to be loved the less because I love you the more [i.e., so intensely]?" There may be an actual comparison here. If Paul's love for the Corinthians exceeded the love of a father for his children, how could they love him less than children love their father? In other words, Paul is seeking a response of filial love to his paternal affection (cf. 11:11).

16–18 Whether or not the Corinthians loved Paul the less for his intense love for them

("Be that as it may"), all were agreed that he himself (note *egō*) had not proved a financial strain on the church. Yet the rumor had circulated at Corinth that because Paul was unscrupulous by nature (*hyparchōn panourgos,* v.16), he had exploited the church's generosity and had gained surreptitiously through his agents what he had declined to accept personally. The collection for the poor at Jerusalem was simply a convenient way to fulfull his covert wish to live at the church's expense. There is no explicit reference in these verses to a charge of financial fraud, but the context renders this interpretation likely. The alternative would be to regard the exploitation (*pleonekteō,* vv.17, 18; cf. 2:11; 7:2) as the psychological pressure to which Paul allegedly subjected the Corinthians by refusing to exercise his personal right to remuneration and yet requesting generous contributions to the collection he was organizing.

Since Paul knew the charge had been maliciously made and was couched in general terms, he refutes it first by indirectly appealing to the Corinthians to adduce specific evidence (v.17) and then by referring to a particular occasion on which his chief agent had been sent to Corinth on a mission involving finance (v.18a). If Titus was guiltless, so too was Paul, for all their conduct had been governed by the same principles (v.18b).

Which visit of Titus does Paul refer to? Either the visit alluded to in 8:6a when he commenced the collection or the visit mentioned in 8:16–24 when he completed the collection. On either view, the mention of "our brother" in 12:18 requires explanation. Scholars who place 2 Corinthians 10–13 before 2 Corinthians 1–9 as a part of the "severe letter" and the defenders of the epistle's integrity generally prefer the first view. Those who regard chapters 10–13 as written some time later than chapters 1–9 tend to favor the second proposal.

Notes

---

14 Considered in the light of 13:1, 2, the statement "I am ready to visit you for the third time" cannot refer to two prior occasions on which Paul, though willing to visit Corinth or having prepared or decided to do so, had failed to carry through his purpose. If he had here appealed to his unfulfilled good intentions, he would have been liable to a just charge of fickleness (cf. 1:17). Nor were the previous visits implied in 12:14 simply "epistolary" visits (i.e., the "previous letter" and 1 Corinthians) or one actual and one "epistolary" visit. Paul had made two personal visits to Corinth before writing this letter—his founding visit (Acts 18:1–18) and the "painful visit" (see Introduction, 7.a). What would have been a third visit he had earlier cancelled lest it prove to be a second painful visit (1:23; 2:1).

---

2. *Fears about the unrepentant*

12:19–21

> [19]Have you been thinking all along that we have been defending ourselves to you? We have been speaking in the sight of God as those in Christ; and everything we do, dear friends, is for your strengthening. [20]For I am afraid that when I come I may not find you as I want you to be, and you may not find me as you want me to be. I fear that there may be quarreling, jealousy, outbursts of anger, factions, slander, gossip, arrogance and disorder. [21]I am afraid that when I come again my God will humble me before you, and I will be grieved over many who have sinned earlier and have not repented of the impurity, sexual sin and debauchery in which they have indulged.

19 Paul repudiates the suggestion, which might readily have occurred to any Corinthian, that he had all along been seeking to defend his conduct and reputation before a panel of Corinthian judges. It was to God or to Christ, not to the Corinthians, that Paul was ultimately accountable (cf. Rom 14:10; 1 Cor 4:3–5; 2 Cor 5:10), so that self-defense before men was never his primary concern. He had been speaking as a man in Christ whose words and motives were open before God (cf. 2:17; 5:11). His aim in all his relations with the Corinthians—especially his correspondence—was not personal vindication but their edification.

20,21 As the NIV rightly recognizes, Paul expresses here a threefold fear, though the verb *phoboumai,* "I am afraid" (v.20) occurs only once. Defined in general terms in the light of v.19, this fear was his apprehension that the present letter might not be wholly successful and that the Corinthians by harboring Judaizing intruders and persisting in sin would contribute to weakening, not consolidating, their church fellowship.

The first object of Paul's deep concern was the outcome of his impending visit to the Corinthians (v.20a). Would they be mutually disappointed and embarrassed—Paul, by the church's questioning of his apostleship and their refusal to break with sins of the spirit (v.20b) and of the flesh (v.21b), and the Corinthians, by Paul's vigorous exercise of church discipline (cf. 1 Cor 4:21; 5:3–5)? Second, the apostle is fearful that the sins that seemed endemic to Corinth (cf. 1 Cor 1:11, 12, 31; 3:3; 4:6; 5:2, 11; 8:1; 11:18; 14:33, 40) should still be rife as a consequence of the unrest and disorder created by the Palestinian intruders (v.20b).

Third, Paul fears a repetition of humiliation under God's hand (see note) that he had experienced on his second visit (2:1) as a result of certain unrepentant Corinthians (v.21). Any future humiliation would stem from his acute disappointment at the Corinthians' preference for domineering false apostles (11:20) and their supercilious attitude towards him (cf. 1 Cor 4:18, 19), as well as from his grief (*pentheō,* cf. 1 Cor 5:2) over those who had consistently rejected his call to holiness and were continuing unrepentant in their earlier gross sexual sins. These Corinthian libertines may have asserted that since " 'food [was] for the stomach and the stomach for food' " (1 Cor 6:13a, NIV), it followed as a natural corollary that the satisfaction of other physical appetites was equally inevitable and desirable—"the body is meant for immorality" (cf. 1 Cor 6:13b).

Notes

21 Πάλιν (*palin*, "again") probably should be construed with the entire clause that follows ("I fear lest again when I come my God should humiliate me in your presence") rather than simply with ταπεινώσῃ (*tapeinōsē,* "will humble") or ἐλθόντος (*elthontos*). In this humiliation (caused by Corinthian disloyalty and sin) God would be the agent only in the sense that he permitted it and would use it to remind Paul of his personal impotence and the all-surpassing divine power (cf. 4:7, 10, 11).

3. *Warning of impending discipline*

13:1–4

[1]This will be my third visit to you. "Every matter must be established by the testimony of two or three witnesses." [2]I already gave you a warning when I was

> with you the second time. I now repeat it while absent: On my return I will not spare those who sinned earlier or any of the others, [3]since you are demanding proof that Christ is speaking through me. He is not weak in dealing with you, but is powerful among you. [4]For to be sure, he was crucified in weakness, yet he lives by God's power. Likewise, we are weak in him, yet by God's power we will live with him to serve you.

1,2 After expressing his personal forebodings about the forthcoming third visit (12:20, 21), Paul issues two direct warnings on the basis of those fears: "Every matter must be established by the testimony of two or three witnesses" (v.1) and "On my return I will not spare those who sinned earlier or any of the others" (v.2).

What are the "two or three witnesses"? Some believe Paul is referring to the legal strictness that would apply to the judicial investigation he or the assembled church (cf. Matt 18:15–20; 1 Cor 5:3–5) would conduct at Corinth: unsubstantiated accusations against Paul or any Corinthian would be ruled out of court. Others find a reference to Paul's three comings to Corinth (two actual, one promised) as three separate witnesses at whose testimony justice would certainly fall on the dissidents at Corinth on the imminent third visit. A third view sees in the "three witnesses" the threefold testimony or warning that Paul would not spare the Corinthians: (1) either 1 Corinthians 4:21 or the warning given on the second (= painful) visit; (2) the present warning in v.2b; and (3) either the third visit or Paul himself absent in Macedonia. On a fourth but improbable interpretation, the witnesses are not visits or warnings but people—i.e., Timothy, Titus, and Paul. Whether the second or third view is preferred, the general import is clear: "Sufficient warning has been given; punishment is imminent."

"Those who sinned earlier" are the immoral persons of 12:21b who did not repent during Paul's "painful visit" and were evidently still indulging in their sexual sins. "All the rest" ("any of the others," NIV) are probably those Corinthians who had been adversely influenced by the false apostles and were arrogantly fomenting unrest within the church (12:20b). Both groups here receive their final warning. If they remained unrepentant, he would be harsh in his use of authority (cf. v.10; 1 Cor 4:21), perhaps handing the wrongdoers over to Satan "for the destruction of the flesh" (= illness leading to death, unless there was repentance, 1 Cor 5:5; cf. 11:30).

3 It would seem that in their immaturity the Corinthians were unimpressed by Christlike gentleness and meekness (10:1) but were overawed by arbitrary displays of power (11:20). In their misguided judgment, Paul's gentle demeanor, so unlike the temperament of the intruding false apostles, raised doubts about his claim to apostolic authority. He needed to give them some proof that Christ in his resurrection power was speaking through him. His reply was that, though he had previously been "weak" in the Corinthian estimation (10:1, 10), his impending severity would afford the proof they demanded that he was a spokesman of Christ—Christ, who was not weak in dealing with them but was powerful among them. The Corinthians had in effect challenged Christ (cf. 1:1), who would not disappoint them as he exhibited his resurrection power through his apostle.

4 The relationship between Christ and Paul with regard to weakness and power is now clarified. Jesus Christ was crucified "because of [*ek;* see note] weakness." This weakness was not, of course, physical frailty or moral impotence, but rather the "weakness" of nonretaliation or nonaggressiveness before men and the "weakness" of obedience to God. Christ's "weakness" in assuming the poverty of earthly existence (8:9) and in humbling himself and becoming obedient even to the point of death on a cross (Phil 2:8), was, however, the most perfect evidence of strength. The person who is "weak" in man's estimation because he seeks to do God's will is in fact supremely strong. But that "weakness" of Christ is past. Now he lives a resurrection life sustained by God's power, "the Spirit of holiness" (Rom 1:4).

As a result of being in Christ (*en autō*, "in him"), Paul shared in the weakness of his crucified Master. As a result of his fellowship with Christ (*sun autō*, "with him"), he shared in the mighty power of his risen Lord, a power imparted by God. From a human standpoint, the nonretaliation and nonassertiveness that had marked Paul's conduct on his second visit to Corinth (cf. 10:1, 10) were simply weakness. But on his forthcoming visit, God's power would be vigorously displayed through him in his dealings with the Corinthians (*eis hymas;* NIV renders this "to serve you").

Notes

4 The preposition ἐκ (*ek*, lit. "out of") in the phrase ἐξ ἀσθενείας (*ex astheneias*, "in weakness") indicates cause; see RHG, p. 598, BAG, p. 234 s.v. ἐκ 3f., and N. Turner, *A Grammar of New Testament Greek* by J.H. Moulton. vol. 3. Syntax (T. & T. Clark: Edinburgh, 1963), pp. 259, 260.

4. *A plea for self-examination*

13:5–10

[5]Examine yourselves to see whether you are in the faith; test yourselves. Do you not realize that Christ Jesus is in you—unless, of course, you fail the test? [6]And I trust that you will discover that we have not failed the test. [7]Now we pray to God that you will not do anything wrong. Not that people will see that we have stood the test but that you will do what is right even though we may seem to have failed. [8]For we cannot do anything against the truth, but only for the truth. [9]We are glad whenever we are weak but you are strong; and our prayer is for your perfection. [10]This is why I write these things when I am absent, that when I come I may not have to be harsh in my use of authority—the authority the Lord gave me for building you up, not for tearing you down.

5,6 Rather than demanding proof (*dokimē*) that Christ was speaking through Paul (v.3), the Corinthians ought to be examining and testing (*dokimazō*) their own selves. The repeated *heautous* ("yourselves") is in each case emphatic by position. Paul continues like this: "Don't you know yourselves [*heautous*] sufficiently well to recognize that Christ Jesus lives within each of you [cf. Rom 8:9] and that therefore you are in the faith?" Although for the sake of emphasis he adds "unless, of course, you fail the test [*adokimoi*]," he does not believe the Corinthians are counterfeit and knows that no Corinthian is likely to form such a conclusion about himself.

As v.6 implies, the Corinthians' belief in the genuineness of their faith carried with it the proof of the genuineness of Paul's apostleship and gospel, for he had become their father in Christ Jesus through the gospel (1 Cor 4:15). They themselves as men and women in Christ formed the verification of his credentials (cf. 3:2, 3). Only if they doubted their own salvation should they doubt Paul's claim to be a true "apostle of Christ Jesus" (1:1). If they did not fail the test, neither did he (v.6).

7 Again, as in 3:1; 5:12; 12:19, Paul anticipates and answers the objection that he had been commending or defending himself. His chief desire and his prayer to God were not for his vindication (though he was concerned about this, v.6) but for their avoidance of wrongdoing, both for the sake of their life in Christ and so that they would not need to see his severity (vv.2, 10). The wrong they might do would certainly include a refusal to repent of sin (12:20, 21) and to repudiate the visitors from Palestine. It would be better that the Corinthians did what they knew to be good and right, even if this were to place Paul seemingly in the wrong, than that they should do something wrong. Paul did not expect to be shown up as counterfeit (*adokimoi*), but even such a price would be worth paying if it guaranteed that the Corinthians would do good. Not dissimilar is the sentiment expressed in Romans 9:3.

8 This verse, which has the appearance of being proverbial, may in this context bear one of two meanings. (1) Paul's concern was that truth, especially the truth of the gospel (cf. 4:2; 6:7), should prevail at all costs—even if it involved his exposure as a false apostle and counterfeit Christian (vv.6, 7). He would never be able to bring himself to hinder the advance of the truth or to propagate falsehood, such as a "different gospel" (11:4), without first changing his identity as an apostle. (2) Paul did not need to exercise his apostolic authority where "truth" already existed, but was able and willing, if necessary, to act decisively to establish "truth," i.e., to restore the Corinthians to wholeness (v.9b).

9,10 Paul's sole concern was to further and consolidate the truth of the gospel (cf. 1 Cor 9:16). So he was happy whenever his converts gave evidence of robust and mature Christian character. If the Corinthians were strong in Christ, there would be no occasion for him to use his apostolic authority harshly. He would be able to come to them in the "weakness" of a "gentle spirit" (1 Cor 4:21). Such "weakness" on his part as a result of "strength" on their part would make him rejoice. In fact, his prayer was precisely for the restoration of the Corinthians to spiritual strength and wholeness (*katartisis;* cf. v.11; 1 Cor 1:10; Gal 6:1).

If 12:20, 21 expresses Paul's fears about what he would find at Corinth on his arrival, 13:10 indicates his hope in this respect. But even here a veiled warning is registered. While the Lord had not invested Paul with apostolic authority primarily for the negative work of tearing down, if destruction proved to be a necessary prelude to the positive task of construction, it would be reluctantly undertaken—and with the same authority (cf. 10:8).

Was Paul's final visit to Corinth actually an unpleasant one? Though direct evidence is lacking, we have several indications that it was not unsuccessful. First, during the visit (which lasted three months according to Acts 20:2, 3, probably in the winter of A.D. 56–57) he wrote the Epistle to the Romans. This letter seems to betray some apprehension for the future (Rom 15:30, 31) but none for the present. Second, Paul would hardly have planned to visit Rome and then do pioneer evangelism in the west (Rom 15:24, 28), if the church in the city he was writing from was in a state of disorder and disloyalty. Third, it is clear from Romans 15:26, 27 that the Corinthians heeded Paul's appeal in 2 Corinthians 8–9 and completed their collection for the saints at Jerusalem. Twice Paul notes that they "were pleased" to contribute, scarcely an appropriate description unless the church in Corinth was in harmony with the promoter of the collection. Fourth, the very preservation of 2 Corinthians (presumably at Corinth) argues in favor of the success of the visit promised in it.

D. *Conclusion*

13:11–13

11Finally, brothers, good-by. Aim for perfection, listen to my appeal, be of one mind, live in peace. And the God of love and peace will be with you.
12Greet one another with a holy kiss. All the saints send their greetings.
13May the grace of the Lord Jesus Christ, and the love of God, and the fellowship of the Holy Spirit be with you all.

11 In closing, Paul issues a final appeal couched in general terms. The Corinthian believers were to strive to achieve that perfection or restored strength for which Paul himself was praying (v.9b). They were to heed his call for a break with all idolatry (6:14–7:1), for warm hospitality to be shown the three delegates, for a generous and prompt contribution to the Jerusalem relief fund (chapters 8, 9), and for a changed attitude toward him (chapters 10–13). They were also to agree in the Lord (cf. 1 Cor 1:10; Phil 4:2) and so live in peace without divided loyalties (11:2, 3; 12:20).

If in the concluding promise Paul is stressing love and peace as characteristics of God (cf. Rom 5:8; 1 Cor 14:33), the meaning will be: "[If you] aim for perfection. . . , then [*kai*] the God of love and peace will be with you." But if love and peace are here viewed as God's gifts ("the God who imparts love and peace"), Paul is indicating the divine resources that will enable the Corinthians to follow his injunctions.

12 Evidently the early church invested the kiss, a common form of salutation in the Orient, with a special and sacred significance (cf. Rom 16:16; 1 Cor 16:20; 1 Thess 5:26; 1 Peter 5:14). It expressed union and fellowship within the one family of God, and perhaps also was a sign of mutual forgiveness and reconciliation that was exchanged before the Lord's Supper was celebrated (cf. Matt 5:23, 24; 1 Cor 16:20b, 22).

The "saints" referred to may well be the Philippians, but they could be the Thessalonians or Bereans, depending on the place where this Epistle was written (see Introduction, 5). Like the "holy kiss," this epistolary greeting was an expression of unity within the one body of Christ.

13 Paul grounds his pastoral appeal for unity of spirit and for the rejection of discord (vv.11, 12) in the theological doctrine of the Trinity. The grace of Christ banishes self-assertiveness and self-seeking, the love of God puts jealousy and anger to flight, while the fellowship created by the Spirit (see note) leaves no room for quarreling and factions (cf. 12:21).

This embryonic Trinitarian formulation is noteworthy for the unusual "economic" order of Son, Father, Spirit. It is through the grace shown by Christ (8:9) in living and dying for men that God demonstrates his love (Rom 5:8) and the Spirit creates fellowship (Eph 4:3). This order also reflects Christian experience.

Notes

11 If **παρακαλεῖσθε** (*parakaleisthe*) is construed as a middle (rather than a passive, "be exhorted" = "listen to my appeal," NIV), it will mean "exhort (or, comfort) one another."

13 Since the first two genitives (**τοῦ κυρίου Ἰησοῦ Χριστοῦ**, *tou kyriou Iēsou Christou*, and **τοῦ θεοῦ**, *tou theou*) are clearly subjective ("the grace shown by the Lord Jesus Christ," "the love displayed by God"), it is more likely that the third genitive (**τοῦ ἁγίου πνεύματος**, *tou hagiou pneumatos*) is also subjective ("the fellowship engendered by the Holy Spirit"; cf. Eph 4:3) than that it is objective ("participation in the Holy Spirit"). But in defense of the latter view, see C.K. Barrett, in loc.

GALATIANS

James Montgomery Boice

GALATIANS

Introduction

1. The Historical Setting
2. Who Were the Galatians?
3. The Jerusalem Council
4. Date and Place of Writing
5. Authorship
6. Bibliography
7. Outline of the Book

Not many books have made such a lasting impression on men's minds as the Epistle of Paul to the Galatians, nor have many done so much to shape the history of the Western world. Galatians has been called the "Magna Carta of Christian liberty," and this is quite correct. For it rightly maintains that only through the grace of God in Jesus Christ is a person enabled to escape the curse of his sin and of the law and to live a new life, not in bondage or license, but in a genuine freedom of mind and spirit through the power of God. Because of this powerful truth, Galatians was the cornerstone of the Protestant Reformation. Luther especially loved it. He called it his Catherine von Bora, for, he said, "I am wedded to it." In Luther's hands the book became a mighty weapon in the Reformation arsenal.

Paul regarded the thesis of Galatians—salvation by the grace of God through faith in the Lord Jesus Christ—as the indispensible foundation of Christian life and conduct, while Luther, by rediscovering and teaching it, restored to the church its spiritual heart and freedom. The thesis of Galatians is no less important for our time than it was in Paul's day and in Luther's day.

1. The Historical Setting

In the decade or so surrounding the year A.D. 50, the infant church was drifting by degrees and at times almost unnoticeably toward its first great doctrinal crisis. When the gospel was being preached primarily to Jews by Jews, the development of the church progressed smoothly. But as the ambassadors of Christ pushed out into largely Gentile communities and the gospel began to take root there, questions arose regarding a Christian's relationship to the law of Moses and to Judaism as a system. Was the church to open her doors wide to all comers, regardless of their relationship to the particularized traditions of Judaism? Were her boundaries to be as wide as the human race? Or was she to be only an extension of Judaism to the Gentiles?

In more particular terms, was it necessary for a Gentile believer to observe the law of Moses in order to become a Christian? Should a Gentile be circumcised? Questions like these must have been raised with increasing force throughout the Roman Empire, wherever the church of Jesus Christ camped on Gentile soil.

Galatians is a record of the form this struggle took in one area of Asia Minor. But it is also a reflection of the way in which the issue was being debated and handled in Jerusalem and at Antioch in Syria. Acts supplements this information. Was it right for Gentile and Jewish Christians to eat together? And could they eat the same food? Was an orthodox Jew contaminated by such fellowship, as Jewish traditions declared, or was he not? For a time, debate seemed to move in a direction destructive of Christian unity and of the survival of the gospel of grace, but Paul almost singlehandedly withstood this trend and turned the tide. At Jerusalem the question was taken up formally in council, and Paul's approach was upheld (Acts 15:1–29).

As the apostle to the Gentiles, Paul had deliberately not brought up questions of conformity to Jewish law when presenting the gospel in non-Jewish communities. He had followed this practice in Galatia on each of two occasions when he had preached there (cf. 4:13). As Paul preached it, salvation is never to be achieved by any amount of conformity to rules and regulations, even God-given regulations. Law condemns. Consequently, if there is to be salvation for sinful men, it must come in another way entirely. God has offered this other way through Jesus Christ. Jesus died for sin. Now God offers righteousness freely to all who put their trust in him.

Paul had taught this gospel to the Galatians, as he had to Gentiles in other places, and it had been well received. He had been detained in Galatia unexpectedly because of a repulsive illness, but instead of rebuffing him, as they might have done, the Galatians actually embraced both himself and the gospel willingly (4:13–15). These former pagans (4:8) were now baptized (3:27) and received the Holy Spirit, who began to work miracles among them (3:5). In accordance with his usual custom, Paul established churches in Galatia and then moved on. He visited the area again at least once afterward.

Some time later, however, Paul received word that the Galatian believers were on the point of departing from the faith they had previously received so openly. Conservative Jewish teachers who were legalizers had arrived from Jerusalem claiming to be from James, the Lord's brother, and had begun to teach that Paul was wrong in his doctrine. They contended that Gentiles had to come under the law of Moses to be saved. It was not enough for them to have Christ; they must have Moses too. To grace must be added circumcision.

Paul was immediately filled with righteous indignation. He saw in a moment that if the views of the legalizers prevailed, grace and the cross of Jesus Christ would be emptied of all value (5:2–4). Moreover, Christianity would lose its distinctive character and soon become little more than a minor sect of Judaism. In righteous anger, Paul wrote this letter to reprove legalism and regain the Galatian churches.[1]

It is evident that Paul had heard of three distinct charges made by his Jewish opponents, the first being directed against him personally. He was an apostle. He had been

[1]It is argued by Luetgert (*Gesetz und Geist: Eine Untersuchung zur Vorgeschichte des Galaterbriefs*, "Beitraege zur Forderung christlicher Theologie," 22.6, 1919) and Ropes (*The Singular Problem of the Epistle to the Galatians*, "Harvard Theological Studies," 14, 1929), who accepts Luetgert's views with some modification, that it cannot be assumed that the attacks made against Paul in Galatia came from one source only, that is, only from the Judaizers. Ropes suggests that there was also a party that argued for the right of Christians to neglect moral discipline and to do as they pleased. Ropes feels that the arguments of Galatians are directed against both parties, more or less alternatively, and that the book can therefore be dated fairly late. This theory has not received any general acceptance by scholars, most of whom have recognized that it is much easier to account for Paul's warning against license in the Christian life as an answer to attacks against him by the legalizers ("This is where your gospel leads, Paul") than as replies to an entirely new set of problems and party about which we otherwise know nothing.

called by Christ and had come speaking those doctrines that had been revealed to him by Christ. Now enemies were saying that he was not an apostle and that the gospel he preached had not been revealed by God. Paul had not lived with Jesus when Jesus was here on earth, as had the "true" apostles. He was not one of the Twelve. Actually, they asserted, he was merely an evangelist who, after he had received some knowledge of Christianity, turned to his own devices and, in order to please the Gentiles, taught an easy gospel that was opposed to that of the apostolic model (1:10). They said that Paul must teach as the disciples taught or be rejected.

Paul answers the accusation by retelling the story of his life, particularly as it was related to the other twelve apostles (chapters 1, 2). He replies that (1) his teaching is not dependent on other human authorities—this is what makes him an apostle, for the teaching of an apostle must come directly from God, (2) his authority had been acknowledged by the other apostles on each occasion on which they had come in contact, and (3) he had proved his worth by remaining firm at Antioch when others, including even Peter and Barnabas, had wavered. It is the glory of Paul's reply in this section of the letter that he is able to assert his own authority as an apostle without diminishing either the authority or reputation of those who were apostles before him.

The second charge directed against Paul by the legalizers was that his gospel was not the true gospel. Obviously, this charge was closely related to the first, for since Paul was a "false" apostle it followed to their way of thinking that his teaching was not true teaching. Paul taught that the law could be set aside, but this was wrong, they said. God's law is eternal and it can never be set aside. All who have ever been saved have been saved by keeping the law. Moreover, it is perfectly evident from all that is known of the life of Jesus that Jesus himself kept the law. The disciples did likewise. Who, then, was Paul to dismiss the requirements of the law for salvation?

Paul answers this charge by showing that the issue is not one of who does or does not keep the law, but rather of the true basis on which God reckons a sinful man righteous. At this point of his letter (chapters 3, 4) Paul appeals both to the personal experience of the Galatians and to Scripture, showing, primarily from the case of Abraham, that God accounts a person righteous on the basis of faith rather than works. This imputed righteousness obviously does not come either from the law or circumcision, for God had declared Abraham righteous on the basis of faith years before either circumcision or the law were given.

Finally, the opponents of Paul charged that the gospel he preached led to loose living. By stressing the law, Judaism had stressed morality. Jews looked down on Gentile sin and excesses. But what would happen if the law should be taken away? Clearly, lawlessness and immorality would increase, the legalizers argued.

Paul replies that this is not true (chapters 5, 6). It is not true because Christianity does not lead the believer away from the law into nothingness. It leads him to Jesus Christ, who, in the person of the Holy Spirit, comes to dwell within him and furnishes him with the new nature that alone is capable of doing what God desires. The change is internal. So it is from within rather than without that the Holy Spirit produces the fruit that is "love, joy, peace, patience, kindness, goodness, faithfulness, gentleness, and self-control" (5:22, 23). Life in the Spirit is free from and above the kind of religion that would result in either legalism or license. It is true freedom—a freedom to serve God fully, unencumbered by the shackles of sin or regulations.

2. Who Were the Galatians?

There would seem to be few difficulties in relating a book with such a clear message to its time. But this is not true of Galatians. In fact, from the historian's point of view, few NT books contain so many problems. We do not know for certain when the letter was written, where it was written, or even (which is a more serious problem) to whom it was written. Each of these questions has been the subject of intense debate and has led to the production of much scholarly material.

The people who first became known as Galatians came from the barbarian tribal stock known as Celts, one branch of which Julius Caesar knew in France as the Gauls. Some of these had invaded Macedonia and later Asia Minor in the third century B.C. in order to establish themselves there. In popular speech, these Gauls were distinguished from the West-European Gauls by the term "Gallo-Graecians," from which the name "Galatians" comes. At first the tribes were dramatically successful. They laid the whole country west of the Taurus river under tribute and, according to Livy (*History of Rome,* 38:16), even forced the Syrian kings to submit for a time to their terms. However, in 230 B.C., the Gauls were decisively defeated by Attalus I, king of Pergamum, and then were increasingly confined to a small territory in the north. This region was the first to become known as Galatia. Its principle cities were Ancyra (now the capital of modern Turkey), Pessinus, and Tavium.

With the coming of the Romans, conditions did not change markedly for these Galatians. True, they were conquered by the Roman Consul Manlius in 189 B.C., but even then they were permitted to maintain much of their independence and to be governed in part by their own princes. This system worked so well from the Roman point of view that later, upon the death of Amyntas, the territory of the Galatians was incorporated into a much larger Roman province to which the old ethnic name, Galatia, was extended. This province, established in 25 B.C., contained the districts of Lycaonia and Isauria as well as portions of Pisidia and Phrygia. In particular, the cities of Pisidian Antioch, Iconium, Derbe and Lystra—cities Paul visited on his first missionary journey—belonged to it.

To the Christians in which of these areas was Paul writing? Or, to state the question another way, in what sense does Paul use the name Galatia? Was he writing to Christians in northern, ethnic Galatia? Or was he writing to Christians in the southern, Roman province? Paul can hardly have written to both areas, because the letter implies that the churches of Galatia were all founded at about the same time. But in the light of Paul's missionary journeys, this is impossible for both north and south Galatia.

Until the eighteenth century, no commentator ever seriously disputed the idea that Paul's letter was written to Christians living in northern Galatia. Indeed, it was not until the nineteenth century that the contrary view began to make progress in the English-speaking world.[2]

---

[2]The theory that Galatians was written to Christians living in the southern edges of the Roman province of Galatia was first suggested by Schmidt, who was answered by Michaelis in his *Einleitung in die goettlichen Schriften des Neuen Bundes* (4th ed., 1788; trans. into English as *Introduction to the New Testament* by Herbert Marsh). The theory was adopted by Thiersch (*The Church in the Apostolic Age,* 1852), Perrot (*De Galatia Provincia Romana,* 1867), Renan (*Saint Paul,* 1869), Hausrath (*A History of the New Testament Times: The Time of the Apostles,* Vol. 3, 1895), and Ramsay, who became the great defender of this view in the English language (*The Church in the Roman Empire,* 1893; *Studia Biblia et Ecclesiastica,* Vol. 4, 1896; *Historical Commentary on*

True, the Book of Acts contains no record of Paul's having founded churches in this area. But Acts 16:6 and 18:23 at least open the possibility, if not the probability, that he may have done so. The former verse says that Paul and Timothy, who were traveling together at the time, went through "the region of Phrygia and Galatia." When they were forbidden by the Holy Spirit to preach the word in Asia, they passed by and came to Mysia and Troas. In Acts 18:23 we are told that Paul later went "throughout the region of Galatia and Phrygia, strengthening all the disciples." The work in Galatia was therefore placed in this period by the early commentators.

There was much to recommend this view. First, it gave the oldest and most obvious meaning to the word "Galatia." Second, it seemed to fit in with the Book of Acts, for by it Paul was allowed to make the two visits to Galatia implied in the letter before writing to these Galatians. Third, certain details of the book were explained by what was thought to be the warmhearted but fickle nature of the Gaulish people and by the vice these barbarians were assumed to be subject to. It was no small matter, moreover, that this had been the view of the early church and was thus almost sanctified by antiquity.

In the last century, however, largely because of extensive textual work and the archaeological examination of Asia Minor by Ramsay (*St. Paul the Traveler and the Roman Citizen,* London, 1895; *An Historical Commentary on St. Paul's Epistle to the Galatians,* New York, 1900), the view quickly gained backing that Paul had not written to Christians in the northern, ethnic Galatia at all—in fact, that he had never been there—but rather that he had written to Christians in the southern area of the Roman province, i.e., to Christians living primarily in those cities Paul had visited on his first missionary journey. A number of very impressive arguments were raised in support of this position.

1. The argument that had initially gripped Ramsay was that the southern Galatia theory made greater sense of Paul's travels than the hypothesis of a journey into central Asia Minor. Such a journey in itself was improbable for a man whose major desire was obviously to establish churches in the chief cities of the empire. But even more importantly, it did not make sense of the moves Luke portrays Paul as having made during the second missionary journey. Paul had left the cities of Derbe and Lystra on this journey and had apparently turned northwestward along one of the great Roman roads that linked Syria with Greece. Being forbidden by the Holy Spirit to preach either in Asia to the south or Bithynia to the north (Acts 16:6, 7), Paul and his companion, Timothy, pressed on through Iconium and Antioch of Pisidia to Troas, where for the first time on the journey they encountered an open door before them into Greece. On this journey they would have passed through areas of Phrygia and Roman Galatia, as Acts 16:6 indicates; but they would have had to take a most unlikely detour of about three hundred miles to have entered ethnic Galatia and to have preached there. The difficulty of assuming that Paul traveled three hundred miles to preach in Galatia is further increased when we take into account the probability that Paul went there originally as a sick man (4:13).

Galatians, 1900; and various articles in *The Expositor* and *The Expository Times*). It has since been held by Bacon, Burton, Duncan, Emmet, Guthrie, and others in their commentaries.

The traditional view is held by Davidson (*An Introduction to the Study of the New Testament,* 2nd ed., 1882), Lightfoot (*The Epistle of St. Paul to the Galatians,* 1865), Godet (*Introduction to the New Testament: I, The Epistles of St. Paul,* 1894), Moffatt (*An Introduction to the Literature of the New Testament,* 1911), Feine, Behm, Kummell (*Introduction to the New Testament,* 14th ed., 1966), and by Oepke, Schlier, and others in their commentaries.

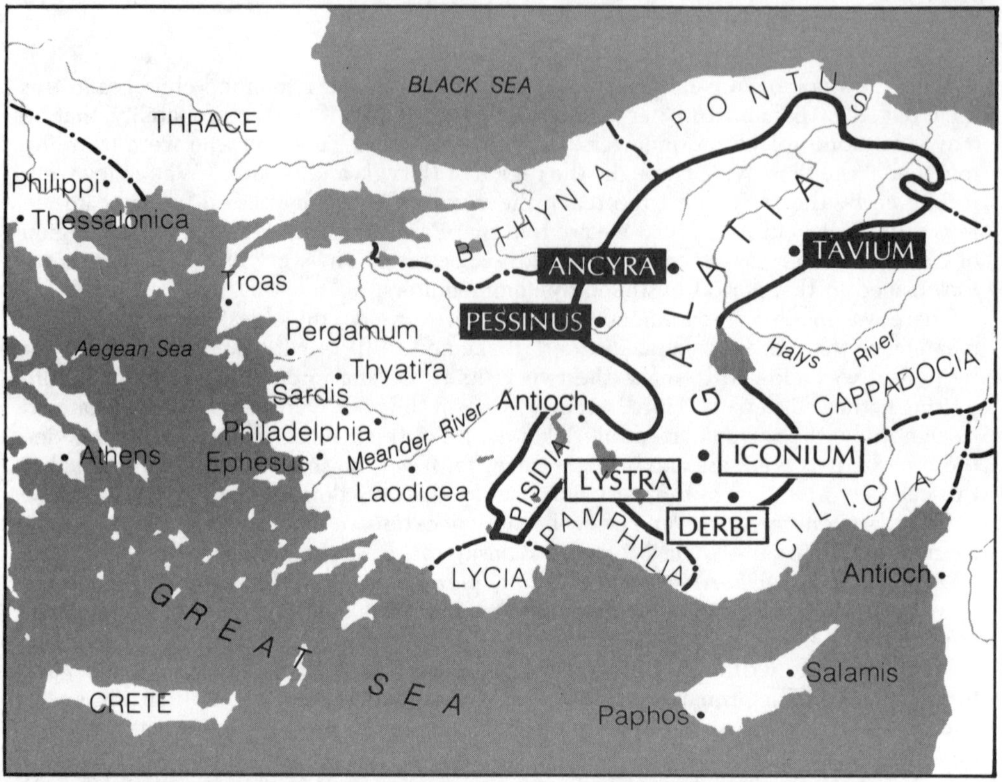

THE CITIES POSSIBLY INVOLVED IN THE "NORTHERN" AND "SOUTHERN" GALATIAN THEORIES.

The next journey, indicated in Acts 18:23, suggests that Paul strengthened the disciples along a general route from Antioch to Ephesus. But, once again, this does not suggest a long journey deliberately taken across difficult mountain passages to Turkey's central plains.

The major objection to Ramsay's handling of the passages in Acts is that in speaking of the regions of Phrygia and Galatia, Acts 16:6 seems to differentiate the two, and that if they are to be separated, in this verse at least Galatia cannot be the Roman province (which included Phrygia). Ramsay's reply (pp. 401ff.), followed by Askwith, was that both terms are adjectives, rather than proper names, and that the phrase should therefore properly be translated "the Phrygic-Galatic region." This he understood to mean the area of the Roman province of Galatia inhabited by Phrygians.

2. Ramsay also recognized that even if the references to Galatia in Acts could be interpreted as implying a visit by Paul to northern Galatia—which, of course, he disputed—this in itself would not necessarily mean that Paul wrote his letter to the people there unless it could be shown also that Paul used the terms "Galatia" and "Galatians" in the same way Luke used them. This means that if Luke used local, ethnic names (as he seems to have done), it would have to be shown that Paul used local, ethnic names, too. Did he? Apparently not, for Paul seems to have preferred provincial titles, especially when referring to groups of churches. Thus Paul writes of the churches of Macedonia (2 Cor 8:1), Asia (1 Cor 16:19), and Achaia (2 Cor 1:1). He also speaks of Judea, Syria, and Cilicia, but never of Lycaonia, Pisidia, Mysia, and Lydia (which are not Roman

names). The presumption that he is also using the Roman title in speaking of Galatia is therefore strong.

Ramsay strengthened this argument by showing that if, as he maintained, Paul was writing to the churches of Derbe, Lystra, Iconium, and Pisidian Antioch, then there was actually no other name than "Galatians" by which Paul could have identified them collectively.

3. Ramsay's third major argument was that nothing we know about either the people or churches of northern Galatia supports the northern Galatia hypothesis. We know of no churches at all in the north at this early date, either as mentioned in the New Testament or outside it, and what information we do have seems to point to the establishing of churches (which, moreover, remained relatively weak) fairly late in early church history. By contrast, we do have a record of the founding of the strong, important churches of the southern region, into which all that Paul tells us about his initial preaching to the Galatians fits nicely.[3] From his knowledge of the history of this period and of the Galatian people, Ramsay also argued that no special traces of the supposed fickleness, drunkenness, revelings, superstitions, or contact with Judaism by the northern Galatians can be documented.

Other arguments have also been raised in support of the south Galatian theory.

4. If Paul established a series of important churches in north Galatia, it is a serious and most unnatural matter for Luke to neglect to say so, particularly when he mentions Paul's supposed passage through this region. The argument that in writing Acts Luke was anxious to get Paul on to Troas and therefore does not mention them is hardly convincing, because Luke could have told everything necessary about the founding of these churches in a single sentence. The reply that he fails to mention them because of the troubles that developed in Galatia is equally unconvincing in view of the fact that Luke reports troubles elsewhere.

5. It is more natural to suppose that the legalistic party would have pursued Paul first in the southern region of Galatia, where Paul had early established good churches, than that they would have bypassed these bastions of "Paulinism" in order to push on over the remote northern platèau to less important strongholds. We know from Acts that Paul had already met with Jewish opposition in the south of Galatia, which was not far from Jerusalem. What is more natural than that the legalists should first go there if Jews in any sizeable number were turning from Judaism to Christianity?

6. When Luke reports the list of those who accompanied Paul to Jerusalem with the long-awaited gift of the Gentile churches (Acts 20:4), there is one companion (Timothy), and perhaps a second (Gaius), from the south Galatian region. Paul had solicited funds in Galatia (1 Cor 16:1–4). It is generally assumed that those traveling with him were something like delegates to the Jerusalem churches. It seems reasonable to assume then, against this background, that Timothy and Gaius (from southern Galatia) were the Galatian delegates, particularly since no delegates are mentioned as having been present from the north. This argument is somewhat weakened by the fact that no delegate is listed as having come from southern Greece where Paul obviously also solicited funds (1 Cor 16:1), but Titus could have represented this area.

---

[3]Arguing somewhat the reverse of this, Conway notes that if Galatians is written to the northern churches, as some indicate, then there is a strange lack of any reference to Christians in Derbe, Lystra, Iconium, and Antioch by Paul, in spite of Paul's habit of frequently directing thankful words to other "first fruit" churches ("The Galatian Churches," ITQ, 14, 1919, pp. 15–28).

7. In writing to the Galatians, Paul mentions Barnabas several times without bothering to explain who he is (2:1, 9, 13). This is natural only if Barnabas were known to the Galatians. Since Barnabas accompanied Paul only on the first missionary journey, when Paul visited southern Galatia, and not on the second or third journeys, nothing but an identification of the Galatians with Christians in the cities of the south seems possible. But some point out that Paul also mentions Barnabas to the Corinthians without explaining who he is (1 Cor 9:6). However, the situations are not entirely identical. The Corinthian letter does not imply that the believers in Corinth knew Barnabas personally, while at least one of the references in Galatians suggests that the Galatians did ("even [such a man as] Barnabas," 2:13). Besides, we cannot even be sure that Barnabas did not visit Corinth sometime after having separated from Paul, in which case the Corinthians would have known him.

8. Finally, in writing of the Jerusalem conference, Paul argues that he did not give place to the legalizers even for an hour so that "the truth of the gospel might remain with you [i.e., with the Galatians]." If this is to be understood literally, it means that Paul must already have preached to the Galatians by the time of the conference, i.e., on his first missionary journey, which involved southern (but not northern) Galatia.

It might be assumed from a first presentation of this evidence that the arguments in favor of the southern Galatia theory are overwhelming as opposed to the traditional view, but it is only fair to state that while the south Galatia theory has captured the attention of what seems today to be a majority of scholars, not all have been persuaded by it. Those who are not persuaded follow in the steps of Lightfoot who presented a classic statement of the traditional view (pp. 1–35) before the appearance of Ramsay's massive examination.

Today the arguments for the traditional view are as follows:

1. The southern Galatia hypothesis does not take Luke's terminology seriously enough. Luke does not refer to those living in the cities of Derbe, Lystra, Iconium, and Pisidian Antioch as Galatians when he describes Paul's work there. He used geographical titles—Pamphilia (Acts 13:13), Pisidia (Acts 13:14), and Lycaonia (Acts 14:6). It is strange to think that he is not, therefore, still using geographical terminology when he refers to Galatia a few chapters later.

2. Paul assumes in his letter that all, or at least most, of the Galatians are Gentiles. But this does not seem to fit conditions in the south where, according to Acts, there was a large Jewish population. Moreover, if the churches of Galatia possessed large numbers of Jews, it is hard to see how the situation of a later drifting into Judaism by Paul's converts could have occurred at all, particularly in a manner that would have surprised him. Indeed, the issue of a Christian's relationship to the law of Moses would have had to be faced from the start. Against this view it is argued that we have no way of knowing how many Jews became part of the churches in the southern cities. Certainly many opposed Paul (Acts 13:43–52; 14:1–7, 19). It may even be, as Rendall maintains, that the work in Galatia was the first really Gentile-oriented work and resulted in the first truly Gentile churches.[4]

3. Paul's account of his work in Galatia does not tally with what Luke tells us of Paul's work in Derbe, Lystra, Iconium, and Antioch. So Paul must be speaking of another area. As an example, there is his reference to his sickness, which is totally disregarded in Acts.

---

[4]Rendall, "The First Galatian Ministry," Exp., 6th series, 3 (1901), pp. 241–256.

This argument is weakened, however, by the observation that Luke obviously does not include everything in his narration and that an argument from silence, which this is, is at best a probability.

4. It is said that Paul could not have spoken of Barnabas as he did, i.e., as less than an equal, if Barnabas had been a cofounder with Paul of the Galatian churches. Since Barnabas was a cofounder of the churches in the south, the reference in Galatians must be to those in the northern area.

5. Finally, it is said that Paul does not necessarily use the titles of Roman provinces in speaking of churches in those provinces. E.g., in 1 Thessalonians 2:14 Paul speaks of "God's churches in Judea." Does this mean that Paul was restricting his references to churches in the strict Roman province? Is Galilee excluded? Is he not also thinking of a wider area? One may agree that perhaps this is true. But it may also be that Paul *is* thinking specifically of Judea, for he mentions the killing of the Lord Jesus by the Jewish rulers (which occurred in Judea) just a verse later (1 Thess 2:15). In any case, a departure from Paul's customary usage in referring to this one area does not cast much doubt on a practice he almost invariably seems to follow elsewhere.

Was Galatians written, then, to Christians living in the old, ethnic Galatia? Or was it written to Christians in provincial Galatia, in the cities of Derbe, Lystra, Iconium, and Antioch? The answer is that the matter cannot yet be regarded as fully certain, though the weight of probability now lies on the side of the southern-Galatia hypothesis. Given the desire of Paul to visit the large Roman cities, the general movement of Paul and Timothy suggested by Luke in Acts, and the vast knowledge we have of the southern churches versus all lack of information about churches in the north, the likelihood that Jewish legalizers would come first to the southern cities, and Paul's general preference for Roman titles especially in referring to area churches, the theory of visits by Paul to the southern churches should be preferred.

3. The Jerusalem Council

What visit to Jerusalem is Paul referring to in the first part of chapter 2?

The difficulty is this. In Acts, Luke records three visits of Paul to Jerusalem prior to his final visit, at which time he was arrested and eventually sent to Rome. There is a visit referred to in Acts 9:26–30. This occurred shortly after his conversion. There is also a visit referred to in Acts 11:27–30. This is generally referred to as the "famine visit" because its purpose was to send material relief to those in Jerusalem who were suffering from a famine. Finally, there is a third visit, mentioned in Acts 15:1–29, when a church council decided the question of Gentile adherence to the law in favor of the gospel, taught by Paul and Barnabas, of freedom from law. Over against this testimony in Acts, however, Paul records but two visits in Galatians, the second of which seems to fit better with Luke's third visit than with the second. Consequently we need either to identify Paul's second visit with Luke's second, with obvious difficulties involved; or we need to identify Paul's second visit with Luke's third, at the same time explaining why Paul neglected to mention the second in writing to the Galatians. On the surface this neglect is difficult to understand, simply because Paul seems to be chronicling all contacts with the Jerusalem apostles in order to refute the charges of the legalizers.

In the opinion of this writer, the case for identifying the Jerusalem visit of Galatians 2:1–10 with the council meeting of Acts 15 is strongest, above all because of the striking coincidence of circumstances. A strong and classical treatment of this argument is that of Lightfoot (pp. 123–128). In the first place, there is the coincidence of *geography.* In both accounts, communications take place between Jerusalem and Antioch. The false brethren have their headquarters in the first city but cause trouble in the second. In both accounts, Paul and Barnabas apparently go to Jerusalem from Antioch and return to Antioch after the council. The *time* is the same, or at least not inconsistent. The *participants* are the same. There are the legalizers who are causing the trouble, Paul and Barnabas who are representatives of the church at Antioch, and the Jerusalem apostles, primarily Peter and James. The *subject of dispute* is the same. The *character of the conference* is the same. Finally, the *results* are the same. In each case, the victory goes to Paul with the result that the Gentiles in Antioch, Syria, and Cilicia are officially pronounced free from obligation to conform to Jewish customs and maintain the law.

Lightfoot, who presents this evidence, concludes that a combination of circumstances so striking is not likely to have occurred twice within the space of just a few years. Besides, he adds, there is absolutely no correspondence between what Paul tells us of his visit and what Luke writes of the so-called "famine visit," which is the only other option (p. 124).

There are, however, obvious difficulties in linking Galatians 2 with Acts 15, and these are so weighty in the opinion of some scholars that they prefer nearly any other solution.[5]

First, there are apparent discrepancies. Acts gives the impression that Paul and Barnabas presented their case publicly before an assembled council of apostles and elders. But Galatians tells of a private meeting in which the dispute seems to be resolved between a small group of those who were considered leaders. Galatians says Titus accompanied Paul and Barnabas to Jerusalem. But Acts does not mention Titus. Finally, in Galatians Paul writes that he and Barnabas went up to Jerusalem by revelation, whereas in Acts Luke indicates that they went there as a result of a decision reached by the leaders of the church in Antioch.

Although discrepancies should not be passed over lightly, at the same time it is not difficult to see how they may be resolved. Every great public meeting is accompanied by private meetings. Titus is not mentioned by Luke because he did not become an issue, which is precisely the point Paul makes in Galatians ("not even Titus, who was with me, was compelled to be circumcised," 2:3). And concerning the revelation to send Paul to Jerusalem, this is no more than an alternate way of telling what happened, since the church at Antioch undoubtedly prayed about who their representatives should be and believed that they were responding to God in commissioning Paul and Barnabas. A

---

[5]Calvin linked Galatians 2 with Paul's famine visit of Acts 11. In more recent times the view is advanced by Weber (*Die Abfassung des Galaterbriefs vor dem Apostelkonzil,* 1900, p. 347) and by others who adopted it as an alternative to the views of the Tübingen school, which pitted Acts 15 and Galatians 2 against one another as Pauline and Petrine interpretations of the same event. The identification of Acts 11 with Galatians 2 is also made by Ramsay ("On the Interpretation of Two Passages in the Epistle to the Galatians," Exp., 5th series, 2, 1895, pp. 103–115), and Bird ("The Problem of Acts and Galatians," CBQ, 8, 1946, p. 259) and by Neil, Tenney, and Stott, in their commentaries.

Rendall ("St. Paul and the Galatian Judaizers," Exp., 3rd series, 10, 1889, pp. 51–64, 107–122), Burton ("Those Trouble-Makers in Galatia," BW, 53, 1919, pp. 555–560 and *The Epistle to the Galatians*), Dibelius ("Das Apostelkonzil," TLZ, 72, 1947, pp. 193–198), as well as Ridderbos, Stamm, and Lightfoot in their commentaries, support identification of the events of Galatians 2 with the Acts 15 council.

similar contrast between two ways of narrating the same event is seen in a comparison of Acts 9:29, 30 with Acts 22:17, 18.

More serious than these problems is the failure of Paul to mention either the decrees of the council or the visit to Jerusalem mentioned in Acts 11. Why should he not mention the decrees of the council? At first sight, this seems almost inexplicable, for, as Neil maintains (p. 14), it is most unlikely that Paul would have neglected to appeal to the council if, at the time of writing this letter, he held such a trump card in his hand. If the matter had already been decided, why did Paul not simply quote the council?

When looked at a bit deeper, however, Paul's failure to quote the council's decrees is understandable. First, the decrees were not so significant as this line of arguing implies. They were addressed to "the Gentiles in Antioch and Syria and Cilicia" to start with, not to Gentiles throughout the whole Roman world. Second, they were a compromise. They freed the Gentiles from adherence to the law, but they added certain restrictions for conscience' sake. Paul could very well have agreed with the decrees at the time they were devised but later, when writing to the Galatians, he could have considered the restrictions a dangerous concession likely to be misunderstood. The most impressive explanation of why he may have omitted reference to the decrees is that in quoting them he would have seemed to be conceding the very thing his enemies were insisting on—i.e., the authority of the Jerusalem apostles as greater than his own. In any case, Paul shows that the other apostles did agree with him regarding circumcision and actually supported him in his ministry.

Finally, if the council of Acts 15 is to be identified with the council of Galatians 2:1–10, why is it that Paul neglects to mention the visit to Jerusalem that Luke records in Acts 11? Isn't this dishonest? Or, to put it another way, doesn't this play into the hands of Paul's enemies? It is probably impossible to say exactly why Paul neglected to mention this visit, if the visit of Galatians 2 is indeed the visit of Acts 15, but there may be an explanation in the circumstances. The time of the Acts 11 visit was a time of turmoil and political agitation against the apostles, in which James the son of Zebedee was killed by Herod and Peter was imprisoned. Because of that, it is probable that every Christian of any rank had fled the city. Some evidence for this is found in Acts 11 itself, because no mention is made there of the Twelve nor is any meeting between Paul and the apostles recorded. Instead, Luke writes that the money for famine relief was delivered into the hands of "the elders." It also seems that this would be a most inauspicious time, if not an impossible time, for the full-scale discussion of so momentous an issue as Gentile adherence to the law and to circumcision.

Much of the difficulty inherent in this point vanishes when the student of Galatians realizes that Paul is not attempting to give a full account of all his activities during the early years of his ministry. Rather, he is attempting to answer specific criticisms directed against him by the legalizers. The first criticism is that he got his gospel from others and (the legalizers would add) got it imperfectly. Paul answers this by showing that in the early years he was not influenced by the Jerusalem apostles at all—either before, during, or after his conversion. This is the argument of the historical parts of chapter 1. On the other hand, Paul was not preaching something different from the gospel preached by the other apostles, as the legalists had also maintained. That criticism is handled in chapter 2. Neither of these points requires a rehearsal of events connected with the famine visit.

There are certain advantages to the Acts 11 theory, set forth well by many who adhere to it. On the whole, however, it is better to identify Galatians 2 with Acts 15, imagining two views of the same incident (one public and one private) rather than identifying two totally dissimilar accounts in which two totally different objectives for the visits are given.

4. Date and Place of Writing

Under the northern Galatia hypothesis a fairly late date is required for the writing of the letter; that is, a date subsequent to the events of Acts 18:23. But if the southern hypothesis is held, the possibilities begin earlier and are of wider scope. Unfortunately, it is impossible, even after identifying the council of Galatians 2 with that of Acts 15, to date the letter precisely and determine the place of its writing.

Several factors enter into an approximation of the date if the above conclusions are valid. First, the letter must have been written after the Jerusalem Council described in Acts 15, which in its turn is to be dated approximately fourteen or seventeen years after Paul's conversion. The usual dating of this council is A.D. 48 or 49. Hence, A.D. 48 becomes a *terminus a quo* for Paul's writing. Second, the visit of Peter to Antioch during which he was opposed by Paul (Gal 2:11–14) most naturally follows the council, though there are voices to the contrary. If this is so, then the earliest date is pushed back somewhat toward the end of Paul's stay in Antioch as described in Acts 15:35. Third, since Paul seems to be at liberty at the time of writing Galatians, the *terminus ad quem* is clearly the moment he lost that liberty during the final visit to Jerusalem, recorded in Acts 21 (approximately A.D. 58). Within these limits there are roughly eight or nine years in which Paul made two missionary journeys and in which the letter could have been written. This range can be narrowed somewhat by assuming that Paul had visited the Galatians twice before writing to them, once on the first missionary journey and once on the second (cf. Gal 4:13); for in that case, Galatians must have been written after Paul's arrival at Corinth on his second journey.

The most likely possibilities for a more precise placing of the book, as Burton states them (p. xlvii), are: (1) Corinth in the period of Acts 18:1–17, either before or after the writing of 1 Thessalonians, (2) Antioch in the period of Acts 18:22, (3) Ephesus in the period covered by Acts 19, or (4) Macedonia or Achaia in the period covered by Acts 20:1–3. Ephesus about the year A.D. 52 seems a likely possibility in view of Paul's lengthy stay there.

Fuller discussions of the matters of dating occur in Burton, pp. xliv–liii; Lightfoot, pp. 36–56; Ridderbos, pp. 31–35; Tenney, pp. 58–63; Guthrie, pp. 27–37; Stamm, pp. 438–441; and others, as well as in the various NT introductions.

5. Authorship

Of the traditional Pauline books few have been so unquestioningly accepted as genuine as the Book of Galatians. Paul, as author, is mentioned by name not only at the beginning (1:1) but also toward the end of the letter (5:2), and the whole from beginning to end breathes such an intensely personal and unconsciously autobiographical note that only a genuine historical situation involving the true founder of the Gentile mission within the Church accounts for it. Thus, even at the height of the highly critical period of NT scholarship in Germany in the nineteenth century, the Tübingen school and others consistently maintained the Pauline authorship of Galatians along with 1 and 2 Corinthians and Romans. The only noticeable exceptions are Bauer and the so-called

"Dutch school" of the late nineteenth century, headed by Loman, Pierson, Naber, Van Manen, and the Swiss scholar Steck. But their views are now generally discredited.

Quotations from Galatians or apparent allusions to it occur in 1 Peter, The Epistle of Barnabas, 1 Clement, the Epistle of Polycarp to the Philippians, Justin Martyr, Irenaeus, Clement of Alexandria, and Origen. The book is listed as Pauline in the Marcionite and Muratorian canons. A full listing of early allusions to Galatians may be found in Lightfoot (pp. 58–62).

6. Bibliography

The following is a select bibliography of commentaries or works on Galatians available to the English reader. References to other works as well as to the abundant periodical literature will be found throughout the commentary.

Askwith, E.H. *The Epistle to the Galatians: An Essay on Its Destination and Date.* New York: Macmillan, 1899.

Barclay, William. *Flesh and Spirit: An Examination of Galatians 5:19–23.* Nashville: Abingdon, 1962.

———. *The Letters to the Galatians and Ephesians,* "The Daily Study Bible." ICC. Edinburgh: St. Andrew Press, 1954.

Burton, Ernest de Witt. *A Critical and Exegetical Commentary on the Epistle to the Galatians,* Edinburgh: T. & T. Clark, 1921.

Calvin, John. *The Epistles of Paul the Apostle to the Galatians, Philippians and Colossians.* Grand Rapids: Eerdmans, 1965. Original edition, 1548.

Cole, R.A. *The Epistle of Paul to the Galatians,* TNTC. London: Tyndale, 1965.

Guthrie, Donald. *Galatians,* NCB. Camden, N.J.: Nelson, 1969.

Lightfoot, J.B. *The Epistle of St. Paul to the Galatians.* Grand Rapids: Zondervan, 1957. Original edition, 1865.

Luther, Martin. *A Commentary on St. Paul's Epistle to the Galatians.* Westwood, N.J.: Revell, 1953. Original edition, 1535.

Neil, William. *The Letter of Paul to the Galatians,* "The Cambridge Bible Commentary." Cambridge: Cambridge University Press, 1967.

Ramsay, Michael M. *An Historical Commentary on St. Paul's Epistle to the Galatians.* New York: G.P. Putnam's Sons, 1900.

Ridderbos, Herman N. *The Epistle of Paul to the Churches of Galatia,* NIC. Grand Rapids: Eerdmans, 1953.

Ropes, James H. *The Singular Problem of the Epistle to the Galatians,* "Harvard Theological Studies," 14. Cambridge, Mass.: Harvard, 1929.

Stamm, Raymond T., and Blackwelder, Oscar Fisher. *The Epistle to the Galations,* IB, vol. 10. New York: Abingdon, 1953.

Stott, John R.W. *The Message of Galatians,* "The Bible Speaks Today." Downers Grove, Ill.: Inter-Varsity Press, 1968.

Tenney, Merrill C. *Galatians: The Charter of Christian Liberty.* Grand Rapids: Eerdmans, 1950.

Williams, A. Lukyn. *The Epistle of Paul the Apostle to the Galatians,* "The Cambridge Bible for Schools and Colleges." Cambridge: Cambridge University Press, 1911.

7. Outline of the Book

Introduction (1:1–10)
- A. Salutation (1:1–5)
- B. The Reason for the Letter (1:6–9)
- C. Transition (1:10)

I. Paul's Defense of His Apostleship (1:11–2:21)
- A. Thesis: Paul's Gospel Received Directly From God (1:11, 12)
- B. Paul's Personal History (1:13–24)
  1. Paul's early years and conversion (1:13–17)
  2. Paul's early years as a Christian (1:18–24)
- C. Paul's Relationship to the Other Apostles (2:1–21)
  1. The council at Jerusalem (2:1–5)
  2. Paul and the pillar apostles (2:6–10)
  3. Peter comes to Antioch (2:11–14)
  4. Justification by faith alone (2:15–21)

II. Paul's Defense of the Gospel (3:1–4:31)
- A. The Doctrinal Issue: Faith or Works (3:1–5)
- B. The Doctrinal Argument (3:6–4:7)
  1. Sons of Abraham (3:6–9)
  2. The law's curse (3:10–14)
  3. The seed of Abraham (3:15–18)
  4. Law versus covenant (3:19–22)
  5. Heirs with Abraham (3:23–29)
  6. Heirs of God (4:1–7)
- C. Paul's Appeal to the Galatians (4:8–31)
  1. A return to bondage (4:8–11)
  2. Their past and present relationships (4:12–20)
  3. An appeal from allegory (4:21–31)

III. The Call to Godly Living (5:1–6:10)
- A. Summary and Transition (5:1)
- B. The Danger of Falling From Grace (5:2–12)
- C. Life in the Spirit (5:13–26)
  1. Liberty is not license (5:13–18)
  2. The works of the flesh (5:19–21)
  3. The fruit of the Spirit (5:22–26)
- D. Two Practical Exhortations (6:1–10)
  1. Bearing one another's burdens (6:1–5)
  2. The use of money (6:6–10)

Conclusion (6:11–18)

Text and Exposition

Introduction (1:1–10)

A. *Salutation*

1:1–5

[1]Paul, an apostle—sent not from men nor by man, but by Jesus Christ and God the Father, who raised him from the dead— [2]and all the brothers with me,

To the churches in Galatia:

[3]Grace and peace to you from God our Father and the Lord Jesus Christ, [4]who gave himself for our sins to rescue us from the present evil age, according to the will of our God and Father, [5]to whom be glory for ever and ever. Amen.

An opening salutation consisting of the author's name, the name of those to whom he is writing, and (in most cases) an expression of good wishes on the recipient's behalf is characteristic of most ancient letters, Paul's included. But Paul's opening remarks also generally breathe something of the content and tone of the letter or, at the very least, employ explicitly Christian terms as greetings. None of Paul's opening remarks are more characteristic of the letter to follow than those in Galatians. The usual elements are present—the writer's name, the name of the recipients, and a wish for grace and peace on their behalf—but there are a brevity and vigor of expression that immediately plunge the reader into the heart of the Epistle and that reflect Paul's concern. Most surprisingly, there is no expression of praise for these churches—elsewhere a normal procedure (Rom, 1 and 2 Cor, Eph, Phil, Col, 1 and 2 Thess).

Of particular importance is Paul's abrupt restatement of his claim to be an apostle, precisely the point that had been denied by those who were subverting the Galatians. In these few verses the three major themes of the letter—the source of authority in religion, the doctrine of grace, and the promise of full deliverance from sin's power—are tied together in a way that relates all solely to the sovereign and gracious will of God.

1 By adding the word "apostle," Paul at once highlights his claim to be commissioned by Jesus to preach the gospel with authority and to plant Christianity. It was this commission that had been challenged by the Galatian legalizers. In early use of Greek, the word "apostle" (*apostolos*) was used of a naval expedition, commissioned to represent Greek interests in foreign service. In Greek-speaking Judaism it was used of authorized representatives, either an individual or a body of persons. With the coming of Christ, the word was applied to those commissioned by Christ as bearers of the gospel. It is this sense, coupled with the idea of the full authority deriving from Christ, that prevails in all seventy-nine instances of the term in the NT.

It would seem from the opening chapter of Acts (vv.21–26) that two major prerequisites for being an apostle were: (1) to have been an eyewitness of Christ's ministry from the time of the baptism by John up to and including the resurrection, and (2) to have been chosen for the office by the risen Lord. At first the number of those so commissioned was twelve (Matthias having been chosen to replace Judas), but there is no indication either in Acts or elsewhere that the number was always so limited. Paul obviously claimed to have fulfilled the conditions as the result of his Damascus experience; and Luke, who clearly endorses Paul's claim, also speaks of Barnabas as being called to this office. Other examples are: James, the Lord's brother (suggested by the phrase "then to *all* the apostles," which follows mention of James in 1 Corinthians 15:7), and Silvanus (1 Thess 2:7, cf. 1:1).

The difficulty was not that the office could not be extended by the Lord to others in addition to the Twelve—this was possible—but rather that Paul, according to his enemies, did not meet the conditions. They could claim that he had never met Jesus. Certainly he had not been an eyewitness of Christ's ministry. They could claim that he had never received a commission. It would be easy, for instance, to contrast Paul's description of his Damascus experience with the very formal and official action of the Twelve in choosing Matthias. Paul answered by entirely overlooking the matter of his not being an eyewitness of the whole of Christ's earthly ministry, though undoubtedly he considered his Damascus experience to be the equivalent of this, and by denying that his status had relation to men or to the decisions of men at all. Instead, Paul's claim was that his apostleship came to him directly from and through God the Father and the Lord Jesus Christ.

Paul's specific choice of words is of interest, for he employs two prepositions (*apo* and *dia*) to deny that his call to apostleship came either "from" or "through" man. Thus, as Lightfoot notes (in loc.): "In the first clause he distinguishes himself from the false apostles, who did not derive their commission from God at all [whereas] in the second he ranks himself with the Twelve, who were commissioned directly" by him.

On the positive side, Paul stresses that his call came rather from God himself through the Lord Jesus Christ. Here the preposition *apo* is dropped, but the effect is not to eliminate the truth that the call is "from" God. That much is obvious. Rather, the single preposition anchors Paul's call in the historical experience on the Damascus road in which Jesus, through whom the call came, appeared to him. By linking both the Father and the Son under one preposition, Paul also stresses that there is no difference between them so far as the appointment of the apostolate is concerned. Reference to the resurrection stresses the important point that it was by the risen and glorified Lord of the church that Paul was commissioned.

The gospel committed to Paul is a great gospel to possess. Anchored in history, it has been articulated and communicated to believers of all times by those who were specifically chosen by the risen Lord and were empowered by him for this task. It is the logical outcome of the principles stated here that for the NT as well as for the OT, "prophecy never had its origin in the will of man, but men spoke from God as they were carried along by the Holy Spirit" (2 Peter 1:21).

2 From Paul's normal habit of including the names of his fellow missionaries at the beginning of his letters (1 and 2 Cor, Phil, Col, 1 and 2 Thess, Philem) as well as from the fact that he usually refers to the Christians in the place from which he is writing in different terms, it would appear that "the brothers" mentioned here are his fellow missionaries, though their actual identity cannot be known until the date and place of writing are determined. The interesting point is that Paul does not name these fellow missionaries, as he does elsewhere, not wanting to give the impression that his gospel requires additional support. It was, after all, received directly from God. At the same time, he wishes to remind the Galatians that the gospel that had been preached to them, far from being a Pauline oddity, is actually the received doctrine of all the Christian church and its missionaries.

3 Paul's nearly standard formula of Christian blessing and greeting—"grace and peace to you from God our Father and the Lord Jesus Christ"—seems particularly appropriate at the start of this letter. Normally, Paul alters the traditional Greek greeting (*charein*, a verb) to the important Christian word "grace" (*charis*, a noun). This is always striking. But it is doubly striking here, inasmuch as it occurs in a letter to churches where the sufficiency of salvation by grace was being questioned and perhaps even denied. In the same way, "peace" (*eirēnē*, the Greek equivalent of the Hebrew word *shalom*) is also especially appropriate, for it denotes that state of favor and well-being into which men are brought by Christ's death on the cross and in which they are kept by God's persevering grace. To choose law, as the Galatians were doing, is to fall from grace. To live by works is to lose the peace with God that was purchased for believers by Christ's atonement.

It is characteristic of Paul to join the names of the Father and Son together in the statement that they are the source of grace and peace, as he does here. But the inversion of the order—"by Jesus Christ and God the Father" (v.1)—to "from God our Father and the Lord Jesus Christ" (v.3) heightens the effect. It is a good equivalent of Jesus' words "Father, . . . you are in me and I am in you" (John 17:21) and thus a good statement of the full divinity of Jesus.

4 To the doctrines of the Christian faith already stated in germinal form—the source of authority in religion, the person and character of God, the divinity of Christ, the resurrection, grace, and peace—Paul now adds a statement affirming the substitutionary death of the Lord Jesus Christ and its outcome in the deliverance of men from sin. All this, he asserts, is according to the will of the Father. It is hard to imagine a statement better calculated to oppose any intrusion of the will or supposed merits of man in the matter of attaining salvation. This phrase, which does not occur in other Pauline greetings, is undoubtedly added for the sake of the erring Christians in Galatia.

Salvation begins in the eternal counsels of God. It is a matter of his will and not of the will of man. As Paul says elsewhere, "It does not, therefore, depend on man's desire or effort, but on God's mercy" (Rom 9:16). The will of God to save men leads next to the coming of the Lord Jesus Christ with its focus in his substitutionary death for sinners. Finally, the goal is articulated; for the death of the Lord Jesus Christ, which originated in the will of the Father, was designed to "rescue us from the present evil age." The word "rescue" or "deliver" (*exelētai*) denotes not a "deliverance from" but a "rescue from the power of." Thus, it strikes the keynote of the latter, ethical section of the letter, peaking in the great challenge at the beginning of chapter 5—"It is for freedom that Christ has set us free. Stand firm, then, and do not let yourselves be burdened again by a yoke of slavery" (v.1). The deliverance is conceived of here, not as a deliverance out of the present evil world (though that will also be true eventually), but as a deliverance from the power of evil and the values of the present world-system through the power of the risen Christ within the Christian.

5 It is not customary for Paul to include a doxology at the beginning of a letter, but the doxology that occurs here serves an important purpose. It sets the gospel, centering in the preeminence of the Lord Jesus Christ and his work, above any human criticism or praise. The fact that the glory of God and the giving of glory to God will last forever (literally, "unto the ages of ages") contrasts markedly with "the present evil age," which is passing away.

Notes

1 The bearing of the significance of the office of the apostle on the Book of Galatians is discussed at length by Lightfoot (pp. 92–101) and Burton (pp. 363–384) in their commentaries.

In the NT ἀπό (*apo*) means "from" with reference to the source, i.e., "he went up *out of* the water" (Matt 3:16). Διὰ (*dia*), as distinguished from *apo,* means "through" and denotes the agent or instrument by which the action takes place. It is used often of Christ, "through" whom we are saved (John 3:17) and receive other blessings (Rom 5:1). The change from "men" (plural) to "man" (singular) is probably stylistic, though there may be a veiled reference to a person who had been influential in Paul's life, either Barnabas (Zahn) or Ananias (Sanday), as some have argued.

2 The distinction in Phil 4:21, 22 between "the brothers who are with me" and the Christians who were part of the local church at Rome seems to support the conclusion that the "brothers" of Galatians 1:2 are Paul's fellow missionaries. The emphatic "all," which modifies "brothers," has the effect of highlighting the unanimity with which these fellow missionaries supported Paul in his case against the Jerusalem legalizers.

4 Ὑπὲρ (*hyper,* "for") habitually denotes substitution. So, for example, professional letter writers would close their document with their name, adding, "I wrote on behalf of [*hyper*] him who does not know letters." This phrase had the effect of legalizing the document. In the NT the substitutionary idea is clear in the use of the word *hyper* by Caiaphas to argue that it was necessary "that one man die *for* the people" (John 11:50) and in Paul's statement that "one died *for* all, and therefore all died" (2 Cor 5:14). Paul's phrase in Galatians is identical with that found in 1 Corinthians 15:3, where the fundamental affirmations of the gospel are set out (cf. also Gal 2:20, Rom 5:6, 8).

4,5 The contrast between the present and future ages is even more sharp in Ephesians 2:2–7, in which the nature of the ages is related to the past, present, and future life of the Christian. For a fuller discussion see Burton (pp. 426–432).

B. *The Reason for the Letter*

1:6–9

[6]I am astonished that you are so quickly deserting the one who called you by the grace of Christ and are turning to a different gospel— [7]which is really no gospel at all. Evidently some people are throwing you into confusion and are trying to pervert the gospel of Christ. [8]But even if we or an angel from heaven should preach a gospel other than the one we preached to you, let him be eternally condemned! [9]As we have already said, so now I say again: If anybody is preaching to you a gospel other than what you accepted, let him be eternally condemned!

At this point Paul would normally introduce an expression of praise for the Christians of the church to which he is writing, followed sometimes by a mild suggestion of that which is not so praiseworthy. But here, instead of an expression of praise, there is an abrupt and indignant cry of astonishment at what seems to be happening among the Galatians. Paul had delivered to them the one gospel of salvation by grace through faith in Jesus Christ. They had received it. But now, according to reports that had come to him, Paul has reason to believe that the Christians of Galatia are on the point of turning from the gospel of Christ to embrace something that was no gospel at all, but only legalism. So in this brief expression of his feelings, Paul declares his astonishment at this almost inconceivable turn of events, pronounces a judgment upon any who would pervert the gospel of grace, and reiterates that there is only one gospel that makes salvation possible.

6 The agitation Paul feels is shown by the tone and vocabulary of these verses. But his words also show why he is so stirred. He is agitated, first, because the Galatians are "deserting" (*metatithesthe*) the one who had called them to faith in Christ Jesus. It is not simply that they "had been removed" to another and errant, though partially valid expression of the Christian faith, as the KJV translation might suggest. The problem was that they were "deserting" the Christian camp altogether. The Greek word is "a colorful one," as Guthrie notes, "used both of military revolt and of a change of attitude" (in loc.). Moreover, since the verb is probably in the middle voice, rather than the passive, it is not even possible for the Galatians to claim that their conduct was the result of outside influences. This is something they were doing to themselves and were responsible for. The only ray of hope is that they were still only in the process of deserting and could possibly be reclaimed.

Second, there is a tragic personal element in the way Paul describes their condition. It is not merely that they have deserted an idea or a movement; rather, they have deserted the very one who had called them to faith. This one is God the Father. Embracing legalism means rejecting God, according to Paul's reasoning, because it means substituting man for God in one's life. It is significant that once again even in the space of a few words ("who called you by the grace of Christ") Paul reiterates the true nature of the gospel: (1) it is of God, for God does the calling, and (2) it is of grace rather than of merit.

Third, Paul explains his agitation by the fact that the Galatians were deserting God "so quickly" (*houtōs tacheōs*). This phrase could have several meanings, some of them bearing on the date of the writing of the letter, but it is probably best to see it merely as a general reference to the Galatians' deserting the faith soon after their conversion.

Finally, Paul's agitation results from the fact that by embracing legalism the Galatians have actually turned their back on the gospel in order to embrace "a different gospel," which, however, does not even deserve to be called by that name.

7 Here the opening clause implies a correction or explanation of what was previously written. Paul has just spoken of "a different gospel" the Galatian Christians were turning to, but if that phrase were left without any comment, it might suggest that there are after all various gospels among which a Christian may choose. This is the opposite of what Paul is saying. So he adds that though he said "a different gospel" actually there cannot be another gospel as long as the gospel is understood to be God's way of salvation in Christ. The gospel is one. Therefore any system of salvation that varies from it is counterfeit. In the Greek text of vv.6, 7 the two words translated "another" in KJV are not the same and are used in a specific way to make this distinction.

Paul now mentions the false teachers for the first time, though not by name, presumably because he does not want anyone to think his remarks were originating from a dislike of certain personalities rather than from concern for the truth. He objects to two aspects of the conduct of these teachers: (1) they were perverting the gospel and (2) they were troubling the church. These two always go together. Thus, as Stott notes,

> To tamper with the gospel is to trouble the Church. . . . Indeed, the Church's greatest troublemakers (now as then) are not those outside who oppose, ridicule and persecute it, but those inside who try to change the gospel. . . . Conversely, the only way to be a good churchman is to be a good gospel-man. The best way to serve the Church is to believe and to preach the gospel (in loc.).

8 The logical objection to what Paul has been saying is that the teaching he calls the gospel is not actually *the* gospel, but only the gospel of Paul. If this is the case, then the Galatians must evaluate the source of the teaching they had received, taking into account that they, the legalizers, were the official representatives of the Jerusalem apostles, while Paul was not. Paul wards off this accusation, arguing that ultimately the human source does not matter, nor would it matter even if the source were an "angelic" one. Satan can disguise himself as "an angel of light," as can his ministers (2 Cor 11:14, 15). So the Galatians must learn to evaluate their teachers. Besides, they must learn that any attempt to alter the true gospel is culpable and that any who go about teaching another gospel will be condemned.

The vehemence with which Paul denounces those who teach another gospel (literally, he says, "Let them be damned") has bothered some commentators, as well as other readers of the letter. But this shows how little the gospel of God's grace is understood and appreciated and how little many Christians are concerned for the advance of biblical truth.

The word translated "eternally condemned" (*anathema*) is related to the Hebrew word *herem* and is used of that which is devoted to God, usually for destruction. In spiritual terms it means damnation. We must not think, however, that in speaking in this way Paul is merely giving vent to an intemperate outburst or even merely to partially justified anger. For one thing, he is impartial in expressing his judgment. He has not named names. He has even included himself in the ban, should he do otherwise in his preaching than he has done thus far. Moreover, he is universal in his judgment. His words include "anybody" who should so teach (v.9).

How can it be otherwise? If the gospel Paul preaches is true, then both the glory of Jesus Christ and the salvation of men are at stake. If men can be saved by works, Christ has died in vain (Gal 2:21); the cross is emptied of meaning. If men are taught a false gospel, they are being led from the one thing that can save them and are being turned to destruction (cf. Matt 18:6).

9 No doubt Paul repeats the *anathema* primarily for the sake of emphasis. But the restatement involves three alterations that tie it more closely to the situation in Galatia: (1) "The one we preached" is changed to "what you accepted"; (2) the element of improbability is lessened—"we or an angel from heaven" being changed to "anybody"; and (3) the thought of future possibility—"if we . . . should preach"—is replaced by present supposition.

Notes

6 If οὕτως ταχέως (*houtōs tacheōs*) is to be tr. "so soon" or "so quickly," then the comparison is between the time of Paul's having preached the gospel to the Galatians and the time of his writing to them. If one is to understand the phrase as "so rashly" or "so precipitously," then it refers to the quickness of their departure from the faith after the legalizers had begun to preach circumcision (cf. 1 Tim 5:22; 2 Thess 2:2).

7 The specific nature of the distinction between the two Greek words for "other" that occur here (ἕτερος, *heteros,* and ἄλλος, *allos*) has been the subject of sharp debate between Lightfoot (in

loc.), who takes the position reflected in this commentary, and Ramsay (in loc.), who claimed that Lightfoot's views were the result of a theological bias. Lightfoot took the first of the two words for "other" (*heteros*) as denoting that which is entirely different, i.e., not even of the same species. The second word (*allos*) he interpreted as numerically different but, nevertheless, of the same kind. This would give the meaning that there is only one gospel and that in deserting the gospel that Paul had taught to them the Galatians were deserting the Christian faith altogether. Ramsay simply inverted the two, claiming support from classicial Gr. authors (Homer, Plato, Aristotle). In his view, there would be a number of gospels and Paul would merely be recalling the Galatians to the best and purest form of Christianity.

Unfortunately for Ramsay's view, a close examination of the classical passages reveals that most are indecisive. Besides, there is a glaring failure to take full account of the important LXX texts and NT passages. In these cases the use of the two words is apparently often indistinguishable, but not always. And when a distinction is clearly made, it is on the side of Lightfoot's interpretation. Thus, in 1 Cor 15:39, 40 there is a distinction between various kinds of flesh (of men, beasts, fish, and birds) in which the word *allos* is used, and another categorical distinction between earthly bodies and the body of the resurrection in which the word *heteros* is employed. This is precisely the distinction Paul makes in Galatians, and it is this view rather than Ramsay's that best explains the abrupt and anguished tone of Paul's letter. In addition to the commentaries, see Ramsay, "On the Interpretation of Two Passages in the Epistle to the Galatians," Exp., 5th series, 2 (1895), pp. 115–118. For a recent thorough discussion of the problem, see Burton (pp. 420–422).

8 Paul's use of the phrase παρ' ὃ (*par' ho*, "contrary to") in reference to teaching other than that which conveys the true gospel, strengthens the view taken above regarding Paul's use of the words **ἕτερος** (*heteros*) and **ἄλλος** (*allos*). Although παρά (*para*) has other uses, it almost certainly means "contrary to" in this context. The so-called "gospel" of the legalizers is therefore totally other and contrary to the gospel Paul had received by revelation.

C. *Transition*

1:10

[10]Am I now trying to win the approval of men, or of God? Or am I trying to please men? If I were still trying to please men, I would not be a servant of Christ.

Having given the reason for writing his letter, Paul now moves to a statement of his first important thesis (vv.11, 12). But first, he makes a transition. The connective particle *gar* links the verse with the preceding, while the repeated use of "men" and the mention of "Christ" also join it loosely with what follows.

10 Paul had been accused of being a pleaser of men by his enemies, who no doubt also implied that he was such at the expense of the truth (cf. 2 Cor 10; Gal 6:12). Would his enemies dare to say this now, Paul asks, after he has written so sharply? Do men-pleasers pronounce *anathemas* against those who teach false gospels? On the other hand, Paul's words cannot be read as justification of the belligerent and fault-finding attitude so often found among religious crusaders. For one thing, he does not say that he is never concerned with pleasing men. Actually, he did strive to please men sometimes (1 Cor 9:19–22), though not where the gospel was at stake. He is merely saying that he did not please men *as opposed to* pleasing God. Besides, the statement that he does not please men is related here to the present moment and subject, as the prominently placed "now" (*arti*) indicates. The sense is this: "Have I made myself clear enough about Christ's gospel? Can anyone *now* charge that I seek to please men in presenting *it*?"

The incongruity of this thought is strengthened by the following sentence, in which Paul mentions being "a servant of Christ." Jesus had said, "No one can serve two masters" (Matt 6:24). Thus, when faced with the necessity of making a choice, Paul chose to stand with him whose slave he had become. The choice of the word "slave" is interesting because the letter is about freedom. It is an early indication of the true though paradoxical teaching that real freedom is to be found in bondage—bondage to Christ.

I. Paul's Defense of His Apostleship (1:11–2:21)

A. *Thesis: Paul's Gospel Received Directly From God*

1:11, 12

[11]I want you to know, brothers, that the gospel I preached is not something that man made up. [12]I did not receive it from any man, nor was I taught it; rather, I received it by revelation from Jesus Christ.

Important points have already been made in the introduction to Galatians, but with these two verses the reader comes to its first important thesis. Paul has spoken of the gospel (vv.6–9), stating clearly that there is only one gospel. But certain questions might be asked: "Why should your gospel be normative, Paul? Why not another gospel? Or, if it is true that there can be only one *gospel,* why should not some entirely other teaching be normative?" Paul's answer is to stress the origin of his teaching, which did not have human origins as did other religious teaching. On the contrary, it was divine in origin, having been received by Paul directly from God. Throughout the remainder of this chapter and all of chapter 2 Paul defends this thesis by an appeal to his own religious experience.

11 The verb introducing this verse (*gnōrizō*) means "to make clear," "to certify," and has the effect of suggesting a somewhat formal statement to follow. Indeed, this is what does follow. For just as v.1 advanced Paul's claim to apostleship by denying alleged inadequate sources for that apostleship and affirming the true one, so this section denies inadequate sources for the gospel, while affirming that the gospel Paul preached came directly from God by revelation.

Paul denies three possible sources for his teaching. First, he denies that it was "according to man" (*kata anthrōpon*). This phrase may mean that the source of the gospel was not according to man or to human authority. But it is more likely that the phrase is more general and simply means "human" or, as NIV has it, "something that man made up." This is patently true, for the centrality of a cross and a resurrection do not figure in man-made religion. Man seems always to prefer what flatters him and affirms human goodness.

12 Paul also denies that his teaching was "received from man." This is a different denial from that in v.11. Both *para* (the preposition) and *paralambanō* (the verb) refer to the transmission of religious teaching. According to Gerhardsson and others of the Scandinavian school, these even belong to a set of technical words used of the process of memorization by which rabbis passed along rabbinic traditions to students. Paul uses the verb in this sense in 1 Corinthians 15:1, 3 to indicate that the basic facts of Christ's life—his death, burial, and resurrection—were received by him and passed on intact to his hearers. Important as this type of transmission may be, however, this was simply not the way Paul received his message.

Finally, Paul adds that he was not "taught" the gospel either. This phrase denies instruction as the channel through which he came to the truth. This may be the way the vast majority of Christians come to receive the gospel, ourselves included. It was certainly true of the Galatians, since Paul had himself instructed them. But it was not the way Paul himself had received the truth. He now adds the positive side of his thesis, saying that the gospel came to him by revelation.

The revelation of the Christian gospel to Paul, an unexpected unfolding of what had been secret, was a distinctive experience, paralleled only by the experience of those who were apostles before him. It can never be ours. Nevertheless, the gospel that was the product of that experience is unique and is ours; in fact, it is ours precisely because its source was not Paul but God himself. And Christians value it properly only when they make it an integral part of their lives and share it with others.

Notes

12 Ιησοῦ Χριστοῦ ("of Jesus Christ") may be either an objective or a subjective genitive. If it is objective, Paul is claiming that Jesus was himself the content of the revelation he received, and God the Father would therefore be considered the source. If the genitive is subjective, Jesus is the source of the revelation. Obviously both interpretations are valid. Either one would be appropriate in the context.

B. *Paul's Personal History* (1:13–24)

1. *Paul's early years and conversion*

1:13–17

> [13]For you have heard of my previous way of life in Judaism, how I violently persecuted the church of God and tried to destroy it. [14]I was advancing in Judaism beyond many Jews of my own age and was extremely zealous for the traditions of my ancestors. [15]But when God, who set me apart from birth and called me by his grace, was pleased [16]to reveal his Son in me so that I might preach him among the Gentiles, I did not consult any man. [17]I did not go up to Jerusalem to see those who were apostles before I was. Instead, I went immediately into Arabia and later returned to Damascus.

Paul has written that his gospel did not have its source in men. But how is he to prove this to the Galatian churches? The answer is by appeal to his personal history. Hence, in the remainder of the chapter Paul shows that the conditions of his life before his conversion, at his conversion, and within a reasonable period after his conversion were not such that he could have received the gospel from others, particularly the Jerusalem apostles. On the contrary, the very isolation of his life at this period (criticized by the legalizers) shows that the gospel must have come to him directly from God, as he has indicated.

13 The first part of this cumulative argument concerns Paul's former life in Judaism, before his conversion to Christianity. At this point, so far was he from coming under Christian influences that he actually was opposing the church and persecuting it.

The word Paul used for his former "way of life" (*anastrophē*) is singularly appropriate to the Jewish faith. Judaism was not a mask to be donned or doffed at will, as was the case with so many of the pagan religions. Judaism was a way of life, involving all of life, and Paul is correct in describing it as his exclusive sphere of existence before his conversion. His brief reference to his former life is somewhat augmented by his lengthier descriptions elsewhere, particularly in Philippians 3:4–6. There Paul shows that he was (1) a Jew by birth—indeed, of the best stock of Israel; (2) by choice, a Pharisee, i.e., of the strictest sect of Judaism; and (3) in conduct, exceedingly zealous, a zeal demonstrated by his persecution of the church and his rigid adherence to the law. "You have heard" suggests that these facts were known to the Galatians long before any question had been raised about Paul's teaching.

Two aspects of his former life are specifically brought forward in his review of it. First, he persecuted the church (v.13). Second, he advanced in the traditions of Judaism well beyond those of his own age among his countrymen (v.14). In both of these aspects Paul was fanatical. He demonstrated his fanaticism against the church by the violence of his persecution (literally, *kath' hyperbolēn,* "to an extraordinary degree" or "beyond measure") and by his actual endeavor to destroy it (cf. Acts 8:1–4; 9:1, 2, 13, 14; 22:4, 5). The same word for "destroy" (*portheō*) is used of Paul in Acts 9:21 and later on in this chapter (v.23).

14 The zeal that fired Paul in his missionary efforts also existed before his conversion. It was an aspect of his personality. But before his Damascus experience this zeal was devoted to advancing as a Pharisee in Judaism. This he did beyond his own contemporaries. To advance in the "traditions" of his fathers would have meant much time spent in memorizing the Torah and the rabbinical traditions accompanying it. "Traditions," strictly speaking, are the latter. With such a background no one could claim that Paul did not know Judaism or the OT. Nor could one claim that during this period he had subtly received his instruction in Christianity from others.

15,16 No man possessing such characteristics and engaged in zealous persecution of the church is about to be converted by someone else or by human testimony. God himself must accomplish his conversion. This is precisely what happened in Paul's case. Thus, Paul begins to speak of his conversion, pointing out that God did it entirely apart from any human agent. The reference is to Paul's Damascus experience described in Acts 9:1–19; 22:1–16; and 26:9–18. The contrast in subjects between vv.13, 14 on the one hand, and 15, 16 on the other hand, is interesting. In the first section Paul himself is the subject. The pronoun is "I." "*I* persecuted the church," he says. "*I* was advancing in Judaism." In the second section, God is the subject, and his grace is emphasized.

There are three things Paul says God did for him. First, God *set him apart from birth.* Paul's words parallel Jeremiah's description of his own calling (Jer 1:5) and may, indeed, consciously reflect them. The emphasis is on God's grace in electing Paul to salvation and to the apostleship. Second, God *called Paul by grace.* This is a reference to his conversion, the moment in which Paul became aware of God's work in him.

Third, God *revealed his Son in Paul* (v.16). This phrase may have two senses. It may refer to Paul's sudden realization of what God had done in his life, namely, that God had placed the life of the Lord Jesus Christ within him. In this case, it seems merely to repeat point two from a slightly different perspective. Or it may refer to the revalation of Jesus Christ through Paul to others. In this case, there is a three-step historical progression, ending with Paul's actual entering into his ministry in fulfillment of his call (so Lightfoot, in loc.). In spite of the weighty testimony of Lightfoot and the obvious appeal of a three-part progression, the first of these two possible meanings should probably be preferred. Thus, though Paul does speak of his ministry of preaching to the Gentiles, his phrasing indicates that God revealed his Son in him "in order that" this might take place; i.e., Paul was converted so that he might become the apostle to the Gentiles. Besides, in the context of this chapter the sequel to the call is not preaching but rather a departure from Damascus for a time of inner searching and meditation in Arabia.

God's revelation of Jesus in Paul was essentially an inner revelation concerning who Jesus was and what his life, death, and resurrection signified. This became so much a part of him, even at this early stage of his Christian experience, that he immediately began to make the revelation of Christ known to others. What grace this demonstrates! Paul, the chief opponent of Christianity in the apostolic era, now turned preacher of what he once tried to destroy! Was this change accomplished by men? No! Hence, even in his conversion (as in the period before his conversion) Paul could not have received from others the gospel that he preached.

17 Finally, just as Paul did not receive his gospel from men before or at the time of his conversion, so neither did he not receive it from them afterward. The second half of vv.16, 17 shows that he did not consult men, particularly the Jerusalem apostles, but went instead into Arabia. It was not until after three years (v.18) that he went up to Jerusalem and met Peter.

Notes

13 Burton calls attention to two notable aspects of Paul's phrase "the church of God": (1) the use of the singular to denote not a local body but rather the Christian community at large; and (2) the characterization of this community as God's church. He writes, "The first of these facts shows that Paul had not only formed the conception of churches as local assemblies and communities of Christians (vv.2, 22), but had already united these local communities in his thought into one entity—the church. The second fact shows that this body already stood in his mind as the chosen people of God, and indicates how fully, in his thought, the Christian church had succeeded to the position once occupied by Israel" (in loc.). For a fuller discussion of the church, see the extended note in Burton (pp. 417–420) and Schmidt (*Theological Dictionary of the New Testament,* ed. by Kittel, 3:501–536). These considerations show what a remarkable contrast there is in this verse between Christianity and the Judaism Paul had left.

A fuller discussion of the elements of Paul's life before his conversion may be found in Tenney (pp. 68–87).

15,16 The connecting particle and adverb that begin v.15 may be tr. either "but when" or "and when." The former brings out the abrupt change resulting from Paul's conversion and is, in fact, the force that another conjunction (ἀλλὰ, *alla*) has in Paul's parallel account of his conversion in Phil 3:7. In this case, however, the argument Paul advances is cumulative rather than contrasting, with the result that the translation "and when" should be preferred. The point is that in his conversion, as well as before, Paul was free from human influences.

17 Paul does not say what he did in Arabia or even what particular area of Arabia he visited in order to sort out his thoughts about Christianity, but the natural surmise would be an area not too far from Damascus (cf. Lightfoot for the view that Paul visited Sinai, pp. 87–90). His Damascus experience would have shown Paul that he had been wrong about Jesus. However, the replacement of his Jewish world and life view by a Christian theology would have been the work of more than a long weekend. Some have imagined a contradiction between what Paul writes here and what Luke writes in Acts 9, where Arabia is not even mentioned. But this is unjustified. Luke leaves room for an Arabian sojourn between v.22 and v.23, and he can be excused for omitting it if nothing of historical importance occurred during those months or years. Seen from the other side, Luke's omission suggests that Paul went into Arabia to think and study rather than to preach, for Luke would probably have mentioned the journey if Paul had established churches there. The same conclusion follows from the wording of Galatians, because Paul says that the trip was connected with the fact that for a considerable period he conferred with no one (vv.16, 17).

---

2. *Paul's early years as a Christian*

1:18–24

[18]Then after three years, I went up to Jerusalem to get acquainted with Peter and stayed with him fifteen days. [19]I saw none of the other apostles—only James, the Lord's brother. [20]I assure you before God that what I am writing you is no lie. [21]Later I went to Syria and Cilicia. [22]I was personally unknown to the churches of Judea that are in Christ. [23]They only heard the report: "The man who formerly persecuted us is now preaching the faith he once tried to destroy." [24]And they praised God because of me.

18 Three years passed, but it is hard to be specific about the time. The Jewish mode of reckoning does not indicate precisely how long this period was. It may have been only one full year plus parts of two others. Nor does Paul's wording indicate the point from which the three years or parts of three years are to be reckoned. Is it from the time of his return to Damascus? Or is Paul reckoning from his conversion? The importance of the conversion plus the fact that it has just been mentioned probably means that the three years are to be counted from that time, in which case (if Paul's conversion occurred in A.D. 32, as there is reason to believe), the visit to Jerusalem referred to here would have been near A.D. 35. This is the visit mentioned by Luke in Acts 9:26–29. But again it is impossible to be certain of the dating.

What is certain is the general drift of Paul's argument. He has been stressing that none of the apostles were in touch with him in order to impart the gospel to him either before, during, or immediately following his conversion. Now he is adding that in addition to that a considerable length of time passed before he even met one of the disciples in Jerusalem. What is more, even then he stayed no more than a fortnight and met only Peter and James.

Why did Paul go to meet Peter? It has been said that the two great apostles probably did not spend the entire fifteen days talking about the weather. No doubt they talked about Christ, and Paul used the occasion to enrich his already firm grasp of the gospel by the stories Peter could tell of the life and actual teachings of Jesus. There is no reason to think that Paul denied the importance of knowing these things. On the other hand, the wording of the text in Galatians suggests that Paul went up primarily to get acquainted with Peter (cf. Burton). The Greek verb (*historeō*) is the word from which we get our word "history." It suggests the telling of a story. Paul would have told his story, Peter his. So the two leading apostles—Paul, the apostle to the Gentiles, and Peter, the apostle to the Jews—became acquainted and encouraged each other in their forthcoming work. For the point of Paul's argument, it is important to note that this was a private visit and not one designed to secure the support of any human authorities.

19 Perhaps Paul's legalizing opponents would take advantage of this admission of a visit to Peter to attempt to show that Paul was dependent on the Jerusalem apostles after all. Well, let them! Paul will even admit that he also saw James, the brother of the Lord, who was later to play such an important part in the Jerusalem Council. A reading of Acts 9:26–29 might suggest that Paul was introduced to all the apostles by Barnabas, but he is affirming that, in point of fact, he met only two.

20 The foregoing are facts, whatever anyone else may say, and here Paul affirms quite solemnly that the account he has given is accurate (for other instances of similarly strong assertions, see Rom 9:1; 2 Cor 1:23; 11:31; 1 Thess 2:5; 1 Tim 2:7). The assertion can be made to apply in a general way to the entire account preceding it, but it is best explained as Paul's answer to a specific charge that he had been misrepresenting his relationship to the Twelve. That Paul seems to be answering specific charges should be borne in mind when we meet some difficulties later in fitting his remarks into a full chronology. Machen observed years ago in the Sprunt lectures that here in Galatians each historical event seems to be related in order to answer a specific argument raised by Paul's opponents and not to provide a full chronology of the preceding years (*The Origin of Paul's Religion,* [1921. Reprint, Grand Rapids: Eerdmans, 1947], pp. 85, 86).

21 Strict chronology is not the main concern in this verse either; if that were so, the correct order of the areas Paul visited would be Cilicia and then Syria, as indicated by Acts 9:30; 11:25, 26. Actually, he is merely indicating that in the next period of his life he worked, not in the immediate area of Jerusalem—in Judea, where one might suppose him to have been under the authority and subject to the review of the other apostles—but far away from Jerusalem in the regions of Syria and Cilicia where he was by necessity his own authority. Tarsus, Paul's hometown, was in Cilicia. According to Acts 11:25, Barnabas went there to get Paul when he needed his help for the work in Antioch. Antioch was the capital of Syria. Here Paul carried on a long and fruitful ministry after Barnabas's call.

22 As a result of his work in the north and of his paying no new visits to Jerusalem, Paul was personally unknown to the Christians who lived in Judea. "Unknown"! It is a striking word to use of the man who, after Jesus himself, has probably influenced the world more than any other who has ever lived. No doubt, Paul could have been an instant celebrity. Instead, he worked for long years in relative obscurity. It was only after a very long period that Paul began his famed missionary journeys in response to the call of the Holy Spirit through the Christians at Antioch.

23,24 The word "only" (v.23) warns us that we are not to take this sentence as a summary of an exciting and well-attended report that we might assume to have been on the mind of everyone in Judea during the years of Paul's Cilician and Syrian ministry. The opposite is the case. The Christians had heard of Paul's conversion—at the time it happened. But after that he apparently dropped so completely from sight that he was almost forgotten. The only report heard was that the one who long ago was persecuting the church is now preaching the gospel. This sense of the verse is also demanded by the flow of Paul's argument, which is to stress his isolation from everything happening in Jerusalem. Would that there were more such contentment among Christians today—the contentment to be unknown!

There would be, if this were the goal—to have God glorified (v.24). Too often those in prominent places within the church seek their own glory in Christian service rather than the glory of God.

Notes

19 It is uncertain from the Gr. precisely to what the words εἰ μὴ (*ei mē,* "except") refer. If they refer only to the verb εἶδον (*eidon,* "I saw"), then the sentence itself does not necessarily designate James as an apostle. If they refer to the whole of the preceding statement, then James is numbered among them. In this case, however, as Burton notes (in loc.), the view that would make the exception refer to only part of the preceding clause is excluded, for Paul can hardly mean that of all the people in Jerusalem at the time of his visit he saw none but Peter and James. James, the brother of the Lord (also mentioned later in chapter 2), was therefore considered an apostle, a fact supporting the view that the apostolate was broader than the very limited circle of the Twelve, even apart from Paul's claim to be numbered with them. Lightfoot has a lengthy note on James as well as the other "pillar" apostles (pp. 292–374).

Ἀδελφός (*adelphos,* "brother") can mean (1) a true brother born of the same father and mother, (2) a stepbrother, and (3) a cousin. But there is no reason to take the word in any other than the first and most natural sense here, particularly as Mark 6:3 indicates that as many as six other children had been born to Mary. It may have been this family relationship that compelled Paul to make James's acquaintance. The theory that these were sons and daughters of Joseph by a former marriage is purely a product of Roman Catholic thinking regarding the supposed perpetual virginity of Mary rather than the product of sound exegesis or even probability (cf. Lightfoot, pp. 252–291).

C. *Paul's Relationship to the Other Apostles* (2:1–21)

1. *The council at Jerusalem*

2:1–5

1 Fourteen years later I went up again to Jerusalem, this time with Barnabas. I took Titus along also. 2 I went in response to a revelation and set before them the gospel that I preach among the Gentiles. But I did this privately to those who seemed to be leaders, for fear that I was running or had run my race in vain. 3 Yet not even Titus, who was with me, was compelled to be circumcised, even though he was a Greek. 4 [This matter arose] because some false brothers had infiltrated our ranks to spy on the freedom we have in Christ Jesus and to make us slaves. 5 We did not give in to them for a moment, so that the truth of the gospel might remain with you.

Chapter 2 begins a significantly different section of Paul's argument. There is a connection, of course. Paul is still speaking of his apostolic authority. But now he wants to demonstrate the essential unity existing between himself and the Twelve, whereas in chapter 1 his focus was on his independence from them. There are four important differences between the first ten verses of this chapter and those preceding it: (1) There is a new subject—not the source of Paul's gospel, but the nature of the gospel itself centered in the issue of circumcision for Gentiles; (2) there is a new aspect of Paul's relationship to the Twelve—not independence from them, as during the early years of his ministry, but harmony and cooperation; (3) there is a new period of Paul's ministry and of early church history; and (4) there is a new conclusion—namely, that in the essential content of the gospel and of the plan for missionary activity, Paul and the Twelve were one.

This is also the first point historically at which Paul came into sharp conflict with the heresy now troubling the Galatian churches. What was to be done about this distinct point of view? Was it a minor matter to be passed over quickly? Was it an issue on which to seek compromise? Should a battle be fought? It would seem that few besides Paul and perhaps Barnabas recognized the full importance of the issue at the time. So it is to Paul's steadfastness in conflict that Christians owe, humanly speaking, the continuation of the full gospel of grace in subsequent church history. The issue is important today because many would claim that doctrine is not of great importance, that compromise should always be sought, and that the value of human works alongside the reality of grace should be recognized.

1 In spite of Paul's seeming to date the period of three years from the time of his conversion, rather than from his return to Damascus (1:17, 18), it is most probable that the fourteen years mentioned here are to be reckoned from the end, not the beginning, of the first three years. Lightfoot rightly notes that the argument seems to demand this interpretation and the language suggests it. The point is obviously not how long after his conversion Paul made this visit, but how long after last seeing the apostles he went up to Jerusalem. Besides, Paul undoubtedly thought of the years of labor in Syria and Cilicia as a block of time or a set period of his ministry, and his point is that these years were broken only by the trouble from the legalizers and by the revelation to go up to Jerusalem to argue the cause of Gentile liberty. The most probable dating would place Paul's conversion at approximately A.D. 32; the visit to see Peter, in A.D. 35; and the council, in A.D. 49. (The correctness of these dates depends, of course, on the actual date of Christ's crucifixion.)

Barnabas and Titus accompanied Paul, though Luke does not mention the presence of Titus in his account of the council. There seems to be an order in the delegation from Antioch. Paul went up, accompanied by Barnabas, and taking Titus along. The order would therefore be: Paul, Barnabas, and Titus. The presence of Titus is best explained by Paul's desire for a test case, as shown by vv.3–5.

2 Luke says that Paul and Barnabas went up to Jerusalem as the result of a decision by the "brothers" at Antioch. Yet there is no real contradiction between Luke's account and Paul's statement about his having gone up by revelation. Either the church at Antioch itself prayed about what should be done and then commissioned Paul and Barnabas in response to what they believed God revealed they should do, or else the revelation was a parallel and confirming one to Paul. It makes little difference whether the revelation prompted or else confirmed the church's decision. Undoubtedly, Paul mentions the matter only to emphasize once again that at no time, either earlier or at this late point, was he at the call of the other apostles. On the contrary, his movements as well as his gospel are to be attributed directly to the revealed will of God.

The discussion of Paul's experiences in Jerusalem will go on as far as v.10 but the essence of the matter and its outcome are already suggested in the second half of this statement. Paul spoke privately to those who were the apparent leaders of the Jerusalem church, for he wished to avoid public remarks or a decision, whether valid or not, that could harm the work he had already done or was planning to do among the Gentiles. The phrase "for fear that I was running or had run my race in vain" must be taken in this sense, for the only other possibility—"for fear I had been mistaken about the gospel" —is inconceivable in view of Paul's previous insistence upon the divine source and truthfulness of his teaching. Here was a great issue, and Paul recognized that the decision reached could have terrible consequences for the church's missionary outreach—if the doctrine of grace were not boldly and clearly upheld. What happened at the council, then? Obviously, Paul's point was upheld; for the present tense of the verb "to preach" shows that the gospel preached by Paul in the early years was the gospel still being preached by him years later.

3–5 In the context of relating his contacts with the apostolic leaders at Jerusalem Paul now introduces an instance in which he claims to have defended the purity of the gospel from the encroachments of those who would have mixed aspects of the Mosaic law with grace as the way of salvation. This incident was the attempt of the Jewish legalists to force the rite of circumcision on Titus. The outcome of the struggle, as Paul said, was a successful defense of the gospel.

It would seem that the facts of such an event would be beyond question, but this is not the case. Either because of Paul's care in handling a difficult and delicate situation or merely from the fact that the grammar of the passage has suffered in his dictation, commentators from the time of Marcion to the present have been puzzled about what Paul was actually trying to say. Does Paul say that he refused to yield to the demands laid upon him, as most of the translations indicate? Or does he maintain that for a short time he did in fact yield? To whom is Paul referring in v.5, to the apostles or to the false brothers of v.4? Finally, can we even be sure that Titus was not circumcised, since even such careful commentators as Bacon ("The Reading *hois oude* in Gal 2:5," JBL, 42, 1923, pp. 69–80) and Lake ("Was Titus Circumcised?" Exp., 7th series [1], 1906, pp. 236–245) have maintained that he was? These questions have immense bearing on the relationship of Paul to the apostles at Jerusalem, the character of Paul himself, and the general defense of Christian liberty against a reactivation of law.

One source of these problems lies in the fact that the Greek MSS of Galatians vary greatly in rendering v.5. Some omit the words "to whom" and also the negative. In these MSS the sentence reads very smoothly: "But on account of the false brothers. . .we yielded for a time." That would mean that Paul allowed Titus to be circumcised, either giving in to the legalizers who demanded that he yield (so Tertullian and Zahn) or to the apostles who requested him to yield (Bacon), in order that in some way the truth of the gospel might continue with the Gentile Christians. In favor of this reading are the authority of some MSS and good syntax.

On the other hand, there are major difficulties. First, it is hard to see how Paul could admit that he yielded to the demands to have Titus circumcised and still maintain that he had defended the "truth of the gospel." Paul speaks of the gospel again and again in these chapters (1:6, 9, 11; 2:2, 5). How could he have been so certain that he had defended the gospel if, in fact, Titus had been circumcised? Again, Paul's description of the legalistic party is so vehement that it is hard to believe, if only for this reason, that he submitted to them even for a time. Paul says that these men were traitors, "false brothers," and that they had sneaked into the Christian camp to "spy on" the liberty of Christians. Their intention was to bring the Galatians into slavery to the law.

The other possible reading of the text is to retain both the words "to whom" and the negative. This gives the translation "to whom we did not give the subjection demanded even for an hour." With this approach, the phrase itself is clear enough and seems, at least on the surface, to be in keeping with the tone of the Epistle. But by doing this, we create another problem. For if one begins the phrase with the words "to whom," it is impossible to complete the sense of v.4, and the entire verse stands as an anacoluthon, that is, as a series of phrases without a grammatical relationship to the passage.

What are we to do in such circumstances? It is the contention of this writer that the more difficult reading should stand in spite of the anacoluthon. This view is supported by the best principles of textual criticism and by a reconstructed syntax for the passage.

Four factors require the decision to retain the words "to whom" and the negative: (1) They have the best support, being found in most of the Greek uncials and the Chester Beatty papyri. (2) There is absolutely no reason for demanding perfect grammar when approaching a text of Scripture. Difficult grammatical structure is an explanation of the variants resulting from attempts to amend it, but it is not susceptible to rejection solely on grounds of being nongrammatical. (3) Paul's writings give evidence of other cases in which we may observe the results of scribes or commentators who eliminated a negative, thereby supposing themselves to be improving the text (cf. variants on Gal 5:8 and Rom 5:14). (4) The most difficult reading of a text is most likely to be the correct one, for variants are then best explained as attempts to improve the text and eliminate the difficulty. It follows that the reading "to whom" and the negative may be accepted as that of the original autograph and that the variant readings must be explained as alterations aimed at eliminating the problems raised by its interpretation.

To retain the words "to whom" and the negative is, however, also to retain the difficulty of relating v.4 to the passage. In general, there have been three major approaches to doing this: (1) attempts to relate the anacoluthon of v.4 to some following word in the passage, (2) those attempting to make it limit something that precedes, and (3) those which make it limit something to be supplied from the preceding (cf. Burton, pp. 79–82, for full details). The best interpretation is that v.4 is related to the thought of pressure being applied to Paul by the leaders at Jerusalem in deference to the false brothers, yet successfully resisted by Paul in defense of Gentile liberty.

Here the weight of the historical context is impressive. There is the picture of the apostles at Jerusalem, wavering on neutral ground, tending to advise compliance on Paul's part, and then finally coming out for Paul by declaring openly for freedom from the law. This attitude is suggested in the following verses, both in the attitude of reserve Paul seems to have encountered at Jerusalem (2:6, 9) and in the related wavering of Peter at Antioch. Moreover, this fits in with the fact of greatest certainty; namely, that the conflict was primarily between the false brothers and Paul and that in the end (whether wavering before that time or not) the apostles stood solidly with Paul and Barnabas. Such a view would permit us to translate v.4 nearly as it stands, though introducing the word "that" to indicate the relationship of the verse to something understood from the preceding—"And that for the sake of the false brethren." The NIV takes this general approach when it translates, "[This matter arose] because some false brothers had infiltrated our ranks."

Paul's references to the false brothers in v.4 entail a military metaphor, used to indicate the subversive and militant nature of the evil that Paul was fighting. The term "false brothers" (*pseudadelphous*) is used only twice in the NT (here and in 2 Cor 11:26). In each case Paul uses the term of those who are not in fact Christians, though pretending to be so. The overtone is that of a traitor or spy. "Infiltrated" (*pareisaktous*) is used in the same way, as in 2 Peter 2:1, where we are told of those who will "secretly introduce" destructive heresies to weaken and ruin the church. In the LXX reading of 2 Samuel

10:3, "spy" (*kataskopeō*) is used of the servants of David who, according to his enemies, had come "to search the city, and to spy it out, and to overthrow it." Similarly, Paul speaks of the desire of the legalizers "to make us slaves" (*katadoulōsousin*), in the manner of those who would take a city by stealth or force in order to place the inhabitants in chains.

Paul's defense of the gospel he had received from God was not made for any personal or selfish reasons, but "so that the truth of the gospel might remain" with believers (v.5). The word "truth" has a decided emphasis in contrast to the falseness mentioned in the preceding verse. Therefore, it cannot mean only "the truths" of the gospel or even "the true message" of the gospel; it must mean "the true gospel" as opposed to "the false gospel" being taught by the false brothers. There is also a possibility that Paul is thinking of his earlier reference to that other gospel, which is really "no gospel at all" (1:6, 7).

The idea of the true gospel is prominent and very significant, so much so that many have seen the necessity of rounding out the phrase in their commentaries. Ridderbos has "its true, unmodified content." Lightfoot says, "the gospel in its integrity." Calvin writes, "its genuine purity, or, which means the same thing, its pure and entire doctrine." This is the issue! The gospel in its entirety, or that which is no gospel at all! It is the importance of this issue that made Paul adamant in his relationship to all others, Christians and non-Christians, and that must make all who know the Lord Jesus Christ and who love the gospel equally adamant in their thought, speech, and writings at the present time.

Notes

1 The words "then" (ἔπειτα, *epeita*) and "again" (πάλιν, *palin*) have been taken as indicating that this was a *second* visit to Jerusalem, i.e., the visit immediately following the first trip to see Peter. This is a possible interpretation, of course, but in themselves the words do not necessarily imply this. *Epeita* need not be any more than a general particle of chronological succession, indicating that the events of chapter 2 happened after those of chapter 1. And *palin* means "again" much more than it means "a second time." The verse does not rule out the possibility that the famine visit of Acts 11 intruded between the two visits mentioned in this letter.

3 Why "not even" (ἀλλ' οὐδὲ, *all' oude*)? The answer depends on the significance of Titus's having been with Paul and, thus, on Paul's intention in having Titus accompany him. Lightfoot suggests two possible answers: (1) that Titus, who was Paul's companion, would be in constant contact with Jewish Christians and might well have adopted a conciliatory attitude toward them, and (2) that great pressure had been brought to bear on Titus by the legalistic party. These suggestions cannot be separated from the significance of Titus's presence as a test case. If we consider that Titus had been brought to Jerusalem mainly for the purpose of this dispute, then Paul's "not even" would effectually say, "And they were so far from winning their case that not even Titus, whom I had brought along for just this purpose, was compelled to be circumcised. How, then, can they think to require the same thing of you?"

"Being a Gentile" (Ἕλλην ὤν, *Hellēn ōn*) is added for argumentative effect; for, taken together with the fact of Titus's presence with Paul, it points up the significance of the event. In English tr. this might best be captured by the reading "though he was a Gentile" (NIV: "even though he was a Greek").

2. *Paul and the pillar apostles*

2:6–10

6As for those who seemed to be important—whatever they were makes no difference to me; God does not judge by external appearance—those men added nothing to my message. 7On the contrary, they saw that I had been given the task of preaching the gospel to the Gentiles, just as Peter had been given the task of preaching the gospel to the Jews. 8For God, who was at work in the ministry of Peter as an apostle to the Jews, was also at work in my ministry as an apostle to the Gentiles. 9James, Peter and John, those reputed to be pillars, gave me and Barnabas the right hand of fellowship when they recognized the grace given to me. They agreed that we should go to the Gentiles, and they to the Jews. 10All they asked was that we should continue to remember the poor, the very thing I was eager to do.

6 As in v.4, the construction is again broken, with the result that the first six words of the Greek text (followed by an interjection concerning God's refusal to judge by appearances) are left hanging. Undoubtedly, Paul wished to revert to the subject of v.2 in order to point out that, having laid before the pillar apostles the gospel he had been preaching, he found they had nothing to add to his message. If he had continued v.6 in this way, without the interrupted thought and the new beginning, the words "and from those who seemed to be important" (Gr.) would have been followed by a phrase like "I received nothing." Instead, Paul's thought is interrupted, and he hastens to add that whatever the historical advantages of the original apostles might have been in that they had known Jesus after the flesh (this is the force of the imperfect "were"), this was not important either to him or to God—and they added nothing to his message.

Four times in this chapter—once earlier (v.2), twice in this verse, and once later (v.9)—Paul refers to the three major figures at Jerusalem in an unusual way. The persons in question are James, Peter, and John, as is apparent from v.9. They are described as "those who seemed to be leaders," "those who seemed to be important," and "those reputed to be pillars." Why this unusual and perhaps even differential way of referring to them?

Most commentators are reluctant to admit that Paul may be deprecating in any way those who were apostles before him. Some, like Burton, deny it outright, pointing out (quite properly) that Paul's obvious intention in these verses is to show his unity with the apostles both in spirit and doctrine. He argues that it is not likely that Paul would speak poorly of them in the same context. Other commentators admit the slightly deflating tone of these expressions but refer them to something other than Paul's own opinion of the apostles—that is, either to the exaggerated claims concerning them made by the legalizers or to the exaggerated views entertained by the Galatians or both (cf. Lightfoot, Guthrie, Ridderbos, Stott, and others). Over against these views needs to be placed the fact that a very good case can be made for the existence of a real though balanced note of disparagement on Paul's own part and for this in itself being the best explanation for the grammatical difficulties throughout the passage.

First, while it is true that the phrase "those of reputation" (*hoi dokountes*)—"those who seemed to be important," NIV—is not necessarily deprecating, nevertheless it can convey this meaning. Lightfoot (in loc.) gives several examples from Plato. More pertinent is the fact that this sense of the word occurs again in Galatians—"If anyone thinks he is something when he is nothing, he deceives himself" (Gal 6:3).

Second, the very repetition of the phrase in the Greek text seems ominous. It is hard to explain exactly why this is so, but the effect of the repetition is much like the effect of Antony's repetition of the word "honorable" concerning Brutus in his eulogy at the funeral of Julius Caesar in Shakespeare's play. The more he speaks the word, the less honorable Brutus and the other conspirators appear.

Third, the expression Paul uses grows fuller and slightly stronger with each repetition. The apostles are at first called "those who seemed to be leaders." Next, they are "those who seemed to be important." Finally, they are "those reputed to be pillars," at which point the veiled reference is dropped and those of reputation are named—James, Peter, and John. Cole, who notes this progression, observes that it is as if "Paul's rising indignation is finding the studied courtesy of 2:2 impossible to maintain" (in loc.).

Fourth, the story of Peter's conduct at Antioch, which immediately follows this section, lends credence to the feeling that Paul's disappointment with the conduct of those who should have been leaders in this great crisis of faith and doctrine but who failed to take the lead is increasingly spilling over into the letter as he retells and (to some extent) relives the events of the council. According to this interpretation, Paul felt that the Jerusalem apostles did not perform on a level commensurate with the reputation they held, either at the council or (in Peter's case) after it. If they had been alert to the issue, the legalizers would not have succeeded even to the degree they did.

Fifth, the delicate situation lying behind these verses alone explains the grammatical difficulties. To understand them, one must see Paul as torn between a desire to stress the basic unity that did exist between himself and the Twelve and the need to be honest in indicating that, so far as he was concerned, the apostles did not perform well in the crisis. Thus, his initial allusion to the apostles in v.2 seems to him on second thought to be too vague. He breaks in with the Titus incident, but again not indicating clearly enough that it was the apostles who for the sake of harmony were urging that Titus be circumcised. Finally, Paul picks up the matter of the apostles again (v.6) and eventually names them (v.9), this time indicating that those who were reported to be "pillars" almost failed to do the work of supporting the gospel.

Looked at grammatically, the entire passage from v.2 to v.10 is a problem. But if these verses are considered against the historical context just outlined, they not only make sense but also greatly increase admiration for the apostle Paul. How many men would be able to strike such an emotional balance in as highly charged a situation as this and at the same time make the points they need to make in writing?

Paul has done the following: (1) recognized the position and authority of the Jerusalem apostles without diminishing his own authority in the slightest; (2) indicated, in opposition to the exaggerated claims about them made by the legalizers, that the apostles were men after all and hence not always perfect in their initial reactions or conduct; (3) decisively separated the gospel and policies of the Twelve, for all their weaknesses, from the gospel and policies of the legalizers; and (4) taken note of the fact that he and the Twelve, rather than the legalizers and the Twelve, stood together. Eventually, he will even show that the agreement between himself and the Twelve was cordial both in relation to their respective spheres of ministry ("James, Peter and John . . . gave me and Barnabas the right hand of fellowship") and in regard to the special obligation of the Gentiles toward the Jerusalem poor ("the very thing I was eager to do").

So far as the gospel Paul preached was concerned, the Jerusalem conference had two results. Negatively, the Twelve "added nothing" to Paul. Paul's gospel was complete because received by revelation. Positively, however, the "pillars" extended to Paul the right hand of fellowship—that is, they recognized that all of them had been entrusted with the same gospel and that they differed only in respect to the different fields they had been assigned to preach it in.

7 There is minor support for this interpretation of the conference in Paul's use of the aorist participle "having seen," or "when they had seen." It implies a change of mind by the Twelve as a result of Paul and Barnabas's having reported on all that God had done through them among the Gentiles (cf. Acts 15:4). At first they were skeptical and uncertain, but later they came to stand with Paul. The participle gives the reason for the step taken in v.9—i.e., having seen the results of their ministries, the Twelve gave Paul and Barnabas "the right hand of fellowship."

KJV contains an unfortunate rendering at this point in the letter, because the phrases "the gospel of the uncircumcision" and "the gospel of the circumcision" suggest two different gospels, which was a thought not at all in Paul's mind. The NIV guards against this error by rendering the same words "the gospel to the Gentiles" and "the gospel to the Jews." But in this case, Paul's direct allusion to the underlying issue of circumcision vanishes.

8 Just as the gospel is one gospel, no matter to whom preached, so also are the commissioning and enabling of those who preach it one. The reason is that the one who commissioned and empowered both Peter and Paul is God.

9 The exact use and order of the names of the leading apostles in this verse should not escape notice. First, the order obviously corresponds to the relative positions and work of James and Peter as recorded in Acts. Peter was the great missionary. Hence, when Paul is speaking of the ministry to the Jews, Peter is prominent and James is not mentioned (vv.7, 8). In dealing with a particular and official act of the Jerusalem church, however, James (who apparently presided at the council) is mentioned in the first position with the names of Peter and John following. Lightfoot (in loc.) also points out, no doubt rightly, that the fact that James is first called "James, the Lord's brother" (1:19) but here only "James" is explained clearly by the Acts narrative. At the earlier visit to Jerusalem there were two prominent Jameses in the city—James, the Lord's brother, and James, the son of Zebedee. So, in describing that visit, Paul identifies the proper James. By the time of this visit (the visit of Acts 15), James, the son of Zebedee, had been put to death by Herod.

10 Paul had already shown a concern for the poor at the time of the famine visit when he traveled to Jerusalem with Barnabas as a representative of the church at Antioch (Acts 11:27–30). At the time of the council he was reminded of this good work and encouraged to pursue it. Out of this request, with which he was in great sympathy, arose the collection from among the Gentile churches that occupied so large a part in Paul's later thought and writings (cf. Acts 24:17; Rom 15:26; 1 Cor 16:3, 4; 2 Cor 8 and 9). The change from the plural first person ("we") to the singular ("I") may reflect Paul and Barnabas's parting company by the time the collection was actually taken up.

Notes

6 Δοκέω (*dokeō*) is an old Gr. verb to which the noun δόξα (*doxa,* "glory") is related. It means "to believe" or "to think," but intransitively "to have the appearance of" or "to seem." It is this second meaning that occurs in Galatians. In later years the verb usually meant "to hold an opinion of" and then "to hold [only a good] opinion of." Here the use is neutral and related primarily to external circumstances.

9 Γνόντες (*gnontes,* tr. "recognized" but literally "knowing") differs from ἰδόντες (*idontes,* "saw," v.7) in pointing to an internal conviction as opposed to an external awareness of a situation. The apostles "saw" that Paul's ministry had been blessed by God, for there were many converts. Out of this awareness grew the deeper conviction that the grace of God was with him. The change of "Cephas" to "Peter" and the placing of Peter before James in some MSS is a corruption of the Western text made for ecclesiastical purposes. This change of "Cephas" to "Peter" also occurs at 1:18, 2:11, 14 in these MSS.

---

3. *Peter comes to Antioch*

2:11–14

> [11]When Peter came to Antioch, I opposed him to his face, because he was in the wrong. [12]Before certain men came from James, he used to eat with the Gentiles. But when they arrived, he began to draw back and separate himself from the Gentiles because he was afraid of those who belonged to the circumcision group. [13]The other Jews joined him in his hypocrisy, so that by their hypocrisy even Barnabas was led astray.
>
> [14]When I saw that they were not acting in line with the truth of the gospel, I said to Peter in front of them all, "You are a Jew, yet you live like a Gentile and not like a Jew. How is it, then, that you force Gentiles to follow Jewish customs?

The account of the Jerusalem Council is followed immediately by another historical incident, the last in Paul's series, in which he dramatically supports his claim to possess an authority equal to and independent of that of the other apostles. In the opening part of this chapter, Paul has demonstrated his essential unity with those who were apostles before him. Now he shows that he stood so firmly grounded in the gospel that he opposed even Peter, contradicting him publicly when Peter's conduct at Antioch threatened to compromise that gospel.

For some reason, Peter had left the Jewish community at Jerusalem and had gone to the Gentile city of Antioch in Syria. If this event took place after the council, the visit may have originated in Peter's desire to see what Paul had reported concerning the work of God there, but it is impossible to be certain. Whatever the reason, at Antioch Peter discovered a community of Jewish and Gentile Christians living together and, in particular, eating together in apparent disregard of Jewish dietary customs. This was probably against the practice then prevailing in Jerusalem even after the council, but God had already shown Peter what he was to do in such situations. God had told Peter in the vision of the great sheet, "Do not call anything impure that God had made clean" (Acts 10:15). So Peter, no doubt remembering this and being impressed with the example of Jewish/Gentile harmony, joined with other Jews in eating with his Gentile brothers. According to Paul, Peter did this for some time, because the imperfect tense of the verb implies that he ate with the Gentiles not once, on a single occasion, but on a regular basis, habitually. In this decision, Peter went beyond the letter of the decrees of the council, for though the council had acknowledged the right of freedom from the law for Gentiles, it had nevertheless retained the observance of the law for Jews. Now Peter was declaring that the Jew as well as the Gentile was free from Mosaic legislation.

After a time, some influential Jews arrived in Antioch from Jerusalem, giving out that they were representatives of James. They were the legalists or, at the very least, strict

Jews. Peter's practice shocked them. Not only was his conduct not required by the Jerusalem agreement, they might have argued, it was actually contrary to it; for Peter was encouraging a disregard of the Mosaic law by Jewish believers. These persons brought such pressure to bear on Peter that though he was unconvinced by their views, he nevertheless gradually detached himself from the Gentile fellowship and began to eat with Jews only. Moreover, his conduct drew others away with him so that when Paul returned (it is hard to understand how he could have been present during these events and have let them go as far as they did without protest), he found a church divided and the Gentiles under an unwarranted pressure either to accept the division or to conform to the legalistic standards of Judaism as the means of avoiding it.

What did Paul do? Since the schism was public, Paul confronted Peter publicly, charging him with inconsistency and stating once again that the works of the law have no place in God's plan of salvation through the death of Christ. From this response, the Galatians were to realize that Paul was not a self-appointed apostle, nor even a worker appointed and approved by the Twelve. He was rather a full apostle in his own right, who could therefore speak with full authority even, if necessary, in opposition to another apostle.

11 It is not known exactly when Peter came to Antioch, but the flow of events suggests that it was after the council. It is true that the verb "had come" allows the view that Paul is here reverting to an earlier incident; if this is so, then Peter's defense of Paul at Jerusalem in Acts 15 naturally reflects their earlier confrontation and conversation at Antioch. Some have defended this view on the basis that Peter could not have acted as he did following the council. But this overlooks both the reality of human inconsistency (even among the best people) and the fact that the Antioch incident reflects an entirely new situation. There was: (1) a new issue—foods rather than circumcision; (2) a new area of the faith—Christian living rather than the basis of salvation; and (3) a new subject—Jewish liberty rather than the liberty of Gentile Christians. This dispute could have followed naturally upon the compromise reached at the council.

12 Here is the reason why Peter was in the wrong or stood condemned. It was not, it must be noted, a case of Peter's simply making an honest mistake. The Peter who had received the vision prior to going to the house of Cornelius and who had defended Paul at the council was not fooled by the arguments of the legalizers. The difficulty was that he gradually gave in to pressure exerted by the legalizers, even though he knew what was right. In other words, Peter played the hypocrite. "The same Peter who had denied his Lord for fear of a maid-servant now denied Him again for fear of the circumcision party" (Stott, in loc.).

13 Unfortunately, conduct such as Peter's is not inconsequential, neither in his day nor now. So one is not surprised to read that other Jews, including Barnabas, were led away by his dissimulation. If Peter had been a lesser man or less prominent, the defection might have been less serious. But this was Peter, the pillar apostle, the companion of the Lord during his earthly ministry!

What Peter did moved others. It is obvious that any Christian must give heed to his actions and the greater the position or responsibility, the more important those actions become.

14 Paul has already shown that he opposed Peter to his face because he was wrong (v.11), but we are not to think that he did this because he loved exposing error or, even less, because he loved an argument or wanted to enhance his own prestige. Paul's real concern was for the truth of the gospel. It was not a matter of personalities. To the Corinthians he wrote, "What, after all, is Apollos? And what is Paul?" (1 Cor 3:5). It is not a matter of trivial forms or ceremonies. What was at stake was the gospel itself. Hence, Paul acted out of the very concern that Peter lacked.

This is the second time that Paul has spoken of "the truth of the gospel" (vv.5, 14)—the good news that men and women do not become accepted with God because of anything they have done or can do but solely on the basis of God's grace shown in the death and resurrection of Jesus Christ. Moreover, on the basis of this death all who believe become fully accepted by God and are accepted equally. Peter's conduct compromised this principle, for it implied that there could be a superiority in some Christians based on race or traditions.

It is not enough merely to understand and accept the gospel, as Peter did, nor even to defend it, as he did at Jerusalem. A Christian must also practice the gospel consistently, allowing it to regulate all areas of his conduct.

Notes

---

11 This section of the letter has always been the basis of dispute for historical and doctrinal reasons, though the events themselves should be clear. In the Rom. church there have been various attempts to defend Peter from the charge of hypocrisy. Some have argued that another Peter, rather than Simon Peter, is indicated. Some have taught that the debate was staged in order to dramatize the issue for the edification of the Antiochian Christians. In the 19th century these verses became a primary basis for the historical reconstruction of early church history by Baur and others of the Tübingen school. According to this school, the gospels of Peter and Paul were in antithesis in the Hegelian sense and were synthesized into early Catholicism. This view is unsupported by the context. The point of the passage is not that there was an antithesis between the two great apostles. They were actually one. The point is that Peter did not live up to his convictions and, therefore, needed to be straightened out by Paul.

12 There is no doubt that those who came from Jerusalem belonged to the circumcision party, but nothing more may be inferred from Paul's statements. That they came from James does not necessarily imply that theirs was an official visit. Even less does it suggest that James endorsed their position. Lightfoot argues that they may well have come vested with some powers they proceeded to abuse.

---

4. *Justification by faith alone*

2:15–21

15"We who are Jews by birth and not 'Gentile sinners' 16know that a man is not justified by observing the law, but by faith in Jesus Christ. So we, too, have put our faith in Christ Jesus that we may be justified by faith in Christ and not by observing the law, because by observing the law no one will be justified.

17"If, while we seek to be justified in Christ, it becomes evident that we ourselves are sinners, does that mean that Christ promotes sin? Absolutely not! 18If I rebuild what I destroyed, I prove that I am a lawbreaker. 19For through the law I died to the law so that I might live for God. 20I have been crucified with Christ and I no longer live, but Christ lives in me. The life I live in the body, I live by faith in the Son of God, who loved me and gave himself for me. 21 I do not set aside the grace of God, for if righteousness could be gained through the law, Christ died for nothing!"

The verses that conclude this chapter contain capsule statements of some of the most significant truths of Christianity. In particular, Paul clearly states the doctrine of justification by grace through faith and defends it over against the traditional objection that justification by faith leads to lawlessness. The words "justify" and "justification" occur in these verses for the first time—the verb, three times in v.16 and once in v.17; the noun, in v.21—as Paul now begins to develop the message that is central to the letter, to his gospel, and indeed to Christianity generally. This statement flows out of the situation at Antioch and anticipates the fuller argument of the same doctrine occurring in chapters 3 and 4. "After working through the rest of the Epistle, one turns back to [these verses] and finds in [them] the whole truth in embryo," as Ramsay states.

15 It is impossible to say precisely where Paul's remarks to Peter on the occasion of Peter's hypocrisy at Antioch leave off and Paul's direct remarks to the Christians of Galatia begin. In trying to answer that question, one is faced with the same kind of problem faced by interpreters of some parts of John's Gospel. Some commentators end the direct quotation at v.14. Others, like the NIV, carry it to the end of the chapter. Most likely, the truth lies in Paul's gradually moving away from the situation at Antioch but doing it so naturally that he himself was unconcerned with and perhaps even unaware of the transition. At the beginning, he speaks of "you" (meaning Peter) and "we" (meaning himself, Peter, and other Jews), undoubtedly with the situation at Antioch in mind. Later he is probably thinking of the broader situation that faced the Gentile churches.

The argument is addressed to Jews at this point, and the words "who are" must be supplied—"we *who are* Jews by nature." Paul is speaking of natural-born Jews; that is, those who possessed the advantages of a privileged birth and a revealed religion. These are great advantages, as Paul admits elsewhere (cf. Rom 3:1, 2; 9:4, 5). But even so great advantages as these are inadequate for achieving a state of righteousness before God. Even Jews must be saved through faith. It is folly, therefore, to attempt to reestablish Judaism as a base for Christianity.

In Jewish speech the phrase "Gentile sinners" was used seriously as an opposite concept to all that being Jewish implied. In Paul's mouth, the phrase has an ironic ring.

16 This is one of the most important verses in the Epistle. As already noted, it contains the first mention of the words "justify" or "justification." "Law" is mentioned for the first time. This is also the first place in the letter in which "faith" is brought forward as the indispensible channel of salvation.

"Justify" (*dikaioō;* noun, *dikaiōsunē;* adjective, *dikaios*) is a forensic term borrowed from the law courts. It means "to declare righteous or innocent." The opposite of "to justify" is "to condemn" or "to pronounce guilty." Such a term involves an objective standard, and since righteousness is understood to be the unique characteristic of God, that standard must be the divine standard. In themselves, all persons fall short of this standard—"For all have sinned and fall short of the glory of God" (Rom 3:23). But in Christ, God declares all righteous who believe, imputing divine righteousness to them. In this sense, justification does not express an ethical change or influence (though ethical changes follow); rather, it expresses the judicial action of God apart from human merit according to which the guilty are pardoned, acquitted, and then reinstated as God's children and as fellow heirs with Jesus Christ.

This experience does not happen automatically to all men. It is true that God justifies, but he does so only as he unites a man or woman to Christ, a union that takes place only through the channel of human faith. Faith is the means, not the source, of justification. Faith is trust. It begins with knowledge, so it is not blind. It builds on facts, so it is not speculation. It stakes its life on the outcome, so it is not impractical. Faith is trusting Christ and proving his promises. The expression in the middle of v.16, literally "we have believed *into* Christ," implies an act of personal commitment, not just assenting to the facts concerning Christ, but actually running to him for refuge and seeking mercy.

It is also implied in this commitment that a person will turn his back on the only other apparent possibility—the attempt to be justified by works done in obedience to formal statutes from whatever source. It is important to note that the article is not present in the phrases "observing law" or "works of law." This means that Paul's emphasis is not on the Jewish law, the law of Moses, at all, though it includes it, but rather on any system of attempting to please God by good deeds. "Works of law" are "deeds of men." The introduction of the article into the KJV, RSV, and NIV texts is a defect in these versions.

The threefold repetition of the doctrine of justification by faith in this one verse is important, because it shows the importance the apostle gives to the doctrine. Besides, the three phrases increase in emphasis. The first is general. Paul says, "A man is not justified by observing . . . law, but by faith in Jesus Christ." A man is *any* man, anyone. The second phrase is particular and personal. "We, too, have put our faith in Christ Jesus that we may be justified by faith in Christ and not by observing the law." This phrase involves Paul himself, as well as all who stand with him in the faith. The final statement is universal: "By observing the law no one will be justified." The words are literally "all flesh," i.e., mankind without exception. This universal application of the teaching is heightened by the fact that Paul apparently quotes from Psalm 143:2 (as he also does in Rom 3:20), thereby, adding the stamp of a more general, biblical principle to his statements.

17 In Paul's day, as today, arguments were directed against this way of salvation. So in this verse and the ones following Paul begins to answer these objections, first noting the main argument of his opponents and then revealing the argument by which he refutes theirs.

There have been many interpretations of this sentence, because the wording contains several ambiguities. Is Paul speaking hypothetically or is he referring to actual experience? He obviously denies the conclusion that Christ is the minister of sin, but does he also deny that "we ourselves . . . are found sinners" (KJV)? In what sense is sin mentioned? The importance of these questions is seen in the various interpretations that have grown out of an attempt to answer them.

1. A very ancient view, held by many of the early church fathers and by most of the Reformation theologians, is that the words "sinners" and "sin" must be taken in the same sense and that, as a result, the words "absolutely not" (*mē genoito*) deny both of the phrases in which the two words occur. According to this view, Paul is answering an objection based on two premises: (a) that it is necessary to abandon the law in order to be justified by faith, and (b) that abandoning the law is sin. Moreover, he must be arguing that to abandon the law is not sin; so Christ is not a minister of sin. The major difficulty with this view is that it does not do justice to Paul's regular usage of the phrase *mē genoito*, a phrase regularly employed to deny a conclusion falsely based on a true

premise. It also forms an awkward introduction to the verse that follows, as Lightfoot notes.

2. Lightfoot takes "sinners" in the same sense as "sinners" in v.15, with the conclusion that Paul is referring to Jews taking a place with "Gentile sinners" in the desire to be justified by faith; that is, taking a position with them outside the law. According to this view, Paul would be admitting the first point—that Jews become "Gentile sinners" in seeking to be justified by faith ("there is no difference," Rom 3:22)—but would be denying the conclusion that the legalizers sought to derive from it; namely, that Christ thereby becomes the encourager of sin. This is a possible interpretation, but it is slightly academic and is well removed from the situation at Antioch.

3. A third interpretation is that Paul is referring precisely to the situation at Antioch, indicating that he and Peter (as well as other Jews) became violators of the law, sinners, by eating with Gentiles. Nevertheless, Paul argues, Christ would hardly be called a minister of sin by Peter because they did that.

4. Some refer the sense of "sinners" to the actual practice of sin by Christians after their conversion, but this is extraneous to the context.

5. A final interpretation is that Paul refers to the standard antinomian objection to the doctrine of justification by faith which, significantly enough, he also deals with elsewhere. This view is adopted by Ridderbos, Stamm, and Stott (in loc.). According to this interpretation, Paul would be answering the objection that to eliminate the law entirely as he is doing is to encourage godless living, living without norms. The argument would go, "Your doctrine of justification by faith is dangerous, for by eliminating the law you also eliminate a man's sense of moral responsibility. If a person can be accounted righteous simply by believing that Christ died for him, why then should he bother to keep the law or, for that matter, why should he bother to live by any standard of morality? There is no need to be good. The result of your doctrine is that men will believe in Christ but thereafter do as they desire." Paul's reply is abrupt. The form of his expression suggests that he was aware of the possibility that a Christian can (and that all Christians do) sin. But this is not the result of the doctrine of justification by faith, and therefore Christ is not responsible for it. Such a thought is abhorrent. "Absolutely not!" "God forbid!" If there is sin, as Paul acknowledges indirectly in the next verse, man himself is responsible ("I am a lawbreaker").

This view is preferred by the present writer because it reflects Paul's arguments elsewhere (cf. Rom 6–8) and it best explains the presence of the following verses, as the commentary indicates.

Why is it that Paul can reply so vigorously to the objection that his gospel promotes antinomianism, especially since he seems to admit that those who have been justified by faith do sin? The answer is that the objection totally misunderstands the nature of man's justification. In the eyes of legalizers, justification by faith is nothing more than a legal fiction by which men and women are accounted righteous when in fact they are not. But justification is not a legal fiction. It is true that men are accepted by God as righteous when they are not, but this takes place only because God has first joined them to Christ and this in its turn implies a real transformation. They are "in Christ," says Paul. Consequently, they are "a new creation" (2 Cor 5:17; Gal 6:15). Obviously, to return to the old way of life after such a change is inconceivable.

18 The interpretation of this verse is not difficult if the interpretation of v.17 given above is valid. The legalizers had accused Paul of encouraging sin because Paul's doctrine throws over the law for God's grace. This Paul denied. Nevertheless, he replies, sin could be encouraged if having once come to God by faith in Jesus Christ the one coming should then return to law as a basis for the relationship. This is an argument *e contrario.* It refers to a stituation precisely like that one into which Peter had fallen. How is it that returning to law promotes sin? It is likely, in view of the following verses, that Paul is thinking here of the great sinfulness of turning from the Savior (whom the law anticipated) to mere ordinances. For a similar argument, see Hebrews 6:4–6.

19 The "we" of v.17 (which included both Paul and Peter) has changed to the "I" of v.18. This personal form of expression now continues as Paul begins to unfold the full nature of the justification that is his because of his being "in Christ." In this verse "I" is emphatic by being in the first position in the sentence. It contrasts with the similar position given to "in Christ," which (in the Greek text) begins v.20.

Paul has argued that if he should return to law after having come to God through faith in Christ, he would make himself a transgressor. But this is not what he does. Actually, the opposite is true, because in coming to God in Christ he died to the law so completely that he could not possibly return to it. "Through the law" probably justifies seeing in this brief sentence a capsule version of Paul's explanation of the law's purpose as developed at greater length in Romans 7. The law cannot bring life, for no one has ever fulfilled it. Law brings death, for by it all stand condemned. Nevertheless, even in doing this, law performs a good function. For in the very act of destroying all hope for salvation by human works, law actually opens the way to discovering new life in God. It is only when a man will die to his own efforts to achieve salvation that he will receive the gift of salvation that God offers.

20 This same point Paul now repeats in greater detail, with the name of Christ prominent. He has died to law so that he might live for God, but this is true only because he has been joined to the Lord Jesus Christ by God the Father. Jesus died; so did Paul. Jesus rose again; so did Paul. The resurrection life he is now living he is living through the presence of the Lord Jesus Christ within him. There are different ways in which Paul's references to having died and come to life in Christ may be taken; he himself uses the images in different ways. He may be referring to the participation of Christians in the benefits of Christ's experiences, as Burton notes (in loc.). This would mean that Christians experience death and new life because Jesus experienced death and new life for them. He may be referring to Christian experiences analogous to those that Christ endured. Philippians 3:10 and Romans 8:17 would be examples of this usage. Finally, he may be referring to an actual participation of the believer in Christ's death and resurrection conceived on the basis of the mystical union of the believer with the Lord (cf. Rom 6:4–8; Col 2:12–14, 20; 3:1–4). This last view is the hardest to understand, but it is the one involved here.

What does it mean to be "in Christ"? It means to be so united to Christ that all the experiences of Christ become the Christian's experiences. Thus, his death for sin was the believer's death; his resurrection was (in one sense) the believer's resurrection; his ascension was the believer's ascension, so that the believer is (again in one sense) seated with Christ "in the heavenly realms" (so Eph 2:6). This thought is particularly evident in Paul's use of the perfect tense in speaking of his having been crucified with Christ. The perfect refers to something that has happened in the past but whose influence continues into the present. Therefore, Paul cannot be speaking of a present experience of Christ's crucifixion, in whatever sense it may be conceived, but rather to Christ's death itself. He died with Christ; that is, his "old man" died with Christ. This was arranged by God so that Christ, rather than the old Paul, might live in him.

In one sense, Paul is still living. But he adds that the life he lives now is lived "by faith." It is a different life from the life in which he was striving to be justified by law. In another sense, it is not Paul who is living at all, but rather Christ who lives in him.

21 The last sentence of the chapter is introduced abruptly and from a new point of view. In the preceding verses Paul has answered the objections of his critics. Now he objects to their doctrine, showing that if they are right, then Christ has died in vain. The heart of Christianity lies in the grace of God and in the death of Jesus Christ. So, as Stott notes,

> If anybody insists that justification is by works, and that he can earn his salvation by his own efforts, he is undermining the foundations of the Christian religion. He is nullifying the grace of God (because if salvation is by works, it is not by grace) and he is making Christ's death superfluous (because if salvation is our own work, then Christ's work was unnecessary) (in loc.).

Paul's logic is incontrovertible. Yet many still pursue the fallacious logic of the legalizers. They suppose that to earn their salvation is somehow praiseworthy and noble, when actually it is vainglorious and ignoble. True nobility (and humility) is to accept what God offers. One must either receive God's offer of salvation or insult him.

Notes

16 The last phrase of v.16 must be regarded as a quotation from Ps 143:2, even though the text is cited loosely: (1) The introductory ὅτι (*hoti*) alone would suggest this, for it is Paul's most general form of introducing an OT reference; (2) the Hebraism, οὐ. . .πᾶσα (*ou. . .pasa*), also suggests it; (3) since the words merely repeat what has gone before, they would be redundant and superfluous were Paul not reinforcing his own statements by an appeal to Scripture.

"Law" (νόμος, *nomos*) is a prominent concept in this letter, being the opposite of faith as the means of salvation. In the NT, "law" can mean: "a single statute" ("But if her husband dies, she is released from that law," Rom 7:3); "divine law" in the specific sense of the law given through Moses (Gal 3:17); "God's revealed will," including both the Mosaic precepts and the principles behind these precepts (Rom 2:14); and "the single underlying principle behind the given law" ("The entire law is summed up in a single command: 'Love your neighbor as yourself,' " Gal 5:14). The word occurs again at 2:19, 21; 3:2, 5, 10–13, 17–19, 21, 23, 24; 4:4, 5, 21; 5:3, 4, 14, 18, 23; 6:2, 13.

In classical Gr. πίστις (*pistis*) has two meanings: on the one hand, "trustworthiness" or "faithfulness" and, on the other, "confidence" in someone or "trust." Both ideas also exist in the Heb root אמן (*'mn*), which generally underlies *pistis* in LXX. In the NT the religious sense of faith as belief and trust in God is prominent, though other meanings persist. Faith is primarily "acceptance of the gospel message concerning Jesus Christ and the committal of one's self . . . to him or to God as revealed in him," as Burton observes (in loc.). In these verses, just as he has refuted the idea of being justified by works of law in three successive clauses, so does Paul also emphasize three times that only "through faith" and "out of faith" in Christ can men be justified.

19 The law may be said to lead the sinner to Christ in two ways. First, the law bears evidence of its transitory character in that it contains elements that can be fulfilled only by Christ. Since the law's sacrifices and types foreshadowed Christ, to receive him when he appeared was only an act of obedience to law. The second way in which the law may be said to lead to Christ, the point Paul makes here, is that it enhances the sin of the one who tries to live by it and thereby drives him to the cross in desperation (so Rom 5:20 and other passages).

20 That Paul speaks in such a brief context both of the love and the sacrifice of Christ should in itself dispel any thought that his is a harsh legalistic interpretation of Christ's death. Paul twice acknowledges that Christ did what he did "for me," and adds that it was for love. The combination is so important to Paul that it is difficult to find a reference to the love of God in his writings in which the cross is not prominent.

II. Paul's Defense of the Gospel (3:1–4:31)

A. *The Doctrinal Issue: Faith or Works*

3:1–5

> [1]You foolish Galatians! Who has bewitched you? Before your very eyes Jesus Christ was clearly portrayed as crucified. [2]I would like to learn just one thing from you: Did you receive the Spirit by observing the law, or by believing what you heard? [3]Are you so foolish? After beginning with the Spirit, are you now trying to attain perfection by human effort? [4]Have you suffered so much for nothing—if it really was for nothing? [5]Does God give you his Spirit and work miracles among you because you observe the law, or because you believe what you heard?

The apostle has been defending the gospel of grace from the very beginning of this letter, but till now it has been done from the point of view of his own experience and calling. These had been challenged. So Paul begins by insisting that God rather than man has called him and given him his message. In speaking of his own experiences, however, Paul has gradually worked around to talking about the gospel itself, and this has brought him to the place where he is now set for a theological—or, better, a scriptural—defense of the gospel. So he returns to the Galatians themselves and to the point at which the doctrine of justification through faith bore down upon their own experience.

1 This is the first time since 1:11 that Paul has addressed the Galatians by name. Now it is by the impersonal term "Galatians" rather than by the word "brothers" he used earlier and it sets a sober tone for the formal argument to follow.

Three things are inexplicable in regard to the Galatians' conduct, according to vv.1–4. First, Paul says, their conduct is irrational or foolish. The word used here is not *mōros*, so often used in Christ's parables (Matt 5:22; 7:26; 25:2ff.). *Mōros* refers to one who is mentally deficient or who plays the fool, particularly in the moral or spiritual realm. In Galatians the word is *anoētos* which, quite differently, suggests the actions of one who can think but fails to use his powers of perception (so also at Luke 24:25; Rom 1:14; 1 Tim 6:9; Titus 3:3). This term was clearly suggested to Paul by the trend of his thought at the end of the previous chapter—namely, that a doctrine of salvation by works foolishly denies the necessity for grace and declares the death of the Lord Jesus Christ unnecessary. A doctrine leading to such a conclusion is irrational. Yet this is what the Galatians were on the verge of embracing. They were being intellectually inconsistent, self-contradictory. How can such nonsense be explained? Paul suggests facetiously that perhaps they have been placed under a spell by some magician.

Second, the conduct of the Galatians is inexplicable because the true gospel has been so clearly preached to them. Undoubtedly, Paul is referring to his own preaching, arguing that the gospel had been made as clear by him as if he had posted it on a public bulletin board. Moreover, he had not obscured it by nonessentials. For the heart of the gospel Paul preached is—and always must be—"Christ crucified." The perfect tense of this verb is important, for it refers to an act completed in the past but which nevertheless has continuing significance.

2 The third reason for the incomprehensible nature of the Galatians' defection is that it was so totally contrary to their initial experiences of Christianity. How did they begin? This is what Paul would like to hear from them. Did they receive the Holy Spirit by living up to some formal statutes? Or did they enter into the Christian life simply by believing and receiving what they heard concerning the death of the Lord Jesus Christ? The form of the question (literally, "This only do I wish to learn from you") suggests that so long as they are in their present confused state, Paul does not want to hear anything other than the most basic answer to this most basic question.

3 Paul presupposes their answer, which is obviously that they became Christians only through faith, through believing what they heard. The conclusion follows that, having begun by faith, they must continue in faith. It cannot be otherwise, because the two ways—faith versus works—are in conflict. Paul emphasizes this conflict by three sets of comparisons: (1) works versus hearing, (2) law versus faith, and (3) spirit versus flesh. The last antithesis will come to prominence in the ethical section of the letter where the works of the flesh and the fruit of the Spirit are contrasted.

4 There is some ambiguity in the question "Have you suffered so much for nothing...?" It may imply actual suffering, as the English word generally does. Or it may refer simply to the Galatians' previous spiritual experiences. NEB takes this approach by translating, "Have all your great experiences been in vain . . . ?" Neither view makes a great deal of difference for interpreting the letter as a whole, but the latter seems to fit the immediate context better. In this case, the experiences of the Galatians are further amplified by the reminder in v.5 that God was working miracles in their midst through the power of his Holy Spirit.

5 Nothing must be allowed to obscure the point Paul is making, so once more he voices the test question of v.2. There are some differences, however. First, v.2 presents the question from the point of view of the Galatians, asking on what basis it was that they received God's Spirit. Verse 5 looks at the matter from God's point of view, asking on what basis God is working miracles among them. The two verses also differ in that the past tense of v.2, which looks back to the initial moment of the Galatians' faith in Christ, gives way to present participles in v.5. The present participles ("gives" and "works") anticipate the end of the argument, for it is evident that blessing in the Christian life comes just as the Christian life began—through faith, and not as the result of any human attainments.

Many outlines have been given of the verses that follow. A helpful outline is to be found in the very antithesis that Paul develops in this section. Is a person justified by "observing law" or by believing what was heard? With this question in mind, Paul begins to discuss the alternatives—dealing first with faith, then with law, then faith, then law, and so on. The diagram suggests the flow of the argument.

In the first three sections the contrast is absolute. In the last three sections the contrast begins to slip into each section; thus, we have "transgressions" versus "promise," "pedagogue" versus "heirs," and "bondage" versus "freedom."

The Test Question:

Believing what was heard or	**"observing the law"?**
The true gospel	The legalizers' "gospel"
3:6-9 Faith ("Abraham")	3:10-14 Law (the "curse")
3:15-18 Faith ("covenant")	3:19-22 Law ("trangressions")
3:23-29 Faith ("heirs")	4:1-7 Law ("bondage")

Notes

1 The "folly" of the Galatians has been taken by some as additional evidence that they were inhabitants of northern Galatia—i.e., country simpletons rather than the more sophisticated people of the southern Asia Minor coast. Doing this attributes characteristics to the Galatians that we have no means of verifying, as Ramsay observes. It also overlooks the truth that "natural man," regardless of his imagined sophistication or lack of it, is foolish spiritually. As a result of such reasoning, Luther thought that the Galatians were Germans. One might equally see them as Americans, French, or any other nationality a person happens to be. The vacillation of the Galatians may also be compared to the action of the people of Lystra, who tried to worship Paul as a god but, after the Jewish intervention, stoned him (Acts 14:13, 19).

The word "portrayed" (**προγράφω**, *prographō*) has three senses: (1) "to write out beforehand," (2) "to write for public reading," and (3) "to write at the head of the list." The first sense is often used in reference to prophecy, but is inappropriate here. The third does not occur in the NT.

3 Burton considers the use of **σάρξ** (*sarx*) in this verse to be physical—i.e., that in which the circumcision the Galatians were urged to accept took place. This is the true sense in 6:13, but here the contrast is better understood as being between the work of the Holy Spirit of God and that of which man by himself is capable.

5 The phrase **ἐξ ἀκοῆς πίστεως** (*ex akoēs pisteōs*) can be variously tr., depending on whether "hearing" and/or "faith" is taken either actively or passively. The best meaning is "a hearing of the gospel accompanied by faith" (Burton). This sense is preserved in NIV, although the precise antithesis between "works" and "hearing" as well as between "law" and "faith" is obscured.

B. *The Doctrinal Argument* (3:6–4:7)

1. *Sons of Abraham*

3:6–9

6Consider Abraham: "He believed God, and it was credited to him as righteous-
ness." 7Understand, then, that those who believe are children of Abraham. 8The

Scripture foresaw that God would justify the Gentiles by faith, and announced the gospel in advance to Abraham: "All nations will be blessed in you." [9]So those who have faith are blessed along with Abraham, the man of faith.

Paul now turns to the first section of the alternating argument that will occupy him as far as 4:7. The issue is scriptural, for he is concerned to show that not only the experience of the Galatians but also the words of the OT support his teaching that the means of entering into salvation is faith. Abraham is his example.

Paul's statements presuppose a knowledge of Abraham by the Galatians, and it is not difficult to imagine how the Christians of Galatia had come by it. If Paul had preached among the Galatians for any length of time, he would undoubtedly have taught Christian theology in part on the basis of Abraham's life. If the churches of Galatia were the churches of the south, there was undoubtedly a large Jewish population in the area with which Christians must at least have had some contact and with whose history they must have been familiar. Most significant, however, is the probability that the obligation to become "sons" of Abraham through circumcision formed the central argument of the legalizers' teaching. This argument would have focused on Genesis 12 and 17 and would have advanced the position that no one could be blessed by God who was not part of the company to whom God's promises were made. It would have added that one entered this company solely through circumcision. These arguments Paul encounters head on, for he shows that even Abraham was blessed through faith, not circumcision.

6 The particle beginning this verse (*kathōs*) is generally used to introduce a new idea but is, nevertheless, one that is linked to the thoughts preceding. In this case, Paul links up his OT example to the Galatians' spiritual experience, showing that what they had known to be true in their own lives was also true for others and is confirmed scripturally.

To appeal to Abraham is more than to appeal to just any historical example, because Abraham was the acknowledged father and prototype of Israel. Abraham was the man God started with. He had come from a pagan ancestry beyond the river Euphrates (Josh 24:1, 2), but God had called him and had made a covenant with him. It was from Abraham that the Jewish people came. All Jews, including Paul's opponents, would look back to Abraham as their father in the faith and as their example. This is what gives the patriarch his importance for Paul's argument. How, then, did Abraham receive God's blessing? How was he justified? Paul answers by a quotation of Genesis 15:6, noting that Abraham "believed God" and that "it was credited to him as righteousness."

What does Paul understand to have been imputed to Abraham as righteousness? The answer depends on what definition of "righteousness" he is using. Righteousness may be either a forensic term (denoting a right standing before the law) or a right relationship, in this case to God. If the latter definition is taken, then "faith" is the key factor, and Paul's point is that Abraham's trusting attitude toward God was accepted by God as righteousness. In this view of justification, there is no difficulty with a so-called "legal fiction." But if the forensic use predominates, then it must be God's own righteousness that is imputed to Abraham in place of his own, which was inadequate. If there were nothing else to go on than Genesis 15:6, the second of these two uses might be preferable. But in view of Paul's development of the doctrine elsewhere, the first must be accepted. It is only by thinking of God's righteousness actually being credited to our account that Paul can say, as he does, for instance, in 2 Corinthians 5:21: "God made him [Christ] who had no sin to be sin for us, so that in him we might become the righteousness of God."

These two views are not in opposition, of course, for justification does bring one into a right relationship with God out of which ethical changes follow. The changes result from one's being placed "in Christ," as Paul has shown.

7 One example does not make a case, however. So Paul continues his argument with a sentence linking the situation of Abraham to the present. He means, "Since Abraham was saved by faith, his true children are, therefore, even now, those who are saved by faith, as he was." The background is undoubtedly the claim of the Judaizers that one became a genuine son of Abraham by circumcision and subsequent obedience to the law. The phrase "sons of Abraham" (RSV) is discussed at considerable length by both Lightfoot (pp. 158–164) and Burton (pp. 156–159).

Furthermore, this verse is an important one for linking the two covenants, that of the OT and that of the NT. To this end Paul eliminates the article from the word "faith," thus stressing that Abraham's faith was of the same kind as Christian faith and placing the phrase "those who believe" or "those who are characterized by faith" in the first and prominent position. Marcion objected to this joining of the two covenants (he stressed their opposition) and, therefore, quite predictably eliminated vv.6–9 from his canon.

8 The particle (*de*) that introduces v.8 is continuative, for Paul wishes to refer to Scripture as evidence of what he has already concluded in v.7. The quotation, from Genesis 12:3, makes two points: (1) that the blessing promised to Abraham was from the beginning intended to include the Gentiles as well as the Jews, and (2) that the gospel promise preceded everything else in God's dealings with his people, including the giving of the law, as he will show later (v.17). The use of this verse is not "proof-texting." If that were the case, the sentence would have been introduced with a stronger conjunction, perhaps *hoti.* Instead, the reference is introduced only in support of a conclusion reached on other grounds.

The unusual way the OT is cited here makes this an important verse assessing the value given the OT by Paul and other NT writers. The unusual feature is that the Scriptures are personified, Paul writing that "the Scripture foresaw that God would justify the Gentiles by faith, and announced the gospel in advance to Abraham." Paul views the Scriptures as if they were God speaking. Another example is Romans 9:17, in which Paul writes: "For the Scripture says to Pharaoh: I raised you up for this very purpose." As Warfield observes,

> It was not, however, the Scripture (which did not exist at the time) that, foreseeing God's purposes of grace in the future, spoke these precious words to Abraham, but God himself in his own person. . . . It was not the not yet existent Scripture that made this announcement to Pharaoh, but God himself through the mouth of his prophet Moses. These acts could be attributed to "Scripture" only as the result of such a habitual identification, in the mind of the writer, of the text of Scripture with God as speaking, that it became natural to use the term "Scripture says," when what was really intended was "God, as recorded in Scripture, said" (*The Inspiration and Authority of the Bible,* 2nd ed. [Nutley, N.J.: Presbyterian and Reformed Publishing Company, 1948], pp. 299, 300).

These verses, along with others, highlight an absolute identification of Scripture with the words of God in the minds of the NT writers and are important biblical support for the historical Christian belief in the total inspiration of the Bible and its authority.

9 The reader is now at the peak of the first section of Paul's argument. It is a throwback to the question of v.5. Who are the ones who enter into spiritual blessing? The answer is: Those characterized by the approach of faith are blessed along with Abraham, who had faith. Besides, since the blessing of Abraham is declared to have been intended for the Gentiles also, how could the Gentiles be blessed except by faith? To have been blessed in any other way would have involved their ceasing to be Gentiles.

Notes

8 The highly condensed phrase ἐν σοὶ (*en soi*, "in you") in reference to Abraham may be variously interpreted: (1) It can refer to physical descent from Abraham, the view undoubtedly taken by the legalizers. According to this view, the Gentiles could experience salvation only by joining themselves to Abraham and his descendents through the rite of circumcision. (2) It can mean merely that the Gentiles would experience blessing through what Abraham did ("because of you"). This meaning does not decide the dispute between Paul and the legalizers one way or the other. (3) It can refer to a spiritual union with Abraham achieved by believing in God, as Abraham himself did. By this means, one becomes part of the great company of those characterized by their trust in God. Paul takes the phrase in this last sense.

2. *The law's curse*

3:10–14

[10]All who rely on observing the law are under a curse, for it is written: "Cursed is everyone who does not continue to do everything written in the book of the Law." [11]Clearly no one is justified before God by the law, because, "The righteous will live by faith." [12]The law is not based on faith; on the contrary, "The man who does these things will live by them." [13]Christ redeemed us from the curse of the law by becoming a curse for us, for it is written: "Cursed is everyone who is hanged on a tree." [14]He redeemed us in order that the blessing given to Abraham might come to the Gentiles through Christ Jesus, so that by faith we might receive the promise of the Spirit.

Having established his doctrine of justification by faith positively, Paul now turns to its negative counterpart: the impossibility of justification by law. Significantly enough, he rests his case on the statements of the law itself, contending that those wishing to live by the law are bound by their own principles to these statements. Three points follow: (1) Those living under the principle of law are under the law's curse, for the law pronounces a curse upon all who fail to keep the law in its entirety; (2) no one is justified by law, since the law itself teaches that men are justified by faith; and (3) no mixture of these principles is possible, for they are mutually exclusive. To this argument Paul adds a full reference to the work of Christ. It is twofold: a work of redemption from the curse the law has imposed on everybody and a work of blessing by which the promise of the Spirit made to Abraham is fulfilled for all who believe on Christ as Savior.

10 In the first four verses of Paul's formal argument (vv.6–9) he has cited two OT texts: Genesis 15:6 in v.6 and Genesis 12:3 in v.8. Now he quotes from the OT three more times in vv.10–12, in each case demonstrating that an attempt to live by law, rather than producing a blessing, actually brings a curse. Why is this so? First of all, because the law demands perfection, as Deuteronomy 27:26 declares. The law is not a collection of stray and miscellaneous parts, some of which may be conveniently disregarded. It is a whole, and must be kept in all its parts if it is to be considered kept at all. The point is not that justification cannot come by keeping the law, at least theoretically, but that a curse is attached to any failure to keep it, no matter how small. Since all fail, all are under the curse. Paul is assuming the universality of sin in this quotation.

The idea that men could be under a curse as a result of God's judgment has appeared so offensive to some commentators that they have tried to avoid the difficulty by stressing that the curse referred to is the curse "of the law" rather than the curse "of God." But this is unsatisfactory. It must be agreed, as Stamm and Burton (who take this approach in their commentaries) maintain, that Paul does attach this curse to the logical and ultimate extension of the law (cf. Burton, "Redemption from the Curse of the Law," AJT, 11, 1907, pp. 624–646). Paul's phrase is always "the curse of the law," rather than "the curse of God." Still, the law is God's law, an extension of his character and will, and it is a failure to keep the law that brings man under God's wrath. There is another way to avoid the wrath of God, as Paul has shown. There is mercy in the work of Christ. Nevertheless, if a man will not come to God on the basis of the atonement made by Christ, he must be judged by his works measured against the law's standard and be condemned.

It is true as a principle, as v.12 says, that "the man who does these things will live by them." But no one does them perfectly. And so the law cannot bring life. Its purpose is to condemn and by condemning to point man in his desperation to the Savior.

11 One must not think that the law did nothing but condemn during all the centuries between the giving of the law through Moses and the coming of Jesus. On the contrary, the law itself showed the way of salvation. Paul proves this by a quotation of Habakkuk 2:4—"The righteous will live by faith"—one of the few OT verses in which faith is presented as the means of salvation. It has been argued that Paul misrepresents Habakkuk's meaning. But if "the righteous" in Habakkuk 2:4 means those who are standing in a right relationship to God rather than those who are literally righteous before the law, as there is every reason to believe, then Habakkuk's view is certainly in accord with Paul's position here. Habakkuk is thinking of the temporal ills resulting from the Chaldean invasion. Paul is thinking in a more general spiritual context. Yet the basic position is the same. It is by faith that a man stands in a right relationship to God and lives before him.

12 But perhaps both are needed, both faith and law? Not so, says Paul. For faith excludes law, and law by its very nature excludes faith. He quotes the law itself (Lev 18:5) to support this position. Mentally we are to supply "the law says that" after "on the contrary."

13 If these principles are true and if they support the topic sentence of v.10—"all who rely on observing the law are under a curse"—then the condition of man under law is obviously hopeless. If there is to be hope, it must come from a different direction entirely. Abruptly, therefore, and without any connecting particle, Paul introduces the work of Christ through which the curse of the law has been exhausted and in whom all who believe find salvation.

This is the first time Christ has been mentioned since the opening verse of the chapter, but now both he and his work are prominent. Christ is the only possible means of redemption.

The two ways of understanding the "curse" of v.10 (the curse of the law exclusive of the curse of God and the curse of the law which contains within it the idea of divine disapproval) lead to two ways of understanding the "us" of v.13. If redemption is from the curse of the law only, then "us" refers most naturally to Jews who have been living under a serious misconception concerning God and his true nature (so Burton). But if, on the contrary, the curse involves the true anathema of God, then "us" must correctly refer to both Jew and Gentile since both have received deliverance through Christ. This latter view is demanded by the context, for Paul will go on to show that the purpose of Christ's death was that the blessing given Abraham might come upon both Jew and Gentile.

To redeem (*exagorazō*) means "to buy out of slavery" by paying a price. Christ paid this price by dying (cf. 1 Peter 1:18, 19; Acts 20:28). Another way of saying the same thing is to say that Christ became "a curse for us," which Paul does. But what does this mean? In what sense could Jesus become a curse? Paul's quotation from Deuteronomy 21:23—"Cursed is everyone who is hanged on a tree"—suggests that Jesus passed under the law's curse in a technical way by virtue of the particular means by which he was executed. Thus, having violated the law in one part—through no fault of his own—he became technically guilty of all of it and bore the punishment of God's wrath for every violation of the law by every man. This may be in the back of Paul's mind as a particular form of rabbinical argument (hence, the quotation) but it does not do full justice to the situation as Paul describes it. The curse of the law is not a technical, still less an imaginary, thing. The curse is real. Jesus bore this real curse on our behalf. The preposition (*hyper*) indicates this by showing that Jesus took our place in dying. No doubt there is more to this than anyone can understand completely, at least in this life. Yet it can be understood in part both through the illustration of the OT sacrifices and in Christ's cry of dereliction from the cross—"My God, my God, why have you forsaken me?" (Matt 27:46). The idea of the curse of sin being borne away by an innocent substitute is best seen in the instruction concerning the scapegoat found in Leviticus 16:5ff.

14 Paul concludes this section of the argument with a twofold statement of the purpose for which Jesus Christ redeemed man through his death. The two clauses (introduced by *hina*, "in order that") relate to the statement "Christ redeemed us from the curse of the law," rather than to any subordinate element of the sentence. The two purposes are these: first, that the blessing of Abraham (Paul is referring to justification, as in vv.8, 9) might come to Gentiles as well as Jews, and second, that all might together receive the gift of the Holy Spirit. These last two clauses, stating the purpose for which Christ redeemed men from the curse, are coordinate. That is, they express the same reality from two perspectives. Both return to the point from which Paul's argument started—namely, that the blessing of Abraham, seen today in the reception of the Holy Spirit, is received through faith and through faith only.

Notes

10 "Law" (νόμος, *nomos*) refers to the law of Moses. But the principle of living by law goes beyond this restricted reference, particularly when Paul uses the phrase "works of law" as he does in vv.2, 5, 10. In this case one might tr. "the law principle" or "legalism."

It is quite true, as many have pointed out, that the word "all" (πᾶς, *pas*, "everything," NIV) does not occur in the original text of Deut 27:26—"Cursed be he who does not confirm the words of this law by doing them" (RSV). But the "all" is implied and, indeed, does appear in the following v. KJV inserts it in italics. Paul probably fuses the two vv. in his quotation.

13 Three Gr. words are habitually tr. "redemption" in the English NT: λυτρόω (*lutroō*, "to loose" or "set free"), ἀγοράζω (*agorazō*, "to buy in the marketplace"), and ἐξαγοράζω (*exagorazō*, "to buy out of the marketplace"). The last of these words, which occurs here, can mean either "to redeem" (as in redeeming a slave) or "to buy up." Paul's thought is expressed in the former meaning, with the thought that Jesus paid the price men could not pay and thus set them free from sin's bondage. Burton and others fail to see the vicarious aspect of the atonement by insisting that the death of Christ was basically only a disclosure of God's true attitude toward men.

Christ became a curse for us. Ridderbos states (in loc.):

> From all this it should be apparent how little justice modern theological thought does to Paul's presentation of these matters when, for example, it talks of a God who does not deal with people on "a basis of legalism" and of a Christ who has set people free from the "fiction" of a curse of God. The reference to Deuteronomy 21 is intended precisely to point out the reality of the curse and, in connection with it, to set forth Christ's redemption as a satisfaction of the justice of God.

Lightfoot has a discussion of this v. from the perspective of Jewish interpretations of it (pp. 152–154).

---

3. *The seed of Abraham*

3:15–18

> 15 Brothers, let me take an example from everyday life. Just as no one can set aside or add to a human covenant that has been duly established, so it is in this case. 16 The promises were spoken to Abraham and to his seed. The Scripture does not say "and to seeds," meaning many people, but "and to your seed," meaning one person, who is Christ. 17 What I mean is this: The law, introduced 430 years later, does not set aside the covenant previously established by God and thus do away with the promise. 18 For if the inheritance depends on the law, then it no longer depends on a promise; but God in his grace gave it to Abraham through a promise.

At the close of the preceding section Paul introduced the idea of God's promise to Abraham. Now he picks up this idea once more and develops it in relation to the giving of the law. This is the third section of his alternating answer to the question of v.2: "Did you receive the Spirit by observing the law, or by believing what you heard?"

Paul's opponents were not ready to admit that Abraham was justified by faith in God's promise. But even if he were, they might argue, still the giving of the law at a later time changed the basis for man's entrance into salvation. Anticipating this objection, Paul draws on the acknowledged character of human wills and covenants so as to show that no new development could change the promise made to Abraham.

15 "Brothers" introduces a change of tone on the apostle's part, in contrast to the somewhat distant and formal beginning of chapter 3 (cf. 4:31; 6:1). It is as though he now invites the erring Galatians to reason along with him as he uses an analogy. "Let me take an example from everyday life" (literally, "I speak as a man," *kata anthrōpon legō*) does not indicate a lowering of the tone of the argument, still less an appeal to human authority rather than God's. It means that Paul is borrowing an illustration from human relationships (so also at Rom 3:5; 6:19; 1 Cor 9:8; cf. Paul's use of marriage laws in Rom 7:1–3).

Commentators have found difficulty in Paul's use of the word "covenant" (*diathēkē*) in this verse because the word can mean either "agreement" or "will." Ramsay, for instance, argues strongly for the idea of a "will," noting that in human affairs only a will has the permanent character Paul alludes to in this passage. Others observe that in LXX *diathēkē* always has the sense of a covenant between God and man and that Paul has just been thinking of God's covenant with Abraham. But is it necessary to choose between the two meanings? Perhaps not. In English one has to choose between them simply because there are two separate words. But in the Greek language, with one word, it is possible to use both ideas. That this is the case here seems to be supported by: (1) Paul's custom of playing on words elsewhere (e.g., Gal 5:12), (2) the same double meaning in Hebrews 9:15–20, and (3) the particular nature of the "covenant" made by God with Abraham. Paul is alluding to the promise of a universal blessing both to Jew and Gentile through Abraham's seed (Gen 12:2, 3) which he conceives as the offer of justification to all men through Christ. But if this is so, Paul certainly also has in mind the formal enactment of the covenant by the ceremony recorded in Genesis 15. This was a unilateral agreement. That is, it did not depend on any condition to be fulfilled by Abraham.

In Abraham's day an oath was sometimes confirmed by a ceremony in which animals were cut into two parts along the backbone and placed in two rows, the rows facing each other across a space marked off between them. The parties to the oath walked together into the space between the parts and spoke their promises there. This oath would be especially sacred because of the shed blood. It was this ceremony God enacted with Abraham (Gen 15). But it had this exception: In the case of God's covenant with Abraham, God alone passed between the pieces of the slain animals, thereby signifying that he alone stood behind the promises. The author of Hebrews captures this sense of the covenant by saying, "When God made his promise to Abraham, since there was no one greater for him to swear by, he swore by himself, saying, 'I will surely bless you and give you many descendants.' And so after waiting patiently, Abraham received what was promised" (Heb 6:13–15).

The idea of a will is not far removed from this type of covenant, save in the matter of the death of the testator, which obviously cannot apply to God. Paul's point is simply that the promise of justification through faith first made to Abraham is permanent. If a human will or agreement cannot be added to or annulled—he is not even thinking of the possibility of altering a contract by mutual consent, since two parties are not involved in this agreement—how much less can there be alteration in the solemn promises made to Abraham and his seed by the living God!

16 Verse 16 appears to be a parenthesis, and a difficult one at that. But by showing the scope of the promises made to Abraham, it is actually essential to Paul's argument. The truth is seen in this way. If the promises made to Abraham were made only to Abraham and his immediate descendants, they might well be considered fulfilled even before the giving of the law; the law would simply inaugurate a new era in God's dealings with mankind. But the promises were not fulfilled in the period before the giving of the law, Paul argues. They were embodied in the coming Redeemer through whom the fullness of blessing was to come. That Redeemer was Christ. Consequently, God's blessing of justification by grace through faith spans the ages; and the law, whatever else one might think of it, must be seen to have served only an interim function.

When Paul speaks of "seed" in the singular as opposed to "seeds," he poses a further difficulty for commentators. For the singular form has a collective significance and does, in fact, generally denote more than one person. The nearest English equivalent is the word "offspring." What is the explanation? The one completely invalid explanation of Paul's procedure is that he did not know Greek accurately. On the contrary, he knew it as well as anybody and certainly knew that "seed" generally referred to many persons. Indeed, he himself so uses the word elsewhere (Rom 4:16–18; 9:6–8). It is not much better to say that Paul merely descends to a typically rabbinical form of argument in speaking to those with this background. The best explanation is that Paul is simply pointing out that the singular word—"seed" rather than "children," "descendants," or some such plural word—*is* appropriate, inasmuch as Israel had always believed that the ultimate messianic blessing would come through a single individual.

The essential point is that the promises made to Abraham cannot be considered fulfilled solely in the period prior to the giving of the law on Sinai and hence must be in effect eternally.

17 The 430 years comes from Exodus 12:40, which in the Greek text is given as the period between Abraham and Moses rather than, as in versions based on the Hebrew text, as the period during which the people were slaves in Egypt. The difference is of no consequence from the viewpoint of Paul's argument, because his point depends only on the historical sequence. If God had been blessing Abraham and his posterity through the way of promise for 430 years and if he was to do the same for all men through Christ and his posterity, how could the giving of the law annul this promise? It could not, as even the human analogy of covenants and wills shows. Therefore, the law cannot add to, nor subtract from, God's first and only way of salvation.

18 This verse adds an objective as well as temporal reason why the giving of the law cannot change the promise. Promise and law are antithetical by nature. They can be neither mingled together nor combined. This point is a restatement in a slightly different context of the point made in v.12. In the last phrase the words "to Abraham" are emphasized, thereby once again driving all discussion of how men and women enter into a right relationship with God to its original source. The word "gave" (*kecharistai*) is important, because it emphasizes that salvation is both a free gift (*kecharistai* is based on the word for grace) and permanent (the perfect tense). Whatever may be said about the law, this much is certain: God saved Abraham through promise, not law, and the original way of salvation is still operative.

Notes

15 In the Gr. of Paul's day, διαθήκη (*diathēkē*) apparently meant "a will" and nothing more, though it had also meant "a covenant" to the classical writers. In the LXX, on the other hand, in which it occurs over 300 times, it also always means a covenant, being a tr. of the Heb. term בְּרִית (*berith*). This does not mean that the word is used in the normal sense of an agreement between two parties, however. At times it does mean this (see Gen 17:13; 21:27, 32, *passim*), particularly when the agreement is reached between men. But in reference to God and his

covenants, the thought is almost always that of a unilateral pledge or promise. This is suggested even in the fact that it is the word *diathēkē* that is used to translate ברית (*berith*) rather than the apparently more available word συνθήκη (*synthēkē*), which involved mutuality. As Ridderbos notes, "It is not the idea of parity, or even that of reciprocity, but that of validity which determines the essence of the covenant-idea" (in loc.).

16 Of the major interpretations of what Paul meant by his stress on the sing. σπέρμα (*sperma*), rather than pl. σπέρματα (*spermata*), the following are prominent: (1) The contrast is between the spiritual posterity of Abraham, the family of Christians, and the other families descended from him after the flesh (so Augustine, Irenaeus, Oldhausen, Alford, and others). (2) This is a purely rabbinical form of argument—in other words, a grammatically insupportable quibble (Meyer, cf. Neil). (3) The stress is not on the particular form of the word but on the fact that a sing. noun of some kind is used (Lightfoot). (4) The reference is to Christ and his posterity collectively considered (Burton; see extended note, pp. 505–510). That Paul is appealing to the generally accepted idea that all the blessings were to be wrapped up in a single deliverer is well stated by Gardiner ("Note on Galatians 3:16," BS, 36, 1879, pp. 23–27).

---

4. *Law versus covenant*

3:19–22

19 What, then, was the purpose of the law? It was added because of transgressions until the Seed to whom the promise referred had come. The law was put into effect through angels by a mediator. 20 A mediator, however, does not represent just one party; but God is one.

21 Is the law, therefore, opposed to the promises of God? Absolutely not! For if a law had been given that could impart life, then righteousness would certainly have come by the law. 22 But the Scripture declares that the whole world is a prisoner of sin, so that what was promised, being given through faith in Jesus Christ, might be given to those who believe.

Paul has proved, at least to his own satisfaction and perhaps even to that of the Galatians, that the way of salvation is by means of the promise received through faith. But the legalizers might object that the approach he has taken has actually proved too much. He has demonstrated that the way of salvation is by promise and that the law brings a curse. But if this is so, it would seem to follow (1) that the law has no purpose at all in the scheme of salvation, or (2) that it is actually opposed to it. This would be an intolerable conclusion for most persons, particularly those Jews whose life had been dominated by the law for centuries. Paul answers these charges by denying both conclusions and by establishing God's true purpose in giving the law. He declares that the law was given not to save man but rather to reveal his sin, that it was temporary, and that it was inferior to the promise because, unlike the promise, it was given through a mediator.

19 To the question "What, then, was the purpose of the law?" Paul provides as his first answer the truth that the law "was added because of transgressions." On the surface the sense is ambiguous. The phrase can mean either that the law was given to restrain transgressions (which is the natural function of law) or that the law was given to make the transgressions known, even in one sense to encourage them or to provoke them to a new intensity. In view of Paul's choice of the word "transgressions" (*parabasis*) rather than "sin" (*hamartia*) in this context and of his discussion of the purpose of the law elsewhere, the latter is the only real possibility. In Romans, Paul argues that "through

the law we become conscious of sin" (3:20) and that "where there is no law there is no transgression" (4:15). The point is that though sin was in the world before the giving of the law, sin was not always known as such. The law reveals sin *as sin.* Hence, it may be said that it is the law that turns sin into transgression—transgression of law—and even accentuates it (Rom 5:20). In this act, law performs the function of showing man's need of a Savior.

The second half of v.19 carries the thought a bit further to show that the giving of the law was temporary ("until the Seed to whom the promise referred had come") and inferior (because "put into effect through angels by a mediator"). Here the mediator is doubtlessly Moses who, as an agent of a mediated revelation, is brought forward in contrast to Abraham, to whom God made promises directly. The role of angels in the giving of the law is suggested in Deuteronomy 33:2 and Psalm 68:17 and is referred to explicitly in Acts 7:53 and Hebrews 2:2.

20 This verse is probably the most obscure verse in Galatians, if not in the entire NT. Lightfoot notes that there have been over 250 interpretations of it; Fricke raises the figure to 300. The difficulty lies in the abrupt, aphoristic character of the verse and in the necessity to relate to Paul's context whatever interpretation may be given of it. The most important interpretations fall into three categories:

1. Those that take Paul's reference to a "mediator" in a general sense. According to this approach, Paul is introducing a general principle in support of the point made at the end of the preceding verse. Mediators always act between parties. Hence, since Moses was a mediator of the law, it follows that he acted between God and the people and that the law thereby came to man indirectly. The last phrase would suggest that in giving the promise to Abraham (see vv.15–18) God acted directly and unilaterally.

2. Those that take the reference to a "mediator" as a specific reference to Moses. This view has support in the fact that Paul has been talking about Moses and that he uses the direct article ("the mediator") in this verse, though the direct article in itself does not necessarily imply an individual. This approach can obviously lead to an interpretation very similar to that given above. However, it can also lead to other views, such as that of Forbes, in which Moses is contrasted with Christ as one who was unable to be a mediator of "a perfectly united body" (cf. "*Brevia*—Galatians 3:20," Exp., 3rd series, 4, 1886, pp. 150–156).

3. Those that refer "the mediator" to Christ (Jerome, Chrysostom and, in more recent times, Cole). This has support in the fact that Paul employs these same terms of Christ in another passage (1 Tim 2:5), but this view does not relate well to the context. If it is right, Paul would be acknowledging that even in Christianity there is a mediator, Christ; but he would be adding that since Christ is God as well as man, in Christ God is therefore still dealing with man directly.

Whatever the details of the interpretation—and there probably will never be perfect agreement on Paul's precise meaning—the general thought seems to be that the promise must be considered superior to the law because the law is one-sided. The law was mediated, and this means that man was a party to it. The promise, on the other hand, is unilateral; man is not a party to it. This thought is intended to reinforce what Paul has said earlier about the unconditional and unilateral nature of the promises.

21 The second apparent conclusion from Paul's doctrine of justification, as the legalizers would note, is that the law becomes evil because it is in opposition to grace as the true means of salvation. But this does not follow, Paul replies. Actually, it is an abhorrent idea, because it suggests a conflict within the nature of God, who gave both the law and the promise. True, the law increases transgressions (Rom 5:20). In a sense it even kills, as Paul argues elsewhere (Rom 7:7–11). Still, the law is not bad. It is good. In fact, it is so good that if a man could do what the law requires, he would find life (Lev 18:5; cf. Gal 3:12).

22 This being impossible, however, the law fulfills its actual function by shutting all humanity up within the bounds of acknowledged sin (cf. note on v.23). It condemns them so that they might turn from attempts to please God through legalism and instead receive the promise of God through faith in Jesus Christ. In the first part of this verse Paul gives a capsule statement of the major truths of the first three chapters of Romans: the law shows that all—the immoral person, the ethical person, and the religious person—have sinned and need a Savior. The second half of the verse reminds us that there is indeed a Savior and that it had always been God's purpose to save a great company through faith in him. Seen from this angle, even the law flowed from God's grace, because it prepared men and women to receive the Lord Jesus Christ when he came. In the last phrase, "faith," the sole means of grace, is again prominent.

Notes

19 The inferiority of law to promise is stated in a slightly different but parallel way in 2 Cor 3:12–18.

22 It is a bit unusual for Paul to use the comprehensive and neuter term τὰ πάντα (*ta panta*) in this v. (literally, "But the Scripture has confined *all things* under sin"), since he might be supposed to be referring exclusively to human beings and even more particularly to Jews. Paul may have been thinking of the involvement of the whole of creation in the effects of man's sin. He does so elsewhere (Rom 8:22). Yet this is so far from the context and from Paul's tone of argument that it seems best merely to interpret *ta panta* in a personal way. In this case it would have been used by Paul to make the reference as comprehensive as possible—that is, of both Jews and Gentiles—though how the law applies to the Gentile world is not stated. Lightfoot notes that the neuter is naturally used when the most comprehensive term is desired (1 Cor 1:27; Eph 1:10; Col 1:20).

5. *Heirs with Abraham*

3:23–29

23Before this faith came, we were held prisoners by the law, locked up until faith should be revealed. 24So the law was put in charge to lead us to Christ that we might be justified by faith. 25Now that faith has come, we are no longer under the supervision of the law.

26You are all sons of God through faith in Christ Jesus, 27for all of you who were united with Christ in baptism have been clothed with Christ. 28There is neither Jew nor Greek, slave nor free, male nor female, for you are all one in Christ Jesus. 29If you belong to Christ, then you are Abraham's seed, and heirs according to the promise.

The closing section of chapter 3 follows directly upon what Paul has said regarding the true purpose of the law. Still, a change has taken place, and this change justifies our taking these verses as a new step in Paul's argument. Before, he has been concerned with the law's true purpose, which is to lead men to Christ. Now, though he begins with this point, he soon moves on to the idea of a change of status for those who have passed from being under the bondage of the law to being sons in Christ. Before, we were prisoners, shut up under the law as under a guardian. Now we are sons, being reconciled to God and being made one with one another and with all who throughout history have been justified on the basis of God's promise.

23 The proper understanding of the phrase "before this faith came" is found in the fact that the definite article occurs before the word "faith," a fact obscured by KJV. It is true that Paul can refer to faith generically as that on which every successful approach to God is founded. But this is not his meaning here. By "this faith" he means "the Christian faith," that faith he has just spoken of in v.22—faith in Jesus Christ as Savior (cf. 1 Tim 4:1 for a similar usage). This faith is like the faith exercised by Abraham. But it is different in that it relates to the explicit revelation of Christ in time and to the distinct Christian doctrines concerning him. Faith waited for this complete revelation. Paul's point is that the law was intended to function only during this 1,500-year period of anticipation.

While the law was here, however, it did serve a purpose; and that purpose was to *hold us prisoner, locking us up* until Christ should be revealed. The second of these two words (*sunkleiō*) has already occurred in v.22. It means "to confine." The first word (*phroureō*) is similar. It means "to hold in custody" (cf. 1 Peter 1:5). Most likely Paul is thinking here that the law, like a jailer, has kept men locked up and therefore out of trouble till Christ, the liberator, should come to set them free. However, it is also possible that he intends the reference more generally, inasmuch as the next verse speaks of a different kind of confinement entirely.

24 It is unfortunate that KJV refers to the law as a "schoolmaster" and that NIV finds it necessary to work around the operative term by speaking of our being put under "charge" or "supervision" (v.25). The term is *paidagōgos,* which means "a child-custodian" or "child-attendant." The pedagogue was a slave employed by wealthy Greeks or Romans to have responsibility for one of the children of the family. He had charge of the child from about the years six to sixteen and was responsible for watching over his behavior wherever he went and for conducting him to and from school. The pedagogue did not teach. Therefore the translation "schoolmaster" is wrong; if Paul had meant this, he would have used *didaskalos* rather than *paidagōgos.* Paul's point is that this responsibility ceased when the child entered into the fullness of his position as a son, becoming an acknowledged adult by the formal rite of adoption by his father (see on 4:1–7). "To Christ" is not to be taken in a geographic sense as though the pedagogue was conducting the child to a teacher, as some have implied. The reference, as in the preceding verse, is temporal; it means "until we come of age at the time of the revelation of our full sonship through Christ's coming."

The next phrase (literally, "in order that by faith we might be justified") gives the ultimate objective of the law in its role of pedagogue. The emphasis is on justification rather than faith, for Paul has already shown that faith is the only means to salvation.

25 The two most important points of the previous verses are repeated for emphasis: first, the time element—we were under the law as pedagogue *until* the faith should come, but *now* no longer; second, the reference to the fully revealed faith of Christianity (again with the definite article). No doubt, the experience of passing from law to promise needs to be repeated in everyone who comes to faith in Christ Jesus, for the law condemns in order that faith might make alive. But Paul does not have this thought in view here. He is thinking historically, stressing that the reign of law has ended for those believers who now through the coming of Jesus have become mature sons of God.

26 But what are the actual results of this passage from the reign of law to grace through faith in Jesus Christ? In the final verses of the chapter Paul lists three of them.

First, through faith in Christ all who believe become "sons of God"—that is, those who have passed through spiritual infancy into full maturity as justified persons. In view of Paul's previous reference to the pedagogue, the mention of full-grown sons is particularly appropriate. Still we must not think of this as a matter of growth alone. To be a true son of God is to be one who is justified by faith in Christ and who has therefore passed into a new and right relationship to God. Before, the person was under law. Now he is under grace. Before, he was under the curse. Now he is the recipient of God's paternal favor.

In this verse emphasis falls on the word *pantes* ("you . . . *all*"), which at the same time becomes very personal by the change from the first person (in v.25) to the second person. All are included in these statements, the Galatians particularly.

27 This new relationship is not something natural to men, as though all automatically were or became God's sons. The fatherhood of God and the universal brotherhood of men are not NT concepts. True, God has a relationship to all men as Creator. Paul can say, as he did in speaking to the Athenians, "We are his children [literally, 'begotten ones']" (Acts 17:28). But a creature is not necessarily a son. In fact, he can become a son only through union by faith with that unique Son of God, Christ Jesus.

Baptism signifies this transforming identification with Christ. So Paul refers to it here. Paul is not now contradicting all he has previously taught about the means of salvation, as if he were suggesting that baptism will now replace circumcision as a saving sacrament or ordinance. No one is saved by baptism. Indeed, Paul mentions baptism only once in the paragraph, but faith five times. Rather baptism is an outward sign of the union that already exists through faith. To be "clothed with Christ" means to become like Christ. If Paul is thinking of the theatre, where this word was employed, he means that one is identified with Christ on the world stage.

28 Second, through faith in Jesus Christ all who believe become one with each other so that, in one sense, there is now "neither Jew nor Greek, slave nor free, male nor female," but all are "one in Christ Jesus." In what sense is this true? Clearly, it does not mean that differences of nationality, status, and sex cease to exist. A Jew remains a Jew; a Gentile, a Gentile. One does not lose his identity by becoming a Christian. Paul simply means that having become one with God as his sons, Christians now belong to each other in such a way that distinctions that formerly divided them lose significance.

Race is the first example, for Paul writes that there is neither Jew nor Greek. In Paul's day there was a deep division between the two. It was national in many respects, but the depth of the feeling (at least from the Jewish perspective) came from the fact that it was also religious. The Gentile was among the *goyim.* He was uncircumcised and therefore no child of Abraham. He did not have the law or the cermonies. He was not of the covenant. This barrier Paul now claims to have been broken down in Christ (cf. Eph 2:11–18). Today this principle must be extended to deny the significance of all racial barriers. In Christ there must be neither black nor white, Caucasian nor Oriental, nor any other such distinction.

Social status is a second example, for there is neither "slave nor free." Again, this is not meant to deny that in actual fact there are social distinctions among men. It is merely meant to affirm that for those who are united to Christ these things do not matter. In fact, when such distinctions no longer matter, when men treat each other as true brothers in Christ regardless of their social standing, then the power of such distinctions is broken and a basis is laid for social change. On this pattern the ideal church should be composed of members from all spectra of society: wealthy and poor, educated and uneducated, straight and long-hair, management and labor, and so on.

There is also the example of sex, for Paul declares that there is neither "male nor female." It is hard to imagine how badly women were treated in antiquity, even in Judaism, and how difficult it is to find any statement about the equality of the sexes, however weak, in any ancient texts except those of Christianity. The Jew prayed, "I thank God that thou hast not made me a woman" (common morning prayer). Josephus wrote, "Woman is inferior to man in every way" (*Contra Apion,* 2:24). The Gentile world had similar expressions. But Paul reverses this. Indeed, in this statement we have one factor in the gradual elevation and honoring of women that has been known in Christian lands.

When Paul concludes this breakdown of the distinctions that are superseded by Christianity, he speaks of the fact that all who are in Christ are "one," using the masculine form of the numeral. The distinction is not between masculine and feminine, as if Paul were reinstating male superiority again after having denied it, but between masculine and neuter; that is, between a unified personality and a unified organization. Paul is, therefore, not thinking of a unified church structure but of the church as the living body of Christ. In this body all are truly one in and with one another. The only permissible distinctions are those of function (cf. 1 Cor 12).

29 Third, through faith in Jesus Christ all who believe also become one with those who have been saved by faith throughout the long history of salvation. Thus, by union with Christ, believers become "Abraham's seed, and heirs according to the promise." Here that which Paul had previously declared to be Christ's—the inheritance of the promise made to Abraham (3:16)—he now applies to the Christian church as a whole by virtue of its actually being Christ's body. The verse carries the thought back to the beginning of the chapter.

The use of the word "seed" without the article is of great importance, for it keeps the necessity of a union with Christ constantly before the Galatians. The prize the legalizers had been holding before the eyes of the Galatian Christians and by which they had hoped to win them to the ceremonial aspects of Judaism was the possibility of becoming part of the seed of Abraham. They meant physical seed. Paul now replies that what the legalizers were offering through circumcision was actually already theirs in Christ. But it was only theirs in him. He is *the* seed to whom the promises were made. Believers enter into the promises by entering into him, thereby also becoming spiritual seed to God.

This last section of the chapter has been filled with references to Jesus Christ. He is mentioned six times, and the point of each reference is that Christians receive all that is of value spiritually by virtue of their attachment to him. Stott has noted,

> This is a three-dimensional attachment which we gain when we are in Christ—in height, breadth and length. It is an attachment in "height" through reconciliation to the God who, although radical theologians repudiate the concept and we must be

> careful how we interpret it, is a God "above" us, transcendent over the universe He has made. Next, it is an attachement in "breadth," since in Christ we are united to all other believers throughout the world. Thirdly, it is an attachment in "length," as we join the long, long line of believers throughout the whole course of time.

It is through faith in Christ and in Christ alone that we find ourselves.

Notes

23 Συγκλείω (*sunkleiō*) occurs in Gr. from the time of Herodotus with various senses, but its primary meaning is "to shut up" or "to confine." In this v., as a present participle, it means "holding in confinement," suggesting that men were already in bondage to sin even before the law's coming. Φρουρέω (*phroureō*) means "to confine," primarily by military guards. When applied to a city, the word is used both of keeping enemies out and of keeping the citizens in (Acts 9:24; 2 Cor 11:32). Paul uses it of God's keeping power over his saints (Phil 4:7), as does Peter (1 Peter 1:5).

27 Much has been written in recent years about the baptismal references by Paul, some seeing allusions to immersion in the "putting on" of Christ, others to putting on white baptismal gowns after the ceremony, or similar things. But it is hard to believe that the ceremony of baptism had become so fixed at this early date as to make the allusions obvious or to require us to prescribe primarily ceremonial thoughts to this passage. Paul is not dealing with cermony here. If anything, he is dismissing ceremonies. His point is simply the overriding necessity of a faith-union with Christ, which is what baptism signifies. Actually, "baptism" speaks of identification, just as cloth is identified with the color of the dye it is dipped into. This understanding of baptism is supported by the most natural uses of the verb ἐνδύω (*enduō*) ("to put on"). The verb refers to taking on a certain role, as in a play or in other social relations. It is used of a goddess who takes on the form of an old woman (cf. MM). Paul uses it of assuming the character of Christ in Rom 13:12–14, Col 3:9–14, and 1 Thess 5:8.

6. *Heirs of God*

4:1–7

> 1What I am saying is that as long as the heir is a child, he is no different from a slave, although he owns the whole estate. 2He is subject to guardians and trustees until the time set by his father. 3So also, when we were children, we were enslaved by the basic principles of the world. 4But when the time had fully come, God sent his Son, born of a woman, born under law, 5to redeem those under law, that we might receive the full rights of sons. 6Because you are sons, God sent the Spirit of his Son into our hearts, the Spirit who calls out, "*Abba,* Father." 7So you are no longer a slave, but a son; and since you are a son, God has made you also an heir.

For the final time Paul contrasts the condition in which believers found themselves before Christ's coming with the position they enjoy now. The difference between these verses and those that conclude chapter 3 is in emphasis. Before, Paul had been stressing the temporal nature of the change, showing what they *were then* in contrast to what they *are now.* At this point he dwells on their status, showing that whereas they were previously *slaves,* they had now become *sons* of their heavenly Father. This development flows from the thought of the pedagogue in vv.23–29. It is the last stage in the six-part alternating argument (see on 3:1–5).

1 The English reader will miss the flavor of these verses unless he realizes that the moment of growing up was a very definite one in antiquity and that it involved matters of great religious and legal importance. For instance, in Judaism a boy passed from adolescence to manhood shortly after his twelfth birthday, at which time he became "a son of the law." In the Greek world the minor came of age later, at about eighteen, but there was the same emphasis on an entering into full responsibility as an adult. At this age, at the festival of the *Apatouria,* the child passed from the care of his father to the care of the state and was responsible to it.

Under Roman law there was also a time for the coming of age of a son. But the age when this took place may not have been as fixed as is often assumed (cf. Lightfoot), with the result that the father may have had discretion in setting the time of his son's maturity. If this is so, it leads one to think that Paul is referring primarily to the Roman custom as he observed that a child is under guardians and trustees "until the time set by his father." A Roman child became an adult at the sacred family festival known as the *Liberalia,* held annually on the seventeenth of March. At this time the child was formally adopted by the father as his acknowledged son and heir and received the *toga virilis* in place of the *toga praetexta* which he had previously worn. A sense of the moving nature of this moment can be gleaned from the description of the coming of age of Marcellus in the opening pages of *The Robe* by Lloyd Douglas.

This is the general background (whether of Greek law, Roman law, or both) of Paul's words in these verses.

When the child was a minor in the eyes of the law—it is this word that Paul actually uses—his status was no different from that of a slave, even though he was the future owner of a vast estate. He could make no decisions; he had no freedom. On the other hand, at the time set by his father the child entered into his responsibility and freedom. The application of the illustration is obvious as Paul applies it to the inferior condition of a person under law, both a "minor" and a "slave," and to the new freedom and responsibility that come to him in Christ.

2 It is interesting that here Paul drops the term "pedagogue" he had used earlier, and speaks instead of "guardians" (*epitropous*) and "trustees" (*oikonomous*). Too much should not be read into the change, but the fact that these refer to legal functions should not be missed either. It is status that Paul is thinking of.

3 Paul now applies the illustration in the way already indicated. Before Christ came we were children and slaves, slaves to the "basic principles" or "elemental spirits" of the world.

There has been much debate about the proper understanding of Paul's phrase at this point, and rightly so, for it contains a reference difficult to identify. There are three major interpretations. First, the reference to "basic principles" or "elemental spirits" (one word in Greek) may be taken as referring to the elementary stages of religious experience common to all men. This is the view of Burton, Ridderbos, and other commentators. The word itself might suggest this, for the word is *stoicheia* and can mean "alphabet." This, or a meaning closely related to it, is involved at Hebrews 5:12 and may be involved in Colossians 2:8 and 20. If this is Paul's meaning, then he will be referring to the elemental stages of Jewish and Gentile religious experience his readers have gone through in the past but which have now been superseded by Christ's coming. The advantage of this view is that it can apply to both Jew and Gentile. The disadvantage is that it is hard to see how Paul could have considered pagan ideas of religion in any way a rudimentary preparation for the coming of the Christian gospel.

The second interpretation (Lightfoot, Stott, Tenney) is that Paul is again referring to the law of Israel. This view is consistent with Paul's earlier teaching about the law—that it holds us in bondage (cf. 3:23). But in this case there are two further difficulties: (1) It does not seem to apply to the Gentiles, for the difficulty of the Gentiles is not that they were under law in the past but that they were in danger of falling under it in the present; and (2) it does not explain why or how Paul could add the phrase "of the world" to the term *stoicheia.* All Jewish thought would emphasize the other-worldly character of the law resulting from its divine origin.

The third view is based on an entirely different meaning of the word *stoicheia* (Guthrie, Neil, and others). The word can mean "elements" in the same way twentieth-century man speaks of the chemical elements the world is made of. In ancient times, the elements were not regarded in the abstract way people today regard them. For one thing, there were fewer of them—earth, fire, air, and water. For another, they had been associated from the dawn of civilization with the gods. It would seem that in Paul's time this exceedingly early and primitive view had been expanded to the point at which the *stoicheia* also referred to the sun, moon, stars, and planets—all of them associated with gods or goddesses and, because they regulated the progression of the calendar, also associated with the great pagan festivals honoring the gods. In Paul's mind these gods were demons. Hence, he would be thinking of a demonic bondage in which the Galatians had indeed been held prior to the proclamation of the gospel.

There is some support for this position because in the verses that follow, Paul goes on to speak of these three crucial subjects in quick succession: (1) "those who by nature are not gods," presumably false gods or demons; (2) "those weak and miserable principles," again *stoicheia;* and (3) "days and months and seasons and years" (vv.9, 10). No doubt Paul would think of these demons in ways entirely different from the former thinking of the Galatians, but the idea of a spiritual warfare against demons would not be alien to the world view he found in the Bible and to which he adhered (cf. Rom 8:38, 39; Eph 6:10–12). Thus, this whole issue takes on a cosmic and spiritual significance. The ultimate contrast to freedom in Christ is bondage to Satan and the evil spirits.

4 But God has set men free! "But God. . . ." These are wonderful words, because they show that the entry of the Christian message is at the same time the turning point of history. Apart from these words, life offers no future hope for any man. Man is lost, without hope and without God. But God has intervened in a way that brings an effective and complete salvation.

What God has done, Paul now spells out in two propositions. First, "God sent his Son." From the human point of view, that this happened in the fullness of time ("when the time had fully come," NIV) can be seen in historical factors. It was a time when the *pax Romana* extended over most of the civilized earth and when travel and commerce were therefore possible in a way that had formerly been impossible. Great roads linked the empire of the Caesars, and its diverse regions were linked far more significantly by the all-pervasive language of the Greeks. Add the fact that the world was sunk in a moral abyss so low that even the pagans cried out against it and that spiritual hunger was everywhere evident, and one has a perfect time for the coming of Christ and for the early expansion of the Christian gospel.

Viewed theologically, however, it may also be said that the time was full because God himself had filled it with meaning.

5 Specifically, God sent his Son "to redeem" those who were under the law's bondage and to provide the basis by which God is able "to adopt" them as sons. Men are in need of both actions. Redemption is mentioned here for the first time since 3:13 and is particulary appropriate in view of the imagery Paul is using. Redemption means "to buy out of slavery" (cf. note on 3:13). Men were slaves either to the law, as Jews, or to the elemental spirits of the universe, as Gentiles. Christ paid the price of their redemption and set them free. Moreover, it is through him that men have the adoption. That is, they move not only from bondage into freedom, they also move into the great household of God where all are free men and all are also "heirs of God and co-heirs with Christ" (Rom 8:17). Observe the subtle link between the central ideas of this verse and the phrase "weak and miserable (literally, *poor*) principles" of v.9. The opposing powers are "weak" because they are unable to redeem and "poor" because unable to provide the adoption.

And who is the one through whom this great salvation comes? It is striking how much of the important Christian teaching about Jesus is revealed in these two verses (vv.4, 5). He is divine, for he is God's "Son." This speaks of an ontological relationship existing from eternity (Phil 2:5–11; Col 1:15). He is human, for he was "born" of a woman. He was "under law"; that is, he was born into Israel and thus within God's historical stream of salvation. It may even be, as some have suggested, that Paul here alludes to the virgin birth—born "of a woman." For though Paul does not speak of the virgin birth directly either here or elsewhere, this alone does not prove that he was not aware of it or may not occasionally allude to it, as here. Indeed, if Paul traveled with Luke, who had undoubtedly investigated the birth stories, it is inconceivable that he who was "the apostle of the Gentiles" would not have known of them also.

6 Paul has already pointed out the first great redemptive act of God in history: God sent his Son. Here he adds the second act: "Because you are sons, God sent the Spirit of his Son into our hearts, the Spirit who calls out, '*Abba,* Father.' " In other words, to the other doctrines of the faith already spilling over from vv.4, 5 Paul now adds Trinitarian teaching, for he is telling us that salvation consists in its fullness of acts by God the Father in sending both God the Son and God the Holy Spirit. Moreover, this salvation is both objective and subjective. For God the Father sent the Son in order that believers might have the *position* of sons and He sent his Spirit so that they might have the *experience* of the same reality. We should notice that the gift of God's Spirit is not something the child of God is to strive after as if, having been given his salvation, he must now work to realize it or achieve it on a higher level. The Spirit is the gift of God to every believer because he is a son.

How does the Christian experience what is his objectively? Paul suggests that this is primarily through the reality of God's presence made known to him in prayer. Before, he was alienated from God, who indeed did not even hear him. Now, being made a member of his family, the Christian is permitted and even urged to cry, "Father." "*Abba*" is the Aramaic diminutive for "Father," perhaps suggesting the overtones of the English word "Daddy" (cf. note on this verse). It was the word Jesus habitually used in his prayers to the Father and which he passed on to those who through him became God's children.

7 This verse sums up all that Paul has said previously. Formerly slaves, Christians are now both sons and heirs. It is also connected with the previous verse, for Paul teaches that the use of the intimate word "*Abba*" in prayer, provided only by the work of the Holy Spirit within, is proof on the subjective level of sonship. The change from the plural of v.6 to the singular of v.7 brings the argument home to the individual reader. Each reader should therefore ask, "Do I know the reality of such an internal witness by God's Spirit? Am I assured of these things?"

In the Greek the final words of this section are "through God" (*dia Theou*). Their position emphasizes them. Confidence in such matters as Paul has just dealt with comes, therefore, not from looking to man, but from looking to God and from receiving through faith what he has done in sending the Lord Jesus Christ to die for the believer and in sending the Holy Spirit to live within him.

Notes

1 The word the NIV tr. "child" is νήπιος (*nēpios*), which can mean either "babe" or "minor." At times Paul uses it with the first meaning, as in 1 Cor 3:1, 2, where he speaks of having fed those who were spiritual babes with milk rather than with solid food. If he is thinking along the same lines here, this is an additional reason for seeing the στοιχεῖα (*stoicheia*) of v.3 as pertaining to the ABC's of religious thinking. On the other hand, *nēpios* in the sense of "minor" seems to fit the context with less stretching. Paul's main point is that before the coming of Christ men and women had not reached that coming of age God intended for them.

3 Many studies have been made of the στοιχεῖα (*stoicheia*). For an excellent study that ends in support of the first of the three views given here, see Burton (pp. 510–518). Many modern commentators take the third view.

4 The same movement of thought from what the Christian was before Christ's coming to what he has become as a result of it, and turning in the same way on the phrase "But . . . God," occurs in Eph 2:1–7.

6 It is not always recognized how unusual the addressing of God as "Father" was in antiquity nor what an unforgettable impression Jesus' habitual mode of praying made on his followers. Lohmeyer, in a book called "*Our Father*" (New York: Harper & Row, 1965), and Jeremias, in an essay entitled "Abba" in *The Central Message of the New Testament* (New York: Charles Scribner's Sons, 1965), both point out that in Jesus' day (1) no one ever addressed God directly as "My Father," because it would have been thought disrespectful; (2) Jesus always used this form of address in praying, much to the amazement of his disciples; and (3) Jesus authorized his disciples to use this form of address after him, and they did.

In one sense, of course, the title "Father" for God is as old as religion. Homer wrote of "Father Zeus, who rules over the gods and mortal men." Aristotle explained that this was right, for "paternal rule over children is like that of a king over his subjects" and "Zeus is king of us all." In Israel God was called "Father" of the nation and the nation his child (cf. Exod 4:22; Ps 103:13; Isa 64:8; Jer 3:19; Hos 11:1).

The point, however, is that none of this was *personal.* God was never considered to be father of the individual. And in Christ's day the distance between man and God was actually widening in popular thought rather than growing narrower. Jesus completely reversed this trend. This so impressed the disciples that, not only do all four Gospels record his use of this address, they also report that he did so in all his prayers (Matt 11:25; 26:39, 42; Mark 14:36; Luke 23:34; John 11:41; 12:27; 17:1, 5, 11, 21, 24, 25). The only exception is one that actually enforces the significance of the phrase, for it was the cry wrung from Christ's lips at the moment in which he was made sin for mankind and in which the relationship to the Father that had been his was temporarily broken (Matt 27:46).

It may be sentimentalizing the word "*Abba*" to tr. it "Daddy," but it should not be forgotten that the word is a diminutive and implies intimacy. The early church fathers—Chrysostom,

Theodor of Mopsuestia, and Theodoret of Cyprus, who came from Antioch (where Aramaic was spoken and who probably had Aramaic-speaking nurses in their childhoods)—unanimously testify that *Abba* was the address of a small child to his father (J. Jeremias, *The Lord's Prayer*, trans. J. Reumann [Philadelphia: Fortress Press, 1964], p. 19).

C. *Paul's Appeal to the Galatians* (4:8–31)

1. *A return to bondage*

4:8–11

> [8]Formerly, when you did not know God, you were slaves to those who by nature are not gods. [9]But now that you know God—or rather are known by God—how is it that you are turning back to those weak and miserable principles? Do you wish to be enslaved by them all over again? [10]You are observing special days and months and seasons and years! [11]I fear for you, that somehow I have wasted my efforts on you.

At this point the formal argument for salvation by grace rather than by works is finished, but Paul seems unwilling to end the discussion without a direct and, indeed, rather lengthy appeal to the Galatians. Paul reminds his converts of their former bondage in paganism and expresses his astonishment that they could even consider a return to such slavery. In view of this possibility, he expresses concern that his labors among them may have been to no purpose.

8 For the third time (3:23ff., 4:1ff., and now) Paul speaks of the former enslaved state of the Galatians, and for the third time he has a very good reason. In these verses the point is made to establish the folly of their proposed actions in returning to the law's bondage.

It has already been shown that the former state of the Galatians, indeed of all who are not yet Christians, was one of bondage and immaturity (3:23, 4:1). But this is not all that can be said. That highly undesirable former state was also one of ignorance of the true God in which the pagans worshiped those who were not gods. The reference is clearly to the idols of paganism, which, in typically Jewish idiom, Paul terms "no gods." This ignorance was actually one cause of their bondage to paganism.

9 That the Galatians had been in bondage through ignorance of the true God is no surprise to Paul. It is only what would be expected. But that they should return to their former bondage after having been delivered from such ignorance by God himself—this *is* astonishing and, indeed, totally incomprehensible. The astonishment involved in the question is more prominent in Greek than in most English translations, for it spans both vv.8 and 9. A cumbersome but suggestive translation would be, "But how can it be that, on the one hand, having formerly been in ignorance of God and therefore enslaved to those who are not gods and, on the other hand, having come to know God or (which is more to the point) being known by him, you are now returning anew to those weak and bankrupt elements which once controlled you?"

There are three causes for Paul's astonishment: (1) the Galatians were going back to what they had already been through—that is, not to a new error but to an old one; (2) they were turning from reality to nonreality; the absence of the article before the word "God" stresses a qualitative contrast between the true God revealed in Jesus Christ and the "no gods"; and (3) this was done after they had actually come to "know" God in a real way. Paul uses the verb *ginōskō* ("to know intimately and on a personal level") at this point rather than *oida* ("to know factually") or *oraō* ("to know through perceiving something").

It is characteristic of Paul's understanding of man's total spiritual depravity and of the electing grace of God that he corrects himself so as not to leave the impression that it is possible for any man to come to know God by his own efforts. The truth of the matter is that God comes to know us. That is, he takes the initiative in salvation with the result that we come to know him only because we are first known of him. Again, the word "known" does not refer to factual knowledge, for God always possesses that. It refers rather to the fact that through Christ the individual Christian has become an object of God's personal recognition and favor.

We have already seen why the elemental spirits or principles the Galatians were in the process of turning to are "weak and miserable" (literally, "powerless and bankrupt"). They are weak because they are unable to set men free, as Christ has done by redeeming them. They are bankrupt because they have no wealth by which they can provide an inheritance.

10 The Judaizers were probably not intentionally trying to enslave the Galatians and it is even more probable that the Galatians did not regard their current drift toward legalism as a return to slavery. Yet that is precisely what it was, as Paul reminds them.

In view of the context of the struggle in Galatia, there can be little doubt that the observances the Galatians were succumbing to were Jewish observances. "Days" would refer to sabbath days, including also those feasts that fell on specified dates in the calendar. "Months" refers to celebrations tied to the recurring monthly cycle, such as those connected with the appearances of the new moon and which Isaiah ridiculed (Isa 1:14). "Seasons" refers to seasonal events of more than one day's duration—the feasts of Tabernacles, Passover, etc. "Years" most naturally refers to the recurring years of Jubilee. What is most significant, however, about this listing of the Jewish observances is not that Paul opposed them (it is easy to see how they might be opposed pragmatically as but one step in a full return to Jewish legalism—circumcision and a full keeping of the rabbinic traditions), but that he regards them in exactly the same light as the pagan festivals—that is, as under the control of and involving interaction with the demonic spirits.

This does not, of course, mean that Paul would attribute the origin of the law, which includes the religious feasts, to Satan. Far from it. The law is good and from God. Nevertheless, even the law, when distorted into a way of trying to earn salvation, can be used by Satan to increase man's bondage. That Paul, the Jew, would even consider the Jewish observances in the same context as the pagan festivals shows the intensity of his estimate of the deadly character of legalism.

11 Can the reader have missed that point? If so, it comes to him once again as the same Paul who speaks elsewhere of the fact that nothing can ever separate the Christian from the redeeming love of God (Rom 8:35–39) and who expresses confidence that the work begun in the Christian by God will be continued till the day of Christ (Phil 1:6) now voices the thought that his labor in bringing the gospel to the people of Galatia might be wasted. This is not, to be sure, the same thing as saying that a Christian can lose his salvation. Indeed, even the Galatians have not gone that far. They have only begun to observe the feasts; they have not been circumcised (5:2). Nevertheless, they are wavering ("turning," present tense, in v.9), and their wavering is inexplicable and inexcusable.

It can only be, as Peter is later to write of other unfruitful Christians, that they are "nearsighted and blind" and have "forgotten" that they were cleansed from old sins (2 Peter 1:9).

Notes

8 Paul's full teaching concerning the Gentiles' knowledge or lack of knowledge of God is in Romans 1:18–23. It may be summed up by saying that the Gentiles were capable of knowing *about* God in two respects—his existence and his power (Rom 1:20)—but not knowing him personally. Moreover, what they did not know they distorted, so that they ended by worshiping the creature rather than the Creator. For this they are held accountable and are judged.

10 Barton has used the reference to ἐνιαυτούς (*eniautous,*) in an ingenious way to help establish the date of the writing of Galatians ("The Exegesis of *eniautous* in Galatians 4:10 and Its Bearing on the Date of the Epistle," JBL, 33, 1914, pp. 118–126). He argues that the reference to "years" must correspond to a real fact in the life of the Galatian churches and that this must mean they were then in the process of observing a sabbatical year or had just recently observed one. Since such a year occurred in A.D. 53–54, when Paul was in Ephesus, this must mean that the Epistle was composed there either during those years or shortly thereafter. Although this is ingenious, it rests on doubtful premises. It can have weight only if the same dating is derived from other sources.

On the Christian observance of days in the light of Paul's prohibition, see Origin, *Contra Celsus,* 8:21-23.

2. *Their past and present relationships*

4:12–20

[12]I plead with you, brothers, become like me, for I became like you. You have done me no wrong. [13]As you know, it was because of an illness that I first preached the gospel to you. [14]Even though my illness was a trial to you, you did not treat me with contempt or scorn. Instead, you welcomed me as if I were an angel of God, as if I were Christ Jesus himself. [15]What has happened to all your joy? I can testify that, if you could have done so, you would have torn out your eyes and given them to me. [16]Have I now become your enemy by telling you the truth?

[17]Those people are zealous to win you over, but for no good. What they want is to alienate you [from us], so that you may be zealous for them. [18]It is fine to be zealous, provided the purpose is good, and to be so always and not just when I am with you. [19]My dear children, for whom I am again in the pains of childbirth until Christ is formed in you, [20]how I wish I could be with you now and change my tone, because I am perplexed about you!

If the reader is inclined to think Paul has been impersonal in dealing with the problems at Galatia, that he has been arguing as a scholar and not as a pastor, the present passage should disabuse him of this idea. It is true that Paul has dealt with the issues facing the Galatians as doctrinal ones and has even been somewhat distant in addressing his converts. The most endearing he has been is in calling them "brothers" (1:11; 3:15), but this was certainly a common enough term within the Christian community. Now, however, all this changes and the deep pastoral concern of Paul for the Galatians, which has stood behind even his staunch biblical and theological discussion, surfaces. In these verses Paul intensifies his appeal to them. He calls them "brothers" once again and then "dear children." The latter, common in John's writings occurs only here in Paul's. Moreover, Paul bases his appeal on their past and present relationship to one another; first their past relationship to him (vv.12–16) and second, his past and present relationship to them (vv.17–20). He contrasts the former with their present actions; the latter he contrasts with the actions of the Judaizers.

12 The opening words of this verse—literally "Become as I [am], for I as you"—are somewhat puzzling, for there is not enough said to know precisely what Paul is referring to. The NEB suggests that Paul is dealing with attitudes. "Put yourselves in my place, my brothers, I beg you, for I have put myself in yours." Cole suggests, "Be as frank and loving with me as I have been with you." Again, as Burton argues, Paul may have been asking the Galatians to enter into the freedom he knows, with the reminder that he had once been in bondage to the law as they are. In the context of Paul's thought in this chapter, it seems that the first part of the appeal must be understood as the third of these suggestions—that is, "Become like me in regard to my full faith in Christ and in my Christian liberty"—while, on the other hand, the second part of the sentence—"for I as you"—is best referred to Paul's identification of himself with the Galatians in order to preach the gospel to them.

This point was one of Paul's evangelistic principles: "To the Jews I became like a Jew, to win the Jews. To those under the law I became like one under the law . . . so as to win those under the law. To those not having the law I became like one not having the law . . . so as to win those not having the law. To the weak I became weak, to win the weak. I have become all things to all men so that by all possible means I might save some" (1 Cor 9:20–22). When Paul went to the Galatians, he did not stand on any special dignity or insist that the Galatians first come to him by becoming Jews. He went to them, becoming like them, in order to win them to Christ.

This is a principle of great importance for all who are trying to witness. As Stott says, "In seeking to win other people for Christ, our end is to make them like us, while the means to that end is to make ourselves like them. If they are to become one with us in Christian conviction and experience, we must first become one with them in Christian compassion" (in loc.). In other words, while witnessing involves doctrine, it also involves the most personal involvement of the witness with those he is witnessing to.

13 "You have done me no wrong" (v.12) really belongs with this and the following verses. Verses 13–15, telling of Paul's original reception by the Galatians on the occasion of his first visit to them, are written to make exactly that point.

How had Paul been received by the Galatians? He recalls that he had been received graciously and with compassion, as if he had been an "angel of God" (v.14). And this was all the more remarkable in that he had not been at his best when among them. He had been ill. In fact, it was only as a result of his illness that he had visited Galatia in the first place. This illness, unpleasant as it was, was a temptation to the Galatians to despise him. Many attempts have been made to identify the precise nature of Paul's illness and link it to the question whether he is writing to Christians in northern or southern Galatia. But it is impossible to be so precise. Some have imagined that Paul was suffering from a form of malaria he had contracted while on the mosquito-infested coast and that he had therefore left the coastal area for the highlands to recuperate there. Others have guessed that Paul is referring to the physical abuse and resulting weakness he had suffered at Lystra (Acts 14:19; 2 Tim 3:11) as a result of which he may have remained longer in southern Galatia than he had intended. Still others have linked Paul's illness to his "thorn in the flesh" (2 Cor 12:7) and to his reference to the desire of the Galatians to give him their eyes (v.15). On the basis of these verses they have supposed that Paul was suffering from an eye disorder, perhaps some form of ophthalmia. That Paul was suffering from bad eyesight is possible (see on 6:11), but it is not necessary to find a reference to that here. The only thing we can say with certainty is that some form of unpleasant illness lay behind Paul's first visit to the Galatians and that, though they could have despised him for his resulting appearance or weakness, they did not and, instead, received him favorably.

14 They actually received him as "an angel of God," that is, as Paul said, "as if I were Christ Jesus himself," so great was their respect for him then. It is noteworthy that though Paul was well aware that he, like the Galatians, was a sinner and though he had been careful even when among them not to allow any conduct on their part that suggested worship (see Acts 14:8–18), nevertheless he does not suggest in this passage that their respect for him as a messenger of God was in error. On the contrary, they were quite right to receive him in this manner. For he came among them as the approved messenger of the Lord Jesus Christ and with the gospel.

Today there are no apostles. But to the degree that ministers and teachers of the Word of God do teach the Word, to that same degree should they be received as the Galatians received the apostle Paul. Ministers should not be received and evaluated on the basis of their personal appearance, intellectual attainments, or winsome manner, but as to whether or not they are indeed God's messengers bearing the word of Christ. If they are, the message is to be received and acted upon, whether it appeals to a particular congregation or not.

15 The Galatians had once had this attitude toward Paul, but their opinion of him had changed. Earlier they had not wronged him; now they have. The joy they had toward him had vanished and now they were apparently regarding him as their enemy. The word translated "joy" is literally "blessedness" (*makarismos*). They had counted themselves blessed as a result of Paul's having preached among them. If one thinks that Paul probably suffered from bad eyesight, then this particular expression of the extent of their joy—"you would have torn out your eyes and given them to me"—would refer to actual conversations they had at the time. If not, then it is just a vivid figure of speech.

16 Why had Paul become their enemy? After their previous reception of him, the only explanation is that he had become an offense to them through telling them the truth. Unfortunately, this is often the case for those who are faithful to Christ's teaching.

17 Paul can appeal, not only to the former attitude of the Galatians, nor only to the contrast between that and their actions in the present, but also to his own attitude toward them. His attitude was guileless and in marked contrast to that of those who had since been attempting to woo the Galatians into legalism.

There are two things Paul notices about the actions of the legalizers: their zeal and their motives. Zeal itself is not bad. Certainly Paul had himself been zealous for the Galatians as he worked among them, and he encourages them to be zealous in regard to the gospel. If zeal is placed at the service of Christ, it is a fine characteristic. In the case of the legalizers, however, this zeal was misdirected. Indeed, it was a zeal by the legalizers in their own cause and for their own glorification, and it had the side effect of alienating the Galatians from both Paul and Christ.

The word translated "zeal" (*zēloō*) can have two meanings, though in Greek thought both probably blended together more than the two do in English. It can mean "to envy." It can also mean "to be deeply concerned for someone to the point of courting their favor." That these do go together is seen in Paul's use of the same word in 2 Corinthians 11:2 in a marriage metaphor: "I am jealous for you with a godly jealousy. I promised you to one husband, to Christ, so that I might present you as a pure virgin to him." This very metaphor may lie behind Paul's thinking in Galatians, for the actions of the legalizers may be compared to those of a seducer who would alienate an engaged woman from her fiancé or a bride from her husband.

There is here an interesting throwback to a previous verse, as Cole notes. When Paul says that the Judaizers "want . . . to alienate you" (literally, "lock you up," *ekkleisai*), he is probably thinking of the function of the law in "locking" men up under sin (*sunkleiomenoi,* 3:23). The locking up was the same action, but the purposes were different. The law served a proper function in locking men up as sinners so that they might find salvation in Christ. The legalizers were trying to lock the Galatians up under law so that they might be separated from Christ and serve their teachers. For the present, the legalizers are courting the Galatians. But the Galatians must take note. When once they are courted and thereby estranged from both Paul and Christ, then the roles will be reversed and the Galatians will find that they must court the legalizers. Failure to maintain Christian liberty always leads to ecclesiastical as well as other forms of bondage.

18 There are three possible meanings of this verse depending on who may be exercising such zeal—whether it is the legalizers, Paul, or the Galatians. (1) It can be the legalizers (Lightfoot, Ridderbos). In this case Paul is saying that he does not begrudge in itself the interest the legalizers are showing in the Galatians and indeed would not begrudge it at all if only it were in a good cause. He himself had shown similar zeal when among them. (2) It can be Paul (Burton). If so, the verse means, "It is only good to be sought after when it is in a good cause, as in the case of my relationship to you both in the past and now." (3) It can refer to the zeal of the Galatians (Cole), which Paul wishes was as intense now in pursuit of the right thing as it was when he was with them.

If it were only a matter of grammar, the first of these interpretations might be preferred. In this case, *zēlousthai* would be passive and the natural reference would be to the legalizers by whom they had "been courted." It is difficult, however, to believe that Paul can now be referring to these enemies of the gospel in a favorable way, especially after his earlier denunciations of them. To speak favorably in even a limited way would undermine his argument. On the other hand, if we are to take the verb as being in the middle voice and apply it to the Galatians who had once exercised zeal in following after the true gospel, then we get a transition that, though somewhat abrupt, nevertheless leads on to the thought of Paul's having been with them in the past and of his wish to be with them once again if possible (v.20).

19 Paul now comes to his main point in referring to the actions and motives of the legalizers. It is that his own attitude to the Galatians was quite different. He had not come to them in order to build up his own personal following, as the false teachers had. He had come to help them: first, to see that they were born again, and second, to labor for them till Christ himself should be formed in them. In calling the Galatians his "dear children" and in speaking of his labor "pains" on their behalf, Paul pictures himself as a mother who went through the pains of childbirth at the time of their conversion to

Christ and who is apparently in labor once again as the result of their apparent defection. It is pedantic and foolish to ask whether Paul is thinking of Christ being formed in the Galatians after their birth or as an embryo before birth, or again whether it is Christ who is being formed or the Galatians. Paul's metaphors are mixed. His point is merely that his pastoral concern matches his evangelistic fervor and, indeed, that neither has diminished because of the Galatians' listening to the legalizers.

20 We do not know why Paul was unable to visit Galatia again at this time, but if he could (he says), he would change his tone. This does not mean that he would change his teaching or be less exacting in expecting them to conform to it, but his approach would be different. He could ask questions. He could find out why they were in the process of turning from freedom to bondage, and so he would no longer be perplexed and perhaps could even speak to them differently as he nevertheless continued to recall them to the gospel.

Notes

13 If πρότερον (*proteron*) could be given its classical meaning with certainty—that is, "on the *first of* my *two* visits"—this verse would be a strong plank in support of the southern-Galatia hypothesis. It would mean that before Paul wrote this letter he had twice visited the churches of Galatia. Moreover, since these trips are difficult to fit in on the grounds of the northern-Galatia hypothesis, it would probably refer to Paul's visits to the southern area on his first missionary journey (once going and once coming back) or on his first and second journeys, in which case the churches to which he is writing would most naturally be those of Iconium, Derbe, Lystra, Antioch in Pisidia, and other unnamed churches in the same area. Unfortunately, the meaning "on the first of two" is not the sole possibility. The word can also mean "formerly," "before," or "originally," and in this case the northern-Galatia theory is at least possible so far as this verse is concerned. It has been argued, however, that in this context *proteron* is superfluous if it does not mean "on the first of two" and, hence, should be given the classical meaning.

For a fuller discussion of Paul's illness, particularly with a view to ancient interpretations, see Lightfoot, pp. 186–191. Ramsay is the most able exponent of the malaria theory. Chafer suggests bodily weakness resulting from the stoning at Lystra ("The Stoning of St. Paul at Lystra, and the Epistle to the Galatians," Exp., 8th series, 6, 1913, pp. 375–384).

14 In Paul's reference to "an angel of God" it is tempting to see an echo of the attempt by the citizens of Lystra to worship Barnabas as Jupiter and Paul as Mercury, after the two apostles had been used to heal the cripple (Acts 14:8–18). In fact, some have found support for the southern-Galatian theory in this reference (Ramsay, Askwith). Actually, Paul's point is quite different. In Acts Paul is appalled at the thought of their actions, while in writing to the Galatians he apparently approves his reception. Clearly, he is approving the latter because he is referring to a reception in which he was recognized as what he really is, namely, a minister of God and of Jesus Christ, and not that which he is not. Besides, he reminds the Galatians that they had received him "as if I were Christ Jesus himself," an impossible expression if he were thinking of their attempt to receive him as one of the Greek gods.

3. *An appeal from allegory*

4:21–31

21Tell me, you who want to be under the law, are you not aware of what the law
says? 22For it is written that Abraham had two sons, one by the slave woman and

the other by the free woman. 23His son by the slave woman was born in the
ordinary way; but his son by the free woman was born as the result of a promise.

24These things may be taken figuratively, for the women represent two cove-
nants. One covenant is from Mount Sinai and bears children who are to be slaves:
This is Hagar. 25Now Hagar stands for Mount Sinai in Arabia and corresponds to
the present city of Jerusalem, because she is in slavery with her children. 26But
the Jerusalem that is above is free, and she is our mother. 27For it is written:

> "Be glad, O barren woman,
> who bears no children;
> break forth and cry aloud,
> you who have no labor pains;
> there are more children of the desolate woman
> than of her who has a husband."

28Now you, brothers, like Isaac, are children of promise. 29At that time the son
born in the ordinary way persecuted the son born by the power of the Spirit. It is
the same now. 30But what does the Scripture say? "Get rid of the slave woman
and her son, for the slave woman's son will never share in the inheritance with the
free woman's son." 31Therefore, brothers, we are not children of the slave woman,
but of the free woman.

Commentators are sometimes embarrassed because Paul's doctrinal argument in the central two chapters of Galatians concludes with an allegory based on what they consider an unjustified use of an OT story. But this is an unnecessary embarrassment, as is also the thought that the allegory was somewhat of an afterthought for Paul, who had, in fact, actually concluded his argument early in the fourth chapter. In one sense, the formal argument did conclude there. What follows (from 4:8 on) is mostly an appeal to the Galatians to remain in that freedom to which God has called them.

However, one may just as well feel that Paul has deliberately saved precisely this argument for his capstone. The advantages are these: (1) The allegory allows Paul to end on a final citation of the law and, in particular, on a passage involving Abraham, who has been his primary example; (2) it allows him to use a method of argument which, we may assume, had been used by the legalizers, thus turning their own style of exegesis against them; (3) it illustrates and reviews all his main points—the radical opposition between the principle of law and the principle of faith, the fact that life under law is a life of bondage and the life of faith is freedom, that the life of faith is a result of the supernatural working of God by means of the Holy Spirit; (4) the story contains an emotional overtone suited both to a wrap-up of the formal argument and to a final personal appeal; and (5) it gives Paul a base upon which to suggest what he had undoubtedly thought but had apparently been reluctant to say previously—that the Galatians should obey God by casting out the legalizers (v.30). Therefore, the allegory effectively ties together both the doctrinal section of the letter and the appeal based on it, while at the same time leading into the ethical section that begins in chapter 5.

Paul introduces the facts of the story itself (vv.21–23), develops the allegory (vv.24–27), and then applies the allegory to the Galatians and indeed to all believers (vv.28–31). The latter section speaks of the supernatural basis of the new life in Christ, the inevitability of persecution for those who stand by the gospel, and the need to so stand.

21 Paul has already appealed to statements of the law to show that the law brings a curse to those who desire to be under it (3:10–14). But that was both indirect and negative. Now he appeals directly and demands that those desiring to be under law hear what the law actually says and retreat from their folly. He does not yet consider that the Galatians have actually rejected the gospel, only that they are desiring to reject it for law.

22 Now Paul turns for the final time to the case of Abraham upon whom the legalizers had undoubtedly based a large part of their argument. Jews derived much satisfaction from their physical descent from Abraham and in many cases certainly considered the promises and blessings of God to be theirs because of it. This outlook had evoked John the Baptist's comment, "Do not think you can say to yourselves, 'We have Abraham as our father.' I tell you that out of these stones God can raise up children for Abraham" (Matt 3:9), and had become the subject of the extended debate between Jesus and the Pharisees recorded in John 8. In that debate Jesus had denied that the Pharisees were descended from Abraham spiritually. The present passage deals with the same issue, only Paul's method of attack is slightly different. Instead of denying outright their descent from Abraham, Paul simply reminds his opponents that Abraham had two sons (Ishmael and Isaac are meant, though Abraham did have other sons later) and asks, in effect, which of these two children the legalizers take after.

23 There were two main differences between these sons. The first is that they were born of different mothers (v.22). One was a free woman, the other a slave. This, according to ancient law, also affected the sons' status. The second difference was in the manner of their conception. Ishamel's was entirely by natural means. Abraham was elderly at the time, about eighty-six years old, but still the conception was natural. In Isaac's case the conception was by means of a miracle; for by this time Abraham had passed the age at which it was normally possible to engender children—he was ninety-nine years old—and Sarah was long past the age of conceiving them. The preposition "through" in Paul's phrase "as the result of [or through] a promise" indicates that the promise of God called life into being. Moreover, in v.29 the phrase "through a promise" becomes "by the power of the Spirit," and this makes the supernatural character of the birth even clearer.

It is apparent that this contrast lends itself well to the very distinction Paul is trying to make between natural or man-made and supernatural or God-made religion. The religion of works and law corresponds to the natural birth of Ishmael. The religion of the Spirit, which is Christianity, corresponds to the supernatural birth of Isaac.

24–26 This basic distinction between the two sons and in the manner of their conception and birth Paul now carries out in more complete spiritual terms, using the historical account as an allegory. This does not mean that Paul's exegesis is fanciful, as some have implied, but only that he uses the story for the sake of its major principle, which he then quite properly applies to the struggle between Judaism and Christianity.

The best way to understand the allegory is to carry it through in parallel columns. Lightfoot argues that the need to do this is suggested by the text itself, for the word *sustoichei* in v.25 (translated "corresponds") refers to things that are in the same column —letters of the alphabet, for instance, or soldiers at attention. Thus we have:

Hagar, the bond woman	Sarah, the free woman
Ishmael, a natural birth	Isaac, a supernatural birth
The old covenant	The new covenant
Earthly Jerusalem	Heavenly Jerusalem
Judaism	Christianity

In this arrangement Hagar, the slave woman, stands for the old covenant enacted at Sinai, while her son, Ishmael, stands for Judaism with her center at earthly Jerusalem. This is one form of religion. On the other hand, Sarah, the free woman, stands for the new covenant enacted on Calvary through the blood of the Lord Jesus Christ, and her son, Isaac, stands for all who have become part of the church of the heavenly Jerusalem through faith in Christ's sacrifice. On the most superficial level, Isaac and Ishmael were alike in that both were sons of Abraham. But on a more fundamental level they were entirely different. In the same way, Paul argues, it is not enough merely to claim Abraham as one's father. Both Christians and Jews did that. The question is: Who is our mother and in what way were we born? If Hagar is our mother, then we were born of purely human means and are still slaves. If our mother is Sarah, then the birth was by promise, and we are free men.

It is significant that when Paul contrasts "the present city of Jerusalem" with "the Jerusalem that is above" he is mixing two metaphors so as to enrich his meaning. Strictly speaking, the phrase "the present city of Jerusalem" should be matched with "the Jerusalem that is to come," and the phrase "the Jerusalem that is above" should be matched with "earthly Jerusalem." These connotations are more or less evident, though unexpressed. But that Paul did not actually say "the Jerusalem that is to come" may be significant; for while it is true that there is a Jerusalem to come (Rev 21:2), it is also true, though in another sense, that this Jerusalem is now present in those born again by God's Spirit.

27 There is no evidence that the verse Paul now quotes (Isa 54:1) was ever associated with the story of Hagar and Sarah and their children; nevertheless, it is highly appropriate. The verse is a prophecy of Jerusalem's restoration following the years of Babylonian captivity and involves the thought that the blessing of the latter years will be greater than that enjoyed formerly. The pre-exilic Jerusalem and the post-exilic Jerusalem correspond, then, to Paul's distinction between the earthly and heavenly Jerusalems and the promise itself to the blessings of God to Israel under the old covenant as contrasted with the greater blessings to the church under the new covenant. The one element common to these verses is the supernatural intervention of God in order to establish Christianity. The new element is the suggestion, soon to be fulfilled, that the numbers of Christians will outnumber those within Judaism.

28 In the third section of this treatment of the Hagar and Sarah story Paul applies the allegory to all Christians, pointing out that because they are like Isaac, who had a supernatural birth, rather than like Ishmael, their experiences will be consistently similar to that of the younger son.

29 In the first place, they must expect to endure persecution from their brother. Paul is referring to an incident in Genesis 21. At the weaning of Isaac, when he was probably about two years of age and his half-brother Ishmael about seventeen, Ishmael "laughed at" or "mocked" Isaac. This was why Sarah asked that Hagar and her son be sent away. So it is today, says Paul. True Christians will be persecuted, as Jesus himself taught (Matt 5:10–12) and the apostles confirm (Phil 1:29; 1 Thess 3:1–4; 2 Tim 3:12; 1 Peter 4:12, 13). And the remarkable thing is that this will not always be by the world but also and indeed more often by their half-brothers—the unbelieving but religious people in the nominal church. This is the lesson of history. It was the Jews who killed the prophets, not the Gentiles. It was the Pharisees and other religious leaders who opposed Jesus and instigated his execution, which was carried out by the Romans. Paul's fiercest opponents were the fanatically religious Judaizers. Today the greatest enemies of the believing church are found among the members of the unbelieving church, the greatest opposition emanating from the pulpits and church hierarchies.

30 Second, the Christians at Galatia must recognize the categorical incompatibility of man-made and God-made religion and respond by casting out the legalizers. Those born after the flesh (v.29) will never share in the inheritance God has reserved for his true children, born after the Spirit. Therefore, Christians are to reject both legalism and those who teach it. It is interesting, as Stott notes, that the verse of Scripture (Gen 21:10) that the Jews undoubtedly interpreted as a statement of the principle of God's rejection of the Gentiles Paul now boldly turns around and applies to the exclusion of unbelieving Jews from Christianity. The procedure would probably have infuriated his opponents, but his point was well taken. God does not look on physical descent but on spiritual affinity. The true sons of Abraham are those who are born of the Spirit.

31 Of such are the Galatians. The "therefore" of this verse is not designed to draw a special conclusion from the verses immediately preceding, but rather to sum up the whole allegory and indeed the whole of Paul's doctrinal argument. The shift to the first person "we," instead of "you" or "they," once again includes both Paul himself and all who embrace the true gospel.

Notes

24 The use of allegory as a tool for interpreting Scripture has had defenders as well as critics. It is important, therefore, in order to assess Paul's use of allegory to determine precisely what he does and to see, in particular, how far removed he is from the totally unrestricted and fanciful use of allegory by such a writer as Philo. In Philo's case, the allegory is the important thing. In Paul's case, the allegory is secondary to the historical sense.

The verb ἀλληγορέω (*allēgoreō*) has two general meanings: (1) "to speak allegorically"—in ancient Gr. this was often the equivalent of "to speak in riddles"; and (2) "to treat allegorically," which means to base an allegorical interpretation or application upon fact. Clearly, it is the latter of these two meanings that is involved in Paul's procedure. What is more, it is also clear that Paul believed his allegorical remarks to be in full harmony with the spiritual truth implicit in the story. So he begins with a statement of the history, then adds his allegory and a practical application.

25 The inherent difficulty of the statement "Now Hagar stands for Mount Sinai in Arabia" has led to four major variants on the text; but the variant leading to the tr. of NIV is to be preferred. The question is: How can Hagar be considered a designation of Sinai? It is hard to suppose that Paul is assuming an historical identification of Hagar and her wanderings with the area of Sinai itself or that Sinai was called Hagar by those living in the area, as Chrysostom suggests. Even if this were true—and there is no evidence for it—it would be unlikely that the Galatians would know about it. The best explanation is simply that Paul wishes to carry through on his allegory, drawing a line from Hagar, who represents the old covenant, to Sinai, where that covenant was established, and beyond it to Jerusalem, where it was centralized at the time of his writing. At that time it was from Jerusalem that the old covenant of law was proceeding, just as it had once proceeded from Sinai.

III. The Call to Godly Living (5:1–6:10)

A. *Summary and Transition*

5:1

[1]It is for freedom that Christ has set us free. Stand firm, then, and do not let yourselves be burdened again by a yoke of slavery.

Paul has already reached two important goals in his appeal to the Galatians. He has defended his apostleship, including a defense of his right to preach the gospel with or without the support of other human authorities (1:11–2:21), and he has defended the gospel itself, showing that it is by grace alone entirely apart from human works that the Christian is freed from the curse of the law and brought into a right relationship with God (3:1–4:31). But there is one more point to be made before Paul concludes his letter: that the liberty into which believers are called is not a liberty that leads to license, as his opponents would charge, but rather a liberty that leads to mature responsibility and holiness before God through the power of the indwelling Holy Spirit. This theme dominates the last two chapters of the Epistle.

1 Before plunging into this third section of his letter, Paul interjects a verse that is at once a summary of all that has gone before and a transition to what follows. It is, in fact, the key verse of the entire Epistle. Because of the nature of the true gospel and of the work of Christ on his behalf, the believer is now to turn away from anything that smacks of legalism and instead rest in Christ's triumphant work for him and live in the power of Christ's Spirit. The best MS evidence divides the verse into two parts—a declaration of Christ's purpose in saving us ("It is for freedom that Christ has set us free") and an appeal based upon that purpose ("Stand firm, then, and do not let yourselves be burdened again by a yoke of slavery")—rather than leaving it as one sentence as does the KJV. Thus, though only loosely connected with the preceding, the first part aptly sums up the message of chapters 3 and 4, while the second part leads into the ethical section. The appeal is for an obstinate perseverance in freedom as the only proper response to an attempt to bring Christians once more under legalism.

Since the Jews of Paul's time spoke of "taking the yoke of the law upon oneself," it is likely that Paul is referring to such an expression here. To the Jews the taking up of the law's yoke was good; indeed, it was the essence of religion. To Paul it was assuming the yoke of slavery. Perhaps Paul was also remembering that Jesus had spoken of Christians taking his yoke upon them (Matt 11:29, 30), but this involves a different kind of service—one that is "easy" and "light"—as the readers of the letter are to see.

Notes

1 The many variants for this text make analysis difficult. But the two most important ones—the position of οὖν (*oun*, "therefore") and the inclusion or exclusion of the relative ᾗ (*hē*, "that") after τῇ ἐλευθερίᾳ (*tē eleutheria*, "for freedom")—when resolved, more or less determine the import of the sentence. The best reading (the one that also best seems to account for the variants) is reflected in the text of NIV and other modern versions. In this reading the relative is omitted and the *oun* follows "stand firm." There are full discussions of these variants in both Burton and Lightfoot (in loc.).

B. *The Danger of Falling From Grace*

5:2–12

[2]Mark my words! I, Paul, tell you that if you let yourselves be circumcised, Christ will be of no value to you at all. [3]Again I declare to every man who lets himself be circumcised that he is obligated to obey the whole law. [4]You who are trying to be justified by law have been alienated from Christ; you have fallen away from grace. [5]But by faith we eagerly await through the Spirit the righteousness for which we hope. [6]For in Christ Jesus neither circumcision nor uncircumcision has any value. The only thing that counts is faith expressing itself through love.

[7]You were running a good race. Who cut in on you and kept you from obeying the truth? [8]That kind of persuasion does not come from the one who calls you. [9]"A little yeast works through the whole batch of dough." [10]I am confident in the Lord that you will take no other view. The one who is throwing you into confusion will pay the penalty, whoever he may be. [11]Brothers, if I am still preaching circumcision, why am I still being persecuted? In that case the offense of the cross has been abolished. [12]As for those agitators, I wish they would go the whole way and emasculate themselves!

The reader is apt to think that in the opening verses of chapter 5 Paul, who seemed to be moving on to the ethical section of his letter, here nevertheless reverts to a theme he has already covered and so departs from his purpose. But to reason this way is to miss an important point—that even the ethical life must begin by recognizing that the foundation of God's dealings with men is grace through faith rather than legalism. "Do you wish to lead a holy life?" Paul seems to be asking. "Then begin with the principles of faith and shun legalism." Holiness will never come as the result of someone insisting on adherence to either man-made or even God-made regulations.

This passage (vv.2–12) makes this point twice: first, from the point of view of those who, like the Galatians, may be about to fall into legalism, thinking it somehow to be a higher good (vv.2–6) and, second, by reference to those who teach such false doctrines (vv.7–12).

2 NIV's "Mark my words!" is actually the word "Behold!" or "Look!" used as an introductory particle. It calls attention to what follows. If the Galatians allow themselves to be circumcised, the result will be that Jesus Christ will profit them absolutely nothing at all. The phrase has the force of a disposition in court of law. Circumcision was, of course, the particular form of legalism that was a problem in Paul's day, and the argument is simply that, circumcision having taken the position it had and signifying what it did, the choice was between Christ and no circumcision at all, or circumcision and no Christ at all. In other words, God would put a minus sign before Christ in the lives of the Galatians if they put a plus sign before anything else.

This explains why Paul is so categorical in condemning the practice of circumcision for the Galatians. It is not that circumcision in itself is that important. In fact, Paul himself had once had Timothy circumcised; just four verses farther on he will declare that "neither circumcision nor uncircumcision has any value." What Paul is condemning is the *theology* of circumcision—namely, the theology that makes works necessary for salvation and seeks to establish conformity to some external standards of behavior as a mark of spirituality.

In this verse the tense of the verb "to be circumcised" is important. It is a present passive (as it is in v.3), which gives the sense, "If you should let yourselves be circumcised." This implies quite clearly that the Galatians had not yet taken this step but rather were just considering it, and therefore their motivation becomes the important thing. It also means that Paul was in no sense condemning those Jewish Christians who had always, as it were, been circumcised. His advice to such is given in 1 Corinthians 7:17–20. If a man who has been circumcised becomes a Christian, he should remain circumcised, not seeking to change his status. If he is uncircumcised, he should remain uncircumcised. The point, once again, is that particular forms of legalism are not themselves the important issues. The issue is works versus grace, or, as we will soon see, spirit versus flesh. Paul's concern was that nothing should cloud perception of this central Christian doctrine.

3 Paul has already given one good reason why the Galatians should remain firm in the freedom Christ has given them: to fall into the practice of circumcision is to lose the value of Christ's death both for salvation and for living the Christian life. Now he adds another: to choose circumcision is to choose legalism, which in turn involves taking on the burden of the whole law. Had the legalizers warned the Galatians that this was involved? One is inclined to doubt it, feeling rather that they were slyly proceeding step by step in their efforts to impose legalistic religion—first the feasts (4:10), then circumcision, and eventually the whole law.

4 Once again Paul reiterates his points, this time dropping the hypothetical "if" for the much stronger statement: "You who are trying to be justified by law have been alienated from Christ; you have fallen away from grace." Have they desired to be saved by legalism? In that case, Christ is of no value to them and the burden of keeping the whole law is theirs.

What does "You have fallen away from grace" mean? Some have taken it as teaching that salvation can be lost. Thus, though this is the only place in Scripture where the phrase occurs, the statement has assumed an importance far beyond Paul's use of it and in a way entirely out of keeping with his context. The phrase does not mean that if a Christian sins, he falls from grace and thereby loses his salvation. There is a sense in which to sin is to fall into grace, if one is repentant. But to fall from grace, as seen by this context, is to fall into legalism. Or to put it another way, to choose legalism is to relinquish grace as the principle by which one desires to be related to God. The article with "grace" distinguishes it as that specific grace of God in Christ that Paul has already stated to be the core of the gospel.

5 The essence of that gospel is now brought forward in the last full statement of the principle of justification by faith in the letter. Up to this point Paul has been talking only of the Galatians, using the pronoun "you." He has been warning them about what they seemed to be doing. Now the pronoun changes to "we" and is placed in an emphatic position—"we wait" and "we hope." It is as if Paul is saying, "But, on the other hand, we Christians do not choose legalism; rather, we wait in faith through the Spirit for the full realization of God's righteousness." Each word in this verse is important and, except for the nontheological words, has already been defined. After "we," which is prominent in the Greek text, comes "through the Spirit." It is a reminder of the electing grace of God in salvation. Next is the phrase "by faith." This is the key word and stands in contrast to flesh, as all should be aware from the arguments of chapters 3 and 4. Circumcision is of the flesh. Faith denotes an entirely different approach. Next, the Christian "waits eagerly" for the full realization of his salvation. He does not *work* for it; he *waits* for it. In the context, "the righteousness for which we hope" does not refer to that imputed righteousness the believer has in the present through faith in Christ's death, though the thought is not far away, but rather (in line with the ethical section to follow) to that actual righteousness the believer is to grow into and which he is to be perfectly conformed to in glory. In the Bible, "hope" refers to that which, though certain, is not yet fully realized.

6 Two more points are made as this verse wraps up the first half of this section. First, as hard as Paul has been on circumcision and as much as it would serve his purpose polemically to downgrade it in preference to uncircumcision, he nevertheless acknowledges that neither circumcision nor uncircumcision in themselves count for anything. This is further evidence that his concern is theological and not ceremonial. It is a similar point to that made about eating meat offered to idols (1 Cor 8:8).

The second point is that true faith, having an ethical side, works itself out "through love." This is what matters—this kind of faith! True, we are saved through faith rather than by works; but faith is no mere intellectual conviction, as if a Christian could do as he wishes so long as he believes properly. This is a horrible idea, as Paul writes elsewhere (Rom 6:1, 2). To believe is to place one's personal confidence in Christ, who loves us and gave himself for us. Therefore, since Christians have learned love in such measure and at such a source, faith must issue in a genuine and self-denying love for others.

It is worth noting that, in making these two points, Paul has come very close to giving a full and extremely beautiful definition of true religion. "In this is the whole of Christianity," says Bengel. The sentence begins with a reference to those who are "in Christ Jesus," so placing the emphasis both in point of order and in importance on God's act of engrafting a person into his Son. It proceeds by repudiating the value of form or ceremony in determining a person's relationship to God. It ends with a unique emphasis upon the combination of faith and love toward both God and man. Paul does not combine the words in this manner anywhere else in his writings.

In vv.5, 6 the three great terms "faith . . . hope . . . and love" appear together (cf. 1 Cor 13; Col 1:4, 5; and 1 Thess 1:3).

7 In the first half of this section the contrast has been between those who desire to add circumcision to Christianity and true believers who trust Christ alone. Paul has indicated the contrast by the pronouns "you" and "we." Now the contrast changes to that between the false teacher or teachers, designated as "the one who is throwing you into confusion," and "I," that is, Paul, who is teaching correctly.

Paul was fond of using athletic imagery to describe the Christian life. To him life is a race, demanding adherence to rules and discipline if the race is to be completed successfully and a prize obtained. Quite often he thinks of himself as the competitor (1 Cor 9:24–27; Gal 2:2; Phil 3:13, 14; 2 Tim 4:7). At other times, as here, he applies it to the life of his converts. The Galatians had begun the race well, Paul testifies. Theirs had not been merely an intellectual assent to certain truths, that is, not mere orthodoxy divorced from Christian life and character. Nor was theirs the life of Christianity without doctrine. This is the full meaning of the phrase "obeying the truth." Theirs was both a head and a heart religion. In spite of this good beginning, however, something had obviously gone wrong. Someone had hindered them. The verb *enkoptō*—a military term—refers primarily to setting up an obstacle or breaking up a road. In this context, it probably refers to the illegal interference of a runner who cuts in ahead of another and thereby disadvantages him. Thus, so it seemed, the situation at Galatia was one in which the Galatians had already ceased, in some measure, to obey the plain truth of the gospel.

8 But what is to be said regarding the false teaching and false teacher or teachers? Much indeed. In three succinct statements Paul traces the origin, results, and end of such doctrine. What is the origin of this teaching? "Well," says Paul somewhat understating the case, "its origins do not lie in the one who calls you." The one who called the Galatians is obviously God (so at 1:6), but Paul does not say that the origin of the false teaching is with Satan, though that may well be the case. The point is simply that the doctrine of salvation by works is not of God but rather proceeds from that which is hostile to God's grace.

9 Second, Paul speaks of the present results of such teaching: it spreads. It is permeating, insidious, and therefore dangerous. No doubt Paul is quoting a proverb at this point, as he also seems to be doing in 1 Corinthians 5:6. But there is no need to identify it as a specific saying of the Lord, as some have done. The point is merely that false teaching, like yeast, grows and affects everything it touches. Therefore, this alone would justify Paul's alarm at the state of affairs in the Galatian churches.

10 That it is the nature of evil to spread does not mean that God will permit evil to triumph ultimately. In fact, its end is the opposite. In completing his analysis of the situation, Paul therefore concludes with an optimistic expression of his confidence that the Galatians will return to a right mind and that the false teacher, whoever he is or however important he may seem to be, will suffer God's judgment. Paul's use of the singular ("the one") must not be overstressed. Some question exists about what the phrase "no other view" refers to. "No other view" from what? From the gospel? From their first opinions formed as the result of Paul's teaching? Or to what Paul has just said regarding the origin and danger of the legalizers' teaching? The answer is not given. Any of the three is possible, and indeed Paul may have all of them in mind.

11 Two personal remarks conclude the section, one in this verse and one in the next. The first presents a difficulty. What does Paul mean by saying, "If I am still preaching circumcision"? This cannot refer to his pre-Christian days only, for there would be no point to the criticism in that case. Besides, Paul links his alleged preaching to times in which he was persecuted as a Christian. But is one to believe that anyone could actually have made that claim in view of Paul's stand on the circumcision issue? Those who feel the force of this objection are inclined to take the verse in the sense of "If I preach circumcision, which everyone knows I do not" (gaining support from the omission of the word "still" in a few ancient MSS), or else by arguing that Paul must have preached circumcision early in his ministry. The most likely explanation is simply that Paul's words are a reply to an accusation that he did preach circumcision when it suited him, however unfounded or unlikely that accusation was. The accusation could have originated from views such as those expressed in 1 Corinthians 7:18 or from the fact that Paul had once encouraged Timothy to be circumcised.

The "offense [*skandalon*] of the cross" is an important concept in Paul and is a highly important reference in this context. The Greek word means a "trap," "snare," or "temptation." Paul uses it in the sense of that which is so offensive to the natural mind that it arouses fierce opposition. But why should Paul link his refusal to approve circumcision for Gentiles to the offense of the cross? Obviously, for the same reason that he opposed circumcision or any other work of the flesh generally. All these things—feasts, circumcision, ceremonies, legal observances, or anything symbolizing external religion today—are of man and are part of a system that seeks to attain standing before God through merit. In opposition to this, the cross proclaims man's complete ruin in sin, to the degree that nothing he does or can do can save him, and thus also proclaims man's radical need for God's grace. The natural man does not understand such teaching (1 Cor 2:14) and, in fact, hates it, because it strips away any pretense of spiritual achievement. It is "only by the gift of God's Spirit," as Cole maintains, that "that which was once a 'trap' to him become[s] his greatest boast and glory" (on Gal 6:14).

12 The second of Paul's personal remarks concerns the legalizers. It is his wish, expressed somewhat obliquely, that they would not stop with circumcision in their zeal for ordinances but rather would go on to castration. Sacral castration was known to citizens of the ancient world; it was frequently practiced by pagan priests as in the cult of Attis-Cybele, which was prominent in Asia. But for Paul to compare the ancient Jewish rite of circumcision to pagan practices even in this way is startling. For one thing, it puts the efforts of the Judaizers to have the Gentiles circumcised on the same level as abhorred pagan practices. For another, it links their desire for circumcision to that which even in Judaism disbarred one from the congregation of the Lord (Deut 23:1).

To many in our day Paul's expression sounds coarse and his wish reprehensible. But we may be sure that Paul did not speak out of a malicious spirit or in ill temper. He spoke out of a concern for the gospel of grace and for God's truth. As Stott says, "If we were as concerned for God's church and God's Word as Paul was, we too would wish that false teachers might cease from the land" (in loc.).

Notes

6 The first part of v.6 occurs again in 6:15 and in 1 Cor 7:19, in which verses the second part may be found to parallel the phrase "faith expressing itself through love." The phrase is therefore more or less synonymous with "a new creation" (6:15) and "keeping God's commands" (1 Cor 7:19).

The verb **ἐνεργουμένη** (*energoumenē,* here tr. "expressing itself") has been the subject of substantial debate within Catholicism and between others and Catholic theologians. If the verb is passive, as most Catholics maintain, then the phrase means that faith is inspired by love; that is, love comes first, faith stemming from it. This, while linguistically possible, is not Paul's meaning. If the verb is in the middle voice, as it seems to be elsewhere in the NT, then the thought is as tr. in NIV. This links up with two of Paul's basic thoughts expressed elsewhere: first, that love is the fulfillment of the law (Rom 13:10), and second, that faith leads to the development of the fruit of the Spirit in which love is prominent (Gal 5:22). It is through love that faith reveals and proves itself, as the Epistle of James indicates.

10 In line with the theories of the Tübingen school, Meyer has suggested somewhat more recently (*Ursprung und Anfaenge des Christentums,* III, 1923, p. 434) that the unnamed "one who is throwing you into confusion" was Peter. Some other German scholars agree. The idea that Paul is referring to Peter conflicts not only with all we know of Peter from Acts but also with the letter to the Galatians itself. Thus, though Paul speaks of his one sharp confrontation with Peter, everything both in Acts and Galatians indicates that in the essentials of the faith Paul and "the apostle to the circumcision" were one.

C. *Life in the Spirit* (5:13–26)

1. *Liberty is not license*

5:13–18

> 13You, my brothers, were called to be free. But do not use your freedom to indulge your sinful nature; rather, serve one another in love. 14The entire law is summed up in a single command: "Love your neighbor as yourself." 15If you keep on biting and devouring each other, watch out or you will be destroyed by each other.
>
> 16So I say, live by the Spirit, and you will not gratify the desires of your sinful nature. 17For the sinful nature desires what is contrary to the Spirit, and the Spirit what is contrary to the sinful nature. They are in conflict with each other, so that you do not do what you want. 18But if you are led by the Spirit, you are not under law.

Paul has already spoken of freedom several times in this letter (2:4; 4:26, 31; 5:1). From one point of view, Galatians is almost entirely about freedom. Still, up to this point, Paul has not yet defined it, at least not in practical terms dealing with the ethical life. Now he does so, showing not only the true nature of Christian freedom but also that it is only through the life of the Spirit and by the Spirit's power that the Christian can live for God and not fulfill the desires of his sinful nature. Negatively, freedom in Christ is not license. Positively, it is service both to God and man. It expresses itself in the great Christian virtues. This latter point is emphasized by two contrasting catalogs of the works of the flesh versus the fruit of the Spirit.

One reason why Paul adds this section to his letter is to show what he means by "faith expressing itself through love" (v.6). Another is apparently to counter developing strife and divisiveness in the churches of Galatia (so Cole), for the verses speak of a "biting," "devouring," and "destroying" of each other that seems to have been taking place. The greatest reason, however, is undoubtedly Paul's desire to complete his portrait of true Christianity by showing that the freedom we have been called to in Christ is a responsible freedom that leads to holiness of life. Called to freedom? Yes! But this is a freedom to serve God and others as love dictates! That Paul would have had this point uppermost in mind is evident from the apparent and quite understandable fear within Judaism that a faith without law would not be sufficiently strong to resist the ethical debauchery of paganism.

13 Verse 13, like v.1, is transitional and marks a new beginning. The fact that "you" is emphasized in the Greek by being placed first in the sentence (cf. NIV) shows that Paul is building on the confidence expressed earlier as to what side the Galatians are on (v.10); the language of the verse shows that Paul is echoing the original challenge of v.1: "It is for freedom that Christ has set us free." On the other hand, while in the first instance Paul followed his statement with a warning about falling again into slavery, in this case the warning is changed into the demand not to allow this freedom to become an excuse for sinful self-indulgence. Here the contrast is between indulgence and the serving of one another in love.

Paul says that the Christian is not to allow this freedom—the articles emphasize that this is the freedom in Christ Paul has been writing about—to become a beachhead for the armies of indulgence to gain a foothold in his life. The first meaning of the Greek word *aphormē* originally means "a starting point or base of operations for an expedition," then an "opportunity" or "pretext" (so 2 Cor 11:12). When Paul speaks of *sarx* ("flesh"; "sinful nature" in NIV) he means all that man is and is capable of as a sinful human being apart from the unmerited intervention of God's Spirit in his life (see comment on v.16).

It is ironical that, having urged the Galatians not to become slaves to law, Paul should now encourage them to become slaves of one another—for that is what the verb translated "serve" (*douleuete*) means. It is a paradox, but the paradox is instructive. The Galatians are to be slaves of one another, though this slavery is not at all like the first. In fact—this is the paradox—it is the Christian form of being free. Slavery to sin is involuntary and terrible; a man is born into sin (Ps 51:5) and cannot escape it (Rom 7:18). Slavery to law, which comes by choice, is foolish and burdensome. On the other hand, slavery to one another is voluntary and a source of deep joy. It is possible only because Christians are delivered through the presence and power of the Holy Spirit from the necessity of serving sin in their lives.

14 Throughout his letter Paul has been arguing against law and in defense of the gospel of pure grace. Now, in a most striking fashion, he returns to law and seems to speak favorably of it, stressing that when Christians love and serve others, the law is fulfilled. There is a play on two meanings of the Greek word *peplērōtai,* translated "summed up." On the one hand, it refers to the fact that the law can aptly be summarized by the words of Leviticus 19:18. This idea was a commonplace of rabbinic opinion and Jesus endorsed it in Matthew 22:39 and Luke 10:25–28. On the other hand, the word can also mean "fulfilled" (as in Rom 13:8), and in this sense Paul is suggesting that it is actually out of the new life of love made possible within the Christian community through the Spirit that the law finds fulfillment.

This use of the word "law" is most instructive, because it shows that in spite of all Paul has said, there remains a sense in which the requirements of the law are a proper concern for Christians. This does not mean that the Christian is to make progress in holiness by once again setting up a system of rules and regulations. Nothing in the last half of Galatians or any other part of the NT suggests this. Still, it means that the essential ends of the law will be met in those who, being called by God and being filled with the Spirit, allow God to produce the Spirit's fruit in their character. On this verse, Ridderbos says, "This fulfillment [of the law] remains a divine requirement. But since the law, as demanding agent, cannot effectuate the fulfillment, it is not the imperative of the law but the bond of faith in Christ which forms the ground and origin of the fulfillment of the will of God."

15 It is not hard to imagine the kind of strife that may have been present in the Galatian churches, either strife parallel to that of the Corinthians (1 Cor 1:10–12; 3:1–4) or strife arising directly out of the conflict with the legalizers. Paul does not say precisely what it was. That it was, so far as Paul knew, even then existing is evident from the tense of the verbs. That it was intense seems evident from the verbs themselves as well as by the fact that they move by increasingly strong degrees to a climax.

16 What is the solution to such biting, devouring, and destroying that is all too common among Christian assemblies? The answer, Paul says, is in living by the Spirit. Then, and only then, will one cease to gratify the desires of the flesh. It is the Spirit alone who can keep the believer truly free.

The contrast between *sarx* ("flesh"), on the one hand, and *pneuma* ("spirit"), on the other, is one of the characteristic themes in NT, and particularly Pauline, theology. It is as important, for instance, as the contrast between the works of the law and the hearing of faith which has thus far dominated the letter. In the earliest days of the Greek language *sarx* meant mostly the soft, fleshy parts of the body, like its Hebrew equivalent *basar.* But *sarx* soon came to denote the body as a whole (that is, the material part of a person) and after that, by extension, the whole man as conditioned by a bodily existence and by natural desires. In this sense, it is not bad. But when the word was taken over into the Christian vocabulary, as it was to a large degree by Paul, it came to mean man as a fallen being whose desires even at best originate from sin and are stained by it. Thus, *sarx* came to mean all the evil that man is and is capable of apart from the intervention of God's grace in his life. In this respect *sarx* is synonomous with "the natural man" or "the old nature." Because fallen man is only flesh apart from the intervention of God's Spirit, "old nature" or "sinful nature" (as in NIV) rather than "lower nature" (NEB, Phillips) or "animal nature" is the better translation in these passages.

Sarx also contains thoughts of human limitation, both intellectually (1 Cor 2:14, where, however, the term *psychikos* is used) and morally (Rom 7:18). Thus, that which is flesh is incapable of knowing God apart from special revelation and the redemption that removes the barrier of sin.

The other term is *pneuma,* which is usually translated "spirit." Its meaning in the earliest writers is "wind," "air," "breath," or "life." The word later came to refer to the spirit or incorporeal part of man, which (like breath) leaves him at death. These meanings also occur in the NT. But in biblical texts the emphasis is always on "spirit" as the Spirit of God. Indeed, it is because God breathes his spirit or breath into man that man has breath. The word also refers to the incorporeal part of man (which has God-consciousness) and to incorporeal beings such as angels or demons. In distinctly religious terminology, it is the Spirit of God who takes up residence in Christians to enable them to understand spiritual things (1 Cor 2:14), receive Christ as Savior and Lord, call God "Father" (Rom 8:15; Gal 4:6), and develop a Christian personality. The Spirit, in many characteristic passages, is thus the presence of God in the man, through which fellowship with God is made possible and power given for winning the warfare against sin in the soul.

The Spirit is not natural to man in his fallen state. But this does not mean that by the gift of the Spirit the redeemed man escapes the need to struggle against sin. The Spirit simply makes victory possible and that only to the degree that the believer "lives by the Spirit" or "walks" in him. The present tense of the verb "walk" (*peripateite*) points to a continuing condition or need for it. That the word is an imperative demonstrates the necessity of a choice.

17 A characteristic of the contrast between flesh and spirit—Paul has stressed the contrast by eliminating the articles before each word in v.16—is that the two principles are in deep and irreconcilable conflict. In the sense in which Paul uses the words, the flesh does no good and does not desire good, whereas the spirit does no evil and, indeed, opposes anything that does not please God. A fuller discussion of this same principle occurs in Romans 7.

The last clause of v.17 may mean one of three things: (1) the sinful nature keeps you from doing the good you desire, (2) the Spirit keeps you from doing the evil you desire, or (3) each nature hinders the desires of the other (so Burton). In view of the parallel statements in Romans 7:15, 16, probably the first should be preferred, especially since the next verse goes on to speak of the victory that can be attained by the Spirit's power.

Some have maintained that there is no conflict within the Christian because of the supposition that the old nature governed by the flesh has been eradicated. But this is not true according to this and other passages. Naturally, the flesh is to become increasingly subdued as the Christian learns by grace to walk in the Spirit. But it is never eliminated. So the Christian is never released from the necessity of consciously choosing to go in God's way. There is no escape from the need to depend on God's grace.

18 This final verse of the section is best taken as a summary in which Paul reminds the Galatians that, though he is now talking of the need to live a godly life, he is not thereby reverting to legalism. Life by the Spirit is neither legalism nor license—nor a middle way between them. It is a life of faith and love that is above all of these false ways. Being led by the Spirit does not imply passivity but rather the need to allow oneself to be led. Responding to the Spirit is described by three mutually interpreting words in vv.16, 18, and 25—"walk" (RSV), "led," and "live."

Notes

16 There are many excellent and detailed studies of the terms "flesh" and "spirit" by which the brief study here may be amplified. Foremost among them are the comprehensive studies in TDNT and the briefer but excellent studies in BAG. See also the extended notes by Burton in his commentary (pp. 486–495) and the opening chapter of Barclay's *Flesh and Spirit* (pp. 9–22).

17 Burton takes ἵνα (*hina*, "so that") in this verse as final rather than consecutive. But this, while the most common and natural use, does not give the best sense. According to this use, it is necessary to have both flesh and spirit as a common subject, which is not natural for Paul. Nor do the results fit the context. On the other hand, if *hina* is consecutive, being used to introduce a loosely connected clause, then a meaning is allowed that is characteristic of Paul (so Rom 7) and prepares for v.18. Ridderbos has a note on this meaning in which he finds a weakened but consecutive coloring of *hina* elsewhere in the NT.

2. *The works of the flesh*

5:19–21

[19]The acts of the sinful nature are obvious: sexual immorality, impurity and debauchery; [20]idolatry and witchcraft; hatred, discord, jealousy, fits of rage, selfish ambition, dissensions, factions [21]and envy; drunkenness, orgies, and the like. I warn you, as I did before, that those who live like this will not inherit the kingdom of God.

That spirit and flesh are in conflict is now illustrated by contrasting lists of the works of the flesh and of the fruit of the Spirit. Paul has both in mind as he begins to write this section. At the same time, the lists are more than a mere proof of what he has written earlier. For by raising these particulars of conduct, he also provides a checklist for measuring the conduct of those who consider themselves spiritual. If one's conduct is characterized by the traits in the first list, then he is either not a believer or else a believer who is not being led by God's Spirit. The same standards of evaluation hold true for churches.

19 When Paul says that the acts of the flesh are obvious, he does not mean that they are all committed publicly where they may be seen. Some are, some are not. Instead, he means that it is obvious to all that such acts originate with the sinful nature, and not with the nature given believers by God. Here the full scope of the word "flesh" becomes evident (if it was not so before), for the list does not contain only the so-called "fleshly" sins. It contains sins that emanate from every part of human nature.

It is impossible to tell whether Paul was thinking in categories of sin as he wrote. But whether or not he did, four divisions in his list are obvious: first, three sins that are violations of sexual morality; second, two sins from the religious realm; third, eight sins pertaining to conduct in regard to other human beings—i.e., social sins; and finally, there are two typically pagan sins—drunkenness and the revellings accompanying it. These divisions are indicated by appropriate punctuation in NIV and other modern versions.

The first three words, then, cover sexual sins. They are obviously intended to be somewhat comprehensive and inclusive. "Sexual immorality" or "fornication" (*porneia*) is the broadest term, denoting any immoral sexual intercourse or relationships. It probably derives from the words meaning "prostitution" and "prostitute." In starting with this vice, Paul begins with what was acknowledged to be the most open and shameless vice of the Greek and Roman world. "Impurity" (*akatharsia*) originally meant the state of being dirty but later developed ethical overtones, referring to a person who was either morally or ceremonially unclean. Paul uses it almost exclusively of moral impurity and perhaps of unnatural vice. "Debauchery" (*aselgeia*) is an "open and reckless contempt of propriety" (so Lightfoot). In this regard it is a fitting term for what is probably intended to be a climax of several evils. The same words occur in 2 Corinthians 12:21.

20 Sexual sins are not the only sins of the flesh, however. Paul goes on to list two sins of religion: "idolatry" (*eidōlolatria*), a worship of the creature rather than the Creator, and "witchcraft" (*pharmakeia*), a secret tampering with and at times a worship of the powers of evil. These two terms are also arranged in an ascending horror of evil and indicate that the works of the flesh include offenses against God as well as against ourselves or our neighbors.

Neighbors are in view in the third section of Paul's list, since this section includes much of what would today be called social offenses. Most of the words are self-explanatory. "Hatred" (*echthrai*, the first of several words occurring in plural form to denote multiple manifestations of the quality) means "enmities" such as those between classes, nations, and individuals. It is these enmities that have been broken down for those who are in Christ (Gal 3:28; Eph 2:14–16). "Discord" (*eris*) is the natural outcome of hatred both in the world and in the church. Four out of six of Paul's uses of the word are connected with church life. "Jealousy" (*zēlos*) and "fits of rage" (*thumoi*) can denote both good and bad qualities. There is a godly zeal as well as righteous anger. When zeal or anger originate from selfish motives and hurt pride, they are evil and harm others, as Paul implies here. "Selfish ambition" (*eritheiai*) may be translated in many ways: contention, strife, selfishness, rivalry, intrigues. Its basic meaning is a selfish and self-aggrandizing approach to work. This and the preceding three words occur in the same order in 2 Corinthians 12:20. "Dissensions" (*dichostasiai*) and "factions" (*haireseis*) denote a state of affairs in which men are divided and feuds flourish.

21 "Envy" (*phthonoi*) is so closely related to "jealousy" (*zēlos*) that it is hard to tell the difference between them, except for the fact that *phthonoi* is always bad, whereas *zēlos* is not. This set of words, beginning with "hatred," shows the flesh to be responsible for that breakdown in interpersonal relationships seen in all strata of society.

The final grouping is concerned with sins of alcohol: "drunkenness" (*methai*) and "orgies" (*kōmoi*). They denote pleasures that have degenerated to debauchery. There are more items that could be mentioned, for when Paul adds "and the like," he indicates that the list is not exhaustive.

Paul adds a solemn warning, saying that those who habitually practice such things will never inherit God's kingdom. This does not mean that if a Christian falls into sin through getting drunk, or some such thing, he thereby loses his salvation. The tense of the verb (present) indicates a habitual continuation in fleshly sins rather than an isolated lapse, and the point is that those who continually practice such sins give evidence of having never received God's Spirit. When Paul says that he warned the Galatians of this previously (presumably when he was among them), he reveals that his preaching was never what one might call mere evangelism but that it always contained a strong dose of the standard of morality expected from Christians.

The reference to the kingdom of God introduces an entirely new and large subject and one that it is an important and complex idea in the New Testament. Here, however, Paul is doubtlessly thinking of God's kingdom only in an eschatological sense. The phrase "will not inherit" carries the thought back to Paul's words about Abraham in chapter 3. The point is that those who keep on living in the flesh give evidence that they are not Abraham's seed and therefore will not inherit salvation.

Notes

19 The KJV of this passage contains two words not in the best MSS and therefore not discussed here: "adultery" (at the very beginning of the list) and "murders" (after the word "envy" [φθόνος, *phthonos*]). They are not inappropriate, since Paul himself indicates that the list is not complete, but they were apparently not in the list as Paul wrote it. For a fuller discussion of the fifteen works of the flesh see Barclay (*Flesh and Spirit,* pp. 23–62), Burton (pp. 304–310), Stamm (pp. 561–564), as well as the various lexicons and theological dictionaries.

21 The "kingdom of God" (βασιλεία θεοῦ, *basileia theou*) is the rule of God, which has, therefore, both a present (the rule of God in men's hearts) and a future aspect (the anticipated coming of God in power at the end of the age). The term is prominent in the Gospels and in Acts; and even Paul uses it frequently (Rom 14:17; 1 Cor 4:20; 6:9; 15:24, 50; 2 Thess 1:5), though in Paul the idea of the kingdom is not dominant.

3. *The fruit of the Spirit*

5:22–26

22But the fruit of the Spirit is love, joy, peace, patience, kindness, goodness, faithfulness, 23gentleness and self-control. Against such things there is no law. 24Those who belong to Christ Jesus have crucified their sinful nature with its passions and desires. 25Since we live by the Spirit, let us keep in step with the Spirit. 26Let us not become conceited, provoking and envying each other.

Paul continues the contrast between the natural productions of the flesh and Spirit he had begun in v.19. Here, however, he speaks of the "fruit" of the Spirit (using both a new term and the singular form) in contrast to the "works" (v.19) of which the flesh is capable. The term "works" (*erga*) already has definite overtones in this letter. It refers to what man can do, which, in the case of the works of the law (2:16, 3:2, 5, 10), has already been shown to be inadequate. The fruit of the Spirit, on the other hand, suggests that which is a natural product of the Spirit rather than of man, made possible by the living relationship between the Christian and God (cf. 2:20; John 15:1–17). The singular form stresses that these qualities are a unity, like a bunch of grapes instead of separate pieces of fruit, and also that they are all to be found in all Christians. In this they differ from the "gifts" of the Spirit, which are given one by one to different people as the church has need (1 Cor 12).

The nine virtues that are the Spirit's fruit hardly need classification, though they seem to fall into three categories of three each. The first three appear to "comprise Christian habits of mind in their more general aspect," as Lightfoot notes. Their primary direction is God-ward. The second set primarily concerns the Christian in his relationship to others and are social virtues. The last three concern the Christian as he is to be in himself.

22 It is appropriate that "love" (*agapē*) should head the list of the Spirit's fruit—every Christian feels this—for "God is love" (1 John 4:8) and, therefore, the greatest of these is love (1 Cor 13:13). In biblical texts it is the association of *agapē* with God that gives the word its distinctive character. Divine love is unmerited (Rom 5:8), great (Eph 2:4), transforming (Rom 5:5), and unchangeable (Rom 8:35–39). It is this love that sent Christ to die for sinful men and that perseveres with men in spite of their willfulness and love of sin. Now because the Spirit of Christ (who is characterized by love) is living within the Christian, the believer is to show love both to other Christians and to the world. By this, men are to know that Christians are indeed Christ's disciples (John 13:35).

"Joy" (*chara*) is the virtue in the Christian life corresponding to happiness in the secular world. On the surface they seem related. But happiness depends on circumstances, whereas joy does not. In the NT a form of the word "joy" becomes a typical—and the most popular—Christian greeting (Matt 28:9; Luke 1:28; Acts 15:23; 2 Cor 13:11; James 1:1). Joy is particularly full when what was lost spiritually is found (Luke 15:6, 7, 9, 10, 32).

The second of the two most popular Christian greetings is "peace" (*eirēnē*). It is roughly the equivalent of the Hebrew *shalom.* But, though it is related to this word, it also means more. Above all, peace is God's gift to man, achieved by him at the cross of Christ. It is peace with God (Rom 5:1) and is to express itself both in peace of mind (Phil 4:6, 7) and in a very practical peace between all those who know God. This latter peace should be seen, as Barclay notes: in the home (1 Cor 7:12–16), between Jew and Gentile (Eph 2:14–17), within the church (Eph 4:3; Col 3:15), and indeed in the relationships of the believer with all men (Heb 12:14). Moreover, Christians are to strive for it (1 Peter 3:11). The importance of this word is evident from its frequent and extensive occurrence in the NT—eighty times and in every book.

"Patience" (*makrothumia*) is the quality of putting up with others, even when one is severely tried. The importance of patience is evidenced by its being most often used of the character of God, as in the great text from Joel: "Return to the LORD, your God, for he is gracious and merciful, *slow to anger,* and abounding in steadfast love, and repents of evil" (2:13, RSV).

"Kindness" (*chrēstotēs*) is the divine kindness out of which God acts toward men. It is what the OT means when it declares that "God is good," as it so frequently does. The Christian is to show kindness by behaving toward others as God has behaved toward him.

"Goodness" (*agathōsunē*) is hard to define, just as in English. However, though it is related to "kindness" (above), it differs from it in being a more active term and being often directed toward that which does not merit the action. The primary idea seems to be generosity that springs from kindness.

The last three virtues are concerned with the Christian man primarily as he is to be in himself, though these virtues naturally affect others also. He is to be characterized by "faithfulness" (*pistis*). This word also means faith, as KJV translates it here, but in this list it undoubtedly means that which makes a person one on whom others can rely—trustworthiness or reliability. It is the word by which a faithful servant is described (Luke 16:10–12), including servants of the gospel and of Christ (1 Tim 1:12; 2 Tim 2:2). It describes the character of a person who will die for his confession of Christ (Rev. 2:10; 3:14). It goes without saying that it is also descriptive of the character of Christ, the faithful witness (Rev 1:5), and of God the Father, who always acts faithfully toward his people (1 Cor 1:9; 10:13; 1 Thess 5:24; 2 Thess 3:3).

23 "Gentleness" (*prautēs*) describes the person who is so much in control of himself that he is always angry at the right time and never angry at the wrong time (Aristotle, *Nicomachean Ethics*, IV, 5, 1–4), just like Moses, who is praised for being the gentlest or meekest among his contemporaries (Num 12:3). This is the spirit in which to learn (James 1:21) and in which discipline must be applied and faults corrected (Gal 6:1). It is also the virtue for meeting opposition (2 Tim 2:25) and giving a Christian witness (1 Peter 3:15, 16).

"Self-control" (*enkrateia*) is the quality that gives victory over fleshly desires and which is therefore closely related to chastity both in mind and conduct. As Barclay says (in loc.), "*Enkrateia* is that great quality which comes to a man when Christ is in his heart, that quality which makes him able to live and to walk in the world, and yet to keep his garments unspotted from the world."

These are the qualities of the life that has been claimed by Jesus Christ and is Spirit-led. "Against such things there is no law" (v.23b). The last clause is most likely an understatement used for rhetorical effect. The law, as Paul has said, was given to restrain evil; but these qualities do not need to be restrained. Hence, no law opposes them. There may also be a sense, however, in which Paul is suggesting that the law cannot be *against* such as live in this manner because of the very fact that by being so led they are in principle fulfilling all that the law requires.

24 It should be evident to the reader of Galatians that the warfare between the flesh and the Spirit is both intense and unremitting. The qualities of each are fundamentally opposed; it may therefore well be, as Paul seems to have said earlier (v.17), that the one who is caught in the warfare cannot do the good he would like to do. How, then, is victory to be achieved? What must the believer do to triumph? In the final verses of this chapter Paul gives two answers.

First, he reminds his readers that when they came to Christ, they repented fully of the works of the flesh and indeed turned their backs on them forever. This act they must sustain. In speaking of this radical repentance, Paul uses the vivid image of crucifixion. This is an image he has used in other places; it was a favorite with him. But here he uses it in a slightly different way from the way he used it in Romans 6:6 or Galatians 2:20, for example. In these other instances, the verb is in the passive voice ("was crucified," "have been crucified"), and the reference is to what has been done for the believer as a result of Christ's death. But in this passage the verb is in the active voice ("have crucified") and points rather to what the believer has himself done and must continue to regard as being done. The proper term to describe this act is repentance. Thus the believer in Christ has already repented of his former way of life to the degree of actually having executed the old nature. This does not mean that the battle is thereby over forever. As in an actual crucifixion, life lingers even though the criminal has been nailed to the cross. Nevertheless, the believer is to regard the decisive act as having been done. He is not to seek to remove from the cross what has once been nailed there.

25 Next, Paul reminds believers that if they have been made alive by the Spirit—which, of course, they have if they are truly believers—they are also to walk by the Spirit. The Spirit leads; they are to follow. Indeed, they are to get in line with him or keep in step (*stoichōmen*). The verb is also used of those who walk in the steps of the faith of Abraham by believing as he believed (Rom 4:12) or obeying the truth of the gospel (Gal 6:16).

26 It is hard to tell whether this verse belongs with the preceding section or with what follows. Certainly, it is the first of a number of specific actions that should characterize those who are being led by the Spirit. But, on the other hand, it is also a return to the theme of v.15 and, therefore, a summation. The direct address ("brothers") in the next verse has the effect of beginning a new section. Perhaps the verse is best seen as a reference to the situation Paul knew to be existing in Galatia and hence a direct attempt to discourage pride and dampen party spirit. Walking by the Spirit is the ultimate solution to such evils.

Notes

22 A very full study of the terms in this list of virtues may be found in Barclay's work, *Flesh and Spirit,* pp. 63–127. Also valuable are Burton (pp. 314–318), Stamm (pp. 565–570) and, for individual words, the various lexicons and theological dictionaries. Burton has extended notes on "love" (pp. 519–521) and "peace" (pp. 424–426).

D. *Two Practical Exhortations* (6:1–10)

1. *Bearing one another's burdens*

6:1–5

> 1 Brothers, if a man is trapped in some sin, you who are spiritual should restore him gently. But watch yourself; you also may be tempted. 2 Carry each other's burdens, and in this way you will fulfill the law of Christ. 3 If anyone thinks he is something when he is nothing, he deceives himself. 4 Each man should test his own actions. Then he can take pride in himself, without comparing himself to somebody else, 5 for each man should carry his own load.

In the verses closing chapter 5, Paul has contrasted the works of the flesh and the fruit of the Spirit, concluding that Christians are to live Spirit-led lives. But what does it mean to live a life characterized by love, joy, peace, patience, and the other virtues? To those who might prefer a mystical experience or a flight of fancy at this point it comes as a shock to find Paul returning at once to the most down-to-earth subjects—personal relationships (vv.1–5) and the use of money (vv.6–10)—and to find him measuring spirituality by action in these areas.

It is easy to talk about the fruit of the Spirit while doing very little about it. So Christians need to learn that it is in the concrete situations, rather than in emotional highs, that the reality of the Holy Spirit in their lives is demonstrated.

1 The first situation is one that, more than any other, inevitably reveals the real character and spiritual maturity of a believer. Paul imagines a hypothetical situation—which is, however, not at all infrequent—in which one believer unexpectedly learns that another believer is trapped in some sin. What is he to do? Is he to overlook the sin? Does love mean that he is to refuse to face the facts? Or should he expose the sin openly and so gain for himself a reputation for superior holiness? Paul shows that a Spirit-led person should not proceed in either of these ways. In presenting the proper course of action, he shows what to do, who should do it, and finally how it should be done.

First, Paul shows what should be done. He says that Christians are to restore the person who has fallen into sin. The verb (*katarizō*) is a medical term used in secular Greek for setting a fractured bone. What is wrong in the life of the fallen Christian is to be set straight. It is not to be neglected or exposed openly.

Second, Paul says that the work of restoring must be done by those who are spiritual. This word "spiritual" (*pneumatikos*) cuts two ways. On the one hand, it is obviously related to Paul's use of it at the end of chapter 5. It is as much as to say, "Do you consider yourself to be a spiritual instead of a carnal Christian? Well, then, here is a way you can test it. Restoring an erring brother is exactly the kind of thing that spiritual Christians do." On the other hand, Paul is reminding his readers that only those who are genuinely led of the Spirit have the maturity to deal with sin in others. Every Christian should desire such maturity and be mature.

Third, Paul says that the restoration should be made "gently" (using the same word he used in the list of virtues in 5:22) and with the consciousness that none, no matter how spiritual, have immunity from temptation and that all can fall. Stott's comments (in loc.) are valuable:

> If we walked by the Spirit we would love one another more, and if we loved one another more we would bear one another's burdens, and if we bore one another's burdens we would not shrink from seeking to restore a brother who has fallen into sin. Further, if we obeyed this apostolic instruction as we should, much unkind gossip would be avoided, more serious backsliding prevented, the good of the Church advanced, and the name of Christ glorified.

2 The second practical example of spirituality is the bearing of one another's burdens. Four times in the letter Paul uses the word "bearing" (*bastazō*). In 5:10 it is the Judaizer who is to bear his judgment. At 6:5 each Christian is to bear his own load. At the very end, 6:17, he will speak of bearing the marks of Jesus Christ on his body. In this verse the reference is to helping another Christian—sharing his load—whenever temptations oppress him or life depresses him. Here Paul returns quite deliberately to the thought of love being the fulfillment of the law, for the "law of Christ" is the new commandment

(John 13:34) fulfilled in part at least by such actions. "If you must needs impose *burdens* on yourselves, let them be the burdens of mutual sympathy. If you must needs observe a *law*, let it be the law of Christ" (Lightfoot, in loc.).

3 Two errors might keep a believer from fulfilling this role. The first is conceit, that is, thinking himself to be more important than he is. The implication seems to be that if the Christian neglects to bear another's burdens or refuses to bear them, it is because he thinks himself above it. But this is to be self-deceived, for, measured by God's standards, no one amounts to anything. Paul's statement has more force in Greek even than in English: "thinks" (*dokei*) contrasts sharply with "is" (*ōn*, "being"), and "something" (*tis*) contrasts with "nothing" (*mēden*). The first part of the contrast is the one by which Paul described the Jerusalem pillars in chapter 2 (vv.2, 6, 9), but he refrained from saying that these men were nothing, though, in fact, apart from the grace of God, this was true. A positive statement of the same principle occurs in Romans 12:3.

4 The second error that might keep a believer from bearing the burdens of another Christian is to be always comparing himself and his own work with others. This can be harmful both in a positive sense ("I am doing better than they are"—the very conceit Paul has just warned against) and in a negative sense ("I am unable to do anything; everyone else is much better"). To counter both these forms of the error, Paul suggests that each believer has a task from the Lord and is responsible only to the Lord for doing it. To use others as a norm is a kind of escape. When a Christian has his eyes on God rather than on other Christians, then in his own eyes he will at best be an unprofitable servant (Luke 17:10) and God himself will receive glory (2 Cor 10:12–18).

5 In other words, the duty of a Christian is to carry his own load. There is no contradiction between this verse and v.2, as KJV seems to suggest, for different words are used for what one is to bear. The word in v.2 is *barē*, which means "heavy burdens"—those that are more than a man should carry. The word in this verse is *phortion*, a common term for a man's "pack." Each Christian has his own work to do, so let him take pride in how he does it.

Notes

1 There is a closer connection between the example given in this verse and the preceding injunctions than most EV indicate. After "brothers," the Gr. has the introductory concessive clause ἐὰν καὶ (*ean kai*), which has (in this case) the effect of stressing the following situation as an exception that is in some sense extreme. The effect is as follows: Having spoken of the need to walk by the Spirit and having encouraged his readers so to walk, Paul now says, in effect, "Nevertheless, if a believer should disregard this injunction and fail so to walk, thereby falling into sin, you who do walk by the Spirit should restore him." A similar use of *ean kai* occurs in 1 Cor 7:11. For a full discussion see Burton (in loc.).

"Trapped" ("overtaken," KJV) does not refer to being caught in some sin, though the context implies that the sin has come to light somehow, but rather to being overcome by it (cf. Robb, "Gal. 6:1," ExpT, 57, 1945–46, p. 222, and Burton).

5 It is difficult to establish a precise distinction between βάρη (*barē*) and φορτίον (*phortion*). But such distinctions as there are seem to be between a load that is burdensome and one that is a

man's normal work to carry (cf. Hall, ExpT, 34, 1922-23, p. 563, and Jones, ExpT, 34, 1922-23, p. 333). *Phortion* is thus used of the cargo of a ship in the sense of that which the ship is designed to carry (cf. Acts 27:10).

---

2. *The use of money*

6:6–10

[6]Anyone who receives instruction in the word must share all good things with his instructor.

[7]Do not be deceived: God cannot be mocked. A man reaps what he sows. [8]The one who sows to please his sinful nature, from that nature will reap destruction; the one who sows to please the Spirit, from the Spirit will reap eternal life. [9]Let us not become weary in doing good, for at the proper time we will reap a harvest if we do not give up. [10]Therefore, as we have opportunity, let us do good to all people, especially to those who belong to the family of believers.

The second area to which Paul seeks to apply the life of the Spirit in a practical way is the use of money; indeed, few things more clearly disclose the priorities of the heart than this. Many commentators hesitate to relate this entire section to the use of money, believing that vv.7–9 cannot be written primarily of material things. But while it is true that the section as a whole goes beyond the use of money, nevertheless, at least three factors indicate that Paul was thinking primarily of money as he wrote it. First, although vv.7–9 expand on the theme of v.6 in general ways, v.10 returns to it; for the phrase "do good to all" is most certainly a euphemism for giving alms. This indicates that a concern for financial matters never entirely leaves Paul's mind. Second, v.7 is a proverb Paul used on at least one other occasion to encourage generous giving (2 Cor 9:6). The presumption is that giving is also uppermost in his mind here. Finally, we have the fact that giving is important to Paul at this time even apart from the situation in Galatia, for the collection for the Jerusalem poor is part of his policy and the admonition to proceed with the collection is fresh in his mind as a result of the Jerusalem council (Gal 2:10). Seen in this light, the passage may even be an indirect allusion to the collection, as Cole speculates.

Three uses of money are mentioned: (1) the support of the teacher in a Christian congregation, (2) the use of money to build up the life of the Spirit rather than to feed the flesh, and (3) the spending of money to help others, particularly Christians. The principle that ties all three points together is that enunciated in the proverb: reaping is in proportion to sowing. Thus, a man will get out of his effort what he puts into it.

6 The reference to the one who is taught in the word (*katēchoumenos ton logon*) probably does not imply a fully developed catechetical system such as prevailed in the church later on, but it does point to a class of paid teachers at a surprisingly early date. Paul's policy was apparently to preach the gospel without receiving money, preferring to earn his living as a tentmaker. But this was in pioneer work. As soon as possible he seems to have established a more fixed structure. So here as elsewhere (1 Cor 9:11, 14; 1 Tim 5:17, 18; cf. Luke 10:7), he indicates that a workman is worthy of his pay.

To support the Lord's servants is not, however, a grim duty, though some congregations seem to treat it as such. Instead, Paul speaks of it as sharing; it is a "fellowship" or a "partnership" (*koinōneō*). As the teacher shares the good things of the Word, so the congregation is to share all good things with the teacher.

7 The special advice of v.6 is now enlarged to benevolence in general, and the principle that ties everything together is stated. What a man sows he reaps. This is an immutable law of God, which the phrase "God cannot be mocked" emphasizes. Consequently, though a man may fool himself (by sowing little but expecting much), he cannot fool God and the results of his poor sowing will be manifest.

8 This is true especially in Christian living. If a man spends his money on what gratifies his fleshly nature, he will reap a fleshly harvest. And since the flesh is mortal and will one day pass away, the harvest will pass away also. On the other hand, if a man uses his money to promote spiritual causes and to feed his spiritual nature, the resulting harvest will remain. Two factors give the primary application of this principle as Paul intends it to be applied here: (1) he is still dealing with money, and (2) he has just been dealing with the spiritual character of the Christian. It is obvious, however, that the principle also applies more broadly. It applies to others than the individual himself, for instance. Thus, as in the case of ministers, if congregations refuse to support them and so forfeit good teaching, preferring to spend their money on themselves, the results will be corruption. But if, on the other hand, they support good teachers, a spiritual harvest will result. The principle also applies to the use of time, the use of the mind, and other matters.

9 The great hindrance to such good sowing is weariness that results in discouragement and eventually in giving up. Four months elapse between planting and harvest (John 4:35); and, while it is true that in spiritual sowing the results occasionally come sooner, it is also true that more often the results take much longer. Two imperatives govern Paul's warning: "do not be weary" and "do not faint." These are not identical but are directed against the temptations to become discouraged and give up (cf. Smith, "Gal. 6:9," ExpT, 13, 1901–02, p. 139). The best reason for resisting them is that if the necessary preparation is done, the harvest is sure.

One cannot help feeling that Paul may be talking to himself as he thinks of the extensive but thus far unrewarding efforts he expended on the churches of Galatia. The change to the first person plural supports this supposition.

10 Finally, Paul speaks broadly about the obligation to do good to all men, returning, however, primarily to the thought of giving money. But suppose a Christian is very limited in his resources? In that case, says Paul, he is to give to Christian causes especially, knowing that if they are not supported by Christians, they will not be supported at all. If he has unlimited funds, he can give to every valid charity that comes along.

Two parts of this verse are of special interest. First, Paul speaks of the "family of believers." This really means "those who have become related to us by believing in Christ" and points to a relationship transcending all others. In one sense, this is a narrow company made up of those who should have preference in Christian giving and other kinds of welldoing. On the other hand, the phrase includes all who so believe. Therefore, giving should not be unduly restricted by denomination or party loyalty.

The other point of special interest is Paul's mention of "time" (*kairos*, translated "time" in v.9 and "opportunity" in v.10). *Kairos* denotes "the right time" or "the proper time" for anything; consequently a time that occurs only once before it is lost forever. No one can hope to reap the harvest before the time appointed for it by God (v.9). But if he does not seize the time appointed him for sowing, he will reap no harvest at all (v.10).

Notes

6 It is difficult to speculate on why Paul places such emphasis on the use of money, devoting five verses to it, but the following are possibilities: (1) He may have been dealing with a situation in the churches of Galatia we otherwise know nothing about. The delicacy of the situation may have made a more direct reference unwise or impossible. (2) The subject may have been high on Paul's list of priorities in dealing with any church. Certainly, the lengthy discussions about money in the Corinthian letters, written about this time, suggest it. (3) Being aware that the use of money is an excellent indication of the priorities held by anyone, Paul may simply have seized upon this subject as a way of sharpening the contrast between the works of the flesh and the fruit of the Spirit made earlier. It is also possible that all three reasons are involved.

10 That Paul distinguishes between all men and those of the family of believers (who have a first claim on the Christian) supports the view of the present writer that the verses are primarily dealing with money. It is hard to see how Paul could make the distinction if the reference is merely to good deeds, even less if he were thinking of people's spiritual welfare. But if he is thinking of financial support, the distinction is understandable; in time of need a Christian can hardly expect to receive help from non-Christians.

Conclusion

6:11–18

11See what large letters I use as I write to you with my own hand!

12Those who want to make a good impression outwardly are trying to compel you to be circumcised. The only reason they do this is to avoid being persecuted for the cross of Christ. 13Not even those who are circumcised obey the law, yet they want you to be circumcised that they may boast about your flesh. 14May I never boast except in the cross of our Lord Jesus Christ, through which the world has been crucified to me, and I to the world. 15Neither circumcision nor uncircumcision means anything; what counts is a new creation. 16Peace and mercy to all who follow this rule, even to the Israel of God.

17Finally, let no one cause me trouble, for I bear on my body the marks of Jesus.

18The grace of our Lord Jesus Christ be with your spirit, brothers. Amen.

The apostle has said nearly everything he wishes to say, and the letter is drawing to a close. But in ending it he first takes the pen from the hand of his amanuensis and adds a summary of the letter in his own handwriting. The summary contains a fresh warning against the legalizers, a restatement of the basic principle that Christianity is internal and supernatural rather than external and human (as the legalizers were trying to make it), a final reference to his own suffering for the cause of Christ, and a benediction. The somewhat abrupt ending has the effect of leaving the great issue of the letter—faith or works—sharply before the Galatians.

11 There can be little doubt that Paul took the pen in his own hand at this point and an almost equal lack of doubt that he did so for at least two purposes: (1) to authenticate the letter, as he seems also to have done on other occasions (cf. 1 Cor 16:21; Col 4:18; 2 Thess 3:17), and (2) to emphasize his main points. There is less agreement about the meaning of the words "large letters." On the one hand, some, among them certain of the reformers (Luther, Calvin), refer them to the size of the letter: that is, "See what a lengthy letter I have written." But grammar and comparative brevity of the letter argue against this. On the other hand are the majority of scholars who correctly see a reference to the size of the letters Paul was inscribing but who, nevertheless, disagree on their significance.

Deissmann believed that this was a reference to the awkward writing of a working man, whose hands had become disfigured by toil (*Light from the Ancient East,* pp. 166, 167; *Paul,* p. 49). This seems unconvincing and even a bit snobbish. Besides, while it is probably true that Paul did not write with quite the degree of polish of a professional scribe, this alone seems hardly to account either for his large letters or his emphasis on them. The second and more general assumption is that Paul increased the size of his letters for emphasis much as in contemporary printing a paragraph is italicized or set in boldface. This view accords with the tone of this section in which the main points of the letter are reiterated to impress them on the minds of the Galatians. A third and very intriguing view is that Paul may have been writing with large letters due to poor eyesight. The case for this view, which involves both the "thorn in the flesh" passage in 2 Corinthians 12:7 and the reference to "eyes" in Galatians 4:15, is presented by Clemens ("St. Paul's Handwriting," ExpT, 24, 1912–13, p. 380) and other scholars.

12 For the last time Paul speaks of the legalizers, this time warning the Galatians about what they were attempting to do and why they were doing it.

The object of this legalistic activity, Paul says, is "to make a good impression outwardly." The Greek for this phrase is richer than any single English translation can make it. For one thing, the verb translated "to make a good impression" (*euprosōpēsai*) carries overtones of insincerity. They were not what they seemed. For another, the impression they desired to make was both before men and in external matters. The word that suggests this is the crucial term "flesh" (*sarx*), which has appeared throughout the letter. Flesh refers to men, whom the legalizers wanted to impress, and to circumcision, which had become the touchstone of their religion. In contrast to this, Christianity consists in a desire to please God on the part of those who, as a result of his grace, have become new creatures (vv.14, 15).

But why did the legalizers persevere so strongly in their error if, indeed, as Paul claims, it is an error? There are two reasons. First, they desired to escape the persecution that attached to Christ's cross. It is not even so much Christ himself who is the problem here, as Paul expresses it, for a Christ who is a teacher (but only a teacher) can well be assimilated by Judaism or by any other religion. The difficulty is the cross, because the cross speaks of the necessity of a divine death as the only solution to the sin of man. To have the cross is to have three disquieting and humiliating doctrines: (1) man is a sinner; (2) his sin brings him under the curse of God, which curse Christ bore; and (3) nothing man can do can earn salvation, for if this were possible, the cross would have been unnecessary. These doctrines humble men. Consequently, men hate the cross and actively persecute those who proclaim it.

13 Second, the legalizers persevered in their error because of their desire to boast that they had been able to win over the Galatians for Judaism. There were two things wrong with this. (1) It was an attempt to win others to that which was itself bankrupt; for not even those who were circumcised (that is, Jews) were able to keep the law. (2) It was based on pride. The legalizers wanted to boast in the flesh of the Galatians. This means that they wanted to boast in the number of circumcisions, much as David had boasted in the two hundred foreskins of the Philistines. They were trophy hunters and wanted to be able to report on mass "conversions" in Galatia. The humbling parallel would be in the tendency to take pride in counting the number of "decisions for Christ" or "baptisms" today.

14 Over against all such improper and sinful boasting, Paul sets an entirely different boasting of his own. It is a boasting "in the cross of our Lord Jesus Christ." So important is this cause of boasting that, says Paul, it is inconceivable that he could boast in anything else. It is striking how much of the gospel is involved in this statement. The cross speaks of the atonement necessitated by man's sin (see above on v.12). The full name of the Savior speaks of the significance of his person and the role he played, meaning literally "God who saves, the Messiah." Finally, the pronoun "our" speaks of the personal aspects of Christ's redemption, for it becomes "ours" through the response of faith.

The legalizers had a motive for their actions. Well, so did Paul. Only his motive was not that of a fear of persecution or of a desire to boast in statistics. He was boasting in the cross of Christ because of what the cross had accomplished in his life. As Paul looks back on his life he realizes that before his conversion he was exactly like the legalizers. Once he, too, was ruled by externals. He, too, gloried in human attainment (Phil 3:3–6). But when he met Jesus, all this passed for him, so much so that he is able even to apply the bold image of crucifixion to it. The world with its selfish and fleshly attitudes was crucified to him and he to the world. In its place came Christ alone—Christ, who is everything.

15 The summary is brief. Neither circumcision nor uncircumcision count for anything as a means of salvation (cf. 5:6 and 1 Cor 7:19). The only thing that counts is to be born again, to become a new creation. This comes about not by observing the law in any form but by receiving and stepping out upon the truth of the gospel.

16 Has anyone yet missed the point? If so, Paul will state it once again in even starker language—"Peace and mercy to all who follow this rule, even to the Israel of God" (cf. the blessings of Pss 125:5; 128:6). This statement makes three points: (1) the peace and mercy of God are given only to those who adhere to this gospel; (2) all who believe the gospel, so it is implied, have an obligation to continue walking in it; and (3) these, and these only, are the true Israel. In this verse "rule" (*kanon*) clearly refers to the heart of the gospel just enunciated; but it may also be applied to the "canon" of Scripture (as the church later used the word) and to the whole of Christian doctrine. It is sometimes said that those who are concerned with the essence of the gospel and with true doctrine are the disrupters of the church, but Paul says the opposite. The truth is that the gospel is the real promoter of peace and is the channel of God's mercy. There can be no peace or mercy for the church when those responsible for following this "rule" depart from it.

17 Paul's last words are a request and a final benediction. The request is that henceforth he be not troubled with the kind of problem that had erupted in the Galatian churches. This can hardly mean that Paul did not want to hear about such problems if they occurred. If they did occur he would want to combat them. Nor can it mean that he did not want further trouble from the legalizers; for they would certainly cause trouble, regardless of his wishes, and he could hardly direct an appeal to them anyway. Instead, the appeal is to the churches themselves and is that they might no longer trouble him by giving way to the legalistic heresies. The reason, Paul says, is that he has suffered enough already. It would be far better if the churches he founded at such cost would assume their own share of suffering, above all by resisting the kind of teaching that the legalizers upheld and therefore, if necessary, by enduring whatever persecution might follow.

The "marks of Jesus" refer to the scars Paul bore on his body as the result of the persecutions he had endured for the sake of his Lord. These marks revealed his relationship to Christ, just as the "marks" (*stigmata*) of a slave revealed his ownership. A list of the experiences that might have caused such scars occurs in 2 Corinthians 6:4–6 and 11:23–30. These genuine and honorable marks in the body contrast strikingly with the ritualistic and now meaningless mark (circumcision) the legalizers wished to impose on the Galatians.

18 Paul ends the letter as he had begun it, upon the single and glorious note of God's grace, expressing the wish that this grace might abide with the spirits of the Galatians. Paul's legacy is, therefore, a wish that the grace of God would be increasingly realized and that whatever external marks there might be, would be received, not as an effort to impress God ritualistically, but as a natural result of true Christian service. The church will always know great days when these are the two distinguishing marks of God's people.

Notes

13 "Those who are circumcised" may denote either: (1) Gentiles who have become circumcised, (2) the legalizers, or (3) all Jews generally. The first possibility is ruled out by 5:3, which indicates that the legalizers had not yet succeeded in having the Gentiles circumcised. The second is improbable, since (in addition to grammatical considerations, cf. Burton) Paul would be unlikely to make such a new and unsupported claim—that the legalizers failed to keep the law—this late in his letter. The third possibility is used by Paul elsewhere (Rom 2:17–29) and fits well in the context. Thus, Paul would be pointing out that neither the legalizers, who were Jews, nor those Jews to whom they would boast keep the law; yet, they would glory in this one external adherence to it on the part of the Galatians.

16 There are two ways in which the "and" (*καί, kai*) of this verse may be taken. It may be a simple connective, in which case Paul's final words would be directed to all who among the Gentiles walk according to the truth of the gospel *and* to Israel. This would not mean "unbelieving Israel," of course. It would refer to Christian Judaism. But it would, nevertheless, be somewhat of an olive-branch stretched out to the Jewish side of Christianity. On the other hand, *kai* may have the sense of "even," in which case there would not be two parties and two benedictions (as Burton holds) but one group containing both Jews and Gentiles, which Paul now designates as God's Israel. This second use is much bolder, but it is probably the one in view here. One can hardly suppose Paul to be distinguishing two distinct branches of Christianity now after his lengthy insistence upon one gospel throughout the letter and his closing insistence upon the one rule by which those who believe the gospel are to walk. The point is that a true Jew is not one who is a child of Abraham according to the flesh, but rather a child of God through the new birth by grace according to God's Spirit.

We want to hear from you. Please send your comments about this book to us in care of zreview@zondervan.com. Thank you.

ZONDERVAN®

GRAND RAPIDS, MICHIGAN 49530 USA

ZONDERVAN.COM/
AUTHORTRACKER